To Fritzy Schachner, 1907–1996

Acknowledgment is gratefully extended to:

John Whited, Ellie Gorinstein, Jerry Houle II, McGladrey, Hendrickson and Pullen, Kathy Zukowski, The Broward Community College Central Campus Library, and Mr. John Williams, president of the Scrabble® Association of America, in the original edition, and

Carol Cole, whose dedication and hard work made this new edition possible.

Cheri and James Williamson, whose help and dedication have been invaluable.

Marcy J. Goldberg, for her detailed suggestions, and Victor Scudiery, who has always kept the faith.

CONTENTS

FOREWORD

We are the species that uses language, and that is enough to set us apart from all other creatures.

—JOHN CIARDI

Little did the inventor of Scrabble® know in 1931 that by the 1990s there would be 35 million leisure Scrabble® players enjoying the game in the United States and Canada. Or that 100 million sets would be sold worldwide since the popular word game was first developed and originally named Lexiko. Nor did the inventor know that his world game would become the most popular word game of all time, spawning world championships in twenty-two nations.

With the increase in popularity of the Scrabble® board game came the proliferation of dictionaries, word books, and word finders. And among those available, one of the most popular of all, is our own Official Scrabble® Word-Finder. This new edition, the first in ten years, has some important new features.

First and foremost, *The Official Scrabble® Word-Finder,* Second Edition, has been brought up to speed to match *The Official Scrabble® Players Dictionary*, Third Edition. This means that words that have been dropped or added (and fall into one of our categories) have been added or subtracted correspondingly in our Word-Finder. In addition, we have included a new section, "Ten Tips for a Better Game," and, for the first time, have listed all 955 three-letter words in a separate chapter. The Quick-Check Usage Guide has also been expanded to include technological words and sporting words.

If you are one of the tens of thousands of users of our *Official Scrabble® Word-Finder*, you will be pleased to have this updated edition. And, if you are a newcomer to this publication, I am sure you will find it beneficial to your knowledge of the game of Scrabble® and the enjoyment the world's most popular word game brings to your life.

—RWS

INTRODUCTION

*Respect for the word—to employ wit
with scrupulous care and heartfelt love of truth—
is essential . . . .*

—DAG HAMMARSKJÖLD
MARKINGS

This book is the product of a loser—me—a frustrated Scrabble® player, who has been beaten game after game by a person with whom I dearly love to play. She always seems to beat the clock and find the unusual word and the highest-scoring combination of letters, leading to my almost certain defeat. This has been going on for years, and I suspect I'm not alone. Scrabble® has been the most popular word game since its invention by Alfred Butts, at the time an out-of-work architect, during the Great Depression. Mr. Butts counted the letters used on the front page of *The New York Times* and produced what was eventually released commercially as Criss-Cross Words. It became Scrabble® in 1948 and has since then sold more than 90 million copies worldwide.

Scrabble®'s fun to play, win or lose, but who wants to lose? Who enjoys watching the score mount against him as round by round the reservoir of unused letters is depleted? Who enjoys scrambling through a dictionary, trying to memorize esoteric words? No one except a masochist. So, if you want to be a winner, this book is for you.

I began by considering ways of rearranging the dictionary of acceptable Scrabble® words to suit my number one need as a player: constructing the highest-scoring word in the shortest possible time. The word lists in this book are the result of that effort.

Word-Finder (Chapter 1) is a powerful new tool providing quick access to thousands of high-scoring words. For each letter of the alphabet (except vowels) there are three lists:

1. Words beginning with that letter

2. Words ending with that letter

3. Words having that letter in approximately the middle of the word

In Chapter 2 you'll find a listing of all "legal" two-letter words (based on standard Scrabble® rules) for those tough situations that arise during play.

In Chapter 3, we provide an alphabetical listing of two-letter words that can be made into a new word with the addition of one letter. For quick recognition. the letter to be added stands apart from the original two-letter word.

Prefixes, suffixes, and plurals can be a boon to the Scrabble® player and in Chapter 4 we provide a review of the rules for their use. Again, for easy reference, the base word shown is detached from the new addition.

Everyone who has played Scrabble® has experienced an opponent who uses a word drawn from his or her special knowledge. Little-known legal, medical, military, and other specialized words are, if contested, time consuming to check, and, if not challenged, can be very successful for the player using them. In Chapter 5 we present a new kind of word list, a Quick-Check Usage Guide covering the various categories.

Now that you know how the *Official Scrabble® Word-Finder* works, you should be aware of some other aspects of the game and the word use that affects it.

Players of Scrabble® must, in the interests of their continued friendship and the nonviolent settlement of arguments, have a mutually agreeable dictionary at hand. Since dictionaries vary enormously from publisher to publisher and editor to editor, the agreement of the "standard" or dictionary of play must be made at the outset of any game. The *Word-Finder* is not such a dictionary and does not cover every "legal" word nor provide definitions of the words included, although it does contain approximately 60,000 words culled from the complete *Official Scrabble® Players Dictionary.*

There are also many acceptable variations of play. Only those actually playing the game can decide by which set of rules they wish to test their vocabulary strength against their opponents. There are also interpretations of rules, both official and those agreed upon by the players. One of the most controversial areas in interpretation of the rules in "designated foreign words." For instance, *oui* (yes) is not found in the

Oxford dictionaries, and the word *si* is shown as a musical note in the full *Oxford*. However, in *Funk & Wagnalls, si* is shown as meaning "yes" in Portuguese, Italian, and Spanish as well as an alternate for *ti* (musical note), and *oui* (yes in French) is permissible for "yes." You can see that with that degree of variation some discussion before the start of play is necessary to agree upon the interpretation of the rules. The *Word-Finder* does not provide a set of rules nor does it attempt to interpret the rules.

Another factor determining the acceptability of words is the particular set of rules chosen by the participants before play begins. The official rules may be used or the rules for any of the many games, such as "theme" Scrabble® , solitaire, clock-racing or timed play, foreign, or even "sex" Scrabble®. The game you choose to play will, of course, affect the "legality" or acceptability of words used in play, the *Word-Finder* may not always prove useful in these more unconventional games.

Now go forth, *Official Scrabble® Word-Finder* in hand, and with a new sense of confidence. I'm sure these word lists will prove as useful for you as they have been for me.

—RWS

P.S. While compiling this book I became fascinated with certain interesting facts and statistics about our language and its cataloging. For instance, there are eighty-two two-letter words in our general use language and seven hundred seventy-nine three-letter words. There are twenty-four kinds of antelope, twenty-eight words for types of carriages, one hundred thirty-seven listings of foreign, domestic, and ancient coins in the dictionary, and fourteen words meaning prostitute, including some that you would probably have never hear of regardless of your sexual proclivities. Whole dictionaries exist on the subject of underground language like *A Dictionary of Historical Slang* and *A Dictionary of the Underworld.* Words from the American West and words used in obsolete English are cataloged by the thousands in volumes of their own. There are dictionaries of usage, of style, of diplomacy, of dates—even of narcotics. And just in case you are feeling smug because you have a so-called unabridged, remember that *The Oxford English Dictionary,* in eleven volumes weighing one hundred thirty-two pounds, has 500,000 entries.

Increasing your word power will not just make you a better Scrabble®
player, it will enrich your knowledge and understanding of the world in
which we live. One method of vocabulary building is to play Scrabble®
using the *Official Scrabble® Word-Finder* in combination with the *Official Scrabble® Players Dictionary*. The *Word-Finder* will guide your
play and help you obtain the highest possible score, while the dictionary will teach you the meaning of a word that may be new to your
vocabulary. Learning the idea behind unfamiliar words will facilitate
adding those words to your vocabulary—permanently.

Ten Tips for a Better Game

1. Memorize two-letter words to improve your game.

2. Learn the following twelve *q* words that do not have a *u* in them (*q* is worth ten points on its face):

   FAQIR
   QAID
   QAT
   QATS
   QOPH
   QAIDS
   QANAT
   QINDAR
   QINTAR
   QOPHS
   QWERTY
   TRANQ

3. Learn three-letter words. There are 955.

4. Move tiles around on your rack frequently.

5. Try not to duplicate letters on your rack unless it is an *e*.

6. Save better combinations of letters on your rack when possible.

7. Watch for *AID* and *AT*, which are helpful to opponents for dumping *O*s.

8. Once you find a good play, look for an even better one.

9. Always look at the board to see if your opponent's last move has changed your options.

10. Watch for words that can rid you of bad letters (low scoring and difficult).

Word-Finder

Words listed in this section are arranged alphabetically and according to the number of letters they contain. High-scoring words are shown in boldface type (10–14 points), extra high-scoring words (15 points or more) are shown with an asterisk in addition to the boldface type. Words with the value of 3 points or less are not shown at all. The vowels have been omitted in Word-Finder as separate categories because most words contain them; their inclusion would make the book cumbersome and difficult to use. Also, having been assigned the most numerous allotment of letters in the game, vowels have the lowest point value (based on face value of the letter). With your highest point-value letters and Word-Finder to maximize your score, you will most certainly use the vowels you are holding.

Based on the standard Scrabble® rules, the following words will also not be contained in Word-Finder since their use is not "legal" in normal play:

Capitalized words

Hyphenated words

Prefixes and suffixes (standing alone)

Abbreviations

Words requiring an apostrophe

The maximum length of words shown in Word-Finder is eight letters (the maximum letters held at any one time, plus one letter on the board). The skilled vocabularist and experienced player will, at times, construct longer words out of existing words already on the board, but *The Scrabble® Word-Finder* is designed to be a *quick* reference to locate as high a scoring word as possible in the shortest possible time.

Here's the most effective way to use the Word-Finder. First, turn to the list based on the letter you plan to build onto. You'll notice that the

list has three sections: words beginning with that letter, words ending with that letter, and words containing that letter in the middle. Thus, you have a variety of word suggestions built around your key letter. All you have to do is choose the highest-scoring word that fits the other letters on your rack.

B

BAAL	**BEAK**	BIRR	BONY	BRUT	**BADDY**
BAAS	BEAM	BISE	BOOB	BUBO	BADGE
BABA	BEAN	**BISK**	**BOOK**	BUCK	**BADLY**
BABE	BEAR	BITE	BOOM	**BUFF**	*BAFFY
BABU	BEAT	BITT	BOON	BUHL	BAGEL
BABY	BEAU	*BIZE	BOOR	BUHR	**BAGGY**
BACH	**BECK**	BLAB	BOOT	BULB	BAIRN
BACK	BEEF	BLAE	BORA	**BULK**	**BAITH**
BADE	BEEN	BLAH	BORE	BULL	*BAIZA
BAFF	BEEP	BLAM	BORN	**BUMF**	*BAIZE
BAHT	BEER	BLAT	BORT	**BUMP**	**BAKER**
BAIL	BEET	BLAW	**BOSK**	BUND	BALAS
BAIT	BELL	BLEB	BOSS	BUNG	**BALDY**
BAKE	BELT	BLET	BOTA	**BUNK**	BALER
BALD	BEMA	BLIN	BOTH	BUNT	**BALKY**
BALE	BEND	BLIP	BOTT	BUOY	**BALLY**
BALL	BENE	BLOB	BOUT	BURA	BALMY
BALM	BENT	BLOC	BOWL	BURD	BALSA
BAND	BERG	BLOT	*BOXY	BURG	BANAL
BANE	BERM	BLOW	BOYO	BURL	BANCO
BANG	BEST	BLUB	*BOZO	BURN	**BANDY**
BANI	BETA	BLUE	BRAD	BURP	**BANJO**
BANK	BETH	BLUR	BRAE	BURR	BANNS
BARB	**BEVY**	BOAR	BRAG	BURY	**BANTY**
BARD	BHUT	BOAT	BRAN	BUSH	BARBE
BARE	BIAS	**BOCK**	BRAT	**BUSK**	BARDE
BARF	BIBB	BODE	BRAW	BUSS	BARER
BARK	BICE	**BODY**	BRAY	BUST	BARGE
BARM	BIDE	**BOFF**	BRED	BUSY	BARIC
BARN	BIER	**BOGY**	BREE	BUTE	**BARKY**
BASE	**BIFF**	BOIL	BREN	BUTT	**BARMY**
BASH	**BIKE**	BOLA	BREW	*BUZZ	**BARNY**
BASK	BILE	BOLD	BRIE	BYRE	BARON
BASS	**BILK**	BOLE	BRIG	BYRL	BARRE
BAST	BILL	BOLL	BRIM	BYTE	**BARYE**
BATE	BIMA	BOLO	BRIN		BASAL
BATH	BIND	BOLT	BRIO	BABEL	BASED
BATT	BINE	**BOMB**	BRIT	**BABKA**	BASER
BAUD	BINT	BOND	BROO	BABOO	BASES
BAND	BIRD	BONE	BROS	BABUL	BASIC
BAWL	**BIRK**	BONG	BROW	**BACCA**	BASIL
BEAD	BIRL	**BONK**	BRRR	BACON	BASIN

BISTRO	**BODIED**	BORIDE	BRASIL	**BRUMAL**	BURGLE
*BITCHY	BODIES	BORING	**BRASSY**	*BRUMBY	BURGOO
BITING	BODILY	**BORROW**	**BRATTY**	**BRUNCH**	BURIAL
BITTED	**BODING**	BORSCH	BRAVER	BRUNET	BURIED
BITTEN	BODKIN	BORSHT	BRAWLY	**BRUSHY**	BURIER
BITTER	**BOFFIN**	*BORZOI	**BRAWNY**	BRUTAL	BURIES
*BIZONE	BOGGED	BOSKER	BRAYER	**BRYONY**	**BURKER**
*BLABBY	**BOGGLE**	BOSKET	*BRAZEN	**BUBALE**	**BURLAP**
BLAMER	BOGIES	**BOSOMY**	*BRAZER	**BUBBLE**	**BURLER**
BLANCH	*BOHUNK	*BOSQUE	*BRAZIL	*BUBBLY	**BURLEY**
BLASTY	BOILER	BOSTON	BREACH	BUCCAL	**BURNER**
*BLAZER	BOLERO	BOTANY	**BREADY**	BUCKER	BURNET
*BLAZON	BOLETE	*BOTCHY	BREAST	BUCKET	BURNIE
BLEACH	BOLIDE	BOTFLY	BREATH	BUCKLE	BURRED
BLEARY	*BOLLIX	BOTHER	BREECH	BUDDER	BURRER
BLENCH	*BOLLOX	BOTTLE	BREEKS	BUDDLE	**BURROW**
BLENDE	BOLSHY	BOTTOM	*BREEZE	BUDGER	BURSAR
BLENNY	BOLSON	BOUBOU	*BREEZY	BUDGET	BURTON
BLIMEY	BOLTER	BOUCLE	BREGMA	BUDGIE	BUSBOY
BLINIS	*BOMBAX	BOUFFE	BREVET	BUFFER	BUSHEL
*BLINTZ	BOMBER	BOUGHT	BREWER	BUFFET	**BUSHER**
BLITHE	*BOMBYX	BOUGIE	BREWIS	BUGEYE	**BUSHWA**
*BLOCKY	BONACI	BOULLE	BRIARD	BUGGED	BUSIED
BLONDE	BONBON	BOUNCE	BRIBEE	BUGGER	BUSIER
BLOODY	BONDER	BOUNCY	BRIBER	BUGLER	BUSIES
BLOOEY	BONDUC	BOUNTY	*BRICKY	BUGSHA	**BUSILY**
BLOOIE	BONIER	BOURNE	BRIDAL	BULBEL	BUSING
BLOOMY	BONING	BOURSE	**BRIDGE**	BULBIL	BUSKER
BLOTCH	BONITA	BOUTON	BRIDLE	BULBUL	BUSKIN
BLOTTO	BONITO	BOVINE	**BRIGHT**	BULGER	**BUSMAN**
BLOTTY	BONNET	BOWERY	BRINER	BULGUR	BUSSED
BLOUSE	BONNIE	BOWFIN	**BRIONY**	BULLET	BUSSES
BLOUSY	BONSAI	BOWING	BROACH	BUMBLE	BUSTER
*BLOWBY	*BONZER	BOWLEG	BROCHE	BUMKIN	BUSTIC
BLOWER	BOOBOO	BOWLER	BROGAN	BUMMED	BUSTLE
BLOWSY	BOODLE	BOWMAN	BROGUE	BUMMER	BUTANE
BLOWUP	BOOGER	BOWPOT	BROKEN	BUMPER	BUTENE
*BLOWZY	BOOGEY	*BOWWOW	BROKER	*BUNCHY	BUTLER
BLUELY	BOOGIE	BOWYER	BROLLY	BUNDLE	BUTTER
BLUEST	BOOHOO	*BOXCAR	BROMAL	BUNGEE	BUTTON
BLUESY	BOOKER	*BOXFUL	BROMIC	BUNGLE	**BUYOUT**
BLUING	BOOKIE	*BOXIER	BROMID	BUNION	*BUZUKI
BLUISH	BOOMER	*BOXING	BROMIN	BUNKER	*BUZZER
BLUNGE	BOOTEE	BOYARD	BRONCO	BUNKUM	**BYELAW**
BLURRY	BOOTIE	BOYISH	*BRONZE	BUNTER	**BYGONE**
BOATEL	*BOOZER	BRACER	*BRONZY	BUPPIE	**BYLINE**
BOATER	BOPEEP	BRAGGY	BROOCH	*BUQSHA	**BYNAME**
BOBBER	BOPPER	BRAHMA	BROODY	BURBLE	**BYPASS**
BOBBIN	BORAGE	BRAINY	BROOMY	BURBLY	**BYPAST**
BOBBLE	BORANE	BRAISE	BROTHY	BURBOT	*BYPATH
BOBCAT	BORATE	*BRAIZE	BROWNY	BURDEN	*BYPLAY
BOCCIA	BORDEL	BRANCH	BROWSE	BURDIE	**BYRNIE**
BOCCIE	BORDER	BRANDY	BRUCIN	BUREAU	**BYROAD**
BODEGA	BOREAL	BRANNY	BRUISE	BURGEE	**BYSSUS**
BODICE	BOREEN	BRASHY	BRULOT	BURGER	*BYTALK

*BYWORD	BANDANA	BASTING	BECRAWL	*BEJEWEL	BESTEAD
*BYWORK	*BANDBOX	BASTION	BECRIME	BELABOR	BESTIAL
*BYZANT	BANDEAU	BATCHER	*BECROWD	BELACED	BESTREW
	BANDIED	*BATFISH	BECRUST	BELATED	BESTROW
BAALISM	BANDIES	*BATFOWL	BECURSE	BELCHER	BESWARM
BABASSU	BANDORA	BATHING	BEDDING	BELDAME	BETAINE
BABBITT	BANDORE	BATHMAT	BEDEMAN	BELIEVE	*BETAXED
BABBLER	BANEFUL	BATHTUB	BEDEVIL	BELLBOY	*BETHANK
BABESIA	*BANGKOK	*BATHYAL	BEDFAST	BELLEEK	*BETHINK
*BABICHE	BANKING	BATISTE	BEDGOWN	BELLHOP	BETHORN
*BABYISH	BANKSIA	BATLIKE	BEDIGHT	BELLIED	*BETHUMP
BACALAO	BANNING	BATSMAN	BEDIRTY	BELLIES	BETIMES
BACCARA	*BANNOCK	BATTEAU	*BEDIZEN	BELLMAN	BETOKEN
BACCATE	*BANQUET	BATTERY	BEDLAMP	BELOVED	BETROTH
*BACCHIC	BANSHEE	BATTIER	BEDLESS	BELTING	BETTING
*BACKFIT	BANSHIE	BATTING	BEDLIKE	*BELTWAY	BETWEEN
*BACKHOE	BANTENG	BATTLER	BEDMATE	BELYING	*BETWIXT
*BACKING	BAPTISE	BATWING	BEDOUIN	BEMADAM	BEVELER
*BACKLIT	BAPTISM	BAUSOND	BEDPOST	BENCHER	BEVOMIT
*BACKLOG	BAPTIST	*BAUXITE	BEDRAIL	BENEATH	*BEWEARY
*BACKOUT	*BAPTIZE	*BAWCOCK	BEDRAPE	BENEFIC	*BEWITCH
*BACKSAW	BARBATE	BAWDIER	*BEDROCK	BENEFIT	*BEWORRY
*BACKSET	BARBELL	BAWDIES	BEDROLL	BENEMPT	*BEZIQUE
BADGING	BARBULE	*BAWDILY	BEDROOM	BENISON	*BEZZANT
BADLAND	BARCHAN	*BAWDRIC	BEDSIDE	BENOMYL	*BHEESTY
BADNESS	BAREFIT	BAWSUNT	BEDSORE	BENTHAL	BHISTIE
*BAFFIES	BARGAIN	BAYONET	*BEDTICK	BENTHIC	*BIAXIAL
*BAFFLER	BARGING	*BAYWOOD	BEDTIME	BENTHOS	BIBASIC
BAGASSE	BARILLA	*BAZOOKA	BEDUNCE	*BENZENE	*BIBBERY
BAGGAGE	*BARKEEP	BEADIER	BEDWARD	*BENZINE	BIBBING
BAGGING	BARLESS	BEADILY	*BEDWARF	*BENZOIN	*BIBCOCK
BAGPIPE	BARMAID	BEADING	BEEFALO	*BENZOLE	BIBELOT
BAGSFUL	BARONET	BEADMAN	BEEFIER	*BENZOYL	BIBLESS
*BAGWORM	BARONNE	BEAMIER	*BEEFILY	BEPAINT	*BIBLIKE
BAHADUR	*BAROQUE	BEAMILY	*BEEHIVE	*BEQUEST	BIBLIST
*BAILIFF	*BARRACK	BEAMISH	BEELIKE	BEREAVE	BICOLOR
BAILOUT	BARRAGE	BEANBAG	BEELINE	BERETTA	BICORNE
BAIRNLY	BARRIER	BEANERY	*BEESWAX	BERGERE	*BICYCLE
*BAKLAVA	BARRING	BEARCAT	BEETLER	*BERHYME	BIDARKA
*BAKLAWA	BARROOM	BEARHUG	BEEYARD	BERLINE	BIDDING
BALANCE	BARTEND	BEARISH	*BEFLECK	BEROBED	BIFILAR
BALCONY	BARWARE	BEASTIE	BEGGARY	BERSEEM	BIFOCAL
BALDIES	BASCULE	BEASTLY	BEGGING	BERSERK	BIGFOOT
BALDISH	BASEMAN	*BEATIFY	BEGLOOM	BESCOUR	BIGGEST
BALDRIC	*BASENJI	BEATING	BEGONIA	BESEECH	BIGGETY
BALEFUL	*BASHFUL	BEATNIK	BEGORAH	BESHAME	BIGGING
BALLADE	*BASHLYK	BEBEERU	BEGORRA	BESHOUT	BIGGISH
BALLAST	BASILAR	BEBLOOD	BEGRIME	*BESHREW	BIGGITY
BALLIES	BASILIC	BECAUSE	BEGROAN	BESIDES	BIGHEAD
BALLOON	BASINET	*BECHALK	BEGUILE	BESIEGE	BIGHORN
BALLUTE	BASMATI	*BECHARM	BEGUINE	BESLIME	BIGNESS
BALNEAL	BASSIST	BECLASP	*BEHAVER	BESMEAR	BIGOTED
BALONEY	BASSOON	*BECLOAK	*BEHOOVE	BESMILE	BIGOTRY
BAMBINO	BASTARD	BECLOUD	BEIGNET	*BESMOKE	*BIKEWAY
BANDAGE	BASTILE	BECLOWN	*BEJESUS	*BESPEAK	BILAYER

BILIARY	BLABBER	BLUEISH	*BOOKFUL	*BOXFISH	BRICOLE
BILIOUS	*BLACKEN	*BLUEJAY	BOOKING	*BOXHAUL	BRIDLER
BILLBUG	*BLACKLY	*BLUFFER	*BOOKISH	*BOXIEST	BRIDOON
BILLIES	BLADDER	BLUNDER	BOOKLET	*BOXLIKE	BRIEFER
BILLING	BLAMING	BLUNGER	*BOOKMAN	*BOXWOOD	*BRIEFLY
BILLION	BLANKET	BLURTER	*BOOMBOX	*BOYCHIK	BRIGADE
*BILLOWY	*BLANKLY	BLUSHER	BOOMIER	BOYCOTT	BRIGAND
BILOBED	BLARNEY	BLUSTER	*BOOMKIN	*BOYHOOD	BRIMFUL
BILSTED	BLASTER	BOARDER	BOOMLET	BRABBLE	BRIMMED
BILTONG	BLASTIE	BOARISH	BOONIES	BRACERO	BRIMMER
BIMETAL	BLATANT	BOASTER	BOORISH	BRACHET	BRINDED
BIMODAL	BLATHER	BOATFUL	BOOSTER	BRACING	BRINDLE
BINDERY	BLATTED	BOATING	BOOTERY	*BRACKEN	BRINGER
BINDING	BLATTER	BOATMAN	BOOTIES	*BRACKET	BRINIER
BINNING	*BLAUBOK	*BOBBERY	BOOTLEG	BRADAWL	BRINIES
BINOCLE	*BLEAKLY	BOBBIES	BORACES	BRADOON	BRINING
*BIOCHIP	BLEATER	BOBBING	BORACIC	BRAGGER	BRINISH
BIOCIDE	BLEEDER	*BOBECHE	BORDURE	BRAIDER	BRIOCHE
BIOGENY	BLELLUM	BOBSLED	BOREDOM	BRAILLE	*BRIQUET
BIOHERM	BLEMISH	BOBSTAY	BORNEOL	BRAKING	BRISKET
BIOLOGY	BLENDER	BOBTAIL	BORNITE	BRALESS	*BRISKLY
BIOMASS	*BLESBOK	BODHRAN	BOROUGH	BRAMBLE	BRISSES
BIONICS	BLESSED	*BOFFOLA	BORSCHT	*BRAMBLY	BRISTLE
BIONOMY	BLESSER	BOGBEAN	BORSTAL	*BRANCHY	BRISTLY
BIOPSIC	BLETHER	BOGGIER	BOSCAGE	BRANDER	BRISTOL
BIOPTIC	*BLIGHTY	BOGGING	BOSKAGE	BRANNED	BRITSKA
BIOTICS	BLINDER	BOGGISH	*BOSQUET	BRANNER	BRITTLE
BIOTITE	BLINDLY	BOGGLER	BOSSDOM	BRASIER	BRITTLY
BIOTOPE	BLINKER	*BOGYISM	BOSSIER	BRASSIE	*BRITZKA
BIOTRON	*BLINTZE	*BOGYMAN	BOSSIES	BRATTLE	*BROADAX
BIOTYPE	BLISTER	BOHEMIA	BOSSISM	BRAVADO	BROADEN
BIPARTY	BLITHER	*BOILOFF	BOTANIC	*BRAVERY	BROADLY
BIPLANE	BLOATER	BOLETUS	BOTCHER	BRAVEST	BROCADE
BIPOLAR	*BLOCKER	BOLIVAR	BOTONEE	BRAVING	*BROCKET
BIRCHEN	BLOOMER	BOLIVIA	BOTTLER	BRAVURA	BROCOLI
BIRDING	BLOOPER	BOLLARD	BOTULIN	BRAWLER	BROIDER
BIRDMAN	BLOSSOM	BOLOGNA	BOUCHEE	BRAWLIE	BROILER
BIRETTA	*BLOTCHY	BOLONEY	BOUDOIR	*BRAZIER	BROKAGE
BIRLING	BLOTTED	BOLSHIE	BOULDER	*BRAZING	BROKING
BISCUIT	BLOTTER	BOLSTER	BOUNCER	BREADTH	BROMATE
BISMUTH	BLOUSON	BOMBARD	BOUNDEN	BREAKER	BROMIDE
BISNAGA	*BLOWFLY	BOMBAST	BOUNDER	*BREAKUP	BROMINE
BISTATE	BLOWGUN	BOMBING	*BOUQUET	*BREATHY	BROMISM
BISTORT	BLOWIER	*BONANZA	BOURBON	BRECCIA	*BROMIZE
BITABLE	*BLOWOFF	BONDAGE	BOURDON	*BRECHAM	BRONCHI
BITTERN	BLOWOUT	BONDING	BOURREE	BRECHAN	BRONCHO
BITTIER	BLOWSED	BONDMAN	*BOWHEAD	BREEDER	*BRONZER
BITTING	*BLOWZED	BONESET	*BOWKNOT	BREVIER	BROODER
*BITTOCK	BLUBBER	BONFIRE	BOWLDER	*BREVITY	BROOKIE
BITUMEN	BLUCHER	BONIEST	BOWLESS	BREWAGE	BROTHEL
*BIVALVE	BLUDGER	BONKERS	*BOWLFUL	*BREWERY	BROTHER
*BIVINYL	BLUECAP	*BONNOCK	*BOWLIKE	BREWING	BROUGHT
BIVOUAC	BLUEFIN	BOOBISH	BOWLINE	BRIBERY	BROWNIE
*BIZARRE	BLUEGUM	BOODLER	BOWLING	BRIBING	BROWSER
*BIZNAGA	BLUEING	BOOKEND	*BOWSHOT	*BRICKLE	BRUCINE

BRUISER	BULLIES	BUSSING	*BACKRUSH	BANDITRY	BARRATRY
BRUITER	BULLION	BUSTARD	*BACKSEAT	BANDSMAN	BARRETOR
BRULYIE	BULLISH	BUSTIER	*BACKSIDE	BANGTAIL	BARRETRY
*BRULZIE	*BULLOCK	BUTANOL	*BACKSLAP	BANISHER	BARRETTE
BRUSHER	BULLOUS	BUTCHER	*BACKSLID	BANISTER	BARSTOOL
BRUSHUP	BULLPEN	BUTLERY	*BACKSPIN	*BANJOIST	BARTERER
*BRUSQUE	BULRUSH	BUTTALS	*BACKSTAY	*BANKBOOK	BARTISAN
BRUTELY	*BULWARK	BUTTERY	*BACKSTOP	*BANKCARD	*BARTIZAN
*BRUTIFY	BUMBLER	BUTTIES	*BACKWARD	BANKNOTE	BARYTONE
BRUTING	BUMBOAT	*BUTTOCK	*BACKWASH	BANKROLL	BASALTES
BRUTISH	BUMMEST	BUTTONY	*BACKWOOD	*BANKRUPT	BASEBALL
BRUTISM	BUMMING	BUTYRAL	*BACKWRAP	*BANKSIDE	BASEBORN
*BRUXISM	*BUMPKIN	BUTYRIC	*BACKYARD	BANNERET	BASELESS
BUBALIS	BUNDIST	BUTYRIN	BACTERIA	BANNEROL	BASELINE
BUBBLER	BUNDLER	*BUTYRYL	BACTERIN	BANTERER	BASEMENT
BUBINGA	BUNGLER	*BUYBACK	BACULINE	BANTLING	BASENESS
BUBONIC	BUNRAKU	*BUZZARD	*BADGERLY	BAPTISIA	*BASICITY
*BUCKEEN	BUNTING	*BUZZWIG	BADINAGE	*BAPTIZER	BASIDIUM
*BUCKEYE	BUOYAGE	BYLINER	*BADMOUTH	BARATHEA	BASIFIER
*BUCKISH	BUOYANT		BAGHOUSE	BARBARIC	BASILARY
*BUCKLER	BURBLER	*BAASKAAP	*BAGPIPER	BARBASCO	BASILICA
*BUCKRAM	*BURDOCK	*BABBLING	BAGUETTE	BARBECUE	BASILISK
*BUCKSAW	BURETTE	BABIRUSA	*BAIDARKA	*BARBEQUE	BASINFUL
BUCOLIC	BURGAGE	*BABUSHKA	BAILMENT	*BARBERRY	*BASKETRY
BUDDIED	BURGEON	*BABYHOOD	BAILSMAN	BARBETTE	*BASOPHIL
BUDDIES	BURGESS	BACCARAT	*BAKEMEAT	BARBICAN	BASSINET
BUDDING	BURGHER	*BACCATED	*BAKESHOP	BARBICEL	BASSNESS
BUDGING	BURGLAR	*BACCHANT	*BAKSHISH	BARBITAL	BASSWOOD
BUDLESS	BURGOUT	*BACCHIUS	BALANCER	BARBLESS	BASTARDY
BUDLIKE	BURKITE	*BACHELOR	*BALDHEAD	*BARBWIRE	BASTILLE
*BUDWORM	BURLESK	BACILIAR	BALDNESS	*BAREBACK	*BATHETIC
*BUFFALO	BURNING	BACILLUS	BALDPATE	BAREBOAT	BATHLESS
*BUFFIER	BURNISH	*BACKACHE	*BALDRICK	BAREFOOT	*BATHROBE
*BUFFOON	BURNOUS	*BACKBEAT	BALEFIRE	BAREHEAD	*BATHROOM
BUGABOO	BURNOUT	*BACKBEND	BALISAUR	BARENESS	BATTALIA
BUGBANE	BURRIER	*BACKBITE	BALKLINE	BARESARK	BATTENER
BUGBEAR	BURRING	*BACKBONE	BALLGAME	BARGELLO	BATTERIE
BUGGERY	BURRITO	*BACKCAST	*BALLHAWK	BARGEMAN	BATTIEST
BUGGING	BURSARY	*BACKCHAT	BALLISTA	BARGHEST	*BAUDEKIN
BUGLOSS	BURSATE	*BACKDATE	BALLONET	BARGUEST	BAUDRONS
BUGSEED	BURSEED	*BACKDOOR	BALLONNE	BARITONE	BAUHINIA
BUILDER	BURSERA	*BACKDROP	BALLOTER	BARKLESS	BAWDIEST
BUILDUP	BURSTER	*BACKFILL	*BALLPARK	BARLEDUC	BAYADEER
BUIRDLY	BURTHEN	*BACKFIRE	BALLROOM	BARNACLE	BAYADERE
BULBLET	BURWEED	*BACKFLOW	*BALLYHOO	BARNYARD	*BAYBERRY
BULBOUS	BUSHIDO	*BACKHAND	BALLYRAG	BAROGRAM	BDELLIUM
BULIMIA	BUSHIER	*BACKHAUL	BALMORAL	BARONAGE	*BEACHBOY
BULIMIC	*BUSHILY	*BACKLAND	BALSAMIC	BARONESS	BEADIEST
BULKAGE	BUSHING	*BACKLASH	BALUSTER	BARONIAL	*BEADLIKE
BULLACE	BUSHMAN	*BACKLESS	BANALITY	*BAROUCHE	BEADROLL
BULLATE	*BUSHPIG	*BACKLIST	*BANALIZE	BARRABLE	BEADSMAN
BULLBAT	BUSHTIT	*BACKMOST	BANAUSIC	BARRANCA	*BEADWORK
BULLDOG	*BUSHWAH	*BACKPACK	BANDAGER	BARRANCO	BEAMIEST
BULLIED	BUSIEST	*BACKREST	BANDANNA	BARRATER	BEAMLESS
BULLIER	BUSLOAD	*BACKROOM	BANDEROL	BARRATOR	*BEAMLIKE

BEANBALL	BEGETTER	BEROUGED	*BIFACIAL	BIRACIAL	*BLENCHER
BEANLIKE	*BEGGARLY	BERRETTA	*BIFIDITY	BIRADIAL	*BLESBUCK
BEANPOLE	BEGINNER	*BESCORCH	BIFORATE	BIRAMOSE	BLESSING
BEARLIKE	BEGIRDLE	BESCREEN	*BIFORKED	BIRAMOUS	BLINDAGE
BEARSKIN	BEGLAMOR	BESETTER	*BIFORMED	*BIRDBATH	*BLINKARD
*BEATIFIC	BEGORRAH	*BESHADOW	BIGAMIES	BIRDCAGE	BLISTERY
BEATLESS	BEGOTTEN	*BESHIVER	BIGAMIST	BIRDCALL	*BLIZZARD
BEAUCOUP	BEGRUDGE	BESHROUD	BIGAMOUS	*BIRDFARM	*BLOCKADE
*BEAUTIFY	BEGUILER	BESIEGER	BIGARADE	*BIRDLIKE	*BLOCKAGE
*BEBOPPER	*BEHAVIOR	BESLAVED	BIGAROON	BIRDLIME	*BLOCKISH
BECARPET	*BEHEMOTH	*BESMIRCH	*BIGEMINY	BIRDSEED	BLONDISH
*BECHAMEL	BEHOLDEN	*BESMOOTH	*BIGMOUTH	BIRDSEYE	BLOODFIN
*BECHANCE	BEHOLDER	BESMUDGE	BIGNONIA	BIRDSHOT	BLOODIED
*BECKONER	*BEJABERS	BESOOTHE	*BIHOURLY	BIRDSONG	BLOODIER
BECLAMOR	*BEJEEZUS	BESOUGHT	*BIJUGATE	BIRRETTA	BLOODIES
*BECLOTHE	*BEJUMBLE	BESPOUSE	*BIJUGOUS	*BIRTHDAY	BLOODILY
*BECOMING	*BEKNIGHT	BESPREAD	BILABIAL	BISECTOR	BLOODING
*BECOWARD	BELABOUR	BESPRENT	BILANDER	*BISEXUAL	BLOODRED
BECUDGEL	BELIEVER	BESTIARY	*BILBERRY	BISTOURY	*BLOOMERY
*BEDABBLE	*BELIQUOR	BESTOWAL	BILINEAR	*BITCHERY	*BLOSSOMY
*BEDARKEN	BELITTLE	BESTRIDE	BILLETER	BITEWING	BLOTLESS
*BEDAZZLE	BELLBIRD	BETATRON	*BILLFISH	BITINGLY	BLOTTIER
*BEDCHAIR	BELLOWER	BETATTER	BILLFOLD	*BITSTOCK	BLOTTING
*BEDCOVER	BELLPULL	BETELNUT	BILLHEAD	BITTIEST	BLOVIATE
BEDEAFEN	BELLWORT	BETHESDA	*BILLHOOK	*BIUNIQUE	*BLOWBACK
BEDESMAN	*BELLYFUL	BETRAYAL	BILLIARD	BIVALENT	*BLOWBALL
*BEDFRAME	BELTLESS	BETRAYER	*BILLYCAN	*BIVALVED	*BLOWDOWN
BEDIAPER	BELTLINE	BEUNCLED	BILOBATE	*BIWEEKLY	*BLOWFISH
*BEDIMPLE	BEMADDEN	BEVATRON	BIMANOUS	*BIYEARLY	*BLOWHARD
*BEDMAKER	BEMINGLE	BEVELLER	BIMANUAL	*BLACKCAP	*BLOWHOLE
BEDOTTED	BEMUDDLE	BEVERAGE	BIMENSAL	*BLACKFIN	BLOWIEST
BEDPLATE	BEMURMUR	BEWAILER	BIMESTER	*BLACKFLY	*BLOWPIPE
*BEDQUILT	*BEMUZZLE	BEWILDER	*BIMETHYL	*BLACKGUM	*BLOWTUBE
*BEDRENCH	*BENDWAYS	*BEWINGED	BINAURAL	*BLACKING	*BLUBBERY
BEDRIVEL	BENDWISE	*BEWRAYER	*BINDWEED	*BLACKISH	BLUDGEON
BEDSHEET	*BENEDICK	BHEESTIE	BINNACLE	*BLACKLEG	BLUEBALL
BEDSONIA	BENEDICT	*BIACETYL	BINOMIAL	*BLACKOUT	BLUEBELL
BEDSTAND	*BENEFICE	BIANNUAL	BIOASSAY	*BLACKTOP	BLUEBILL
BEDSTEAD	*BENJAMIN	BIASNESS	BIOCLEAN	BLAMABLE	BLUEBIRD
BEDSTRAW	BENTWOOD	BIATHLON	*BIOCYCLE	*BLAMEFUL	*BLUEBOOK
*BEDWARDS	*BENZIDIN	BIBULOUS	*BIOETHIC	*BLANCHER	BLUECOAT
BEEBREAD	*BENZOATE	BICAUDAL	BIOGENIC	BLANDISH	*BLUEFISH
*BEECHNUT	*BEPIMPLE	*BICHROME	BIOLOGIC	BLASTEMA	BLUEGILL
*BEEFCAKE	*BEQUEATH	*BICKERER	BIOLYSIS	BLASTIER	BLUEHEAD
BEEFIEST	BERASCAL	BICOLOUR	*BIOMETRY	BLASTING	*BLUEJACK
BEEFLESS	BERBERIN	*BICONVEX	BIOPLASM	*BLASTOFF	BLUELINE
*BEEPWOOD	BERBERIS	*BICUSPID	BIOSCOPE	BLASTOMA	BLUENESS
BEESWING	BERCEUSE	*BICYCLER	*BIOSCOPY	BLASTULA	BLUENOSE
BEETROOT	*BERDACHE	*BICYCLIC	BIOTICAL	*BLATANCY	BLUESMAN
BEFINGER	BEREAVER	*BIDARKEE	*BIOTOXIN	BLATTING	BLUESTEM
*BEFLOWER	BERGAMOT	BIDDABLE	BIOVULAR	*BLAZONER	*BLUETICK
BEFOULER	BERIBERI	BIDENTAL	BIPAROUS	*BLAZONRY	BLUEWEED
BEFRIEND	BERINGED	BIENNALE	BIPARTED	*BLEACHER	BLUEWOOD
BEFRINGE	BERMUDAS	BIENNIAL	*BIPHASIC	*BLEAKISH	*BLUSHFUL
*BEFUDDLE	BERNICLE	BIENNIUM	*BIPHENYL	BLEEDING	BLUSTERY

BOARDING	BOOKREST	*BOYARISM	BRINIEST	BULLETIN	BUTYLENE
BOARDMAN	*BOOKSHOP	*BOYCHICK	BRISANCE	BULLFROG	BUTYRATE
*BOARFISH	*BOOKWORM	BRABBLER	BRISLING	BULLHEAD	BUTYROUS
BOASTFUL	BOOMIEST	BRACELET	*BRITCHES	BULLHORN	*BUZZWORD
BOATBILL	*BOOMTOWN	*BRACHIAL	*BRITZSKA	BULLIEST	BYSTREET
*BOATHOOK	*BOONDOCK	*BRACHIUM	*BROACHER	*BULLNECK	
BOATLIKE	*BOOTJACK	BRACIOLA	*BROADAXE	BULLNOSE	K B AR
BOATLOAD	BOOTLACE	BRACIOLE	BROADISH	BULLPOUT	M B IRA
BOATSMAN	BOOTLESS	*BRACKISH	BROCATEL	BULLRING	B IB B
BOATYARD	*BOOTLICK	BRACONID	BROCCOLI	BULLRUSH	CO B B
BOBBINET	BORACITE	BRACTLET	*BROCHURE	BULLSHOT	*JI B B
*BOBOLINK	*BORDEAUX	BRAGGART	*BROCKAGE	BULLWEED	KO B O
*BOBWHITE	BORDELLO	BRAGGEST	BROGUERY	BULLWHIP	MA B E
*BOCACCIO	BORDERER	BRAGGING	BROGUISH	*BULLYBOY	SI B B
BODEMENT	BORECOLE	BRAIDING	BROIDERY	BULLYRAG	VI B E
BODILESS	BOREHOLE	BRAINIER	BROMELIN	*BUMBLING	CA B O B
*BODINGLY	BORESOME	BRAINILY	*BROMIDIC	*BUNCOMBE	KA B A B
BODYSUIT	BORINGLY	BRAINISH	*BRONCHIA	BUNDLING	KA B O B
*BODYSURF	BORROWER	BRAINPAN	*BRONCHUS	BUNGALOW	KI B B E
*BODYWORK	*BOSCHBOK	*BRAKEAGE	*BRONZING	BUNGHOLE	KI B B I
*BOEHMITE	*BOSHVARK	*BRAKEMAN	BROOKITE	BUNGLING	KI B EI
*BOGEYMAN	BOTANICA	*BRANCHIA	BROOKLET	*BUNKMATE	NA B O B
BOGGIEST	BOTANIES	BRANDISH	*BROUGHAM	BUNTLINE	NO B LE
*BOHEMIAN	BOTANISE	BRANNING	*BROUHAHA	*BUOYANCE	PI B AL
BOISERIE	BOTANIST	BRANTAIL	*BROWBAND	*BUOYANCY	RA B AT
*BOLDFACE	*BOTANIZE	BRASILIN	*BROWBEAT	BURDENER	RE B AR
BOLDNESS	*BOTCHERY	BRASSAGE	BROWLESS	BURGLARY	RE B UY
*BOLLOCKS	*BOTHRIUM	BRASSARD	BROWNIER	BURGONET	TA B UN
*BOLLWORM	BOTONNEE	BRASSART	*BROWNISH	BURGRAVE	YO B B O
BOLTHEAD	BOTRYOID	BRASSICA	BROWNOUT	*BURGUNDY	BAB B LE
BOLTHOLE	BOTRYOSE	BRASSISH	BRUCELLA	BURNABLE	B A B IED
BOLTONIA	BOTRYTIS	BRATTICE	BRUNETTE	BURNOOSE	B A B IES
BOLTROPE	BOTTOMER	BRAUNITE	*BRUNIZEM	BURRIEST	B A B OOL
BOMBESIN	*BOTTOMRY	*BRAZENLY	BRUSHIER	BURROWER	B A B OON
*BOMBLOAD	BOTULISM	*BRAZILIN	*BRUSHOFF	BURSITIS	BIB B ED
*BOMBYCID	*BOUFFANT	*BREACHER	*BRYOLOGY	BURSTONE	BIB B ER
BONDMAID	*BOUGHPOT	*BREADBOX	*BRYOZOAN	*BUSHBUCK	BOB B ER
BONDSMAN	BOUGHTEN	BREADNUT	BUBALINE	BUSHELER	BOB B IN
*BONEFISH	BOUILLON	*BREAKAGE	*BUCKAROO	*BUSHFIRE	BOB B LE
BONEHEAD	BOUNDARY	*BREAKING	*BUCKAYRO	BUSHGOAT	BOB CAT
BONELESS	BOURGEON	BREAKOUT	*BUCKBEAN	BUSHIEST	B UB ALE
BONEMEAL	BOURTREE	BREATHER	*BUCKEROO	BUSHLAND	BUB B LE
BONEYARD	BOUSOUKI	BREEDING	*BUCKSHEE	BUSHLESS	*BUB B LY
BONGOIST	*BOUTIQUE	BRETHREN	*BUCKSHOT	*BUSHLIKE	CA B ALA
*BONHOMIE	*BOUZOUKI	*BREVETCY	*BUCKSKIN	BUSINESS	CA B ANA
*BONIFACE	*BOVINELY	*BREVIARY	*BUCKTAIL	BUSTLINE	CA B B IE
BONINESS	*BOVINITY	*BRICKBAT	BUDDLEIA	BUSULFAN	CA B LET
BONSPELL	*BOWFRONT	BRIDALLY	BUDGETER	*BUSYBODY	CA B MAN
BONSPIEL	*BOWINGLY	BRIDGING	*BUFFETER	BUSYNESS	CE B OID
*BONTEBOK	*BOWLLIKE	BRIEFING	*BUFFIEST	*BUSYWORK	CO B ALT
*BOOGYMAN	*BOWSPRIT	BRIGHTEN	BUGHOUSE	BUTANONE	COB B ER
*BOOKCASE	*BOXBERRY	*BRIMFULL	*BUHLWORK	*BUTCHERY	COB B LE
BOOKLORE	*BOXBOARD	BRIMLESS	BUILDING	BUTTONER	CO B NUT
*BOOKMARK	*BOXINESS	*BRIMMING	*BULKHEAD	BUTTRESS	*CO B WE B
*BOOKRACK	*BOXTHORN	BRINDLED	*BULLDOZE	BUTYLATE	CU B ISM

CU B IST	*HY B RID	RA B IES	SU B ITO	B O B STAY	GA B B LER
CU B OID	HY B RIS	RE B AIT	SU B LET	B O B TAIL	GA B ELLE
CY B ORG	*JA B B ER	RE B ATE	SU B LOT	B U B ALIS	GA B FEST
DA B B ER	*JA B IRU	RE B ATO	SU B MIT	B U B B IES	GI B B ING
DA B B LE	*JI B B ER	RE B ECK	SU B NET	B U B B LER	GI B B OSE
DE B ARK	*JO B B ER	RE B ILL	SU B ORN	B U B INGA	GI B B OUS
DE B ATE	*JU B B AH	RE B IND	SU B PAR	B U B ONIC	GO B B LER
DE B EAK	*JU B HAH	RE B ODY	SU B SEA	CA B ARET	GO B IOID
DE B ONE	*JU B ILE	RE B OIL	SU B SET	CA B B AGE	GO B ONEE
DE B RIS	*KA B AKA	RE B OOK	SU B TLE	CA B B ALA	HA B ITAN
DE B TOR	KA B ALA	RE B OOT	SU B UR B	CA B B ING	HA B ITAT
DE B UNK	*KA B AYA	RE B ORE	SU B WAY	*CA B EZON	HA B ITUE
DI B B ER	*KA B IKI	RE B ORN	TA B ARD	CA B ILDO	HA B ITUS
DI B B LE	*KA B UKI	*RE B OZO	TA B B ED	CA B INET	HE B ETIC
*DI B B UK	KE B B IE	RE B UFF	TA B B IS	CA B LING	*HI B ACHI
DO B B ER	*KE B LAH	RE B UKE	TA B LET	*CA B OM B A	HO B B IES
DO B B IN	*KI B B EH	RE B URY	TA B OUR	CA B OOSE	HO B B LER
DO B LON	KI B B LE	RI B ALD	TA B ULI	CI B OULE	*HO B B NO B
DU B B ER	*KI B ITZ	RI B AND	TU B ATE	CO B B IER	*HO B LIKE
DU B B IN	*KI B LAH	RI B B ED	TU B B ED	CO B B LER	HO B NAIL
*DY B B UK	*KI B OSH	RI B B ER	TU B B ER	CU B B AGE	HO B OISM
FA B LER	KO B OLD	RI B B ON	TU B FUL	CU B B ING	*JA B B ING
FA B RIC	*KY B OSH	RI B IER	TU B IST	*CU B B ISH	*JI B B ING
FI B B ER	LA B IAL	RI B LET	TU B ULE	CU B ICAL	*JI B B OOM
FI B RIL	LA B IUM	RI B OSE	VI B IST	CU B ICLE	*JO B B ERY
FI B RIN	LA B OUR	RO B ALO	VI B RIO	*CU B ICLY	*JO B B ING
GA B B ED	LA B RET	RO B AND	WA B B LE	DA B B LER	*JO B LESS
GA B B ER	LA B RUM	RO B B ED	*WA B B LY	DA B STER	*JO B NAME
GA B B LE	LI B B ER	RO B B ER	*WE B FED	DE B ACLE	*JU B ILEE
GA B B RO	LI B IDO	RO B B IN	WO B B LE	DE B ASER	*KA B ALAH
GA B IES	LI B LA B	RO B UST	*WO B B LY	DE B ATER	*KE B B OCK
GA B ION	LO B ATE	RU B ACE	YA B B ER	*DE B AUCH	*KE B B OCK
GA B OON	LO B B ED	RU B ATO	*ZE B ECK	DE B ONER	*KI B B ITZ
GI B B ER	LO B B ER	RU B B ED	*ZI B ETH	*DE B OUCH	*KI B B UTZ
GI B B ET	LO B ULE	RU B B ER	B A B ASSU	DE B RIDE	LA B ARUM
GI B B ON	LU B B ER	RU B B LE	BAB B ITT	DE B RIEF	LA B ELER
GI B LET	LU B RIC	RU B IED	BA B B LER	DI B ASIC	LA B ELLA
GI B SON	MO B LED	RU B IER	BA B ESIA	DI B B ING	LA B IATE
GO B ANG	NE B ULA	RU B IES	*B A B ICHE	DI B B LER	LA B ORER
GO B B ED	NE B ULE	RU B IGO	*B A B YISH	DO B B IES	LA B ROID
GO B B ER	NE B ULY	RU B OFF	B E B EERU	DU B B ING	LI B ELEE
GO B B LE	NO B ODY	RU B OUT	B E B LOOD	DU B IETY	LI B ELER
GO B IES	NU B B IN	RU B RIC	B I B ASIC	DU B IOUS	LI B ERAL
GO B LET	NU B B LE	SA B B AT	*B I B B ERY	FA B LIAU	LI B ERTY
GO B LIN	NU B B LY	SA B B ED	B I B B ING	FA B LING	LI B RARY
GO B ONY	NU B ILE	SA B INE	*B I B COCK	FA B ULAR	LI B RATE
HA B ILE	PA B LUM	SO B B ER	B I B ELOT	FE B RILE	LO B ATED
HA B OO B	PE B B LE	SO B EIT	B I B LESS	FI B ROID	LO B B ING
HO B B IT	*PE B B LY	SO B FUL	*B I B LIKE	FI B ROIN	LO B B YER
HO B B LE	PU B LIC	SU B B ED	B I B LIST	FI B ROMA	LO B EFIN
HO B NO B	RA B ATO	SU B DE B	*B O B B ERY	FI B ROUS	LO B ELIA
*HU B B LY	RA B B ET	SU B DUE	B O B B IES	GA B B ARD	LO B STER
*HU B B UB	RA B B IN	*SU B FIX	B O B B ING	GA B B ART	LO B WORM
*HU B CAP	RA B B IT	SU B GUM	*B O B ECHE	GA B B IER	*MO B B ISH
HU B RIS	RA B B LE		B O B SLED	GA B B ING	

MO B ILIS	SA B B ING	SU B SIST	*BAB B LING	CRI B ROUS	GLO B ULAR
MO B OCRA	SE B ACIC	SU B SITE	BAR B ARIC	*CRI B WORK	GLO B ULIN
NE B B ISH	SE B ASIC	SU B SOIL	BAR B ASCO	CUM B ERER	GOM B ROON
NI B B ILE	SI B LING	SU B SUME	BAR B ECUE	CUM B ROUS	GOR B ELLY
NI B B LER	SO B ERLY	SU B TASK	*BAR B EQUE	*CUP B OARD	*GOR B LIMY
*NI B LICK	SU B ACID	SU B TEEN	*BAR B ERRY	CUR B SIDE	GRA B B IER
NI B LIKE	SU B ADAR	SU B TEND	BAR B ETTE	*CYM B ALER	GRA B B ING
NO B B IER	SU B ALAR	SU B TEST	BAR B ICAN	*CYM B ALOM	GRA B B LER
NO B B ILY	SU B AREA	*SU B TEXT	BAR B ICEL	*CYM B IDIA	*GRUB B WORM
NO B B LER	SU B ARID	SU B TILE	BAR B ITAL	*CYM B LING	GUM B OTIL
NO B LEST	SU B ATOM	SU B TONE	BAR B LESS	DA B B LING	*HAG B ERRY
NU B B IER	SU B B ASE	SU B TYPE	*BAR B WIRE	*DAY B REAK	HAR B ORER
NU B B LES	SU B B ASS	SU B UNIT	B EE B READ	*DEW B ERRY	HER B ARIA
PA B ULUM	SU B B ING	SU B VENE	B ER B ERIN	DIA B ETES	HER B IEST
*PI B ROCH	SU B CELL	SU B VERT	B ER B ERIS	DIA B ETIC	HER B LESS
PU B ERTY	SU B CLAN	*SU B ZERO	B IL B ERRY	DIA B LERY	*HER B LIKE
PU B LISH	SU B CODE	*SU B ZONE	*BLU B BERY	DIA B OLIC	*HO B B YIST
RA B B ITY	SU B COOL	TA B ANID	B OB B INET	DIO B OLON	HOT B LOOD
RA B B LER	SU B CULT	TA B ARET	B OM B ESIN	DIS B OSOM	*HUM B LEST
RA B B ONI	SU B DEAN	TA B B IED	*BOMB B LOAD	DIS B URSE	*HUM B LING
RE B ATER	SU B DUAL	TA B B IES	*BOMB B YCID	*DOG B ERRY	*JA B B ERER
RE B EGIN	SU B DUCE	TA B B ING	*BOX B ERRY	DOU B LING	*JAM B OREE
RE B IRTH	SU B DUCT	TA B ETIC	*BOX B OARD	DOU B LOON	*JAW B ONER
RE B LEND	SU B DUER	TA B LEAU	B RA B B LER	DOU B LURE	*KAB B ALAH
RE B LOOM	SU B ECHO	TA B LING	*BUM B LING	DOU B TFUL	*KEY B OARD
RE B OANT	SU B EDIT	TA B LOID	*CAB B ALAH	DRA B NESS	KOL B ASSI
RE B OARD	SU B ERIC	TA B ORER	*CAM B OGIA	DRI B B LER	LAM B ASTE
RE B OUND	SU B ERIN	TA B ORET	*CAR B AMIC	DRI B B LET	*LAM B ENCY
RE B REED	SU B FILE	TA B ORIN	*CAR B AMYL	DRU B B ING	LAM B IEST
RE B UILD	SU B FUSC	TA B OULI	*CAR B ARYL	*DUMB B ELL	*LAM B KILL
RE B UKER	SU B GOAL	TA B ULAR	CAR B INOL	*DUMB B CANE	*LAM B LIKE
RI B B AND	SU B HEAD	TO B ACCO	CAR B OLIC	*DUMB B HEAD	*LAM B SKIN
RI B B IER	SU B IDEA	TU B AIST	*CAR B ONYL	DUM B NESS	LAP B OARD
RI B B ING	SU B ITEM	TU B B ING	*CAR B OXYL	FAU B OURG	LAR B OARD
RI B B ONY	*SU B JECT	*TU B IFEX	CAR B URET	*FEE B LISH	LEE B OARD
RI B LESS	*SU B JOIN	TU B LIKE	CAT B RIER	FLA B ELLA	LIM B LESS
RI B LIKE	SU B LATE	TU B ULAR	*CHU B ASCO	*FOG B OUND	LIM B TEST
RI B WORT	SU B LIME	TU B ULIN	*CIM B ALOM	FOR B IDAL	*LOB B YGOW
RO B B ERY	SU B LINE	VE B ROSE	CLU B A B LE	FOR B ORNE	*LO B B YISM
RO B B ING	SU B MENU	VI B RANT	*CLU B B ING	*FRA B JOUS	*LO B B YIST
RO B OTRY	SU B MISS	VI B RATE	*CLU B FOOT	*FRI B B LER	LUM B ERER
RO B USTA	SU B ORAL	VI B RATO	*CLU B HAND	*FUR B ELOW	*MOP B OARD
RU B A B OO	SU B OVAL	VI B RION	*CLU B HAUL	GAL B ANUM	*MOR B IFIC
RU B ASSE	SU B PART	WA B B LER	CLU B ROOT	GAM B ESON	*MUL B ERRY
RU B B ERY	SU B PENA	*WE B B ING	CO B B IEST	GAM B USIA	*MYO B LAST
RU B B ING	SU B PLOT	*WE B FOOT	COM B ATER	*GAR B ANZO	NO B B IEST
RU B B ISH	SU B RACE	WE B LESS	COM B INER	GAR B LESS	NON B ASIC
RU B DOWN	SU B RENT	*WE B LIKE	*COM B INGS	GAR B OARD	NON B EING
RU B ELLA	SU B RING	WE B STER	*COM B LIKE	GER B ILLE	*NON B LACK
RU B EOLA	SU B RULE	*WE B WORM	*COW B ERRY	GI B B SITE	NON B RAND
RU B IEST	SU B SALE	*WE B WORM	CRA B MEAT	GLA B ELLA	NU B B IEST
RU B IOUS	SU B SECT	WO B B LER	*CRA B WISE	GLA B RATE	NUM B ERER
SA B ATON	SU B SERE	*ZE B B RASS	*CRI B B AGE	GLA B ROUS	*NUM B FISH
SA B AYON	SU B SIDE	*ZE B RINE	*CRI B B ING	GLI B NESS	NUM B NESS
SA B B ATH	SU B SIDY	*ZE B ROID	*CRI B B LED	GLO B ATED	NUT B ROWN

PAN B ROIL	*SNO B B ERY	TUR B INAL	GLO B	KEDA B	SU B DE B
PEG B OARD	SNO B B IER	TUR B OCAR	GRA B	KERO B	SU B UR B
PLE B EIAN	*SNO B B ILY	TUR B OFAN	GRU B	NA B O B	SUPER B
*POT B ELLY	*SNO B B ISH	*TUR B OJET	HER B	NAWA B	B ATHTU B
PRE B ASAL	SNO B B ISM	*VAM B RACE	*JAM B	PLUM B	CORNCO B
PRE B LESS	SNU B NESS	*VER B ALLY	*JI B B	REDU B	COULOM B
PRE B OUND	SOM B RERO	*VER B ATIM	KER B	REHA B	*COWHER B
PRO B A B LE	SOM B ROUS	VER B IAGE	KNO B	RHOM B	*COXCOM B
*PRO B A B LY	SOR B ITOL	VER B LESS	LAM B	RHUM B	DISTUR B
PUR B LIND	*SOW B ELLY	VER B OTEN	LIM B	SAHI B	*FLU B DU B
*QUI B B LER	SOW B READ	*WAX B ERRY	NUM B	SCRU B	*HO B B NO B
RA B B ITER	STA B LEST	*ZAI B ATSU	PLE B	SHRU B	MINICA B
*RA B B ITRY	STA B LING	*ZOM B IISM	SCA B	SLUR B	MINILA B
RAM B UTAN	STA B LISH		SI B B	*SQUA B	PEDICA B
RAW B ONED	STI B NITE	B AR B	SLA B	*SQUI B	PERTUR B
REA B SOR B	STU B B IER	BIB B	SLO B	THRO B	POTHER B
*RED B RICK	*STU B B ILY	B LA B	SLU B	THUM B	PROVER B
*REO B JECT	STU B B ING	B LE B	SNI B	*ZINE B	REPLUM B
REO B TAIN	STU B B ORN	B LO B	SNO B	B AO B A B	RHU B AR B
*RHA B DOME	SU B B REED	B LU B	SNU B	B EDAU B	SANDDA B
RI B B IEST	*SUN B AKED	B OM B	SOR B	B EDUM B	*SUCCUM B
RUB B ABOO	SUN B ATHE	B OO B	STA B	B ICAR B	*TAXICA B
RUM B LING	*SUN B LOCK	B UL B	STO B	CHERU B	*WASHTU B
SA B B ATIC	SUN B URST	CHU B	STU B	*CO B WE B	*CATACOM B
SAW B ONES	*SYM B IONT	CLU B	SWA B	CONFA B	*CHORIAM B
*SCA B BARD	*SYM B IOTE	CO B B	SWO B	*CORYM B	CORNCRI B
SCA B IOSA	*SYM B OLIC	COM B	TOM B	DENUM B	*DIVE B OM B
SCA B IOUS	TAG B OARD	CRA B	VER B	DESOR B	*DOORJAM B
SCA B LAND	TAM B OURA	CRI B	WOM B	HA B OO B	*DOORKNO B
*SCA B LIKE	TAR B OOSH	CUR B	B LUR B	HO B NO B	*FIRE B OM B
SCA B ROUS	TEA B ERRY	DAR B	CA B O B	*HU B B U B	*FORELIM B
*SEA B EACH	TEA B OARD	DAU B	CARO B	LI B LA B	*HECATOM B
SEA B OARD	THE B AINE	DRA B	CELE B	MIDRI B	LANDGRA B
SEA B ORNE	TOL B OOTH	DRI B	CHIM B	MIHRA B	*MEMSAHI B
*SKY B ORNE	TOM B LESS	DRU B	CLIM B	MILNE B	REA B SOR B
*SLA B ERY	*TOM B LIKE	DUM B	CLOM B	PREFA B	SILLA B U B
SLA B B ING	TRA B EATE	FLA B	COOM B	RECOM B	SILLI B U B
SLA B LIKE	TRI B ASIC	FLU B	CRUM B	RESOR B	SPARERI B
*SLO B B ERY	*TRI B RACH	FOR B	CURE B	REVER B	*SU B SHRU B
*SLO B B ISH	TRI B UNAL	GAM B	DEMO B	SCARA B	*SYLLABUB
SLU B B ING	TUB B ABLE	GAR B	KA B A B	SERDA B	*WELLCUR B
SLY B OOTS	TUM B LING	GLI B	KA B O B	SKI B O B	

C

CACA	CAIN	CALX	CARD	CASA	CAVY
CADE	CAKE	CAME	CARE	CASE	CEDE
CADI	CAKY	CAMP	CARK	CASH	CEDI
CAFE	CALF	CANE	CARL	CASK	CEIL
CAFF	CALK	CANT	CARN	CAST	CELL
CAGE	CALL	CAPE	CARP	CATE	CELT
CAGY	CALM	CAPH	CARR	CAUL	CENT
CAID	CALO	CAPO	CART	CAVE	CEPE

CERE	**COAX**	CRAB	CAIRD	**CAULK**	*CHEVY
CERO	**COBB**	CRAG	CAIRN	CAUSE	*CHEWY
CESS	COCA	CRAM	**CAJON**	**CAVED**	CHIAO
CETE	**COCK**	CRAP	**CAKEY**	**CAVER**	*CHICK
CHAD	COCO	CRAW	**CALIF**	CAVIE	CHICO
CHAM	CODA	CREW	**CALIX**	**CAVIL**	CHIDE
CHAO	CODE	CRIB	CALLA	CEASE	**CHIEF**
CHAP	COED	CRIS	**CALVE**	**CEBID**	**CHIEL**
CHAR	**COFF**	CROC	*CALYX	**CECUM**	**CHILD**
CHAT	COFT	CROP	CAMAS	CEDAR	**CHILE**
CHAW	COHO	CROW	CAMEL	CEDER	**CHILI**
CHAY	COIL	CRUD	CAMEO	CEIBA	**CHILL**
CHEF	COIN	CRUS	**CAMPI**	CELEB	**CHIMB**
CHEW	COIR	**CRUX**	**CAMPO**	CELLA	**CHIME**
*CHEZ	**COKE**	CUBE	**CAMPY**	CELLO	**CHIMP**
CHIA	COLA	**CUFF**	CANAL	CELOM	**CHINA**
CHIC	COLD	CUIF	**CANDY**	CENSE	**CHINE**
CHIC	COLE	**CUKE**	CANER	CENTO	**CHINK**
CHIN	COLT	CULL	CANID	CEORL	**CHINO**
CHIP	COLY	CULM	CANNA	CERED	**CHIRK**
CHIT	COMA	CULT	**CANNY**	CERIA	**CHIRM**
CHON	**COMB**	CURB	CANOE	CERIC	**CHIRO**
CHOP	COME	CURD	CANON	CESTA	**CHIRP**
CHOW	**COMP**	CURE	CANSO	CESTI	**CHIRR**
CHUB	CONE	CURF	CANST	**CHAFE**	**CHIVE**
CHUG	CONI	CURL	CANTO	*CHAFF	*CHIVY
CHUM	**CONK**	CURN	**CANTY**	**CHAIN**	*CHOCK
CIAO	CONN	CURR	CAPER	**CHAIR**	**CHOIR**
CINE	CONY	CURT	CAPON	**CHALK**	**CHOKE**
CION	COOF	**CUSK**	CAPUT	**CHAMP**	*CHOKY
CIRE	**COOK**	CUSP	CARAT	**CHANG**	**CHOLO**
CIST	COOL	CUSS	CARBO	**CHANT**	**CHOMP**
CITE	COON	CUTE	CARER	**CHAOS**	**CHOOK**
CITY	COOP	CYAN	CARET	**CHAPE**	**CHORD**
CLAD	COOT	**CYMA**	**CAREX**	**CHAPT**	**CHORE**
CLAG	COPE	**CYME**	CARGO	**CHARD**	**CHOSE**
CLAM	**COPY**	CYST	CARLE	**CHARE**	**CHOTT**
CLAN	CORD	*CZAR	**CARNY**	**CHARK**	*CHUCK
CLAP	CORE	CABAL	CAROB	**CHARM**	**CHUFA**
CLAW	**CORK**	**CABBY**	CAROL	**CHARR**	*CHUFF
CLAY	CORM	CABER	CAROM	**CHART**	**CHUMP**
CLEF	CORN	CABIN	CARPI	**CHARY**	**CHUNK**
CLEW	CORY	CABLE	**CARRY**	**CHASE**	**CHURL**
CLIP	COSH	**CABOB**	CARSE	**CHASM**	**CHURN**
CLOD	COSS	CACAO	CARTE	**CHEAP**	**CHURR**
CLOG	COST	**CACHE**	**CARVE**	**CHEAT**	**CHUTE**
CLON	COSY	**CADDY**	CASED	**CHEEK**	**CHYLE**
CLOP	COTE	CADET	**CASKY**	**CHEEP**	*CHYME
CLOT	COUP	CADGE	CASTE	**CHEER**	CIBOL
CLOY	COVE	**CADGY**	CASUS	CHELA	CIDER
CLUB	COWL	CADRE	**CATCH**	**CHERT**	CIGAR
CLUE	**COWY**	CAGER	CATER	**CHESS**	CILIA
COAL	COXA	**CAGEY**	**CATTY**	**CHEST**	*CIMEX
COAT	*COZY	**CAHOW**	CAULD	**CHETH**	**CINCH**

CIRCA	CLOWN	CONIC	CRAAL	CRUMP	CYDER
CIRRI	*CLOZE	CONIN	CRACK	CRUOR	*CYLIX
CISCO	CLUCK	CONKY	CRAFT	CRUSE	CYMAR
CISSY	CLUMP	CONTE	CRAKE	CRUSH	CYMOL
CITER	CLUNG	CONTO	CRAMP	CRUST	CYNIC
CIVET	CLUNK	CONUS	CRANE	CRWTH	CYTON
CIVIC	COACH	COOCH	CRANK	CRYPT	CABALA
CIVIE	COACT	COOEE	CRAPE	CUBBY	CABANA
CIVIL	COALA	COOER	CRASH	CUBEB	CABBIE
*CIVVY	COALY	COOEY	CRASS	CUBER	CABLET
CLACH	COAPT	COOKY	CRATE	CUBIC	CABMAN
CLACK	COAST	COOLY	CRAVE	CUBIT	CACHET
CLADE	COATI	COOMB	CRAWL	CUDDY	CACHOU
CLAIM	COBBY	COOPT	*CRAZE	CUING	CACKLE
CLAMP	COBIA	COPAL	*CRAZY	CUISH	CACTUS
CLANG	COBLE	COPEN	CREAK	CULCH	CADDIE
CLANK	COBRA	COPER	CREAM	CULET	CADDIS
CLARO	COCCI	COPRA	CREDO	CULEX	CADENT
CLARY	*COCKY	COPSE	CREED	CULLY	CADGER
CLASH	COCOA	CORAL	CREEK	CULPA	CAECUM
CLASP	CODEC	CORBY	CREEL	CULTI	CAEOMA
CLASS	CODED	CORER	CREEP	CUMIN	CAESAR
CLAST	CODEN	CORGI	CREME	CUPEL	CAFTAN
CLAVE	CODER	CORKY	CREPE	CUPID	CAGIER
CLAVI	*CODEX	CORNU	CREPT	CUPPA	CAGILY
CLEAN	CODON	CORNY	CREPY	CUPPY	CAGING
CLEAR	COGON	CORPS	CRESS	CURCH	CAHIER
CLEAT	COHOG	CORSE	CREST	CURDY	CAHOOT
CLEEK	COIGN	COSEC	CRICK	CURER	CAIMAN
CLEFT	COLIC	COSET	CRIED	CURET	*CAIQUE
CLEPE	COLIN	COSEY	CRIER	CURIA	*CAJOLE
CLERK	COLLY	COSIE	CRIES	CURIE	CALAMI
CLICK	COLOG	COSTA	CRIME	CURIO	CALASH
CLIFF	COLON	COTAN	CRIMP	CURLY	CALCAR
CLIFT	COLOR	COTTA	CRIPE	CURRY	CALCES
CLIMB	*COLZA	COUCH	CRISP	CURSE	CALCIC
CLIME	COMAL	COUDE	CROAK	CURST	CALESA
CLINE	COMBE	COUGH	CROCI	CURVE	CALICO
CLING	COMBO	COULD	CROCK	CURVY	CALIPH
CLINK	COMER	COUNT	CROFT	CUSEC	CALKER
	COMET	COUPE	CRONE	CUSHY	CALKIN
CLIPT	*COMFY	COURT	CRONY	CUSSO	CALLAN
CLOAK	COMIC	COUTH	CROOK	CUTCH	CALLER
CLOCK	*COMIX	COVEN	CROON	CUTES	CALLET
CLOMB	COMMA	COVER	CRORE	CUTEY	CALLOW
CLOMP	COMMY	COVET	CROSS	CUTIE	CALLUS
CLONE	COMPO	COVEY	CROUP	CUTIN	CALORY
CLONK	COMPT	COVIN	CROWD	CUTIS	CALPAC
CLOOT	COMTE	COWER	CROWN	CUTTY	*CALQUE
CLOSE	CONCH	COWRY	*CROZE	CUTUP	CALVES
CLOTH	CONDO	COYLY	CRUCK	CYANO	CAMAIL
CLOUD	CONEY	COYPU	CRUDE	CYCAD	CAMASS
CLOUR	CONGA	*COZEN	CRUEL	CYCAS	CAMBER
CLOUT	CONGE	*COZEY	CRUET	CYCLE	CAMBIA
CLOVE	CONGO	*COZIE	CRUMB	CYCLO	CAMERA

CAMION	CARBOY	CASUAL	CEREUS	*CHEEKY	CHORUS
CAMISA	CARCEL	CATALO	CERING	CHEERY	CHOSEN
CAMISE	CARDER	*CATCHY	CERIPH	CHEESE	*CHOUGH
CAMLET	CARDIA	CATENA	CERISE	CHEESY	CHOUSE
CAMPER	CAREEN	CATGUT	CERITE	CHEGOE	CHOUSH
CAMPUS	CAREER	CATION	CERIUM	*CHEMIC	CHOWSE
CANAPE	CARESS	CATKIN	CERMET	*CHEQUE	CHRISM
CANARD	CARFUL	CATLIN	CEROUS	CHERRY	CHROMA
CANARY	CARHOP	CATNAP	CERTES	CHERTY	CHROME
CANCAN	CARIBE	CATNIP	CERUSE	CHERUB	CHROMO
CANCEL	CARIES	CATSUP	CERVID	CHESTY	*CHUBBY
CANCER	CARINA	CATTED	*CERVIX	CHETAH	*CHUCKY
CANCHA	CARING	CATTIE	CESIUM	CHEVRE	*CHUFFY
CANDID	CARLIN	CATTLE	CESTOS	CHEWER	*CHUKAR
CANDLE	CARMAN	CAUCUS	CESTUS	CHIASM	*CHUKKA
CANDOR	CARNAL	CAUDAD	CESURA	CHIAUS	*CHUMMY
CANFUL	CARNET	CAUDAL	CETANE	*CHICHI	*CHUNKY
CANGUE	CARNEY	*CAUDEX	*CHABUK	CHICLE	*CHURCH
CANINE	CARNIE	CAUDLE	*CHACMA	*CHICLY	*CHYMIC
CANING	CAROCH	CAUGHT	CHADAR	CHIDER	CICADA
CANKER	CAROLI	CAULES	CHADOR	CHIELD	CICALA
CANNED	CARPAL	CAULIS	CHAETA	CHIGOE	CICELY
CANNEL	CARPEL	CAUSAL	CHAFER	CHILDE	CICERO
CANNER	CARPER	CAUSER	*CHAFFY	CHILLI	CILICE
CANNIE	CARPET	CAUSEY	CHAINE	CHILLY	CILIUM
CANNON	CARPUS	CAVEAT	CHAISE	CHIMAR	CINDER
CANNOT	CARREL	CAVERN	*CHAKRA	CHIMER	CINEMA
CANOLA	CARROM	CAVIAR	CHALAH	CHIMLA	CINEOL
CANOPY	CARROT	CAVIES	CHALEH	*CHINCH	*CINQUE
CANTER	CARTEL	CAVING	CHALET	*CHINKY	CIPHER
CANTIC	CARTER	CAVITY	*CHALKY	CHINTS	CIRCLE
CANTLE	CARTON	CAVORT	CHALLA	*CHINTZ	CIRCUS
CANTON	CARTOP	CAYMAN	CHALLY	*CHIPPY	*CIRQUE
CANTOR	CARVEL	CAYUSE	CHALOT	CHIRAL	CIRRUS
CANTUS	CARVEN	CEBOID	*CHAMMY	*CHIRPY	CISTUS
CANULA	CARVER	CEDING	*CHAMPY	CHIRRE	CITHER
CANVAS	CASABA	CEDULA	CHANCE	CHISEL	CITIED
CANYON	CASAVA	CEILER	*CHANCY	CHITAL	CITIES
CAPFUL	CASBAH	CELERY	CHANGE	CHITIN	CITIFY
CAPIAS	CASEFY	CELIAC	CHANTY	CHITON	CITING
CAPITA	CASEIN	CELLAR	CHAPEL	CHITTY	CITOLA
CAPLET	CASERN	CEMENT	CHARAS	*CHIVVY	CITOLE
CAPLIN	CASHAW	CENOTE	CHARGE	CHOANA	CITRAL
CAPOTE	CASHEW	CENSER	CHARRO	CHOICE	CITRIC
CAPPED	CASHOO	CENSOR	CHARRY	*CHOKER	CITRIN
CAPPER	CASING	CENSUS	CHASER	*CHOKEY	CITRON
CAPRIC	CASINO	CENTAL	CHASSE	CHOLER	CITRUS
CAPRIS	CASITA	CENTER	CHASTE	CHOLLA	CIVICS
CAPSID	CASKET	CENTRA	CHATTY	CHOOSE	CIVISM
CAPTAN	*CASQUE	CENTRE	CHAUNT	CHOOSY	*CLAMMY
CAPTOR	CASSIA	CENTUM	CHAWER	CHOPIN	CLAMOR
CARACK	CASSIS	CERATE	*CHAZAN	*CHOPPY	*CLAQUE
CARAFE	CASTER	CERCIS	CHEAPO	CHORAL	CLARET
CARATE	CASTLE	CERCUS	*CHEBEC	CHOREA	CLASSY
CARBON	CASTOR	CEREAL	CHEDER	CHORIC	CLAUSE

CLAVER	COBNUT	COLLOP	COOKIE	COSIES	*CRAPPY
CLAVUS	*COBWEB	COLONE	COOLER	COSIGN	CRASES
CLAWER	COCAIN	COLONI	COOLIE	COSILY	CRASIS
*CLAXON	COCCAL	COLONY	COOLLY	COSINE	CRATCH
CLAYEY	COCCIC	COLOUR	COOLTH	COSMIC	CRATER
CLEAVE	COCCID	COLTER	COOMBE	COSMOS	CRATON
CLENCH	COCCUS	COLUGO	COOPER	COSSET	CRAVAT
CLEOME	*COCCYX	COLUMN	COOTER	COSTAR	CRAVEN
CLERGY	COCHIN	COLURE	COOTIE	COSTER	CRAVER
CLERIC	COCKER	COMAKE	COPALM	COSTLY	CRAWLY
CLERID	COCKLE	COMATE	*COPECK	COTEAU	CRAYON
CLEVER	*COCKUP	COMBAT	COPIED	COTING	*CREAKY
CLEVIS	COCOON	COMBER	COPIER	COTTAR	CREAMY
CLICHE	CODDED	COMEDO	COPIES	COTTER	CREASE
CLIENT	CODDER	COMEDY	COPING	COTTON	CREASY
*CLIFFY	CODDLE	COMELY	COPLOT	COTYPE	CREATE
*CLIMAX	CODEIA	COMETH	COPPED	COUGAR	CRECHE
CLINAL	CODEIN	COMFIT	COPPER	COULEE	CREDAL
CLINCH	CODGER	COMING	COPPRA	COUNTY	CREDIT
CLINGY	*CODIFY	COMITY	COPRAH	COUPLE	CREEPY
CLINIC	CODING	COMMIE	COPTER	COUPON	CREESE
*CLIQUE	CODLIN	COMMIT	COPULA	COURSE	CREESH
*CLIQUY	COELOM	*COMMIX	*COQUET	COUSIN	CRENEL
CLITIC	COEMPT	COMMON	CORBAN	COUTER	CREOLE
CLIVIA	COERCE	COMOSE	CORBEL	COVERT	CREPEY
CLOACA	COEVAL	COMOUS	CORBIE	COVING	CREPON
CLOCHE	COFFEE	COMPEL	CORDER	COWAGE	CRESOL
CLODDY	COFFER	*COMPLY	CORDON	COWARD	CRESYL
CLOGGY	COFFIN	CONCHA	CORING	*COWBOY	CRETIC
CLONER	COFFLE	*CONCHY	CORIUM	COWIER	CRETIN
CLONIC	COGENT	CONCUR	CORKER	COWMAN	CREWEL
CLONUS	COGGED	CONDOM	CORMEL	COWPAT	*CRIKEY
*CLOQUE	COGITO	CONDOR	CORNEA	COWPEA	*CRIMPY
CLOSER	COGNAC	CONFAB	CORNEL	COWPIE	CRINGE
CLOSET	*COGWAY	CONFER	CORNER	*COWPOX	CRINUM
CLOTHE	COHEAD	CONFIT	CORNET	COWRIE	CRIPES
CLOTTY	COHEIR	CONGEE	CORNUS	COYDOG	CRISIS
CLOUDY	COHERE	CONGER	CORODY	COYISH	CRISPY
CLOUGH	COHORT	CONGOU	CORONA	COYOTE	CRISTA
CLOVEN	COHOSH	CONIES	CORPSE	COYPOU	CRITIC
CLOVER	COHOST	CONINE	CORPUS	*COZIED	*CROAKY
*CLUBBY	COHUNE	CONING	CORRAL	*COZIER	CROCUS
*CLUMPY	COIFFE	CONIUM	CORRIE	*COZIES	*CROJIK
CLUMSY	COIGNE	CONKER	CORSAC	*COZZES	CROSSE
*CLUNKY	COILER	CONNED	CORSET	*CRABBY	CROTCH
CLUTCH	COINER	CONNER	*CORTEX	*CRACKY	CROTON
COALER	COITUS	CONOID	CORTIN	CRADLE	CROUCH
COARSE	*COJOIN	CONSOL	CORVEE	CRAFTY	CROUPE
COATEE	COLDLY	CONSUL	CORVES	CRAGGY	CROUPY
COATER	COLEAD	CONTRA	CORVET	CRAMBE	CROUSE
*COAXAL	COLEUS	*CONVEX	*CORYMB	CRAMBO	*CROWDY
*COAXER	COLIES	*CONVEY	*CORYZA	CRANCH	CROWER
COBALT	COLLAR	CONVOY	COSHER	CRANIA	CRUCES
COBBER	COLLET	COOKER	COSIED	*CRANKY	CRUDDY
COBBLE	COLLIE	*COOKEY	COSIER	CRANNY	CRUISE

*CRUMBY	CURLEW	CABOOSE	CALUMET	CAPELIN	CARNIES
*CRUMMY	CURRAN	*CACHEXY	CALUMNY	CAPERER	*CARNIFY
CRUNCH	CURRIE	*CACHING	*CALVARY	CAPITAL	CAROACH
CRURAL	CURSED	*CACIQUE	CALYCES	CAPITOL	CAROCHE
CRUSET	CURSER	*CACKLER	CALYCLE	CAPLESS	CAROLER
CRUSTY	CURSOR	*CACODYL	CALYPSO	CAPORAL	CAROLUS
CRUTCH	CURTAL	CADAVER	*CALZONE	*CAPOUCH	CAROTID
CRYPTO	CURTLY	CADDICE	CAMBIAL	CAPPING	CAROTIN
CUBAGE	CURTSY	CADDISH	*CAMBISM	CAPRICE	CAROUSE
CUBING	CURULE	CADELLE	CAMBIST	CAPRINE	CARPALE
CUBISM	CURVEY	CADENCE	*CAMBIUM	*CAPROCK	CARPING
CUBIST	CUSCUS	*CADENCY	*CAMBRIC	*CAPSIZE	CARPOOL
CUBOID	CUSHAT	*CADENZA	CAMELIA	CAPSTAN	CARPORT
CUCKOO	CUSHAW	CADMIUM	CAMISIA	CAPSULE	*CARRACK
CUDDIE	CUSPID	CAESIUM	CAMORRA	CAPTAIN	CARRELL
CUDDLE	CUSPIS	CAESTUS	*CAMPHOL	CAPTION	CARRIED
CUDDLY	CUSSER	CAESURA	*CAMPHOR	CAPTIVE	CARRIER
CUDGEL	CUSTOM	*CAFFEIN	CAMPIER	CAPTURE	CARRIES
CUESTA	CUSTOS	CAGEFUL	*CAMPILY	*CAPUCHE	CARRION
CUISSE	CUTEST	CAGIEST	CAMPING	CARABAO	CARROCH
CULLAY	CUTESY	CAISSON	CAMPION	CARABID	CARROTY
CULLER	CUTLAS	*CAITIFF	CAMPONG	CARABIN	CARRYON
CULLET	CUTLER	*CAJAPUT	CANAKIN	CARACAL	*CARSICK
CULLIS	CUTLET	*CAJOLER	CANASTA	CARACOL	CARTAGE
CULTCH	CUTOFF	*CAJUPUT	CANDELA	CARACUL	CARTOON
CULTIC	CUTOUT	CALAMUS	CANDENT	CARAMBA	CARVING
CULTUS	CUTTER	CALANDO	CANDIDA	CARAMEL	*CARWASH
CULVER	CUTTLE	*CALCIFY	CANDIED	*CARAPAX	CASCADE
CUMBER	CYANIC	CALCINE	CANDIES	CARAVAN	CASCARA
CUMMER	CYANID	CALCITE	CANDLER	CARAVEL	CASEASE
CUMMIN	CYANIN	CALCIUM	CANDOUR	*CARAWAY	CASEATE
CUNDUM	CYBORG	CALDERA	CANELLA	CARBARN	CASEOSE
CUNEAL	CYCLER	CALDRON	CANIKIN	CARBIDE	CASEOUS
CUNNER	*CYCLIC	CALECHE	CANNERY	CARBINE	CASERNE
CUPFUL	CYESIS	CALENDS	CANNIER	CARBORA	CASETTE
CUPOLA	CYGNET	CALIBER	CANNILY	CARCASE	*CASHBOX
CUPPED	*CYMBAL	CALIBRE	CANNING	CARCASS	CASHIER
CUPPER	CYMENE	CALICES	CANNOLI	CARDIAC	CASSABA
CUPRIC	CYMLIN	CALICHE	CANNULA	CARDING	CASSATA
CUPRUM	CYMOID	CALICLE	CANONRY	CARDOON	CASSAVA
CUPULA	CYMOSE	CALIPEE	CANSFUL	CAREFUL	CASSINO
CUPULE	CYMOUS	CALIPER	CANTALA	CARFARE	*CASSOCK
CURACY	*CYPHER	CALLANT	CANTATA	CARIBOU	CASTING
CURAGH	CYPRES	CALLBOY	CANTDOG	CARICES	*CASTOFF
CURARA	CYPRUS	CALLING	CANTEEN	CARIOCA	CASUIST
CURARE	CYSTIC	CALLOSE	CANTHUS	CARIOLE	CATALOG
CURARI	CABARET	CALLOUS	CANTINA	CARIOUS	CATALPA
CURATE	CABBAGE	CALOMEL	CANTRAP	CARITAS	CATARRH
CURBER	CABBALA	CALORIC	CANTRIP	CARLESS	CATAWBA
CURDLE	CABBING	CALORIE	CANVASS	CARLINE	CATBIRD
CURFEW	*CABEZON	CALOTTE	*CANZONA	CARLING	CATBOAT
CURING	CABILDO	CALOYER	*CANZONE	CARLISH	CATCALL
CURITE	CABINET	*CALPACK	CAPABLE	CARLOAD	CATCHER
CURIUM	CABLING	CALTRAP	CAPELAN	CARMINE	*CATCHUP
CURLER	*CABOMBA	CALTROP	CAPELET	CARNAGE	CATCLAW

CATECHU	CENTNER	*CHAPMAN	CHETRUM	CHORALE	CITADEL
CATERAN	CENTRAL	*CHAPPED	*CHEVIED	CHORDAL	CITATOR
CATERER	CENTRIC	CHAPTER	*CHEVIES	CHORIAL	CITHARA
CATFACE	CENTRUM	CHARADE	*CHEVIOT	CHORINE	CITHERN
CATFALL	CENTURY	CHARGER	*CHEVRON	CHORING	CITHREN
*CATFISH	CERAMAL	CHARIER	*CHEWINK	CHORION	*CITIZEN
CATHEAD	CERAMIC	*CHARILY	CHIASMA	*CHORIZO	CITRATE
CATHECT	CERATED	CHARING	*CHIBOUK	CHOROID	CITRINE
CATHODE	CERATIN	CHARIOT	CHICANE	CHORTLE	CITROUS
CATLIKE	CEROTIC	CHARISM	CHICANO	CHOUSER	CITTERN
CATLING	CERTAIN	*CHARITY	*CHICKEE	*CHOWDER	*CIVILLY
CATMINT	*CERTIFY	*CHARKHA	*CHICKEN	CHRISOM	CLABBER
CATSPAW	CERUMEN	*CHARLEY	*CHICORY	*CHRISTY	CLACHAN
CATTAIL	CERVINE	CHARLIE	*CHIEFLY	*CHROMIC	*CLACKER
CATTALO	CESSION	CHARMER	*CHIFFON	*CHROMYL	CLADIST
CATTERY	CESSPIT	CHARNEL	CHIGGER	CHRONIC	CLADODE
CATTIER	CESTODE	CHARPAI	CHIGNON	CHRONON	CLAIMER
CATTILY	CESTOID	*CHARPOY	CHILIAD	*CHUCKLE	CLAMANT
CATTING	*CEVICHE	*CHARQUI	CHILLER	*CHUDDAH	CLAMBER
CATTISH	CHABLIS	CHARRED	CHILLUM	CHUDDAR	CLAMMED
*CATWALK	*CHABOUK	CHARTER	*CHIMBLY	CHUDDER	CLAMMER
CAUDATE	*CHAFFER	CHASING	CHIMERA	CHUGGER	CLAMOUR
CAULINE	*CHAFING	CHASSIS	CHIMERE	*CHUKKAR	CLAMPER
CAULKER	*CHAGRIN	CHASTEN	*CHIMING	CHUNTER	CLANGER
CAUSING	*CHALAZA	CHATEAU	*CHIMLEY	*CHURCHY	CLAPPER
CAUSTIC	*CHALCID	CHATTED	*CHIMNEY	CHURNER	*CLAQUER
CAUTERY	CHALICE	CHATTEL	*CHINCHY	CHUTIST	CLARIES
CAUTION	*CHALLAH	CHATTER	CHINNED	CHUTNEE	*CLARIFY
CAVALLA	CHALLIE	*CHAUFER	CHINONE	*CHUTNEY	CLARION
*CAVALLY	CHALLIS	*CHAYOTE	*CHINOOK	*CHUTZPA	CLARITY
*CAVALRY	CHALLOT	*CHAZZAN	*CHINTZY	*CHYMIST	CLARKIA
CAVEMAN	CHALONE	*CHAZZEN	*CHIPPED	*CHYMOUS	CLASHER
CAVETTO	*CHALOTH	CHEAPEN	*CHIPPER	CIBOULE	CLASPER
CAVIARE	*CHALUTZ	CHEAPIE	*CHIPPIE	*CICHLID	CLASSER
CAVILER	*CHAMADE	*CHEAPLY	CHIRPER	CICOREE	CLASSES
CAYENNE	*CHAMBER	CHEATER	CHIRRUP	CIGARET	CLASSIC
*CAZIQUE	*CHAMFER	*CHECKER	CHITLIN	CILIARY	CLASSIS
CEDILLA	CHAMISE	*CHECKUP	CHITTER	CILIATE	CLASTIC
CEILING	CHAMISO	CHEDDAR	*CHIVARI	CINDERY	CLATTER
CELADON	CHAMOIS	CHEDITE	*CHLAMYS	CINEAST	CLAUCHT
CELESTA	*CHAMPAC	CHEEPER	CHLORAL	CINEOLE	CLAUGHT
CELESTE	*CHAMPAK	CHEERER	CHLORIC	CINERIN	CLAVATE
CELLIST	*CHAMPER	CHEERIO	CHLORID	*CIPHONY	CLAVIER
CELLULE	CHANCEL	*CHEERLY	CHLORIN	CIPOLIN	*CLAYISH
CELOSIA	CHANCRE	*CHEETAH	*CHOKING	CIRCLER	CLAYPAN
CEMBALO	CHANGER	*CHEFDOM	CHOLATE	CIRCLET	CLEANER
CENACLE	CHANNEL	CHELATE	CHOLENT	CIRCUIT	CLEANLY
CENSUAL	CHANSON	CHELOID	CHOLERA	CIRRATE	CLEANSE
CENSURE	CHANTER	CHEMISE	CHOLINE	CIRROSE	CLEANUP
CENTARE	*CHANTEY	*CHEMISM	*CHOMPER	CIRROUS	CLEARER
CENTAUR	CHANTOR	CHEMIST	CHOOSER	CIRSOID	CLEARLY
CENTAVO	*CHANTRY	*CHEQUER	*CHOOSEY	CISSOID	CLEAVER
CENTILE	CHAPATI	*CHERISH	CHOPINE	CISTERN	CLEMENT
CENTIME	CHAPEAU	CHEROOT	*CHOPPED	CISTRON	CLERISY
CENTIMO	CHAPLET	*CHERVIL	*CHOPPER	CITABLE	*CLERKLY

*CLICKER	*COCKILY	COLLIES	CONCAVE	CONTENT	CORNUTE
CLIMATE	*COCKISH	COLLINS	CONCEAL	CONTEST	CORNUTO
CLIMBER	*COCKNEY	COLLOID	CONCEDE	*CONTEXT	COROLLA
CLINGER	*COCKPIT	COLLUDE	CONCEIT	CONTORT	CORONAL
CLINKER	*COCKSHY	COLOBUS	CONCENT	CONTOUR	CORONEL
CLIPPER	COCOMAT	COLOGNE	CONCEPT	CONTROL	CORONER
*CLIQUEY	COCONUT	COLONEL	CONCERN	CONTUSE	CORONET
CLIVERS	COCOTTE	COLONIC	CONCERT	CONVECT	CORPORA
CLOBBER	*COCOYAM	COLONUS	CONCHIE	CONVENE	CORRADE
*CLOCKER	CODABLE	COLORED	CONCISE	CONVENT	CORRECT
CLOGGER	CODDING	COLORER	CONCOCT	CONVERT	CORRIDA
CLONING	CODDLER	COLUMEL	CONCORD	CONVICT	CORRODE
CLONISM	CODEINA	*COMAKER	CONCUSS	*CONVOKE	CORRODY
CLOSEST	CODEINE	COMATIC	CONDEMN	*COOKERY	CORRUPT
CLOSING	*CODFISH	*COMATIK	CONDIGN	COOKIES	CORSAGE
CLOSURE	CODICES	COMBINE	CONDOLE	COOKING	CORSAIR
CLOTTED	CODICIL	COMBUST	CONDONE	COOKOUT	CORSLET
CLOTURE	CODLING	COMEDIC	CONDUCE	*COOKTOP	CORTEGE
CLOUTER	CODRIVE	COMETIC	CONDUCT	COOLANT	CORULER
CLOWDER	COELIAC	COMFIER	CONDUIT	COOLIES	CORVINA
CLUBBER	COELOME	COMFORT	CONDYLE	COOLISH	CORVINE
CLUBMAN	COENACT	*COMFREY	CONFECT	COONCAN	COSIEST
CLUMBER	COENURE	COMICAL	CONFESS	COONTIE	COSMISM
CLUNKER	*COEQUAL	COMITIA	CONFIDE	COOPERY	COSMIST
CLUPEID	COERCER	COMMAND	CONFINE	COPAIBA	*COSSACK
CLUSTER	COERECT	COMMATA	CONFIRM	COPEPOD	COSTARD
*CLUTCHY	COESITE	COMMEND	*CONFLUX	COPIHUE	COSTATE
CLUTTER	*COEXERT	COMMENT	CONFORM	COPILOT	COSTIVE
CLYPEUS	*COEXIST	COMMIES	CONFUSE	COPIOUS	COSTREL
CLYSTER	*COFFRET	COMMODE	CONFUTE	*COPPERY	COSTUME
COACHER	COFOUND	*COMMOVE	CONGEAL	*COPPICE	COTERIE
COACTOR	*COGENCY	COMMUNE	CONGEST	COPPING	COTHURN
COAEVAL	COGGING	COMMUTE	CONGIUS	*COPYBOY	COTIDAL
COAGENT	COGNATE	*COMPACT	CONICAL	*COPYCAT	COTTAGE
COALBIN	COGNISE	*COMPANY	CONIFER	COPYIST	COTTIER
*COALBOX	*COGNIZE	COMPARE	CONIINE	*COQUINA	COTTONY
COALIER	COHABIT	COMPART	*CONJOIN	*COQUITO	COUCHER
*COALIFY	COHERER	COMPASS	*CONJURE	CORACLE	COUGHER
COALPIT	COINAGE	COMPEER	CONNATE	CORANTO	COULDST
COAMING	COINFER	COMPEND	CONNECT	CORBEIL	COULOIR
*COANNEX	COINTER	COMPERE	CONNING	CORBINA	COULOMB
COARSEN	COITION	COMPETE	CONNIVE	CORDAGE	COULTER
COASTAL	COLDISH	COMPILE	CONNOTE	CORDATE	COUNCIL
COASTER	COLICIN	*COMPLEX	*CONQUER	CORDIAL	COUNSEL
COATING	*COLICKY	COMPLIN	CONSENT	CORDING	COUNTER
*COAXIAL	COLITIS	COMPLOT	CONSIGN	CORDOBA	COUNTRY
COBBIER	COLLAGE	COMPONE	CONSIST	COREIGN	COUPLER
COBBLER	COLLARD	COMPORT	CONSOLE	CORKAGE	COUPLET
COCAINE	COLLATE	COMPOSE	CONSORT	CORKIER	COURAGE
COCCOID	COLLECT	COMPOST	CONSULT	CORNCOB	COURANT
COCHAIR	COLLEEN	COMPOTE	CONSUME	CORNFED	COURIER
COCHLEA	COLLEGE	COMPUTE	CONTACT	CORNICE	COURLAN
*COCKADE	COLLIDE	COMPLIN	CONTAIN	CORNIER	COURSEP
*COCKEYE	COLLIED	COMRADE	CONTEMN	CORNILY	COURTER
*COCKIER	COLLIER	CONATUS	CONTEND	CORNROW	COURTLY

COUTEAU	CRAWLER	CROWDER	CULTURE	CUTLERY	*CACHEPOT
COUTHIE	CREAMER	CROWDIE	CULVERT	CUTLINE	*CACHEXIA
COUTURE	CREASER	CROWNER	CUMARIN	CUTOVER	*CACHUCHA
COUVADE	CREATIN	CROWNET	*CUMQUAT	CUTTAGE	*CACOMIXL
COVERER	CREATOR	*CROZIER	*CUMSHAW	CUTTIES	CADASTER
COVERUP	CREDENT	CRUCIAL	CUMULUS	CUTTING	CADASTRE
COVETER	CREEPER	CRUCIAN	CUNEATE	*CUTWORK	CADUCEUS
COWBANE	CREEPIE	*CRUCIFY	CUNNING	CUTWORM	*CADUCITY
COWBELL	CREMATE	CRUDITY	*CUPCAKE	CUVETTE	CADUCOUS
*COWBIND	CRENATE	CRUELTY	CUPELER	CYANATE	*CAFFEINE
*COWBIRD	CREOSOL	CRUISER	*CUPLIKE	CYANIDE	CAGELING
*CQWEDLY	CRESSET	CRULLER	CUPPING	CYANINE	CAGINESS
*COWFISH	CRESTAL	CRUMBER	CUPRITE	CYANITE	*CAJOLERY
*COWFLAP	CREVICE	CRUMBLE	CUPROUS	CYCASIN	*CAJOLING
*COWFLOP	CREWMAN	*CRUMBLY	CUPSFUL	CYCLASE	*CAKEWALK
COWGIRL	CRIBBER	*CRUMBUM	CUPULAR	*CYCLERY	*CALABASH
*COWHAGE	*CRICKET	CRUMMIE	CURABLE	*CYCLING	CALADIUM
*COWHAND	*CRICKEY	CRUMPET	CURACAO	CYCLIST	CALAMARI
*COWHERD	CRICOID	CRUMPLE	CURACOA	*CYCLIZE	*CALAMARY
*COWHIDE	CRIMMER	*CRUMPLY	CURATOR	*CYCLOID	CALAMINE
COWIEST	CRIMPER	*CRUNCHY	CURBING	CYCLONE	CALAMINT
*COWLICK	CRIMPLE	CRUNODE	CURCUMA	*CYCLOPS	CALAMITE
COWLING	CRIMSON	CRUPPER	CURDIER	*CYMLING	*CALAMITY
*COWPLOP	CRINGER	CRUSADE	CURDLER	CYNICAL	CALATHOS
*COWPOKE	CRINGLE	CRUSADO	CURETTE	CYPRESS	CALATHUS
COWRITE	CRINITE	CRUSHER	CURIOSA	CYPRIAN	CALCANEA
*COWSHED	CRINKLE	CRUSILY	CURIOUS	CYPSELA	CALCANEI
*COWSKIN	*CRINKLY	CRUSTAL	CURLING	CYSTEIN	CALCEATE
COWSLIP	CRINOID	*CRUZADO	CURRACH	CYSTINE	*CALCIFIC
*COXALGY	CRIOLLO	*CRYBABY	CURRAGH	CYSTOID	CALCSPAR
*COXCOMB	CRIPPLE	CRYOGEN	CURRANT	*CZARDAS	*CALCTUFA
COYNESS	CRISPEN	*CRYPTIC	CURRENT	*CZARDOM	*CALCTUFF
*COZENER	CRISPER	CRYSTAL	CURRIED	*CZARINA	CALCULUS
*COZIEST	CRISPLY	CTENOID	CURRIER	*CZARISM	CALDARIA
CRABBER	CRISSUM	*CUBBISH	CURRISH	*CZARIST	CALENDAL
*CRACKER	CRITTER	CUBICAL	CURSING	CABALISM	CALENDAR
*CRACKLE	CRITTUR	CUBICLE	CURSIVE	CABALIST	CALENDER
*CRACKLY	CROAKER	*CUBICLY	CURSORY	CABALLED	*CALFSKIN
*CRACKUP	CROCEIN	*CUCKOLD	CURTAIL	*CABBALAH	CALIFATE
CRADLER	CROCHET	CUDBEAR	CURTAIN	CABERNET	*CALIPASH
CRAMMED	CROCINE	CUDDIES	CURTATE	CABESTRO	CALISAYA
CRAMMER	*CROCKET	CUDDLER	CURTESY	*CABEZONE	CALLALOO
CRAMPIT	CROFTER	CUDWEED	CURVING	*CABLEWAY	*CALLBACK
CRAMPON	CROOKED	CUIRASS	CUSHIER	*CABOCHED	CALLIOPE
CRANIAL	CROONER	CUISINE	*CUSHILY	*CABOCHON	CALLIPEE
CRANING	CROPPED	CUITTLE	CUSHION	CABOODLE	CALLIPER
CRANIUM	CROPPER	CULICID	CUSTARD	*CABOSHED	CALMNESS
CRANKLE	CROPPIE	CULLIED	CUSTODY	CABOTAGE	*CALORIZE
*CRANKLY	*CROQUET	CULLIES	*CUTAWAY	CABRESTA	*CALOTYPE
CRANNOG	*CROQUIS	CULLION	*CUTBACK	CABRESTO	*CALTHROP
CRAPPIE	CROSIER	CULOTTE	*CUTBANK	CABRETTA	CALUTRON
CRASHER	CROSSER	CULPRIT	CUTDOWN	CABRILLA	CALVADOS
CRAUNCH	CROSSLY	CULTISH	CUTESIE	CABRIOLE	CALVARIA
CRAVING	CROUTON	CULTISM	CUTICLE	CABSTAND	*CALYCATE
CRAWDAD	CROWBAR	CULTIST	CUTLASS	*CACHALOT	*CALYCEAL

*CALYCINE	*CAPACITY	CARINATE	CATEGORY	CENTRIST	*CHARCOAL
*CALYCULI	*CAPESKIN	*CARMAKER	CATENARY	CENTROID	CHARIEST
*CALYPTER	*CAPEWORK	CARNAUBA	CATENATE	CENTUPLE	*CHARISMA
*CALYPTRA	CAPITATE	CARNIVAL	CATENOID	*CEPHALAD	*CHARLADY
*CAMBOGIA	CAPITULA	CAROLLED	CATERESS	*CEPHALIC	*CHARLOCK
CAMELEER	*CAPMAKER	CAROTENE	*CATFIGHT	*CEPHALIN	*CHARMING
CAMELLIA	CAPONATA	CAROUSAL	CATHEDRA	CERAMIST	CHARRIER
CAMISADE	CAPONIER	CAROUSEL	CATHETER	CERASTES	CHARRING
CAMISADO	*CAPONIZE	CAROUSER	*CATHEXIS	CERATOID	CHARTIST
CAMISOLE	*CAPRICCI	CARRIAGE	*CATHOLIC	CERCARIA	CHASSEUR
CAMOMILE	*CAPRIFIG	CARRIOLE	CATHOUSE	CEREBRAL	CHASTISE
*CAMPAGNA	CAPRIOLE	*CARRITCH	CATNAPER	CEREBRUM	*CHASTITY
*CAMPAIGN	CAPSICIN	CARROTIN	CATTIEST	CEREMENT	*CHASUBLE
*CAMPFIRE	*CAPSICUM	CARRYALL	CATTLEYA	*CEREMONY	*CHATCHKA
*CAMPHENE	CAPSOMER	CARRYOUT	CAUDATED	CERNUOUS	*CHATCHKE
*CAMPHINE	CAPSTONE	CARTLOAD	CAUDILLO	*CEROTYPE	CHATTING
CAMPIEST	CAPSULAR	CARTOONY	CAULDRON	CERULEAN	*CHAUFFER
CAMPOREE	CAPTIOUS	*CARTOUCH	CAULICLE	CERUSITE	CHAUNTER
CAMPSITE	CAPTURER	CARUNCLE	*CAULKING	CERVELAS	CHAUSSES
*CAMSHAFT	*CAPUCHIN	*CARYATIC	CAUSABLE	CERVELAT	*CHEAPISH
CANAILLE	*CAPYBARA	CARYATID	CAUSALLY	*CERVICAL	*CHECHAKO
CANALISE	CARABINE	CARYOTIN	CAUSERIE	CESAREAN	*CHECKOFF
*CANALIZE	CARACARA	CASCABEL	*CAUSEWAY	CESARIAN	*CHECKOUT
CANALLED	CARACOLE	CASCABLE	CAUTIOUS	CESSPOOL	*CHECKROW
CANALLER	CARAGANA	*CASEBOOK	CAVALERO	CETACEAN	*CHEDDITE
CANCELER	CARAGEEN	CASELOAD	CAVALIER	CETOLOGY	*CHEEKFUL
CANCROID	CARANGID	CASEMATE	CAVATINA	*CHACONNE	*CHEERFUL
*CANDIDLY	CARAPACE	CASEMENT	CAVEATOR	*CHADARIM	CHEERIER
*CANEPHOR	CARASSOW	*CASEWORK	*CAVEFISH	*CHAINMAN	*CHEERILY
CANEWARE	*CARBAMIC	*CASEWORM	CAVELIKE	*CHAINSAW	CHEERLED
CANFIELD	*CARBAMYL	*CASHBOOK	*CAVICORN	*CHAIRMAN	CHELATOR
CANINITY	*CARBARYL	CASHLESS	CAVILLER	*CHALAZIA	*CHELIPED
CANISTER	CARBINOL	*CASHMERE	*CAVITARY	CHALDRON	*CHEMICAL
CANITIES	CARBOLIC	CASIMERE	CAVITATE	CHALLIES	*CHEMURGY
CANNABIC	*CARBONYL	CASIMIRE	CAVORTER	*CHALLOTH	CHENILLE
CANNABIN	*CARBOXYL	CASSETTE	CEINTURE	*CHAMBRAY	*CHENOPOD
CANNABIS	CARBURET	CASTANET	CELERIAC	*CHAMFRON	*CHESSMAN
CANNELON	*CARCAJOU	*CASTAWAY	CELERITY	*CHAMPION	CHESTFUL
CANNIBAL	CARCANET	CASTEISM	*CELIBACY	*CHANCERY	CHESTNUT
CANNIEST	*CARDAMOM	CASTRATE	CELIBATE	*CHANCIER	*CHEVALET
CANNIKIN	CARDAMON	CASTRATO	CELLARER	*CHANCILY	*CHEVERON
CANNONRY	*CARDAMUM	CASUALLY	CELLARET	CHANDLER	*CHIASMUS
CANOEIST	CARDCASE	CASUALTY	CELLMATE	*CHANFRON	*CHICANER
CANONESS	CARDIGAN	*CATACOMB	CELLULAR	CHANTAGE	*CHICCORY
CANONISE	CARDINAL	CATALASE	CEMENTER	CHANTIES	*CHICKORY
CANONIST	CARDIOID	CATALYST	CEMENTUM	*CHAPATTI	*CHICKPEA
*CANONIZE	CARDITIS	*CATALYZE	*CEMETERY	*CHAPBOOK	CHICNESS
CANOODLE	CAREENER	CATAMITE	CENOBITE	*CHAPERON	*CHIEFDOM
CANOROUS	CAREERER	CATAPULT	*CENOTAPH	*CHAPITER	CHIGETAI
CANTICLE	CAREFREE	CATARACT	CENSURER	*CHAPLAIN	*CHILDBED
CANTONAL	CARELESS	CATBRIER	CENTAURY	*CHAPPATI	*CHILDING
CANTRAIP	CARESSER	*CATCHALL	CENTESIS	*CHAPPING	*CHILDISH
CANULATE	CARETAKE	*CATCHFLY	CENTIARE	*CHAQUETA	*CHILIASM
CANVASER	CAREWORN	*CATECHIN	CENTRING	*CHARACID	CHILIAST
*CANZONET	CARILLON	*CATECHOL	CENTRISM	*CHARACIN	*CHILIDOG

*CHILOPOD	*CHUCKLER	*CLASSIFY	*COACHMAN	*COEFFECT	COLLIDER
*CHIMAERA	*CHUGALUG	CLASSILY	COACTION	*COEMBODY	COLLIERY
*CHIMBLEY	*CHUMSHIP	CLASSISM	*COACTIVE	*COEMPLOY	COLLOGUE
*CHIMERIC	*CHURCHLY	CLASSIST	COADMIRE	COENAMOR	*COLLOQUY
*CHINBONE	CHURNING	CLATTERY	*COAGENCY	COENDURE	COLLUDER
CHINLESS	*CHUTZPAH	CLAUSTRA	COAGULUM	COENURUS	COLLUVIA
CHINNING	*CHYMOSIN	*CLAVICLE	COALESCE	*COENZYME	COLLYRIA
*CHIPMUCK	CIBORIUM	CLAWLESS	*COALFISH	*COEQUATE	COLOBOMA
*CHIPMUNK	*CICATRIX	*CLAWLIKE	COALHOLE	COERCION	COLOCATE
*CHIPPING	CICERONE	*CLAYBANK	COALIEST	*COERCIVE	COLONIAL
CHISELER	CICISBEO	*CLAYLIKE	COALLESS	*COEVALLY	COLONISE
*CHITCHAT	CILANTRO	*CLAYMORE	*COALSACK	*COEVOLVE	COLONIST
CHITLING	CILIATED	*CLAYWARE	COALSHED	*COEXTEND	*COLONIZE
CHITOSAN	*CIMBALOM	CLEANSER	COALYARD	*COFACTOR	*COLOPHON
*CHIVALRY	*CINCHONA	CLEARING	*COANCHOR	COGITATE	COLORADO
*CHIVAREE	CINCTURE	CLEAVAGE	COAPPEAR	*COGNIZER	COLORANT
*CHLOASMA	CINEASTE	CLEIDOIC	COASSIST	COGNOMEN	COLORFUL
CHLORATE	CINERARY	CLEMATIS	COASSUME	COGNOVIT	COLORING
CHLORDAN	CINGULUM	*CLEMENCY	COASTING	*COGWHEEL	COLORISM
CHLORIDE	CINNABAR	*CLENCHER	COATLESS	COHERENT	COLORIST
CHLORINE	CINNAMON	CLERICAL	*COATRACK	COHERING	*COLORIZE
CHLORITE	*CINNAMYL	*CLERIHEW	COATROOM	COHESION	COLORMAN
CHLOROUS	*CINQUAIN	*CLERKDOM	COATTAIL	*COHOBATE	COLOSSAL
*CHOCKFUL	CIOPPINO	*CLERKISH	COATTEND	COHOLDER	COLOSSUS
*CHOIRBOY	CIRCLING	CLEVEITE	COATTEST	*COIFFEUR	*COLOTOMY
*CHOLERIC	*CIRCUITY	CLINALLY	COAUTHOR	*COIFFURE	COLOURER
CHOOSING	CIRCULAR	*CLINCHER	COBBIEST	COINCIDE	COLPITIS
*CHOPPING	CIRRIPED	*CLIPPING	*COBWEBBY	COINHERE	COLUBRID
CHORAGUS	CISLUNAR	*CLIQUISH	*COCCIDIA	COINMATE	*COLUMBIC
*CHORALLY	CISTERNA	CLITELLA	COCINERA	COINSURE	COMANAGE
CHORDATE	CITATION	CLITORIS	*COCKAPOO	COINVENT	COMATOSE
CHOREGUS	CITEABLE	*CLOCHARD	*COCKATOO	COISTREL	COMATULA
*CHOREMAN	CITREOUS	CLODPATE	*COCKBILL	COISTRIL	COMBATER
CHOREOID	*CITYFIED	CLODPOLE	*COCKBOAT	*COKEHEAD	COMBINER
*CHORIAMB	*CITYWARD	CLODPOLL	*COCKCROW	COLANDER	*COMBINGS
CHORIOID	*CITYWIDE	CLOISTER	*COCKEREL	*COLDCOCK	*COMBLIKE
CHORTLER	*CIVICISM	CLOSEOUT	*COCKIEST	COLDNESS	*COMEBACK
CHOUSING	CIVILIAN	CLOTHIER	*COCKLIKE	COLEADER	COMEDIAN
*CHOWCHOW	CIVILISE	CLOTHING	*COCKLOFT	COLESEED	COMEDIES
*CHOWTIME	*CIVILITY	CLOTTING	*COCKSHUT	COLESLAW	*COMEDOWN
CHRESARD	*CIVILIZE	CLOUDLET	*COCKSPUR	COLESSEE	*COMEMBER
*CHRISMON	CLADDING	*CLOWNERY	*COCKSURE	COLESSOR	*COMETHER
CHRISTEN	CLAIMANT	*CLOWNISH	*COCKTAIL	COLEWORT	*COMFIEST
CHRISTIE	*CLAMBAKE	CLUBABLE	COCOBOLO	COLICINE	COMINGLE
*CHROMATE	*CLAMMING	*CLUBBING	COCREATE	*COLIFORM	*COMMANDO
*CHROMIDE	CLAMORER	*CLUBBISH	*CODEBOOK	COLINEAR	*COMMENCE
*CHROMING	*CLAMWORM	*CLUBFOOT	CODEBTOR	COLINIES	*COMMERCE
*CHROMITE	CLANGOUR	*CLUBHAND	CODELESS	COLISEUM	COMMONER
*CHROMIUM	CLANNISH	*CLUBHAUL	CODERIVE	COLISTIN	*COMMONLY
*CHROMIZE	CLANSMAN	CLUBROOT	CODESIGN	COLLAGEN	COMMUNAL
*CHROMOUS	CLAPTRAP	CLUELESS	CODIFIER	COLLAPSE	COMMUTER
*CHRONAXY	CLARENCE	*CLUMPISH	CODIRECT	COLLARET	*COMPADRE
*CHTHONIC	CLARINET	CLUPEOID	*CODPIECE	COLLATOR	COMPARER
*CHUBASCO	CLASSICO	CLUSTERY	CODRIVER	COLLEGER	COMPILER
*CHUCKIES	CLASSIER	CLUTTERY	COEDITOR	COLLEGIA	COMPLAIN

COMPLEAT	*CONQUEST	*COPYHOLD	*COSTMARY	CRANKOUS	*CRONYISM
*COMPLECT	*CONQUIAN	*COPYREAD	COSTUMER	*CRANKPIN	*CROOKERY
COMPLETE	CONSERVE	*COQUETRY	*COSTUMEY	CRANNIED	CROPLAND
*COMPLICE	CONSIDER	*COQUETTE	COTENANT	CRANNIES	CROPLESS
*COMPLIED	CONSOLER	*COQUILLE	COTHURNI	CRANNOGE	*CROPPING
COMPLIER	CONSOMME	CORACOID	COTILLON	*CRAPPING	CROSSARM
COMPLIES	CONSPIRE	CORDELLE	*COTQUEAN	*CRAVENLY	CROSSBAR
COMPLINE	CONSTANT	CORDLESS	COTTAGER	*CRAWFISH	*CROSSBOW
COMPOSER	CONSTRUE	*CORDLIKE	COTYLOID	*CRAWLWAY	CROSSCUT
*COMPOUND	CONSUMER	CORDOVAN	*COUCHANT	*CRAYFISH	CROSSING
COMPRESS	CONTAGIA	CORDUROY	*COUCHING	*CREAMERY	CROSSLET
COMPRISE	CONTEMPT	CORDWAIN	COULDEST	CREATINE	CROSSTIE
*COMPRIZE	CONTINUA	*CORDWOOD	COULISSE	CREATION	*CROSSWAY
COMPUTER	CONTINUE	COREDEEM	COUMARIN	CREATIVE	*CROTCHET
CONATION	CONTINUO	CORELATE	COUMAROU	CREATURE	CROUPIER
CONCEDER	CONTRACT	CORELESS	COUNTESS	CREDENCE	CROUPOUS
*CONCEIVE	CONTRAIL	COREMIUM	COUNTIAN	CREDENDA	*CROWFOOT
CONCERTO	CONTRARY	CORKIEST	COUPLING	*CREDENZA	*CROWSTEP
*CONCHOID	CONTRAST	*CORKLIKE	COURANTE	CREDIBLE	CRUCIATE
*CONCLAVE	CONTRITE	*CORKWOOD	COURANTO	CREDITOR	CRUCIBLE
CONCLUDE	CONTRIVE	CORNBALL	COURSING	CREEPAGE	*CRUCIFER
CONCRETE	CONVENER	*CORNCAKE	COURTESY	CREMAINS	*CRUCIFIX
CONDENSE	CONVENOR	CORNCRIB	COURTIER	CREMATOR	CRUDITES
CONDOLER	CONVERGE	CORNEOUS	COUSCOUS	CRENATED	CRUISING
CONDONER	CONVERSE	*CORNETCY	COUSINRY	CRENELLE	CRUMBIER
CONDUCER	*CONVEXLY	*CORNHUSK	COVALENT	CREODONT	*CRUMHORN
CONELRAD	*CONVEYER	*CORNICHE	COVENANT	CREOLISE	*CRUNCHER
CONENOSE	*CONVEYOR	CORNICLE	COVERAGE	*CREOLIZE	CRUSADER
CONEPATE	*CONVINCE	CORNIEST	COVERALL	CREOSOTE	CRUSTOSE
CONEPATL	*CONVOKER	CORNMEAL	COVERING	CRESCENT	*CRUZEIRO
CONFEREE	*CONVOLVE	CORNPONE	COVERLET	*CRESCIVE	*CRYOGENY
*CONFERVA	CONVULSE	CORNUTED	COVERLID	CRESTING	CRYOLITE
CONFETTO	COOINGLY	*CORONACH	*COVERTLY	*CRESYLIC	*CRYONICS
CONFIDER	*COOKBOOK	CORONARY	COVETOUS	CRETONNE	CRYOSTAT
CONFINER	COOKLESS	CORONATE	*COWARDLY	CREVALLE	CRYOTRON
CONFLATE	*COOKSHOP	CORONOID	*COWBERRY	CREVASSE	CTENIDIA
*CONFLICT	*COOKWARE	COROTATE	COWINNER	CREWLESS	CUBATURE
*CONFOCAL	COOLDOWN	CORPORAL	*COWORKER	*CREWMATE	*CUBICITY
CONFOUND	COOLNESS	CORPSMAN	*COXALGIA	*CREWNECK	CUBICULA
CONFRERE	COONSKIN	CORRIDOR	*COXSWAIN	*CRIBBAGE	*CUBIFORM
CONFRONT	COOPTION	CORRIVAL	*COZENAGE	*CRIBBING	*CUCUMBER
CONFUTER	COPARENT	CORSELET	*COZINESS	*CRIBBLED	CUCURBIT
CONGENER	COPASTOR	CORSETRY	CRABMEAT	CRIBROUS	CUDGELER
CONGLOBE	COPATRON	CORTISOL	*CRABWISE	*CRIBWORK	*CUFFLESS
CONGRATS	COPEMATE	CORUNDUM	*CRACKING	CRICETID	CULICINE
CONGRESS	COPLANAR	CORVETTE	*CRACKNEL	CRIMINAL	CULINARY
*CONICITY	*COPPERAH	*CORYBANT	*CRACKPOT	CRIPPLER	CULPABLE
CONIDIUM	COPPERAS	*CORYPHEE	CRAGSMAN	CRISPATE	CULTIGEN
CONIOSIS	COPREMIA	COSCRIPT	*CRAMMING	CRISTATE	CULTIVAR
*CONJUGAL	COPRINCE	COSECANT	*CRAMOISY	CRITERIA	CULTRATE
*CONJUNCT	COPULATE	COSIGNER	CRAMPOON	*CRITIQUE	CULTURAL
*CONJURER	*COPURIFY	COSINESS	CRANIATE	CROCEINE	CULVERIN
*CONJUROR	*COPYBOOK	COSMETIC	CRANKIER	*CROCKERY	CUMBERER
CONNIVER	*COPYDESK	COSMICAL	*CRANKILY	CROCOITE	CUMBROUS
CONODONT	*COPYEDIT	COSTLESS	*CRANKISH	*CROMLECH	CUMULATE

CUNEATED	*CYMOGENE	S C OFF	BA C KER	DE C KER	*JI C AMA
CUNEATIC	*CYNICISM	S C OLD	*BA C KUP	DE C KLE	*JO C KEY
*CUNIFORM	CYNOSURE	S C ONE	BE C ALM	DE C OCT	*JO C OSE
*CUPBOARD	*CYPRINID	S C OOP	BE C AME	DE C REE	*JO C UND
CUPELLER	CYSTEINE	S C OOT	BE C KET	DE C URY	*KE C KLE
*CUPIDITY	CYSTITIS	S C OPE	BE C KON	DI C AST	*KI C KER
CUPREOUS	CYTASTER	S C ORE	BE C LOG	DI C ING	*KI C KUP
CUPULATE	CYTIDINE	S C ORN	BE C OME	DI C KER	*KU C HEN
CURARINE	*CYTOGENY	S C OUR	BI C ARB	*DI C KEY	LA C HES
*CURARIZE	*CYTOKINE	S C OUT	BI C EPS	DI C KIE	LA C IER
CURASSOW	*CYTOLOGY	S C OWL	BI C KER	DI C TUM	LA C ILY
CURATIVE	CYTOSINE	S C RAG	BI C ORN	DO C ENT	LA C ING
CURBSIDE	*CZAREVNA	S C RAM	BI C RON	DO C ILE	LA C KER
CURCULIO	*CZARITZA	S C RAP	BO C CIA	DO C KER	*LA C KEY
CURDIEST		S C REE	BO C CIE	DO C KET	LA C TAM
CURELESS		S C REW	BU C CAL	DO C TOR	LA C TIC
CURLICUE	S C AB	S C RIM	BU C KER	DU C KER	LAC UNA
*CURLYCUE	S C AD	S C RIP	BU C KET	DU C KIE	LA C UNE
*CURRENCY	S C AG	S C ROD	BU C KLE	DU C TAL	LE C HER
CURRICLE	S C AM	S C RUB	BU C KRA	FA C ADE	LE C TIN
CURRIERY	S C AN	S C RUM	C A CHET	FA C ETE	LE C TOR
CURRYING	S C AR	S C UBA	C A CHOU	FA C EUP	LI C HEE
*CURTALAX	S C AT	S C UDO	C A CKLE	FA C IAL	LI C HEN
CURTNESS	S C OP	S C UFF	C A CTUS	FA C IES	LI C KER
CUSHIEST	S C OT	S C ULK	CIC ADA	FA C ILE	LIC TOR
*CUSHIONY	S C OW	S C ULL	CIC ALA	FA C ING	LO C ALE
CUSPIDAL	S C UD	S C ULP	CIC ELY	FA C TOR	LO C ATE
CUSPIDOR	S C UM	S C URF	CIC ERO	FA C ULA	LO C HAN
CUSSEDLY	S C UP	S C UTA	CO C AIN	FE C IAL	LO C KER
CUSSWORD	S C UT	S C UTE	CO C CAL	*FE C KLY	LO C KET
CUSTODES	S C ALD	S C ENIC	CO C CIC	FE C ULA	LO C KUP
CUSTOMER	S C ALE	S C ALDIC	CO C CID	FE C UND	LO C ULE
CUSTUMAL	S C ALL	S C EPTIC	CO C CUS	*FI C KLE	LO C UST
*CUTCHERY	S C ALP	SCIATIC	*CO C CYX	FU C OID	LU C ENT
CUTENESS	S C ALY	YE C H	CO C HIN	FU C OSE	LU C ERN
CUTGRASS	S C AMP	YO C K	CO C KER	FU C OUS	LU C KIE
CUTICULA	S C ANT	YU C A	CO C KLE	*HA C KEE	LY C EUM
CUTINISE	S C APE	YU C H	*CO C KUP	*HA C KER	LY C HEE
*CUTINIZE	S C ARE	YU C K	CU C KOO	*HA C KLE	*MI C KEY
CUTPURSE	S C ARF	DE C AF	CY C LER	*HA C KLY	*MO C KUP
CUTTABLE	S C ARP	DI C TY	*CY C LIC	*HE C KLE	MU C LUC
CUTWATER	S C ART	FI C US	DA C KER	HE C TIC	NA C HAS
*CYANAMID	S C ARY	*KI C KY	DA C OIT	HE C TOR	NA C HES
CYANOGEN	S C ATT	MA C ON	DA C TYL	*HI C CUP	NE C KER
CYANOSIS	S C AUP	MI C HE	DE C ADE	*HI C KEY	NE C TAR
*CYCLAMEN	S C AUR	NA C HO	DE C AMP	*HO C KER	NI C ETY
*CYCLECAR	S C ENA	NI C AD	DE C ANE	*HO C KEY	NI C KEL
*CYCLICAL	S C END	RE C CE	DE C ANT	*HU C KLE	NI C KER
*CYCLITOL	S C ENE	SI C KO	DE C ARE	*JA C ANA	NI C KLE
CYLINDER	S C ENT	SO C KO	DE C EIT	*JA C KAL	NO C ENT
*CYMATIUM	S C HAV	WA C KO	DE C ENT	*JA C KER	NU C HAL
*CYMBALER	S C HMO	*YE C CH	DE C ERN	*JA C KET	NU C LEI
*CYMBALOM	S C HUL	*YE C HY	DE C IDE		*PA C IFY
*CYMBIDIA	S C HWA	*YU C CH	DE C ILE		PA C ING
*CYMBLING	S C ION	*YU C KY	DE C KEL		

PA C KER	RE C TAL	TE C HIE	*BU C KLER	DE C LINE	*JA C INTH
PA C KET	RE C TOR	TE C TAL	*BU C KRAM	DE C ODER	*JA C KASS
*PA C KLY	RE C TUM	TE C TUM	*BU C KSAW	DE C OLOR	*JA C KDAW
PE C HAN	RE C TUS	TI C KER	BU C OLIC	DE C ORUM	*JA C KIES
PE C KER	RE C USE	TI C KET	*CA C HEXY	DE C OYER	*JA C KLEG
PE C TEN	RI C HEN	TI C TAC	*CA C HING	DE C REER	*JA C KPOT
PE C TIN	RI C HES	TI C TOC	*CA C IQUE	DE C RIAL	*JA C OBIN
PI CARA	RI C HLY	TI C KLE	*CA C KLER	DE C RIED	*JA C OBUS
PI CARO	RI C ING	TO C HER	*CA C ODYL	DE C RIER	*JA C ONET
*PI C KAX	*RI C KEY	TO C SIN	CI C OREE	DE C ROWN	*JO C ULAR
PI C KER	RI C RAC	TU C HUN	*CI C HLID	*DE C RYPT	*KA C HINA
PI C KET	RO C HET	TU C KER	CO C AINE	DE C UMAN	*KI C KIER
PI C KLE	RO C KER	TU C KET	COC C OID	DE C UPLE	*KI C KOFF
*PI C KUP	RO C KET	TY C OON	COC C OON	DE C URVE	LA C IEST
PI C NIC	RO C OCO	VA C ANT	CO C HAIR	DI C IEST	LA C ONIC
PI C RIC	RU C HED	VA C UUM	CO C HLEA	DI C KENS	*LA C QUER
PO C KET	RU C KLE	VE C TOR	*CO C KADE	DI C LINY	*LA C QUEY
PU C KER	RU C KUS	VI C ING	*CO C KEYE	DI C OTYL	LA C TARY
RA C EME	SA C BUT	VI C TIM	*CO C KIER	DI C TATE	LA C TASE
RA C HET	SA C HET	VI C TOR	*CO C KILY	DI C TIER	LA C TATE
RA C HIS	SA C KER	VI C UNA	*CO C KISH	DI C TION	LA C TEAL
RA C IAL	*SA C QUE	*WI C KER	*CO C KNEY	*DI C YCLY	LA C TEAN
RA C IER	SA C RAL	*WI C KET	*CO C KPIT	DO C ETIC	LA C TONE
RA C ILY	SA C RED	*WI C OPY	*CO C KSHY	*DO C KAGE	LA C UNAR
RA C ING	SA C REM	*ZE C HIN	CO C OMAT	DU C HESS	*LE C HERY
RA C ISM	SA C RUM	BA C ALAO	CO C ONUT	DU C KIER	LE C TERN
RA C IST	SA C ULE	BA C CARA	CO C OTTE	DU C KIES	LE C TION
RA C KER	SE C ANT	BA C CATE	*CO C OYAM	*DU C KPIN	LE C TURE
RA C KET	SE C EDE	*BA C CHIC	*CU C KOLD	DU C TILE	LI C ENCE
RA C KLE	SE C ERN	*BA C KFIT	CY C ASIN	DU C TING	LI C ENTE
RA C OON	SE C OND	*BA C KHOE	CY C LASE	DU C TULE	LI C ENSE
RE C ALL	SE C PAR	*BA C KING	*CY C LERY	FA C IEND	*LI C HTLY
RE C ANE	SE C RET	*BA C KLIT	*CY C LING	FA C TION	LI C KING
RE C ANT	SE C TOR	*BA C KLOG	CY C LIST	FA C TOID	LO C ALLY
RE C AST	SE C UND	*BA C KOUT	*CY C LIZE	*FA C TORY	LO C ATER
RE C EDE	SE C URE	*BA C KSAW	*CY C LOID	FA C TUAL	LO C ATOR
RE C ENT	SI C KEE	*BA C KSET	CY C LONE	FA C TURE	*LO C KAGE
RE C EPT	SI C KIE	BE C AUSE	*CY C LOPS	*FA C ULTY	*LO C KBOX
RE C ESS	SI C KLE	*BE C HALK	DA C OITY	FI C TILE	LO C KNUT
RE C HEW	SI C KEN	*BE C HARM	DE C ALOG	FI C TION	LO C KOUT
RE C IPE	*SI C KLY	BE C LASP	DE C ANAL	*FI C TIVE	*LO C KRAM
RE C ITE	SO C AGE	*BE C LOAK	DE C APOD	*FO C ALLY	LO C OISM
RE C KON	SO C CER	BE C LOUD	DE C AYER	FO C USER	LO C ULAR
RE C LAD	SO C IAL	BE C LOWN	DE C EASE	*FU C HSIA	LO C ULUS
RE C OAL	SO C KET	BE C RAWL	DE C EIVE	*FU C HSIN	LO C USTA
RE C OCK	SO C MAN	BE C RIME	*DE C ENCY	*HA C HURE	LU C ARNE
RE C ODE	SU C CAH	*BE C ROWD	DE C IARE	*HA C KBUT	LU C ENCE
RE C OIL	SU C COR	BE C RUST	DE C IBEL	*HA C KLER	LU C ENCY
RE C OIN	SU C KER	BE C URSE	DE C IDER	*HA C KMAN	LU C ERNE
RE C OMB	SU C KLE	BI C OLOR	DE C IDUA	*HA C KNEY	LU C IFER
RE C OOK	TA C KER	BI C ORNE	DE C IMAL	*HA C KSAW	*LY C HNIS
RE C OPY	*TA C KEY	*BI C YCLE	*DE C KING	*HE C KLER	*MA C AQUE
RE C ORD	TA C KLE	*BU C KEEN	DE C LAIM	HE C TARE	*MA C CHIA
RE C ORK	TA C TIC	*BU C KEYE	DE C LARE	*HI C KORY	*MA C HZOR
RE C OUP	TE C HED	*BU C KISH	DE C LASS	*JA C AMAR	

*MA C UMBA	PO C OSIN	SA C C ATE	TI C KING	*DU C KWALK	*ZE C CHINO
*MI C RIFY	PS C HENT	*SA C KBUT	TI C KLER	*DU C TWORK	*ZU C CHINI
*MI C ROHM	PU C C OON	*SA C KFUL	TO C CATA	*FO CAC CIA	C RU C K
*MO C KERY	*PU C KERY	SA C KING	*VA C AN CY	*HI C COUGH	NAT C H
*MU C KIER	*PU C KISH	SA C LIKE	VA C C INA	*JA C KROLL	PIS C O
*MU C KILY	RA C C OON	SA C RING	VA C C INE	*JO C KETTE	REC C E
*MY C OPOD	RA C EMI C	SA C RIST	*VA C UITY	*KI C KBALL	SPA C Y
NA C ELLE	*RA C EWAY	SE C EDER	VA C UOLE	*KI C KIEST	WRI C K
NE C KING	RA C IEST	SE C LUDE	VA C UOUS	*LE C YTHIS	*YE C C H
NE C KTIE	*RA C KETY	SE C ONDE	*VI C ARLY	*LO C KDOWN	*YU C C H
NE C ROSE	*RA C KFUL	SE C ONDO	*VI C EROY	MA C ARONI	BO C C IA
NE C TARY	*RA C QUET	SE C RE CY	VI C INAL	MA C AROON	BO C C IE
NI C OTIN	RE C ARRY	SE C RETE	VI C IOUS	*MA C CABAW	BU C C AL
NI C TATE	RE C EIPT	SE C TARY	VI C OMTE	*MA C CABOY	CAL C I C
NO C TUID	RE C EIVE	SE C TILE	*VI C TORY	*MA C COBOY	C O C CAL
NO C TULE	RE C EN CY	SE C TION	VI C TUAL	MA C ERATE	C OC C I C
NO C TURN	RE C HART	SE C ULAR	VI C UGNA	MA C RURAN	C OC C ID
NO C UOUS	RE C HEAT	SE C URER	VO C ABLE	MA C ULATE	C OC C US
NU C LEAL	*RE C HE CK	*SI C KBAY	*VO C ABLY	*ME C HANI C	*C O C CYX
NU C LEAR	RE C ITAL	*SI C KBED	VO C ALI C	ME C ONIUM	FAL C ES
NU C LEIN	RE C ITER	*SI C KISH	*VO C ALLY	MI C ROBAR	FRA C TI
NU C LEON	RE C LAIM	SI C KOUT	VO C ODER	MI C ROBUS	GLU C AN
NU C LEUS	RE C LAME	SO C AGER	*WI C KAPE	MI C RODOT	*HI C C UP
NU C LIDE	RE C LASP	SO C C AGE	*WI C KING	MO C C ASIN	*KIM C HI
PA C HISI	RE C LEAN	SO C IETY	*WI C KIUP	*MU CHACHO	LOU C HE
*PA C HU CO	RE C LINE	*SO C KEYE	*WI C KYUP	MU C ILAGE	MUD CAT
*PA C IFI C	RE C LUSE	*SO C KMAN	*YA C HTER	*NI C KELI C	PAS C AL
*PA C KAGE	RE C OLOR	SU C C EED	*ZA C ATON	NU C LEOID	PRE C UT
*PA C KING	RE C OUNT	SU C C ESS	*ZE C C HIN	*PA C HALI C	REE C HY
*PA C KMAN	RE C OUPE	SU C C ORY	BA C C ARAT	*PA C HINKO	SIT C OM
*PA C KWAX	RE C OVER	SU C C OTH	*BA C CATED	*PE C CABLE	SO C C ER
PA C TION	RE C RATE	SU C C OUR	*BA C CHANT	*PE C CANCY	SPA C EY
PE C CANT	RE C ROSS	SU C C UBA	*BA C C HIUS	PE C ORINO	SU C C AH
*PE C CARY	RE C ROWN	*SU C C UMB	*BA C KBEAT	*PI C IFORM	SU C C OR
*PE C CAVI	RE C RUIT	SU C C USS	*BA C KCAST	PI C OMOLE	*WHA C KO
*PE C KISH	*RE C TIFY	SU C KLER	*BA C KCHAT	*PY C NOSIS	*ZIN C I C
PE C TASE	RE C TORY	SU C RASE	*BA C KDATE	*PY C NOTI C	BA C C ARA
PE C TATE	*RE C TRIX	SU C ROSE	*BA C KFLOW	RA C HILLA	BA C CATE
*PE C TIZE	RE C URVE	SU C TION	*BA C KHAUL	RE C AMIER	*BA C C HI C
*PI C ACHO	RE C USAL	SY C OSIS	*BA C KLAND	*RE C YCLER	BAR C HAN
PI C ADOR	RE C YCLE	TA C HISM	*BA C KROOM	RO C AILLE	*BIO C HIP
PI C COLO	RI C C TUS	TA C HIST	*BA C KRUSH	SA C C ULAR	BOU C HEE
PI C EOUS	RI C INUS	*TA C HYON	*BA C KWRAP	SA C C ULUS	*BOY C HIK
*PI C KAXE	RI C KETS	TA C KIER	BI C AUDAL	SE C ALOSE	CAT C LAW
*PI C KEER	*RI C KETY	*TA C KIFY	*BI C YCLI C	SO C KLESS	C HI CANO
*PI C KIER	*RI C KSHA	*TA C KILY	*C OC C IDIA	SU C C INCT	*C HI C KEE
*PI C KING	RI C OTTA	TA C KLER	*C OCKAPOO	SU C C INI C	C OA C TOR
*PI C KOFF	*RO C KABY	TA C NODE	*DA C TYLI C	*SU C C INYL	C OC C OID
PI C OLIN	*RO C KERY	TA C TFUL	DE C OUPLE	SU C C ORER	C OC C OON
PI C OTEE	RO C KIER	TA C TILE	DE C URIES	SU C C UBUS	C ON C HIE
*PI C QUET	RO C KOON	TA C TION	*DI C HOTI C	*TA C HISME	*C RI C KEY
PI C RATE	RU C HING	TA C TUAL	*DI C HROI C	TE C TONI C	DEI C ING
PI C RITE	RU C TION	TE C HNI C	DI C ROTI C	*TU C KSHOP	DEI C TI C
PI C TURE	SA C ATON	TE C TITE	DI C TIEST	*VA C C INEE	FRA C TAL
*PO C HARD	SA C C ADE	*TE C TRIX	*DI C YCLI C	*VA C C INIA	FRA C TUS

KAT C INA	BER C EUSE	*CHA C ONNE	DIS C LAIM	GOL C ONDA	NAR C OSIS
*KEY C ARD	*BES C ORCH	*CHE C HAKO	*DIS C LIKE	GRA C EFUL	NAR C OTI C
*KIM C HEE	BES C REEN	*CHE C KOFF	DIS C LOSE	GRA C ILIS	NAS C EN C E
*MA C C HIA	*BIA C ETYL	*CHE C KOUT	DIS C OLOR	GRA C IOSO	*NAS C EN CY
MAR C ATO	BIO C LEAN	*CHE C KROW	DIS C OUNT	GRA C IOUS	NES C IENT
*MAT C HUP	*BIO C YCLE	*C HI C ANER	DIS C OVER	GUA C HARO	*NEW C OMER
MID C ULT	*BIT C HERY	*C HI C CORY	DIS C REET	*HAT CHECK	NON C LING
MIS C ODE	*BLA C KCAP	*C HI C KORY	DIS C RETE	*HAT C HERY	NON C OLOR
NON C OLA	*BLA C KFIN	*C HI C KPEA	DIS C ROWN	*HAT C HING	NON C RIME
NUT C ASE	*BLA C KFLY	*C HI C NESS	DRA C AENA	*HAT C HWAY	*NUN C HAKU
PE C C ANT	*BLA C KGUM	*CHO C KFUL	DRA C ONIC	*HEN C HMAN	PAN C ETTA
*PE C C ARY	*BLA C KING	*C HU C KIES	DUE C ENTO	HER C ULES	PAN C REAS
*PE C C AVI	*BLA C KISH	*CHU C KLER	DUL C ETLY	*HI C COUGH	PAR C ENER
PI C C OLO	*BLA C KLEG	*C IN C HONA	DUL C IANA	*HOA C TZIN	*PAR C HESI
POR C INO	*BLA C KOUT	C IN C TURE	DUL C IMER	*HOT C HPOT	*PAR C HISI
PRA C TI C	*BLA C KTOP	C IR C LING	DUL C INEA	*HYA C INTH	*PAY C HECK
PRE C ODE	*BLO C KADE	*C IR C UITY	*DUT C HMAN	*JUN C TION	*PEA C EFUL
PRE C OUP	*BLO C KAGE	C IR C ULAR	FAL C ATED	*JUN C TURE	*PEA C ENIK
*PSY C HI C	*BLO C KISH	*CLO C HARD	*FAL C HION	*KAT C HINA	*PEA C OCKY
PU C C OON	*BOS C HBOK	*COA C HMAN	FAL C ONER	*KER C HIEF	*PEC C ABLE
RA C C OON	*BOT C HERY	C OA C TION	FAL C ONET	*KNA C KERY	*PEC C ANCY
RAN C HMA	*BOY C HICK	*C OA C TIVE	*FAL C ONRY	*KNI C KERS	*PEN C HANT
RI C C TUS	BRA C ELET	*COC C IDIA	FAN C IFUL	*KNO C KOFF	PEN C ILER
SA C C ADE	*BRA C HIAL	C ON C EDER	*FAR C ICAL	*KNO C KOUT	*PER C EIVE
SA C C ATE	*BRA C HIUM	*C ON C EIVE	*FAS C I C LE	*KNU C KLER	PIA C ULAR
*SAL C HOW	BRA C IOLA	C ON C ERTO	*FEN C EROW	LAN C ELET	PIE C RUST
*SHI C KER	BRA C IOLE	*C ON C HOID	*FEN C IBLE	LAN C IERS	*PIL C HARD
SME C TI C	*BRA C KISH	*C ON C LAVE	*FIS C ALLY	LAR C ENER	*PIN C HBUG
SO C C AGE	BRA C ONID	C ON C LUDE	*FLA C KERY	*LAT C HKEY	PIS C ATOR
*SPA C KLE	BRA C TLET	C ON C RETE	FLE C TION	LEA C HATE	*PIT C HIER
*STA C KUP	*BRI C KBAT	C OS C RIPT	*FLI C HTER	LEU C EMIA	*PIT C HILY
*STO C KMA	BRO C ATEL	*COU C HANT	*FLI C KERY	*LIN C HPIN	*PIT C HMAN
SUB C ODE	BRO C C OLI	*COU C HING	*FOR C EFUL	LUN C HEON	*PIT C HOUT
SUB C ULT	*BRO C HURE	*C RA C KING	*FOR C IBLE	LUS C IOUS	PLA C ABLE
SU C C EED	*BRO C KAGE	*C RA C KNEL	*FOR C IPES	*LYN C HING	PLA C ATER
SU C C ESS	BRU C ELLA	*C RA C KPOT	FRA C TION	*LYN C HPIN	PLA C EMAN
SU C C ORY	*BUN C OMBE	C RI C ETID	FRA C TURE	*MAC C ABAW	PLA C ENTA
SU C C OTH	*BUT C HERY	C RO C EINE	FRI C ANDO	*MAC C ABOY	PLE C TRON
SU C C OUR	C AL C ANEA	*C RO C KERY	FRI C TION	*MAC C OBOY	PLE C TRUM
SU C C UBA	C AL C ANEI	C RU C IATE	*FRU C TIFY	*MAR C HESA	PLI C ATED
*SU C C UMB	C AL C EATE	C RU C IBLE	FRU C TOSE	*MAR C HESE	POA C EOUS
SU C C USS	*C AL C IFI C	*C RU C IFER	FUN C TION	*MAT C HBOX	*POE C HORE
TO C C ATA	C AL C SPAR	C RU C IFIX	FUR C RAEA	*MER C HANT	PRA C TI C E
VA C C INA	*C AL C TUFA	C UR C ULIO	*FUR C ULUM	*MER C IFUL	PRA C TISE
VA C C INE	*C AL C ULIO	*C UT C HERY	*GIM C RACK	*MIS C ARRY	*PRE C HECK
*ZE C C HIN	C AL C ULUS	*DAB CHICK	GLA C IATE	*MIS C HIEF	*PRE C HILL
*ZOE C IUM	C AN C ELER	DEA C ONRY	GLU C AGON	MO C C ASIN	*PRE C IEUX
BAC C ARAT	C AN C ROID	DES C RIBE	GLU C INUM	*MOS C HATE	PRE C IN C T
*BAC C ATED	*CAR C AJOU	DES C RIER	GLY C ERIN	*MOU C HOIR	PRE C IOUS
*BAC C HANT	C AR C ANET	DIA C ETYL	GLY C EROL	*MUN C HIES	PRE C ITED
*BAC C HIUS	C AS C ABEL	DIA C ONAL	*GLY C ERYL	*MUN C HKIN	PRE C LEAN
*BEA C HBOY	C AS C ABLE	DIE C IOUS	*GLY C OGEN	MUS C ADET	PRE C LEAR
*BED C HAIR	*CAT C HALL	DIO C ESAN	*GLY C ONI C	*MUT C HKIN	PRE C LUDE
*BED C OVER	*CAT C HFLY	DIS C IPLE	*GLY C OSYL	NAR C EINE	*PRE C RASH
*BEE C HNUT	C ER C ARIA		*GOD C HILD	NAR C ISSI	PRI C IEST

*PRI C KIER	SPE C IATE	TIE C LASP	*WAT C HDOG	GAMI C	BROMI C
*PRI C KING	*SPE C IFIC	TIN C TURE	*WAT C HEYE	GENI C	BUSTI C
PRO C AINE	SPE C IMEN	TOP C ROSS	*WAT C HFUL	HAVO C	CALC I C
*PRO C HAIN	SPE C IOUS	TOR C HERE	*WAT C HMAN	HEMI C	C ALPA C
*PRO C HEIN	SPE C TATE	TOR C HIER	*WAT C HOUT	HUMI C	C ANTI C
PRO C LAIM	SPE C TRAL	TRA C HEID	*WEL C OMER	LILA C	C APRI C
PRO C URAL	SPE C TRUM	*TRA C HOMA	*WIT C HERY	LINA C	C ELIA C
PRO C URER	SPE C ULUM	*TRA C HYTE	*WIT C HING	LOTI C	*C HEBE C
*PUN C HEON	SPI C C ATO	*TRA C KAGE	*WRA C KFUL	LUDI C	*C HEMI C
PUN C TATE	SPI C IEST	*TRA C KING	*WRE C KAGE	LYRI C	C HORI C
PUN C TUAL	SPI C ULUM	*TRA C KMAN	*WRE C KFUL	LYTI C	*C HYMI C
PUN C TURE	STA C CATO	*TRA C KWAY	*WRE C KING	MAFI C	C ITRI C
*PUR C HASE	*STI C KFUL	TRA C TATE	*ZE C C HINO	MAGI C	C LERI C
*QUA C KERY	STI C KIER	TRA C TILE	*ZIN C KING	MALI C	C LINI C
*QUA C KISH	*STI C KILY	TRA C TION	*ZIR C ONIA	MANI C	C LITI C
*QUA C KISM	STI C KLER	TRE C ENTO	*ZIR C ONI C	MEDI C	C LONI C
*QUI C KSET	*STI C KMAN	TRI C HINA	*ZOO C HORE	MELI C	COC C I C
RAN C HERO	STI C KOUT	TRI C HITE	*ZU C C HINI	MESI C	C OGNA C
RAS C ALLY	*STI C KPIN	TRI C HOID	BLO C	MIMI C	C ORSA C
REA C C EDE	STI C TION	*TRI C HOME	C HI C	MUSI C	C OSMI C
REA C C ENT	STO C CADO	*TRI C KERY	CRO C	PANI C	C RETI C
REA C C EPT	STO C CATA	TRI C KIER	DIS C	PUBI C	C RITI C
REA C C USE	*STO C KADE	*TRI C KILY	FIS C	PUDI C	C ULTI C
REA C TANT	*STO C KCAR	*TRI C KISH	FLI C	PYRI C	C UPRI C
REA C TION	STO C KIER	TRI C OLOR	HUI C	RABI C	C YANI C
REA C TIVE	*STO C KILY	TRI C ORNE	LAI C	REBE C	*C Y C LI C
*REO C CUPY	*STO C KING	TRI C TRA C	MAR C	RELI C	C YSTI C
RES C HOOL	*STO C KISH	*TRI C YCLE	NAR C	RUNI C	DEIFI C
RES C REEN	STO C KIST	*TRO C HAI C	PYI C	SALI C	*DEZIN C
RES C RIPT	*STO C KPOT	TRO C HILI	SPE C	SERA C	DYADI C
RES C ULPT	STU C C OER	TRO C HLEA	SPI C	SONI C	FABRI C
SA C C ULAR	SUB C ASTE	TRO C HOID	SYN C	STOI C	FENNE C
SA C C ULUS	SUB C AUSE	*TRU C KAGE	TAL C	SUMA C	FERRI C
*SAN C TIFY	*SUB C HIEF	*TRU C KFUL	TOR C	TARO C	FILMI C
SAN C TION	SUB C LASS	*TRU C KING	*ZIN C	TELI C	FISTI C
SAN C TITY	*SUB C LERK	TRU C KLER	*ZOI C	TONI C	FORMI C
SAR C ENET	SUB C UTIS	*TRU C KMAN	BARI C	TOPI C	FROLI C
*SAU C EBOX	SU C CINCT	*VA C C INEE	BASI C	TORI C	FUNGI C
SAU C EPAN	SU C C INIC	*VA C C INIA	BORI C	TOXI C	FUSTI C
SEA C OAST	*SU C CINYL	VAS C ULAR	BRON C	TRIA C	GALYA C
SEA C RAFT	SU C C ORER	*VAS C ULUM	C ERI C	TUNI C	GARLI C
*SEE CAT CH	SU C C UBUS	*VIN C HECK	CIVI C	TYPI C	GEODI C
SEI C ENTO	SUI C IDAL	*VIN C IBLE	C ODE C	VATI C	GESTI C
SEL C OUTH	SUL C ATED	*VIN C ULUM	C OLI C	VINI C	GNOMI C
*SHA C KLER	*SUN C HOKE	*VIS C A C HA	C OMI C	*XEBE C	GOTHI C
*SHU C KING	SUR C EASE	VIS C ERAL	C ONI C	XENI C	GUAIA C
SME C TITE	*SYN C ARPY	VIS C OUNT	C OSE C	XERI C	GWEDU C
*SMO C KING	SYN C LINE	*VIZ C A C HA	C UBI C	YOGI C	HAEMI C
*SNI C KERY	*SYN C YTIA	*VOI C EFUL	C USE C	*ZEBE C	HAPTI C
SOO C HONG	TEA C HING	*VOL C ANI C	C YNI C	BARDI C	HE C TI C
SOR C ERER	TEO C ALLI	*VUL C ANI C	DARI C	BEYLI C	HELIA C
SOU C HONG	TER C ELET	*WAH C ONDA	DOMI C	BIOPI C	HERDI C
SPA C EMAN	*THI C KISH	*WAR C RAFT	DURO C	BIOTI C	HEROI C
SPA C IOUS	*THI C KSET	*WAT C H CRY	FRAN C	BONDU C	*HYDRI C

*HYPNI C	THORI C	DINERI C	PHRENI C	TITANI C	DIDA C TI C
LA C TI C	*THYMI C	DISOMI C	PIRATI C	*TRAFFI C	DIETETI C
LENTI C	TI C TA C	DO C ETI C	PLASTI C	TRIADI C	*DIHYDRI C
LIMBI C	TI C TO C	DRASTI C	*PLUMBI C	TROPHI C	DIMETRI C
LIMNI C	TOLUI C	*DYNAMI C	POLEMI C	VENATI C	DIOPTRI C
LITHI C	TOMBA C	FANATI C	POLITI C	VERIDI C	*DIPHASI C
LUBRI C	TRAGI C	FARADI C	POSTDO C	*VIVIFI C	DIURETI C
LUETI C	TROPI C	FATIDI C	POTAMI C	VO C ALI C	DOMESTI C
MANIA C	VIATI C	FRANTI C	PRA C TI C	*XANTHI C	DRA C ONI C
MANIO C	VITRI C	FUMARI C	PRIAPI C	*YASHMA C	DRAMATI C
MANTI C	*ZIN C I C	*FUTHAR C	PROSAI C	BALSAMI C	*DYSGENI C
MASTI C	*ZODIA C	*FUTHOR C	PRUSSI C	BANAUSI C	*DYSLEXI C
METRI C	*BA C C HI C	GASTRI C	PSALMI C	BARBARI C	FARADAI C
MIOTI C	BALDRI C	GENERI C	*PSY C HI C	BARLEDU C	*FEBRIFI C
MOSAI C	BASILI C	GENETI C	PYRETI C	*BATHETI C	FORENSI C
MU C LU C	*BAWDRI C	GEORGI C	*PYRRHI C	*BEATIFI C	FRENETI C
MYOTI C	BENEFI C	*GLYPTI C	*QUADRI C	*BI C Y C LI C	*FULMINI C
MYSTI C	BENTHI C	GNATHI C	*QUANTI C	*BIOETHI C	GALA C TI C
*MYTHI C	BIBASI C	GNOSTI C	*QUARTI C	BIOGENI C	GALVANI C
NASTI C	BIOPSI C	*GRAPHI C	*QUINTI C	BIOLOGI C	GEODESI C
NITRI C	BIOPTI C	*GYNE C I C	RA C EMI C	*BIPHASI C	GEODETI C
NOETI C	BIVOUA C	*HALAKI C	RAGADI C	*BROMIDI C	GEOPONI C
NORDI C	BORA C I C	HEBETI C	*RHOMBI C	*C AL C IFI C	GERMANI C
NOSTO C	BOTANI C	HEDONI C	*SAPPHI C	C ANNABI C	GERONTI C
PARSE C	BUBONI C	HEMATI C	SATANI C	C ARBOLI C	GIGANTI C
PELVI C	BU C OLI C	HEPATI C	S C ALDI C	*C ARYATI C	*GLY C ONI C
PEPTI C	BULIMI C	HERETI C	S C EPTI C	*C ATHOLI C	*HABBINI C
*PHOBI C	BUTYRI C	*JURIDI C	S C IATI C	C ELERIA C	*HAEMATI C
PHONI C	C ALORI C	*KERAMI C	SEBA C I C	*C EPHALI C	*HAGGADI C
PHOTI C	*C AMBRI C	KINESI C	SEBASI C	*C HIMERI C	*HARMONI C
*PHYSI C	C ARDIA C	KINETI C	SELENI C	*C HOLERI C	HERALDI C
PI C NI C	C AUSTI C	LA C ONI C	SEMATI C	*C HTHONI C	*HERMETI C
PI C RI C	C ENTRI C	LUNATI C	SHELLA C	C LEIDOI C	HIDROTI C
POETI C	C ERAMI C	MALEFI C	SHOEPA C	C OSMETI C	HIERATI C
PRATI C	C EROTI C	MASONI C	SILI C I C	*C RESYLI C	HISTORI C
PUBLI C	*C HAMPA C	*MEDEVA C	*SKEPTI C	C UNEATI C	*HOLOZOI C
*PYKNI C	C HLORI C	MELANI C	SME C TI C	*DA C TYLI C	*HOMEOTI C
*QUINI C	*C HROMI C	MELODI C	SPASTI C	DALMATI C	*HORRIFI C
RI C RA C	C HRONI C	METOPI C	SPATHI C	DALTONI C	*HYDRONI C
RUBRI C	C LASSI C	MOLLUS C	SPHENI C	DEMONIA C	*HYDROPI C
RUSTI C	C LASSI C	*MORPHI C	SPHERI C	DESERTI C	*HYLOZOI C
S C ENI C	C OELIA C	MOTIVI C	SPLENI C	DEUTERI C	*HYPNOTI C
SEPTI C	C OLONI C	MOTORI C	STANNI C	DIABETI C	*HYPOTHE C
SORBI C	C OMATI C	*MUNTJA C	STROBI C	DIABOLI C	*HYSTERI C
STATI C	C OMEDI C	NEMATI C	STYPTI C	DIALOGI C	LEPROTI C
STERI C	C OMETI C	NEPHRI C	SUBERI C	DIALYTI C	*LEUKEMI C
SYNDI C	*C RYPTI C	NERITI C	SUBFUS C	DIATOMI C	LIMNETI C
TA C TI C	DEI C TI C	NUMERI C	TABETI C	DIATONI C	LOGISTI C
TAMBA C	*DELPHI C	*PA C IFI C	TE C HNI C	*DI C HOTI C	MAGNETI C
TANNI C	DEMONI C	PARETI C	TEREBI C	*DI C HROI C	*MAGNIFI C
TANRE C	DEMOTI C	PARODI C	TETANI C	DI C ROTI C	MAIEUTI C
TARMA C	DEONTI C	PAROTI C	THERIA C	*DI C Y C LI C	*MAJESTI C
TENRE C	DIBASI C	PELAGI C	THERMI C		MANGANI C
THETI C	DIMERI C	PHALLI C	THIONI C		MARGARI C

*MECHANIC	NONMUSIC	*PHTRALIC	REPUBLIC	STOMATIC	TELLURIC
MEDALLIC	*NONOHMIC	*PHTRISIC	*RHEMATIC	SUBOPTIC	TERRIFIC
*MELLIFIC	*NONTOXIC	PLATINIC	RHETORIC	*SUBPUBIC	*THEMATIC
MERISTIC	*PACHALIC	PLATONIC	*RHYTHMIC	SUBSONIC	TOREUTIC
MESMERIC	PALLADIC	POLLINIC	ROMANTIC	SUBTONIC	TRIBASIC
METALLIC	PANOPTIC	*POLYZOIC	RUTHENIC	SUBTOPIC	TRICTRAC
*METHODIC	PARANOIC	*PONTIFIC	SABBATIC	SUBTUNIC	TRISOMIC
MNEMONIC	PARANOIC	POPLITIC	*SALVIFIC	SUCCINIC	*TROCHAIC
*MOLYBDIC	*PARHELIC	*POSTSYNC	SANDARAC	SULFONIC	TURMERIC
MONASTIC	*PASHALIC	POTASSIC	SANTALIC	SULFURIC	*TYMPANIC
*MORBIFIC	*PATHETIC	*PREMEDIC	SARDONIC	*SYLLABIC	TYRANNIC
*MYOGENIC	PENTOMIC	*PROLIFIC	SEMANTIC	*SYLVATIC	*VIBRONIC
NARCOTIC	PERIODIC	*PROXEMIC	SEMIOTIC	*SYMBOLIC	VILLATIC
NEOTERIC	PERIOTIC	PULMONIC	SIMONIAC	SYNDETIC	*VOLCANIC
NEURITIC	PERISARC	PURPURIC	*SIPHONIC	*SYNECTIC	*VULCANIC
NEUROTIC	PETROLIC	*PYCNOTIC	*SLIVOVIC	*SYSTEMIC	*ZIRCONIC
*NICKELIC	*PHENETIC	*PYKNOTIC	*SPAGYRIC	*TAGMEMIC	*ZOOGENIC
NITROLIC	*PHENOLIC	*PYOGENIC	*SPECIFIC	TALMUDIC	
NONBASIC	*PHONETIC	*QUIDNUNC	SPONDAIC	TECTONIC	
NONIONIC	*PHREATIC	*QUIXOTIC	SPORADIC	TELESTIC	

D

DACE	DEAL	*DEXY	DIVA	DOSE	DUAL
DADA	DEAN	DHAK	DIVE	DOSS	DUCE
DADO	DEAR	DHAL	DJIN	DOST	DUCI
DAFF	DEBT	DHOW	DOAT	DOTE	DUCK
DAFT	DECK	DIAL	DOCK	DOTH	DUCT
DAHL	DECO	DICK	DODO	DOTY	DUDE
DAIS	DEED	DIDO	DOER	DOUM	DUEL
DALE	DEEM	DIDY	DOES	DOUR	DUET
DAME	DEEP	DIED	DOFF	DOUX	DUFF
DAMN	DEER	DIEL	DOGE	DOVE	DUIT
DAMP	DEET	DIET	DOGY	DOWN	DUKE
DANG	DEFI	DIKE	DOIT	*DOXY	DULL
DANK	DEFT	DILL	DOJO	DOZE	DULY
DARB	DEFY	DIME	DOLE	*DOZY	DUMA
DARE	DEIL	DINE	DOLL	DRAB	DUMB
DARK	DEKE	DING	DOLT	DRAG	DUMP
DART	DELE	DINK	DOME	DRAM	DUNE
DASH	DELF	DINT	DONA	DRAT	DUNG
DATA	DELL	DIOL	DONE	DRAW	DUNT
DATE	DEME	DIPT	DONG	DRAY	DUPE
DATO	DEMO	DIRE	DOOM	DREE	DURA
DAUB	DEMY	DIRK	DOOR	DREG	DURE
DAUT	DENE	DIRL	DOPA	DREK	DURN
DAVY	DENT	DIRT	DOPE	DREW	DURO
DAWK	DENY	DISC	DOPY	DRIB	DURR
DAWN	DERE	DISH	DORE	DRIP	DUSK
DAWT	DERM	DISS	DORK	DROP	DUTY
DAZE	DESK	DITA	DORM	DRUB	DYAD
DEAD	DEVA	DITE	DORR	DRUM	DYER
DEAF	DEWY	DITZ	DORY	DUAD	DYKE

DYNE	DEITY	DINGE	**DOOMY**	DRIVE	DAEDAL
DACHA	**DEKKO**	DINGO	***DOOZY**	DROIT	DAEMON
DADDY	DELAY	**DINGY**	DOPER	DROLL	DAGGER
*DAFFY	DELLY	**DINKY**	**DOPEY**	DRONE	DAGGLE
DAGGA	DELTA	DIODE	**DORKY**	DROOL	**DAGOBA**
DAILY	DELVE	**DIPPY**	**DORMY**	DROOP	**DAHLIA**
DAIRY	DEMIT	DIPSO	DORSA	DROPT	**DAHOON**
DAISY	**DEMOB**	DIRER	DORTY	DROSS	**DAIKER**
DALLY	DEMON	DIRGE	DOSER	**DROUK**	**DAIKON**
DAMAN	DEMOS	DIRTY	DOTAL	DROVE	DAIMEN
DAMAR	DEMUR	DISCI	DOTER	DROWN	DAIMIO
DANCE	DENIM	DISCO	DOTTY	DRUID	DAIMON
DANDY	DENSE	**DISHY**	DOUCE	**DRUNK**	**DAIMYO**
DANIO	***DEOXY**	DISME	**DOUGH**	DRUPE	**DAINTY**
DARER	DEPOT	**DITCH**	DOUMA	DRUSE	**DAKOIT**
DARIC	**DEPTH**	DITSY	DOURA	**DRYAD**	DALASI
DASHI	DERAT	DITTO	DOUSE	DRYER	**DALEDH**
DASHY	DERAY	DITTY	DOVEN	**DRYLY**	**DALETH**
DATER	**DERBY**	***DITZY**	**DOWDY**	**DUCHY**	DALLES
DATTO	DERMA	DIVAN	DOWEL	***DUCKY**	DALTON
DATUM	DERRY	DIVOT	DOWER	**DUDDY**	**DAMAGE**
DAUBE	**DESEX**	***DIVVY**	DOWIE	DULIA	**DAMASK**
DAUNT	DETER	DIWAN	**DOWNY**	DULLY	**DAMMAR**
DAVEN	**DETOX**	**DIXIT**	**DOWRY**	DULSE	**DAMMED**
DAVIT	DEVEL	***DIZEN**	DOWSE	**DUMKA**	**DAMMER**
DAWEN	DEVIL	***DIZZY**	**DOXIE**	**DUMMY**	**DAMNED**
DEAIR	DEVON	**DJINN**	DOYEN	**DUMPY**	DAMNER
DEALT	DEWAN	**DOBBY**	**DOYLY**	DUNAM	**DAMPEN**
DEARY	DEWAR	DOBIE	***DOZEN**	DUNCE	**DAMPER**
DEASH	***DEWAX**	DOBLA	***DOZER**	**DUNCH**	**DAMPLY**
DEATH	**DEXIE**	DOBRA	**DRAFF**	**DUNGY**	**DAMSEL**
DEAVE	DHOLE	DODGE	DRAFT	DUOMO	DAMSON
DEBAR	DHOTI	**DODGY**	DRAIL	DUPER	DANCER
DEBIT	DHUTI	DOEST	DRAIN	DUPLE	DANDER
DEBUG	DIARY	DOETH	**DRAKE**	DURAL	DANDLE
DEBUT	***DIAZO**	**DOGEY**	DRAMA	DUROC	DANGER
DEBYE	DICER	DOGGO	**DRANK**	DURRA	DANGLE
DECAF	**DICEY**	**DOGGY**	DRAPE	DURST	**DANISH**
DECAL	***DICKY**	DOGIE	DRAVE	DURUM	**DAPHNE**
DECAY	DICOT	DOGMA	DRAWL	DUSTY	**DAPPED**
DECOY	DICTA	DOILY	DRAWN	**DUTCH**	**DAPPER**
DECRY	**DICTY**	DOING	DREAD	DUVET	**DAPPLE**
DEDAL	DIDIE	DOLCE	DREAM	**DWARF**	DARING
DEEDY	DIDST	DOLLY	DREAR	DWELL	**DARKEN**
DEFAT	DIENE	DOLMA	DRESS	DWELT	**DARKLE**
DEFER	**DIGHT**	DOMAL	DREST	DWINE	**DARKLY**
DEFOG	DIGIT	**DOMIC**	DRIED	**DYING**	DARNED
DEGAS	**DIKER**	DONEE	DRIER	DYNEL	DARNEL
DEGUM	DILDO	DONGA	DRIES	**DABBER**	DARNER
DEICE	DILLY	DONNA	DRIFT	**DABBLE**	DARTER
DEIFY	DIMER	DONOR	DRILL	**DACKER**	DARTLE
DEIGN	**DIMLY**	DONSY	DRILY	DACOIT	**DASHER**
DEISM	DINAR	DONUT	**DRINK**	**DACTYL**	DASSIE
DEIST	DINER	DOOLY	DRIPT	DADDLE	**DATARY**

DATCHA	DEFANG	DENTAL	DEXTRO	DINGLE	DOBLON
DATING	DEFEAT	DENTIL	*DEZINC	DINGUS	DOCENT
DATIVE	DEFECT	DENTIN	DHARMA	DINING	DOCILE
DATURA	DEFEND	DENUDE	DHARNA	DINKEY	DOCKER
DAUBER	DEFIED	DEODAR	DHOOLY	DINKLY	DOCKET
DAUBRY	DEFIER	DEPART	DHOORA	DINKUM	DOCTOR
DAUTIE	DEFIES	DEPEND	DHOOTI	DINNED	DODDER
DAWTIE	DEFILE	DEPERM	DHURNA	DINNER	DODGEM
DAYBED	DEFINE	DEPICT	DIACID	DIOBOL	DODGER
*DAYFLY	DEFLEA	DEPLOY	DIADEM	DIOECY	DOFFER
*DAZZLE	DEFOAM	DEPONE	DIALER	DIOXAN	DOGDOM
DEACON	DEFORM	DEPORT	DIALOG	*DIOXID	DOGEAR
DEADEN	DEFRAY	DEPOSE	DIAMIN	DIOXIN	DOGGED
DEADLY	DEFUND	DEPUTE	DIAPER	*DIPLEX	DOGGER
DEAFEN	DEFUSE	DEPUTY	DIAPIR	DIPLOE	DOGIES
DEAFLY	*DEFUZE	DERATE	DIATOM	DIPNET	DOGLEG
DEARIE	DEGAGE	DERIDE	*DIAZIN	DIPODY	DOGNAP
DEARLY	DEGERM	DERIVE	DIBBER	DIPOLE	DOILED
DEARTH	DEGREE	DERMIS	DIBBLE	DIPPED	DOITED
DEASIL	DEGUST	DERRIS	*DIBBUK	DIPPER	DOLING
DEATHY	DEHORN	DESALT	DICAST	DIPSAS	DOLLAR
DEBARK	DEHORT	DESAND	DICIER	*DIQUAT	DOLLOP
DEBASE	DEICER	DESCRY	DICING	DIRDUM	DOLMAN
DEBATE	DEIFIC	DESERT	DICKER	DIRECT	DOLMEN
DEBEAK	DEIXIS	DESIGN	*DICKEY	DIRELY	DOLOUR
DEBONE	*DEJECT	DESIRE	DICKIE	DIREST	DOMAIN
DEBRIS	DEKARE	DESIST	DICTUM	DIRHAM	DOMINE
DEBTOR	DELATE	DESMID	DIDACT	DIRNDL	DOMING
DEBUNK	DELEAD	DESORB	DIDDLE	DISARM	DOMINO
DECADE	DELETE	*DESOXY	DIDDLY	DISBAR	DONATE
DECAMP	DELICT	DESPOT	DIDIES	DISBUD	DONJON
DECANE	DELIME	DETACH	DIETER	DISCUS	DONKEY
DECANT	DELIST	DETAIL	DIFFER	DISMAL	DONNED
DECARE	DELUDE	DETAIN	DIGAMY	DISMAY	DONNEE
DECEIT	DELUGE	DETECT	DIGEST	DISOWN	DONSIE
DECENT	DELUXE	DETENT	DIGGED	DISPEL	*DONZEL
DECERN	DELVER	DETEST	DIGGER	DISSED	DOODAD
DECIDE	DEMAND	DETICK	DIGLOT	DISSES	DOOFUS
DECILE	DEMARK	DETOUR	*DIKDIK	DISTAL	DOOLEE
DECKEL	DEMAST	DEVEIN	DIKTAT	DISTIL	DOOLIE
DECKER	DEMEAN	DEVEST	DILATE	DISUSE	*DOOZER
DECKLE	DEMENT	DEVICE	DILLED	DITHER	*DOOZIE
DECOCT	DEMIES	DEVISE	DILUTE	DIURON	DOPANT
DECODE	DEMISE	DEVOID	DIMITY	DIVERT	DOPIER
DECREE	DEMODE	DEVOIR	DIMMED	DIVEST	DOPING
DECURY	DEMOTE	DEVOTE	DIMMER	DIVIDE	DORADO
DEDANS	DEMURE	DEVOUR	DIMOUT	DIVINE	DORBUG
DEDUCE	DENARY	DEVOUT	DIMPLE	DIVING	DORIES
DEDUCT	DENGUE	DEWIER	DIMPLY	*DJEBEL	DORMER
*DEEJAY	DENIAL	DEWILY	DIMWIT	DJINNI	DORMIE
DEEPEN	DENIED	DEWLAP	DINDLE	*DJINNY	DORMIN
DEEPLY	DENIER	DEWOOL	DINERO	DOABLE	DORPER
DEEWAN	DENIES	DEWORM	DINGER	DOBBER	DORSAD
DEFACE	DENNED	DEXIES	DINGEY	DOBBIN	DORSAL
DEFAME	DENOTE	DEXTER	DINGHY	DOBIES	DORSEL

DORSER	**DRIVEN**	DURESS	DATEDLY	DECRIED	DEMOTIC
DORSUM	**DRIVER**	DURIAN	DAUBERY	DECRIER	DEMOUNT
DOSAGE	DROGUE	DURING	DAUNDER	**DECROWN**	DENDRON
DOSSAL	**DROLLY**	DURION	DAUNTER	*DECRYPT	*DENIZEN
DOSSEL	DROMON	DURNED	DAUPHIN	DECUMAN	DENNING
DOSSER	DRONER	DUSTER	*DAYBOOK	DECUPLE	**DENSIFY**
DOSSIL	DRONGO	DUSTUP	*DAYGLOW	DECURVE	**DENSITY**
DOTAGE	**DROOPY**	**DYABLE**	**DAYLILY**	DEERFLY	DENTINE
DOTARD	**DROPSY**	DYADIC	DAYLONG	DEFACER	DENTIST
DOTIER	**DROSKY**	*DYBBUK	DAYMARE	DEFAMER	DENTOID
DOTING	**DROSSY**	DYEING	DAYROOM	DEFAULT	DENTURE
DOTTED	**DROUTH**	DYNAST	DAYSIDE	DEFENCE	DENUDER
DOTTEL	**DROVER**	DYNEIN	DAYSMAN	DEFENSE	DEODAND
DOTTER	**DROWND**	DYNODE	DAYSTAR	DEFIANT	DEODARA
DOTTLE	**DROWSE**	DYVOUR	DAYTIME	DEFICIT	DEONTIC
DOUBLE	**DROWSY**	**DABBLER**	*DAYWORK	DEFILER	DEORBIT
DOUBLY	DRUDGE	**DABSTER**	*DAZZLER	DEFINER	DEPAINT
DOUCHE	**DRUGGY**	DACOITY	DEADEYE	DEFLATE	DEPLANE
DOUGHT	**DRUMLY**	DADAISM	DEADPAN	DEFLECT	DEPLETE
DOUGHY	**DRYISH**	DADAIST	DEAFISH	DEFOCUS	DEPLORE
DOURAH	**DRYLOT**	*DAGLOCK	DEALING	DEFORCE	DEPLUME
DOURLY	**DUALLY**	DAGWOOD	DEANERY	DEFRAUD	DEPOSAL
DOUSER	**DUBBER**	*DAKOITY	DEARIES	*DEFROCK	DEPOSER
DOVISH	**DUBBIN**	DALAPON	DEATHLY	DEFROST	DEPOSIT
DOWERY	**DUCKER**	DALLIER	DEBACLE	DEFUNCT	DEPRAVE
DOWNER	**DUCKIE**	DAMAGER	DEBASER	DEGAUSS	DEPRESS
DOWSER	DUCTAL	DAMMING	DEBATER	*DEGLAZE	DEPRIVE
DOYLEY	DUDDIE	*DAMNIFY	*DEBAUCH	DEGRADE	DEPSIDE
*DOZIER	DUDEEN	DAMOSEL	DEBONER	DEHISCE	DERAIGN
*DOZILY	DUDING	*DAMOZEL	*DEBOUCH	DEICIDE	DERIDER
*DOZING	**DUDISH**	DAMPING	DEBRIDE	DEICING	DERIVER
DRABLY	DUELER	*DAMPISH	DEBRIEF	DEICTIC	DERMOID
DRACHM	DUELLI	DANDIER	DECALOG	DEIFIED	DERNIER
*DRAFFY	DUELLO	DANDIES	DECANAL	DEIFIER	DERRICK
DRAFTY	DUENDE	DANDILY	DECAPOD	DEIFORM	DERVISH
DRAGEE	DUENNA	DANDLER	DECAYER	*DEJECTA	DESCANT
DRAGGY	**DUFFEL**	DANGLER	DECEASE	DELAINE	DESCEND
DRAPER	**DUFFER**	DANSEUR	DECEIVE	DELATOR	DESCENT
DRAPEY	**DUFFLE**	DAPHNIA	*DECENCY	DELAYER	DESERVE
DRAWEE	DUGONG	DAPPING	DECIARE	DELEAVE	DESIRER
DRAWER	**DUIKER**	DAPSONE	DECIBEL	DELIGHT	DESMOID
DRAWLY	DULCET	DARBIES	DECIDER	DELIMIT	DESPAIR
DREAMT	**DUMBLY**	DAREFUL	DECIDUA	DELIVER	DESPISE
DREAMY	**DUMDUM**	DARESAY	DECIMAL	DELOUSE	DESPITE
DREARY	**DUMPER**	DARIOLE	*DECKING	*DELPHIC	DESPOIL
DREGGY	DUNITE	*DARKISH	DECLAIM	DELTOID	DESPOND
DREICH	DUNLIN	DARNING	DECLARE	DELUDER	DESSERT
DREIDL	DUNNED	DARSHAN	DECLASS	DEMAGOG	DESTAIN
DREIGH	DUNNER	DASHEEN	DECLINE	DEMERGE	DESTINE
DRENCH	DUOLOG	DASHIER	DECODER	DEMERIT	DESTINY
DRESSY	**DUPERY**	*DASHIKI	DECOLOR	DEMESNE	DESTROY
DRIEST	DUPING	DASHPOT	DECORUM	DEMETON	DESUGAR
DRIFTY	*DUPLEX	DASTARD	DECOYER	DEMIGOD	DETENTE
DRIPPY	DUPPED	DASYURE	DECREER	DEMIREP	DETERGE
DRIVEL	DURBAR	DATABLE	DECRIAL	DEMONIC	DETINUE

DIATONIC	*DIMETHYL	DISGUISE	DIURESIS	DOMINIUM	*DOWNPLAY
DIATRIBE	DIMETRIC	DISHERIT	DIURETIC	DONATION	DOWNPOUR
*DIAZEPAM	DIMINISH	*DISHEVEL	DIVAGATE	DONATIVE	DOWNSIDE
*DIAZINON	*DIMMABLE	DISHIEST	DIVALENT	DONENESS	*DOWNSIZE
DICHASIA	DINGDONG	*DISHLIKE	*DIVEBOMB	DONNERED	*DOWNTICK
*DICHOTIC	DINKIEST	DISHONOR	DIVERTER	DONNIKER	DOWNTROD
*DICHROIC	DINOSAUR	*DISHWARE	DIVIDEND	*DOOMSDAY	DOWNTURN
DICROTAL	DIOBOLON	DISINTER	DIVIDING	DOOMSTER	*DOWNWARD
DICROTIC	DIOCESAN	*DISJOINT	DIVIDUAL	DOORBELL	*DOWNWASH
DICTATOR	DIOECISM	*DISJUNCT	DIVINING	*DOORJAMB	*DOWNWIND
DICTIEST	DIOICOUS	DISKETTE	DIVINISE	*DOORKNOB	DOWSABEL
*DICYCLIC	DIOLEFIN	DISLIKER	*DIVINITY	DOORLESS	*DOXOLOGY
DIDACTIC	DIOPSIDE	DISLODGE	*DIVINIZE	DOORNAIL	*DOZINESS
*DIDACTYL	DIOPTASE	DISLOYAL	DIVISION	DOORPOST	DRABNESS
DIDAPPER	DIOPTRIC	DISMOUNT	*DIVISIVE	DOORSILL	DRACAENA
*DIDYMIUM	*DIPHASIC	DISORDER	DIVORCEE	DOORSTEP	DRACONIC
*DIDYMOUS	*DIPHENYL	*DISPATCH	DIVORCER	DOORSTOP	*DRAFFISH
*DIDYNAMY	DIPLEGIA	DISPENSE	DIVULGER	DOORYARD	DRAFTING
DIECIOUS	*DIPLEXER	DISPERSE	*DIZYGOUS	DOPAMINE	DRAGGIER
DIELDRIN	*DIPLOIDY	DISPIRIT	*DJELLABA	*DOPEHEAD	DRAGGING
*DIEMAKER	DIPLOMAT	DISPLACE	DOCILITY	DOPESTER	DRAGLINE
DIERESIS	DIPLOPOD	DISPLANT	*DOCKHAND	DOPINESS	DRAGONET
*DIESTOCK	DIPLOSIS	DISPLODE	*DOCKLAND	*DORMANCY	DRAGROPE
DIESTRUM	*DIPPABLE	DISPLUME	*DOCKSIDE	DORMIENT	DRAGSTER
DIESTRUS	*DIPSTICK	DISPOSAL	*DOCKYARD	DORMOUSE	DRAINAGE
DIETETIC	DIPTERAL	DISPOSER	DOCTORAL	DORSALLY	DRAMATIC
*DIFFRACT	DIPTERAN	DISPREAD	DOCTRINE	DOSSERET	DRAMMING
*DIFFUSER	DIPTERON	*DISPRIZE	DOCUMENT	DOTATION	*DRAMMOCK
*DIFFUSOR	DIRECTOR	DISPROOF	DODDERER	DOTINGLY	*DRAMSHOP
DIGAMIES	DIRENESS	DISPROVE	*DOGBERRY	DOTTEREL	*DRAUGHTY
DIGAMIST	DIRIMENT	DISPUTER	*DOGESHIP	DOTTIEST	DRAWBACK
DIGESTER	DISABUSE	*DISQUIET	*DOGFIGHT	DOUBLING	DRAWBORE
DIGESTOR	DISAGREE	DISROBER	*DOGGEDLY	DOUBLOON	*DRAWDOWN
DIGGINGS	DISALLOW	DISSEISE	DOGGEREL	DOUBLURE	DRAWTUBE
DIGITATE	DISANNUL	*DISSEIZE	DOGGIEST	DOUBTFUL	DREADFUL
*DIGITIZE	DISARMER	DISSERVE	DOGGONED	*DOUGHBOY	DREAMFUL
DIHEDRAL	DISARRAY	DISSUADE	DOGHOUSE	DOUGHIER	DREDGING
DIHEDRON	DISASTER	DISTANCE	DOGNAPER	DOUGHNUT	DRENCHER
*DIHYBRID	DISBOSOM	DISTASTE	*DOGSBODY	DOUPIONI	DRESSAGE
*DIHYDRIC	DISBURSE	DISTAVES	DOGTOOTH	DOURNESS	DRESSING
DILATANT	DISCIPLE	DISTINCT	*DOGWATCH	*DOUZEPER	DRIBBLER
DILATATE	DISCLAIM	DISTRACT	DOLDRUMS	DOVECOTE	DRIBBLET
DILATION	*DISCLIKE	DISTRAIN	DOLERITE	*DOVELIKE	DRIFTAGE
DILATIVE	DISCLOSE	DISTRAIT	DOLESOME	DOVETAIL	DRIFTPIN
DILATORY	DISCOLOR	DISTRESS	DOLOMITE	DOWNBEAT	DRILLING
DILIGENT	DISCOUNT	DISTRICT	DOLOROUS	DOWNCAST	DRIPLESS
DILUTION	DISCOVER	DISTRUST	*DOMELIKE	*DOWNCOME	DRIPPING
DILUTIVE	DISCREET	DISULFID	*DOMESDAY	*DOWNFALL	DRIVELER
DILUVIAL	DISCRETE	DISUNION	DOMESTIC	*DOWNHAUL	*DRIVEWAY
DILUVIAN	DISCROWN	DISUNITE	DOMICILE	*DOWNHILL	DROLLERY
DILUVION	DISENDOW	DISUNITY	DOMINANT	DOWNIEST	*DROPHEAD
DILUVIUM	*DISFAVOR	DISVALUE	DOMINATE	DOWNLAND	*DROPKICK
DIMERISM	*DISFROCK	DITHEISM	DOMINEER	*DOWNLINK	DROPPING
*DIMERIZE	DISGORGE	DITHEIST	*DOMINICK	DOWNLOAD	DROPSHOT
DIMEROUS	DISGRACE	DITHERER	DOMINION	*DOWNPIPE	DROPWORT

*DROUGHTY	DURATION	BE D BUG	DUD DIE	MA D RAS	RA D IUS
DRUBBING	DURATIVE	BE D DED	DUD EEN	MA D URO	*RA D JUM
DRUDGERY	DUSTHEAP	BE D DER	DUD ING	*ME D FLY	RA D OME
DRUGGIST	DUSTIEST	*BE D ECK	DUD ISH	*ME D ICK	RA D ULA
DRUIDESS	DUSTLESS	BE D ELL	FE D ORA	ME D IA D	RE D ACT
DRUIDISM	DUSTLIKE	BE D LAM	FI D DLE	ME D IAL	RE D ATE
DRUMBEAT	*DUTCHMAN	BE D PAN	FI D GET	ME D IAN	RE D BAY
DRUMFIRE	DUTIABLE	BE D RID	FO D DER	ME D INA	RE D BUD
*DRUMFISH	DUVETINE	BE D RUG	FO D GEL	ME D LAR	RE D BUG
*DRUMHEAD	*DUVETYNE	BE D SIT	FU D DLE	MI D AIR	RE D CAP
DRUMLIER	*DWARFISH	BE D UIN	GA D DED	*MI D WAY	RE D DED
*DRUMLIKE	*DWARFISM	BE D UMB	GA D DER	MO D ERN	RE D DEN
DRUMMING	DWELLING	BI D DEN	GA D FLY	MO D EST	RE D DER
DRUMROLL	*DYESTUFF	BI D DER	GA D GET	*MO D IFY	RE D DLE
DRUNKARD	*DYNAMISM	BO D EGA	GA D OID	MO D ULE	RE D EAR
DRUPELET	DYNAMIST	BO D ICE	GI D DAP	MO D ULO	RE D EEM
DRUTHERS	DYNATRON	BO D IED	GO D DAM	MU D CAT	RE D EFY
DRYPOINT	*DYSGENIC	BO D IFS	GO D DED	NI D GET	RE D ENY
DRYSTONE	*DYSLEXIA	BO D ILY	GO D OWN	NI D IFY	RE D EYE
DUBONNET	*DYSLEXIC	BO D ING	GO D SON	NI D ING	RE D FIN
*DUCKBILL	*DYSPEPSY	BO D KIN	GO D WIT	NO D DED	RE D IAL
*DUCKIEST	DYSPNOEA	BU D DER	HA D ITH	NO D DER	RE D LEG
*DUCKLING	*DYSTAXIA	BU D DLE	*HA D JEE	NO D DLE	RE D OCK
*DUCKTAIL	DYSTOCIA	BU D GET	HA D RON	NO D OSE	RE D ONE
*DUCKWALK	DYSTONIA	BU D GIE	HE D DLE	NO D OUS	RE D OUT
*DUCKWEED	DYSTOPIA	CA D DIE	HE D GER	NO D ULE	RE D OWA
DUCTLESS		CA D DIS	HI D DEN	NU D EST	RE D RAW
*DUCTWORK	LU D E	CA D ENT	HI D ING	NU D GER	RE D TOP
*DUDISHLY	NA D A	CA D GER	HO D DEN	NU D ISM	RE D UCE
DUECENTO	PA D I	CE D ING	HO D DIN	NU D IST	RI D DED
DUELLING	RE D-D	CE D ULA	HU D DLE	NU D ITY	RI D DEN
DUELLIST	RU D D	CO D DED	HY D RIA	NU D NIK	RI D DLE
DUETTIST	SU D D	CO D DER	*HY D RIC	PA D AUK	RI D ENT
DULCETLY	CO D EC	CO D DLE	HY D RID	PA D DER	RI D GEL
DULCIANA	CO D ED	CO D EIA	*JA D ISH	PA D DLE	RI D GIL
DULCIMER	GA D ID	CO D EIN	*JU D DER	PA D NAG	RI D ING
DULCINEA	GO D ET	CO D GER	*JU D GER	PA D OUK	RI D LEY
DULLNESS	HO D AD	*CO D IFY	*JU D OKA	PE D ALO	RO D ENT
*DUMBBELL	LU D IC	CO D ING	*KE D DAH	PE D ANT	RO D MAN
*DUMBCANE	MO D EM	CO D LIN	KI D DER	PE D ATE	RU D DER
*DUMBHEAD	MUD D Y	CU D DIE	KI D DIE	PE D LAR	RU D DLE
DUMBNESS	*NU D ZH	CU D DLE	KI D NAP	PI D DLE	RU D EST
*DUMFOUND	RE D ID	CU D DLY	KI D NEY	PI D DLY	SA D DEN
*DUMMKOPF	RE D ON	CU D GEL	*KI D VID	PI D GIN	SA D DLE
*DUMPCART	RE D UB	DAD-DLE	LA D DER	PO D ITE	SA D ISM
DUMPIEST	RE D UX	DE D ANS	LA D DIE	PO D IUM	SA D IST
DUMPLING	SI D ED	DE D UCT	LA D IES	PO D SOL	SA D DHU
DUNELAND	SO D OM	DI D ACT	LA D ING	*PO D ZOL	SE D ATE
DUNGAREE	WI D ER	DI D DLE	LA D INO	PU D DLE	SE D ILE
DUNGHILL	WO D GE	DI D DLY	LA D LER	PU D DLY	SE D UCE
DUODENUM	BA D DIE	DI D IES	LA D RON	RA D DLE	SI D DUR
DUOLOGUE	BA D GER	DO D DED	LE D GER	RA D IAL	SI D ING
DUOPSONY	BA D MAN	DO D GEM	LO D GER	RA D IAN	SI D LER
*DUPLEXER	BE D AMN	DO D GER	MA D DED	RA D ISH	SO D DED
DURABLES	BE D AUB				

SO D DEN	BE D POST	D U D GEON	KI D DIES	PE D ICEL	RO D LIKE	
SO D IUM	BE D RAIL	FA D ABLE	KI D DING	PE D ICLE	RO D SMAN	
SO D OMY	BE D RAPE	FA D DIER	*KI D DISH	PE D LARY	RU D DIER	
SU D ARY	*BE D ROCK	FA D DING	*KI D DUSH	PE D LERY	RU D DILY	
SU D DEN	BE D ROLL	*FA D DISH	*KI D LIKE	PE D OCAL	*RU D DOCK	
SU D SER	BE D ROOM	FA D DISM	*KI D SKIN	PI D DLER	RU D ERAL	
TE D DER	BE D SIDE	FA D DIST	LA D ANUM	*PI D DOCK	RU D ESBY	
TE D IUM	BE D SORE	FE D AYEE	LA D LING	PO D AGRA	SA D DLER	
TI D BIT	*BE D TICK	FE D ERAL	LA D RONE	PO D LIKE	SA D IRON	
TI D DLY	BE D TIME	FI D DLER	LA D YBUG	PU D DING	SA D NESS	
TI D IED	BE D UNCE	FI D EISM	LA D YISH	PU D DLER	SE D ARIM	
TI D IER	BE D WARD	FI D EIST	*LA D YKIN	*PU D ENCY	SE D UCER	
TI D IES	*BE D WARF	*FI D GETY	LI D LESS	RA D IANT	SI D EARM	
TI D ILY	BI D ARKA	FI D GING	LO D GING	RA D IATE	SI D EBAR	
TI D ING	BI D DING	GA D DING	LY D DITE	RA D ICAL	SI D ECAR	
TO D DLE	BO D HRAN	GA D ROON	MA D HOUS	RA D ICEL	SI D EMAN	
VA D OSE	BU D DIED	GA D WALL	MA D RIGA	RA D ICES	SI D EWAY	
VO D OUN	BU D DIES	*GI D DYAP	*MA D ZOON	RA D ICLE	SO D DING	
WA D DER	BU D DING	*GI D DYUP	ME D DUSA	*RA D JALE	TA D POLE	
WA D DIE	BU D GING	GO D DESS	*ME D EVAC	RE D BAIT	TE D IOUS	
WA D DLE	BU D LESS	GO D DING	*ME D IACY	RE D BIRD	TI D DLER	
WA D DLY	BU D LIKE	GO D HEAD	ME D IATE	RE D BONE	TI D ERIP	
WA D MAL	*BU D WORM	GO D HOOD	MI D CULT	RE D COAT	TI D EWAY	
WA D MEL	CA D AVER	GO D LIER	MI D LAND	RE D DEST	TI D IEST	
WA D MOL	CA D DICE	GO D LIKE	MI D LIFE	RE D DING	TO D DIES	
WA D SET	CA D DISH	GO D LING	MI D LING	RE D DISH	TO D DLER	
WE D DER	CA D ELLE	GO D ROON	*MI D RIFF	RE D FISH	VE D ALIA	
WE D ELN	CA D ENCE	GO D SEND	*MI D SHIP	RE D HEAD	VE D ETTE	
WE D GIE	*CA D ENCY	GO D SHIP	*MI D SIZE	RE D LINE	VI D ETTE	
WI D DER	*CA D ENZA	GU D GEON	MI D SOLE	RE D NECK	VI D ICON	
WI D DIE	CA D MIUM	HA D ARIM	*MI D WEEK	RE D NESS	VI D UITY	
WI D DLE	CE D ILLA	HA D DEST	*MI D WIFE	RE D OUBT	WA D ABLE	
WI D EST	CO D ABLE	*HA D DOCK	MO D ERNE	RE D OUND	WA D DIED	
WI D GET	CO D DING	HE D GING	MO D ISTE	RE D POLL	WA D DIES	
WI D ISH	CO D DLER	HE D ONIC	MO D ULED	RE D RAFT	WA D DING	
YO D LER	CO D EINA	HI D ABLE	MU D DIED	RE D REAM	WA D DLER	
*ZA D DIK	CO D EINE	HI D ALGO	*MU D FISH	RE D RESS	WA D MAAL	
*ZO D IAC	*CO D FISH	HI D EOUS	MU D FLAT	RE D RIED	WA D MOLL	
*ZY D ECO	CO D ICES	HI D EOUT	MU D HOLE	RE D RIES	WE D DING	
BA D GING	CO D ICIL	*HO DAD DY	*MU D PACK	RE D RILL	WI D ENER	
BA D LAND	CO D LING	HU D DLER	*MU D ROCK	RE D RIVE	WI D EOUT	
BA D NESS	CO D RIVE	*HY D ATID	NO D DIES	RE D ROOT	WI D GEON	
BE D DING	CU D BEAR	HY D RANT	NO D DING	RE D SKIN	WI D OWER	
BE D EMAN	CU D DIES	HY D RASE	NO D ICAL	RE D TAIL	YO D ELER	
BE D EVIL	CU D DLER	HY D RATE	NU D NICK	RE D UCER	*ZA D DICK	
BE D FAST	CU D WEED	*HY D RIDE	PA D DIES	RE D WARE	*ZE D OARY	
BE D GOWN	D A D AISM	*HY D ROID	PA D DING	RE D WING	BE D OTTED	
BE D IGHT	D A D AIST	*HY D ROPS	PA D DLER	RE D WOOD	BE D SHEET	
BE D IRTY	D E D LICE	*HY D ROUS	*PA D DOCK	RI D ABLE	BE D STAND	
*BE D IZEN	D I D DLER	*HY D ROXY	PA D RONE	RI D DING	BE D STEAD	
BE D LAMP	D I D DLEY	*JA D EITE	*PA D LOCK	RI D DLER	BI D DABLE	
BE D LESS	D O D DERY	*JO D HPUR	PA D RONE	RI D GIER	BO D YSUIT	
BE D LIKE	D O D GING	*JU D OIST	*PA D SHAH	RI D GING	BU D DLEIA	
BE D MATE	D O D GING	*KA D DISH	PE D AGOG	RI D OTTO	*CO D EBOOK	
BE D OUIN	D O D OISM		PE D ICAB	RO D LESS	CO D ESIGN	

CO D IRECT	RE D EMAN D	FI D D LY	SO D D ED	*HA D D OCK	TAR D YON
CO D RIVER	*RE D SHIFT	FO D D ER	SO D D EN	HOO D IER	TI D D LER
DO D DERER	RE D START	FOO D IE	SOR D I D	HU D D LER	TOA D IE D
FA D D IEST	RE D UCTOR	FU D D LE	SOR D OR	HUN D RE D	TO D D IES
*GO D CHILD	RI D D ANCE	GA D D ED	STU D LY	*KA D D ISH	TO D D LER
HI D ROTIC	RU D D IEST	GA D D ER	SU D D EN	KI D D IES	TUR D INE
*HYD RACID	SA D D LERY	GI D D AP	TE D D ER	KI D D ING	*TWI D D LY
*HY D ROSKI	SA D D LING	GO D D AM	TI D D IE	*KI D D ISH	WA D D IE D
*KI D NAPEE	SI D EBAN D	GO D D ED	TO D D LE	*KI D D USH	WA D D IES
*LA D YBIR D	SI D EWAR D	HE D D LE	WA D D ER	KIN D RE D	WA D D ING
*LADYHOO D	SO D D ENLY	HI D D EN	WA D D IE	LEA D MAN	WA D D LER
ME D ALIST	SO D OMIST	HO D D EN	WA D D LE	LY D D ITE	WE D D ING
ME D ALLIC	*SO D OMIZE	HO D D IN	WA D D LY	ME D D USA	WOO D IES
ME D IALLY	TI D ELAN D	HON D LE	WE D D ER	MIN D SET	*ZA D D ICK
ME D IANLY	*VI D EOTEX	HU D D LE	WI D D ER	MIS D EE D	*BAI D ARKA
ME D IATOR	*WI D EBAND	*JU D D ER	WI D D IE	MIS D IAL	*BAL D HEA D
ME D ICAI D	BAL D Y	*KE D D AH	WI D D LE	MU D D IE D	BAL D NESS
ME D ICARE	BIN D I	KI D D ER	WOO D IE	NAN D INA	BAL D PATE
ME D ICATE	BUN D T	KI D D IE	*ZA D D IK	NO D D IES	*BAL D RICK
ME D ICINE	CLA D E	LA D D ER	BAL D IES	NO D D ING	BAN D AGER
ME D IOCRE	CON D O	LA D D IE	BAN D IE D	NON D RUG	BAN D ANNA
ME D ITATE	HOO D Y	MA D D ED	BE D D ING	PA D D IES	BAN D EROL
ME D TEVAL	MU D D Y	NO D D ED	BI D D ING	PA D D ING	BAN D ITRY
ME D USOI D	NER D Y	NO D D ER	BIR D ING	PA D D LER	BAN D SMAN
MI D BRAIN	RAN D Y	NO D D LE	BLU D GER	*PA D D OCK	BAU D RONS
*MI D FIEL D	REA D D	NOO D GE	BON D ING	PAN D IE D	BAW D IEST
MI D POINT	WOO D Y	NOR D IC	BU D D IE D	PE D D LER	BEA D IEST
MI D RANGE	BA D D IE	PA D D ER	BU D D IE D	PER D URE	*BEA D LIKE
*MI D SIZE D	BE D D ED	PA D D LE	BU D D IES	PI D D LER	BEA D ROLL
MI D STORY	BE D D ED	PE D D LE	BU D D ING	*PI D D OCK	BEA D SMAN
MO D ALITY	BE D D ER	PI D D LE	CA D D ICE	PRE D IVE	*BEA D WORK
MO D ELING	BI D D EN	PI D D LY	CA D D ISH	PU D D ING	*BEN D WAYS
MO D ELIST	BI D D ER	PU D D LE	CAN D IE D	PU D D LER	BEN D WISE
MO D ELLE D	BU D D ER	PU D D LY	CLA D IST	RAN D IER	*BER D ACHE
MO D ELLER	BU D D LE	RA D D LE	CO D D ING	REA D IE D	BI D D ABLE
MO D ERATE	CA D D IE	RE D D ED	CO D D LER	RE D D EST	*BIN D WEE D
MO D ERATO	CA D D IS	RE D D EN	COR D ING	RE D D ISH	*BIR D BATH
*MO D IFIE D	CAN D I D	RE D D ER	CU D D IES	RE D D ISH	BIR D CAGE
MO D IOLUS	CAU D A D	RE D D LE	CU D D LER	REE D ILY	BIR D CALL
MO D ULATE	CHA D AR	RI D D ED	DEO D AN D	REE D MAN	*BIR D FARM
MU D D IEST	CHA D OR		DI D D LER	RI D D LER	*BIR D LIKE
MUDGUARD	CO D D ED	RI D D EN	DI D D LEY	RI D D LER	BIR D LIME
MU D SLI D E	CO D D ER	RI D D ER	DO D D ERY	ROA D BE D	BIR D SEE D
MU D STONE	CO D D LE	RI D D LE	FA D D IER	RU D D IER	BIR D SEYE
PA D D LING	COY D OG	ROA D EO	FA D D ING	*RU D D OCK	BIR D SHOT
PE D ALLE D	CU D D IE	ROA D IE	*FA D D ISH	SA D D LER	BIR D SONG
*PE D DLERY	CU D D LE	RU D D ER	FA D D ISM	SAR D ANA	BLU D GEON
PE D D LING	CU D D LY	RU D D LE	FA D D IST	SEE D BE D	*BOL D FACE
*PO D OCARP	DA D D LE	SA D D EN	FI D D LER	SEE D PO D	BOL D NESS
PU D D LING	DI D D LE	SA D D HU	GA D D ING	SO D D ING	BON D MAI D
RA D ICAN D	DI D D LY	SA D D LE	*GI D D YAP	STU D IE D	*BOR D EAUX
RA D WASTE	DO D D ER	SEI D EL	*GI D D YUP	SUN D ECK	BOR D ERER
RE D AMAGE	DOO D AD	SEN D UP	GO D D ESS	STU D IE D	BRI D ALLY
RE D ECI D E	DU D D IE	SI D D UR	GO D D ING	SUN D ECK	BRI D GING
RE D EFECT	FI D D LE	SMI D GE	HA D D EST	SWI D D EN	BU D D LEIA

BUN D LING	D EE D LESS	*HAN D CUFF	HEA D RACE	LOR D LESS	PEN D ULUM
BUR D ENER	D EN D RITE	*HAN D FAST	HEA D REST	LOR D LIER	PIE D FORT
CAL D ARIA	D EN D ROI D	*HAN D GRIP	HEA D ROOM	LOR D LIKE	PIE D MONT
*CAN D IDLY	D OD D ERER	*HAN D HELD	HEA D SAIL	LOR D OSIS	PIN D LING
*CARDAMOM	D OL D RUMS	*HAN D HOL D	*HEA D SHIP	LOR D SHIP	PLE D GEOR
CAR D AMON	D RE D GING	*HAN D ICAP	HEA D SMAN	LOU D NESS	PLE D GING
*CAR DA MUM	D RU D GERY	HAN D IEST	*HEA D STAY	*MAI D HOO D	PON D ERER
CAR D CASE	D UO D ENUM	HAN D LING	*HEA D WIN D	*MAN D RAKE	*PON D WEE D
CAR D IGAN	FA D D IEST	HAN D LIST	*HEA D WORD	MU D D IEST	POW D ERER
CAR D INAL	FAL D ERAL	HAN D LOOM	*HEA D WORK	ME D ALIST	PRA D ITOR
CAR D IOI D	FAL D EROL	*HAN D MADE	*HEB D OMA D	ME D ALLIC	PRE D ATOR
CAR D ITIS	FAN D ANGO	*HAN D MAI D	HEE D LESS	ME D IALLY	PRE D RILL
CAU D ATE D	*FEE D BACK	*HAN D OVER	HER D LIKE	ME D IANLY	PRI D EFUL
CAU D ILLO	*FEE D HOLE	HAN D RAIL	HER D SMAN	ME D IATOR	PRO D IGAL
*CHA D ARIM	FEL D SPAR	*HAN D SEWN	HIN D ERER	ME D ICAID	PRO D ROME
CLA D D ING	*FOL D AWAY	*HAN D SFUL	HIN D MOST	ME D ICARE	PRO D UCER
CLO D PATE	FOL D BOAT	HAN D SOME	*HOL D BACK	ME D ICATE	PRU D ENCE
CLO D POLE	FOL D EROL	*HAN D WORK	*HOL D FAST	ME D ICINE	PU D D LING
CLO D POLL	FON D LING	*HAN D WRIT	*HOL D OVER	ME D TEVAL	PUN D ITRY
COA D MIRE	FON D NESS	*HAN D YMAN	HOO D IEST	ME D IOCRE	*PYO D ERMA
COE D ITOR	*FOO D WAYS	*HAR D BACK	HOO D LESS	ME D ITATE	*QUA D PLEX
*COL D COCK	FOR D LESS	HAR D BALL	*HOO D LIKE	ME D USOID	*QUA D RANS
COL D NESS	GAR D ENER	HAR D BOOT	*HOO D WINK	MI D BRAIN	*QUA D RANT
CON D ENSE	GAR D ENIA	HAR D CASE	KIN D LESS	MI D POINT	*QUA D RATE
CON D OLER	GAR D YLOO	HAR D CORE	KIN D LING	MI D RANGE	*QUA D RIGA
CON D ONER	GEN D ARME	HAR D E D GE	KIN D NESS	MI D STORY	*QUA D ROON
CON D UCER	GEO D ESIC	HAR D ENER	LAB D ANUM	MO D ALITY	*QUI D D ITY
COR D ELLE	GEO D ETIC	*HAR D HACK	LAN D FALL	MO D ELING	*QUI D NUNC
COR D LESS	GIL D HALL	*HAR D HEA D	LAN D FILL	MO D ELLE D	RAN D IEST
*COR D LIKE	GLA D D EST	HAR D IEST	LAN D FORM	MO D ELLER	RAN D OMLY
COR D OVAN	GLA D D ING	HAR D LINE	LAN D GRAB	MO D ERATE	*RAN D PICK
COR D UROY	GLA D IATE	HAR D NESS	*LAN D LA D Y	MO D ERATO	REA D D ICT
COR D WAIN	GLA D IEST	HAR D NOSE	LAN D LESS	MO D IFIE D	REA D IEST
*COR D WOOD	GLA D IOLA	*HAR D SHIP	LAN D LINE	MO D IOLUS	*REA D JUST
CRE D EN D A	GLA D IOLI	*HAR D TACK	LAN D LOR D	MO D ULATE	REE D BIR D
*CRE D ENZA	GLA D NESS	*HAR D WARE	*LAN D MARK	*MOL D WARP	*REE D BUCK
CRE D IBLE	GLA D SOME	*HAR D WIRE	LAN D MASS	*MOR D ANCY	REE D LIKE
CRE D ITOR	GOA D LIKE	*HAR D WOOD	LAN D SI D E	MU D DIEST	REE D LING
CRU D ITES	*GOL D FISH	*HAV D ALAH	*LAN D SKIP	MU D GUARD	REN D ERER
CUR D IEST	GOO D NESS	*HEA D ACHE	LAN D SLI D	MU D STONE	REN D IBLE
*D AN D RUFF	*GOO D WIFE	*HEA D ACHY	LAN D SLIP	NEE D IEST	*REN D ZINA
*D AN D YISH	GOO D WILL	*HEA D BAN D	LAN D SMAN	NEE D LESS	RHO D AMIN
*D AN D YISM	*GRA D IENT	*HEA D FISH	LAN D WAR D	NEE D LING	RI D D ANCE
*D AY D REAM	GRA D UAN D	HEA D GATE	LAR D IEST	NON D AIRY	ROA D KILL
D EA D BEAT	GRA D UATE	HEA D GEAR	LAR D LIKE	NON D ANCE	ROA D LESS
D EA D BOLT	GRI D IRON	HEA D HUNT	LAU D ABLE	PA D D LING	*ROAD SHOW
D EA D ENER	*GRI D LOCK	HEA D IEST	LAU D ANUM	PAN D ANUS	ROA D SI D E
D EA D FALL	GUI D ANCE	*HEA D LAMP	LAU D ATOR	*PAN D EMIC	*ROAD WORK
D EA D HEA D	*GUI D EWAY	HEA D LAN D	LEA D IEST	PAN D ERER	ROA D STER
D EA D LIER	*HAB D ALAH	HEA D LESS	LEA D SMAN	*PAN D OWDY	RON D ELET
D EA D LIFT	HAN D BALL	HEA D LINE	LEA D LESS	PAR D ONER	*ROW D YISH
D EA D LINE	HAN D BELL	*HEA D LOCK	*LEA D WORK	*PE D D LERY	*ROW D YISM
*D EA D LOCK	HAN D BILL	HEA D LONG	LEA D WORT	PE D D LING	RU D D IEST
D EA D NESS	*HAN D BOOK	HEA D MOST	LEW D NESS	*PEN D ENCY	SA D D LERY
D EAD WOOD	HAN D CART	HEA D NOTE	LOA D STAR		

SA D D LING	SUB D URAL	**WIL D LING**	BIR D	KIN D	SEN D
SAN D ARAC	SUN D ERER	**WIL D NESS**	BOL D	LAI D	SHA D
*SAN D BANK	SUN D RESS	*WILD WOOD	BON D	LAN D	SHE D
SAN D BURR	SUN D RIES	*WILD WOOD	BRA D	LAR D	SHO D
*SAN D FISH	SUN D ROPS	WIN D BURN	BRE D	LAU D	SIL D
SAN D IEST	*SVE D BERG	*WIN D FALL	BUN D	LEA D	SKI D
SAN D LIKE	SYN D ESIS	*WIN D FLAW	BUR D	LEN D	SLE D
SAN D LING	SYN D ETIC	WIN D GALL	CAI D	LEU D	SNE D
SAN D PEEP	SYN D ROME	WIN D IEST	CAR D	LEW D	SOL D
SAN D PILE	TEN D ANCE	WIN D LASS	**CHA D**	LIE D	SOR D
SAN D SHOE	TEN D ENCE	WIN D LESS	CLA D	LOA D	SPE D
SAN D SOAP	TEN D ENCY	WIN D LING	CLO D	LOR D	SPU D
SAN D SPUR	TEN D ERER	WIN D MILL	COE D	LOU D	STU D
*SAN D WICH	TEN D ERLY	*WIN D PIPE	COL D	MAI D	SU D D
SAN D WORM	*TOA D FISH	*WIN D SOCK	COR D	MEA D	SUR D
SAN D WORT	*TOA D FLAX	*WIN D SURF	CRU D	MEE D	TEN D
SAR D ONIC	TOA D LESS	*WIND WAR D	CUR D	MEL D	THU D
*SAR D ONYX	TOA D LIKE	*WIND WAR D	D EA D	MEN D	TIE D
SEA D ROME	*TOA D YISH	WON D ERER	D EE D	MIL D	TOA D
*SEE D CAKE	TOA D YISM	WON D ROUS	D IE D	MOL D	TOL D
SEE D CASE	*TRA D EOFF	*WOO D BIND	D UA D	MOO D	TRA D
SEE D IEST	TRA D ITOR	WOO D BINE	D YA D	NAR D	TRO D
SEE D LESS	TRA D UCER	*WOO D CHAT	FAR D	NEE D	TUR D
SEE D LIKE	TRU D GEON	*WOO D COCK	FEE D	NER D	VEL D
SEE D LING	TRU D GING	WOO D IEST	FEN D	NUR D	VEN D
SEE D SMAN	TWA D DLER	WOO D LAN D	FEO D	PAI D	VOI D
SEE D TIME	TWI D DLER	*WOO D LARK	FEU D	PAR D	WAN D
*SHA D BLOW	VEN D ETTA	WOO D LESS	FIN D	PEN D	WAR D
*SHA D BUSH	VEN D EUSE	WOO D LORE	FLE D	PIE D	WEE D
*SHA D CHAN	VEN D IBLE	WOO D NOTE	FOL D	PLE D	WEL D
*SHA D DOCK	*VEN D IBLY	WOO D PILE	FON D	PLO D	WEN D
SHA D IEST	*VER D ANCY	*WOO D RUFF	FOO D	PON D	**WHI D**
*SHA D OWER	VER D ERER	*WOO D SHED	FOR D	POO D	WIL D
*SHA D RACH	VER D EROR	*WOO D SHED	FUN D	PRO D	WIN D
SHE D ABLE	VER D ITER	WOO D SMAN	GAU D	QAI D	WOA D
SHE D D ING	VIN D ALOO	*WOO D WIND	GEL D	QUA D	WOL D
*SHE D LIKE	VOI D ANCE	*WOO D WORK	GIL D	QUI D	WOO D
*SHU D D ERY	VOI D NESS	*WOO D WORM	GIR D	QUO D	WOR D
*SKY D IVER	WAN D ERER	*WOR D BOOK	GLA D	RAI D	**WYN D**
SLE D D ING	WAN D EROO	WOR D IEST	GLE D	RAN D	YAL D
*SLI D EWAY	*WAR D ENRY	WOR D LESS	GOA D	REA D	YAR D
SMI D GEON	WAR D RESS	*WOR D PLAY	GOL D	RE D D	YAU D
SO D D ENLY	WAR D ROBE	*YAR D BIR D	GOO D	REE D	YEL D
SOL D ERER	WAR D ROOM	YAR D LAN D	GOW D	REN D	YIR D
SOL D IERY	*WAR D SHIP	*YAR D WAN D	GRA D	RIN D	YON D
SPA D EFUL	WEE D IEST	*YAR D WORK	GRI D	ROA D	BASE D
SPA D ICES	WEE D LESS		GUI D	ROO D	BEAR D
SPA D ILLE	*WEE D LIKE	BAL D	HAN D	RU D D	BIEL D
STE D FAST	WEL D LESS	BAN D	HAR D	RYN D	**BIFI D**
*STU D BOOK	*WEL D MENT	BAR D	HEE D	SAI D	**BIPE D**
STU D D ING	*WHO D UNIT	BAU D	HEL D	SAN D	**BIPO D**
*STU D FISH	*WIL D FIRE	BAW D	HER D	SAR D	BLAN D
STU D IOUS	*WIL D FOWL	BEA D	HIN D	SCA D	BLEE D
*STU D WORK	WIL D LAN D	BEN D	HOL D	SCU D	BLEN D
SUB D EPOT	*WIL D LIFE	BIN D	HOO D	SEE D	BLIN D

BLON D	GEOI D	PAGE D	STAI D	**BEHEA D**	**D AMME D**
BLOO D	GLAN D	PAGO D	STAN D	**BEHEL D**	**D AMNE D**
BLUE D	GLEE D	**PAVI D**	STEA D	**BEHIN D**	**D APPE D**
BOAR D	GONA D	PILE D	STEE D	**BEHOL D**	D ARNE D
BORE D	GOUR D	PINE D	STIE D	BELAU D	**D AYBE D**
BOUN D	GRAN D	PLAI D	STOO D	BESTU D	**D EFEN D**
BOVI D	GREE D	PLEA D	SWAR D	BETTE D	**D EFIE D**
BRAI D	GRIN D	PLIE D	SWOR D	**BEYON D**	**D EFUN D**
BRAN D	GUAR D	POIN D	SYNO D	**BIBBE D**	D ELEA D
BREA D	GUIL D	POLE D	TABI D	**BIFOL D**	**D EMAN D**
BREE D	HALI D	POUN D	TEII D	BINNE D	D ENIE D
BROA D	*HEXA D	PRIE D	TEIN D	BITTE D	D ENNE D
BROO D	HOAR D	PROU D	TEPI D	**BO D IE D**	**D EPEN D**
BUIL D	**HO D A D**	PSEU D	THIR D	**BOGGE D**	D ESAN D
CAIR D	**HOME D**	**PYOI D**	TIMI D	**BOYAR D**	**D ESMI D**
CANI D	HOUN D	RABI D	TIRE D	BRIAR D	D EVOI D
CASE D	**HUMI D**	RANI D	TREA D	**BROMI D**	**D IACI D**
CAUL D	**HYOI D**	RAPI D	TREN D	**BUGGE D**	**D IGGE D**
CAVE D	*JEHA D	REA D D	TRIA D	**BUMME D**	D ILLE D
CEBI D	**JERI D**	REBI D	TRIE D	BURIE D	**D IMME D**
CERE D	*JIHA D	RE D I D	TRUE D	BURRE D	D INNE D
CHIL D	**KNEA D**	RESI D	TUMI D	BUSIE D	*D IOXI D
CHOR D	LAIR D	RESO D	TWEE D	BUSSE D	**D IPPE D**
CLOU D	**LAKE D**	REWE D	**TYPE D**	**BYROA D**	D ISBU D
CO D E D	LAME D	RIGI D	VALI D	*BYWOR D	D ISSE D
COUL D	LATE D	ROSE D	**VAPI D**	CANAR D	**D OGGE D**
CREE D	LIAR D	ROUN D	VIAN D	**CAN D I D**	D OILE D
CRIE D	**LIKE D**	SALA D	VIRI D	CANNE D	D OITE D
CROW D	LINE D	SAPI D	**VIVI D**	**CAPPE D**	D ONNE D
CUPI D	LIPI D	SARO D	WEAL D	CAPSI D	D OO D A D
CYCA D	LIVI D	SAYI D	WEIR D	CATTE D	D ORSA D
D REA D	LOVE D	SCAL D	WIEL D	**CAU D A D**	D OTAR D
D RIE D	LUCI D	SCEN D	WISE D	**CEBOI D**	D OTTE D
D RUI D	LURI D	SCOL D	WOAL D	**CERVI D**	**D ROWN D**
D RYA D	LUTE D	SCRO D	WORL D	**CHIEL D**	D UNNE D
FARA D	LYAR D	SHAR D	WOUL D	CITIE D	**D UPPE D**
FAUL D	MAUN D	SHEN D	WOUN D	CLERI D	D URNE D
FELI D	MENA D	SHER D	WRIE D	COCCI D	FANNE D
FETI D	MONA D	SHIE D	YAIR D	**CO D DE D**	FANTO D
FIEL D	**MOPE D**	SHRE D	YAUL D	**COGGE D**	FATTE D
FIEN D	MOUL D	SI D E D	YIEL D	**COHEA D**	FECUN D
FIOR D	MOUN D	**SKAL D**	*ZOOI D	COLEA D	FERVI D
FIRE D	**MOVE D**	**SKIE D**	**BABIE D**	CONNE D	FETTE D
*FJEL D	**MUCI D**	SLOI D	**BAGGE D**	CONOI D	FINNE D
*FJOR D	MURI D	**SLOJ D**	BALLA D	**COPIE D**	FITTE D
FLIE D	**MYOI D**	SLOY D	BANNE D	**COPPE D**	FOETI D
FLUI D	**MYSI D**	SNOO D	BARIE D	COSIE D	FOGGE D
FOUN D	NAIA D	SOLE D	BARRE D	**COWAR D**	FORBI D
FRAU D	**NAKE D**	SOLI D	BATTE D	*COZIE D	FRIEN D
FREE D	NALE D	SOUN D	**BAYAR D**	CUBOI D	FRIGI D
FREM D	NICA D	SPEE D	BE D DE D	CUPPE D	FUCOI D
FRIE D	NITI D	SPEN D	BE D RI D	CURSE D	FUGGE D
FRON D	NOMA D	SPIE D	BEGGE D	CUSPI D	FULGI D
GA D I D	NOSE D	*SQUA D	BEGIR D	CYANI D	FUNNE D
GELI D	NOTE D	*SQUI D	BEGLA D	CYMOI D	FURRE D

GABBE D	JERRI D	MORBI D	RAPPE D	SACRE D	TOLUI D
GA D DE D	JETTE D	MUCOI D	RATTE D	SAGGE D	TOMCO D
GA D OI D	*JOCUN D	MUGGE D	REBIN D	SAIYI D	TOMME D
GAGGE D	*JUGGE D	MUMME D	RECLA D	SALPI D	TOPPE D
GAMME D	KELOI D	MUSCI D	RECOR D	SAPPE D	TOROI D
GANOI D	KENNE D	*MUSJI D	RE D BU D	SAYYI D	TORPI D
GAPPE D	*KEPPE D	MYRIA D	RE D DE D	SCHRO D	TORRI D
GARRE D	*KEYPA D	*MYXOI D	REFEE D	SCREE D	TOTTE D
GASSE D	*KI D VI D	NAPPE D	REFFE D	SCRIE D	TOWAR D
GELLE D	KITTE D	NAVAI D	REFIN D	SEABE D	TOXOI D
GEMME D	KOBOL D	NEREI D	REFOL D	SECON D	TREPI D
GERUN D	LAGEN D	NETTE D	REFUN D	SECUN D	TRIFI D
GIGGE D	LAGGE D	NIMRO D	REGAR D	SHAIR D	TRIPO D
GINNE D	LAMME D	NITRI D	REGIL D	SHALE D	TUBBE D
GOBBE D	LAMPA D	NO D DE D	RELEN D	SHIEL D	TUNNE D
GO D DE D	LAPPE D	NORME D	RELIE D	SHOUL D	TUPPE D
GRAVI D	*LAZIE D	NUTTE D	RELOA D	SHREW D	TURBI D
GROUN D	LEAVE D	PALLE D	REMAN D	SHROU D	TURGI D
GUMME D	LEGEN D	PALLI D	REMEN D	SIALI D	TUTTE D
GUNNE D	LEGGE D	PANNE D	REMIN D	SINNE D	VANNE D
GUTTE D	LETTE D	PARRE D	REMOL D	SIPPE D	VARIE D
HAGGE D	LEVIE D	PATTE D	REPAI D	SO D DE D	VATTE D
HAIRE D	LIGAN D	PAVEE D	REPAN D	SOGGE D	VAWAR D
HALOI D	LILIE D	PEGGE D	REPPE D	SOLAN D	VERBI D
HAMME D	LIMPI D	PENNE D	REREA D	SOPPE D	VESPI D
HAPPE D	LIPOI D	PENTA D	RESAI D	SOR D I D	VETTE D
HATRE D	LIPPE D	PEPPE D	RESEE D	SOTTE D	VIROI D
HATTE D	*LIQUI D	PEPTI D	RESEN D	SPARI D	VISAR D
*HAZAR D	*LIZAR D	PERIO D	RESOL D	SPREA D	VISCI D
HEMME D	LOBBE D	PETAR D	RETAR D	STOLI D	*VIZAR D
HEMOI D	LOGGE D	PETTE D	RETOL D	STOUN D	WAGGE D
HEPTA D	LOOSE D	*PHYSE D	RETTE D	STRAN D	WANNE D
HERAL D	LOPPE D	PIGGE D	REVVE D	STROU D	WARRE D
HERBE D	LOTTE D	PINNE D	REWAR D	STUPI D	*WEBFE D
HIPPE D	LUGGE D	PIPPE D	REWEL D	SUBBE D	WETTE D
HISPI D	MA D DE D	PITIE D	REWIN D	SULFI D	*WICKE D
HOGGE D	MAENA D	PITTE D	REWOR D	SUMME D	WIGGE D
HOLAR D	MALFE D	PLACI D	RIBAL D	SUNNE D	WINNE D
HONIE D	MALTE D	PLATE D	RIBAN D	SUPPE D	WITTE D
HOOPE D	MANNE D	PLEIA D	RIBBE D	SWOUN D	*WIZAR D
HOOVE D	MANTI D	PONGI D	RI D DE D	TABAR D	WONNE D
HORRI D	MAPPE D	PONIE D	RIFFE D	TABBE D	WOOLE D
HOTBE D	MARAU D	POPPE D	RIGGE D	TAGGE D	*XYLOI D
HOTRO D	MARRE D	POTTE D	RIMME D	TANNE D	YAPPE D
HOTTE D	*MASJI D	PREME D	RIPPE D	TAPPE D	YESSE D
HUGGE D	MATTE D	PSOCI D	RITAR D	TARRE D	YIPPE D
HUMME D	*MAZAR D	PUGGE D	ROBAN D	TATTE D	*ZONKE D
HUTTE D	ME D IA D	PUNNE D	ROBBE D	TECHE D	*ZYGOI D
*HYBRI D	MELOI D	PUPPE D	ROTUN D	TETRA D	BA D LAN D
HY D RI D	METHO D	PURRE D	RUBBE D	THREA D	BAN D IE D
*JAGGE D	MILOR D	PUTRI D	RUBIE D	TI D IE D	BARMAI D
*JAMME D	MISA D D	RAGGE D	RUCHE D	TINEI D	BARTEN D
JARRE D	MOBLE D	RAMME D	RUGGE D	TINNE D	BASTAR D
JASSI D	MONIE D	RAMRO D	RUTTE D	TIPPE D	BAUSON D
JEREE D	MOPPE D	RANCI D	SABBE D	TOGGE D	*BAYWOO D

BEBLOO D	*CHEVIE D	D ENTOI D	FRITTE D	*JETTIE D	MISREA D
BECLOU D	CHILIA D	D EO D AN D	FROGGE D	*JOLLIE D	MISSEN D
*BECROW D	CHINNE D	D ERMOI D	FROSTE D	*JUGHEA D	MISSHO D
BE D WAR D	*CHIPPE D	D ESCEN D	FROWAR D	*KATY D I D	MISTEN D
BEEYAR D	CHLORI D	D ESMOI D	FUNGOI D	*KEFLOO D	MISWOR D
BELACE D	*CHOPPE D	D ESPON D	GABBAR D	*KEYCAR D	MO D ULE D
BELATE D	CHOROI D	D IALLE D	GARLAN D	*KEYWOR D	MONACI D
BELLIE D	*CICHLI D	D IAMON D	GESSOE D	KILORA D	MONEYE D
BELOVE D	CIRSOI D	D IAPSI D	*GIZZAR D	KIN D RE D	MU D D IE D
BEROBE D	CISSOI D	D IEHAR D	GLENOI D	KNEEPA D	MUMMIE D
BESTEA D	CLAMME D	D IPLOI D	GLOBOI D	KNOTTE D	MUSTAR D
*BETAXE D	CLOTTE D	D ISBAN D	GLOCHI D	LABROI D	MYELOI D
BIGHEA D	CLUPEI D	D ISCAR D	GLORIE D	LAGGAR D	NEGROI D
BIGOTE D	COCCOI D	D ISCOI D	GLUTTE D	LALLAN D	NEUROI D
BILOBE D	COFOUN D	D ISCOR D	GNARRE D	LANATE D	NOCTUI D
BILSTE D	COLLAR D	D ISPEN D	GOBIOI D	LANGUI D	NONACI D
BLATTE D	COLLIE D	D ISTEN D	GO D HEA D	LANIAR D	NONFOO D
BLESSE D	COLLOI D	D OGSLE D	GO D HOO D	LANYAR D	NONPAI D
BLOTTE D	COLORE D	D OGWOO D	GO D SEN D	LATERA D	NONSKE D
BLOWSE D	COMMAN D	D OLLIE D	GOLIAR D	LEEWAR D	NONSKI D
*BLOWZE D	COMMEN D	D ONNER D	GORMAN D	LENTOI D	NONWOR D
BOBSLE D	COMPEN D	D RAMME D	GRAN D A D	LEOPAR D	NORLAN D
BOGWOO D	CONCOR D	D ROMON D	GRINNE D	LEOTAR D	NOTEPA D
BOLLAR D	CONTEN D	D ROPPE D	GRIPPE D	LEPORI D	NUTWOO D
BOMBAR D	COPEPO D	D RUMME D	GUISAR D	LIANOI D	PAGURI D
BOOKEN D	CORNFE D	D RYLAN D	GUMWEE D	LIMITE D	PAN D IE D
*BOWHEA D	COSTAR D	D UELLE D	GUMWOO D	LINGCO D	PAROTI D
*BOXWOO D	*COWBIN D	D ULLAR D	GURNAR D	LINSEE D	PARRIE D
*BOYHOO D	*COWBIR D	*D YEWEE D	HAGGAR D	LITHOI D	PARTIE D
BRANNE D	*COWHAN D	*D YEWOO D	HALBER D	LOBATE D	PAYLOA D
BRIGAN D	*COWHER D	FACIEN D	HALYAR D	LOGWOO D	PEASCO D
BRIMME D	*COWSHE D	FACTOI D	HAPLOI D	LOWBRE D	PERACI D
BRIN D E D	CRAMME D	FANCIE D	HARRIE D	LOWLAN D	PERCOI D
BU D D IE D	CRAW D A D	FANFOL D	HATBAN D	LUNATE D	*PEROXI D
BUGSEE D	CRICOI D	FARMAN D	HAYSEE D	LYRATE D	PERPEN D
BULLIE D	CRINOI D	FATBIR D	HELIPA D	*LYCOPO D	*PHASMI D
BURSEE D	CROOKE D	FATHEA D	*HEXAPO D	MALLAR D	PHONIE D
BURWEE D	CROPPE D	FATWOO D	HISTOI D	MANGOL D	*PHYTOI D
BUSLOA D	CTENOI D	FENLAN D	*HOGWEE D	MANHOO D	PIEBAL D
BUSTAR D	*CUCKOL D	FERRIE D	HOLLAN D	MANKIN D	PIGWEE D
*BUZZAR D	CU D WEE D	FIBROI D	HOMINI D	MANSAR D	PINFOL D
CAN D IE D	CULICI D	FILARH D	*HOPHEA D	MANWAR D	PINGUI D
CARABI D	CULLIE D	FLAC D I D	HOPTOA D	MARRIE D	PINHEA D
CARLOA D	CURRIE D	*FLAMME D	HOTHEA D	MASTOI D	PINWEE D
CAROTI D	CUSTAR D	*FLAPPE D	HUN D RE D	MATTOI D	PITHEA D
CARRIE D	*CYCLOI D	FLATBE D	HUSBAN D	*MAYWEE D	PLACAR D
CATBIR D	CYSTOI D	FLATTE D	HYALOI D	*MAZZAR D	PLACOI D
CATHEA D	D AGWOO D	*FLIPPE D	*HY D ATI D	MEGAPO D	PLAFON D
CERATE D	D ASTAR D	FLUORI D	*HY D ROI D	MELAME D	PLANNE D
CESTOI D	D ECAPO D	FOOTPA D	*HYPNOI D	MERMAI D	PLASMI D
*CHALCI D	D ECRIE D	FORFEN D	*JARHEA D	MI D LAN D	PLASTI D
*CHAPPE D	D EFRAU D	FORWAR D	*JAYBIR D	MINUEN D	PLATTE D
CHARRE D	D EIFIE D	FOULAR D	*JEOPAR D	MISBIN D	PLEOPO D
CHATTE D	D ELTOI D	FRACTE D	*JERREE D	MIS D EE D	PLOTTE D
CHELOI D	D EMIGO D	FRETTE D	*JETBEA D	MISLEA D	*PLYWOO D

*POCHAR D	RIMLAN D	SPATTE D	TOGATE D	*BACKYAR D	BULLHEA D
POLLAR D	RIPCOR D	SPIROI D	TOWHEA D	*BAL D HEA D	BULLWEE D
*POLYPO D	ROA D BE D	SPITTE D	TOWMON D	*BANKCAR D	BUSHLAN D
PONIAR D	ROSEBU D	SPOROI D	TRAMME D	BAREHEA D	*BUZZWOR D
*POPEYE D	SAGGAR D	SPURRE D	TRAPPE D	BARNYAR D	CABALLE D
POPPIE D	SALLIE D	*SQUALI D	TRIACI D	BASSWOO D	*CABOCHE D
PORTEN D	SAPHEA D	STAGGE D	TRICLA D	*BECOWAR D	*CABOSHE D
POTHEA D	SAPWOO D	STARRE D	TRIFOL D	BE D OTTE D	CABSTAN D
POULAR D	SARCOI D	STEMME D	TRIMME D	BE D STAN D	CANALLE D
PREAGE D	SATYRI D	STEPPE D	*TRIOXI D	BE D STEA D	CANCROI D
PREBEN D	SCANNE D	STEROI D	TRIPPE D	BEEBREA D	CANFIEL D
PREBIN D	SCARRE D	STEWAR D	TROLAN D	*BEEFWOO D	CARANGI D
PREMOL D	SCATTE D	STIPEN D	TROTTE D	BEFRIEN D	CAR D IOI D
PREPAI D	SCIURI D	STIRRE D	TWINNE D	BEROUGE D	CAROLLE D
PREPPE D	SCUMME D	STOPPE D	TWITTE D	BESHROU D	CARTLOA D
PRESOL D	SEABIR D	STORIE D	TWOFOL D	BESLAVE D	CARYATI D
PRETEN D	SEAFOO D	STU D IE D	*TYPHOI D	BESPREA D	CASELOA D
PRIMME D	SEAWAR D	STUMME D	VANWAR D	*BEWINGE D	CATENOI D
PROBAN D	SEAWEE D	STUNNE D	VISCOI D	*BICUSPI D	CAU D ATE D
PROCEE D	SEE D BE D	STYLOI D	WA D D IE D	*BIFORKE D	CENTROI D
PROPEN D	SEE D PO D	SUBACI D	WARHEA D	*BIFORME D	*CEPHALA D
PROPPE D	*SHAMME D	SUBARI D	WARLOR D	BILLFOL D	CERATOI D
PROTEI D	SHINNE D	SUBHEA D	*WAXWEE D	BILLHEA D	*CHARACI D
PROTEN D	*SHIPPE D	SUBTEN D	*WAYWAR D	BILLIAR D	CHEERLE D
PSYLLI D	*SHOPPE D	SUCCEE D	WEARIE D	*BIND WEE D	*CHELIPE D
PUTTIE D	SHOTTE D	SULPHI D	WEASAN D	BIPARTE D	*CHENOPO D
PYRALI D	SIALOI D	SUMMAN D	*WEAZAN D	BIR D SEE D	*CHIL D BE D
*PYRAMI D	*SICKBE D	SUNBIR D	*WEEKEN D	*BIVALVE D	*CHILOPO D
*QUERIE D	SIGANI D	SUNLAN D	WERGEL D	*BLINKAR D	CHOREOI D
*QUINOI D	SIGMOI D	SUNWAR D	WERGIL D	*BLIZZAR D	CHORIOI D
*QUITTE D	SILURI D	SUSPEN D	WESSAN D	BLOO D IE D	CHRESAR D
RAGWEE D	SIMIOI D	SWAGGE D	WETLAN D	BLOO D RED	CILIATE D
RALLIE D	*SIXFOL D	SWANNE D	*WHIPPE D	*BLOWHAR D	CIRRIPE D
REA D IE D	SKINNE D	SWATTE D	WHIRRE D	BLUEBIR D	*CITYFIE D
REBLEN D	*SKIPPE D	*SYLPHI D	*WHIZZE D	BLUEHEA D	*CITYWAR D
REBOAR D	*SKYWAR D	*SYRPHI D	WILLIE D	BLUEWEE D	*CLOCHAR D
REBOUN D	SLAPPE D	TABANI D	WITHRO D	BLUEWOO D	*CLUBHAN D
REBREE D	SLATTE D	TABBIE D	WOOLLE D	BOATLOA D	CLUPEOI D
REBUIL D	SLIMME D	TABLOI D	WORRIE D	BOATYAR D	COALSHE D
RE D BIR D	SLIPPE D	TALIPE D	WORSTE D	BOLTHEA D	COALYAR D
RE D HEA D	SLITTE D	TALLIE D	*XIPHOI D	*BOMBLOA D	COATTEN D
RE D OUN D	SLOPPE D	TANKAR D	*YCLEPE D	*BOMBYCI D	*COEXTEN D
RE D RIE D	SLOTTE D	TANYAR D	YEAREN D	BON D MAI D	*COKEHEA D
RE D WOO D	SLUGGE D	TARRIE D	*ZEBROI D	BONEHEA D	COLESEE D
REFOUN D	SLUMME D	TARWEE D	*ZINCKE D	BONEYAR D	COLUBRI D
REGRIN D	SLURRE D	*TAXPAI D	*ZINCOI D	BOTRYOI D	*COMPLIE D
REPLEA D	SMARAG D	TELFOR D	*ZONATE D	*BOXBOAR D	*COMPOUN D
RESCIN D	SMUTTE D	TENFOL D	*BABYHOO D	BRACONI D	*CONCHOI D
RESOUN D	SNAPPE D	TETCHE D	*BACCATE D	BRASSAR D	CONELRA D
RESPON D	SNIPPE D	THEROI D	*BACKBEN D	BRIN D LE D	CONFOUN D
RETREA D	SONHOO D	THINNE D	*BACKHAN D	*BROWBAND	*COPYREA D
REWOUN D	*SOZZLE D	THYROI D	*BACKLAN D	*BULKHEA D	*COPYROL D
REYNAR D	SPANNE D	TIERCE D	*BACKSLI D		CORACOI D
*RHIZOI D	SPAROI D	TOA D IE D	*BACKWAR D		*COR D WOO D
RIBBAN D	SPARRE D	TOEHOL D	*BACKWOO D		*CORKWOO D

CORNUTE D	FAIRLEA D	*HAN D HEL D	*LA D YBIR D	*MO D IFIE D	PINNATE D
CORONOI D	FALCATE D	*HAN D HOL D	*LA D YHOO D	*MONKHOO D	PINNIPE D
COTYLOI D	*FARMHAN D	*HAN D MAI D	*LAMPYRI D	MONOACI D	PLASMOI D
COVERLI D	*FARMYAR D	*HANGBIR D	LAN D LOR D	MOONSEE D	PLAYLAN D
CRANNIE D	*FILMCAR D	*HAR D HEA D	LAN D SLI D	MOONWAR D	PLICATE D
*CRIBBLE D	FILMLAN D	*HAR D HEA D	LAN D WAR D	MOORLAN D	PLOWLAN D
CRICETI D	FIREBIR D	*HARDWOO D	LAPBOAR D	*MOPBOAR D	*PLUMIPE D
CROPLAN D	*FIREWEE D	*HASHHEA D	LATEWOO D	MORIBUN D	*POKEWEE D
CUNEATE D	*FIREWOO D	*HAULYAR D	LEEBOAR D	MU D GUAR D	POLEWAR D
*CUPBOAR D	*FISHPON D	*HAWKEYE D	*LEFTWAR D	MULTIFI D	*POLY D IR D
CUSSWOR D	FISSIPE D	*HAWKWEE D	LEMUROI D	MULTIPE D	*POLYPOI D
*CYANAMI D	*FIVEFOL D	*HAYFIEL D	LIBELLE D	MURAENI D	*PON D WEE D
*CYPRINI D	FLANCAR D	*HEA D BAN D	LIMULOI D	MURIATE D	*PORKWOO D
D ANEGEL D	*FLATHEA D	HEA D LAN D	LINEATE D	MUTINIE D	POSTCAR D
D ANEWEE D	FLATLAN D	*HEA D WIN D	LINEBRE D	*MYRIAPO D	POSTPAI D
D EA D HEA D	*FLAXSEE D	*HEAD WOR D	LIVERIE D	*MYRIOPO D	POTSHAR D
D EAD WOO D	*FOGBOUN D	*HEB D OMA D	LOANWOR D	NAILFOL D	POTSHER D
*D EATHBE D	*FOOTHOL D	HELICOI D	LOCOWEE D	NAILHEA D	PREBOUN D
*D ECKHAN D	*FOREFEN D	HEMATOI D	LONGHAN D	NEATHER D	PRECITE D
D EERWEE D	*FOREHAN D	*HIGHBRE D	LONGHEA D	*NECKBAN D	PRESCIN D
D EERYAR D	*FOREHEA D	*HIGHLAN D	LOPSI D E D	NINEBAR D	PRETTIE D
D EFERRE D	FORELAN D	*HIGHROA D	LOVEBIR D	NINEFOL D	PRISMOI D
*D EFLEXE D	FORESAI D	*HOGSHEA D	*LUNKHEA D	NONBRAN D	PROFOUN D
D EMURRE D	*FOREWOR D	*HOMEBRE D	LYREBIR D	NONFLUI D	PROPOUN D
D EN D ROI D	*FOREYAR D	HOMELAN D	*MAGICKE D	NONRATE D	PROTOPO D
D ENTATE D	*FOURFOL D	*HOMEWAR D	*MAIDHOO D	NONRIGI D	*PROTOXI D
D ETERRE D	*FOXHOUN D	HOMINOI D	MAINLAN D	NONSOLI D	PTEROPO D
D EVILLE D	*FREEHAN D	HONORAN D	MALPOSE D	NONVALI D	*PULPWOO D
*D IHYBRI D	*FREEHOL D	HOTBLOO D	MANIFOL D	NOSEBAN D	PURBLIN D
D IPLOPO D	FREELOA D	HUMANOI D	*MANYFOL D	NUCLEOI D	PUREBRE D
D ISPREA D	FURIBUN D	*HUMIFIE D	MARIGOL D	*PACIFIE D	PYRENOI D
D ISULFI D	GALLIAR D	*HY D RACI D	MASTHEA D	PAILLAR D	RACEMOI D
*D IVI D EN D	GANGLAN D	*HYPOACI D	MEATHEA D	PALMATE D	RA D ICAN D
*D OCKHAN D	GAPESEE D	*HYRACOI D	ME D ICAI D	PANELLE D	RAFTERE D
*D OCKLAN D	GARBOAR D	*JACQUAR D	ME D USOI D	PARANOI D	RAILBIR D
*D OCKYAR D	GASIFIE D	*JAILBIR D	MELANOI D	*PARKLAN D	RAILHEA D
D OGGONE D	GATEFOL D	*JEREMIA D	METALLE D	PARO D IE D	RAILROA D
D ONNERE D	GEEPOUN D	*JIGGERE D	*MI D FIEL D	PAROTOI D	RAINBAN D
D OORYAR D	GILTHEA D	*JUNKYAR D	*MI D SIZE D	PASSBAN D	RAINBIR D
*D OPEHEA D	GIRLHOO D	*KAILYAR D	*MILKMAI D	PASSWOR D	RAPESEE D
D OWNLAN D	GLOBATE D	*KALEYAR D	*MILKSHE D	PE D ALLE D	RAVELLE D
D OWNLOA D	GOALWAR D	*KEESHON D	*MILKWEE D	PEGBOAR D	RAWBONE D
D OWNTRO D	GOATHER D	KERATOI D	*MILKWOO D	PELLUCI D	REARWAR D
*D OWNWAR D	*GO D CHIL D	*KEYBOAR D	MILLEPE D	PENNATE D	REASCEN D
*D OWNWIN D	GOURMAN D	*KILOBAU D	MILLIAR D	PEREOPO D	RE D EMAN D
*D ROPHEA D	GRA D UAN D	*KINGBIR D	MILLIPE D	PERIO D I D	RE D UVII D
*D RUMHEA D	GRAND DAD	*KINGHOO D	MILLPON D	PETALOI D	REE D BIR D
D RUNKAR D	*GRAN D KI D	*KINGWOO D	MISAWAR D	PHORONI D	REE D BIR D
*D UCKWEE D	GROUPOI D	*KNAPWEE D	MISBRAN D	*PHOSPHI D	REFERRE D
*D UMBHEA D	GRUELLE D	*KNOTWEE D	MISBUIL D	*PHYLLOI D	REMANNE D
*D UMFOUN D	*GULFWEE D	LABELLE D	MISFIEL D	*PILCHAR D	REPETEN D
D UNELAN D	GUTTATE D	LABIATE D	MISPLEA D	PILEATE D	RERECOR D
FACETTE D	*GYNECOI D	LACERTI D	MISSOUN D	PINELAN D	REREMIN D
*FAHLBAN D	HALLIAR D	LACEWOO D	MISSPEN D	PINEWOO D	REREWAR D
			MO D ELLE D		RESINOI D

RESPREA D	SCLEREI D	*SKINHEA D	STINKAR D	TETRACI D	*VIVERRI D
RETHREA D	SCLEROI D	SLIPSHO D	STRIPPE D	TETRAPO D	WATERBE D
RETINOI D	SCOREPA D	SLUGABE D	SUBACRI D	*TETROXI D	*WAVEBAN D
REVEREN D	*SCRAPPE D	SLUGGAR D	SUBBREE D	THEROPO D	*WELLHEA D
REVULSE D	SCURRIE D	SLUMLOR D	SUBFIEL D	THINCLA D	*WHIPCOR D
*RHIZOPO D	SEABOAR D	SNAPWEE D	SUBFLUI D	THOUSAN D	*WI D EBAN D
*RHOMBOI D	*SELFHOO D	SNOWBIR D	*SUBHUMI D	*THYREOI D	*WIFEHOO D
RICEBIR D	*SELFWAR D	SNOWLAN D	SUBTREN D	*TICKSEE D	WIL D LAN D
*RICHWEE D	SEMIARI D	SNOWMOL D	SUBWORL D	TI D ELAN D	*WIL D WOO D
RIVERBE D	SEMIBAL D	*SNOWSHE D	SULCATE D	*TIGHTWA D	*WILLYAR D
*ROCKWEE D	SEMIHAR D	*SOFTHEA D	*SUMPWEE D	TILTYAR D	*WIN D WAR D
ROOTHOL D	SEMIWIL D	*SOFTWOO D	*SUNBAKE D	TIMECAR D	*WOO D BIN D
ROSEWOO D	*SERFHOO D	SOLENOI D	SUNSCAL D	TOOLHEA D	WOO D LAN D
RUBICUN D	SERRANI D	*SOLIQUI D	SUPERA D D	TOOLSHE D	*WOO D SHE D
RUNROUN D	SESAMOI D	SONGBIR D	SUPERBA D	TOTALLE D	*WOO D WIN D
SALMONI D	*SHAMMIE D	SOREHEA D	SURFBIR D	TRACHEI D	*WOOLSHE D
SARABAN D	*SHEETFE D	*SOUFFLE D	SURROUN D	TRAMROA D	*WORKLOA D
SASSWOO D	*SHEPHER D	SOURWOO D	*SWANHER D	TRICHOI D	WORMSEE D
SATINPO D	SHETLAN D	SOWBREA D	SYNAPSI D	TRILOBE D	*WORMWOO D
SAUROPO D	SHIPLOA D	SPHENOI D	SYNERGI D	TRIPLOI D	*WRETCHE D
*SCABBAR D	*SHIPYAR D	SPHEROI D	TACHINI D	TROCHOI D	*YAR D BIR D
SCABLAN D	SI D EBAN D	*SPHINGI D	TAGBOAR D	TROLLIE D	YAR D LAN D
*SCAFFOL D	SI D EWAR D	SPLEN D I D	TAILSKI D	TRUEBRE D	*YAR D WAN D
*SCAPHOI D	*SILKWEE D	*SQUIFFE D	TAILWIN D	TUBEROI D	
*SCHIZOI D	SILUROI D	STAGGAR D	TAMARIN D	VERECUN D	
SCIAENI D	SINUSOI D	STAN D AR D	TEABOAR D	*VAGABON D	
SCINCOI D	SISTROI D	STEA D IE D	*TEAKWOO D	VILIPEN D	
SCIUROI D	*SKEWBAL D	STENOSE D	TEENAGE D	*VINEYAR D	

F

FACE	FAUN	FETE	FIST	FLOW	FORM
FACT	FAWN	FEUD	FIVE	FLUB	FORT
FADE	FAUX	FIAR	FIXT	FLUE	FOSS
FADO	FAVA	FIAT	*FIZZ	FLUX	FOUL
FAIL	FAVE	FICE	FLAB	FOAL	FOUR
FAIN	*FAZE	FICO	FLAG	FOAM	FOWL
FAIR	FEAL	FIDO	FLAK	FOGY	*FOXY
FAKE	FEAR	FIEF	FLAM	FOHN	*FOZY
FALL	FEAT	FIFE	FLAN	FOIL	FRAE
FALX	FECK	FILA	FLAP	FOIN	FRAG
FAME	FEED	FILE	FLAT	FOLD	FRAP
FANE	FEEL	FILL	FLAW	FOLK	FRAT
FANG	FEET	FILM	FLAX	FOND	FRAY
FANO	FELL	FILO	FLAY	FONT	FREE
FARD	FELT	FIND	FLEA	FOOD	FRET
FARE	FEME	FINE	FLED	FOOL	FRIT
FARL	FEND	FINK	FLEE	FOOT	*FRIZ
FARM	FEOD	FIRE	FLEW	FORA	FROE
FARO	FERE	FIRM	FLEX	FORB	FROG
FASH	FERN	FIRN	FLEY	FORD	FROM
FAST	FESS	FISC	FLIC	FORE	FROW
FATE	FETA	FISH	FLIP	FORK	FRUG

FUCI	FAUNA	FILLE	**FLUKE**	FREER	***FUZEE**
FUEL	**FAUVE**	FILLO	***FLUKY**	**FREMD**	***FUZIL**
FUGU	**FAVOR**	**FILLY**	**FLUME**	FRENA	***FUZZY**
FUJI	**FAVUS**	**FILTH**	**FLUMP**	FRERE	**FYTTE**
FULL	**FAWNY**	**FILUM**	FLUNG	**FRESH**	**FABLER**
FUME	FEASE	FINAL	**FLUNK**	FRIAR	**FABRIC**
FUMY	FEAST	**FINCH**	FLUOR	FRIED	**FACADE**
FUND	***FEAZE**	**FINER**	**FLUSH**	FRIER	**FACETE**
FUNK	**FECAL**	FINIS	FLUTE	FRIES	**FACEUP**
FURL	**FECES**	**FINNY**	**FLUTY**	FRILL	**FACIAL**
FURY	***FEEZE**	FIORD	**FLUYT**	FRISE	**FACIES**
FUSE	FEIGN	***FIQUE**	***FLYBY**	**FRISK**	**FACILE**
FUSS	FEINT	FIRED	**FLYER**	**FRITH**	**FACING**
*FUTZ	FEIST	FIRER	**FLYTE**	FRITT	**FACTOR**
*FUZE	FELID	**FIRRY**	**FOAMY**	***FRITZ**	**FACULA**
*FUZZ	FELLA	**FIRST**	**FOCAL**	***FRIZZ**	**FADING**
FYCE	**FELLY**	**FIRTH**	**FOCUS**	**FROCK**	**FAECES**
FYKE	FELON	**FISHY**	**FOEHN**	FROND	FAERIE
FABLE	**FEMME**	**FITCH**	**FOGEY**	FRONS	**FAGGOT**
FACER	**FEMUR**	**FITLY**	**FOGGY**	FRONT	**FAILLE**
FACET	**FENCE**	**FIVER**	FOGIE	FRORE	**FAIRLY**
FACIA	**FENNY**	***FIXER**	FOIST	**FROSH**	***FAJITA**
FADDY	**FEOFF**	***FIXIT**	FOLIA	FROST	**FAKEER**
FADER	FERAL	***FIZZY**	FOLIO	**FROTH**	***FAKERY**
FADGE	FERIA	***FJELD**	***FOLKY**	**FROWN**	**FAKING**
FAENA	**FERLY**	***FJORD**	**FOLLY**	***FROZE**	**FALCES**
FAERY	**FERMI**	**FLACK**	FONDU	FRUIT	**FALCON**
FAGIN	**FERNY**	FLAIL	**FOOTY**	**FRUMP**	**FALLAL**
FAGOT	**FERRY**	FLAIR	FORAM	**FRYER**	**FALLEN**
FAINT	**FESSE**	**FLAKE**	**FORAY**	**FUBSY**	**FALLER**
FAIRY	FETAL	***FLAKY**	**FORBY**	**FUCUS**	**FALLOW**
FAITH	**FETCH**	**FLAME**	**FORCE**	**FUDGE**	**FALSIE**
FAKER	FETID	**FLAMY**	FORDO	FUGAL	**FALTER**
*FAKEY	FETOR	**FLANK**	**FORGE**	**FUGGY**	**FAMILY**
FAKIR	**FETUS**	**FLARE**	FORGO	FUGIO	**FAMINE**
FALSE	FEUAR	**FLASH**	***FORKY**	**FUGLE**	**FAMING**
FANCY	**FEVER**	**FLASK**	**FORME**	FUGUE	**FAMISH**
FANGA	**FIBER**	**FLAWY**	FORTE	**FULLY**	**FAMOUS**
FANNY	**FIBRE**	***FLAXY**	**FORTH**	**FUMER**	**FANDOM**
FANON	**FICHE**	**FLEAM**	**FORTY**	**FUMET**	**FANEGA**
FANUM	**FICHU**	**FLECK**	**FORUM**	FUNGI	FANION
*FAQIR	**FICIN**	FLEER	FOSSA	FUNGO	***FANJET**
FARAD	**FICUS**	FLEET	FOSSE	***FUNKY**	**FANNED**
FARCE	**FIDGE**	**FLESH**	FOUND	**FUNNY**	FANNER
FARCI	FIELD	**FLICK**	FOUNT	FURAN	**FANTOD**
FARCY	FIEND	FLIED	**FOVEA**	FUROR	**FANTOM**
FARER	**FIERY**	FLIER	**FOYER**	**FURRY**	***FAQUIR**
FARLE	**FIFER**	FLIES	FRAIL	***FURZE**	**FARCER**
FATAL	**FIFTH**	FLING	**FRAME**	***FURZY**	**FARCIE**
FATLY	**FIFTY**	FLINT	**FRANC**	FUSEE	**FARDEL**
FATTY	**FIGHT**	FLOUR	**FRANK**	FUSEL	**FARFAL**
FATWA	FILAR	FLOUT	FRASS	FUSIL	**FARFEL**
FAUGH	**FILCH**	**FLOWN**	FRAUD	**FUSSY**	**FARINA**
FAULD	FILER	**FLUFF**	**FREAK**	**FUSTY**	**FARING**
FAULT	FILET	FLUID	FREED	FUTON	**FARMER**

FARROW	FESTAL	**FITFUL**	**FLURRY**	FORINT	**FROLIC**
FASCES	**FESTER**	**FITTED**	FLUTER	**FORKER**	**FROSTY**
FASCIA	FETIAL	FITTER	**FLUTEY**	**FORMAL**	*FROTHY
FASTEN	**FETICH**	*FIXATE	*FLYBOY	**FORMAT**	*FROUZY
FATHER	**FETING**	*FIXITY	FLYING	**FORMEE**	**FROWST**
FATHOM	**FETISH**	*FIXURE	**FLYMAN**	**FORMER**	*FROWSY
FATING	**FETTED**	*FIZGIG	*FLYOFF	**FORMIC**	*FROWZY
FATTED	FETTER	*FIZZER	*FLYSCH	**FORMOL**	*FROZEN
FATTEN	**FETTLE**	*FIZZES	*FLYWAY	**FORMYL**	**FRUGAL**
FATTER	**FEUDAL**	*FIZZLE	**FOAMER**	*FORNIX	**FRUITY**
FAUCAL	**FIACRE**	*FLABBY	**FODDER**	FORRIT	*FRUMPY
FAUCES	**FIASCO**	**FLACON**	**FODGEL**	**FORTES**	**FRYPAN**
FAUCET	**FIBBER**	**FLAGGY**	**FOEMAN**	FORTIS	**FUCOID**
FAULTY	**FIBRIL**	**FLAGON**	FOETAL	*FORWHY	**FUCOSE**
FAVELA	**FIBRIN**	**FLAKER**	**FOETID**	FOSSIL	**FUCOUS**
FAVISM	**FIBULA**	*FLAKEY	FOETOR	**FOSTER**	**FUDDLE**
FAVOUR	*FICKLE	**FLAMBE**	FOETUS	**FOUGHT**	**FUELER**
FAWNER	**FIDDLE**	**FLAMEN**	*FOGBOW	**FOULLY**	**FUGATO**
FEALTY	**FIDDLY**	**FLAMER**	**FOGDOG**	**FOURTH**	**FUGGED**
FEARER	**FIDGET**	**FLANGE**	**FOGGED**	**FOWLER**	**FUHRER**
FECIAL	**FIERCE**	*FLAPPY	**FOGGER**	*FOXIER	**FULFIL**
*FECKLY	**FIESTA**	*FLASHY	**FOIBLE**	*FOXILY	**FULGID**
FECULA	**FIGURE**	**FLATLY**	FOISON	*FOXING	**FULHAM**
FECUND	FILIAL	**FLATUS**	FOLATE	**FRACAS**	**FULLAM**
FEDORA	**FILING**	**FLAUNT**	**FOLDER**	**FRACTI**	**FULLER**
FEEBLE	FILLER	**FLAVIN**	FOLIAR	FRAISE	**FULMAR**
FEEDER	FILLET	**FLAVOR**	**FOLIUM**	**FRAMER**	**FUMBLE**
FEELER	**FILLIP**	*FLAXEN	**FOLKIE**	**FRAPPE**	**FUMIER**
*FEIJOA	**FILMER**	**FLAYER**	*FOLKSY	**FRATFR**	**FUMING**
FEIRIE	**FILMIC**	**FLECHE**	FOLLES	*FRAZIL	**FUNDUS**
FEISTY	FILOSE	*FLECKY	FOLLIS	*FREAKY	**FUNEST**
FELINE	FILTER	**FLEDGE**	**FOLLOW**	**FREELY**	**FUNGAL**
FELLAH	*FILTHY	**FLEDGY**	FOMENT	FREEST	**FUNGIC**
FELLER	**FIMBLE**	**FLEECE**	**FOMITE**	*FREEZE	**FUNGUS**
FELLOE	FINALE	**FLEECH**	**FONDLE**	**FRENCH**	**FUNKER**
FELLOW	**FINDER**	**FLEECY**	**FONDLY**	**FRENUM**	**FUNKIA**
FELONY	**FINELY**	**FLENCH**	**FONDUE**	*FRENZY	**FUNNED**
FEMALE	**FINERY**	FLENSE	**FOODIE**	**FRESCO**	FUNNEL
FENCER	FINEST	*FLESHY	FOOTER	**FRETTY**	FUNNER
FENDER	**FINGER**	**FLETCH**	FOOTLE	**FRIARY**	**FURANE**
FENNEC	FINIAL	**FLEURY**	**FOOTSY**	**FRIDGE**	**FURFUR**
FENNEL	**FINISH**	*FLEXOR	*FOOZLE	**FRIEND**	**FURIES**
FERDAM	FINITE	FLIEST	**FORAGE**	*FRIEZE	**FURLER**
FERINE	**FINNED**	**FLIGHT**	**FORBAN**	**FRIGHT**	**FURORE**
FERITY	**FIPPLE**	**FLIMSY**	**FORBID**	**FRIGID**	**FURRED**
FERLIE	**FIRING**	**FLINCH**	**FORBYE**	*FRIJOL	**FURROW**
FERREL	**FIRKIN**	**FLINTY**	**FORCER**	FRILER	**FUSAIN**
FERRET	**FIRMAN**	*FLIPPY	**FOREBY**	**FRILLY**	**FUSILE**
FERRIC	**FIRMER**	FLOOIE	**FOREDO**	**FRINGE**	**FUSING**
FERRUM	**FIRMLY**	**FLOURY**	**FOREGO**	**FRINGY**	**FUSION**
FERULA	**FISCAL**	**FLOWER**	FOREST	*FRISKY	**FUSSER**
FERULE	**FISHER**	**FLUENT**	**FORGAT**	**FRIVOL**	**FUSTIC**
FERVID	*FISHLY	*FLUFFY	**FORGER**	*FRIZER	**FUTILE**
FERVOR	**FISTIC**	*FLUKEY	**FORGET**	*FRIZZY	**FUTURE**
FESCUE	*FITCHY	*FLUNKY	**FORGOT**	**FROGGY**	*FUZING

*FYLFOT	FARCEUR	FELLATE	*FIEFDOM	FISHING	*FLESHLY
PRINGE	FARCING	FELLIES	FIELDER	FISHNET	*FLEXILE
FABLIAU	FARINHA	FELONRY	FIFTEEN	*FISHWAY	*FLEXION
FABLING	FARMING	FELSITE	*FIFTHLY	FISSATE	*FLEXURE
FABULAR	FARNESS	FELSPAR	FIGHTER	FISSILE	*FLICKER
FACIEND	FARRAGO	FELTING	FIGMENT	FISSION	*FLIGHTY
FACTION	FARRIER	FELUCCA	FIGURAL	FISSURE	FLINDER
FACTOID	FARSIDE	FELWORT	FIGURER	FISTFUL	FLINGER
*FACTORY	FARTHER	FEMINIE	FIGWORT	FISTULA	*FLIPPED
FACTUAL	FASCINE	FEMORAL	FILAREE	*FITCHEE	FLIPPER
FACTURE	FASCISM	FENAGLE	FILARIA	*FITCHET	FLOATEL
*FACULTY	FASCIST	FENCING	FILBERT	*FITCHEW	FLOKATI
FADABLE	FASHION	FENLAND	*FILCHER	FITMENT	FLOOSIE
FADDIER	FASTING	FENURON	FILEMOT	FITNESS	FLOUTER
*FADDISH	FATALLY	FEODARY	FILIATE	FITTEST	FLOWAGE
FADDISM	*FATBACK	*FEOFFEE	FILIBEG	FITTING	*FLOWERY
FADDIST	FATBIRD	*FEOFFER	FILLIES	*FIXATIF	FLUBBER
FAGOTER	FATEFUL	*FEOFFOR	FILLING	*FIXEDLY	*FLUBDUB
FAIENCE	FATHEAD	FERMATA	*FILMDOM	*FIXINGS	*FLUENCY
FAILING	FATIDIC	FERMENT	FILMIER	*FIXTUTE	FLUIDLY
FAILURE	FATIGUE	FERMION	*FILMILY	FLACDID	*FLUMMOX
FAINTER	FATLESS	FERMIUM	FILMSET	FLAGGER	FLUNKER
FAINTLY	FATLIKE	FERNERY	FIMBRIA	FLAGMAN	*FLUNKEY
FAIRIES	FATLING	FERRATE	FINABLE	FLAMBEE	FLUORID
FAIRING	FATNESS	FERRETY	FINAGLE	FLAMEAU	FLUORIN
FAIRISH	FATTEST	FERRIED	FINALIS	FLAMIER	FLUSHER
*FAIRWAY	FATTIER	FERRIES	FINALLY	FLAMING	FLUSTER
FAITOUR	FATTIES	FERRITE	FINANCE	*FLAMMED	FLUTIER
FALAFEL	FATTILY	FERROUS	*FINBACK	FLANEUR	FLUTING
FALBALA	FATTING	FERRULE	FINDING	FLANGER	FLUTIST
FALCATE	FATTISH	FERTILE	FINESSE	FLANKEN	FLUTTER
*FALLACY	FATUITY	FERVENT	*FINFISH	FLANKER	FLUVIAL
*FALLOFF	FATUOUS	FERVOUR	FINFOOT	FLANNEL	*FLUXION
FALLOUT	FATWOOD	FESTIVE	FINICAL	*FLAPPED	*FLYABLE
*FALSIFY	FAUCIAL	FESTOON	*FINICKY	FLAPPER	*FLYAWAY
FALSITY	FAUTEIL	*FETCHER	FINIKIN	FLASHER	*FLYBELT
FAMULUS	*FAUVISM	*FETLOCK	FINLESS	FLATBED	*FLYBLOW
FANATIC	FAUVIST	FETTING	FINLIKE	FLATCAP	*FLYBOAT
FANCIED	FAVELLA	FEUDARY	*FINMARK	FLATCAR	*FLYLEAF
FANCIER	FAVORER	FEUDIST	FINNIER	FLATLET	FLYLESS
FANCIES	*FAZENDA	FEWNESS	FINNING	FLATTED	*FLYOVER
FANFARE	FEARFUL	FEYNESS	FIREARM	FLATTEN	*FLYPAST
FANFOLD	FEASTER	FIANCEE	*FIREBOX	FLATTER	FLYTIER
FANLIKE	FEATHER	FIBROID	FIREBUG	FLATTOP	FLYTING
FANNING	FEATURE	FIBROIN	FIREDOG	FLAUNTY	*FLYTRAP
FANTAIL	FEBRILE	FIBROMA	*FIREFLY	FLAVINE	FOAMIER
FANTASM	FEDAYEE	FIBROUS	FIRELIT	FLAVONE	*FOAMILY
FANTAST	FEDERAL	FICTILE	FIREMAN	*FLAVORY	*FOCALLY
FANTASY	FEEDBAG	FICTION	FIREPAN	FLAVOUR	FOCUSER
FANWISE	*FEEDBOX	*FICTIVE	FIREPOT	FLEABAG	FOGGAGE
FANWORT	FEEDLOT	FIDDLER	FIRSTLY	FLEAPIT	FOGGING
*FANZINE	FEELESS	FIDEISM	*FISHERY	FLEECER	FOGHORN
FARADAY	FEELING	FIDEIST	*FISHEYE	*FLEMISH	FOGLESS
FARADIC	FEIGNER	*FIDGETY	*FISHGIG	FLENSER	*FOGYISM
*FARAWAY	FELAFEL	FIDGING	FISHIER	FLESHER	FOLACIN

FOLDOUT	FORKIER	*FREEWAY	FUMIEST	FAIRNESS	*FATHERLY
FOLIAGE	FORLORN	*FREEZER	FUMULUS	*FAIRYISM	*FATSTOCK
FOLIATE	FORMANT	FREIGHT	FUNCTOR	*FAITHFUL	FATTENER
FOLIOSE	FORMATE	FRESHEN	FUNERAL	FALCATED	FATTIEST
FOLIOUS	*FORMFUL	FRESHET	FUNFAIR	*FALCHION	FAUBOURG
*FOLKISH	FORMULA	*FRESHLY	FUNGOID	FALCONER	FAVONIAN
*FOLKMOT	FORSAKE	FRESNEL	FUNGOUS	FALCONET	FAVORITE
*FOLKWAY	FORTIES	FRETFUL	FUNICLE	*FALCONRY	FAVOURER
FOLLIES	*FORTIFY	FRETSAW	FUNNEST	FALDERAL	*FAWNLIKE
FONDANT	FORTUNE	FRETTED	FUNNING	FALDEROL	FAYALITE
FONDLER	FORWARD	FRETTER	*FURBISH	*FALLAWAY	FEARLESS
FONTINA	FORWENT	FRIABLE	FURCATE	*FALLBACK	FEARSOME
FOOLERY	FORWORN	FRIBBLE	FURCULA	*FALLFISH	FEASANCE
FOOLISH	*FOSSICK	FRIGATE	FURIOSO	FALLIBLE	FEASIBLE
FOOTAGE	FOUETTE	*FRIJOLE	FURIOUS	FALSETTO	FEASTFUL
*FOOTBOY	FOULARD	FRISEUR	FURLESS	FALTBOAT	*FEATHERY
FOOTIER	FOULING	FRISKER	FURLONG	FALTERER	*FEBRIFIC
FOOTING	FOUNDER	FRISKET	*FURMETY	FAMELESS	*FECKLESS
FOOTLER	FOUNDRY	FRISSON	*FURMITY	FAMILIAL	FECULENT
FOOTMAN	FOURGON	FRITTED	FURNACE	FAMILIAR	*FEDERACY
FOOTPAD	FOVEOLA	FRITTER	FURNISH	*FAMILISM	FEDERATE
FOOTSIE	FOVEOLE	*FRIZZER	FURRIER	*FANCIFUL	*FEEBLISH
*FOOTWAY	FOWLING	*FRIZZLE	FURRILY	FANDANGO	*FEEDBACK
*FOOZLER	*FOWLPOX	*FRIZZLY	FURRING	FANEGADA	*FEEDHOLE
*FOPPERY	*FOXFIRE	FROGEYE	*FURROWY	FANFARON	*FELDSHER
*FOPPISH	*FOXFISH	FROGGED	FURTHER	*FANLIGHT	FELDSPAR
FORAGER	*FOXHOLE	FROGMAN	FURTIVE	FANTASIA	*FELICITY
FORAMEN	*FOXHUNT	FROMAGE	FUSCOUS	FANTASIE	FELINELY
FORAYER	*FOXIEST	FRONTAL	FUSIBLE	FARADAIC	FELINITY
FORBADE	*FOXLIKE	FRONTES	FUSILLI	FARADISE	FELLABLE
FORBEAR	*FOXSKIN	FRONTON	FUSSPOT	FARADISM	FELLATIO
FORBODE	*FOXTAIL	FROSTED	FUSTIAN	*FARADIZE	FELLATOR
FORBORE	*FOXTROT	FROUNCE	*FUTHARC	*FARCICAL	FELLNESS
FORCEPS	FRACTAL	FROWARD	*FUTHARK	FAREWELL	*FELLOWLY
FORCING	FRACTED	FROWNER	*FUTHORC	FARINOSE	FELSTONE
FOREARM	FRACTUR	*FROWSTY	*FUTHORK	*FARMHAND	*FELTLIKE
*FOREBAY	FRACTUS	FRUITER	*FUTTOCK	FARMLAND	*FEMINACY
*FOREBYE	FRAENUM	FRUSTUM	FABULIST	*FARMWIFE	FEMININE
FOREGUT	FRAGILE	*FUCHSIA	FABULOUS	*FARMWORK	FEMINISE
FOREIGN	FRAILTY	*FUCHSIN	*FACEDOWN	*FARMYARD	*FEMINISM
FORELEG	FRAKTUR	FUEHRER	FACELESS	FARNESOL	FEMINIST
FOREMAN	FRAMING	FUELLER	FACETIAE	*FAROUCHE	*FEMINITY
*FOREPAW	FRANKER	FUGGING	FACETTED	FARRIERY	*FEMINIZE
FORERUN	*FRANKLY	FUGUIST	*FACIALLY	FARTHEST	*FENCEROW
FORESEE	FRANTIC	FULCRUM	*FACILITY	*FARTHING	*FENCIBLE
FORETOP	FRAUGHT	FULFILL	FACTIOUS	FASCITLE	FENESTRA
FOREVER	FRAYING	FULGENT	*FACTOTUM	FASHIOUS	FENTHION
FORFEIT	*FRAZZLE	FULLERY	FADDIEST	*FASTBACK	*FERACITY
FORFEND	*FRECKLE	FULMINE	*FADEAWAY	FASTBALL	FERETORY
FORGAVE	*FRECKLY	FULNESS	FADELESS	FASTENER	*FEROCITY
FORGERY	FREEBEE	FULSOME	FAGOTING	FASTNESS	FERREOUS
FORGING	FREEBIE	FULVOUS	*FAHLBAND	FASTUOUS	FERRETER
FORGIVE	FREEDOM	FUMARIC	FAINEANT	FATALISM	FERRIAGE
FORGOER	FREEMAN	FUMBLER	FAINTISH	FATALIST	FERRITIN
*FORKFUL	FREESIA	FUMETTE	FAIRLEAD	FATALITY	*FERRYMAN

*FERVENCY	FINISHER	*FLACKERY	*FLEXAGON	FONTANEL	*FORELOCK
FESSWISE	FINITELY	FLAGELLA	*FLEXIBLE	*FOODWAYS	FOREMAST
FESTIVAL	FINITUDE	FLAGGING	*FLEXTIME	*FOOFARAW	*FOREMILK
FETATION	*FINNICKY	FLAGLESS	*FLEXUOSE	*FOOLFISH	FOREMOST
FETERITA	FINNIEST	FLAGPOLE	*FLEXUOUS	*FOOLSCAP	FORENAME
FETIALIS	*FINNMARK	FLAGRANT	*FLICHTER	FOOTBALL	FORENOON
FETICIDE	*FINOCHIO	*FLAGSHIP	*FLICKERY	*FOOTBATH	FORENSIC
*FETOLOGY	*FIREBACK	*FLAMENCO	*FLIMFLAM	FOOTFALL	FOREPART
FETTERER	FIREBALL	FLAMEOUT	*FLINCHER	FOOTGEAR	FOREPAST
FETTLING	FIREBASE	FLAMIEST	*FLINKITE	FOOTHILL	*FOREPEAK
*FEVERFEW	FIREBIRD	FLAMINES	*FLIPPANT	*FOOTHOLD	*FOREPLAY
*FEVERISH	FIREBOAT	FLAMINGO	FLORALLY	FOOTIEST	*FORERANK
FEVEROUS	*FIREBOMB	*FLAMMING	FLOURISH	FOOTLESS	FORESAID
*FIBERIZE	FIREBRAT	FLANCARD	FLOWERER	*FOOTLIKE	FORESAIL
FIBRANNE	*FIRECLAY	FLANERIE	FLOWERET	FOOTLING	FORESEER
FIBRILIA	*FIREDAMP	*FLAPJACK	FLUERICS	*FOOTMARK	*FORESHOW
FIBROSIS	*FIREFANG	FLAPLESS	FLUIDICS	FOOTNOTE	FORESIDE
*FIDELITY	FIREHALL	*FLAPPING	FLUIDISE	*FOOTPACE	*FORESKIN
FIDGETER	FIRELESS	*FLASHGUN	*FLUIDITY	*FOOTPATH	FORESTAL
FIDUCIAL	*FIRELOCK	*FLASHING	*FLUIDIZE	FOOTRACE	FORESTAY
*FIENDISH	*FIREPINK	FLATBOAT	FLUIDRAM	FOOTREST	FORESTER
*FIFTYISH	FIREPLUG	*FLATFISH	*FLUMMERY	FOOTROPE	FORESTRY
FIGEATER	FIREROOM	FLATFOOT	FLUORENE	FOOTSLOG	FORETELL
*FIGHTING	FIRESIDE	*FLATHEAD	FLUORIDE	FOOTSORE	FORETIME
FIGULINE	FIRETRAP	FLATIRON	FLUORINE	FOOTSTEP	FOREWARN
FIGURANT	*FIREWEED	FLATLAND	FLUORITE	FOOTWALL	FOREWENT
FIGURATE	*FIREWOOD	FLATLING	FLUTIEST	FOOTWEAR	*FOREWING
FIGURINE	*FIREWORK	FLATLONG	FLUTTERY	*FOOTWORK	*FOREWORD
FIGURING	*FIREWORM	FLATMATE	*FLUXGATE	FOOTWORN	FOREWORN
FILAGREE	FIRMNESS	FLATNESS	*FLYPAPER	FORBIDAL	*FOREYARD
FILAMENT	*FIRMWARE	FLATTERY	*FLYSPECK	FORBORNE	*FORGIVER
FILARIID	*FISCALLY	FLATTEST	*FLYWHEEL	*FORCEFUL	*FORJUDGE
FILATURE	*FISHABLE	FLATTING	FOAMIEST	*FORCIBLE	*FORKBALL
*FILEFISH	*FISHBOLT	FLATTISH	FOAMLESS	*FORCIPES	*FORKIEST
FILICIDE	*FISHBONE	FLATWARE	*FOAMLIKE	FORDLESS	*FORKLESS
*FILIFORM	*FISHBOWL	*FLATWASH	*FOCACCIA	FOREBEAR	*FORKLIFT
FILIGREE	*FISHHOOK	*FLATWAYS	FOCALISE	FOREBODE	*FORKLIKE
FILISTER	FISHIEST	FLATWISE	*FOCALIZE	*FOREBODY	*FORKSFUL
*FILMCARD	FISHLESS	*FLATWORK	*FOGBOUND	*FOREBOOM	FORMALIN
FILMGOER	*FISHLIKE	*FLATWORM	*FOGFRUIT	FORECAST	*FORMALLY
FILMIEST	FISHLINE	FLAUNTER	FOILSMAN	FOREDATE	*FORMERLY
FILMLAND	*FISHMEAL	FLAVONOL	*FOLDAWAY	*FOREDECK	FORMLESS
FILTERER	*FISHPOLE	FLAVORER	FOLDBOAT	FOREDOOM	*FORMWORK
FILTRATE	*FISHPOND	*FLAVOURY	FOLDEROL	*FOREFACE	FORRADER
FINAGLER	FISHTAIL	FLAWLESS	*FOLKLIFE	FOREFEEL	*FORSAKER
FINALISM	*FISHWIFE	*FLAXSEED	*FOLKLIKE	*FOREFEND	FORSOOTH
FINALIST	*FISHWORM	FLEABANE	*FOLKLORE	FOREFOOT	FORSPENT
FINALITY	FISSIPED	FLEABITE	*FOLKMOOT	FOREGOER	FORSWEAR
*FINALIZE	FISTNOTE	FLEAWORT	*FOLKMOTE	*FOREHAND	FORTIETH
FINEABLE	FITTABLE	FLECTION	*FOLKTALE	*FOREHEAD	FORTRESS
FINENESS	*FIVEFOLD	FLEECING	FOLLICLE	*FOREHOOF	FORTUITY
FINESPUN	*FIVEPINS	FLESHIER	FOLLOWER	*FOREKNOW	*FORTYISH
FINGERER	*FIXATION	*FLESHING	FOMENTER	*FORELADY	*FORZANDO
*FINICKIN	*FIXATIVE	*FLESHPOT	FONDLING	FORELAND	FOSSETTE
*FINIKING	FLABELLA	*FLETCHER	FONDNESS	*FORELIMB	FOSTERER

*FOUGHTEN	FRISETTE	FURANOSE	BU F FI	LI F TER	TU F OLI
FOULNESS	FRITTING	*FURBELOW	GO F ER	LO F TER	TU F TER
FOUNTAIN	FRIVOLER	FURCRAEA	TA F FY	NI F FER	*WA F ERY
*FOURCHEE	*FRIZETTE	*FURCULUM	TA F IA	PI F FLE	*WA F FIE
*FOURFOLD	*FRIZZIER	FURFURAL	WI F TY	PU F FER	*WA F FLE
*FOURPLEX	*FRIZZILY	FURFURAN	BA F FLE	PU F FIN	WA F TER
FOURSOME	*FRIZZLER	FURIBUND	BE F ALL	RA F FIA	*WI F ELY
FOURTEEN	*FROGFISH	FURLAUND	BE F LAG	RA F FLE	WI F ING
*FOURTHLY	FROGGING	*FURLOUGH	BE F LEA	RA F TER	*ZA F FAR
FOVEOLET	*FROGLIKE	*FURMENTY	BE F OOL	RE FACE	*ZA F FER
*FOXGLOVE	*FROMENTY	FURRIERY	BE F ORE	RE F ALL	*ZA F FIR
*FOXHOUND	FRONDEUR	FURRIEST	BE F OUL	RE F EED	*ZA F FRE
*FOXINESS	FRONTAGE	FURRINER	BE F RET	RE F EEL	*ZO F TIG
*FOZINESS	FRONTIER	FURROWER	BI FACE	RE F EEL	*BA F FIES
*FRABJOUS	FRONTLET	FURTHEST	BI F FIN	RE F ELL	*BA F FLER
FRACTION	FROSTBIT	FURUNCLE	*BI F LEX	RE F FED	*BE F LECK
FRACTURE	FROSTING	FUSELADE	BI F OLD	RE F ILE	BI F ILAR
FRAGGING	FROTTAGE	FUSELESS	BI F ORM	RE F ILL	BI F OCAL
FRAGMENT	FROTTEUR	*FUSIFORM	BO F FIN	RE F ILM	*BO F FOLA
FRAGRANT	FROUFROU	FUSILEER	BU F FER	RE F IND	*BU F FALO
*FRANCIUM	*FRUCTIFY	FUSILIER	BU F FET	RE F INE	*BU F FIER
*FRANKLIN	FRUCTOSE	FUTILITY	CA F TAN	RE F IRE	*BU F FOON
FRAULEIN	FRUITAGE	FUTURISM	CO F FEE	RE F LET	*CA F FEIN
*FREAKIER	FRUITFUL	FUTURIST	CO F FER	RE F LEW	*CO F FING
*FREAKILY	FRUITIER	FUTURITY	CO F FIN	*RE F LEX	*CO F FRET
*FREAKISH	FRUITION		CO F FLE	RE F LOW	CO F OUND
*FREAKOUT	FRUITLET	P F FT	DE FACE	*RE F LUX	DE FACER
FREEBASE	*FRUMENTY	P F UI	DE F AME	RE F OLD	DE F AMER
FREEBOOT	FRUSTULE	BA F F	DE F ANG	RE F ORM	DE F AULT
FREEBORN	*FUCHSINE	BI F F	DE F EAT	RE F UEL	DE F ENCE
FREEDMAN	FUELLING	BO F F	DE F ECT	RE F UGE	DE F ENSE
*FREEFORM	*FUELWOOD	BU F F	DE F END	RE F UND	DE F IANT
*FREEHAND	*FUGACITY	CA F F	DE F IED	RE F USE	DE F ICIT
*FREEHOLD	*FUGITIVE	CO F F	DE F IER	RE F UTE	DE F ILER
FREELOAD	FUGLEMAN	CU F F	DE F IES	RI F FED	DE F INER
FREENESS	*FULLBACK	DA F F	DE F ILE	RI F FLE	DE F LATE
FREEWILL	*FULLFACE	DO F F	DE F INE	RU F FLE	DE F LECT
FREMITUS	FULLNESS	DU F F	DE F LEA	*RU F FLY	DE F OCUS
FRENETIC	*FULMINIC	GA F F	DE F OAM	RU F OUS	DE F ORCE
FRENULUM	FUMARASE	GU F F	DE F ORM	SA F ARI	DE F RAUD
*FRENZILY	FUMARATE	HU F F	DE F RAY	SA F EST	*DE F ROCK
*FREQUENT	FUMAROLE	*JI F F	DE F UND	SA F ETY	DE F ROST
FRESCOER	*FUMATOKY	LU F F	DE F USE	SA F ROL	DE F UNCT
*FRESHMAN	FUMELESS	MI F F	*DE F UZE	SI F AKA	DI F FUSE
FRETLESS	*FUMELIKE	MU F F	DI F FER	SI F TER	F I FTEEN
FRETSOME	FUMIGANT	PU F F	DO F FER	SO F FIT	*F I FTHLY
FRETTING	FUMIGATE	RA F F	DU F FEL	SO F TEN	*HA F NIUM
*FRETWORK	*FUMINGLY	RI F F	DU F FLE	SO F TIE	*HU F FISH
*FRIBBLER	*FUMITORY	RU F F	GA F FER	SO F TLY	LE F TIES
FRICANDO	FUNCTION	TE F F	GO F FER	SU F FER	LE F TISH
FRICTION	FUNERARY	TI F F	*GU F FAW	*SU F FIX	LE F TISM
*FRIENDLY	FUNEREAL	TO F F	HA F TER	TA F FIA	LE F TIST
*FRIGHTEN	FUNGIBLE	TU F F	HE F TER	TI F FIN	LI F EFUL
FRILLING	FUNICULI	WA F F	*KA F FIR	TO F FEE	*LI F EWAY
*FRIPPERY	*FUNNYMAN	YA F F	KA F TAN	TU F FET	LI F TMAN

*LI F TO F F	CO F F ER	*CO F F RET	CON F RONT	*MIS F AITH	SNI F F IER
LO F TIER	CO F F IN	*COW F LAP	CON F UTER	*MIS F OCUS	*SNI F F ILY
LO F TILY	CO F F LE	*COW F LOP	*CU F F LESS	*MIS F RAME	*SNI F F ISH
*MA F F ICK	CON F IT	*CU F F LESS	*DA F F ODIL	*MO F F ETTE	SNI F F LER
*MU F F LER	DI F F ER	DI F F USE	DEA F NESS	*MOU F LON	*SNU F F BOX
*RA F F ISH	DI F F USE	*HU F F ISH	*DEI F ICAL	*NEW F OUND	SNU F F IER
RA F F LER	DO F F ER	*MA F F ICK	*DI F F RACT	NON F ATTY	*SNU F F ILY
RE F ENCE	DOO F US	MUD F LAT	*DI F F USER	NON F INAL	SNU F F LER
RE F EREE	DU F F EL	*MU F F LER	*DI F F USOR	NON F LUID	SOL F EGGI
RE F F ING	DU F F LE	NON F ACT	*DIS F AVOR	NON F OCAL	*SOU F F LED
RE F IGHT	DUP F ER	NON F UEL	*DIS F ROCK	*PAR F LESH	*SPI F F ING
RE F INER	GA F F ER	POM F RET	*DOG F IGHT	*PAR F OCAL	*STI F F ISH
RE F LATE	GO F F ER	PRE F ADE	*DRA F F ISH	*PER F ECTA	*STU F F ING
RE F LECT	*GU F F AW	PRE F ILE	DRA F TING	*PER F ECTO	SUB F IELD
RE F LIES	*KA F F IR	PRE F IRE	DRI F TAGE	*PER F ORCE	SUB F LOOR
RE F LOAT	*MED F LY	*RA F F ISH	DRI F TPIN	*PER F UMER	SUB F LUID
RE F OCUS	MUG F UL	RA F F LER	*DUM F OUND	PIL F ERER	*SUB F RAME
RE F ORGE	NI F F ER	RE F F ING	FAN FARON	*PRE F ACER	SU F F ERER
RE F OUND	NON F AN	RI F F ING	*F OG F RUIT	*PRE F IGHT	SU F F LATE
RE F RACT	PAN F RY	RI F F LER	*F OO FARAW	*PRE F IXAL	*SU F F ICER
RE F RAIN	PI F F LE	RU F F IAN	F UR F URAL	*PRE F LAME	*SU F F IXAL
RE F RAMT	PU F F ER	RU F F LER	F UR F URAN	*PRE F OCUS	*SU F F RAGE
RE F RESH	PU F F IN	SA F F RON	GON F ALON	*PRE F RANK	SUL F INYL
RE F RONT	RA F F IA	SUB F ILE	GON F ANON	PRO F ANER	SUL F ONAL
RE F UGEE	RA F F LE	SU F FARI	GOO F BALL	PRO F ILER	SUL F ONIC
RE F USAL	RE F F ED	*SU F F ICE	*GRA F FITO	PRO F ITER	SUL F ONYL
RE F USER	RI F F ED	SU F F USE	GRA F TAGE	PRO F OUND	SUL F URET
RE F UTAL	RI F F LE	SYN F UEL	*GRU F F IER	*PU F F BALL	SUL F URIC
RE F UTER	ROL F ER	TA F F ETA	*GRU F F ILY	*REA F F IRM	SUL F URYL
RI F F ING	RU F F LE	*WA F F LE	*GRU F F ISH	*RIF F RA F F	SUR F ACER
RI F F LER	SO F F IT	*BEE F CAKE	GUL F IEST	ROO F LESS	SUR F BIRD
RI F F LER	SU F F ER	BEE F IEST	*GUL F LIKE	*ROO F LIKE	SUR F BOAT
RI F LERY	*SU F F IX	BEE F LESS	*GUL F WEED	ROO F LINE	*SUR F ISH
RI F LING	TA F F IA	*BEE F WOOD	*GUN F IGHT	ROO F TREE	SUR F IEST
RU F F IAN	TI F F IN	*BOU F FANT	GUN F LINT	RU F F LIER	*SUR F LIKE
RU F F LER	TIT F ER	*BOW FRONT	*HAL F BACK	*RU F F LIKE	SWI F TLET
SA F F RON	TU F F ET	*BU F F ETER	*HAL F BEAK	*RU F F LING	TA F F AREL
SA F ROLE	*WA F F IE	*BU F F IEST	*HAL F LIFE	*SCA F F OLD	TA F F EREL
SI F TING	*WA F F LE	*CA F F EINE	HAL F NESS	*SCO F F LAW	TA F F RAIL
SO F TIES	*ZA F F AR	*CAL F SKIN	*HAL F TIME	*SCU F F LER	TRI F ECTA
SO F TISH	*ZA F F ER	*CAN F IELD	HAL F TONE	SEA F ARER	TRI F OCAL
SU F FARI	*ZA F F IR	*CAT F IGHT	*HAW F INCH	SEA F LOOR	TRI F ORIA
*SU F F ICE	*ZA F F RE	*COE F F ECT	*HAY F IELD	SEA F RONT	TUR F IEST
SU F F USE	*BA F F IES	*COI F F EUR	*HOO F BEAT	SEL F HEAL	TUR F LESS
TA F F ETA	*BA F F LER	*COI F F URE	HOO F LESS	*SEL F HOOD	*TUR F LIKE
*WA F F LER	*BED F RAM	*COM F IEST	*HOO F LIKE	SEL F LESS	*WA F F LING
WA F TAGE	BEE F ALO	CON F EREE	*KA F F IYEH	SEL F NESS	*WAI F LIKE
WA F TURE	BIG F OOT	*CON F ERVA	*KE F F IYEH	SEL F SAME	WAR F ARIN
*WI F EDOM	*BO F F OLA	*CON F TTO	*KIN F OLKS	*SEL F WARD	*WAY F ARER
BA F F LE	*BU F F ALO	CON F IDER	LEA F IEST	*SER F HOOD	*WHI F F LER
BI F F IN	*BU F F IER	CON F INER	LEA F LESS	*SER F LIKE	*WOL F FISH
BO F F IN	*BU F F OON	CON F LATE	*LEA F LIKE	*SHA F TING	*WOL F LIKE
BU F F ER	*CA F F EIN	*CON F LICT	*LEA F WORM	*SHU F F LER	
BU F F ET	*CO F F ING	*CON F OCAL	*MEN F OLKS	SI F F LEUR	BA F F
CO F F EE		CON F OUND	*MID F IELD		
		CON F RERE			

BAR F	LOO F	CLI F F	STU F F	*CASTO F F	*WHEREO F
BEE F	LU F F	DECA F	SWAR F	DEBRIE F	WITLOO F
BI F F	MI F F	DRA F F	THIE F	DISTA F F	*BLASTO F F
BO F F	MU F F	DWAR F	WHAR F	DUSTO F F	*BODYSUR F
BU F F	NAI F	F EO F F	*WHI F F	*F ALLO F F	*BRUSHO F F
BUM F	NEI F	FLU F F	WHOO F	*F IXATI F	*CALCTU F F
CA F F	PEL F	GANE F	BEGUL F	*F LYLEA F	*CHECKO F F
CAL F	POO F	GANO F	BEHOO F	*HANDO F F	*DANDRI F F
CHE F	POU F	GLI F F	BELIE F	HERSEL F	*DANDRU F F
CLE F	PRO F	GONE F	CUTO F F	*HIMSEL F	DISPROO F
CO F F	PU F F	GONI F	*F LYO F F	HISSEL F	*DUMMKOPF
COO F	RA F F	GONO F	GONI F F	*JUMPO F F	*DYESTU F F
CU F F	REE F	GRIE F	HEREO F	*KICKO F F	*F OREHOO F
CUI F	R FI F	GRI F F	*KHALI F	LEADO F F	*HANDCU F F
CUR F	RI F F	GRU F F	*LAYO F F	*LI FTO F F	*KERCHIE F
DA F F	ROL F	*HOW F F	MASSI F	*MASTI F F	*KNOCKO F F
DEA F	ROO F	KALI F	MYSEL F	*MIDRI F F	LANGLAU F
DEL F	RU F F	KENA F	*PAYO F F	NONSEL F	LONGLEA F
DO F F	SEI F	KLOO F	PILA F F	*PICKO F F	MEATLOA F
DU F F	SEL F	MOTI F	PUTO F F	*PLAYO F F	*MISCHIE F
F IE F	SER F	PILA F	REBU F F	*PONTI F F	*MOONCAL F
GA F F	SUR F	POU F F	RELIE F	*RAKEO F F	*RI F FRA F F
GOL F	TE F F	PROO F	REROO F	REPROO F	SANSERI F
GOO F	TI F F	*QUA F F	RIPO F F	RESTA F F	SEMIDEA F
GU F F	TO F F	*QUI F F	RUBO F F	RESTU F F	SHINLEA F
GUL F	TRE F	SCAR F	RUNO F F	SENDO F F	*STANDO F F
HAA F	TU F F	SCO F F	SCLA F F	SHADOO F	*SUBCHIE F
HAL F	TUR F	SCU F F	SCRU F F	SHEREE F	SUNPROO F
HOO F	WA F F	SCUR F	SETO F F	*SHERI F F	TIPSTA F F
HOW F	WAI F	SERI F	SHADU F	*SHOWO F F	*TRADEO F F
HU F F	WOL F	SHEA F	SHARI F	*SHUTO F F	*WEREWOL F
*JI F F	WOO F	SHEL F	SHERI F	*SPINO F F	*WETPROO F
KAI F	YA F F	*SKI F F	*SHRO F F	SPORTI F	*WINDSUR F
KEE F	*ZAR F	SLU F F	TARI F F	SUNROO F	*WOODRU F F
KER F	BLU F F	SNI F F	TIPO F F	*TAKEO F F	YOURSEL F
KHA F	BRIE F	SNU F F	*BAILI F F	THEREO F	
KIE F	CALI F	SPI F F	*BEDWAR F	*THYSEL F	
LEA F	*CHA F F	SPOO F	*BLOWO F F	TURNO F F	
LIE F	CHIE F	STA F F	*BOILO F F	*WAVEO F F	
LOA F	*CHU F F	STI F F	*CAITI F F	*WERWOL F	

G

GABY	GAMA	GARB	GAWK	GENS	GIFT
GADI	GAMB	GASH	GAWP	GENT	GIGA
GAFF	GAME	GASP	GAZE	GENU	GILD
GAGA	GAMP	GAST	GEAR	GERM	GILL
GAGE	GAMY	GATE	GECK	GEST	GILT
GAIN	GANE	GAUD	GEEK	GETA	GIMP
GAIT	GANG	GAUM	GEEZ	GEUM	GINK
GALA	GAOL	GAUN	GELD	GHAT	GIRD
GALE	GAPE	GAUR	GELT	GHEE	GIRL
GALL	GAPY	GAVE	GENE	GIBE	GIRN

GIRO	GREW	GANEV	GHYLL	GLOST	GRAPE
GIRT	GREY	GANJA	GIANT	GLOUT	GRAPH
GIST	GRID	GANOF	GIBER	GLOVE	GRAPY
GIVE	GRIG	GAPER	GIDDY	*GLOZE	GRASP
GLAD	GRIM	GAPPY	GIGAS	GLUER	GRASS
GLED	GRIN	GARNI	GIGHE	GLUEY	GRATE
GLEE	GRIP	GARTH	GIGOT	GLUME	GRAVE
GLEG	GRIT	GASSY	GIGUE	GLUON	GRAVY
GLEN	GROG	GATOR	GILLY	GLYPH	*GRAZE
GLEY	GROT	GAUDY	GIMEL	GNARL	GREAT
GLIA	GROW	GAUGE	GIMME	GNARR	GREBE
GLIB	GRUB	GAULT	GIMPY	GNASH	GREED
GLIM	GRUE	GAUNT	GINNY	GNAWN	GREEK
GLOB	GRUM	GAUSS	GIPON	GNOME	GREEN
GLOM	GUAN	*GAUZE	GIPSY	GOBAN	GREET
GLOP	GUAR	*GAUZY	GIRLY	GODET	GREGO
GLOW	GUCK	GAVEL	GIRON	GODLY	GRIDE
GLUE	GUDE	GAVOT	GIRSH	GOFER	GRIEF
GLUG	GUFF	*GAWKY	GIRTH	GOING	GRIFF
GLUM	GUID	GAWSY	GISMO	GOLEM	GRIFT
GLUT	GULF	GAYAL	GIVEN	GOLLY	GRILL
GNAR	GULL	GAYLY	GIVER	GOMBO	GRIME
GNAT	GULP	*GAZAR	*GIZMO	GONAD	GRIMY
GNAW	GUNK	*GAZER	GLACE	GONEF	GRIND
GOAD	GURU	GECKO	GLADE	GONER	GRIOT
GOAL	GUSH	GEEKY	GLADY	GONIA	GRIPE
GOAT	GUST	GEESE	GLAIR	GONIF	GRIPT
GOBO	GYBE	GEEST	GLAND	GONOF	GRIPY
GOBY	GYRE	GELEE	GLANS	*GONZO	GRIST
GOER	GYRI	GELID	GLARE	GOODY	GRITH
GOGO	GYRO	GEMMA	GLARY	GOOEY	GROAN
GOLD	GYVE	GEMMY	GLASS	GOOFY	GROIN
GOLF	GABBY	GEMOT	*GLAZE	GOONY	GROOM
GONE	GABLE	GENET	*GLAZY	GOOPY	GROPE
GONG	GADDI	GENIC	GLEAM	GOOSE	GROSS
GOOD	GADID	GENIE	GLEAN	GOOSY	*GROSZ
GOOF	GAFFE	GENII	GLEBA	GORAL	GROUP
GOOK	GAGER	GENIP	GLEBE	GORGE	GROUT
GOON	GAILY	GENOA	GLEDE	GORSE	GROVE
GOOP	GALAH	GENOM	GLEED	GORSY	GROWL
GORE	GALAX	GENRE	GLEEK	GOUGE	GROWN
GORP	GALEA	GENRO	GLEET	GOURD	GRUEL
GORY	GALLY	GENUS	GLIAL	GOUTY	GRUFF
GOSH	GALOP	GEODE	GLIDE	GOWAN	GRUME
GOUT	GAMAY	GEOID	GLIFF	GRAAL	GRUMP
GOWD	GAMBA	GERAH	GLIME	GRACE	GRUNT
GOWK	GAMBE	GERMY	GLINT	GRADE	GUACO
GOWN	GAMER	GESSO	*GLITZ	GRAFT	GUANO
GRAB	GAMEY	GESTE	GLOAM	GRAIL	GUARD
GRAD	GAMIC	GETUP	GLOAT	GRAIN	GUAVA
GRAM	GAMIN	GHAST	GLOBE	GRAMA	GUESS
GRAN	GAMMA	GHAUT	GLOGG	GRAMP	GUEST
GRAT	GAMMY	*GHAZI	GLOOM	GRANA	GUIDE
GRAY	GAMUT	GHOST	GLORY	GRAND	GUILD
GREE	GANEF	GHOUL	GLOSS	GRANT	GUILE

GUILT	*GALAXY	GARVEY	GERMEN	GLEETY	GOLDEN
GUIRO	GALENA	GASBAG	GERUND	GLIDER	GOLFER
GUISE	GALERE	GASCON	GESTIC	GLIOMA	GOLOSH
GULAG	GALIOT	GASIFY	GETTER	GLITCH	GOMUTI
GULAR	GALLET	GASKET	GEWGAW	*GLITZY	GONIFF
GULCH	GALLEY	GASKIN	GEYSER	GLOBAL	GONION
GULES	GALLON	GASLIT	GHARRI	GLOBBY	GONIUM
GULFY	GALLOP	GASMAN	GHARRY	GLOBIN	GONOPH
GULLY	GALLUS	GASPER	GHERAO	GLOMUS	GOOBER
GULPY	GALOOT	GASSED	GHETTO	GLOOMY	GOODBY
GUMBO	GALORE	GASSER	GHIBLI	GLOPPY	GOODLY
GUMMA	GALOSH	GASSES	GHOSTY	GLORIA	GOOGLY
GUMMY	GALYAC	GASTER	GIAOUR	GLOSSA	GOOGOL
GUNNY	GALYAK	GATEAU	GIBBER	GLOSSY	GOOIER
GUPPY	GAMBIA	GATHER	GIBBET	GLOVER	GOONEY
GURGE	GAMBIR	GATING	GIBBON	GLOWER	GOONIE
GURRY	GAMBIT	GAUCHE	GIBLET	GLUCAN	GOORAL
GURSH	GAMBLE	GAUCHO	GIBSON	GLUING	GOOSEY
GUSHY	GAMBOL	GAUGER	GIDDAP	GLUMPY	GOPHER
GUSSY	GAMELY	GAVAGE	GIGGED	GLUNCH	GORGER
GUSTO	GAMEST	GAVIAL	GIGGLE	GLUTEI	GORGET
GUSTY	GAMETE	GAWKER	GIGGLY	GLUTEN	GORGON
GUTSY	GAMIER	GAWPER	GIGLET	GLYCAN	GORHEN
GUTTA	GAMILY	GAWSIE	GIGLOT	GLYCIN	GORIER
GUTTY	GAMINE	GAYETY	GIGOLO	GLYCOL	GORILY
GUYOT	GAMING	*GAZABO	GILDER	*GLYCYL	GORING
GYPSY	GAMMED	*GAZEBO	GILLER	GNARLY	GOSPEL
GYRAL	GAMMER	*GAZING	GILLIE	GNATTY	GOSSAN
GYRON	GAMMON	*GAZUMP	GIMBAL	GNAWER	GOSSIP
GYRUS	GANDER	GEEGAW	GIMLET	GNEISS	GOTHIC
GABBED	GANGER	*GEEZER	GIMMAL	GNOMIC	GOTTEN
GABBER	GANGLY	GEISHA	GIMMIE	GNOMON	GOUGER
GABBLE	GANGUE	GELADA	GINGAL	GNOSIS	GOURDE
GABBRO	*GANJAH	GELANT	GINGER	GOALIE	GOVERN
GABIES	GANNET	GELATE	GINGKO	GOANNA	GRABBY
GABION	GANOID	GELATI	GINKGO	GOATEE	GRABEN
GABOON	GANTRY	GELATO	GINNED	GOBANG	GRADER
GADDED	GAOLER	GELDER	GINNER	GOBBED	GRADIN
GADDER	GAPING	GELLED	GIPPER	GOBBET	GRADUS
GADFLY	GAPPED	GEMMED	GIRDER	GOBBLE	GRAHAM
GADGET	GARAGE	GEMOTE	GIRDLE	GOBIES	GRAINY
GADOID	GARBLE	GENDER	GIRLIE	GOBLET	GRAMME
GAFFER	GARCON	GENERA	GITANO	GOBLIN	GRANGE
GAGAKU	GARDEN	GENEVA	GITTIN	GOBONY	GRANNY
GAGGED	GARGET	GENIAL	GIVING	GODDAM	GRANUM
GAGGER	GARGLE	GENIUS	GLACIS	GODDED	GRAPPA
GAGGLE	GARISH	GENTES	GLADLY	GODOWN	GRASSY
GAGING	GARLIC	GENTIL	GLAIRE	GODSON	GRATER
GAGMAN	GARNER	GENTLE	GLAIRY	GODWIT	GRATIN
GAIETY	GARNET	GENTOO	GLAIVE	GOFFER	GRATIS
GAINER	GAROTE	GENTRY	GLAMOR	GOGGLE	GRAVEL
GAINLY	GARRED	GEODIC	GLANCE	GOGGLY	GRAVEN
GAINST	GARRET	GERBIL	GLASSY	GOGLET	GRAVER
GAITER	GARRON	GERENT	*GLAZER	GOITER	GRAVID
GALAGO	GARTER	GERMAN	GLEAMY	GOITRE	GRAYLY

*GRAZER	GUGLET	GALIPOT	GASTRIN	GESTURE	GLEANER
GREASE	GUIDER	GALLANT	GATEMAN	GETAWAY	GLEEFUL
GREASY	GUIDON	GALLATE	GATEWAY	GETTING	GLEEMAN
GREAVE	GUILTY	GALLEIN	GAUDERY	GHARIAL	GLENOID
GREEDY	GUIMPE	GALLEON	GAUFFER	GHASTLY	GLEYING
GREENY	GUINEA	GALLERY	GAUNTRY	*GHERKIN	GLIADIN
GREIGE	GUITAR	GALLETA	GAVOTTE	GHILLIE	GLIMMER
GRELAG	GULDEN	GALLFLY	*GAWKIER	GHOSTLY	GLIMPSE
GREMMY	GULLET	GALLIUM	*GAWKIES	GHOULIE	GLISTEN
GREYLY	GULLEY	GALLNUT	*GAWKISH	GIBBING	GLISTER
GRIEVE	GULPER	GALLOON	GAYNESS	GIBBOSE	*GLITCHY
GRIFFE	GUMMED	GALLOOT	*GAZANIA	GIBBOUS	GLITTER
GRIGRI	GUMMER	GALLOUS	*GAZELLE	*GIDDYAP	GLOATER
GRILLE	GUNDOG	GALLOWS	*GAZETTE	*GIDDYUP	GLOBATE
GRILSE	GUNMAN	GALOSHE	*GEARBOX	GIGABIT	GLOBOID
GRIMLY	GUNNED	*GALUMPH	GEARING	GIGATON	GLOBOSE
GRINCH	GUNNEL	GAMBADE	GELATIN	GIGGING	GLOBOUS
GRINGO	GUNNEN	GAMBADO	GELDING	GIGGLER	GLOBULE
GRIPER	GUNNER	GAMBIER	GELLANT	GILBERT	GLOCHID
GRIPEY	GUNSEL	GAMBLER	GELLING	GILDING	GLONION
GRIPPE	GURGLE	GAMBOGE	GEMINAL	GILLNET	GLORIED
GRIPPY	GURNET	GAMBREL	GEMLIKE	*GIMMICK	GLORIES
GRISLY	GURNEY	GAMELAN	GEMMATE	GIMPIER	GLORIFY
GRISON	GUSHER	GAMIEST	GEMMIER	GINGALL	GLOSSER
GRITTY	GUSSET	GAMMIER	GEMMILY	GINGELI	GLOTTIS
GRIVET	GUSSIE	GAMMING	GEMMING	GINGELY	*GLOWFLY
GROCER	GUTTED	GANACHE	GEMMULE	GINGERY	GLUCOSE
GROGGY	GUTTER	GANGLIA	*GEMSBOK	GINGHAM	GLUEPOT
GROOVE	GUTTLE	GANGREL	GENERAL	GINGILI	GLUTEAL
GROOVY	*GUZZLE	*GANGWAY	GENERIC	GINGIVA	GLUTEUS
GROPER	GWEDUC	GANTLET	GENESIS	GINNING	GLUTTED
GROTTO	GYPPER	GAPOSIS	GENETIC	GINSENG	GLUTTON
GROUCH	GYPSUM	GAPPING	GENETTE	GIPPING	GLYCINE
GROUND	GYRASE	GARBAGE	GENIPAP	GIRAFFE	*GLYPTIC
GROUSE	GYRATE	GARBLER	GENITAL	GIRASOL	GNARRED
GROUTY	GYRENE	GARBOIL	GENITOR	GIRDLER	GNATHAL
GROVEL	GYRING	GARDANT	GENOISE	GIRLISH	GNATHIC
GROWER	GYROSE	GARFISH	GENSENG	GIROSOL	GNAWING
GROWLY	GABBARD	GARGLER	GENTEEL	GISARME	*GNOCCHI
GROWTH	GABBART	GARIGUE	GENTIAN	GITTERN	GNOMISH
GROYNE	GABBIER	GARLAND	GENTILE	*GIZZARD	GNOMIST
GRUBBY	GABBING	GARMENT	GENUINE	*GJETOST	GNOSTIC
GRUDGE	GABBLER	GARNISH	GEODESY	GLACIAL	GOATISH
*GRUFFY	GABELLE	GAROTTE	*GEODUCK	GLACIER	GOBBING
GRUGRU	GABFEST	GARPIKE	GEOLOGY	GLADDEN	GOBBLER
GRUMPY	GADDING	GARRING	GEORGIC	GLADDER	GOBIOID
GRUNGE	GADROON	GARROTE	GERBERA	GLADIER	GOBONEE
GRUNGY	GADWALL	GASEOUS	GERENUK	GLAIKET	GODDESS
GRUTCH	GAGGING	GASKING	GERMANE	GLAIKIT	GODDING
GUAIAC	GAGSTER	GASLESS	GERMIER	GLAMOUR	GODHEAD
GUANAY	GAHNITE	GASOHOL	GERMINA	GLANCER	GODHOOD
GUANIN	GAINFUL	GASSING	GESSOED	GLASSIE	GODLESS
GUENON	GAINSAY	GASTRAL	GESTALT	*GLAZIER	GODLIER
*GUFFAW	GALABIA	GASTREA	GESTAPO	*GLAZING	GODLIKE
GUGGLE	GALILEE	GASTRIC	GESTATE	GLEAMER	GODLING

GODROON	GRANDLY	GRIFFON	GUANASE	GYPLURE	GARDENIA
GODSEND	GRANDMA	GRIFTER	GUANINE	GYPSTER	GARDYLOO
GODSHIP	GRANDPA	GRILLER	GUARANI	GYRATOR	GARGANEY
GOGGLER	GRANGER	GRIMACE	GUARDER	GABBIEST	GARGOYLE
GOLDARN	GRANITA	GRIMIER	GUAYULE	GADABOUT	GAROTTER
GOLDBUG	GRANITE	GRIMING	GUDGEON	GADARENE	GARRISON
GOLDEYE	GRANNIE	GRIMMER	GUERDON	GADGETRY	GARROTER
GOLDURN	GRANOLA	GRINDER	GUESSER	*GADZOOKS	GARROTTE
GOLFING	GRANTEE	GRINNED	GUILDER	GAINLESS	GASALIER
GOLIARD	GRANTER	GRINNER	GUIPURE	GALABIYA	GASELIER
GOLOSHE	GRANTOR	GRIPIER	GUISARD	GALACTIC	GASHOUSE
GOMERAL	GRANULE	GRIPING	GULFIER	GALANGAL	GASIFIED
GOMEREL	GRAPERY	GRIPMAN	GUMBOIL	GALAVANT	GASIFIER
GOMERIL	*GRAPHIC	GRIPPED	GUMBOOT	GALBANUM	GASIFORM
GONDOLA	GRAPIER	GRIPPER	GUMDROP	GALENITE	GASLIGHT
GOODBYE	GRAPLIN	GRIPPLE	GUMLESS	GALIVANT	GASOGENE
GOODIES	GRAPNEL	GRISKIN	GUMLIKE	GALLEASS	GASOLENE
GOODISH	GRAPPLE	GRISTLE	GUMMIER	GALLERIA	GASOLIER
GOODMAN	GRASPER	GRISTLY	GUMMING	GALLIARD	GASOLINE
GOOIEST	GRATIFY	*GRIZZLE	GUMMITE	GALLOPER	GASTIGHT
*GOOMBAH	GRATING	*GRIZZLY	GUMMOSE	GALOPADE	GASTNESS
*GOOMBAY	GRAUPEL	GROANER	GUMMOUS	GALVANIC	GASTRAEA
*GORCOCK	GRAVELY	GROCERY	GUMSHOE	GAMASHES	GASTRULA
GORGING	GRAVEST	GROGRAM	GUMTREE	GAMBESON	*GASWORKS
GORIEST	GRAVIDA	GROMMET	GUMWEED	GAMBUSIA	GATEFOLD
GORILLA	GRAVIES	GROOMER	GUMWOOD	*GAMECOCK	GATELESS
GORMAND	GRAVING	GROOVER	GUNBOAT	GAMENESS	GATELIKE
*GOSHAWK	GRAVITY	GROSSER	GUNFIRE	GAMESMAN	GATEPOST
GOSLING	*GRAVLAX	GROSSLY	GUNLESS	GAMESOME	GATHERER
GOSPORT	GRAVURE	*GROUCHY	GUNLOCK	GAMESTER	GAUNTLET
GOSSIPY	GRAYISH	GROUPER	GUNNERY	GAMINESS	*GAVELOCK
GOSSOON	GRAYLAG	GROUPIE	GUNNING	GAMMADIA	*GAYWINGS
GOTHITE	GRAYOUT	GROUSER	GUNPLAY	GAMMIEST	*GAZOGENE
GOUACHE	*GRAZIER	GROUTER	GUNROOM	GAMMONER	*GAZPACHO
GOULASH	*GRAZING	GROWLER	GUNSHIP	GAMODEME	*GAZUMPER
GOURAMI	GREASER	GROWNUP	GUNSHOT	GANGLAND	GEARCASE
GOURMET	GREATEN	*GROWTHY	GUNWALE	GANGLIAL	GEARLESS
GRABBER	GREATLY	GRUBBER	GURGLET	GANGLIAR	GEEPOUND
GRABBLE	*GRECIZE	GRUDGER	GURNARD	GANGLIER	GELATINE
GRACILE	GREENIE	GRUELER	GUSTIER	GANGLING	GELATING
GRACING	GREENLY	*GRUFFLY	GUSTILY	GANGLION	GELATION
GRACKLE	GREENTH	GRUMBLE	GUTLESS	*GANGPLOW	GELIDITY
GRADATE	GREETER	GRUMMER	GUTLIKE	GANGRENE	GELSEMIA
GRADINE	GREISEN	GRUMMET	GUTSILY	GANGSTER	GEMINATE
GRADING	GREMIAL	GRUMOSE	GUTTATE	GANISTER	GEMMIEST
GRADUAL	GREMLIN	GRUMOUS	GUTTERY	GANTLINE	*GEMOLOGY
GRAFTER	GREMMIE	*GRUMPHY	GUTTIER	GANTLOPE	*GEMSBUCK
GRAINER	GRENADE	GRUNION	GUTTING	*GANYMEDE	GEMSTONE
GRAMARY	GREYHEN	GRUNTER	GUTTLER	GAPESEED	GENDARME
GRAMMAR	GREYISH	GRUNTLE	GUYLINE	*GAPEWORM	GENERATE
GRAMPUS	GRIBBLE	GRUSHIE	*GUZZLER	*GAPINGLY	GENEROUS
GRANARY	GRIDDER	GRUTTEN	*GWEDUCK	*GARBANZO	GENETICS
GRANDAD	GRIDDLE	GRUYERE	GYMNAST	GARBLESS	GENITALS
GRANDAM	GRIEVER	*GRYPHON	GYNECIA	GARBOARD	GENITIVE
GRANDEE	GRIFFIN	GUANACO	*GYNECIC	GARDENER	GENITURE

GENOCIDE	GLABRATE	*GLYCONIC	GRACIOUS	GRIMMEST	GUMMIEST
GENOTYPE	GLACIATE	*GLYCOSYL	GRADIENT	GRIMNESS	GUMMOSIS
GENTRICE	GLADDEST	GNARRING	GRADUAND	GRINDERY	GUMPTION
*GENTRIFY	GLADDING	GNATHION	GRADUATE	GRINNING	*GUNFIGHT
GEODESIC	GLADIATE	GNATHITE	*GRAECIZE	GRIPIEST	GUNFLINT
GEODETIC	GLADIEST	GNATLIKE	*GRAFFITO	GRIPPIER	GUNMETAL
GEOGNOSY	GLADIOLA	GNOMICAL	GRAFTAGE	GRIPPING	*GUNNYBAG
GEOLOGER	GLADIOLI	GOADLIKE	GRAMARYE	*GRIPSACK	GUNPAPER
*GEOMANCY	GLADNESS	GOALLESS	*GRAMERCY	GRISEOUS	GUNPOINT
GEOMETER	GLADSOME	GOALPOST	GRANDAME	GRISETTE	GUNSMITH
GEOMETRY	GLANDERS	GOALWARD	GRANDDAD	*GRIZZLER	*GUNSTOCK
*GEOPHAGY	GLANDULE	*GOATFISH	GRANDDAM	GROGGERY	GURUSHIP
GEOPHONE	GLASNOST	GOATHERD	GRANDEUR	*GROGSHOP	GUSTABLE
*GEOPHYTE	GLASSFUL	GOATLIKE	*GRANDKID	GROMWELL	GUSTIEST
GEOPONIC	GLASSIFR	GOATSKIN	GRANDSIR	*GROSBEAK	GUSTLESS
GEOPROBE	GLASSILY	*GODCHILD	GRANDSON	GROSCHEN	GUTTATED
*GEOTAXIS	GLASSINE	GODLIEST	GRANULAR	GROUNDER	GUTTIEST
GERANIAL	GLASSMAN	GOETHITE	*GRAPHEME	GROUPING	GUTTURAL
GERANIOL	GLAUCOMA	GOLCONDA	GRAPHITE	GROUPOID	*GYMKHANA
GERANIUM	GLAUCOUS	*GOLDFISH	GRAPIEST	GROVELER	GYMNASIA
GERARDIA	*GLAZIERY	GOLGOTHA	GRAPLINE	*GRUBWORM	GYNAECEA
GERBILLE	GLEANING	GOLLIWOG	GRAPPLER	GRUELING	GYNAECIA
GERMARIC	GLEESOME	*GOLLYWOG	GRATEFUL	GRUELLED	*GYNANDRY
GERMFREE	GLEGNESS	GOMBROON	GRATINEE	GRUELLER	*GYNARCHY
GERMIEST	GLIADINE	GONENESS	GRATUITY	GRUESOME	*GYNECIUM
GERMINAL	GLIBNESS	GONFALON	GRAVAMEN	*GRUFFIER	*GYNECOID
GERONTIC	GLIMPSER	GONFANON	*GRAVELLY	*GRUFFILY	*GYNIATRY
GESNERIA	GLISSADE	GONGLIKE	GRAVITAS	*GRUFFISH	GYNOECIA
GESTICAL	GLITTERY	GONIDIUM	GRAVITON	GRUMBLER	GYPSEIAN
GESTURAL	GLOAMING	GONOCYTE	*GRAVLAKS	GRUMMEST	GYPSEOUS
*GHASTFUL	GLOBATED	GONOPORE	*GRAYBACK	*GRUMPHIE	*GYPSYDOM
GHOSTING	GLOBULAR	GOODNESS	*GRAYFISH	*GRUMPISH	*GYPSYISH
GIANTESS	GLOBULIN	*GOODWIFE	GRAYLING	GUACHARO	*GYPSYISM
GIANTISM	GLOOMFUL	GOODWILL	GRAYMAIL	GUAIACOL	GYRATION
GIBBSITE	GLOOMING	GOOFBALL	GRAYNESS	GUAIACUM	*GYRATORY
*GIFTEDLY	GLORIOLE	GORBELLY	*GRAZIOSO	GUAIOCUM	GYROIDAL
GIFTLESS	GLORIOUS	*GORBLIMY	GREEGREE	GUANIDIN	GYROSTAT
*GIFTWARE	GLOSSARY	GORGEOUS	GREENERY	GUARANTY	
*GIGABYTE	GLOSSEME	GORGERIN	*GREENFLY	GUARDANT	N G WEE
GIGANTIC	GLOSSIER	GORINESS	GREENIER	GUARDIAN	N G
GIGAWATT	GLOSSIES	GORMLESS	GREENING	GUERIDON	ULTRUM
GILDHALL	GLOSSINA	GOSPELER	GREENISH	GUERILLA	FU G U
GILTHEAD	*GLOWWORM	GOSSAMER	GREENLET	GUERNSEY	HO G G
*GIMCRACK	*GLOXINIA	GOSSIPER	*GREENWAY	GUIDANCE	JA G G
*GIMMICKY	GLUCAGON	GOSSIPRY	GREETING	*GUIDEWAY	MI G G
GIMPIEST	GLUCINUM	GOSSYPOL	GREWSOME	GUILEFUL	MU G G
GINGELEY	GLUELIKE	GOURMAND	GREYNESS	*GUITQUIT	NO G G
GINGELLY	GLUMNESS	GOVERNOR	GRIDIRON	GULFIEST	VI G A
GINGERLY	GLUTELIN	GOWNSMAN	*GRIDLOCK	*GULFLIKE	VU G G
GINGILLI	GLUTTING	GRABBIER	GRIEVANT	*GULF-	YE G G
GIRASOLE	GLUTTONY	GRABBING	GRIEVOUS	WEED	CA G ER
GIRLHOOD	GLYCERIN	GRABBLER	GRILLADE	GULLABLE	DA G GA
*GIVEAWAY	GLYCEROL	GRACEFUL	GRILLAGE	GULLIBLE	KU G EL
*GIVEBACK	*GLYCERYL	GRACILIS	GRIMACER	GULOSITY	LI G ER
GLABELLA	*GLYCOGEN	GRACIOSO	GRIMIEST	GUMBOTIL	LU G ER

MO G GY	DI G AMY	*JA G GER	NA G GER	RI G GED	WI G WAG
NA G GY	DI G EST	JA G UAR	NE G ATE	RI G GER	*WI G WAM
PA G ER	DI G GED	*JI G GER	NI G GLE	RI G HTO	YO G INI
SA G GY	DI G GER	*JI G GLE	NO G GIN	RI G HTY	YO G URT
VU G GY	DI G LOT	*JI G GLY	NU G GET	RI G OUR	*ZI G ZAG
WI G GY	DO G DOM	*JI G SAW	PA G ING	RU G GED	*ZY G OID
BA G ASS	DO G EAR	*JO G GER	PA G ODA	RU G GER	*ZY G OMA
BA G FUL	DO G GED	*JO G GLE	*PE G BOX	RU G OLA	*ZY G OTE
BA G GED	DO G GER	JU G ATE	PE G GED	RU G OSA	BA G ASSE
BA G GER	DO G LEG	*JU G FUL	PI G EON	RU G OSE	BA G GAGE
BA G GIE	DO G NAP	*JU G GED	PI G GED	RU G OUS	BA G GING
BA G MAN	DU G ONG	KE G LER	PI G GIN	SA G BUT	BA G PIPE
BA G NIO	FA G GOT	LA G END	PI G LET	SA G EST	BA G SFUL
BA G UET	FI G URE	LA G GED	PI G NUS	SA G GAR	*BA G WORM
BA G WIG	*FO G BOW	LA G GER	PI G NUT	SA G GED	BE G GARY
BE G ALL	FO G DOG	LA G OON	PI G OUT	SA G GER	BE G GING
*BE G AZE	FO G GED	LA G UNA	PI G PEN	SE G GAR	BE G LOOM
BE G GAR	FO G GER	LA G UNE	PI G STY	SI G HER	BE G ONIA
BE G GED	FU G ATO	LE G ACY	PO G IES	SI G LOS	BE G ORAH
BE G IRD	FU G GED	LE G ATE	PO G ROM	SI G NAL	BE G ORRA
BE G LAD	G A G AKU	LE G ATO	PU G GED	SI G NEE	BE G RIME
BE G ONE	GA G GED	LE G END	PU G GRY	SI G NER	BE G ROAN
BE G RIM	GA G GER	LE G GED	PU G REE	SI G NET	BE G UILE
BE G ULF	GA G GLE	LE G INS	RA G BAG	SI G NOR	BE G UINE
BI G AMY	GA G ING	LE G ION	RA G GED	SO G GED	BI G FOOT
BI G EYE	G A G MAN	LE G IST	RA G GEE	SU G ARY	BI G GEST
BI G GER	GI G GED	LE G MAN	RA G GLE	TA G GED	BI G GETY
BI G GIE	GI G GLE	LE G ONG	RA G ING	TA G GER	BI G GING
BI G GIN	GI G GLY	LE G UME	RA G LAN	TA G RAG	BI G GISH
BI G WIG	G I G LET	LI G AND	RA G MAN	TE G MEN	BI G GITY
BO G GED	GI G LOT	LI G ASE	RA G OUT	TI G HTS	BI G HEAD
BO G GLE	GI G OLO	LI G ATE	RA G TAG	TI G LON	BI G HORN
BO G IES	GO G GLE	LI G NIN	RA G TOP	TO G ATE	BI G NESS
BU G EYE	GO G GLY	LI G ULA	RE G AIN	TO G GED	BI G OTED
BU G GED	GO G LET	LI G ULE	RE G ALE	TO G GLE	BI G OTRY
BU G GER	GU G GLE	LI G URE	RE G ARD	TU G GER	BO G BEAN
BU G LER	GU G LET	LO G GED	RE G AVE	TU G RIK	BO G GIER
BU G SHA	HA G BUT	LO G GER	RE G EAR	VA G ARY	BO G GING
BY G ONE	HA G DON	LO G GIA	RE G ENT	VA G ILE	BO G GISH
CA G IER	HA G GED	LO G ILY	RE G GAE	VA G INA	BO G GLER
CA G ILY	HA G GIS	LO G ION	RE G ILD	VA G ROM	BO G WOOD
CA G ING	HA G GLE	*LO G JAM	RE G IME	VE G ETE	*BO G YISM
CO G ENT	HE G ARI	LO G WAY	RE G INA	VE G GIE	*BO G YMAN
CO G GED	HE G IRA	LU G GED	RE G ION	VI G OUR	BU G ABOO
CO G ITO	HI G GLE	LU G GER	RE G IVE	WA G GED	BU G BANE
CO G NAC	*HI G HLY	LU G GIE	RE G LET	WA G GER	BU G BEAR
*CO G WAY	*HI G HTH	MA G NET	RE G LOW	WA G GLE	BU G GERY
CY G NET	HO G GED	ME G ASS	RE G NAL	WA G GLY	BU G GING
DA G GER	HO G GER	*MI G HTY	RE G NUM	WA G GON	BU G LOSS
DA G GLE	HO G NUT	MI G NON	RE G RET	WA G ING	BU G SEED
DA G OBA	HO G TIE	MO G GIE	RE G REW	WI G EON	CA G EFUL
DE G AGE	HU G EST	MU G FUL	RE G ROW	WI G GED	CA G IEST
DE G ERM	HU G GED	MU G GEE		WI G GLE	CI G ARET
DE G REE	HU G GER	NA G ANA		WI G GLY	*CO G ENCY
DE G UST	*JA G GED			WI G LET	CO G GING

CO G NATE	HA G GADA	LO G ANIA	PI G NOLI	SA G UARO	NA G GY	
CO G NISE	HA G GARD	LO G BOOK	PI G SKIN	SE G ETAL	SA G GY	
*CO G NIZE	HA G GING	LO G GATS	PI G SNEY	SE G MENT	VU G GY	
*DA G LOCK	*HA G GISH	LO G GETS	PI G WEED	SI G ANID	WI G GY	
DA G WOOD	HA G GLER	LO G GIER	PI G WEED	SI G HTER	WOD G E	
DE G AUSS	HA G RIDE	LO G GING	PO G HORN	SI G HTLY	BA G GED	
*DE G LAZE	HE G UMEN	LO G ICAL	PO G ONIA	SI G MOID	BA G GER	
DE G RADE	*HI G HBOY	LO G IEST	PO G ONIP	SI G NAGE	BA G GIE	
DI G AMMA	*HI G HWAY	LO G ROLL	PU G AREE	SI G NIFY	BE G GAR	
DI G GING	*HO G BACK	LO G WOOD	PU G GIER	SI G NIOR	BE G GED	
DI G ITAL	*HO G FISH	LU G CAIL	PU G GING	SI G NORA	BI G GER	
*DI G NIFY	*HO G LIKE	LU G GAGE	PU G GISH	SI G NORE	BI G GIE	
DI G NITY	HO G MANE	LU G GING	*PU G MARK	SI G NORE	BI G GIN	
*DI G OXIN	HO G NOSE	LU G WORM	RA G GEDY	SI G NORY	BIN G ER	
DI G RAPH	*HO G WASH	MA G NETO	RA G GIES	SU G GEST	BIO G AS	
DI G RESS	*HO G WEED	*MA G NIFY	RA G GING	TA G GING	BO G GED	
DO G BANE	HU G EOUS	ME G AHIT	RA G TIME	TA G LIKE	BO G GLE	
DO G CART	HU G GING	ME G ALIT	RA G WEED	TA G MEME	BOO G EY	
DO G EDOM	HY G EIST	ME G APOD	RA G WORT	TE G ULAR	BU G GED	
DO G FACE	HY G IENE	ME G AVOL	RE G ALER	TE G UMEN	BU G GER	
*DO G FISH	*JA G GARY	ME G AWAT	RE G ALIA	TI G HTEN	BUN G EE	
DO G GERY	*JA G GERY	ME G ILLA	RE G ALLY	TI G RISH	CO G GED	
DO G GIES	*JA G GING	*ME G ILPH	RE G ATTA	TI G RESS	DA G GER	
DO G GING	*JA G LESS	MI G NONN	RE G AUGE	TO G ATED	DA G GLE	
DO G GISH	*JI G ABOO	MI G RAIN	RE G ENCY	TO G GERY	DI G GED	
DO G GONE	*JI G GING	MU G GIES	RE G IMEN	TO G GING	DI G GER	
DO G GREL	*JO G GLER	MU G GING	*RE G LAZE	TO G GLER	DIN G ER	
DO G LIKE	*JU G GING	NA G GING	RE G LOSS	TU G BOAT	DOD G EM	
DO G SLED	*JU G GLER	NE G ATON	RE G NANT	TU G GING	DO G GED	
DO G TROT	*JU G HEAD	NE G ATOR	RE G ORGE	TU G LESS	DO G GER	
DO G VANE	*JU G SFUL	NE G LECT	RE G OSOL	VA G RANT	DRU G GY	
DO G WOOD	*JU G ULUM	NE G LIGE	RE G RADE	VE G ETAL	*FIZ G IG	
FA G OTER	*JU G VLAR	NE G ROID	RE G RAFT	VO G UISH	FO G GED	
FI G HTER	KE G ELER	NE G RONI	RE G RANT	WA G ERER	FO G GER	
FI G MENT	KE G LING	*NI G HTY	RE G RATE	*WA G GERY	FU G GED	
FI G URAL	LA G GARD	NI G GLER	RE G REEN	WA G GING	GA G GED	
FI G URER	LA G GING	NI G HTIE	RE G REET	*WA G GISH	GA G GER	
FI G WORT	LE G ALLY	NI G HTLY	RE G RESS	WA G ONER	GA G GLE	
FO G GAGE	LE G ATEE	NI G RIFY	RE G RIND	WA G SOME	GI G GED	
FO G GING	LE G ATOR	NO G GING	RE G ROOM	WA G TAIL	GI G GLE	
FO G LESS	LE G GIER	PA G EANT	RE G ROUP	*WI G GERY	GI G GLY	
*FO G YISM	LE G GING	*PA G EBOY	RE G ULAR	WI G GIER	GO G GLE	
FU G GING	LE G HORN	PA G URID	RE G ULUS	WI G GING	GO G GLY	
FU G UIST	LE G IBLE	PE G GING	RI G GING	WI G GLER	GU G GLE	
GA G GING	LE G LESS	PE G LESS	RI G HTER	WI G LESS	HA G GED	
GA G STER	LE G LIKE	PE G LIKE	RI G IDLY	*WI G LIKE	HA G GIS	
GI G ABIT	LE G ROOM	PI G BOAT	RI G UTLY	YE G GMAN	HA G GLE	
GI G ATON	LE G UMIN	*PI G FISH	RO G UERY	YO G HURT	HAN G UL	
GI G GING	*LE G WORK	PI G GERY	RO G UISH	*ZY G OSIS	HI G GLE	
GI G GLER	LI G HTEN	PI G GIER	RU G GING	BOO G Y	HO G GED	
GO G GLER	LI G HTER	PI G GIES	RU G LIKE	DAG G A	HO G GER	
HA G ADIC	LI G HTLY	PI G GING	SA G AMAN	DIN G E	HU G GED	
HA G BORN	LI G NIFY	PI G GISH	SA G GARD	DON G A	HU G GER	
*HA G BUSH	LI G NITE	PI G LIKE	SA G GIER	GLO G G	*JA G GED	
*HA G FISH	LI G ROIN	PI G MENT	SA G GING	KLU G E	*JA G GER	
			SA G IEST	MO G GY		

*JAN G LY	WA G G LY	HAN G TAG	SA G G ING	CIN G ULUM	FUN G IBLE
*JI G G ER	WA G G ON	HED G ING	SEA G ULL	*COA G ENCY	*GAD G ETRY
*JI G G LE	WI G G ED	HU G G ING	SER G ING	COA G ULUM	G AN G LAND
*JI G G LY	WI G G LE	*JA G G ARY	STA G ING	CON G ENER	G AN G LIAL
*JO G G ER	WI G G LY	*JA G G ERY	SUB G OAL	CON G LOBE	G AN G LIAR
*JO G G LE	*ZIN G ER	*JA G G ING	SU G G EST	CON G RATS	G AN G LIER
*JU G G ED	BAD G ING	*JI G G ING	SUR G ING	CON G RESS	G AN G LING
LA G G ED	BAG G AGE	*JO G G LER	SWA G G IE	CRA G SMAN	G AN G LION
LA G G ER	BA G G ING	*JU G G ING	SWA G ING	CUD G ELER	*GAN G PLOW
LE G G ED	BAR G ING	*JU G G LER	TA G G ING	CUT G RASS	G AN G RENE
LE G G IN	BE G G ARY	LA G G ARD	TO G G ERY	DAU G HTER	G AN G STER
LO G G ED	BE G G ING	LA G G ING	TO G G ING	DIA G NOSE	G AR G ANEY
LO G G ER	BEI G NET	LAR G EST	TO G G LER	DIA G ONAL	G AR G OYLE
LO G G IA	BER G ERE	LE G G IER	TRI G RAM	*DIA G RAPH	G EO G NOSY
LU G G ED	BI G G EST	LE G G ING	TU G G ING	DIG G INGS	G IN G ELEY
LU G G ER	BI G G ETY	LOD G ING	VER G ING	DIN G DONG	G IN G ELLY
LU G G IE	BI G G ING	LO G G ATS	*WA G G ERY	DIS G OR G E	G IN G ERLY
MO G G IE	BI G G ISH	LO G G ETS	*WA G G ISH	DIS G RACE	G IN G ILLI
MOR G AN	BI G G ITY	LO G G IER	WA G G ING	DIS G UISE	G LE G NESS
MU G G EE	BO G G IER	LO G G ING	*WI G G ERY	*DOG G EDLY	G OL G OTHA
NA G G ER	BO G G ING	LON G IES	WI G G IER	DO G G EREL	G ON G LIKE
NI G G LE	BO G G ISH	LON G ING	WI G G ING	DO G G IEST	G OR G EOUS
NO G G IN	BO G G LER	LU G GAGE	WI G G LER	DO G G ONED	G OR G ERIN
NON G AY	BUD G ING	LU G G ING	WIN G TIP	*DOU G HBOY	G RO G G ERY
NU G G ET	BU G G ERY	LUN G FUL	YE G G MAN	*DOU G HIER	*G RO G SHOP
PE G G ED	BU G G ING	LUN G ING	*BAD G ERLY	DOU G HNUT	*HA G G ADAH
PI G G ED	CLO G G ER	MER G ING	BAN G TAIL	DRA G G IER	*HA G G ADIC
PI G G IE	CO G G ING	MU G G IES	BAR G ELLO	DRA G G ING	*HAN G FIRE
PI G G IN	DI G G ING	MU G G ING	BAR G EMAN	DRA G ONET	HAN G NEST
PU G G ED	DIN G IES	NA G G ING	BAR G HEST	DRA G ROPE	*HED G EHO G
PU G G RY	DOD G ING	*NI G G HTY	BAR G UEST	DRA G STER	*HED G EPI G
PUN G LE	DO G G ERY	NO G G ING	*BE G G ARLY	DUN G AREE	*HEI G HTEN
RA G G ED	DO G G IES	PAN G ENE	BER G AMOT	DUN G HILL	*HU G G ABLE
RA G G EE	DO G G ING	PAR G ING	BIO G ENIC	*DYS G ENIC	*HUN G OVER
RA G G LE	DO G G ISH	PE G G ING	BO G G IEST	FID G ETER	IAN G SHAN
RE G G AE	DO G G ONE	PI G G ERY	BON G OIST	FIN G ERER	*JA G G HERY
RI G G ED	DO G G REL	PI G G IER	*BOO G YMAN	FLA G ELIA	*JAR G ONEL
RI G G ER	DRU G G IE	PI G G IES	*BOU G HPOT	*FLA G SHIP	*JI G G ERED
RU G G ED	FID G ING	PI G G ING	BOU G HTEN	*FOR G IVER	*JIN G OISM
RU G G ER	FO G GAGE	PI G G ISH	BRA G G ART	*FOU G HTEN	*JON G LEUR
SA G G AR	FO G G ING	PLU G OLA	BRA G G EST	*FOX G LOVE	*JUD G MENT
SA G G ED	FOR G ING	PU G G IER	BRA G G ING	FRA G G ING	*JU G G LERY
SA G G ER	FU G G ING	PU G G ING	BRI G HTEN	FRA G MENT	*JU G G LING
SE G G AR	GA G G ING	PU G G ISH	BRO G UERY	FRA G RANT	KAN G AROO
SO G G ED	GI G G ING	PUR G ING	BRO G UISH	*FRI G G ERY	KED G EREE
SYN G AS	GI G G LER	RA G G EDY	BUD G ETER	*FRI G HTEN	*KIN G BIRD
TA G G ED	GO G G LER	RA G G IES	BUN G ALOW	*FRO G FISH	*KIN G BOLT
TA G G ER	G OR G ING	RA G G ING	BUN G HOLE	FRO G G ING	*KIN G FISH
TO G G ED	HA G G ADA	RID G ING	BUN G LING	*FRO G LIKE	*KIN G HOOD
TO G G LE	HA G G ARD	RI G G ING	BUR G LARY		KIN G LESS
TU G G ER	HA G G ING	RIN G GIT	BUR G ONET		*KIN G LIKE
VE G G IE	*HA G G ISH	ROU G ING	BUR G RAVE		*KIN G POST
WA G G ED	HA G G LER	RU G G ING	*BUR G UNDY		*KIN G SHIP
WA G G ER	HAN G DOG	SA G GARD	CHI G ETAI		KIN G SIDE
WA G G LE	HAN G ING	SA G G IER	*CHU G ALUG		*KIN G WOOD

*KNI G HTLY	NON G REEN	SAR G ASSO	TON G UIN G	FAN G	SWA G
LAN G LAUF	NON G UILT	SEA G OIN G	TOU G HIES	FLA G	SWI G
LAN G RA G E	NUT G RASS	SEI G NEUR	*TOU G HISH	FRA G	THU G
LAN G SYNE	PAN G OLIN	SEI G NIOR	TRA G ICAL	FRI G	TIN G
LAN G UA G E	*PAY G RADE	SEI G NORY	TRA G OPAN	FRO G	TON G
LAR G ANDO	PEI G NOIR	SER G EANT	TRI G G EST	FRU G	TRI G
LAU G HIN G	PI G G IEST	SHA G REEN	TRI G G IN G	G AN G	TUN G
LAU G HTER	PIN G RASS	SHI G ELLA	*TRI G LYPH	G LE G	TWI G
*LAW G IVER	PLA G IARY	SIN G SON G	TRI G NESS	G LU G	VAN G
LE G G IERO	PLA G UIN G	SIN G ULAR	TRI G ONAL	G ON G	VU G G
LE G G IEST	PLI G HTER	SLO G G IN G	TRI G RAPH	G RI G	WHI G
LIE G EMAN	PLU G LESS	SLU G ABED	TUN G STEN	G RO G	WIN G
LIN G ERER	*PLU G U G LY	SLU G FEST	TUR G ENCY	HAN G	YAN G
LIN G ERIE	POI G NANT	SLU G G ARD	TWI G LESS	HO G G	YE G G
LIN G IEST	PRE G G ERS	SLU G G IN G	*TWI G LIKE	HON G	ZIN G
LIN G UINE	PRE G NANT	SLU G G ISH	VAN G UARD	HUN G	BEFO G
LIN G UINI	*PRI G G ISH	SMU G G LER	*VEN G EFUL	JA G G	BEIN G
LIN G UIST	PRI G G ISM	SMU G NESS	VER G ENCE	KIN G	BEWI G
LOD G MENT	PRO G ERIA	SNA G LIKE	VIR G INAL	LAN G	BHAN G
LON G BOAT	PRO G G IN G	SNI G G LER	WA G G ONER	LIN G	BOIN G
LON G ERON	PRO G NOSE	SNU G G ERY	*WAY G OIN G	LON G	BOUR G
LON G HAIR	PRO G RADE	SNU G G EST	WEI G ELIA	LUN G	BRIN G
LON G HAND	PRO G RESS	SNU G G IES	*WEI G HMAN	MI G G	CHAN G
LON G HEAD	PU G G AREE	SNU G G IN G	*WEI G HTER	MU G G	CLAN G
LON G HORN	PU G G IEST	SNU G NESS	WI G G IEST	NO G G	CLIN G
LON G LEAF	*PUN G ENCY	SON G BIRD	*WIN G BACK	PAN G	CLUN G
LON G LINE	*PYO G ENIC	*SON G BOOK	WIN G DIN G	PEA G	COHO G
LON G NESS	*QUA G MIRE	SON G FEST	*WIN G EDLY	PIN G	COLO G
LON G SHIP	*QUA G MIRY	SON G LESS	WIN G IEST	PLU G	CUIN G
LON G SOME	RAN G BIRD	SON G LIKE	WIN G LESS	PON G	DEBU G
LON G SPUR	RAN G NAIL	SON G STER	*WIN G LIKE	PRI G	DEFO G
LON G TIME	RAY G RASS	*SPA G YRIC	*WIN G OVER	PRO G	DOIN G
LON G UEUR	REI G NITE	SPY G LASS	WIN G SPAN	PUN G	DYIN G
*LON G WAYS	RIB G RASS	*SRA G BARK	WRI G G LER	QUA G	FLIN G
LON G WISE	RID G IEST	STA G EFUL	*ZI G G URAT	RAN G	FLUN G
*LUN G FISH	RID G LIN G	STA G G ARD	*ZOO G ENIC	RIN G	G LO G G
LUN G WORM	*RIN G BARK	STA G G ART	*ZOO G LOEA	RUN G	G OIN G
LUN G WORT	RIN G BOLT	STA G G ERY		SAN G	G ULA G
MA G ICIAN	RIN G BONE	STA G G IN G	BAN G	SCA G	HYIN G
MA G ISTER	RIN G DOVE	STA G IEST	BER G	SHA G	KIAN G
MA G NESIA	RIN G HALS	STA G NANT	BON G	SHO G	KLON G
MA G NETIC	RIN G LIKE	STA G NATE	BRA G	SIN G	LIAN G
MA G NOLIA	*RIN G NECK	STE G ODON	BRI G	SKA G	LYIN G
*MAN G ABEY	RIN G SIDE	SUB G ENRE	BUN G	SKE G	PIRO G
MAN G OVER	RIN G TAIL	SUB G ENUS	BUR G	SLA G	PRAR G
*MED G EHO G	RIN G TOSS	SUB G RADE	CHU G	SLO G	PRON G
*MED G EHOP	RIN G WORM	*SUB G RAPH	CLA G	SLU G	RENI G
MIS G RADE	ROU G HA G E	SUB G ROUP	CLO G	SMO G	REPE G
*MYO G ENIC	*ROU G HDRY	SUN G LASS	CRA G	SMU G	RERI G
*MYO G RAPH	*ROU G HHEW	SUR G ICAL	DAN G	SNA G	RETA G
NAR G HILE	*ROU G HISH	SWA G G IN G	DIN G	SNO G	RUIN G
NAR G ILEH	ROU G HLE G	TAI G LACH	DON G	SNU G	SCRA G
NEI G HBOR	RYE G RASS	TEI G LACH	DRA G	SON G	SHRU G
NON G ATAL	SAN G AREE	*THU G G ERY	DRE G	STA G	SLAN G
NON G LARE	SAN G UINE	*THU G G ISH	DUN G	SUN G	SLIN G

SLUN G	CAVIN G	*G AZIN G	MIDLE G	REHAN G	TIRIN G
SPAN G	CERIN G	G IVIN G	MIMIN G	REHUN G	TOKIN G
SPRA G	CITIN G	G LUIN G	MININ G	RICIN G	TOLIN G
SPRI G	CODIN G	G OBAN G	MIRIN G	RIDIN G	TONIN G
SPRU G	COMIN G	G ORIN G	MOPIN G	RILIN G	TOPIN G
*SQUE G	CONIN G	G RELA G	MOVIN G	RIMIN G	TOTIN G
STAI G	COPIN G	G UNDO G	MULIN G	RIPIN G	TRUIN G
STAN G	CORIN G	G YRIN G	MURIN G	RISIN G	TUBIN G
STIN G	COTIN G	HALIN G	MUSIN G	RIVIN G	TUNIN G
STUN G	COVIN G	HARIN G	MUSKE G	ROPIN G	TYPIN G
SUIN G	COYDO G	HATIN G	MUTIN G	ROSIN G	VICIN G
SWAN G	CUBIN G	HAVIN G	NAMIN G	ROVIN G	VIKIN G
SWIN G	CURIN G	HAYIN G	NIDIN G	ROWIN G	VININ G
SWUN G	CYBOR G	*HAZIN G	NOSIN G	RULIN G	VISIN G
THIN G	DARIN G	HIDIN G	NOTIN G	SANIN G	VOTIN G
THON G	DATIN G	HIRIN G	NUTME G	SARON G	WADIN G
TWAN G	DEFAN G	HOLIN G	PACIN G	SATAN G	WA G IN G
TYIN G	DIALO G	HOMIN G	PADNA G	SATIN G	WAKIN G
VYIN G	DICIN G	HONIN G	PA G IN G	SAVIN G	WALIN G
WHAN G	DININ G	HOPIN G	PALIN G	SAWLO G	WANIN G
WRAN G	DIVIN G	HOSIN G	PARAN G	SAYIN G	WARIN G
WRIN G	DO G LE G	HOTDO G	PARIN G	SEABA G	WAVIN G
WRON G	DOLIN G	HUMBU G	PAVIN G	SEADO G	*WAXIN G
WRUN G	DOMIN G	*HYPIN G	PENAN G	SEEIN G	WIFIN G
YOUN G	DOPIN G	*JAPIN G	PHOTO G	SERIN G	WI G WA G
BA G WI G	DORBU G	*JOKIN G	PIEIN G	SEWIN G	WILIN G
BAKIN G	DOTIN G	KALON G	PIKIN G	SIDIN G	WININ G
BALIN G	*DOZIN G	KITIN G	PILIN G	SIPIN G	WIPIN G
BANDO G	DUDIN G	LACIN G	PINAN G	SIRIN G	WIRIN G
BANIN G	DU G ON G	LADIN G	PININ G	SITIN G	WISIN G
BARIN G	DUOLO G	LAKIN G	PIPIN G	*SIZIN G	WITIN G
BARON G	DUPIN G	LAMIN G	POKIN G	SKIIN G	WIVIN G
BASIN G	DURIN G	LAPDO G	POLIN G	SLUIN G	YOKIN G
BATIN G	DYEIN G	LASIN G	POSIN G	SOLIN G	*ZAFTI G
BECLO G	FACIN G	LAVIN G	PROLE G	SORIN G	*ZI G ZA G
BEDBU G	FADIN G	LAWIN G	PROLO G	SPRAN G	*ZOFTI G
BEDRU G	FAKIN G	*LAZIN G	PULIN G	SPRIN G	*ZONIN G
BEFLA G	FAMIN G	LE G ON G	PUTLO G	SPRUN G	*BACKIN G
BELON G	FARIN G	LIKIN G	*QUAHO G	STALA G	*BACKLO G
BIDIN G	FATIN G	LIMIN G	*QUOHO G	STRAN G	BAD G IN G
BI G WI G	FETIN G	LININ G	RACIN G	STRIN G	BA G G IN G
BIKIN G	FILIN G	LIVIN G	RA G BA G	STRON G	BANKIN G
BITIN G	FIRIN G	LOSIN G	RA G IN G	STRUN G	BANNIN G
BLUIN G	*FIZ G I G	LOVIN G	RA G TA G	SUNDO G	BANTEN G
BODIN G	FLYIN G	LOWIN G	RAKIN G	TA G RA G	BAR G IN G
BONIN G	FO G DO G	LURIN G	RAPIN G	TAKIN G	BARRIN G
BORIN G	*FOXIN G	LUTIN G	RARIN G	TAMIN G	BASTIN G
BOWIN G	FUMIN G	LYSIN G	RASIN G	TAPIN G	BATHIN G
BOWLE G	FUSIN G	MACIN G	RATBA G	TARIN G	BATTIN G
*BOXIN G	*FUZIN G	MAKIN G	RATIN G	TAUTO G	BATWIN G
BUSIN G	G A G IN G	MASKE G	RAVIN G	THRON G	BEADIN G
CA G IN G	G AMIN G	MATIN G	*RAZIN G	TIDIN G	BEANBA G
CANIN G	G APIN G	MAYIN G	REDBU G	TILIN G	BEARHU G
CARIN G	G ASBA G	*MAZIN G	REDIN G	TIMIN G	BEARIN G
CASIN G	G ATIN G	METIN G	REDLE G	TININ G	BEATIN G

BEDDIN G	CAPPIN G	DI G G IN G	FRAMIN G	*HAPPIN G	LADLIN G
BE G G IN G	CARDIN G	DIMMIN G	FRAYIN G	HARPIN G	LADYBU G
BELTIN G	CARLIN G	DINNIN G	FU G G IN G	HATTIN G	LA G G IN G
BELYIN G	CARPIN G	DIPPIN G	FUNNIN G	*HAWKIN G	LAMMIN G
BETTIN G	CARVIN G	DIRTBA G	FURLON G	HEADIN G	LANCIN G
BIBBIN G	CASTIN G	DISHRA G	FURRIN G	HEARIN G	LANDIN G
BIDDIN G	CATALO G	DISSIN G	G ABBIN G	HEAVIN G	LAPPIN G
BI G G IN G	CATLIN G	DOD G IN G	G ADDIN G	HED G IN G	LAPWIN G
BILLBU G	CATTIN G	DO G G IN G	GA G G IN G	HEELIN G	LASHIN G
BILLIN G	CAUSIN G	DONNIN G	G AMMIN G	HELPIN G	LASTIN G
BILTON G	CEILIN G	DOTTIN G	G APPIN G	HEMA G O G	LATHIN G
BINDIN G	*CHAFIN G	DRAPIN G	G ARRIN G	*HEMMIN G	LEADIN G
BINNIN G	CHARIN G	DRAWIN G	G ASKIN G	HERRIN G	LEANIN G
BIRDIN G	CHASIN G	DRONIN G	G ASSIN G	HILDIN G	LEASIN G
BIRLIN G	*CHIMIN G	DUBBIN G	G EARIN G	*HIPPIN G	LEAVIN G
BITTIN G	*CHOKIN G	DUCTIN G	G ELDIN G	HISSIN G	LE G G IN G
BLAMIN G	CHORIN G	DUMPIN G	G ELLIN G	HOLDIN G	LEMMIN G
BLUEIN G	CLONIN G	DUNNIN G	G EMMIN G	*HOMBUR G	LETTIN G
BOATIN G	CLOSIN G	DUPPIN G	G ENSEN G	HOMOLO G	LICKIN G
BOBBIN G	COAMIN G	DUPTRA G	G ETTIN G	*HOPPIN G	LINSAN G
BO G G IN G	COATIN G	FABLIN G	G IBBIN G	HORSIN G	LIPPIN G
BOMBIN G	CODDIN G	FAILIN G	GI G G IN G	HOTTIN G	LISTIN G
BONDIN G	CODLIN G	FAIRIN G	G ILDIN G	HOUSIN G	LOADIN G
BOOKIN G	*COFFIN G	FANNIN G	G INNIN G	HU G G IN G	LOANIN G
BOOTLE G	CO G G IN G	FARCIN G	G INSEN G	*HUMMIN G	LOBBIN G
BOWLIN G	CONNIN G	FARMIN G	G IPPIN G	HUNTIN G	LOD G IN G
BRACIN G	COOKIN G	FASTIN G	*G LAZIN G	HURLIN G	LO G G IN G
BRAKIN G	COPPIN G	FATLIN G	G LEYIN G	*HUSKIN G	LON G IN G
BRAVIN G	CORDIN G	FATTIN G	G NAWIN G	HUTTIN G	LOOSIN G
*BRAZIN G	COWLIN G	FEEDBA G	G OBBIN G	*JABBIN G	LOPPIN G
BREWIN G	CRANIN G	FEELIN G	G ODDIN G	*JACKLE G	LORDIN G
BRIBIN G	CRANNO G	FELTIN G	G ODLIN G	*JA G G IN G	LOTTIN G
BRININ G	CRAVIN G	FENCIN G	G OLDBU G	*JAMMIN G	LOVEBU G
BROKIN G	CUNNIN G	FETTIN G	G OLFIN G	*JARRIN G	LU G G IN G
BRUTIN G	CUPPIN G	FID G IN G	G OR G IN G	*JESTIN G	LUN G IN G
BUDDIN G	CURBIN G	FILIBE G	G OSLIN G	*JETTIN G	MADDIN G
BUD G IN G	CURLIN G	FILLIN G	G RACIN G	*JIBBIN G	*MAHJON G
BU G G IN G	CURSIN G	FINDIN G	G RADIN G	*JI G G IN G	MAHUAN G
BULLDO G	CURVIN G	FINNIN G	G RATIN G	*JOBBIN G	MAILBA G
BUMMIN G	CUTTIN G	FIREBU G	G RAVIN G	*JOININ G	MAILIN G
BUNTIN G	*CYCLIN G	FIREDO G	G RAYLA G	*JOTTIN G	MANNIN G
BURNIN G	*CYMLIN G	*FISH G I G	*G RAZIN G	*JU G G IN G	MAPPIN G
BURRIN G	DAMMIN G	FISHIN G	G RIMIN G	*KAMPON G	MARKIN G
BUSHIN G	DAMPIN G	FITTIN G	G RIPIN G	KARTIN G	MARLIN G
*BUSHPI G	DAPPIN G	FLAMIN G	G UMMIN G	KEEPIN G	MARRIN G
BUSSIN G	DARNIN G	FLEABA G	G UNNIN G	KE G LIN G	MASKIN G
*BUZZWI G	DAYLON G	FLUTIN G	G UTTIN G	KENNIN G	MATTIN G
CABBIN G	DEALIN G	FLYTIN G	HA G G IN G	*KEPPIN G	MEANIN G
CABLIN G	DECALO G	FO G G IN G	HALVIN G	KIDDIN G	MEETIN G
*CACHIN G	*DECKIN G	FOOTIN G	*HAMBUR G	KILLIN G	MENDIN G
CALLIN G	DEICIN G	FORCIN G	*HAMMIN G	KILTIN G	MER G IN G
CAMPIN G	DEMA G O G	FORELE G	HANDBA G	*KIPPIN G	METRIN G
CAMPON G	DENNIN G	FOR G IN G	HAN G DO G	KITLIN G	*MILCHI G
CANNIN G	DIALIN G	FOULIN G	HAN G IN G	KITTIN G	MILLIN G
CANTDO G	DIBBIN G	FOWLIN G	HAN G TA G	*KNOWIN G	MOLDIN G

MONOLO G	PIPPIN G	RIPPIN G	SIPPIN G	TEASIN G	WHORIN G
MOORIN G	PITTIN G	ROARIN G	SITTIN G	TENSIN G	*WICKIN G
MOPPIN G	PLACIN G	ROBBIN G	SKATIN G	TESTIN G	WI G G IN G
MORNIN G	PLANIN G	ROLLIN G	SLATIN G	THEOLO G	WILDIN G
MOUSIN G	PLATIN G	ROOFIN G	SLAVIN G	TICKIN G	WILLIN G
MUDDIN G	PLUMIN G	ROTTIN G	SLIDIN G	TINNIN G	WINCIN G
MU G G IN G	POPPIN G	ROU G IN G	SLIMIN G	TINTIN G	WINDBA G
MUMMIN G	POSTBA G	ROUTIN G	SMITIN G	TIPPIN G	WINDIN G
MUNTIN G	POSTIN G	RUBBIN G	SMOKIN G	TITHIN G	WINNIN G
MUSTAN G	POTTIN G	RUCHIN G	SOARIN G	TO G G IN G	WITHIN G
NA G G IN G	PRATIN G	RU G G IN G	SODDIN G	TOMMIN G	WITLIN G
NAMETA G	PREPRE G	RUNNIN G	SOLVIN G	TOOLIN G	WITTIN G
NAPPIN G	PRESON G	RUSHIN G	SOPPIN G	TOPPIN G	WONNIN G
NECKIN G	PRICIN G	RUTTIN G	SPACIN G	TOTTIN G	WORDIN G
NERVIN G	PRIMIN G	SABBIN G	SPADIN G	TOURIN G	*WORKBA G
NETTIN G	PROBAN G	SACKIN G	SPAEIN G	TRACIN G	*WORKIN G
NIMMIN G	PROLON G	SACRIN G	SPARIN G	TREPAN G	WRITIN G
NIPPIN G	PROSIN G	SA G G IN G	SPICIN G	TRICIN G	*YAPPIN G
NODDIN G	PROVIN G	SAILIN G	SPIKIN G	TUBBIN G	*YAWPIN G
NO G G IN G	PRUNIN G	SALTIN G	SPILIN G	TU G G IN G	YEALIN G
NONDRU G	PUDDIN G	SALVIN G	SPIRIN G	TUNNIN G	YESSIN G
NOONIN G	PU G G IN G	SANDBA G	SPITIN G	TUPPIN G	*YIPPIN G
NOSEBA G	PULSIN G	SANDHO G	SPUMIN G	TURNIN G	*ZIPPIN G
NOTHIN G	PUNNIN G	SAPLIN G	STA G IN G	TUTTIN G	*BABBLIN G
NURSIN G	PUPPIN G	SAPPIN G	STANIN G	TWININ G	BALLYRA G
NUTTIN G	PUR G IN G	SAUCIN G	STARIN G	VANNIN G	BANTLIN G
*PACKIN G	PURRIN G	SCALIN G	STATIN G	VATTIN G	*BECOMIN G
PADDIN G	PURSIN G	SCARIN G	STOKIN G	VEILIN G	BEESWIN G
PAIRIN G	PUTTIN G	SCORIN G	STONIN G	VEININ G	BIRDSON G
PALLIN G	*QUAHAU G	SCUMBA G	STOPIN G	VER G IN G	BITEWIN G
PANNIN G	*QUOTIN G	SEATIN G	STORIN G	VERSIN G	*BLACKIN G
PAR G IN G	RA G G IN G	SEEMIN G	STYLIN G	VESTIN G	*BLACKLE G
PARKIN G	RAILIN G	SEISIN G	SUBBIN G	VETTIN G	BLASTIN G
PARLIN G	RAISIN G	*SEIZIN G	SUBRIN G	VIEWIN G	BLATTIN G
PARRIN G	RAMMIN G	SEMILO G	SUITIN G	VOICIN G	BLEEDIN G
PARSIN G	RANKIN G	SENSIN G	SUMMIN G	WADDIN G	BLESSIN G
PARTIN G	RAPPIN G	SER G IN G	SUNNIN G	WA G G IN G	BLOODIN G
PASSIN G	RATTIN G	SERVIN G	SUPPIN G	WAITIN G	BLOTTIN G
PASTIN G	READIN G	SETTIN G	SURFIN G	*WALKIN G	BOARDIN G
PATTIN G	REDDIN G	SHADIN G	SUR G IN G	WANNIN G	BRA G G IN G
PEACIN G	REDWIN G	*SHAKIN G	SWA G IN G	WARNIN G	BRAIDIN G
PEDÀ G O G	REEDIN G	SHAMIN G	SWIVIN G	WARRIN G	BRANNIN G
PEELIN G	REFFIN G	SHAPIN G	SYNA G O G	WARTHO G	*BREAKIN G
PE G G IN G	RETTIN G	SHARIN G	TABBIN G	WASHIN G	BREEDIN G
PENNIN G	RETYIN G	SHAVIN G	TABLIN G	WASHRA G	BRID G IN G
PEPPIN G	REVVIN G	SHEBAN G	TA G G IN G	WASTIN G	BRIEFIN G
PERIWI G	RIBBIN G	SHINDI G	TAILIN G	*WAXWIN G	*BRIMMIN G
PETTIN G	RIDDIN G	SHININ G	TALKIN G	*WEBBIN G	BRISLIN G
PFENNI G	RID G IN G	SHORTIN G	TANNIN G	WEDDIN G	*BRONZIN G
PHONIN G	RIFFIN G	SHOVIN G	TAPPIN G	WELTIN G	BUILDIN G
*PICKIN G	RIFLIN G	SHOWIN G	TARRIN G	WESTIN G	BULLFRO G
PIECIN G	RI G G IN G	SIAMAN G	TASTIN G	WETTIN G	BULLRIN G
PI G G IN G	RIMMIN G	SIBLIN G	TATTIN G	WHALIN G	BULLYRA G
PINKIN G	RINNIN G	SIFTIN G	TAUTAU G	WHININ G	*BUMBLIN G
PINNIN G	RINSIN G	SINNIN G	*TAXYIN G	WHITIN G	BUNDLIN G

BUN G LIN G	DRESSIN G	G RIPPIN G	NEEDLIN G	REEDLIN G	*SHOPPIN G
CA G ELIN G	DRILLIN G	G ROUPIN G	NESTLIN G	REFININ G	SHOTTIN G
*CAJOLIN G	DRIPPIN G	G RUELIN G	NIDERIN G	RESPRAN G	*SHOWRIN G
*CAPRIFI G	DROPPIN G	*G UNNYBA G	NONBEIN G	RESPRIN G	*SHRIVIN G
*CAULKIN G	DRUBBIN G	HANDLIN G	NONCLIN G	RESTRIN G	*SHUCKIN G
CENTRIN G	DRUMMIN G	*HATCHIN G	NONUSIN G	RESTRUN G	SHUTTIN G
*CHANCIN G	*DUCKLIN G	HEADLON G	NORTHIN G	RETIRIN G	SIDELIN G
*CHAPPIN G	DUELLIN G	*HED G EHO G	NURSLIN G	REVERIN G	SIDELON G
*CHARMIN G	DUMPLIN G	*HED G EPI G	PADDLIN G	*REVIVIN G	SI G HTIN G
CHARRIN G	DWELLIN G	HIRELIN G	PAINTIN G	RID G LIN G	SIN G SON G
CHATTIN G	*FARTHIN G	HOARDIN G	PANELIN G	RIESLIN G	SKILLIN G
*CHILDIN G	FAUBOUR G	*HUMBLIN G	PARADIN G	RIPPLIN G	*SKIMMIN G
*CHILIDO G	FETTLIN G	*HYDRA G O G	PARASAN G	*ROCKLIN G	SKINNIN G
CHINNIN G	*FI G HTIN G	*JELUTON G	PARAWIN G	ROSESLU G	SKIORIN G
*CHIPPIN G	FI G URIN G	*JU G G LIN G	PEDDLIN G	ROU G HLE G	*SKIPPIN G
CHITLIN G	*FINIKIN G	KAOLIAN G	PETTIFO G	*RUFFLIN G	SKIRTIN G
CHOOSIN G	*FIREFAN G	*KAYAKIN G	*PHILABE G	RUMBLIN G	SLABBIN G
*CHOPPIN G	FIREPLU G	KINDLIN G	*PHILIBE G	RUSTLIN G	SLAPPIN G
*CHROMIN G	FLA G G IN G	KNITTIN G	PHRASIN G	SADDLIN G	SLASHIN G
*CHU G ALU G	*FLAMMIN G	KNOTTIN G	PILOTIN G	SALADAN G	SLATTIN G
CHURNIN G	*FLAPPIN G	LACEWIN G	*PINCHBU G	SANDLIN G	SLEDDIN G
CIRCLIN G	*FLASHIN G	LALLY G A G	PINDLIN G	SAVA G IN G	SLEEPIN G
CLADDIN G	FLATLIN G	LAU G HIN G	PLA G UIN G	SCALAWA G	SLIMMIN G
*CLAMMIN G	FLATLON G	LAYERIN G	PLAITIN G	SCANNIN G	SLIPPIN G
CLEARIN G	FLATTIN G	LEAPFRO G	*PLANKIN G	SCARRIN G	SLITTIN G
*CLIPPIN G	FLEECIN G	LEARNIN G	PLANNIN G	SCATTIN G	SLO G G IN G
CLOTHIN G	*FLESHIN G	*LEFTWIN G	PLANTIN G	SCOLDIN G	SLOPPIN G
CLOTTIN G	FONDLIN G	LE G ATIN G	PLATTIN G	SCOURIN G	SLOTTIN G
*CLUBBIN G	FOOTLIN G	LIFELON G	PLEADIN G	SCOUTIN G	SLUBBIN G
COASTIN G	FOOTSLO G	LI G HTIN G	PLED G IN G	SCRAPIN G	SLU G G IN G
COHERIN G	*FOREWIN G	LIVELON G	PLOTTIN G	*SCUMMIN G	SLUMMIN G
COLORIN G	FRA G G IN G	LOATHIN G	*PLUMBIN G	*SCUPPAU G	SLURRIN G
*COUCHIN G	FRETTIN G	LOLLY G A G	POLLIWO G	SEA G OIN G	*SMOCKIN G
COUPLIN G	FRILLIN G	LORDLIN G	*POLLYWO G	SECURIN G	SMUTTIN G
COURSIN G	FRITTIN G	LUSTRIN G	POSTDRU G	SEEDLIN G	SNAPPIN G
COVERIN G	FRO G G IN G	*LYNCHIN G	*PREPPIN G	SELAPAN G	SNIPPIN G
*CRACKIN G	FROSTIN G	*MAHJON G G	PRESSIN G	SETTLIN G	SNU G G IN G
CRESTIN G	FUELLIN G	MANTLIN G	*PRICKIN G	*SHAFTIN G	SOANNIN G
*CRIBBIN G	G AN G LIN G	MANURIN G	*PRIMMIN G	*SHAMMIN G	SOOCHON G
*CROPPIN G	G ELATIN G	MARBLIN G	PRINTIN G	SHANTUN G	SOOTHIN G
CROSSIN G	G HOSTIN G	*MEALYBU G	PRO G G IN G	SHEALIN G	SOUARIN G
CRUISIN G	*G LADDIN G	*MED G EHO G	*PROPPIN G	SHEARIN G	SOUCHON G
CURRYIN G	G LEANIN G	MIDDLIN G	PUDDLIN G	*SHEEPDO G	SOUNDIN G
*CYMBLIN G	G LOAMIN G	MINUTIN G	PURFLIN G	SHEETIN G	SOUTHIN G
DABBLIN G	G LOOMIN G	MISDOIN G	*QUANDAN G	*SHELVIN G	*SPANKIN G
DEMOTIN G	G LUTTIN G	MISLYIN G	*QUANDON G	*SHEMMIN G	SPARLIN G
DEVISIN G	G NARRIN G	MODELIN G	*QUANTON G	SHIELIN G	SPARRIN G
DIN G DON G	G OLLIWO G	*MONEYBA G	*QUILLIN G	SHILLIN G	SPATTIN G
DIVIDIN G	*G OLLYWO G	MOTORIN G	*QUILTIN G	*SHIMMIN G	*SPEAKIN G
DIVININ G	G RABBIN G	MOULDIN G	*QUISLIN G	SHINNIN G	SPEEDIN G
DOUBLIN G	G RAYLIN G	MOUNTIN G	*QUITTIN G	*SHIPPIN G	SPEERIN G
DRAFTIN G	G REENBU G	MOURNIN G	RALLYIN G	SHIRRIN G	SPELLIN G
DRA G G IN G	G REENIN G	MUTININ G	RATTLIN G	SHIRTIN G	SPHERIN G
DRAMMIN G	G REETIN G	*MYSTA G O G	RAVELIN G	SHITTIN G	*SPIFFIN G
DRED G IN G	G RINNIN G	NAETHIN G	RAVENIN G	SHOOTIN G	SPITTIN G

SPON G IN G	STIRRIN G	SWEETIN G	TRAPPIN G	TWISTIN G	*WHIRRIN G
SPOOLIN G	*STOCKIN G	SWELLIN G	TRAVELO G	TWITTIN G	*WHIZBAN G
SPOONIN G	STOPPIN G	*SWIMMIN G	TRIFLIN G	VAPORIN G	*WHIZZIN G
SPOTTIN G	STRAVAI G	SWIN G IN G	TRI G G IN G	VAULTIN G	WILDLIN G
SPRNNIN G	STRIDIN G	*TACKLIN G	TRIMMIN G	*WAFFLIN G	WIN G DIN G
SPURRIN G	STRIPIN G	TA G ALON G	TRIPLIN G	WAISTIN G	*WITCHIN G
STABLIN G	STUBBIN G	*TEACHIN G	TRIPPIN G	*WAKENIN G	*WRAPPIN G
STA G G IN G	STUDDIN G	TEETHIN G	TRITHIN G	*WATCHDO G	*WRECKIN G
STANDIN G	*STUFFIN G	*THIEVIN G	TROLLIN G	WATERDO G	*WRITHIN G
STARLIN G	STUMMIN G	*THINKIN G	TROTTIN G	WATERIN G	*YACHTIN G
STARRIN G	STUNNIN G	THINNIN G	TROUPIN G	WATERLO G	YEANLIN G
STEADIN G	*SUCKLIN G	TINKLIN G	*TRUCKIN G	*WAY G OIN G	YEARLIN G
STEALIN G	*SVEDBER G	TON G UIN G	TRUD G IN G	*WEAKLIN G	YEARLON G
STEEVIN G	*SWABBIN G	*TORQUIN G	TRUSSIN G	WEANLIN G	YEARNIN G
STEMMIN G	SWA G G IN G	TOWELIN G	TUMBLIN G	*WEEKLON G	*ZINCKIN G
STEPPIN G	SWANNIN G	*TRACKIN G	TURTLIN G	*WHEELIN G	
STERLIN G	SWATTIN G	TRAININ G	TWILLIN G	*WHETTIN G	
*STINKBU G	SWEEPIN G	TRAMMIN G	TWINNIN G	*WHIPPIN G	

H

HAAF	HARP	HERD	HOLK	HULA	HAMAL
HAAR	HART	HERE	HOLM	HULK	*HAMMY
HABU	HASH	HERL	HOLP	HULL	*HAMZA
HACK	HASP	HERM	HOLS	HUMP	HANCE
HADE	HAST	HERN	HOLT	HUNG	HANDY
*HADJ	HATE	HERO	HOLY	HUNH	*HANKY
HAEM	HATH	HERS	HOME	HUNK	HANSA
HAEN	HAUL	HEST	HOMO	HUNT	HANSE
HAET	HAUT	HETH	HOMY	HURL	HAOLE
HAFT	HAVE	HICK	HONE	HURT	*HAPAX
HAHA	HAWK	HIDE	HONG	HUSH	HAPLY
HAIK	*HAZE	HIGH	HONK	HUSK	*HAPPY
HAIL	*HAZY	HIKE	HOOD	HWAN	HARDS
HAIR	HEAL	HILA	HOOF	HYLA	HARDY
HAJI	HEAP	HILI	HOOK	HYMN	HAREM
*HAJJ	HEAR	HILL	HOOP	HYPO	HARPY
HAKE	HEAT	HILT	HOOT	HYTE	HARRY
HALE	HECK	HIND	HOPE	HABIT	HARSH
HALF	HEED	HIRE	HORA	HACEK	HASTE
HALL	HEEL	HISN	HOSE	HADAL	HATCH
HALM	HEFT	HISS	HOST	*HADJI	HATER
HALO	HEIL	HIST	HOUR	HADST	HAUGH
HALT	HEIR	HIVE	HOVE	*HAFIZ	HAULM
HAME	HELD	HOAR	HOWE	HAIKU	HAUNT
HAND	HELL	HOAX	HOWF	HAIRY	HAUTE
HANG	HELM	HOBO	HOWK	*HAJJI	HAVOC
HANK	HELO	HOCK	HOWL	HALER	HAWSE
HANT	HELP	HOER	HOYA	HALID	HAYER
HARD	HEME	HOGG	HUCK	HALLO	*HAZAN
HARE	HEMP	HOKE	HUFF	HALMA	*HAZEL
HARL	HENT	HOLD	HUGE	HALVA	*HAZER
HARM	HERB	HOLE	HUIC	HALVE	HEADY

HEART	HOICK	*HUMPY	HALLOT	HAULMY	HEPTAD
HEAVE	HOISE	HUMUS	*HALLUX	HAUNCH	HERALD
HEAVY	HOIST	HUNCH	HALOID	HAUSEN	HERBAL
HEDER	*HOKEY	*HUNKY	HALTER	HAVING	HERBED
HEDGE	*HOKKU	HURDS	*HALUTZ	HAVIOR	HERDER
HEDGY	HOKUM	HURLY	*HALVAH	*HAWKER	HERDIC
*HEEZE	HOLEY	HURRY	HALVES	*HAWKEY	HEREAT
HEFTY	HOLLA	HURST	HAMATE	*HAWKIE	HEREIN
HEIGH	HOLLO	*HUSKY	HAMAUL	HAWSER	HEREOF
HEIST	HOMED	HUSSY	HAMLET	HAYING	HEREON
HELIO	HOMER	HUTCH	HAMMAL	*HAYMOW	HERESY
*HELIX	HOMEY	*HUZZA	HAMMED	*HAZARD	HERETO
HELLO	HONAN	HYDRA	HAMMER	*HAZIER	HERIOT
HELOT	HONDA	HYDRO	HAMPER	*HAZILY	HERMIT
HELVE	HONER	HYENA	*HAMZAH	*HAZING	HERNIA
HEMAL	HONEY	HYING	HANDLE	*HAZZAN	HEROIC
HEMIC	*HONKY	HYMEN	HANGAR	HEADER	HEROIN
HEMIN	HONOR	HYOID	HANGER	HEALER	HERPES
*HEMPY	HOOCH	HYPER	HANGUL	HEALTH	HETERO
HENCE	HOODY	*HYPHA	HANGUP	HEARER	*HEXADE
HENNA	HOOEY	*HYRAX	HANIWA	HEARSE	*HEXANE
HENRY	HOOKA	HYSON	HANKER	HEARTH	*HEXONE
HERBY	*HOOKY	HABILE	HANKIE	HEARTY	*HEXOSE
HERES	HOOLY	HABOOB	HANSEL	*HEATHY	*HEYDAY
HERMA	HOPER	*HACKEE	HANSOM	HEAUME	*HEYDEY
HERON	*HOPPY	*HACKER	HANTLE	HEAVEN	HIATUS
HERRY	HORAH	*HACKIE	HAPPED	HEAVER	*HICCUP
*HERTZ	HORAL	*HACKLE	HAPPEN	*HECKLE	*HICKEY
HEUGH	HORDE	*HACKLY	HAPTEN	HECTIC	HIDDEN
HEWER	HORNY	HADITH	HAPTIC	HECTOR	HIDING
*HEXAD	HORSE	*HADJEE	HARASS	HEDDLE	HIEMAL
*HEXER	HORST	HADRON	HARBOR	HEDGER	HIGGLE
*HEXYL	HORSY	HAEMAL	HARDEN	HEEDER	*HIGHLY
HIDER	HOSEL	HAEMIC	HARDLY	*HEEHAW	*HIGHTH
HIGHT	HOSTA	HAEMIN	HAREEM	HEELER	*HIJACK
HIKER	HOTCH	HAERES	HARING	HEFTER	HILLER
HILAR	HOTEL	HAFTER	HARLOT	HEGARI	HILLOA
HILLO	HOTLY	HAGBUT	HARMER	HEGIRA	HINDER
HILLY	HOUND	HAGDON	HARMIN	HEIFER	HINGER
HILUM	HOURI	HAGGED	HARPER	HEIGHT	HIPPED
HILUS	HOUSE	HAGGIS	HARPIN	HEINIE	HIPPER
HINGE	HOVEL	HAGGLE	HARROW	HEISHI	HIPPIE
HINNY	HOVER	HAILER	HARTAL	*HEJIRA	HIRING
HIPPO	*HOWFF	HAIRDO	HASLET	HELIAC	HIRPLE
*HIPPY	HOYLE	HAIRED	HASSEL	HELIUM	HIRSEL
HIRER	*HUBBY	*HAKEEM	HASSLE	HELLER	HIRSLE
HISSY	*HUFFY	HALALA	HASTEN	HELMET	HISPID
HITCH	HUGER	HALEST	*HATBOX	HELPER	HISSER
HOAGY	*HULKY	HALIDE	HATFUL	HEMMED	HITHER
HOARD	HULLO	HALING	HATING	HEMMER	HOAGIE
HOARY	HUMAN	HALITE	HATPIN	HEMOID	HOARSE
*HOBBY	HUMIC	HALLAH	HATRED	HEMPEN	*HOAXER
HOCUS	HUMID	HALLEL	HATTED	HEMPIE	HOBBIT
HODAD	HUMOR	HALLOA	HATTER	HENBIT	HOBBLE
HOGAN	*HUMPH	HALLOO	HAULER	HEPCAT	HOBNOB

*HOCKER	HOOTCH	HUNTER	HAIRIER	HARBOUR	*HAYCOCK
*HOCKEY	HOOTER	HURDLE	HAIRNET	HARDHAT	*HAYFORK
HODDEN	HOOVED	HURLER	HAIRPIN	HARDIER	HAYLAGE
HODDIN	HOOVES	HURLEY	*HALACHA	HARDIES	*HAYLOFT
HOGGED	HOPING	HURRAH	*HALAKHA	HARDILY	*HAYRACK
HOGGER	HOPPLE	HURRAY	*HALAKIC	HARDPAN	*HAYRICK
HOGNUT	HORARY	HURTER	HALALAH	HARDSET	HAYRIDE
HOGTIE	HORNET	HURTLE	*HALAVAH	HARDTOP	HAYSEED
HOIDEN	HORRID	HUSKER	HALBERD	HARELIP	*HAYWARD
HOLARD	HORROR	HUSSAR	HALBERT	HARIANA	*HAYWIRE
HOLDEN	HORSEY	HUSTLE	*HALCYON	HARICOT	*HAZELLY
HOLDER	HORSTE	HUTTED	*HALFWAY	*HARIJAN	*HAZIEST
HOLDUP	HOSIER	*HUTZPA	HALIBUT	*HARMFUL	HEADIER
HOLIER	HOSING	*HUZZAH	HALIDOM	HARMINE	HEADILY
HOLIES	HOSTEL	HYAENA	HALITUS	*HARMONY	HEADING
HOLILY	HOSTLY	*HYBRID	HALLOTH	HARNESS	HEADMAN
HOLING	HOTBED	HYBRIS	*HALLWAY	HARPIES	HEADPIN
HOLISM	*HOTBOX	HYDRIA	HALOGEN	HARPING	HEADSET
HOLIST	HOTDOG	*HYDRIC	HALVERS	HARPIST	*HEADWAY
HOLLER	HOTROD	HYDRID	HALVING	HARPOON	*HEALTHY
HOLLOA	HOTTED	HYETAL	HALYARD	HARRIED	HEARING
HOLLOO	HOTTER	HYMNAL	HAMBONE	HARRIER	HEARKEN
HOLLOW	HOUDAH	*HYPHEN	*HAMBURG	HARRIES	HEARSAY
HOLPEN	HOURLY	*HYPING	*HAMMADA	HARSHEN	HEARTEN
HOMAGE	HOUSEL	*HYPNIC	HAMMIER	*HARSHLY	HEATHEN
HOMBRE	HOUSER	HYSSOP	*HAMMILY	HARSLET	HEATHER
HOMELY	*HOWDAH	HABITAN	*HAMMING	*HARUMPH	HEAVIER
HOMIER	HOWLER	HABITAT	*HAMMOCK	HARVEST	HEAVIES
HOMILY	HOWLTT	HABITUE	HAMSTER	*HASHISH	HEAVING
HOMING	HOYDEN	HABITUS	HAMULUS	*HASSOCK	HEBETIC
HOMINY	*HUBBLY	*HACHURE	HANAPER	HASTATE	*HECKLER
HOMMOS	*HUBBUB	*HACKBUT	HANDBAG	HASTING	HECTARE
HONCHO	*HUBCAP	*HACKLER	HANDCAR	HATABLE	HEDGING
HONDLE	HUBRIS	*HACKMAN	HANDFUL	HATBAND	HEDONIC
HONEST	*HUCKLE	*HACKNEY	HANDGUN	*HATCHEL	HEEDFUL
HONIED	HUDDLE	*HACKOUT	HANDIER	*HATCHER	HEELING
HONING	HUGEST	*HACKSAW	HANDILY	*HATCHET	HEGUMEN
HONKER	HUGGED	HADARIM	HANDLER	HATEFUL	*HEIGHTH
*HONKEY	HUGGER	HADDEST	*HANDOFF	HATLESS	*HEIMISH
HONKIE	HUIPIL	*HADDOCK	HANDOUT	HATLIKE	HEINOUS
HONOUR	HULLER	HAEMOID	HANDSAW	*HATRACK	HEIRDOM
HOODIE	HULLOA	*HAFNIUM	HANDSEL	HATSFUL	HEIRESS
HOODOO	HU^MANE	HAGADIC	HANDSET	HATTING	HEISTER
HOOFER	HUMATE	HAGBORN	HANGDOG	*HAUBERK	HEKTARE
*HOOKAH	HUMBLE	*HAGBUSH	HANGING	*HAUGHTY	HELIAST
*HOOKEY	*HUMBLY	*HAGFISH	HANGMAN	HAULAGE	HELICAL
*HOOKUP	HUMBUG	HAGGADA	HANGOUT	HAULIER	HELICES
HOOLIE	HUMMED	HAGGARD	HANGTAG	HAUNTER	HELICON
HOOPED	HUMMER	HAGGING	HANUMAN	*HAUTBOY	HELIPAD
HOOPER	HUMMUS	*HAGGISH	HAPLESS	HAUTEUR	*HELLBOX
HOOPLA	HUMOUR	HAGGLER	HAPLITE	HAVARTI	HELLCAT
HOOPOE	HUMVEE	HAGRIDE	HAPLOID	HAVEREL	HELLERI
HOOPOO	HUNGER	*HAHNIUM	HAPLONT	HAVIOUR	*HELLERY
HOORAH	HUNGRY	HAIRCAP	*HAPPING	*HAWKING	HELLISH
HOORAY	HUNKER	HAIRCUT	HAPTENE	*HAWKISH	HELLUVA

HELOTRY	*HIMSELF	HOLSTER	HOUNDER	*HYMNODY	*HANDBOOK
*HELPFUL	HINDGUT	*HOLYDAY	HOUSING	*HYPERON	HANDCART
HELPING	HIPBONE	HOMAGER	HOVERER	*HYPNOID	*HANDCUFF
HEMAGOG	HIPLESS	*HOMBURG	*HOWBEIT	*HYPOGEA	*HANDFAST
HEMATAL	*HIPLIKE	*HOMEBOY	*HOWEVER	*HYPONEA	*HANDGRIP
HEMATIC	HIPLINE	HOMIEST	HUDDLER	*HYPOXIA	*HANDHELD
HEMATIN	HIPNESS	HOMINES	*HUFFISH	HABANERA	*HANDHOLD
HEMIOLA	HIPPEST	HOMINID	HUGEOUS	*HABBINIC	*HANDICAP
HEMLINE	HIPPIER	*HOMMOCK	HUGGING	*HABDALAH	HANDIEST
*HEMLOCK	*HIPPING	HOMOLOG	*HUMANLY	HABITANT	HANDLING
*HEMMING	*HIPPISH	*HOMONYM	HUMBLER	HABITUAL	HANDLIST
HEMPIER	*HIPSHOT	*HOMOSEX	*HUMDRUM	HABITUDE	HANDLOOM
HENBANE	HIPSTER	HONESTY	HUMERAL	HACIENDA	*HANDMADE
HENCOOP	HIRABLE	HONOREE	HUMERUS	*HACKWORK	*HANDMAID
HENLIKE	HIRCINE	HONORER	*HUMIDLY	HAEMATAL	*HANDOVER
HENNERY	HIRSUTE	HOODIER	HUMIDOR	*HAEMATIC	HANDRAIL
*HENPECK	HIRUDIN	HOODLUM	*HUMMING	HAEMATIN	*HANDSEWN
HEPARIN	HISSELF	HOOKIER	*HUMMOCK	*HAFTARAH	*HANDSFUL
HEPATIC	HISSING	HOOKIES	HUMORAL	*HAFTORAH	HANDSOME
HEPTANE	HISTOID	HOOKLET	HUNDRED	HAGADIST	*HANDWORK
HEPTOSE	HISTONE	HOOSGOW	HUNNISH	*HAGBERRY	*HANDWRIT
HERBAGE	HISTORY	*HOPEFUL	HUNTING	*HAGGADAH	*HANDYMAN
HERBIER	*HITCHER	*HOPHEAD	HURDIES	*HAGGADIC	*HANGBIRD
HERDMAN	HITLESS	HOPLITE	HURDLER	HAIRBALL	*HANGFIRE
HEREDES	HOARDER	*HOPPING	HURLING	HAIRBAND	HANGNAIL
HERETIC	HOARIER	*HOPSACK	HURRIER	HAIRIEST	HANGNEST
HERITOR	HOARILY	HOPTOAD	HURTFUL	HAIRLESS	HANGOVER
HEROINE	HOARSEN	HORDEIN	HUSBAND	*HAIRLIKE	*HANKERER
HEROISM	*HOATZIN	*HORIZON	*HUSHABY	HAIRLINE	*HAPLOIDY
*HEROIZE	HOBBIES	HORNIER	*HUSHFUL	*HAIRLOCK	*HAPTICAL
HERONRY	HOBBLER	HORNILY	HUSKIER	*HAIRWORK	HARANGUE
HERRING	*HOBLIKE	HORNIST	HUSKIES	*HAIRWORM	HARASSER
HERSELF	HOBNAIL	HORNITO	*HUSKILY	*HALAKIST	HARBORER
HESSIAN	HOBOISM	HORRENT	*HUSKING	*HALAKOTH	*HARDBACK
HESSITE	*HODADDY	*HORRIFY	HUSTLER	HALATION	HARDBALL
HETAERA	*HOECAKE	HORSIER	*HUSWIFE	*HALAZONE	HARDBOOT
HETAIRA	HOEDOWN	HORSILY	HUTLIKE	HALENESS	HARDCASE
*HEXAGON	HOELIKE	HORSING	HUTMENT	*HALFBACK	HARDCORE
*HEXAPLA	*HOGBACK	HOSANNA	HUTTING	*HALFBEAK	HARDEDGE
*HEXAPOD	*HOGFISH	HOSIERY	*HUTZPAH	*HALFLIFE	HARDENER
*HEXEREI	*HOGLIKE	HOSPICE	HYALITE	HALFNESS	*HARDHACK
*HEXOSAN	HOGMANE	HOSTAGE	HYALOID	*HALFTIME	*HARDHEAD
*HIBACHI	HOGNOSE	HOSTESS	*HYDATID	HALFTONE	HARDIEST
*HICKORY	*HOGWASH	HOSTILE	HYDRANT	HALIDOME	HARDLINE
HIDABLE	*HOGWEED	HOSTLER	HYDRASE	HALLIARD	HARDNESS
HIDALGO	HOISTER	*HOTCAKE	HYDRATE	*HALLMARK	HARDNOSE
HIDEOUS	HOLDALL	HOTFOOT	*HYDRIDE	HALLOWER	*HARDSHIP
HIDEOUT	HOLDING	HOTHEAD	*HYDROID	*HALOLIKE	*HARDTACK
*HIGHBOY	HOLDOUT	HOTLINE	*HYDROPS	HAMARTIA	*HARDWARE
*HIGHWAY	HOLIBUT	HOTNESS	HYDROUS	*HAMMERER	*HARDWIRE
*HIJINKS	HOLIDAY	HOTSHOT	*HYDROXY	*HAMMIEST	*HARDWOOD
HILDING	HOLIEST	HOTSPUR	HYGEIST	*HAMPERER	HAREBELL
HILLIER	HOLLAND	HOTTEST	HYGIENE	HANDBALL	*HARELIKE
*HILLOCK	HOLLIES	HOTTING	*HYMNARY	HANDBELL	*HARKENER
HILLTOP	HOLMIUM	HOTTISH	*HYMNIST	HANDBILL	

HARLOTRY	HEADRACE	HEMATEIN	HIDROSTS	HOLSTEIN	HOPELESS
HARMLESS	HEADREST	HEMATINE	HIDROTIC	*HOLYTIDE	*HORNBEAM
*HARMONIC	HEADROOM	HEMATITE	*HIERARCH	*HOMEBODY	HORNBILL
HARRIDAN	HEADSAIL	HEMATOID	HIERATIC	*HOMEBRED	*HORNBOOK
HARROWER	*HEADSHIP	*HEMATOMA	*HIGHBALL	HOMELAND	HORNFELS
*HARRUMPH	HEADSMAN	*HEMIPTER	*HIGHBORN	HOMELESS	HORNIEST
*HARUSPEX	*HEADSTAY	*HEMOCOEL	*HIGHBRED	*HOMELIKE	HORNLESS
*HASHEESH	*HEADWIND	*HEMOCYTE	*HIGHBROW	*HOMEMADE	*HORNLIKE
*HASHHEAD	*HEADWORD	*HEMOLYZE	*HIGHBUSH	*HOMEOBOX	*HORNPIPE
HASTEFUL	*HEADWORK	HEMOSTAT	*HIGHJACK	*HOMEOTIC	HORNPOUT
HASTENER	*HEATEDLY	*HEMPIEST	*HIGHLAND	*HOMEPORT	HORNTAIL
*HATCHECK	HEATLESS	*HEMPWEED	*HIGHLIFE	*HOMEROOM	*HORNWORM
*HATCHERY	*HEAVENLY	*HENCHMAN	*HIGHNESS	*HOMESICK	HORNWORT
*HATCHING	*HEAVYSET	*HENEQUEN	*HIGHROAD	HOMESITE	HOROLOGE
*HATCHWAY	*HEBDOMAD	*HENEQUIN	*HIGHSPOT	*HOMESPUN	*HOROLOGY
HATEABLE	HEBETATE	HENHOUSE	*HIGHTAIL	*HOMESTAY	HORRIBLE
*HATMAKER	HEBETUDE	*HENIQUEN	*HIJACKER	*HOMETOWN	*HORRIBLY
HATTERIA	*HEBRAIZE	*HEPATICA	HILARITY	*HOMEWARD	*HORRIFIC
*HAULYARD	*HECATOMB	*HEPATIZE	HILLIEST	*HOMEWORK	HORSECAR
HAUSFRAU	*HECTICAL	*HEPATOMA	HILLSIDE	*HOMICIDE	*HORSEFLY
HAUTBOIS	*HEDGEHOG	HEPTAGON	HILTLESS	HOMILIST	HORSEMAN
*HAVDALAH	*HEDGEHOP	*HEPTARCH	HIMATION	HOMINESS	HORSIEST
*HAVELOCK	*HEDGEPIG	HERALDIC	HINDERER	HOMINIAN	HOSANNAH
*HAVOCKER	*HEDGEROW	*HERALDRY	HINDMOST	HOMINIES	*HOSEPIPE
*HAWFINCH	HEDONICS	HERBARIA	*HIPPARCH	HOMININE	HOSPITAL
*HAWKBILL	HEDONISM	HERBIEST	*HIPPIEST	*HOMINIZE	HOSPITIA
*HAWKEYED	HEDONIST	HERBLESS	HIRAGANA	HOMINOID	HOSPODAR
*HAWKLIKE	HEEDLESS	*HERBLIKE	HIRELING	*HOMOGONY	HOTBLOOD
*HAWKMOTH	HEELBALL	HERCULES	HISTAMIN	*HOMOLOGY	*HOTCHPOT
*HAWKNOSE	HEELLESS	*HERDLIKE	HISTIDIN	*HOMONYMY	HOTELDOM
*HAWKSHAW	*HEGEMONY	HERDSMAN	HISTOGEN	HONEWORT	HOTELIER
*HAWKWEED	HEGUMENE	*HEREDITY	HISTORIC	*HONEYBEE	HOTELMAN
*HAWTHORN	*HEGUMENY	HEREINTO	HITHERTO	*HONEYBUN	HOTHOUSE
*HAYFIELD	*HEIGHTEN	*HERETRIX	HIVELESS	*HONEYDEW	HOTPRESS
*HAYMAKER	HEIRLESS	HEREUNTO	*HIZZONER	*HONEYFUL	*HOUSEBOY
*HAYSTACK	HEIRLOOM	HEREUPON	*HOACTZIN	HONORAND	*HOUSEFLY
*HAZELHEN	*HEIRSHIP	*HEREWITH	HOARDING	HONORARY	HOUSEFUL
*HAZELNUT	HELIACAL	HERITAGE	HOARIEST	HONOURER	HOUSEMAN
*HAZINESS	*HELICITY	*HERITRIX	*HOBBYIST	HOODIEST	HOUSETOP
*HEADACHE	HELICOID	*HERMETIC	*HOCKSHOP	HOODLESS	*HOWITZER
*HEADACHY	*HELICOPT	*HERMITRY	*HOGMANAY	*HOODLIKE	*HUARACHE
*HEADBAND	HELILIFT	HERNIATE	*HOGMENAY	*HOODWINK	*HUARACHO
*HEADFISH	HELIPORT	HEROICAL	*HOGSHEAD	*HOOFBEAT	*HUCKSTER
HEADGATE	HELISTOP	HERSTORY	*HOKINESS	HOOFLESS	HUGENESS
HEADGEAR	HELLBENT	HESITANT	*HOKYPOKY	*HOOFLIKE	*HUGGABLE
*HEADHUNT	HELLFIRE	HESITATE	*HOLDBACK	HOOKIEST	*HUISACHE
HEADIEST	*HELLKITE	*HEXAGRAM	*HOLDFAST	*HOOKLESS	HUMANISE
*HEADLAMP	*HELMINTH	*HEXAMINE	*HOLDOVER	*HOOKLIKE	*HUMANISM
HEADLAND	HELMLESS	*HEXAPODY	HOLELESS	*HOOKNOSE	*HUMANIZE
HEADLESS	*HELMSMAN	*HEXARCHY	HOLINESS	*HOOKWORM	HUMANOID
HEADLINE	HELOTAGE	HIBERNAL	*HOLOGAMY	HOOLIGAN	*HUMBLEST
*HEADLOCK	HELOTISM	*HIBISCUS	HOLOGRAM	HOOPLESS	*HUMBLING
HEADLONG	HELPLESS	*HICCOUGH	*HOLOGYNY	*HOOPLIKE	*HUMIDIFY
HEADMOST	*HELPMATE	*HIDEAWAY	*HOLOTYPE	HOOPSTER	*HUMIDITY
HEADNOTE	*HELPMEET	HIDELESS	*HOLOZOIC	*HOOSEGOW	*HUMIFIED

*HUMILITY B H UT	S H IV	*C H AFF	*C H IVY	S H ADE
*HUMMABLE C H AD	S H MO	C H AIN	*C H OCK	S H ADY
*HUMORFUL C H AM	S H OD	C H AIR	C H OIR	S H AFT
HUMORIST C H AO	S H OE	C H ALK	C H OKE	S H AKE
HUMOROUS C H AP	S H OG	C H AMP	*C H OKY	S H AKO
*HUMPBACK C H AR	S H OO	C H ANG	C H OLO	*S H AKY
*HUMPLESS C H AT	S H OP	C H ANT	C H OMP	S H ALE
*HUNGOVER C H AW	S H OT	C H AOS	C H OOK	S H ALL
HURTLESS C H AY	S H OW	C H APE	C H ORD	S H ALT
*HUSKIEST C H EF	S H RI	C H APT	C H ORE	S H ALY
*HUSKLIKE C H EW	S H UL	C H ARD	C H OSE	S H AME
HUSTINGS *C H EZ	S H UN	C H ARE	C H OTT	S H ANK
*HYACINTH C H IA	S H UT	C H ARK	*C H UCK	S H APE
*HYALOGEN C H IC	T H AE	C H ARM	C H UFA	S H ARD
*HYDRACID C H IN	T H AN	C H ARR	*C H UFF	S H ARE
*HYDRAGOG C H IP	T H AT	C H ART	C H URL	S H ARK
*HYDRANTH C H IT	T H AW	C H ARY	C H URN	S H ARN
*HYDRATOR C H ON	T H EE	C H ASE	C H URR	S H ARP
*HYDROGEL C H OP	T H EM	C H ASM	C H UTE	S H AUL
*HYDROGEN C H OW	T H EN	C H EAP	C H YLE	S H AWL
*HYDROMEL C H UB	T H EW	C H EAT	*C H YME	S H AWM
*HYDRONIC C H UG	T H EY	C H EEK	D H OLE	S H AWN
*HYDROPIC C H UM	T H IN	C H EEP	D H OTI	S H EAF
*HYDROPSY D H AK	T H IO	C H EER	D H UTI	S H EAL
*HYDROSKI D H AL	T H IR	C H ELA	G H AUT	S H EAR
*HYDROSOL D H OW	T H IS	C H ERT	*G H AZI	S H EEN
*HYDROXYL G H AT	T H OU	C H ESS	G H OST	S H EEP
*HYGIEIST G H EE	T H RO	C H EST	G H OUL	S H EER
*HYLOZOIC K H AF	T H RU	C H ETH	G H YLL	S H EET
*HYMENEAL K H AN	T H UD	*C H EVY	K H ADI	S H EIK
*HYMENIUM K H AT	T H UG	*C H EWY	*K H AKI	S H ELF
*HYMNBOOK K H ET	T H US	C H IAO	*K H APH	S H ELL
*HYMNLESS P H AT	W H AM	*C H ICK	K H EDA	S H END
*HYMNLIKE P H EW	W H AP	C H ICO	*K H ETH	S H EOL
*HYOSCINE *P H IZ	W H AT	C H IDE	K H OUM	S H ERD
*HYPERGOL P H ON	W H EE	C H IEF	P H AGE	S H IED
*HYPEROPE P H OT	W H EN	C H IEL	P H ASE	S H IES
*HYPHEMIA P H UT	W H ET	C H ILD	P H IAL	S H IFT
*HYPNOSIS R H EA	W H EW	C H ILE	*P H LOX	S H ILL
*HYPNOTIC R H US	W H EY	C H ILI	P H ONE	S H ILY
*HYPOACID S H AD	W H ID	C H ILL	P H ONO	S H INE
*HYPODERM S H AG	W H IG	C H IMB	P H ONY	S H INY
*HYPOGEAL S H AH	W H IM	C H IME	P H OTO	S H IRE
*HYPOGEAN S H AM	W H IN	C H IMP	*P H PH T	S H IRK
*HYPOGENE S H AT	W H IP	C H INA	P H YLA	S H IRR
*HYPOGEUM S H AW	W H IR	C H INE	P H YLE	S H IRT
*HYPOGYNY S H AY	W H IT	C H INK	*Q H AST	S H IST
*HYPONOIA S H EA	*W H IZ	C H INO	R H EUM	S H IVA
*HYPOPNEA S H ED	W H OA	C H IRK	R H INO	S H IVE
*HYPOPYON S H EW	W H OM	C H IRM	R H OMB	S H LEP
*HYPOTHEC S H IM	W H OP	C H IRO	R H UMB	S H OAL
*HYRACOID S H IN	B H ANG	C H IRP	R H YME	S H OAT
HYSTERIA S H IP	B H OOT	C H IRR	R H YTA	S H OCK
*HYSTERIC S H IT	C H AFE	C H IVE	S H ACK	S H OER

*S H OJI	T H ORN	W H ORT	C H ABLIS	*C H ILIDOG	CO H EIR
S H ONE	T H ORO	W H OSE	*C H ALLA H	C H ITOSAN	CO H ERE
S H OOK	T H ORP	W H OSO	*C H ALOT H	*C H LOASMA	CO H ORT
S H OOL	T H OSE	*W H UMP	C H APATI	*C H OCKFUL	CO H OS H
S H OON	T H RAW	C H ADAR	*C H ARLEY	*C H UGALUG	CO H OST
S H OOT	T H REE	C H ADOR	C H ARLIE	*C H UTZPA H	CO H UNE
S H ORE	T H REW	*C H AKRA	C H ATTED	G H OSTING	DA H LIA
S H ORL	T H RIP	C H ALA H	*C H AZZAN	*P H ILTRUM	DA H OON
S H ORN	T H ROB	C H ALE H	*C H EERLY	P H ORONID	DE H ORN
S H ORT	T H ROE	C H ALLA	*C H EETA H	*P H T H ALIC	DE H ORT
S H OTE	T H ROW	C H EAPO	*C H ERIS H	*P H T H ALIN	FU H RER
S H OTT	T H RUM	C H ETA H	C H ETRUM	*P H T H ISIC	*JO H NNY
S H OUT	*T H UJA	C H EVRE	C H ICANO	*P H T H ISIS	KA H UNA
S H OVE	T H UNK	*C H INC H	*C H ICKEE	*S H ADBUS H	*MA H ZOR
S H OWN	T H URL	*C H IPPY	C H OLENT	*S H ADRAC H	MI H RAB
S H OWY	T H UYA	C H IRAL	*C H OMPER	S H EARING	RE H ANG
S H OYU	T H YME	*C H LINK	*C H UDDA H	S H EENFUL	RE H AS H
S H RED	T H YMI	C H OANA	D H URRIE	*S H EDLIKE	RE H EAR
S H REW	*T H YMY	*C H URC H	G H ARIAL	S H EENFUL	RE H EAT
S H RUB	*W HACK	*K H EDA H	G H OULIE	*S H EEPCOT	RE H EEL
S H RUG	W H ALE	*P H OBIC	*K H IRKA H	*S H EEPIS H	RE H IRE
S H UCK	W H AMO	P HYLLO	*P HARAO H	*S H IITAKE	RE H UNG
S H UNT	W H ANG	*P H YSED	P H ENATE	*S H MALTZY	SC H EMA
S H US H	W H ARF	S H ALEY	*P H ENOXY	S H OELESS	SC H EME
S H UTE	W H AUP	S H AMOS	P H OEBUS	S H OOTOUT	SC H ISM
S H YER	W H EAL	S H ANNY	P H ONIED	S H ORTIS H	SC H IST
S H YLY	W H EAT	S H AUG H	S H ANTI H	S H OWERER	*SC H IZO
T HACK	W H EEL	S H EAT H	S H IATSU	*S H OWRING	*SC H IZY
T HANE	W H EEN	*S H EIK H	*S H IATZU	*S H REWIS H	SC H LEP
T HANK	W H EEP	S H EILA	*S H ICKER	*T H ICKIS H	SC H MOE
T HARM	*W H ELK	S H ELTA	*S H IKKER	*T H IEVIS H	*SC H NOZ
T H EBE	W H ELM	S H ERPA	S H ITAKE	T H INNIS H	SC H OOL
T H EFT	W H ELP	S H EUC H	S H ITTA H	*T HOROUG H	SC H ORL
T H EGN	W H ERE	S H EUG H	*S H LUMPY	*T H UGGIS H	*SC H RIK
T H EIN	*W H IC H	S H IBA H	*S H MALTZ	*T H YMOSIN	SC H ROD
T H EIR	*W H IFF	*S H IVA H	*S H MOOZE	W H ATNESS	*SC H TIK
T H EME	W H ILE	S H LEPP	*S H OWBIZ	*W H EYLIKE	SC H UIT
T H ERE	W H INE	S H LUMP	T H ISTLY	*W H IPLAS H	SC H USS
T H ERM	W H INY	S H MEAR	T H ROUG H	W H ITIEST	SP H ENE
T H ESE	W H IPT	S H NOOK	W H ATSIS	RE H AB	SP H ERE
T H ETA	W H IRL	T HATC H	*W H ITIS H	BE H ALF	SP H ERY
T H EWY	W H IRR	T H LIMB	*W H ORIS H	BE H AVE	*SP H INX
T H ICK	W H IS H	T H LIMP	*C H AINSAW	BE H EAD	TA H INI
T H IEF	*W H ISK	T H OUG H	*C H ALAZIA	BE H ELD	TA H SIL
T H IG H	W H IST	T H RAS H	*C H ALLOT H	BE H EST	VA H INE
T H ILL	W H ITE	T H RES H	*C H APATTI	BE H IND	WA H INE
T H INE	W H ITY	T H RUS H	*C H APPATI	BE H OLD	BA H ADUR
T H ING	*W H IZZ	*W HACKO	*C H ATCH KA	BE H OOF	*BE H AVER
T H INK	W H OLE	*W H AMMO	*C H ATCH KE	BE H OVE	*BE H OOVE
T H IOL	*W H OMP	W H INGE	*C H EAPIS H	BE H OWL	BO H EMIA
T H IRD	W H OOF	*W H OOS H	C H EERLED	*BO H UNK	CO H ABIT
T H IRL	W H OOP	W H INGE	*C H ELIPED	CA H IER	CO H ERER
T H OLE	W H ORE	*W H YDA H	*C H ICKORY	CA H OOT	DE H ISCE
T H ONG	W H ORL		*C H ILDIS H	CO H EAD	GA H NITE

*H A H NIUM	*BUS H WA H	*CAS H MERE	*H IG H BRED	NEP H RITE	RUT H ENIC
*LE H AYIM	*FOX H UNT	CAT H EDRA	*H IG H BROW	NIG H NESS	RUT H LESS
MA H ARAN	GAT H ERE	CAT H ETER	*H IG H BUS H	*NIG H TCAP	SAW H ORSE
*MA H JONG	*H AS H IS H	*CAT H EXIS	*H IG H JACK	NIG H TIES	SIG H LESS
*PA H LAVI	*JAR H EAD	*CAT H OLIC	*H IG H LAND	*NIG H TJAR	*SIG H LIKE
RE H INGE	*LIT H IFY	CAT H OUSE	*H IG H LIFE	*NON HARDY	SIG H TING
RE H OUSE	LIT H OID	*CEP H ALAD	*H IG H NESS	NON H UMAN	SIG H TSEE
SA H IWAL	LUT H IER	*CEP H ALIC	*H IG H ROAD	*NUT HATC H	SIP H ONAL
SA H UARO	MES H IER	*CEP H ALIN	*H IG H SPOT	NUT H OUSE	*SIP H ONIC
*SC H APPE	MES H UGA	*C H T H ONIC	*H IG H TAIL	*PAC HADOM	SIT H ENCE
SC H EMER	MOT H ALL	COT H URNI	H IT H ERTO	*PAC H ALIC	*SUB H UMAN
*SC H ERZO	MUD H OLE	CUS H IEST	H OT H OUSE	*PAC H INKO	*SUB H UMID
*SC H IZZY	NON H EME	*CUS H IONY	*H YP H EMIA	*PAC H OULI	*SUC H LIKE
*SC H LEPP	NON H OME	DAS H IEST	*KAS H RUT H	*PAN H UMAN	SUC H NESS
*SC H LOCK	PIS H OGE	DET H RONE	*KEP H ALIN	PAR H ELIA	*SYP H ILIS
*SC H LUMP	RES H AVE	DIC H ASIA	*KYP H OSIS	*PAR H ELIC	TAC H INID
*SC H MALZ	RES H INE	*DIC H OTIC	LAT H ERER	*PAS H ADOM	*TAC H ISME
SC H MEAR	RES H ONE	*DIC H ROIC	LAT H IEST	*PAS H ALIC	TAC H ISTE
SC H MEER	SON H OOD	*DIP H ASIC	*LAT H WORK	*PAS H ALIK	TAP H OUSE
SC H MOOS	*TAC H YON	*DIP H ENYL	*LEC H AYIM	*PAT H ETIC	TEA H OUSE
*SC H MUCK	*TUG H RIK	DIS H ERIT	LET H ALLY	PAT H LESS	TEP H RITE
SC H NAPS	*ZIT H ERN	*DIS H EVEL	*LET H ARGY	PAT H OGEN	*TIG H TWAD
*SC H NOOK	*BAC H ELOR	DIS H IEST	LIC H ENIN	*P H T H ALIC	TIT H ABLE
*SC H NOZZ	BAG H OUSE	*DIS H LIKE	*LIG H TFUL	*P H T H ALIN	TIT H ONIA
*SC H TICK	*BAT H ETIC	DIS H ONOR	LIG H TING	*P H T H ISIC	TRI H EDRA
SP H ENIC	BAT H LESS	*DIS H WARE	*LIG H TIS H	*P H T H ISIS	WAR H ORSE
SP H ERAL	*BAT H ROBE	DIT H EISM	LIT H ARGE	PIS H OGUE	*WAS H ABLE
SP H ERIC	*BAT H ROOM	DIT H EIST	LIT H EMIA	PIT H LESS	*WAS HBOWL
ST H ENIA	BAU H INIA	DIT H ERER	LIT H OSOL	POS H NESS	WAS H IEST
*VE H ICLE	*BEC H AMEL	DOG H OUSE	LOT H ARIO	POT H OUSE	*WASHROOM
BOT H Y	*BEC H ANCE	FAS H IOUS	LOT H SOME	PRE H UNAN	*WIS H BONE
DAS H I	*BES H ADOW	*FAT H ERLY	LUS H NESS	*PRO H IBIT	WIS H LESS
LAT H I	*BES H IVER	*FIG H TING	*MAC H ISMO	*PUS H BALL	*WIT HDRAW
MIC H E	BES H ROUD	*FIS H BOLT	*MEC H ANIC	*PUS H CART	WIT H ERER
*MYT H Y	BET H ESDA	*FIS H BONE	*MEP H ITIS	*PUS H DOWN	*WIT H OLD
NAC H O	*BIC H ROME	*FIS H BOWL	MES H IEST	PUS H IEST	WIT H IEST
SUS H I	*BIP H ASIC	*FIS H HOOK	*MES H UGA H	*PUS H OVER	*YAC H TING
WAS H Y	*BIP H ENYL	FIS H IEST	*MES H UGGE	RAC H ILLA	*YACHTMAN
*YEC H Y	*BOE H MITE	FIS H LESS	*MES H WORK	RAC H ITIS	*YES H IVA H
BUS H WA	*BON H OMIE	*FIS H LIKE	*MET H INKS	RAS H NESS	*YOG H OURT
*H IG H T H	*BOS H VARK	FIS H LINE	*MET H ODIC	REC H ANGE	BAC H
*JUB H A H	*BOT H RIUM	*FIS H MEAL	*MET H OXYL	REC H ARGE	BAS H
LEC H WE	BUG H OUSE	*FIS H POLE	*MET H YLAL	REC H OOSE	BAT H
LOC H AN	*BUS H FIRE	*FIS H POND	*MIS H MAS H	RED H ORSE	BET H
NAC H AS	BUS H GOAT	FIS H TAIL	*MIS H MOS H	REP H RASE	BLA H
NAC H ES	BUS H IEST	*FIS H WIFE	*MOT H ERLY	RES H APER	BOT H
NOT H ER	BUS H LAND	*FIS H WORM	*MOT H LIKE	RET H READ	BUS H
*QUO H OG	BUS H LESS	*FOX H OUND	*MUCHACHO	RIC H NESS	CAP H
REC H EW	*BUS H LIKE	*FUC H SINE	*MUC H NESS	RIG H TIES	CAS H
RUC H ED	*CAC H ALOT	GAS H OUSE	MUS H ROOM	RIG H TISM	DAS H
TEC H IE	*CAC H EPOT	*H AS H EES H	*MYT H ICAL	RIG H TIST	DIS H
WUT H ER	*CAC H EXIA	*H AS H HEAD	*NAP H T H OL	RUS H IEST	DOT H
BAT H MAT	*CAC H UCHA	H EN H OUSE	NAT H LESS	*RUS H LIKE	FASH
BOD H RAN	*CAS H BOOK	*H IG H BALL	*NEP H RISM		FIS H
*BUS H PIG	CAS H LESS	*H IG H BORN			

GAS H	SUC H	CRUS H	KETC H	*PUJA H	TILT H
GOS H	SUG H	CUIS H	KNIS H	PUNC H	TOOT H
GUS H	SYP H	CULC H	LAIC H	*QUAS H	TORA H
H AS H	TAC H	CURC H	LAIG H	*QUOT H	TORC H
H AT H	TET H	CUTC H	LAIT H	*QURS H	TOUC H
H ET H	TOP H	DEAS H	LARC H	*RAJA H	TOUG H
H IG H	TOS H	DEAT H	LATC H	RALP H	TRAS H
H UN H	TUS H	DEPT H	LAUG H	RANC H	TROT H
H US H	VUG H	DIRT H	LEAC H	RATC H	TRUT H
JOS H	WAS H	DITC H	LEAS H	RAYA H	VETC H
KAP H	WIC H	DOET H	LEEC H	REAC H	VOUC H
KIT H	WIS H	DOUG H	LETC H	RERC H	WATC H
KOP H	WIT H	DUNC H	LOAC H	ROAC H	WAUG H
LAK H	*WYC H	DUTC H	LOAT H	ROTC H	WEIG H
LAS H	YEA H	FAIT H	LOTA H	ROUG H	WELC H
LAT H	YEC H	FAUG H	LOUG H	ROUT H	WELS H
LEC H	YOD H	FETC H	LUNC H	ROWT H	WENC H
LIC H	YOG H	FIFT H	LURC H	SAIT H	*W H IC H
LOC H	YUC H	FILC H	*LYMP H	SANG H	W H IS H
LOT H	BAIT H	FILT H	LYNC H	SAUC H	WIDT H
LUS H	BATC H	FINC H	MARC H	SAUG H	WINC H
MAC H	BEAC H	FIRT H	MARS H	SELA H	WITC H
MAS H	BEEC H	FITC H	MATC H	S HUS H	WOOS H
MAT H	BELC H	FLAS H	MILC H	*SIXT H	WORT H
MES H	BENC H	FLES H	MIRT H	SKOS H	WRAT H
MET H	BERT H	FLUS H	MONT H	SLAS H	WROT H
MOT H	BIMA H	FORT H	MOOC H	SLOS H	*YECC H
MUC H	BIRC H	FRES H	MORP H	SLOT H	YIRT H
MUS H	BITC H	FRIT H	MOUC H	SLUS H	YOUT H
MYT H	BLUS H	FROS H	MOUT H	SMAS H	*YUCC H
NIG H	BOOT H	FROT H	MULC H	SMIT H	*ZILC H
NOS H	BOTC H	GALA H	MUNC H	SNAS H	BANIS H
PAS H	BOUG H	GART H	MUST H	SNAT H	BLANC H
PAT H	BRAC H	GERA H	MUTC H	SOOT H	BLEAC H
PEC H	BRAS H	GIRS H	MYNA H	SOUG H	BLENC H
PIS H	BROT H	GIRT H	MYRR H	SOUT H	BLOTC H
PIT H	BRUG H	GLYP H	NATC H	STAP H	BLUIS H
POO H	BRUS H	GNAS H	NEAT H	STAS H	BOYIS H
POS H	BUMP H	GRAP H	NEIG H	STIC H	BRANC H
PUG H	BUNC H	GRIT H	NORT H	SUBA H	BREAC H
PUS H	BURG H	GULC H	NOTC H	SURA H	BREAT H
*QOP H	BUTC H	GURS H	*NYMP H	SWAS H	BREEC H
RAS H	CATC H	H ARS H	PARC H	SWAT H	BROAC H
RAT H	C HET H	H ATC H	PATC H	SWIS H	BROOC H
RES H	CINC H	H AUG H	PEAC H	SWIT H	BRUNC H
RIC H	CLAC H	H EIG H	PERC H	SYLP H	CALAS H
RUS H	CLAS H	H EUG H	PINC H	SYNC H	CALIP H
RUT H	CLOT H	H ITC H	PITC H	SYNT H	CAROC H
SAS H	COAC H	H OOC H	PLAS H	TEAC H	CASBA H
S HA H	CONC H	H ORA H	PLUS H	TEET H	CERIP H
SIG H	COOC H	H OTC H	POAC H	TENC H	C HALA H
SIN H	COUC H	*H UMP H	POOC H	TENT H	C HALE H
SIT H	COUG H	H UNC H	PORC H	TEUC H	C HETA H
SOP H	COUT H	H UTC H	POUC H	TEUG H	*C H INC H
SOT H	CRAS H	KENC H	*PSYC H	T HIG H	*C H OUG H

C H OUS H	H ALLA H	MULLA H	*S H IVA H	WARMT H	*C H ALOT H
*C H URC H	*H ALVA H	NAUTC H	SIRRA H	WEALT H	*C H EETA H
CLENC H	*H AMZA H	NEWIS H	SKEIG H	*W H IDA H	*C H ERIS H
CLINC H	H AUNC H	NULLA H	*SKETC H	*W H OOS H	*C H UDDA H
CLOUG H	H EALT H	OARAP H	SLATC H	*W H YDA H	*CLAYIS H
CLUTC H	H EART H	PAINC H	SLEIG H	WIDIS H	*COCKIS H
CO H OS H	*H IG H T H	PALIS H	SLEUT H	WINIS H	*CODFIS H
COMET H	*H OOKA H	PARDA H	SLOUC H	WRAIT H	COLDIS H
COOLT H	H OORA H	PARIA H	SLOUG H	WREAT H	COOLIS H
COPRA H	H OOTC H	PARTS H	SMIRC H	WRENC H	*COWFIS H
COYIS H	H OUDA H	PAUNC H	SMOOC H	WRETC H	CRAUNC H
CRANC H	*H OWDA H	PERIS H	SMOOT H	*ZENIT H	*CUBBIS H
CRATC H	H URRA H	PLANC H	SMUTC H	*ZEROT H	CULTIS H
CREES H	*H UZZA H	PLEAC H	SNATC H	*ZIBET H	CURRAC H
CROTC H	*JADIS H	PLENC H	SNEES H	*ZILLA H	CURRAG H
CROUC H	*JARRA H	PLINI H	SNITC H	*ZIZIT H	CURRIS H
CRUNC H	*JOSEP H	PLOUG H	SPEEC H	*BABYIS H	*DAMPIS H
CRUTC H	*JUBBA H	POLIS H	SPILT H	BALDIS H	*DARKIS H
CULTC H	*JUB H A H	POPIS H	SPLAS H	*BATFIS H	DEAFIS H
CURAG H	*KALIP H	POTAS H	SPLOS H	BEAMIS H	*DEBAUC H
DALET H	*KASBA H	PREAC H	*SQUAS H	BEARIS H	*DEBOUC H
DANIS H	*KEBLA H	PRUTA H	*SQUIS H	BEGORA H	DERVIS H
DEART H	*KEDDA H	PUNIS H	*SQUUS H	BENEAT H	DIGRAP H
DETAC H	*K H EDA H	*PUNKA H	STANC H	BESEEC H	*DIMORP H
DOVIS H	KIAUG H	PURDA H	STARC H	BETROT H	*DIPTYC H
DREIC H	*KIBBE H	PUTSC H	STENC H	*BEWITC H	DISTIC H
DREIG H	*KIBLA H	*QUAIC H	STITC H	BIGGIS H	*DOGFIS H
DRENC H	*KIBOS H	*QUAIG H	STRAT H	BISMUT H	DOGGIS H
DROUT H	*KIRSC H	*QUENC H	SUCCA H	BLEMIS H	DOLLIS H
DRYIS H	*KITSC H	*QUITC H	*SUKKA H	BLUEIS H	DONNIS H
DUDIS H	*KLATC H	*QURUS H	SUMAC H	BOARIS H	*DOZENT H
FAMIS H	*KVETC H	RADIS H	SUNNA H	BOGGIS H	DRONIS H
FELLA H	*KYBOS H	RAKIS H	SWART H	BOOBIS H	DULLIS H
FETIC H	LAMED H	RAUNC H	SWATC H	*BOOKIS H	*DUMPIS H
FETIS H	LATIS H	RAVIS H	SWITC H	BOORIS H	*DUSKIS H
FINIS H	LAUNC H	RAWIS H	SWOOS H	BOROUG H	*FADDIS H
FLEEC H	LAVIS H	RE H AS H	TEMPE H	*BOXFIS H	FAIRIS H
FLENC H	LENGT H	RELIS H	TERAP H	BREADT H	FATTIS H
FLETC H	LOOFA H	REWAS H	T H ATC H	BRINIS H	*FINFIS H
FLINC H	LOWIS H	RUPIA H	T H OUG H	BRUTIS H	*FLEMIS H
*FLYSC H	MARIS H	SAMEC H	T H RAS H	*BUCKIS H	*FOLKIS H
FOURT H	MATSA H	*SAMEK H	T H RES H	BULLIS H	FOOLIS H
FRENC H	*MATZA H	SCARP H	T H RUS H	BULRUS H	*FOPPIS H
GALOS H	*MATZO H	SCORC H	TONIS H	BURNIS H	*FOXFIS H
*GANJA H	MENSC H	SCOTC H	TOROT H	*BUS H WA H	*FURBIS H
GARIS H	*MIKVA H	SCOUT H	TOYIS H	CADDIS H	FURNIS H
GLITC H	*MIKVE H	SCUTC H	TREFA H	*CAPOUC H	*GALUMP H
GOLOS H	MINIS H	SEARC H	TRENC H	CARLIS H	GARFIS H
GONOP H	MODIS H	SERAP H	TROUG H	CAROAC H	GARNIS H
GRINC H	MOLLA H	S H AUG H	TROWT H	CARROC H	*GAWKIS H
GROUC H	MOLOC H	S H EAT H	TUSSA H	*CARWAS H	GIRLIS H
GROWT H	MONIS H	*S H EIK H	TUSSE H	CATARR H	GNOMIS H
GRUTC H	MOOLA H	S H EUC H	TWITC H	*CATFIS H	GOATIS H
H ADIT H	MOPIS H	S H EUG H	VANIS H	CATTIS H	GOODIS H
	MULIS H	S H IBA H	WALLA H	*C H ALLA H	*GOOMBA H

GOULAS H	MONARC H	RUTTIS H	TURBIT H	BROADIS H	FLOURIS H
GRAYIS H	*MONKIS H	SABBAT H	TURPET H	BROGUIS H	*FOOLFIS H
GREENT H	MOONIS H	SALTIS H	*TWELFT H	*BROWNIS H	*FOOTBAT H
GREYIS H	MOORIS H	*SAWFIS H	*VAMPIS H	BULLRUS H	*FOOTPAT H
*H AGBUS H	*MUDFIS H	SCRAIC H	VARNIS H	*CABBALA H	FORSOOT H
*H AGFIS H	NEBBIS H	SCRAIG H	*VERMUT H	*CALABAS H	FORTIET H
*H AGGIS H	NEOLIT H	SCRATC H	VOGUIS H	*CALIPAS H	*FORTYIS H
H ALALA H	NOMARC H	SCREEC H	*WAGGIS H	*CARRITC H	*FREAKIS H
*H ALAVA H	NONCAS H	SCROOC H	*WAMPIS H	*CARTOUC H	*FROGFIS H
H ALLOT H	NONSUC H	SCRUNC H	*WARMIS H	*CAVEFIS H	*FURLOUG H
*H ARUMP H	NOURIS H	SELFIS H	*WARPAT H	*CENOTAP H	*GOATFIS H
*H AS H IS H	NUNNIS H	SERFIS H	*WEAKIS H	*C H ALLOT H	*GOLDFIS H
*H AWKIS H	*PADS H A H	SEVENT H	WEARIS H	*C H EAPIS H	*GRAYFIS H
*H EIG H T H	*PANFIS H	S H ANTI H	WENNIS H	*C H ILDIS H	GREENIS H
*H EIMIS H	*PEAKIS H	S H ITTA H	WETTIS H	*C H UTZPA H	*GRUFFIS H
H ELLIS H	*PECKIS H	*SICKIS H	*W H ITIS H	CLANNIS H	*GRUMPIS H
*H IPPIS H	*PEEVIS H	*SKREEG H	*W H ORIS H	*CLERKIS H	GUNSMIT H
*H OGFIS H	*PERKIS H	*SKREIG H	WILDIS H	*CLIQUIS H	*GYPSYIS H
*H OGWAS H	PETTIS H	SLAVIS H	*WIMPIS H	*CLOWNIS H	*H ABDALA H
H OTTIS H	*P H ARAO H	SLOWIS H	*WISPIS H	*CLUBBIS H	*H AFTARA H
*H UFFIS H	*PIBROC H	SOFTIS H	*WOLFIS H	*CLUMPIS H	*H AFTORA H
H UNNIS H	*PIGFIS H	SOTTIS H	*WORMIS H	*COALFIS H	*HAGGADA H
*H UTZPA H	PIGGIS H	SOURIS H	WOTTET H	*COPPERA H	*H ALAKOT H
*JACINT H	*PINFIS H	SPINAC H	*XERARC H	*CORONAC H	*H AS H EES H
*JEWFIS H	*PINKIS H	SPLOTC H	*ZANYIS H	*CRANKIS H	*H AVDALA H
*KADDIS H	PLANIS H	*SQUELC H	*ZAPTIA H	*CRAWFIS H	*H AWFINC H
*K H IRKA H	PLENIS H	*SQUINC H	*ZAPTIE H	*CRAYFIS H	*H AWKMOT H
*KIDDIS H	POORIS H	*SQUOOS H	*BACKLAS H	*CROMLEC H	*H EADFIS H
*KIDDUS H	POTLAC H	STAUNC H	*BACKRUS H	*DA H ABEA H	*H ELMINT H
*KLATSC H	*PREWAS H	STEALT H	*BACKWAS H	*DA H ABIA H	*H EPTARC H
*KURBAS H	PRUDIS H	STENGA H	*BADMOUT H	*DA H ABIE H	*H EREWIT H
LADYIS H	PUBLIS H	STOMAC H	*BAKS H IS H	*DANDYIS H	*H ICCOUG H
LARGIS H	*PUCKIS H	STONIS H	*BEDRENC H	*DEALFIS H	*H IERARC H
LARKIS H	PUGGIS H	STRETC H	BEGORRA H	DEPOLIS H	*H IG H BUS H
*LAZYIS H	*PUNKIS H	STYLIS H	*BE H EMOT H	*DESPATC H	*H IPPARC H
LEFTIS H	*PUPFIS H	SUCCOT H	*BEQUEAT H	*DEVILIS H	H OSANNA H
LONGIS H	*QUAMAS H	SUNBAT H	*BESCORC H	*DIAGRAP H	*H YACINT H
LOUDIS H	*RAFFIS H	SUNFIS H	*BESMIRC H	DIMINIS H	*H YDRANT H
LOUTIS H	RAMMIS H	SWINIS H	*BESMOOT H	*DISPATC H	*JACKFIS H
LUMPIS H	RANKIS H	TALLIS H	*BIGMOUT H	DOGTOOT H	*KABBALA H
MADDIS H	RASPIS H	TALLIT H	*BILLFIS H	*DOGWATC H	*KAFFIYE H
*MAMMOT H	RATFIS H	TANNIS H	*BIRDBAT H	*DOWNWAS H	*KAS H RUT H
MANNIS H	RATTIS H	TARBUS H	*BLACKIS H	*DRAFFIS H	*KEFFIYE H
*MATZOT H	REBIRT H	TARNIS H	BLANDIS H	*DRUMFIS H	*KEYPUNC H
*MAWKIS H	REDDIS H	TARTIS H	*BLEAKIS H	*DWARFIS H	*KINGFIS H
*MAYBUS H	REDFIS H	TEREFA H	*BLOCKIS H	FAINTIS H	*KREPLAC H
*MEGILP H	REFRES H	T H ROUG H	BLONDIS H	*FALLFIS H	*KRYOLIT H
MENORA H	REMATC H	TIGRIS H	*BLOWFIS H	*FEEBLIS H	*LADYFIS H
MESARC H	REPATC H	TOADIS H	*BLUEFIS H	*FEVERIS H	LANGUIS H
MESSIA H	RETEAC H	TONNIS H	*BOARFIS H	*FIENDIS H	*LIG H TIS H
*MEZUZA H	RETOUC H	TOWNIS H	*BONEFIS H	*FIFTYIS H	LIONFIS H
MIDRAS H	REWEIG H	*TOWPAT H	*BRACKIS H	*FILEFIS H	LITTLIS H
*MITSVA H	ROGUIS H	TRIUMP H	BRAINIS H	*FLATFIS H	LIVERIS H
*MITZVA H	ROMPIS H	TUNDIS H	BRANDIS H	FLATTIS H	*LOGOMAC H
*MOBBIS H	RUBBIS H	TURBET H	BRASSIS H	*FLATWAS H	*LUMPFIS H

*LUNGFIS H	*PARAS H A H	RELAUNC H	*S H AMMAS H	STRENGT H	TOVARIS H
*MASTABA H	*PARFLES H	REPOLIS H	*S H EEPIS H	*STUDFIS H	*TRAMPIS H
MEGALIT H	*PARRITC H	*REPROAC H	S H ORTIS H	*SUBEPOC H	*TRIBRAC H
MEGILLA H	PEARLAS H	RESEARC H	*S H REWIS H	*SUBGRAP H	*TRICKIS H
*MES H UGA H	*PENTARC H	*RESKETC H	SISSYIS H	*SUCKFIS H	*TRIGLYP H
*MIDMONT H	PERIANT H	RESMOOT H	*SIXTIET H	*SUNPORC H	TRIGRAP H
*MIDWATC H	*PIPEFIS H	RESTITC H	*SIXTYIS H	*SURFFIS H	*TRIMORP H
*MILKFIS H	*PLUMPIS H	RETRENC H	*SKIRMIS H	*SWAMPIS H	*TRIPTYC H
*MISFAIT H	*POLYMAT H	*ROCKFIS H	*SKITTIS H	SWEETIS H	TRISTIC H
*MIS H MAS H	POORTIT H	ROSEBUS H	SLAPDAS H	TAIGLAC H	*TZITZIT H
*MIS H MOS H	*POTLATC H	ROSEFIS H	*SLOBBIS H	TARBOOS H	*VANQUIS H
*MISMATC H	*PRANKIS H	*ROUG H IS H	SLUGGIS H	TEIGLAC H	*VAPORIS H
*MISPATC H	*PRECRAS H	ROUNDIS H	SMALLIS H	TELEPAT H	*VERANDA H
*MISTEAC H	*PRELUNC H	*ROWDYIS H	*SNAPPIS H	TETRARC H	*VERMOUT H
*MISTOUC H	*PREPUNC H	SAGANAS H	*SNIFFIS H	*T H ICKIS H	*VIGORIS H
*MONKFIS H	*PRIGGIS H	SAILFIS H	*SNOBBIS H	*T H IEVIS H	*WARMOUT H
MONOLIT H	*PURPLIS H	SALTBUS H	SNOUTIS H	T H INNIS H	WATERIS H
MONTEIT H	*QUACKIS H	*SANDFIS H	*SNOWBUS H	*T H OROUG H	*WEAKFIS H
*MOONFIS H	*QUALMIS H	*SANDWIC H	*SPARKIS H	*T H UGGIS H	*W H IPLAS H
*MUSQUAS H	*QUEERIS H	SAVANNA H	*SPOOKIS H	*TICKLIS H	*WOLFFIS H
*MYOGRAP H	*QUIPPIS H	SAWTOOT H	*SQUARIS H	TIGERIS H	*WOMANIS H
NARGILE H	*QUIRKIS H	*SCAMPIS H	*SQUIRIS H	TILEFIS H	WOSTTET H
*NEOMORP H	RAINWAS H	*SCROOTC H	STABLIS H	TINSMIT H	*XENOLIT H
NONESUC H	*RARRUMP H	*SEABEAC H	STANDIS H	*TOADFIS H	*YES H IVA H
NONTRUT H	REATTAC H	*SEECATC H	STEEPIS H	*TOADYIS H	*YOKELIS H
*NUMBFIS H	*REBRANC H	SELCOUT H	*STIFFIS H	TOLBOOT H	*YOUNGIS H
*NUT H ATC H	REFINIS H	*SEMI H IG H	*STOCKIS H	*TOPNOTC H	*ZOOMORP H
*PADIS H A H	REGOLIT H	*S H ADBUS H	STOUTIS H	*TOUG H IS H	
PAGANIS H	*REGROWT H	*S H ADRAC H	STRAMAS H	*TOVARIC H	

J

*JACK	JEHU	JOEY	*JUNK	JAPER	*JIMMY
JADE	JELL	JOHN	JUPE	JAUNT	*JIMPY
JAGG	JEON	JOIN	JURA	*JAWAN	JINGO
JAIL	*JERK	*JOKE	JURY	*JAZZY	JINNI
*JAKE	JESS	*JOKY	JUST	JEBEL	*JIVER
*JAMB	JEST	JOLE	JUTE	*JEHAD	*JIVEY
JANE	JETE	JOLT	JABOT	*JELLY	JNANA
JAPE	JIAO	JOSH	JACAL	*JEMMY	*JOCKO
JARL	*JIBB	JOSS	*JACKY	*JENNY	JOINT
JATO	JIBE	JOTA	JAGER	JERID	JOIST
*JAUK	*JIFF	*JOUK	*JAGGY	*JERKY	*JOKER
JAUP	JILL	JOWL	JAGRA	*JERRY	*JOLLY
JAVA	JILT	JUBA	*JAKES	JESSE	*JOLTY
*JAZZ	*JIMP	JUBE	JALAP	JETON	JONES
JEAN	*JINK	JUDO	JALOP	*JETTY	JORAM
JEEP	JINN	JUGA	*JAMBE	*JEWEL	JORUM
JEER	*JINX	*JUJU	*JAMMY	JIBER	*JOTTY
*JEEZ	JIVE	*JUKE	*JANTY	*JIFFY	JOUAL
JEFE	*JOCK	JUMP	JAPAN	*JIHAD	JOULE

JOUST	*JAZZER	*JOYPOP	*JARRING	*JOINERY	*JAILBIRD
*JOWAR	JEERER	*JUBBAH	*JARSFUL	*JOINING	*JALAPENO
*JOWLY	*JEJUNA	*JUBHAH	*JASMINE	JOINTER	*JALOUSIE
JUDAS	*JEJUNE	*JUBILE	*JAVELIN	*JOINTLY	*JAMBOREE
JUDGE	JENNET	*JUDDER	*JAWBONE	*JOKIEST	*JANIFORM
JUGAL	*JERBOA	*JUDGER	*JAWLIKE	*JOLLIED	*JANISARY
*JUGUM	JEREED	*JUDOKA	*JAWLINE	JOLLIER	*JANIZARY
JUICE	*JERKER	JUGATE	*JAYBIRD	JOLLIES	*JAPANIZE
*JUICY	*JERKIN	*JUGFUL	*JAYWALK	*JOLLIFY	*JAPANNER
JULEP	JERRID	*JUGGED	*JAZZMAN	*JOLLITY	*JAPINGLY
*JUMBO	*JERSEY	*JUGGLE	JEALOUS	*JONQUIL	*JAPONICA
*JUMPY	JESTER	JUGULA	*JEEPERS	JOSTLER	*JARGONEL
JUNCO	JESUIT	*JUICER	*JEEPNEY	*JOTTING	*JAROSITE
*JUNKY	*JETSAM	*JUJUBE	*JEJUNAL	JOURNAL	*JAROVIZE
JUNTA	*JETSOM	*JUMBAL	*JEJUNUM	*JOURNEY	*JAUNDICE
JUNTO	JETTED	*JUMBLE	*JELLABA	JOUSTER	*JAVELINA
JUPON	JETTON	*JUMPER	*JELLIFY	*JOYANCE	*JAWBONER
JURAL	*JEZAIL	JUNGLE	*JEMADAR	*JOYLESS	*JAZZLIKE
JURAT	*JIBBER	*JUNGLY	*JEMIDAR	*JOYRIDE	*JEALOUSY
JUREL	*JICAMA	JUNIOR	*JEOPARD	*JUBILEE	*JEJUNITY
JUROR	*JIGGER	*JUNKER	*JERKIES	*JUDOIST	*JELUTONG
*JUTTY	*JIGGLE	*JUNKET	*JERREED	*JUGGING	*JEOPARDY
*JABBER	*JIGGLY	*JUNKIE	JESSANT	*JUGGLER	*JEREMIAD
*JABIRU	*JIGSAW	JURANT	*JESTFUL	*JUGHEAD	*JEROBOAM
*JACANA	JILTER	JURIES	*JESTING	*JUGSFUL	*JERRICAN
*JACKAL	*JIMINY	JURIST	*JETBEAD	*JUGULAR	*JERRYCAN
*JACKER	JINGAL	JUSTER	*JETLIKE	*JUGULUM	*JESUITRY
*JACKET	*JINGKO	JUSTLE	*JETPORT	*JUJITSU	*JETLINER
*JADISH	JINGLE	*JUSTLY	*JETTED	*JUJUISM	*JETTIEST
JAEGER	*JINGLY	*JABBING	JETTIER	*JUJUIST	*JETTISON
*JAGGED	*JINKER	*JACAMAR	JETTIES	*JUJUTSU	*JEWELLER
*JAGGER	JINNEE	*JACINTH	*JETTING	*JUKEBOX	*JIGGERED
JAGUAR	*JITNEY	*JACKASS	*JEWELER	*JUMBLER	*JINGOISM
JAILER	JITTER	*JACKDAW	*JEWELRY	*JUMBUCK	*JINGOIST
JAILOR	*JOBBER	*JACKIES	*JEWFISH	*JUMPOFF	*JIPIJAPA
*JALOPY	*JOCKEY	*JACKLEG	*JEZEBEL	*JUNIPER	*JIUJITSU
*JAMMED	*JOCOSE	*JACKPOT	*JIBBING	*JUNKMAN	*JIUJUTSU
*JAMMER	*JOCUND	*JACOBIN	*JIBBOOM	*JURIDIC	*JOCKETTE
JANGLE	*JOGGER	*JACOBUS	*JIGGING	*JURYMAN	*JOCOSITY
*JANGLY	*JOGGLE	*JACONET	JILLION	*JUSSIVE	*JOHANNES
*JAPERY	*JOHNNY	*JADEITE	*JIMJAMS	*JUSTICE	*JOHNBOAT
*JAPING	JOINER	*JAGGARY	*JIMMINY	*JUSTIFY	*JOINTURE
*JARFUL	*JOJOBA	*JAGGERY	*JINGALL	*JUVENAL	*JOKESTER
JARGON	*JOKIER	*JAGGING	*JINGLER	*JABBERER	*JOKINESS
JARINA	*JOKING	*JAGLESS	*JITTERY	*JACINTHE	*JOKINGLY
*JARRAH	JOLTER	*JALAPIN	*JIVEASS	*JACKAROO	*JOLLIEST
JARRED	JORDAN	*JALOPPY	JOANNES	*JACKBOOT	*JONGLEUR
*JARVEY	*JOSEPH	*JAMBEAU	*JOBBERY	*JACKEROO	*JOVIALTY
*JASMIN	*JOSHER	*JAMMIES	*JOBBING	*JACKFISH	*JOYRIDER
*JASPER	JOSTLE	*JAMMING	*JOBLESS	*JACKROLL	*JOYSTICK
JASSID	*JOUNCE	*JANGLER	*JOBNAME	*JACKSTAY	*JUBILANT
*JAUNCE	*JOUNCY	JANITOR	*JOCULAR	*JACQUARD	*JUBILATE
*JAUNTY	*JOVIAL	*JARGOON	*JODHPUR	*JACULATE	*JUDGMENT
*JAYGEE	*JOYFUL	*JARHEAD	*JOGGLER	*JAGGHERY	*JUDICIAL
*JAYVEE	*JOYOUS	*JARLDOM	*JOINDER	*JAILBAIT	*JUGGLERY

*JUGGLING	MO J O	SE J ANT	*MA J ESTY	*BAN J AX	*MAH J ONGG
*JUGULATE	PU J A	*BE J ESUS	*MA J ORAM	*FEI J OA	*MIS J UDGE
*JULIENNE	*PU J AH	*BE J EWEL	*MA J ORLY	*GAN J AH	*NON J UROR
*JUNCTION	*CA J OLE	*CA J APUT	*MO J ARRA	*VEE J AY	*PER J URER
*JUNCTURE	*CO J OIN	*CA J OLER	*PY J AMAS	*NON J URY	*PRE J UDGE
*JUNKETER	*DE J ECT	*CA J UPUT	*RE J OICE	*BAN J OIST	*SER J EANT
*JUNKYARD	*FA J ITA	*DE J ECTA	*RE J UDGE	*BEN J AMIN	*SKI J ORER
*JURATORY	*HE J IRA	*HI J INKS	SE J EANT	*CON J UGAL	*VER J UICE
*JUSTNESS	*HI J ACK	*J E J UNAL	SO J OURN	*CON J UNCT	
*JUVENILE	*JO J OBA	*J E J UNUM	*BE J ABERS	*CON J URER	*HAD J
	*J E J UNA	*J U J ITSU	*BE J EEZUS	*CON J UROR	*HA J J
D J IN	*J E J UNE	*J U J UISM	*RE J ACKET	*DIS J OINT	*SVARA J
D J INN	*J U J UBE	*J U J UIST	*RE J UGGLE	*DIS J UNCT	*SWARA J
*F J ELD	*PA J AMA	*J U J UTSU	*PA J AMAED	*FOR J UDGE	
*F J ORD	*RE J ECT	*KA J EPUT	NIN J A	*J IU J ITSU	
*HA J J	RE J OIN	*MA J AGUA	RIO J A	*J IU J UTSU	

K

KAAS	KENT	KIWI	KABAB	KEMPT	KITTY
KADI	KEPI	KNAP	KABAR	KENAF	KLONG
KAGU	KEPT	KNAR	KABOB	KENCH	KLOOF
KAIF	KERB	KNEE	KAFIR	KENDO	KLUGE
KAIL	KERF	KNEW	KAIAK	KERNE	*KLUTZ
KAIN	KERN	KNIT	KALAM	KERRY	*KNACK
KAKA	KETO	KNOB	KALIF	KETCH	KNAUR
KAKI	KHAF	KNOP	KALPA	KETOL	KNAVE
KALE	KHAN	KNOT	*KAMIK	KEVEL	KNEAD
KAME	KHAT	KNOW	*KANJI	KEVIL	KNEEL
KAMI	KHET	KNUR	*KAPOK	KHADI	KNELT
KANA	KIBE	KOAN	KAPPA	*KHAKI	KNIFE
KANE	KICK	KOBO	KAPUT	*KHAPH	KNISH
KAON	KIEF	KOEL	KARAT	KHEDA	*KNOCK
KAPA	KIER	KOHL	KARMA	*KHETH	KNOLL
KAPH	KILL	KOLA	KAROO	KHOUM	KNOSP
KARN	KILN	KOLO	KARST	KIANG	KNOUT
KART	KILO	KONK	KASHA	KIBBE	KNOWN
KAVA	KILT	KOOK	KAURI	KIBBI	KNURL
KAYO	KINA	KOPH	KAURY	KIBEI	KOALA
KBAR	KIND	KORE	*KAYAK	KIBLA	KOINE
KECK	KINE	KOSS	*KAZOO	*KICKY	*KOOKY
KEEF	KING	KOTO	KEBAB	KIDDO	*KOPEK
KEEK	KINK	KRIS	KEBAR	KIDDY	*KOPJE
KEEL	KINO	KUDO	KEBOB	KILIM	KOPPA
KEEN	KIRK	KUDU	KEDGE	KILTY	KORAT
KEEP	KIRN	KURU	KEEVE	KININ	KOTOW
KEET	KISS	KVAS	KEFIR	*KINKY	KRAAL
KEIR	KIST	*KYAK	KELEP	KIOSK	KRAFT
KELP	KITE	KYAR	KELIM	KISSY	KRAIT
KEMP	KITH	KYAT	KELLY	KITER	KRAUT
KENO	KIVA	KYTE	KELPY	KITHE	KREEP

KRILL	KEGLER	KISMAT	KAINITE	*KICKOFF	KNITTER
KRONA	KELOID	KISMET	*KAJEPUT	KIDDIES	*KNOBBLY
KRONE	KELPIE	KISSER	KALENDS	KIDDING	*KNOCKER
KROON	KELSON	KITING	*KALIMBA	*KIDDISH	KNOLLER
KRUBI	KELTER	*KITSCH	*KAMPONG	*KIDDUSH	KNOTTED
*KUDZU	KELVIN	KITTED	KAMSEEN	*KIDLIKE	KNOTTER
KUGEL	KENNED	KITTEL	KANTELE	*KIDSKIN	*KNOWING
KUKRI	KENNEL	KITTEN	KAOLINE	KIESTER	*KNUCKLE
KULAK	*KEPPED	KITTLE	*KARAKUL	KILLDEE	*KNUCKLY
KUMYS	KEPPEN	*KLATCH	*KARAOKE	*KILLICK	*KOKANEE
KURTA	KERMES	*KLAXON	KARTING	KILLING	*KOLACKY
KUSSO	KERMIS	*KLEPHT	*KASHMIR	*KILLJOY	KOLBASI
KVASS	KERNEL	KLUDGE	KASHRUT	*KILLOCK	*KOLKHOS
*KYACK	KERRIA	*KLUTZY	KATCINA	KILOBAR	*KOLKHOZ
*KYLIX	KERSEY	KNAWEL	*KATHODE	KILOBIT	*KOMATIK
KYRIE	KETENE	KNIFER	*KATYDID	KILORAD	KOTOWER
*KYTHE	KETONE	KNIGHT	*KAYAKER	KILOTON	KOUMISS
*KABAKA	KETOSE	KNIVES	*KEBBOCK	KILTING	*KOUMYSS
KABALA	KETTLE	*KNOBBY	*KEBBUCK	*KIMCHEE	*KOUPREY
*KABAYA	*KEYPAD	KNOLLY	KEELAGE	KINDLER	KREMLIN
*KABIKI	KEYSET	KNOTTY	KEELSON	KINDRED	*KREUZER
*KABUKI	*KEYWAY	KNOWER	KEEPING	KINESIC	*KRIMMER
*KAFFIR	*KHALIF	KNURLY	KEESTER	KINESIS	KRULLER
KAFTAN	*KHAZEN	KOBOLD	KEGELER	KINETIC	*KRYPTON
KAHUNA	*KHEDAH	*KOLHOZ	KEGLING	KINETIN	*KUMQUAT
KAINIT	KIAUGH	*KOLKOZ	KEISTER	*KINFOLK	*KUNZITE
KAISER	*KIBBEH	KOODOO	KEITLOA	*KINGCUP	*KURBASH
*KAKAPO	KIBBLE	KOOKIE	KENNING	*KINGDOM	*KVETCHY
KALIAN	*KIBITZ	*KOPECK	KENOSIS	KINGLET	KYANISE
*KALIPH	*KIBLAH	KOPPIE	*KERAMIC	KINGPIN	KYANITE
KALIUM	*KIBOSH	KORUNA	KERATIN	*KINSHIP	*KYANIZE
KALMIA	*KICKER	KOSHER	*KERCHOO	KINSMAN	*KABBALAH
KALONG	*KICKUP	KOUMIS	KERMESS	*KIPPING	*KABELJOU
*KALPAK	KIDDER	*KOUMYS	KERNITE	*KIPSKIN	*KAFFIYEH
KAMALA	KIDDIE	KOUROS	KEROGEN	*KIRKMAN	*KAILYARD
KAMSIN	KIDNAP	KOUSSO	*KERYGMA	KIRMESS	KAISERIN
KANBAN	KIDNEY	*KOWTOW	KESTREL	KISTFUL	*KAKEMONO
KANTAR	*KIDVID	KRAKEN	*KETCHUP	*KITCHEN	*KAKIEMON
KAOLIN	KILLER	KRATER	KETOSIS	KITHARA	*KALEWIFE
KAPUTT	KILLIE	KRONOR	*KEYCARD	KITLING	*KALEYARD
KARATE	KILTER	KRONUR	*KEYHOLE	KITTIES	*KALIFATE
KAROSS	KILTIE	KRUBUT	KEYLESS	KITTING	KALLIDIN
KARROO	*KIMCHI	*KUCHEN	KEYNOTE	*KLATSCH	*KALYPTRA
*KASBAH	KIMONO	KULTUR	KEYSTER	KLAVERN	KAMAAINA
KASHER	KINASE	KUMISS	*KEYWORD	KLEAGLE	*KAMACITE
KATION	KINDLE	KUMMEL	*KHADDAR	*KLEZMER	*KAMIKAZE
KAVASS	KINDLY	KURGAN	*KHALIFA	KLISTER	KANGAROO
KAYLES	KINEMA	*KUVASZ	*KHAMSIN	*KNACKER	KAOLIANG
KEBBIE	KINGLY	*KVETCH	KHANATE	*KNAPPER	*KARYOTIN
*KEBLAH	KIPPEN	*KWACHA	*KHEDIVE	*KNAVERY	*KASHRUTH
*KECKLE	KIPPER	*KWANZA	*KHIRKAH	KNEADER	*KATAKANA
*KEDDAH	*KIRSCH	*KYBOSH	*KIBBITZ	*KNEECAP	*KATCHINA
KEENER	KIRTLE	*KABBALA	*KIBBUTZ	KNEELER	*KAVAKAVA
KEENLY	*KISHKA	*KACHINA	*KICKIER	KNEEPAD	*KAYAKING
KEEPER	*KISHKE	*KADDISH		KNESSET	*KAZACHOK

*KAZATSKI	KINGSIDE	S K EET	*FA K ERY	*RI K SHAW	*ZAI K AI
*KAZATSKY	*KINGWOOD	S K EIN	FA K ING	SO K EMAN	*BAC K FIT
KEDGEREE	*KINKAJOU	S K ELM	*HA K EEM	*TA K EOFF	*BOO K FUL
KEELBOAT	*KINSFOLK	S K ELP	*JO K IER	TA K EOUT	BRO K ING
*KEELHALE	*KIPPERER	S K ENE	*JO K ING	TE K TITE	*COO K TOP
*KEELHAUL	*KIRIGAMI	S K IED	*K A K APO	*TO K AMA K	FLO K ATI
KEELLESS	*KITELIKE	S K IER	LA K ING	*TO K OMA K	*K IC K IER
KEENNESS	*KLYSTRON	S K IES	LE K VAR	*WA K ANDA	LAR K ISH
*KEEPSAKE	*KNACKERY	S K IEY	LI K ELY	*WA K EFUL	*MIS K IC K
*KEESHOND	*KNAPSACK	*S K IFF	LI K EST	WA K ENER	*PEC K ISH
*KEFFIYEH	*KNAPWEED	S K ILL	LI K ING	*ZI K URAT	*PIC K LOC
KENOTRON	*KNEEHOLE	S K IMO	LI K UTA	*CA K EWAL K	*PUN K ISH
*KEPHALIN	*KNEESOCK	S K IMP	*MI K VAH	*CO K EHEAD	*RAC K FUL
KERATOID	*KNICKERS	S K IN K	*MI K VEH	*HO K INESS	RAN K ING
KERATOMA	*KNIGHTLY	S K INT	*MU K LU K	*JO K INESS	*SHI K K ER
KERATOSE	KNITTING	S K IRL	*MU K TU K	*K A K IEMON	SIC K OUT
*KERCHIEF	*KNITWEAR	S K IRR	NE K TON	*MA K EOVER	TIN K LER
KEROSENE	*KNOCKOFF	S K IRT	*PA K EHA	*PY K NOSIS	*TOP K IC K
KEROSINE	*KNOCKOUT	S K ITE	*PI K A K E	*PY K NOTIC	*BACKACHE
*KERPLUNK	*KNOTHOLE	S K IVE	PI K ING	*TA K EAWAY	*BAC K BEAT
*KEYBOARD	KNOTLESS	S K OAL	PO K IER	*YA K ITORI	*BAC K BEND
*KEYNOTER	*KNOTLIKE	S K OSH	PO K IES	*YO K OZUNA	*BAC K BITE
*KEYPUNCH	KNOTTING	S K UL K	*PO K ILY	*ZI K K URAT	*BACKBONE
*KEYSTONE	*KNOTWEED	S K ULL	PO K ING	DE K K O	*BAC K CAST
*KHAMSEEN	*KNUCKLER	S K UN K	*PY K NIC	DOR K Y	*BAC K CHAT
*KIBITZER	*KOHLRABI	*S K YEY	RA K ING	*FOL K Y	*BAC K DATE
*KICKBACK	KOLBASSI	*S K YBOX	RA K ISH	GEE K Y	*BAC K DOOR
*KICKBALL	*KOLINSKI	S K YLIT	RE K NIT	*K IC K Y	*BAC K DROP
*KICKIEST	*KOLINSKY	*S K YHOO K	*SU K K AH	MIN K E	*BAC K FILL
*KICKSHAW	*KOMONDOR	*S K YJAC K	TA K AHE	NAR K Y	*BAC K FIRE
*KIDNAPEE	*KOWTOWER	*S K YLAR K	TA K EUP	SAR K Y	*BAC K FLOW
*KIDNAPER	*KREPLACH	*S K YWAL K	TA K ING	SIC K O	*BAC K HAND
KIELBASA	*KREUTZER	*S K EWBACK	TO K ING	SIL K Y	*BAC K HAUL
KILLDEER	*KRUMHORN	*S K IPJAC K	TS K TS K	SOC K O	*BAC K LAND
KILOBASE	*KRYOLITE	TA K A	VA K EEL	TRI K E	*BAC K LASH
*KILOBAUD	*KRYOLITH	BI K IE	VI K ING	WAC K O	*BAC K LESS
*KILOBYTE	KURTOSIS	CA K EY	*WA K IKI	*YUC K Y	*BAC K LIST
*KILOGRAM	*KYMOGRAM	DE K K O	WA K ING	*CHA K RA	*BAC K MOST
KILOMOLE	*KYPHOSIS	*FA K EY	*WI K IUP	*CRI K EY	*BAC K PAC K
*KILOVOLT	S K AG	K U K RI	*YA K K ER	DAI K ON	*BAC K REST
*KILOWATT	S K AT	SO K OL	YO K ING	*FLA K EY	*BAC K ROOM
KINDLESS	S K EE	TO K ER	*BA K LAVA	FOL K IE	*BAC K RUSH
KINDLING	S K EG	YI K ES	*BA K LAWA	NEC K ER	*BAC K SEAT
KINDNESS	S K EP	*BA K ERY	*BI K EWAY	PIN K EN	*BAC K SIDE
KINESICS	S K EW	BA K ING	*DA K OITY	PIN K ER	*BAC K SLAP
KINETICS	S K ID	BE K ISS	*DU K EDOM	*PIN K EY	*BAC K SLID
*KINFOLKS	S K IM	BE K NOT	HE K TARE	PUN K ER	*BAC K SPIN
*KINGBIRD	S K IN	BI K ING	*JO K IEST	*QUO K K A	*BAC K STAY
*KINGBOLT	S K IP	BI K INI	*JU K EBOX	RUC K LE	*BAC K STOP
*KINGFISH	S K IT	DA K OIT	*K O K ANEE	RYO K AN	*BAC K WARD
*KINGHOOD	S K UA	DE K ARE	LI K ABLE	SIC K EE	*BAC K WASH
KINGLESS	S K ALD	*DI K DI K	*PI K E K AN	SIC K IE	*BACKWOOD
*KINGLIKE	S K ATE	*DI K DIX	PO K IEST	*SPI K EY	*BAC K WRAP
*KINGPOST	S K EAN	DI K TAT	*RA K EOFF	*SU K K AH	*BAC K YARD
*KINGSHIP	S K EEN	FA K EER	RI K ISHA	*YA K K ER	BAL K LINE

*BANK BOOK	*DEC K HAND	*K IC K IEST	*PEA K LI K E	STO K ESIA	BOO K
*BAN K CARD	DIN K IEST	*K IC K SHAW	*PEE K ABOO	*SUC K FISH	BOS K
BAN K NOTE	DIS K ETTE	*K IN K AJOU	*PEN K NIFE	*SUC K LING	BUC K
BAN K ROLL	*DOC K HAND	*LAC K ADAY	*PIC K ADIL	TAC K IEST	BUL K
*BAN K RUPT	*DOC K LAND	LAR K IEST	*PIC K EREL	TAC K LESS	BUN K
*BAN K SIDE	*DOC K SIDE	LAR K SOME	*PIC K ETER	*TAC K LING	BUS K
BAR K LESS	*DOC K YARD	LAR K SPUR	*PIC K IEST	TAL K ABLE	CAL K
*BAS K ETRY	*DUC K BILL	LEA K LESS	*PIC K LOC K	*TAN K LI K E	CAR K
*BEC K ONER	*DUC K IEST	*LEU K EMIA	*PIC K WIC K	*TASKWORK	CAS K
*BIC K ERER	*DUC K LING	*LEU K EMIC	PIN K NESS	*TEAK WOOD	COC K
*BOO K CASE	*DUC K TAIL	LEU K OSIS	PIN K ROOT	*TIC K LISH	CON K
*BOO K LICE	*DUCK WALK	*LIC K SPIT	*POC K ETER	*TIC K SEED	COO K
BOO K LORE	*DUC KWEED	*LIN K WOR K	*POCKMARK	*TIC K TAC K	COR K
*BOOKMARK	*FEC K LESS	*LOC K DOWN	POR K IEST	*TIC K TOC K	CUS K
*BOOK RACK	*FOL K LIFE	*LOC K STEP	*POR KWOOD	TIN K ERER	DAN K
BOO K REST	*FOL K LI K E	*LOO K DOWN	*PUC K ERER	TIN K LING	DAR K
*BOO K SHOP	*FOL K LORE	*LUN K HEAD	*RACK WORK	*TUC K AHOE	DAW K
*BOOKWORM	*FOL K MOOT	*MAC K EREL	RAN K NESS	*TUC K SHOP	DEC K
*BRA K EAGE	*FOL K MOTE	*MAC K INAW	REC K LESS	TUS K LESS	DES K
*BRA K EMAN	*FOL K TALE	*MARK DOWN	REC K ONER	*TUS K LI K E	DHA K
*BUC K AROO	*FOR K BALL	*MAR K EDLY	*RES K ETCH	*VAL K YRIE	DIC K
*BUC K AYRO	*FOR K IEST	*MAR K HOOR	*RIC K RAC K	*WAL K AWAY	DIN K
*BUC K BEAN	*FOR K LESS	*MAR K SMAN	*RIC K SHAW	*WAL K OVER	DIR K
*BUC K EROO	*FOR K LIFT	RIS K LESS	RIS K LESS	*WAL K YRIE	DOC K
*BUC K SHEE	*FOR K LI K E	*MAS K LI K E	*ROC K ABYE	*WEA K ENER	DOR K
*BUC K SHOT	*FOR K SFUL	*MIL K FISH	*ROC K AWAY	*WEA K FISH	DRE K
*BUC K S K IN	*GYM K HANA	*MIL K MAID	ROC K ETER	*WEA K LING	DUC K
*BUC K TAIL	*HACK WORK	*MIL K SHED	*ROC K ETRY	*WEA K NESS	DUS K
*BUL K HEAD	*HAN K ERER	*MIL K WEED	*ROC K FALL	*WEA K SIDE	FEC K
*BUN K ATE	*HAR K ENER	*MIL K WOOD	*ROC K FISH	*WEE K LONG	FIN K
*COC K ATOO	*HAW K EYED	*MIL K WORT	*ROC K LI K E	*WOR K ABLE	FLA K
*COC K APOO	*HAW K BILL	*MON K FISH	*ROC K LING	*WOR K ADAY	FOL K
*COC K BILL	*HAW K LI K E	*MON K HOOD	ROC K ROSE	*WOR K BOAT	FOR K
*COC K BOAT	*HAWKMOTH	*MUC K IEST	*ROC K WEED	*WORK BOOK	FUN K
*COCK CROW	*HAW K NOSE	*MUCK LUCK	*ROCK WORK	*WOR K FARE	GAW K
*COC K EREL	*HAW K SHAW	*MUCK LUCK	*RUCK SACK	*WOR K FOLK	GEC K
*COC K IEST	*HAW K WEED	*MUCK RAKE	*SAC K LI K E	*WOR K LESS	GEE K
*COC K LI K E	*HOC K SHOP	*MUCKWORM	*SAC K SFUL	*WOR K LOAD	GIN K
*COC K LOFT	*HOO K LESS	*MUS K ETRY	*SHA K EOUT	*WOR K MATE	GOW K
*COC K SHUT	*HOO K NOSE	*NEC K BAND	*SHA K IEST	*WOR K SHOP	GUC K
*COC K SPUR	*HOO KWORM	*NEC K LACE	*SHI K AREE	*WORKWEEK	GUN K
*COC K SURE	*HUC K STER	NEC K LESS	SIC K ENER	*ZI K K URAT	HAC K
*COC K TAIL	*HUS K IEST	*NEC K LI K E	*SIC K ERLY		HAN K
*COO K BOOK	*HUS K LI K E	NEC K LINE	SIC K NESS	BAC K	HAW K
COO K LESS	*JAC K AROO	*NEC KWEAR	*SIC K ROOM	BAL K	HEC K
*COO K SHOP	*JAC K BOOT	*NIC K ELIC	SIL K IEST	BAN K	HIC K
*COO K WARE	*JAC K EROO	*NIC K NAC K	*SIL K LI K E	BAR K	HOC K
COR K IEST	*JAC K FISH	*NIC K NAME	*SIL K WEED	BAS K	HOL K
*COR K LI K E	*JAC K ROLL	*PAC K AGER	*SIL K WORM	BEA K	HON K
*COR KWOOD	*JAC K STAY	*PAC K NESS	*SIN K HOLE	BEC K	HOO K
DAN K NESS	*JOC K ETTE	*PAC K SACK	*SMO K EPOT	BIL K	HOW K
DAR K ENER	*JUN K ETER	*PAR K LAND	SNA K EBIT	BIR K	HUC K
DAR K NESS	*JUN K YARD	*PAR K LI K E	SOC K LESS	BIS K	HUL K
*DAR K ROOM	*K IC K BACK	PEA K IEST	SPI K ELET	BOC K	HUN K
*DAR K SOME	*K IC K BALL	PEA K LESS	STA K EOUT	BON K	HUS K

*JACK	PINK	YERK	DRUNK	SLEEK	TUPIK
*JAUK	POCK	YEUK	FLACK	SLICK	TWEAK
*JERK	PORK	YOCK	FLANK	SLINK	*WHACK
*JINK	PUCK	YOLK	FLASK	SLUNK	*WHELK
*JOCK	PUNK	YUCK	FLECK	SMACK	*WHISK
*JOUK	RACK	*ZERK	FLICK	SMEEK	WRACK
*JUNK	RAIK	*ZONK	FLUNK	SMERK	WREAK
KECK	RANK	BATIK	FRANK	SMIRK	WRECK
KEEK	RECK	BAULK	FREAK	SMOCK	WRICK
KICK	REEK	BLACK	FRISK	SNACK	YAPOK
KINK	RICK	BLANK	FROCK	SNARK	BATTIK
KIRK	RINK	BLEAK	GLEEK	SNEAK	*BEDECK
KONK	RISK	BLINK	GREEK	SNECK	*BEMOCK
KOOK	ROCK	BLOCK	HACEK	SNICK	BETOOK
*KYAK	ROOK	BRANK	HOICK	SNOOK	*BEYLIK
LACK	RUCK	BREAK	KAIAK	SNUCK	*BIPACK
LANK	RUSK	BRICK	*KAMIK	SPANK	*BOHUNK
LARK	SACK	BRINK	*KAPOK	SPARK	*BYTALK
LEAK	SANK	BRISK	*KAYAK	SPEAK	CARACK
LEEK	SARK	BROCK	KIOSK	SPECK	*CHABUK
LICK	SEEK	BROOK	*KNACK	SPICK	*COPECK
LINK	SICK	BRUSK	*KNOCK	SPOOK	*CROJIK
LOCK	SILK	CAULK	*KOPEK	SPUNK	DAMASK
LOOK	SINK	CHALK	KULAK	STACK	DEBARK
LUCK	SOAK	CHEEK	*KYACK	STALK	DEBEAK
LUNK	SOCK	*CHICK	*MUJIK	STANK	DEBUNK
LURK	SOOK	CHINK	PLACK	STARK	DEMARK
MACK	SOUK	CHIRK	PLANK	STEAK	DETICK
MARK	SPIK	CHOOK	PLONK	STEEK	*DIBBUK
MASK	SUCK	*CHOCK	PLUCK	STICK	*DIKDIK
MEEK	SULK	*CHUCK	PLUNK	STINK	*DYBBUK
MERK	SUNK	CHUNK	PRANK	STIRK	GALYAK
MICK	TACK	CLACK	PRICK	STOCK	*HIJACK
MILK	TALK	CLANK	PRINK	STOOK	*KALPAK
MINK	TASK	CLEEK	PULIK	STORK	*KOPECK
MIRK	TEAK	CLERK	*QUACK	STUCK	*MEDICK
MOCK	TICK	CLICK	*QUARK	STUNK	*MOUJIK
MONK	TOOK	CLINK	*QUICK	SWANK	*MUKLUK
MOSK	TREK	CLOAK	*QUIRK	SWINK	*MUKTUK
MUCK	TUCK	CLOCK	REINK	TALUK	*MUZHIK
MURK	TURK	CLONK	SAMEK	TAROK	*MUZJIK
NARK	TUSK	CLUCK	SCULK	THACK	NAMLUK
NECK	WACK	CLUNK	SHACK	THANK	NUDNIK
NEUK	WALK	CRACK	SHANK	THICK	PADAUK
NICK	WARK	CRANK	SHARK	THIN	PADOUK
NOCK	WAUK	CREAK	SHEIK	THUNK	REBECK
NOOK	WEAK	CREEK	SHIRK	TORSK	REBOOK
PACK	WEEK	CRICK	SHOCK	TRACK	RECOCK
PAIK	WICK	CROAK	SHOOK	TRAIK	RECOOK
PARK	WINK	CROCK	SHUCK	TRANK	RECORK
PEAK	WONK	CROOK	SIANK	TRICK	REDOCK
PECK	WORK	CRUCK	SKINK	TROAK	RELINK
PEEK	YACK	DRANK	SKULK	TROCK	RELOOK
PERK	YANK	DRINK	SKUNK	TRUCK	REMARK
PICK	YELK	DROUK	SLACK	TRUNK	REPACK

REPAR K	*BITTOC K	*HATRAC K	*PADLOC K	SUNDEC K	*BUSHBUC K
REPER K	*BLAUBO K	*HAUBER K	PARTOO K	TANBAR K	*BUSYWOR K
RERAC K	*BLESBO K	*HAYCOC K	*PAYBAC K	*TIEBAC K	*CA K EWAL K
RESEE K	*BONNOC K	*HAYFOR K	*PEACOC K	TINWOR K	*CASEBOO K
RESOA K	*BOYCHI K	*HAYRAC K	*PETCOC K	TITLAR K	*CASEWOR K
RETAC K	*BULLOC K	*HAYRIC K	*PIDDOC K	*TO K AMA K	*CASHBOO K
RETOO K	*BULWAR K	*HEMLOC K	*PINWOR K	*TO K OMA K	*CHAPBOO K
REWOR K	*BURDOC K	*HENPEC K	*POLLAC K	*TOMBAC K	*CHARLOC K
*RHEBO K	BURLES K	*HILLOC K	*POLLOC K	*TOP K IC K	*CHIPMUC K
*SANJA K	*BUTTOC K	*HOGBAC K	*POTHOO K	*TOPWOR K	*CHIPMUN K
*SCHRI K	*BUYBAC K	*HOMMOC K	*POTLUC K	TRIPAC K	*CLAYBAN K
*SCHTI K	*CALPAC K	*HOPSAC K	*PREBOO K	TUSSOC K	*COALSAC K
SCREA K	*CAPROC K	*HUMMOC K	*PRECOO K	TUSSUC K	*COATRAC K
*SHLOC K	*CARRAC K	*JAYWAL K	PREDUS K	*TZADDI K	*CODEBOO K
*SHMUC K	*CARSIC K	*JUMBUC K	*PREPAC K	*WAESUC K	*COLDCOC K
SHNOO K	*CASSOC K	*K EBBOC K	*PREROC K	*WARLOC K	*COMEBAC K
SHRAN K	*CATWAL K	*K EBBUC K	PRESOA K	*WARWOR K	*COO K BOO K
SHRIE K	*CHABOU K	*K ILLIC K	*PREWOR K	*WAXWOR K	*COPYBOO K
SHRIN K	*CHAMPA K	*K ILLOC K	*PUGMAR K	*WEDLOC K	*COPYDES K
SHRUN K	*CHEWIN K	*K INFOL K	RANSAC K	*WETBAC K	*CORNHUS K
*SHTIC K	*CHIBOU K	*K OMATI K	RATFIN K	*WINNOC K	*CREWNEC K
*SQUAW K	*CHINOO K	*LAVROC K	*RECHEC K	*WRYNEC K	*CRIBWOR K
*SQUEA K	*COMATI K	*LAWBOO K	REDNEC K	*YASHMA K	*DABCHIC K
STREA K	*COSSAC K	*LEGWOR K	REITBO K	*ZADDIC K	*DATABAN K
STREE K	*COWLIC K	LENTIS K	RESPEA K	*BAC K PAC K	*DAYBREA K
STRIC K	*CUTBAC K	*LIMBEC K	RESTAC K	*BALDRIC K	*DEADLOC K
STROO K	*CUTBAN K	LOGBOO K	RESTOC K	*BALLHAW K	*DIESTOC K
STRUC K	*CUTWOR K	*MAFFIC K	RETHIN K	*BALLPAR K	*DIPSTIC K
SUSLI K	*DAGLOC K	*MAMMOC K	RETRAC K	*BAN K BOO K	*DISFROC K
TAMBA K	*DAYBOO K	*MANPAC K	*RIMROC K	*BAREBAC K	*DOMINIC K
*THWAC K	*DAYWOR K	*MArTOC K	*ROEBUC K	BARESAR K	*DOWNLIN K
TOMBA K	DERRIC K	*MENFOL K	ROLLIC K	BASILIS K	*DOWNTIC K
TS K TS K	*DIEBAC K	*MIDWEE K	*ROWLOC K	*BEADWOR K	*DRAMMOC K
TUGRI K	DORNEC K	*MISCOO K	*RUDDOC K	*BENEDIC K	*DRAWBAC K
*YAPOC K	DORNIC K	*MIS K IC K	*RUNBAC K	*BILLHOO K	*DROP K IC K
*YASMA K	*FATBAC K	*MISMAR K	*SAWBUC K	*BITSTOC K	*DUC K WAL K
*ZADDI K	*FETLOC K	MISTEU K	*SCHLOC K	*BLESBUC K	*DUCTWOR K
*ZEBEC K	*FINBAC K	MISTOO K	*SCHMUC K	*BLOWBAC K	*FALLBAC K
*BANG K O K	*FINMAR K	MUDLAR K	*SCHNOO K	*BLUEBOO K	*FARMWOR K
*BANNOC K	*FOSSIC K	*MUDPAC K	*SCHTIC K	*BLUEJAC K	*FASTBAC K
*BARRAC K	*FUTHAR K	*MUDROC K	*SEACOC K	*BLUETIC K	*FATSTOC K
*BASHLY K	*FUTHOR K	*MULLOC K	SEAMAR K	*BOATHOO K	*FEEDBAC K
*BAWCOC K	*FUTTOC K	MULLUS K	SEASIC K	*BOBOLIN K	*FINNMAR K
BEATNI K	*GEMSBO K	*MUNTJA K	*SETBAC K	*BODYWOR K	*FIREBAC K
*BECHAL K	*GEODUC K	NETWOR K	SHASLI K	*BONTEBO K	*FIRELOC K
*BECLOA K	GERENU K	*NIBLIC K	*SHYLOC K	*BOO K MAR K	*FIREPIN K
*BEDROC K	*GIMMIC K	*NITPIC K	*S K YHOO K	*BOO K RAC K	*FIREWOR K
*BEDTIC K	*GORCOC K	NONBAN K	*S K YJAC K	*BOONDOC K	*FISHHOO K
*BEFLEC K	*GOSHAW K	NONBOO K	*S K YLAR K	*BOOTJAC K	*FLAPJAC K
BELLEE K	GUNLOC K	NONPEA K	*S K YWAL K	*BOOTLIC K	*FLATWOR K
BERSER K	*GWEDUC K	NONWOR K	*SOYMIL K	*BOSCHBO K	*FLYSPEC K
*BESPEA K	*HADDOC K	NUDNIC K	SPELUN K	*BOSHVAR K	*FOOTMAR K
*BETHAN K	*HAMMOC K	NUNATA K	SPUTNI K	*BOYCHIC K	*FOOTWOR K
*BETHIN K	*HASSOC K	*NUTPIC K	SUBTAS K	*BUHLWOR K	*FOREDEC K
*BIBCOC K		*PADDOC K	*SUNBAC K	*BULLNEC K	*FORELOC K

*FOREMIL K	*HOLDBAC K	*MISTHIN K	*PREFRAN K	*SHELLAC K	*TAS K WOR K
*FOREPEA K	*HOMESIC K	*MOBSTIC K	*PRINCOC K	*SHERLOC K	*TEAMWOR K
*FORERAN K	*HOMEWOR K	*MOONWAL K	*PULLBAC K	*SHOEPAC K	TELEMAR K
*FORMWOR K	*HOODWIN K	*MOORCOC K	*RACKWORK	*SHOPTAL K	*TEXTBOO K
*FRETWOR K	*HUMPBAC K	*MOSSBAC K	*REAPHOO K	*SIDE K IC K	*TIC K TAC K
*FULLBAC K	*HYMNBOO K	*MUC KLUC K	REATTAC K	*SIDEWAL K	*TIC K TOC K
*GAMECOC K	*JOYSTIC K	NAINSOO K	*REDBRIC K	*SITZMAR K	*TIDEMAR K
*GAVELOC K	*K AZACHO K	*NEWSPEA K	*REDSHAN K	*S K EWBAC K	*TIMEWOR K
*GEMSBUC K	*K ERPLUN K	*NIC K NAC K	*REEDBUC K	*S K IPJAC K	*TIPSTOC K
*GIMCRAC K	*K IC KBAC K	*NONBLAC K	*REEMBAR K	*SLAPJAC K	*TOMAHAW K
*GRAYBAC K	*K INSFOL K	NONSTIC K	*REFUSNI K	*SLOPWOR K	*TOWNFOL K
*GRIDLOC K	*K NAPSAC K	NOTEBOO K	RESTRUC K	*SLOTBAC K	*TRAPROC K
*GRIPSAC K	*K NEESOC K	*PAC K SAC K	*RIC K RAC K	*SNAPBAC K	*TUBEWOR K
*GROSBEA K	*LACEWOR K	*PASHALI K	*RINGBAR K	*SNOWBAN K	*WHITRAC K
*GUNSTOC K	*LANDMAR K	*PASSBOO K	*RINGNEC K	*SNOWPAC K	*WINDSOC K
*HACKWORK	*LATHWOR K	*PAYCHEC K	*ROADWOR K	*SOAPBAR K	*WINGBAC K
*HAIRLOC K	*LAVEROC K	*PEACENI K	*ROCKWORK	*SOFTBAC K	*WIREWOR K
*HALFBAC K	*LEADWOR K	*PIC K LOC K	*ROLLBAC K	*SONGBOO K	*WOODCOC K
*HALFBEA K	*LIFEWOR K	*PIC K WIC K	*ROORBAC K	STEENBO K	*WOODLAR K
*HALLMAR K	*LIMERIC K	*PIGSTIC K	*ROPEWAL K	STEINBO K	*WOODWOR K
*HANDBOO K	*LIN K WOR K	*PINCHEC K	*RUC KSAC K	*STOPBAN K	*WOOLPAC K
*HANDPIC K	LINSTOC K	*PINPRIC K	*SALTWOR K	*STOPCOC K	*WOOLSAC K
*HANDWOR K	*LIPSTIC K	*PIROZHO K	*SANDBAN K	*STUDBOO K	*WOOLWOR K
*HARDBAC K	*LOPSTIC K	*PLAYBAC K	*SCATBAC K	*STUDWOR K	*WORDBOO K
*HARDTAC K	*LOVELOC K	*PLAYBOO K	*SEATWOR K	*SUBBLOC K	*WORK BOO K
*HATCHEC K	*LOVESIC K	*PLOWBAC K	SELAMLI K	*SUBCLER K	*WOR K FOL K
*HAVELOC K	*MAVERIC K	*POCK MAR K	*SHADDOC K	*SUNBLOC K	*WOR K WEE K
*HAYSTAC K	*MEGABUC K	*POLITIC K	*SHAGBAR K	*SWAYBAC K	*YARDWOR K
*HEADLOC K	*MILLWOR K	*PORTAPA K	*SHAMROC K	*TAILBAC K	*YEARHOO K
*HEADWOR K	*MINIPAR K	*POSTMAR K	*SHAMSHLI K	*TAMARAC K	*ZWIEBAC K
*HIGHJAC K	*MISSPEA K	*PRECHEC K	*SHELDUC K	TAMARIS K	

L

LACE	LANE	*LAZY	LEPT	LIFT	LION
LACK	LANG	LEAD	LESS	LIKE	LIRA
LACY	LANK	LEAF	LEST	LILT	LISP
LADE	LARD	LEAK	LEUD	LILY	LIST
LADY	LARI	LEAL	LEVO	LIMA	LITE
LAIC	LARK	LEAN	LEVY	LIMB	LITU
LAID	LASE	LEAP	LEWD	LIME	LIVE
LAIN	LASH	LEAR	LIAR	LIMN	LOAD
LAIR	LASS	LECH	LICE	LIMO	LOAF
LAKE	LAST	LEEK	LICH	LIMP	LOAM
LAKH	LATE	LEER	LICK	LIMY	LOAN
LAKY	LATH	LEET	LIDO	LINE	LOBE
LALL	LATI	LEFT	LIED	LING	LOBO
LAMA	LAUD	LEHR	LIEF	LINK	LOCA
LAMB	LAVA	LEND	LIEN	LINN	LOCH
LAME	LAVE	LENO	LIER	LINO	LOCI
LAMP	LAWN	LENS	LIEU	LINT	LOCK
LAND	LAZE	LENT	LIFE	LINY	LOCO

LODE	**LUTZ**	LATHI	LIANG	LIVRE	LOWSE
LOFT	**LUXE**	**LATHY**	LIARD	LLAMA	LOYAL
LOGE	LWEI	LAUAN	LIBEL	LLANO	LUCES
LOGO	**LYNX**	LAUGH	LIBER	**LOACH**	LUCID
LOGY	LYRE	LAURA	LIBRA	**LOAMY**	**LUCKY**
LOIN	LYSE	LAVER	LIBRI	LOATH	LUCRE
LOLL	LAARI	*LAXLY	**LICHI**	LOBAR	LUDIC
LONE	LABEL	LAYER	**LICHT**	**LOBBY**	**LUFFA**
LONG	LABIA	**LAZAR**	LICIT	LOCAL	LUGER
LOOF	LABOR	**LEACH**	LIDAR	LOCUM	LUMEN
LOOK	LABRA	LEADY	LIEGE	LOCUS	**LUMPY**
LOOM	LACER	**LEAFY**	LIEVE	LODEN	LUNAR
LOON	**LACEY**	**LEAKY**	LIFER	LODGE	**LUNCH**
LOOP	LADEN	LEANT	LIGAN	LOESS	LUNET
LOOT	LADER	LEAPT	LIGER	**LOFTY**	LUNGE
LOPE	LADLE	LEARN	LIGHT	LOGAN	LUNGI
LORD	LAEVO	LEARY	**LIKED**	**LOGGY**	LUPIN
LORE	LAGAN	LEASE	LIKEN	LOGIA	LUPUS
LORN	LAGER	LEASH	LIKER	LOGOS	**LURCH**
LORY	LAHAR	LEAST	LILAC	LOLLY	LURER
LOSE	**LAICH**	LEAVE	LIMAN	LONER	LURID
LOSS	LAIGH	**LEAVY**	LIMBA	LONGE	LUSTY
LOST	LAIRD	LEBEN	LIMBI	**LOOBY**	LUSUS
LOTA	LAITH	LEDGE	LIMBO	LOOEY	LUTEA
LOTH	LAITY	**LEDGY**	**LIMBY**	LOOFA	LUTED
LOTI	**LAKED**	**LEECH**	LIMEN	LOOIE	LYARD
LOUD	LAKER	LEERY	LIMES	LOONY	LYART
LOUP	**LAMBY**	**LEFTY**	**LIMEY**	**LOOPY**	LYASE
LOUR	LAMED	LEGAL	LIMIT	LOOSE	**LYCEA**
LOUT	LAMER	LEGER	LINAC	LOPER	**LYCEE**
LOVE	LAMIA	LEGES	LINDY	**LOPPY**	LYING
LOWE	LANAI	**LEGGY**	LINED	LORAL	*LYMPH
LOWN	LANCE	LEGIT	LINEN	LORAN	**LYNCH**
LUAU	**LANKY**	LEHUA	LINER	LORIS	**LYRIC**
LUBE	LAPEL	LEMAN	LINEY	LORRY	LYSIN
LUCE	LAPIN	LEMMA	LINGA	LOSEL	LYSIS
LUCK	LAPIS	LEMON	LINGO	LOSER	LYSSA
LUDE	LAPSE	LEMUR	LINGY	LOSSY	**LYTIC**
LUES	**LARCH**	LENES	LININ	LOTAH	LYTTA
LUFF	LARDY	LENIS	**LINKY**	LOTIC	LAAGER
LUGE	LAREE	LENSE	LINTY	LOTOS	LABIAL
LULL	LARES	LENTO	LINUM	LOTTE	LABILE
LULU	LARGE	LEONE	LIPID	LOTTO	**LABIUM**
LUMP	LARGO	LEPER	LIPIN	LOTUS	LABOUR
LUNA	**LARKY**	LETCH	**LIPPY**	LOUGH	LABRET
LUNE	LARUM	LETHE	LISLE	LOUIE	**LABRUM**
LUNG	LARVA	LETUP	LITAS	LOUIS	**LACHES**
LUNK	LASER	LEVEE	LITER	LOUPE	LACIER
LUNT	LASSO	LEVEL	LITHE	LOURY	**LACILY**
LUNY	**LATCH**	LEVER	LITHO	LOUSE	LACING
LURE	LATED	LEVIN	LITRE	LOUSY	**LACKER**
LURK	LATEN	LEWIS	LIVEN	LOVED	*LACKEY
LUSH	LATER	**LEXIS**	LIVER	LOVER	LACTAM
LUST	**LATEX**	LIANA	LIVES	LOWER	LACTIC
LUTE	LATHE	LIANE	LIVID	**LOWLY**	LACUNA

LACUNE	LASHER	**LECHWE**	LIGNIN	LITANY	LOONEY
LADDER	LASING	LECTIN	LIGULA	**LITCHI**	LOOPER
LADDIE	LASSIE	LECTOR	LIGULE	LITHIA	*LOOSED
LADIES	LASTER	LEDGER	LIGURE	**LITHIC**	LOOSEN
LADING	LASTLY	**LEEWAY**	**LIKELY**	LITMUS	LOOSER
LADINO	LATEEN	**LEGACY**	**LIKEST**	LITTEN	LOOTER
LADLER	LATELY	LEGATE	**LIKING**	LITTER	**LOPPED**
LADRON	LATENT	LEGATO	**LIKUTA**	LITTLE	**LOPPER**
LAGEND	LATEST	LEGEND	LILIED	**LIVELY**	*LOQUAT
LAGGED	LATHER	LEGGED	**LIMBER**	**LIVERY**	**LORDLY**
LAGGER	LATIGO	LEGGIN	**LIMBIC**	LIVEST	LOREAL
LAGOON	LATINO	LEGION	**LIMBUS**	LIVIER	LORICA
LAGUNA	LATISH	LEGIST	LIMIER	**LIVING**	LORIES
LAGUNE	LATRIA	LEGMAN	LIMINA	**LIVYER**	LOSING
LAKING	LATTEN	LEGONG	LIMING	*LIZARD	LOTION
LALLAN	LATTER	LEGUME	**LIMMER**	LOADER	LOTTED
LAMBDA	LATTIN	**LEKVAR**	LIMNER	LOAFER	**LOUCHE**
LAMBER	LAUDER	LENDER	**LIMNIC**	LOANER	LOUDEN
LAMBIE	LAUNCE	**LENGTH**	**LIMPER**	LOATHE	**LOUDLY**
LAMEDH	**LAUNCH**	LENITY	**LIMPET**	LOAVES	LOUNGE
LAMELY	LAUREL	LENTEN	**LIMPID**	LOBATE	**LOUNGY**
LAMENT	**LAVABO**	LENTIC	**LIMPLY**	**LOBBED**	**LOUVER**
LAMEST	**LAVAGE**	LENTIL	**LIMPSY**	**LOBBER**	LOUVRE
LAMINA	LAVEER	LEPTON	LINAGE	LOBULE	**LOVAGE**
LAMING	**LAVING**	LESION	LINDEN	LOCALE	**LOVELY**
LAMMED	LAVISH	LESSEE	LINEAL	LOCATE	**LOVING**
LAMPAD	**LAWFUL**	LESSEN	LINEAR	**LOCHAN**	**LOWBOY**
LAMPAS	LAWINE	LESSER	LINEUP	**LOCHIA**	**LOWERY**
LANATE	**LAWING**	LESSON	LINGAM	**LOCKER**	**LOWING**
LANCER	**LAWMAN**	LETHAL	LINGER	**LOCKET**	**LOWISH**
LANCET	**LAWYER**	LETTED	LINGUA	**LOCKUP**	**LUBBER**
LANDAU	*LAXITY	LETTER	LINIER	LOCULE	**LUBRIC**
LANDER	**LAYMAN**	LEUCIN	LINING	LOCUST	**LUCENT**
LANELY	*LAYOFF	**LEUKON**	**LINKER**	LODGER	LUCERN
LANGUE	*LAZIED	LEVANT	**LINKUP**	LOFTER	**LUCKIE**
LANGUR	*LAZIER	**LEVIED**	LINNET	LOGGED	**LUETIC**
LANNER	*LAZIES	LEVIER	LINSEY	LOGGER	LUGGED
LANOSE	*LAZILY	LEVIES	LINTEL	LOGGIA	LUGGER
LANUGO	*LAZING	**LEVITY**	LINTER	LOGIER	LUGGIE
LAPDOG	*LAZULI	*LEXEME	LINTOL	**LOGILY**	**LUMBAR**
LAPFUL	**LEACHY**	LIABLE	LIPASE	LOGION	**LUMBER**
LAPPED	LEADEN	LIAISE	LIPIDE	*LOGJAM	*LUMMOX
LAPPER	LEADER	**LIBBER**	LIPOID	**LOGWAY**	**LUMPEN**
LAPPET	LEAGUE	LIBIDO	**LIPOMA**	LOITER	**LUMPER**
LAPTOP	**LEAKER**	**LIBLAB**	**LIPPED**	LOLLER	LUNACY
LANNER	LEALTY	**LICHEE**	**LIPPEN**	LOLLOP	LUNATE
LANOUS	LEANER	**LICHEN**	**LIPPER**	LOMEIN	LUNGAN
LARDER	LEAPER	**LICKER**	*LIQUID	LOMENT	LUNGEE
LARDON	LEARNT	LICTOR	*LIQUOR	LONELY	LUNGER
LARIAT	LEASER	LIENAL	LISPER	LONGAN	**LUNGYI**
LARINE	**LEAVED**	LIERNE	LISSOM	LONGER	LUNIER
LARKER	LEAVEN	LIFTER	LISTEE	**LONGLY**	LUNIES
LARRUP	LEAVER	LIGAND	LISTEL	**LOOFAH**	**LUNKER**
*LARYNX	LEAVES	LIGASE	LISTEN	**LOOKER**	LUNULA
LASCAR	**LECHER**	LIGATE	LISTER	**LOOKUP**	LUNULE

LUPINE	**LAMBERT**	LATRINE	***LEHAYIM**	LIGNIFY	**LITTERY**
LUPOUS	***LAMBKIN**	LATTICE	LEISTER	LIGNITE	**LITURGY**
LURDAN	**LAMBIER**	**LAUGHER**	LEISURE	LIGROIN	**LIVABLE**
LURING	LAMELLA	LAUNDER	**LEMMING**	**LIKABLE**	**LIVENER**
LURKER	**LAMMING**	**LAUNDRY**	**LEMPIRA**	**LIMACON**	LOADING
LUSTER	**LAMPERS**	**LAUWINE**	LEMURES	**LIMBATE**	LOANING
LUSTRA	**LAMPION**	***LAVROCK**	**LENGTHY**	***LIMBECK**	**LOATHER**
LUSTRE	**LAMPOON**	***LAWBOOK**	LENIENT	**LIMBIER**	**LOATHLY**
LUTEAL	**LAMPREY**	**LAWLESS**	LENSMAN	**LIMEADE**	**LOBATED**
LUTEIN	**LAMSTER**	**LAWLIKE**	LENTIGO	LIMIEST	**LOBBING**
LUTEUM	LANATED	**LAWSUIT**	**LENTISK**	LIMINAL	**LOBBYER**
LUTING	**LANCING**	**LAXNESS**	LENTOID	**LIMITED**	**LOBEFIN**
LUTIST	LANDING	***LAYAWAY**	LEONINE	LIMITER	LOBELIA
LUXATE	**LANDMAN**	**LAYETTE**	**LEOPARD**	LIMITES	LOBSTER
***LUXURY**	**LANDMEN**	**LAYOVER**	LEOTARD	***LIMPKIN**	**LOBWORM**
LYCEUM	**LANEWAY**	***LAZARET**	**LEPORID**	**LIMPSEY**	**LOCALLY**
LYCHEE	LANGREL	***LAZIEST**	LEPROSE	LIMULUS	**LOCATER**
LYRATE	LANGUET	***LAZYISH**	**LEPROSY**	LINABLE	**LOCATOR**
LYRISM	LANGUID	**LEACHER**	LEPROUS	LINALOL	**LOCKAGE**
LYRIST	LANGUOR	LEADIER	LESBIAN	LINDANE	***LOCKBOX**
LYSATE	LANIARD	LEADING	LETDOWN	LINEAGE	***LOCKJAW**
LYSINE	**LANIARY**	**LEADMAN**	LETTING	LINEATE	**LOCKNUT**
LYSING	LANITAL	**LEADOFF**	LETTUCE	LINECUT	**LOCKOUT**
LABARUM	LANOLIN	**LEAFAGE**	LEUCINE	LINEMAN	***LOCKRAM**
LABELER	LANTANA	**LEAFIER**	LEUCITE	LINGCOD	**LOCOISM**
LABELLA	LANTERN	**LEAFLET**	LEUCOMA	LINGIER	LOCULAR
LABIATE	**LANYARD**	LEAGUER	**LEUKOMA**	LINGUAL	LOCULUS
LABORER	**LAPIDES**	**LEAKAGE**	**LEVATOR**	LINIEST	LOCUSTA
LABROID	**LAPPING**	LEANING	**LEVELER**	**LINKAGE**	**LODGING**
LACIEST	**LAPWING**	LEARIER	**LEVELLY**	***LINKBOY**	**LOFTIER**
LACONIC	**LARCENY**	LEARNER	**LEVERET**	**LINKMAN**	**LOFTILY**
***LACQUER**	LARDIER	LEASING	**LEVULIN**	LINOCUT	LOGANIA
***LACQUEY**	LARDOON	**LEATHER**	***LEXICAL**	LINSANG	**LOGBOOK**
LACTARY	**LARGESS**	**LEAVING**	***LEXICON**	LINSEED	LOGGATS
LACTASE	**LARGEST**	***LECHERY**	LIAISON	LINTIER	LOGGETS
LACTATE	**LARGISH**	LECTERN	LIANOID	LINURON	**LOGGING**
LACTEAL	**LARKIER**	LECTION	LIBELEE	LIONESS	**LOGICAL**
LACTEAN	**LARKISH**	LECTURE	LIBELER	LIONISE	LOGIEST
LACTONE	LASAGNA	**LEEWARD**	LIBERAL	***LIONIZE**	LOGROLL
LACTOSE	LASAGNE	**LEFTIES**	**LIBERTY**	LIPLESS	**LOGWOOD**
LACUNAR	**LASHING**	**LEFTISH**	**LIBRARY**	**LIPLIKE**	LOLLIES
LADANUM	**LASHINS**	**LEFTISM**	LIBRATE	**LIPPING**	**LONGBOW**
LADLING	**LASHKAR**	**LEFTIST**	LICENCE	***LIQUATE**	LONGIES
LADRONE	LASSOER	**LEGALLY**	LICENSE	***LIQUEFY**	**LONGING**
LADYBUG	LASTING	LEGATEE	LICENTE	***LIQUEUR**	**LONGISH**
LADYISH	LATAKIA	LEGATOR	***LICHTLY**	***LIQUIFY**	**LOOKOUT**
***LADYKIN**	**LATCHET**	LEGGIER	LICKING	LISENTE	LOOSEST
LAGGARD	**LATENCY**	**LEGGING**	LIDLESS	LISSOME	LOOSING
LAGGING	LATERAD	**LEGHORN**	**LIFEFUL**	LISTING	**LOPPING**
LAICISE	LATERAL	**LEGIBLE**	***LIFEWAY**	LITERAL	LORDING
LAICISM	**LATHERY**	LEGLESS	**LIFTMAN**	***LITHIFY**	**LORDOMA**
***LAICIZE**	**LATHIER**	**LEGLIKE**	***LIFTOFF**	**LITHIUM**	LORGNON
LALIAND	**LATHING**	**LEGROOM**	**LIGHTEN**	**LITHOID**	LORIMER
LAMBAST	LATICES	**LEGUMIN**	**LIGHTER**	LITORAL	LORINER
LAMBENT	LATOSOL	***LEGWORK**	**LIGHTLY**	LITOTES	**LOTTERY**

LOTTING	LABDANUM	LANCELET	LATHIEST	LEFTOVER	LIBELIST
LOUDISH	LABELLED	LANCIERS	*LATHWORK	*LEFTWARD	LIBELLED
LOUTISH	LABELLER	LANDFALL	LATINITY	*LEFTWING	LIBELLEE
LOVABLE	LABELLUM	LANDFILL	*LATINIZE	LEGALESE	LIBELLER
LOVEBUG	LABIALLY	LANDFORM	LATITUDE	LEGALISE	LIBELOUS
LOWBALL	LABIATED	LANDGRAB	LATTERLY	LEGALISM	LIBERATE
LOWBORN	LABILITY	LANDLADY	LAUDABLE	LEGALIST	LIBRETTO
LOWBRED	LABORITE	LANDLESS	LAUDANUM	LEGALITY	LICENCEE
*LOWBROW	LABOURER	LANDLINE	LAUDATOR	*LEGALIZE	LICENCER
LOWDOWN	LABRADOR	LANDLORD	LAUGHING	LEGATINE	LICENSEE
LOWLAND	LABRUSCA	*LANDMARK	LAUGHTER	LEGATING	LICENSER
LOWLIFE	LABURNUM	LANDMASS	LAUNCHER	LEGATION	LICENSOR
LOWNESS	LACELESS	LANDSIDE	LAUREATE	LEGENDRY	LICHENIN
LOYALLY	LACELIKE	LANDSKIP	LAVALAVA	LEGERITY	*LICKSPIT
LOYALTY	LACERATE	LANDSLID	LAVALIER	LEGGIEST	LICORICE
*LOZENGE	LACERTID	LANDSLIP	*LAVALIKE	LEGGIERO	LIEGEMAN
LUCARNE	LACEWING	LANDSMAN	LAVATION	*LEKYTHOS	LIENABLE
LUCENCE	LACEWOOD	LANDWARD	LAVATORY	*LEKYTHUS	LIENTERY
LUCENCY	*LACEWORK	LANGLAUF	LAVENDER	LEMNISCI	LIFEBOAT
LUCERNE	LACINESS	LANGRAGE	*LAVEROCK	LEMONADE	LIFELESS
LUCIFER	*LACKADAY	LANGSHAN	LAVISHER	LEMURINE	*LIFELIKE
LUGGAGE	LACONISM	LANGSYNE	*LAWGIVER	LEMUROID	LIFELONG
LUGGING	LACRIMAL	LANGUAGE	*LAWMAKER	LENGTHEN	LIFETIME
LUGSAIL	LACROSSE	LANGUISH	*LAXATION	LENIENCE	*LIFEWORK
LUGWORM	LACTEOUS	LANKNESS	*LAXATIVE	LENIENCY	LIFTGATE
LULLABY	LACUNOSE	LANNERET	LAYABOUT	LENITION	LIGAMENT
LUMBAGO	LADLEFUL	LANOLINE	LAYERAGE	LENITIVE	LIGATION
LUMPISH	*LADYBIRD	LANOSITY	LAYERING	LENTANDO	LIGATURE
LUNATED	*LADYFISH	LANTHORN	*LAYWOMAN	LENTICEL	*LIGHTFUL
LUNATIC	*LADYHOOD	LAPBOARD	*LAZINESS	LEPIDOTE	LIGHTING
LUNCHER	*LADYLIKE	LAPIDARY	*LAZULITE	LEPORINE	*LIGHTISH
LUNETTE	*LADYLOVE	LAPIDATE	*LAZURITE	LEPROTIC	LIGNEOUS
LUNGFUL	*LADYPALM	*LAPIDIFY	LEACHATE	LETHALLY	LIGROINE
LUNGING	*LADYSHIP	LAPIDIST	LEADIEST	*LETHARGY	LIKEABLE
LUNIEST	LAETRILE	LAPILLUS	LEADLESS	LETTERER	LIKENESS
LUPANAR	LAGNAPPE	LARBOARD	LEADSMAN	LEUCEMIA	*LIKEWISE
LUPULIN	LAITANCE	LARCENER	*LEADWORK	LEUKEMIA	LILLIPUT
LURCHER	LAKEPORT	LARDIEST	LEADWORT	*LEUKEMIC	LIMACINE
LUSTFUL	LAKESIDE	LARDLIKE	LEAFIEST	LEUKOSIS	LIMBIEST
LUSTIER	LALLYGAG	LARGANDO	LEAFLESS	LEVANTER	LIMBLESS
LUSTILY	LAMASERY	LARGESSE	*LEAFLIKE	LEVELLER	LIMEKILN
LUSTRAL	LAMBASTE	LARKIEST	*LEAFWORM	LEVERAGE	LIMELESS
LUSTRUM	*LAMBENCY	LARKSOME	LEAKLESS	LEVIABLE	*LIMERICK
LUTEOUS	LAMBIEST	LARKSPUR	LEANNESS	LEVIGATE	LIMINESS
LUTHIER	*LAMBKILL	LARRIGAN	LEAPFROG	LEVIRATE	LIMITARY
LUTHERN	*LAMBLIKE	LARRIKIN	LEARIEST	LEVITATE	LIMNETIC
*LYCHNIS	*LAMBSKIN	LARRUPER	LEARNING	LEVODOPA	LIMONENE
*LYCOPOD	LAMENESS	*LATCHKEY	LEATHERN	*LEVOGYRE	LIMONITE
LYDDITE	LAMENTER	LATEENER	LEATHERY	LEVULOSE	LIMPNESS
LYINGLY	LAMINATE	LATENESS	*LECHAYIM	LEWDNESS	LIMULOID
LYNCEAN	LAMINOSE	LATENTLY	LECITHIN	LEWISITE	LINALOOL
*LYNCHER	LAMINOUS	LATERITE	LECTURER	LEWISSON	*LINCHPIN
LYRATED	LAMISTER	*LATERIZE	*LECYTHIS	LIBATION	LINEABLE
LYRICAL	LAMPPOST	LATEWOOD	*LECYTHUS	LIBECCIO	LINEBRED
LYSOGEN	*LAMPYRID	LATHERER	LEEBOARD	LIBELANT	LINEATED

LINELESS	LOBELINE	*LONGWAYS	LUSCIOUS	C LOD	P LOP
LINELIKE	LOBLOLLY	LONGWISE	LUSHNESS	C LOG	P LOT
LINESMAN	*LOBOTOMY	*LOOKDOWN	LUSTIEST	C LON	P LOW
LINGERER	*LOBSTICK	LOOPHOLE	LUSTRATE	C LOP	P LOY
LINGERIE	LOCALISE	LOOSENER	LUSTRING	C LOT	P LUG
LINGIEST	LOCALISM	LOPSIDED	LUSTROUS	C LOY	P LUM
LINGUINE	LOCALIST	*LOPSTICK	LUTANIST	C LUB	P LUS
LINGUINI	LOCALITE	LORDLESS	LUTECIUM	C LUE	S LAB
LINGUIST	LOCALITY	LORDLIER	*LUTEFISK	F LAB	S LAG
LINIMENT	*LOCALIZE	LORDLIKE	LUTENIST	F LAG	S LAM
LINKSMAN	LOCATION	LORDLING	LUTEOLIN	**F LAK**	S LAP
*LINKWORK	LOCATIVE	LORDOSIS	LUTETIUM	F LAM	S LAT
LINOLEUM	*LOCKDOWN	LORDSHIP	*LUXATION	F LAN	S LAW
LINSTOCK	*LOCKSTEP	LORICATE	*LYCOPENE	F LAP	S LAY
LINTIEST	*LOCOFOCO	LORIKEET	*LYMPHOMA	F LAT	S LED
LINTLESS	LOCOMOTE	LORNNESS	*LYNCHING	F LAW	S LEW
LIONFISH	LOCOWEED	LOSINGLY	*LYNCHPIN	F LAX	S LIM
*LIONIZER	LOCULATE	LOSTNESS	*LYOPHILE	F LAY	S LIP
*LIPOCYTE	LOCUTION	LOTHARIO	LYREBIRD	F LEA	S LIT
LIPOSOME	LOCUTORY	LOTHSOME	LYRICISE	F LED	S LOB
*LIPSTICK	LODESTAR	LOUDNESS	*LYRICISM	F LEE	S LOE
*LIQUIDLY	LODGMENT	LOVEABLE	LYRICIST	F LEW	S LOG
LIRIPIPE	LODICULE	LOVEBIRD	*LYRICIZE	F LEX	S LOP
LISTENER	LOFTIEST	LOVELESS	*LYRIFORM	F LEY	S LOT
LISTLESS	LOFTLESS	LOVELIER	*LYSOGENY	F LIC	S LOW
LITERACY	LOGICIAN	LOVELIES	LYSOSOME	F LIP	S LUB
LITERARY	LOGICISE	LOVELILY	*LYSOZYME	F LUB	S LUF
LITERATE	*LOGICIZE	*LOVELOCK		F LUE	S LUG
LITERATI	LOGINESS	LOVELORN	B LAB	F LUX	S LUM
LITHARGE	LOGISTIC	*LOVESICK	B LAE	G LAD	S LUR
LITHEMIA	LOGOGRAM	LOVESOME	B LAH	G LED	S LUT
LITHOSOL	*LOGOMACH	LOVEVINE	B LAM	G LEE	**B LACK**
LITIGANT	LOGOTYPE	*LOVINGLY	B LAT	G LEG	B LADE
LITIGATE	*LOGOTYPY	LOWLIFER	B LAW	G LEN	B LAIN
LITTERER	LOITERER	*LOWLIGHT	B LEB	G LEY	B LAME
LITTLISH	LOLLIPOP	LOWRIDER	B LET	G LIA	B LAND
LITTORAL	LOLLYGAG	LOYALISM	B LIN	G LIB	**B LANK**
LIVEABLE	*LOLLYPOP	LOYALIST	B LIP	G LIM	B LARE
LIVELONG	LOMENTUM	LUBRICAL	B LOB	G LOB	B LASE
LIVENESS	LONENESS	LUCIDITY	B LOC	G LOM	B LAST
LIVERIED	LONESOME	LUCKLESS	B LOT	G LOP	B LATE
LIVERISH	LONGBOAT	LUCULENT	B LOW	G LOW	*B LAZE
LIVETRAP	LONGERON	*LUKEWARM	B LUB	G LUG	**B LEAK**
*LIVIDITY	LONGHAIR	LUMBERER	B LUE	G LUH	B LEED
*LIVINGLY	LONGHAND	LUMINARY	B LUR	G LUM	B LEEP
*LIXIVIUM	LONGHEAD	LUMINIST	C LAD	G LUT	B LEND
LOADSTAR	LONGHORN	LUMINOUS	C LAG	P LAN	B LENT
LOAMLESS	LONGLEAF	*LUMPFISH	C LAM	P LAT	B LESS
LOANWORD	LONGLINE	LUNARIAN	C LAN	P LAY	B LEST
LOATHFUL	LONGNESS	LUNATION	C LAP	P LEA	B LEAR
LOATHING	LONGSHIP	LUNCHEON	C LAW	P LEB	B LEAT
LOBATION	LONGSOME	*LUNGFISH	C LAY	P LED	**B LIMP**
*LOBBYGOW	LONGSPUR	LUNGWORM	C LEF	P LEW	**B LIMY**
*LOBBYISM	LONGTIME	LUNGWORT	C LEW	P LIE	B LIND
*LOBBYIST	LONGUEUR	*LUNKHEAD	C LIP	P LOD	B LINI

B L INK	C LOMP	F LUYT	P LANE	S LOSH	BU LGER
B L ISS	C LONE	*F LYBY	P LANK	S LOTH	BU LGUR
B L ITE	C LONK	F LYER	P LANT	S LOYD	BU L LET
*B L ITZ	C LOOT	F LYTE	P LASH	S LUFF	BY L INE
B LOAT	C LOSE	G LACE	P LASM	S LUMP	CALAMI
B LOCK	C LOTH	G LADE	P LATE	S LUNG	CA LASH
B LOKE	C LOUD	G LADY	P LATY	S LUNK	CA L CAR
B LOND	C LOUR	G LAIR	P LAYA	S LURB	CA L CES
B LOOD	C LOUT	G LAND	*P LAZA	S LURP	CA L CIC
B LOOM	C LOVE	G LANS	P LEAD	S LUSH	CA LESA
B LOOP	C LOWN	G LARE	P LEAT	S LYPE	CA LICO
B LOWN	*C LOZE	G LARY	P LEBE	*Z LOTY	CA L IPH
B LOWY	C LUCK	G LASS	P LENA	BAL ATA	CA L KER
B L UER	C LUMP	*G LAZE	P LICA	BAL BOA	CA L KIN
B L UET	C LUNG	*G LAZY	P LIED	BAL DLY	CAL LAN
B L UEY	C LUNK	G LEAM	P LIER	BAL EEN	CAL LER
B L UFF	F LACK	G LEAN	P LIES	BAL KER	CAL LET
B L UMP	F LAIL	G LEBA	P LINK	BAL LAD	CAL LOW
B L UNT	F LAIR	G LEBE	P LONK	BAL LER	CAL LUS
B L URB	F LAKE	G LEDE	P LUCK	BAL LET	CA LORY
B L URT	*F LAKY	G LEED	P LUMB	BAL LON	CA LPAC
B L USH	F LAME	G LEEK	P LUME	BAL LOT	CA LVES
B L YPE	F LAMY	G LEET	P LUMP	BAL SAM	CE LERY
C LACH	F LANK	G LIAL	P LUMY	BEL ADY	CE LIAC
C LACK	F LARE	G LIDE	P LUNK	BEL AUD	CEL LAR
C LADE	F LASH	G LIFF	P LUSH	BEL DAM	CI LICE
C LAIM	F LASK	G LIME	P LYER	BEL EAP	CI LIUM
C LAMP	F LAWY	*G LITZ	S LACK	BEL FRY	CO LDLY
C LANG	*F LAXY	G LOAM	S LAIN	BEL IED	CO LEAD
C LANK	F LEAM	G LOAT	S LAKE	BEL IEF	CO LEUS
C LARO	F LECK	G LOBE	S LANG	BEL IER	CO L LAR
C LARY	F LEER	G LOGG	S LANK	BEL IES	COL LET
C LASH	F LEET	G LOOM	S LANT	BEL IKE	CO L LIE
C LASP	F LESH	G LORY	S LASH	BEL IVE	CO L LOP
C LASS	F LICK	G LOSS	S LATE	BEL LOW	CO LONE
C LAST	F LIED	G LOST	S LATY	BEL ONG	CO LONI
C LAVI	F LIER	G LOUT	S LEEK	BEL TER	CO LONY
C LEAN	F LIES	G LOVE	S LEEP	BEL UGA	CO LOUR
C LEAR	F LING	*G LOZE	S LEET	BIL BOA	CO LTER
C LEEK	F LINT	G LUER	S LEPT	BIL KER	CO LUGO
C LEFT	F LOUR	G LUEY	S LICE	BIL LET	CO LURE
C LEPE	F LOUT	G LUON	S LICK	BIL LIE	CU L LAY
C LERK	F LOWN	G LYPH	S LIDE	BIL LON	CU L LER
C LICK	F LUFF	K LONG	S LIER	BIL LOW	CU L LET
C LIFF	F LUID	K LOOF	S LILY	BIL LOW	CU L LIS
C LIFT	F LUKE	K LUGE	S LIME	BO LERO	CU LTCH
C LIMB	*F LUKY	*K LUTZ	S LIMY	BO LETE	CU LTIC
C LIME	F LUME	L LAMA	S LING	BO LIBE	CU LTUS
C LINE	F LUMP	L LANO	S LINK	*BO L LIX	CU LVER
C LING	F LUNG	P LACE	S LIPE	*BO L LOX	DALASI
C LINK	F LUNK	P LACK	S LIPT	BO LSHY	DA LEDH
C LIPT	F LUOR	P LAGE	S LOID	BO LTER	DA LETH
C LOAK	F LUSH	P LAID	S LOJD	BU LBEL	DAL LES
C LOCK	F LUTE	P LAIN	S LOOP	BU LBIL	DALTON
C LOMB	F LUTY	P LAIT	S LOPE	BU LBUL	DE LEAD

DE L ETE	GA L ERE	HO L ILY	MI L LET	PI L LOW	SA L AAM
DE L ICT	GA L LET	HO L ING	MI L NEB	PI L OSE	SA L AMI
DE L IME	GA L LEY	HO L ISM	MI L ORD	PI L OUS	SA L ARY
DE L IST	GA L LON	HO L IST	MI L TER	PILULE	SA L IFY
DE L UDE	GA L LOP	HO L LER	MO L DER	PO L DER	SA L INA
DE L UGE	GA L LUS	HO L LOA	MO L EST	*PO L EAX	SA L INE
DE L UXE	GA L ORE	HO L LOO	MO L INE	PO L EIS	SA L IVA
DE L VER	GA L OSH	HO L LOW	MO L LIE	PO L EYN	SA L LET
D I LATE	GA L YAK	HO L PEN	MO L TEN	PO L ICE	SA L LOW
DI L L ED	GE L ADA	HU L LER	MO L TER	PO L ICY	SA L MON
DO L LAR	GE L ANT	HU L LOA	MU L ETA	PO L ING	SA L OON
DO L LOP	GE L ATE	*JA L OPY	MU L ING	PO L ISH	SA L OOP
DO L MAN	GE L ATI	JI L TER	MU L LEN	PO L ITE	SA L PID
DO L MEN	GE L ATO	JO L TER	MU L LER	PO L ITY	SA L TER
DO L OUR	GE L DER	KA L IAN	MU L LET	PO L LEE	SA L TIE
DU L CET	GE L LED	*KA L IPH	NE L LIE	PO L LEN	SA L UKI
FA L CES	GI L DER	KA L IUM	NE L SON	PO L LER	SA L UTE
FA L CON	GI L LER	KA L MIA	NI L GAI	*PO L LEX	SA L VER
FAL LAL	GI L LIE	KA L ONG	NI L GAU	PO L YPI	SA L VIA
FA L LEN	GO L DEN	*KA L PAK	NU L LAH	PU L LER	SA L VOR
FA L LER	GO L FER	KE L OID	PA L ACE	PU L LET	SC L AFF
FA L LOW	GO L OSH	KE L PIE	PA L AIS	PU L LEY	SC L ERA
FA L SIE	GU L LET	KE L SON	PA L ATE	PU L LUP	SE L DOM
FA L TER	GU L LEY	KE L TER	PA L EST	PU L PAL	SE L ECT
FE L INE	GU L PER	KE L VIN	PA L ISH	PU L PER	SE L LER
FE L LAH	HA L ALA	KI L LER	PA L LED	PU L PIT	SE L SYN
FE L LER	HA L EST	KI L LIE	PA L LET	*PU L QUE	SE L VES
FE L LOW	HA L IDE	KI L TER	PA L LIA	PU L SAR	SH L EPP
FE L ONY	HA L ING	KI L TIE	PA L LID	PU L SER	*SH L OCK
FI L IAL	HA L ITE	*KO L HOZ	PA L LOR	RA L LYE	SH L UMP
FI L LER	HA L LAH	*KO L KOZ	PA L MAR	RE L ACE	SI L AGE
FI L LET	HA L LEL	KU L TUR	PA L MER	RE L ATE	SI L ANE
FI L LIP	HA L LOA	L I L IED	PA L PAL	RE L AUR	SI L ENI
FI L MER	HA L LOO	LO L LER	PA L PUS	RE L END	SI L ENT
FI L MIC	HA L LOT	LO L LOP	PA L TER	RE L ENT	SI L ICA
FI L OSE	HA L LOW	MA L ATE	PA L TRY	RE L EVE	SI L KEN
FI L TER	*HA L LUX	MA L GRE	PE L AGE	RE L ICT	SI L LER
*FI L THY	HA L OID	MA L IGN	PE L ITE	RE L IED	SI L VAN
FO L ATE	HA L TER	MA L INE	PE L LET	RE L IEF	S I L VER
FO L DER	*HA L UTZ	MA L LEI	PE L MET	RE L IER	SO L ACE
FO L IAR	*HA L VAH	MA L LEE	PE L OTA	RE L IES	SO L AND
FO L IUM	HA L VES	MA L LET	PE L TER	RE L INE	SO L ANO
FO L KIE	HE L IAC	MA L OTI	PE L TRY	RE L INK	SO L ATE
*FO L KSY	HE L IUM	MA L TED	PE L VIC	RE L ISH	SO L DAN
FO L LES	HE L LER	MA L TOL	PE L VIS	RE L IST	SO L DER
FO L LIS	HE L MET	ME L DER	PH L EGM	RE L IVE	SO L ELY
FO L LOW	HE L PER	ME L OID	PH L OEM	RE L OAD	SO L EMN
FU L FIL	HI L LER	ME L TER	PI L AFF	RE L OAN	SO L EUS
FU L GID	HI L LOA	ME L TON	PI L EUM	RE L OOK	SO L GEL
FU L LAM	HO L ARD	MI L ADI	PI L EUP	RE L UCT	SO L IDI
FU L LER	HO L DEN	MI L AGE	PI L EUS	RE L UME	SO L ING
FU L MAR	HO L DER	MI L DEN	PI L FER	RI L LET	SO L ION
GA L AGO	HO L DUP	MI L IEU	PI L ING	RO L FER	SO L UTE
*GA L AXY	HO L IER	MI L LER	PI L LAR	RO L LER	SO L VER
GA L ENA	HO L IES			RU L ING	SP L AKE

SP L ASH	VA L VAR	BA L DRIC	BU L L ISH	CH L ORIN	DI L UTER
SP L EEN	VE L ATE	BA L EFU L	*BU L L OCK	CI L IARY	DI L UTOR
SP L ENT	VE L LUM	BAL L ADE	BU L L OUS	CI L IATE	DI L UVIA
SP L ICE	VE L OCE	BAL L AST	BU L L PEN	CO L DISH	DO L EFU L
SP L INE	VE L OUR	BAL L IES	BU L RUSH	CO L ICIN	DO L L IED
SP L INT	VE L URE	BAL L ING	*BU L WARK	*CO L ICKY	DO L L IES
SP L ORE	VE L VET	BAL L OON	BY L INER	CO L ITIS	DO L L ING
SP L OSH	VIL L US	BAL L UTE	CA L AMAR	COL L AGE	DO L L ISH
SU L CUS	VO L ANT	BA L NEA L	CA L AMUS	COL L ARD	DO L PHIN
SU L DAN	VO L ERY	BA L ONEY	CA L ANDO	CO L LATE	*DU L CIFY
SU L FID	VO L LEY	BE L ABOR	*CA L CIFY	COL L ECT	DU L LARD
SU L FUR	VO L OST	BE L ACED	CA L CINE	COL L EEN	DU L L ISH
SU L KER	VO L UTE	BE L ATED	CA L CITE	COL L EGE	DU L NESS
SU L LEN	*VO L VOX	BE L CHER	CA L CIUM	COL L IDE	FA L AFE L
SU L PHA	VU L GAR	BE L DAME	CA L DERA	COL L IED	FA L BALA
SU L TAN	VU L GUS	BE L IEVE	CA L DRON	COL L IER	FA L CATE
SU L TRY	WA L ING	BEL L BOY	CA L ECHE	COL L IES	*FA L LACY
SY L VAN	WA L KER	BEL L EEK	CA L ENDS	COL L INS	*FA L LOFF
SY L VIN	*WA L KUP	BEL L HOP	CA L IBER	COL L OID	FA L LOUT
TA L CUM	WAL L AH	BEL L MAN	CA L IBRE	COL L UDE	*FA L SIFY
TA L ENT	WA L LET	BE L OVED	CA L ICES	CO L OBUS	FA L SITY
TA L ION	WA L LIE	BE L TING	CA L ICHE	CO L OGNE	FE L AFE L
TA L KER	WA L LOP	BI L AYER	CA L ICLE	CO L ONE L	FE L LATE
TA L KIE	WA L LOW	BI L IARY	CA L IPEE	CO L ONIC	FE L L IES
TAL L IS	WA L NUT	BIL IOUS	CA L IPER	CO L ONUS	FE L ONRY
TAL L IT	WA L RUS	BIL L BUG	CA L LANT	CO L ORED	FE L SITE
TAL L OL	WE L DER	BIL L IES	CAL L BOY	CO L ORER	FE L SPAR
TAL L OW	WE L DOR	BIL L ING	CA L L ING	CO L UME L	FE L TING
TA L UKA	WE L KIN	BIL L ION	CAL L OSE	CU L ICID	FE L UCCA
TE L EDU	WE L LIE	BI L OBED	CA L LOUS	CU L L IED	FE L WORT
TE L EGA	WE L TER	BI L STED	CA L OMEL	CU L L IES	FI L AREE
TE L FER	WIL DER	BI L TONG	CA L ORIC	CU L L ION	FI L ARIA
TE L IAL	WIL DLY	BO L ETUS	CA L ORIE	CU L OTTE	FI L BERT
TE L IUM	WIL FUL	BO L IVAR	CA L OTTE	CU L PRIT	*FI L CHER
TE L LER	WIL IER	BO L IVIA	CA L OYER	CU L TISH	FI L EMOT
TE L OME	WIL ILY	BOL L ARD	*CA L PACK	CU L TISM	FI L IATE
TE L SON	WIL ING	BO L IVIA	CA L TRAP	CU L TIST	FI L IBEG
TI L LER	WIL LER	BOL L ARD	CA L TROP	CU L TURE	FI L L IES
TI L TER	WIL LET	BO L OGNA	CA L UMET	CU L VERT	FI L L ING
TO L ANE	WIL LOW	BO L ONEY	CA L UMNY	DA L APON	*FI L MDOM
TO L EDO	WOL FER	BO L SHIE	*CA L VARY	DA L L IER	FI L MIER
TO L LER	WOL VER	BO L STER	CA L YCES	DE L AINE	*FI L MI LY
TO L UIC	WOL VES	BU L B LET	CA L YCLE	DE L ATOR	FI L MSET
TO L UID	*XY L ENE	BU L BOUS	CA L YPSO	DE L AYER	FO L ACIN
TO L UO L	*XY L OID	BU L IMIA	*CA L ZONE	DE L EAVE	FO L DOUT
TO L UY L	*XY L OSE	BU L IMIC	CE L ADON	DE L IGHT	FO L IAGE
TU L ADI	YC L EPT	BU L KAGE	CE L ESTA	DE L IMIT	FO L IATE
VA L GUS	YE L LER	BU L LACE	CE L ESTE	DE L IVER	FO L IOSE
VA L INE	YE L LOW	BU L LATE	CEL L IST	DE L OUSE	FO L IOUS
VA L ISE	YE L PER	BU L L BAT	CEL L ULE	*DE L PHIC	*FO L KISH
VA L LEY	*ZI L LAH	BU L L DOG	CE L OSIA	DE L TOID	*FO L KMOT
VA L OUR	BA L ANCE	BU L L IED	*CH L AMYS	DE L UDER	*FO L KWAY
VA L UER	BA L CONY	BU L L IER	CH L ORAL	DI L ATER	FO L L IES
VA L UTA	BA L DIES	BU L L IES	CH L ORIC	DI L ATOR	FU L CRUM
VA L VA L	BA L DISH	BU L L ION	CH L ORID	DI L UENT	FU L FI L L

FU L GENT	*HA L LWAY	*KI L LJOY	MU L LEIN	PO L EMIC	SA L LIER
FU L LERY	HA L OGEN	*KO L ACKY	MU L LION	PO L ENTA	SA L LIES
FU L MINE	HA L VERS	KO L BASI	MU L LITE	PO L ITIC	SA L LOWY
FU L NESS	HA L VING	*KO L KHOS	*MU L LOCK	PO L LARD	*SA L PINX
FU L SOME	HA L YARD	*KO L KHOZ	MU L TURE	PO L LARD	SA L PIAN
FU L VOUS	HE L IAST	LA L LAND	NE L UMBO	PO L LIST	SA L SIFY
GA L ABIA	HE L ICAL	LO L LIES	NI L GHAI	*PO L LOCK	SA L TANT
GA L ATEA	HE L ICES	LU L LABY	NI L GHAU	PO L LUTE	*SA L TBOX
GA L ILEE	HE L ICON	MA L ACCA	NU L LIFY	PO L OIST	SA L TERN
GA L IPOT	HE L IPAD	MA L AISE	NU L LITY	PO L YCOT	SA L TIER
GA L LANT	*HE L LBOX	MA L AMUT	NY L GHAI	PO L YENE	SA L TILY
GA L LATE	HE L LCAT	MA L ANGA	NY L GHAU	PO L YGON	SA L TINE
GA L LEIN	HE L LERI	MA L APER	PA L ABRA	PO L YMER	SA L TING
GA L LEON	HE L LERY	MA L APRO	PA L ADIN	PO L YMER	SA L TIRE
GA L LERY	HE L LISH	MA L ARIA	PA L ATAL	PO L YOMA	SA L TISH
GA L LETA	HE L LUVA	*MA L ARKY	PA L AVER	*PO L YPOD	SA L TPAN
GA L LFLY	HE L OTRY	MA L AROM	*PA L AZZO	PO L YPUS	SA L UTER
GA L LIOT	*HE L PFUL	MA L EATE	PA L ETOT	PU L LING	SA L VAGE
GA L LIUM	HE L PING	MA L EDIC	PA L ETTE	PU L LMAN	SA L VING
GA L LNUT	HI L DING	MA L EMIU	*PA L FREY	PU L LOUT	SE L ENIC
GA L LOON	HI L LIER	MA L EMUT	PA L IEST	PU L PIER	SE L FDOM
GA L LOOT	*HI L LOCK	MA L ENES	PA L IKAR	PU L PILY	SE L FISH
GA L LOUS	HI L LTOP	MA L IGNE	PAL LIAL	PU L SANT	SE L LOUT
GA L LOWS	HO L DALL	MA L IGNL	PAL LIER	PU L SATE	*SE L TZER
GA L LYAC	HO L DING	MA L IHIN	PAL LIUM	PU L SING	SE L VAGE
GA L OSHE	HO L DOUT	MA L INGE	PAL LMARY	PU L SION	*SH L UMPY
*GA L UMPH	HO L IBUT	MA L ISON	PAL LMATE	PY L ORUS	Si L ENCE
GE L ATIN	HO L IDAY	MA L LEUS	PA L MIER	RA L LIED	SI L ENTS
GE L DING	HO L IEST	MA L POSE	PA L MIST	RA L LIER	SI L ENUS
GE L LANT	HO L LAND	MA L TASE	PA L MYRA	RA L LINE	SI L ICLE
GE L LING	HO L LIES	MA L TIER	PA L OOKA	RE L ABEL	Si L ICON
GI L BERT	HO L MIUM	MA L TIES	PA L PATE	RE L APSE	SI L URID
GI L DING	HO L STER	MA L TOSE	PA L PATE	RE L ATER	SI L VERN
GI L LNET	*HO L YDAY	ME L AMED	PA L SHIP	RE L ATOR	SI L VERY
GO L DARN	*JA L APIN	ME L ANIN	PA L UDAL	RE L AXIN	SI L VICS
GO L DBUG	*JA L OPPY	ME L ILIT	PE L AGIC	RE L EARN	S I L ESIA
GO L DEYE	*JE L LABA	ME L ILOT	PE L ICAN	RE L EASE	*S I L IQUA
GO L DURN	*JE L LIFY	ME L INIT	PE L ISSE	RE L IANT	*S I L IQUE
GO L FING	JI L LION	ME L ODIC	PE L ORIA	RE L IEVE	SO L ACER
GO L IARD	*JO L LIED	ME L ODIE	PE L ORUS	RE L IEVO	SO L ANIN
GO L OSHE	JO L LIER	*MI L CHIG	PE L TAST	RE L IGHT	SO L ANUM
GU L FIER	JO L LIES	*MI L DEWY	PE L TATE	*RE L IQUE	SO L ARIA
*HA L ACHA	*JO L LIFY	MI L FOIL	*PH L EGMY	RI L IEVO	SO L ATIA
*HA L AKHA	*JO L LITY	MI L ITIA	PI L EATE	RI L LING	SO L DIER
*HA L AKIC	KA L ENDS	*MI L KILY	PI L EOUS	RO L LICK	SO L ERET
HA LA L AH	*KA L IMBA	*MI L KMAN	PI L GRIM	RO L LING	SO L FEGE
*HA L AVAH	KI L LDEE	*MI L KSOP	PI L LAGE	RO L LMOP	SO L ICIT
HA L BERD	KI L LING	MI L LIER	*PI L LBOX	RO L LOUT	SO L IDLY
HA L BERT	*KI L LOCK	MI L LINE	PI L LION	RO L LTOP	SO L IDUS
*HA L CYON	KI L OBAR	MI L LION	PI L LORY	RO L LWAY	SO L ITON
*HA L FWAY	KI L OBIT	MI L LRUN	*PI L LOWY	SA L ABLE	SO L OIST
HA L IBUT	KI L ORAD	MI L REIS	PI L SNER	*SA L CHOW	SO L UBLE
HA L IDOM	Ki L OTON	MO L LIES	PO L ARON	SA L ICIN	SO L UBLY
HA L ITUS	KI L TING	*MO L LIFY	*PO L EAXE	SA L IENT	SO L VATE
HA L LOTH	*KI L LICK	MU L ATTO	PO L ECAT	SA L LIED	SO L VENT

SO L VING
*SP L ASHY
SP L EENY
SP L ENIA
SP L ENIC
SP L ICER
SP L ODGE
SP L OTCH
SP L URGE
SP L URGY
SU L CATE
SU L FATE
SO L ID L Y
SU L FIDE
SU L FITE
SU L FONE
SU L FURY
SU L LAGE
SU L PHID
SU L PHUR
SU L TANA
SY L LABI
*SY L PHID
SY L VINE
SY L VITE
TA L ARIA
TA L IFED
TA L IPES
TA L IPOT
TA L KING
TA L LAGE
TA L LBOY
TA L LIED
TA L LIER
TA L LIES
TA L LISH
TA L LITH
TA L LOWY
TA L LYHO
TA L OOKA
TE L AMON
TE L EMAN
TE L EOST
TE L ERAN
TE L ESIS
TE L FORD
TE L LIES
TE L PHER
TI L APIA
TI L LAGE
TI L LING
TI L LITE
TO L IDIN
TO L LAGE
TO L LBAR
TO L LING

TO L L MAN
TO L L WAY
TO L UATE
TO L UENE
TO L UIDE
TO L UO L E
TY L OSIN
VA L ANCE
VA L ENCE
*VA L ENCY
VA L IANT
VA L ID L Y
VA L LATE
VA L ONIA
VA L UATE
VA L VATE
VA L VU LA
VA L VU L E
VE L AMEN
VE L IGER
VE L ITES
VE L OUTE
VI L AYET
VI L LAGE
VI L LAIN
VI L LEIN
*VI L LIFY
VO L ANTE
VO L CANO
VO L LIME
VO L TAGE
VO L UB L E
VO L UTIN
VU L GATE
VU L PINE
VU L TURE
*WA L KING
WA L KOUT
*WA L KWAY
*WA L LABY
WA L L EYE
WA L L IES
*WA L TZER
*WE L CHER
WE L COME
WE L FARE
WE L L IES
WE L SHER
WE L TING
WI L DCAT
WI L DING
WI L DISH
WI L LIEST
WI L L FUL
WI L L IED

WI L L IES
WI L L ING
*WI L LOWY
*WO L FISH
*WO L FRAM
*XY L IDIN
*XY L ITO L
*YC L EPED
*YE L LOWY
*ZE L KOVA
*ZI L L ION
BA L L GAME
*BAL L HAWK
BA L L ISTA
BA L L ONET
BA L L ONNE
BA L L OTER
BA L L ROOM
*BAL L YHOO
BA L L YRAG
BA L MORA L
BE L L BIRD
BE L L OWER
BE L LPUL L
BE L L WORT
*BEL L YFUL
BI L ABIA L
BI L L ETER
*BI L L FISH
BI L L FOLD
BI L L HEAD
*BI L L HOOK
BI L L IARD
*BI L LYCAN
*BO L LOCKS
*BOL L WORM
BO L THO L E
*BU L LDOZE
BU L L ETIN
BU L L EYE
BU L L HEAD
BU L L HORN
BU L L IEST
*BU L LNECK
BU L L NOSE
BU L LPOUT
BU L L RING
BU L L RUSH
BU L L SHIT
BU L L SHOT
BU L L WEED
*BU L L WHIP
*BUL LYBOY
BU L LYRAG

CA L AMARI
CA L DARIA
CA L ENDA L
CA L LALOO
*CA L LBACK
CA L L IPEE
CA L L IPER
*CA L ORIZE
*CA L OTYPE
*CA L YCEAL
CE L L ARER
CE L L ARET
CE L L MATE
CE L LULAR
*CO L DCOCK
CO L EADER
CO L L AGEN
CO L L APSE
CO L L ARET
CO L L ATOR
CO L L EGER
CO L L IDER
CO L L IERY
CO L L OGUE
*CO L LOQUY
CO L L UDER
CO L L UVIA
CO L L YRIA
CO L OBOMA
CO L ONIA L
CO L ORFU L
*CO L ORIZE
CO L ORMAN
CO L OSSA L
CU L TURA L
DE L OUSER
DI L UVIA L
DU L L NESS
FA L DERA L
FA L DERO L
*FA L LAWAY
*FA L LBACK
*FA L L FISH
FE L LAB L E
FE L LATIO
FE L LATOR
FE L L NESS
*FEL LOWLY
*FEL T L IKE
FO L DERO L
FO L L IC L E
FO L LOWER

*FU L LBACK
*FU L LFACE
FU L L NESS
GA L ABIYA
GA L ANGA L
GA L L ERIA
GA L L IARD
GA L L OPER
GE L ATING
GI L DHA L L
GO L L IWOG
*GO L LYWOG
GU L LAB L E
GU L L IB L E
*HA L AZONE
HA L L IARD
*HA L LMARK
HA L LOWER
HE L IACA L
HE L I L IFT
HE L L BENT
HE L L FIRE
*HE L L KITE
HI L L IEST
HI L L SIDE
*HO L OGAMY
*JA L APENO
*JO L L IEST
KA L L IDIN
KI L L DEER
KI L OBASE
*KI L OBAUD
*KI L OBYTE
KO L BASSI
LA L LYGAG
LI L L IPUT
LO L L TPOP
LO L LYGAG
*LO L LYPOP
MA L L EOLI
MA L TREAT
MA L TSTER
MA L VASIA
ME L AMINE
ME L ANIAN
ME L ANISM
ME L ANITE
ME L ANOID
ME L ANOMA
ME L ANOUS
ME L ODEON
ME L ODICA
ME L ODIST
ME L TDOWN

MI L DNESS
MI L EPOST
MI L ESIMO
MI L IARIA
MI L ITANT
MI L ITARY
MI L ITATE
MI L KIEST
*MI L KSHED
*MI L L CAKE
MI L L EPED
MI L L IARE
MI L L IARY
MI L L IBAR
MI L L IEME
MI L L IGA L
MI L L IGA L
*MI L L ILUX
*MI L L IMHO
MI L L INER
*MI L L IOHM
MI L L IPED
MI L L IREM
MI L L POND
MI L L RACE
*MI L LWORK
MO L A L ITY
MO L ARITY
MO L ASSES
MO L DIEST
MO L ECULE
MO L EHI L L
MO L ESKIN
MO L ESTER
MU L ETEER
MU L L IGAN
MU L TIAGE
MU L TICAR
MU L TIFID
MU L TIPED
*MU L TIP L Y
MU L TITON
MU L TIUSE
MY L ONITE
PA L ATIA L
*PA L AZZOS
PA L EOSO L
*PA L IMONY
PA L LADIA
PA L LADIC
PA L LETTE
PA L L IATE
PA L L IEST
PE L LAGRA

PE L LETAL	VO L LEYER	DO L LOV	MOB L ED	WA L LOW	CO L LEEN
PE L LICLE	WA L LAROO	FA L LAL	MO L LIE	WE L LIE	CO L LEGE
PEL LMELL	WA L LOPER	FA L LEN	MU L LEN	WI L LER	CO L LIDE
PE L LUCID	WA L LOWER	FA L LER	MU L LER	WI L LET	CO L LIED
PI L E LESS	*WE L LADAY	FA L LOW	MU L LET	WI L LOW	CO L LIER
PO L LINIA	*WE L LAWAY	FE L LAH	NE L LIE	WOO L ED	CO L LIES
PO L LINIC	WE L LBORN	FE L LER	NU L LAH	YE L LER	CO L LIMN
PO L LIWOG	*WE L LCURB	FE L LOW	PAB LUM	YE L LOW	CO L LINS
PO L LSTER	*WE L LDOER	FI L LER	PA L LED	*ZI L LAH	CO L LOID
*PO L LYWOG	*WE L LHEAD	FI L LET	PA L LET	BA L LADE	CO L LUDE
*PU L LBACK	*WE L LHOLE	FI L LIP	PA L LIA	BA L LAST	CU L LIED
PU L LOVER	WE L LNESS	FO L LES	PA L LID	BA L LIES	CU L LIES
PU L PO LIS	WE L LSITE	FO L LIS	PA L LOR	BA L LING	CU L LION
RA L LYING	*WI LDFOWL	FO L LOW	PE L LET	BA L LOON	*CYC LERY
RA L LYIST	WI L DLAND	FU L LAM	PHY L LO	BA L LUTE	DA L LIER
RE LIAB LY	*WI L LIWAU	FU L LER	PI L LAR	BE L LBOY	DO L LIED
RO L LAWAY	*WI L LIWAW	GA L LET	PI L LOW	BE L LEEK	DO L LIES
*RO L LBACK	WI L LOWER	GA L LEY	PO L LEE	BE L LHOP	DO L LING
*RO L LICKY	*WI L LYARD	GA L LON	PO L LEN	BE L LMAN	DO L LISH
RO L LOVER	WI L LYART	GA L LOP	PO L LER	BIB LIST	DRY LAND
SE LFHEA L	*WI L LYWAW	GA L LUS	*PO L LEX	BI L LBUG	DU L LARD
SH LEMIE L	BA L LAD	GE L LED	PU L LER	BI L LIES	DU L LISH
SI L ICIER	BA L LER	GI L LER	PU L LET	BI L LING	*FA L LACY
SI L ICI LY	BA L LET	GI L LIE	PU L LEY	BI L LION	*FA L LOFF
SI L ICU LA	BA L LON	GU L LET	PU L LUP	*BOI L OFF	FA L LOUT
SI L LABUB	BA L LOT	GU L LEY	RA L LYE	BO L LARD	FE L LATE
SI L LIBUB	BE L LOW	HA L LAH	REP LOT	*BOW LFU L	FE L LIES
SI L VICA L	BI L LER	HA L LEL	RI L LET	BRA LESS	FEN LAND
SO LATION	BI L LET	HA L LOO	RO L LER	BU L LACE	FI L LIES
SO L LERET	BI L LIE	HA L LOT	SA L LET	BU L LATE	FI L LING
SP LENIA L	BI L LON	HA L LOW	SA L LOW	BU L LBAT	FLY LESS
SP LURGER	BI L LOW	*HA L LUX	SE L LER	BU L LDOG	FO L LIES
SU LFINY L	*BO L LIX	HE L LER	SHA LEY	BU L LIED	FU L LERY
SU LFONA L	*BO L LOX	HI L LER	SHE LTA	BU L LIER	GA L LANT
SU LFONY L	BU L LET	HI L LOA	SIA LID	BU L LIES	GA L LATE
SU LFURY L	CA L LAN	HO L LER	SI L LER	BU L LION	GA L LEIN
*SY L LABIC	CA L LER	HO L LOA	SKY LIT	BU L LISH	GA L LEON
SY L LAB LE	CA L LET	HO L LOO	SMI LEY	*BU L LOCK	GA L LERY
*SY L LABUB	CA L LOW	HO L LOW	SUB LOT	BU L LOUS	GA L LETA
SY L LABUS	CA L LUS	HU L LER	SU L LEN	BU L LPEN	GA L LFLY
TA L LNESS	CAP LET	HU L LOA	TA L LIS	BUS LOAD	GA L LIOT
TA L LYMAN	CE L LAR	KI L LER	TA L LIT	CAB LING	GA L LIUM
TE LEPATH	CHA L LA	KI L LIE	TA L LOL	CA L LANT	GA L LNUT
TE LESTIC	CO L LAR	LA L LAN	TA L LOW	CA L LBOY	GA L LOON
*TE LETEXT	CO L LET	LIB LAB	TE L LER	CA L LING	GA L LOOT
TE L LTA LE	CO L LIE	LO L LER	TI L LER	CA L LOSE	GA L LOUS
TE L LURIC	CO L LOP	LO L LOP	TO L LER	CA L LOUS	GA L LOWS
TO L LGATE	COO LTH	MAG LEV	VA L LEY	CE L LIST	GA L LYAC
TU L LIBEE	CU L LAY	MA L LEE	VE L LUM	CE L LULE	GE L LANT
*VA LKYRIE	CU L LER	MA L LEI	VI L LUS	CHO LENT	GE L LING
VE L LEITY	CU L LET	MA L LET	VO L LEY	COA LIER	GI L LNET
VI L LADOM	CU L LIS	MER LOT	WA L LAH	CO L LAGE	GUY LINE
VI L LAGER	DA L LES	MI L LER	WA L LET	CO L LARD	GYP LURE
VI L LAINY	DI L LED	MI L LET	WA L LIE	CO L LATE	HA L LOTH
VI L LATIC	DO L LAR		WA L LOP	CO L LECT	*HA L LWAY

*HE L L BOX	PIG L IKE	TA L L IES	*BEF L OWER	CHE L ATOR	DIA L L IST
HE L L CAT	PI L L AGE	TA L L ISH	BEG L AMOR	*CHE L IPED	DIA L OGER
HE L L ERI	*PI L L BOX	TA L L ITH	BE L L BIRD	*CHI L DBED	DIA L OGIC
HE L L ERY	PI L L ION	TA L L YHO	BE L L OWY	*CHI L DING	DIA L OGUE
HE L L ISH	PI L L ORY	TEA L IKE	BE L L PUL L	*CHI L DISH	DIA L YSER
HE L L UVA	*PI L L OWY	TE L L IES	BE L L WORT	CHI L DREN	DIA L YSIS
HI L L IER	POD L IKE	TIE L ESS	*BE L L YFU L	*CHI L IASM	DIA L YTIC
*HI L L OCK	*PO L L ACK	TI L L AGE	BES L AVED	CHI L IAST	*DIA L YZER
HI L L TOP	PO L L ARD	TI L L ING	BI L L ETER	*CHI L IDOG	DIE L DRIN
HIP L INE	PO L L IST	TI L L ITE	*BI L L FISH	*CHI L OPOD	DIO L EFIN
HO L L AND	*PO L L OCK	TOI L FU L	BI L L FOLD	*CHO L ERIC	DIP L EGIA
HO L L IES	PO L L UTE	TO L L AGE	BI L L HEAD	CIS L UNAR	*DIP L EXER
HOT L INE	POT L INE	TO L L BAR	*BI L L HOOK	COA L ESCE	*DIP L OIDY
*JE L L ABA	POU L TER	TO L L ING	BI L L IARD	*COA L FISH	DIP L OMAT
*JE L L IFY	PRE L IFE	TO L L MAN	*BI L L YCAN	COA L HOLE	DIP L OPOD
*JET L IKE	PU L L ING	TO L L WAY	BIO L OGIC	COA L IEST	DIP L OSIS
JI L L ION	PU L L MAN	TOP L INE	*BO L L OCKS	COA L LESS	DIS L IKER
*JO L L IED	PU L L OUT	VA L L ATE	*BO L L WORM	*COA L SACK	DIS L ODGE
JO L L IER	RAI L BUS	VI L L AGE	*BOW L LIKE	*COA L SHED	DIS L OYA L
JO L L IES	RAI L CAR	VI L L AIN	*BUH L WORK	COA L YARD	*DJE L L ABA
*JO L L IFY	RA L L IED	VI L L EIN	BUI L DING	CO L L AGEN	DRI L L ING
*JO L L ITY	RA L L IER	*VI L L IFY	*BU L L DOZE	CO L L APSE	DRO L L ERY
KI L L DEE	RA L L INE	VO L L IME	BU L L ETIN	CO L L ARET	DUE L L ING
KI L L ING	RAY L IKE	WAI L FU L	BU L L FROG	CO L L ATOR	DUE L L IST
*KI L L OCK	REB L END	*WA L L ABY	BU L L HEAD	CO L L EGER	DU L L NESS
*KI L L ICK	RED L INE	WA L L EYE	BU L L HORN	CO L L EGIA	DUO L OGUE
*KI L L JOY	REP L EAD	WA L L IES	BU L L IEST	CO L L IDER	*DUP L EXER
L AD L ING	REP L UMB	WI L L FU L	BU L L NOSE	CO L L IERY	DWE L L ING
L AL L AND	RES L ATE	WI L L IED	BU L L POUT	CO L L OGUE	*DYS L EXIA
L OL L IES	RI L L ING	WI L L IES	BU L L RING	*CO L L OQUY	*DYS L EXIC
L UL L ABY	RO L L ICK	WI L L ING	BU L L RUSH	CO L L UDER	*FAH L BAND
MA L L EUS	RO L L ING	*WI L L OWY	*BU L L SHIT	CO L L UVIA	FA L L AWAY
*MAP L IKE	RO L L MOP	WIN L ESS	BU L L SHOT	CO L L YRIA	FA L L BACK
MID L IFE	RO L L OUT	WOO L HAT	BU L L WEED	COO L DOWN	*FA L L FISH
MI L L IER	RO L L TOP	WOO L L ED	*BU L L WHIP	COO L NESS	FA L L IBLE
MI L L INE	RO L L WAY	*YE L L OWY	*BU L L YBOY	COP L ANAR	*FAN L IGHT
MI L L ION	SA L L IED	*ZI L L ION	BU L L YRAG	COU L DEST	FE L L ABLE
MI L L RUN	SA L L IER	*ZIP L ESS	*CAB L EWAY	COU L ISSE	FE L L ATIO
MO L L IES	SA L L IES	BAI L MENT	CA L L ALOO	CUR L ICUE	FE L L ATOR
*MO L L IFY	SA L L OWY	BAI L SMAN	*CA L L BACK	*CUR L YCUE	FE L L NESS
MU L L EIN	SCA L EUP	BA L L GAME	CA L L IPEE	*CYC L AMEN	*FEL L OWLY
MU L L ION	SCA L PE L	BA L L IST	CA L L IPER	*CYC L ECAR	FOI L SMAN
MU L L ITE	*SCH L UMP	BA L L ISTA	CA L L IOPE	*CYC L ICAL	FO L L ICLE
*MU L L OCK	SE L L OUT	BA L L ONET	CAU L DRON	*CYC L ITO L	FO L L OWER
NET L ESS	SKI L FU L	BA L L OTER	CAU L ICLE	*DAY L IGHT	*FOO L FISH
NUC L EA L	SOU L FU L	*BA L L PARK	*CAU L KING	*DEA L FISH	*FOO L SCAP
NU L L IFY	SPI L MIN	BA L L ROOM	CE L L ARER	DEC L ARER	FOU L NESS
NU L L ITY	SUB L INE	*BA L L YHOO	CE L L ARET	DEC L ASSE	FRI L L ING
PAI L FU L	SU L L AGE	BA L L YRAG	CE L L MATE	DEC L INER	FUE L L ING
PA L L IA L	SY L L ABI	BAR L EDUC	CE L L ULAR	DEF L ATER	FUG L EMAN
PA L L IER	TAI L FAN	BDE L L IUM	*CHA L AZIA	DEF L ATOR	*FU L L BACK
PA L L ING	TA L L AGE	BEC L AMOR	CHA L DRON	*DEF L EXED	*FU L L FACE
PA L L IUM	TA L L BOY	*BEC L OTHE	CHA L L IES	*DEF L OWER	FU L L NESS
*PAV L OVA	TA L L IED		*CHA L LOTH	DEP L ORER	*FUR L OUGH
PED L ERY	TA L L IER			DIA L L AGE	GA L L EASS

GAL LERIA	*LOW LIGHT	PEL LMEL L	*QUIL LAJA	SHIL L ING	TAIL LIKE
GAL LIARD	MAL LEOLI	PE L LUCID	*QUI L LING	SIA LIDAN	TAILPIPE
GAL LOPER	*MEAL WORM	PEN LIGHT	*QUI LTING	SI L LABUB	TAI LRACE
GAS LIGHT	*MEA LYBUG	PER LUDER	RAC LETTE	SI L LIBUB	TAI LSKID
GEO LOGER	*ME L LIFIC	PHA LANGE	RAI LBIRD	SKE LETON	TAI LSPIN
GIR LHOOD	*MI L LCAKE	*PHA L LISM	RAI LHEAD	SKI L LESS	TAI LWIND
GOAL LESS	MIL LEPED	PHA L LIST	RAI L LERY	*SKI L LFUL	TAL LNESS
GOAL POST	MIL LIARD	PHE LONIA	RAILROAD	*SKU L LCAP	TAL LYMAN
GOAL WARD	MIL LIARE	*PHI LABEG	RA L LYING	*SKY LIGHT	TAR LETAN
GOD LIEST	MIL LIARY	*PHI LIBEG	RA L LYIST	SMA L LAGE	TEL LTALE
GOL LIWOG	MIL LIBAR	*PHI LOME L	REA LISER	SMA L LISH	TEL LURIC
*GOL LYWOG	MIL LIEME	*PHI LTRUM	*REA LIZER	*SMA L LPOX	THA LAMUS
GRIL LADE	MIL LIGAL	*PHY LAXIS	REA LNESS	SMA LTINE	THA L LIUM
GRIL LAGE	*MIL LILUX	*PHY LESIS	·REC LINER	SMA LTITE	THE LITIS
GUI LEFUL	*MIL LIMHO	*PHY L LARY	REC LOTHE	SME LTERY	THO LEPIN
GUL LABLE	MIL LINER	*PHY L LITE	*REF LEXLY	SOI L LESS	TOI LETTE
GUL LIBLE	*MIL LIOHM	*PHY L LODE	REF LOWER	SO L LERET	TOL LGATE
HA L LIARD	MIL LIPED	*PHY L LOID	REF LUENT	SPA LPEEN	TOO LHEAD
*HAL LMARK	MIL LIREM	*PHY L LOME	REP LACER	SPE LAEAN	TOO L LESS
HAL LOWER	MIL LPOND	PIC LORAM	REP LEDGE	SPE L LING	TOO LROOM
*HAP LOIDY	MIL LRACE	PO L LINIA	REP LEVIN	SPI LLAGE	TOO LSHED
HAR LOTRY	*MIL LWORK	PO L LINIC	REP LICON	*SPI L LWAY	*TOP LOFTY
*HAU LYARD	MIS LABEL	PO L LIWOG	REP LUNGE	SPO LIATE	TRI L LION
HEE LBAL L	MUL LIGAN	PO L LSTER	RIF LEMAN	STA L LION	TRI L LIUM
HEE L LESS	NAI LFOLD	*POL LYWOG	ROL LAWAY	STA LWART	TRI LOBAL
HE L L BENT	NAI LHEAD	POO LHAL L	*ROL LBACK	STE L LATE	TRI LOBED
HE L L FIRE	NEG LIGEE	POO LROOM	*ROL LICKY	STE L LIFY	TRO LLIED
*HE L L KITE	*NEW LYWED	POO LSIDE	ROL LOVER	STI LBENE	TRO L LIES
HI L LIEST	NGU LTRUM	POP LITIC	ROU LETTE	STI LBITE	TRO L LING
HI L LSIDE	NIE LLIST	*POT LACHE	SAI LBOAT	STI LETTO	TU L LIBEE
HOO LIGAN	NOB LEMAN	*POT LATCH	SAI LFISH	STI L LMAN	*TWE LVEMO
*HYA LOGEN	NOB LESSE	POU LARDE	SCA LABLE	STO LPORT	*TWI LIGHT
*JAI LBAIT	NON LABOR	POU LTICE	SCA LAWAG	STU LTIFY	TWI L LING
*JAI LBIRD	NON LEAFY	PRE LEGAL	SCA LENUS	STY LISER	VAR LETRY
*JEA LOUSY	NON LEGAL	PRE LIMIT	SCA LEPAN	*STY LIZER	VAU LTING
*JET LINER	NON LOCAL	*PRE LUNCH	SCA LIEST	SUB LEASE	*VEI LEDLY
*JO L LIEST	NUC LEASE	PRO LABOR	SCA L LION	SUB LEVEL	*VEI L LIKE
*KAI LYARD	NUC LEATE	PRO LAMIN	SCH LIERE	SUB LIMER	VE L LEITY
KA L LIDIN	NUC LEOID	PRO LAPSE	*SCH LOCKY	SUB LUNAR	VI L LADOM
KAO LIANG	NUC LEOLE	*PRO LIFIC	SCI LICET	SUN LIGHT	VI L LAGER
KEE LBOAT	NUC LEOLI	PRO LOGUE	SCO LDING	SWE L LING	VI L LAINY
*KEE LHALE	PAI LLARD	PRO LONGE	SCO LIOMA	*SY L LABIC	VI L LATIC
*KEE LHAUL	PAL LADIA	PSA LMIST	SCU LLERY	SY L LABLE	VIO LABLE
KEE L LESS	PAL LADIC	*PSA LMODY	SCU L LION	*SY L LABUB	VIO LATER
KIE LBASA	PAL LETTE	PSI LOCIN	SCU LPTOR	SY L LABUS	VIO LATOR
KI L LDEER	PAL LIATE	PSI LOSIS	SEA LLIKE	TAB LEFUL	VIO LENCE
*KOH LRABI	PAL LIEST	*PSY L LIUM	SEA LSKIN	TAB LETOP	VO L LEYER
LAD LEFUL	PAR LANCE	PUB LICAN	SHA LIEST	*TAI LBACK	WAI LSOME
LAL LYGAG	PAR LANDO	*PUB LICLY	SHA LLOON	TAI LBONE	WA L LAROO
LIL LIPUT	PAR LANTE	*PU LLBACK	*SHE LDUCK	TAI LCOAT	WA L LOPER
LOB LOL LY	PAR LEYER	PU L LOVER	*SHE LFFUL	TAI LGATE	WA L LOWER
LO L LTPOP	PAU LDRON	PYE LITIS	*SHE L LACK	TAI L LAMP	*WAY LAYER
LO L LYGAG	PE LLAGRA	*QUA LMISH	*SHE LVING	TAI L LESS	*WE L LADAY
*LO L LYPOP	PE L LETAL	*QUIL LAIA	SHI LINGI	TAI LLEUR	*WE L LAWAY
LOW LIFER	PE L LICLE	*QUIL LAJA	SHI L LALA		WE L LBORN

*WE L L CURB	DIA L	LU L L	TE L L	CEOR L	GYRA L
WE L L DOER	DIE L	MAI L	TI L L	CHI L L	HADA L
*WE L L HEAD	DI L L	MA L L	TIR L	CHUR L	HAMA L
WE L L HOLE	DIO L	MAR L	TOI L	CIBO L	*HAZE L
WE L L NESS	DIR L	MAU L	TO L L	CIVI L	HEMA L
WE L L SITE	DO L L	MEA L	TOO L	COMA L	*HEXY L
*WHA L EMAN	DUA L	ME L L	VAI L	COPA L	HORA L
WI L L IWAU	DUE L	MER L	VEA L	CORA L	HOSE L
*WI L L IWAW	DU L L	MEW L	VEI L	CRAA L	HOTE L
*WI L L OWER	FAI L	MI L L	VIA L	CRAW L	HOVE L
*WI L L YARD	FA L L	MOI L	VI L L	CREE L	JACA L
WI L L YART	FAR L	MO L L	VIO L	CRUE L	JEBE L
*WI L L YWAW	FEA L	MOO L	VIR L	CUPE L	*JEWE L
WOO L FE L L	FEE L	MU L L	WAI L	CYMO L	JOUA L
*WOO L LIKE	FE L L	NAI L	WA L L	DECA L	JUGA L
*WOO L PACK	FI L L	NI L L	WAU L	DEDA L	JURA L
*WOO L SACK	FOA L	NOE L	WAW L	DEVE L	JURE L
*WOO L SHED	FOI L	NU L L	WEA L	DEVI L	KETO L
*WOO L SKIN	FOO L	NUR L	WEE L	DOMA L	KEVE L
*WOO L WORK	FOU L	PAI L	WE L L	DOTA L	KEVI L
WOU L DEST	FOW L	PA L L	WI L L	DOWE L	KNEE L
*ZEA L OTRY	FUE L	PAW L	WOO L	DRAI L	KNO L L
*ZOO L ATER	FU L L	PEA L	YAW L	DRAW L	KNUR L
*ZOO L ATRY	FUR L	PEE L	YE L L	DRI L L	KRAA L
	GA L L	PIA L	YI L L	DRO L L	KRI L L
BAA L	GAO L	PI L L	YOW L	DROO L	KUGE L
BAI L	GI L L	PO L L	ZEA L	DURA L	LABE L
BA L L	GIR L	POO L	ZI L L	DWE L L	LAPE L
BAW L	GOA L	PU L L	BABE L	DYNE L	LEGA L
BE L L	GU L L	PUR L	BABU L	FATA L	LEVE L
BI L L	HAI L	RAI L	BAGE L	FECA L	L IBE L
BIR L	HA L L	REA L	BANA L	FERA L	LOCA L
BOI L	HAR L	REE L	BASA L	FETA L	LORA L
BO L L	HAU L	RIA L	BASI L	FINA L	LOSE L
BOW L	HEA L	RIE L	BEDE L	F LAI L	LOYA L
BUH L	HEE L	RI L L	BERY L	FOCA L	MAI L L
BU L L	HEI L	ROI L	BETE L	FOSE L	MEDA L
BUR L	HE L L	RO L L	BEVE L	FRAI L	META L
BYR L	HER L	ROT L	*BEZE L	FRI L L	MIAU L
CA L L	HI L L	SAI L	*BEZI L	FUGA L	MODA L
CAR L	HOW L	SA L L	BINA L	FUSI L	MODE L
CAU L	HU L L	SAU L	BORA L	*FUZI L	MOGU L
CEI L	HUR L	SEA L	BOTE L	GAVE L	MOHE L
CE L L	JAI L	SEE L	BOWE L	GAYA L	MO L A L
COA L	JAR L	SE L L	BRAI L	GHOU L	MORA L
COI L	JE L L	SHU L	BRAW L	GHY L L	MORE L
COO L	JI L L	SIA L	BRI L L	GIME L	MOTE L
COW L	JOW L	SI L L	BROI L	G LIA L	MURA L
CU L L	KAI L	SOI L	BUBA L	GNAR L	NASA L
CUR L	KEE L	SOU L	BUTY L	GORA L	NATA L
DAH L	KI L L	TAE L	CABA L	GRAA L	NAVA L
DEA L	KOE L	TAI L	CAME L	GRAI L	NAVE L
DEI L	KOH L	TA L L	CANA L	GRI L L	NERO L
DE L L	L EA L	TEA L	CARO L	GROW L	NEWE L
DHA L	LO L L	TEE L	CAVI L	GRUE L	NICO L

NIDA L	SHE L L	TRAI L	BRASI L	CUPFU L	*FRAZI L
NIHI L	SHEO L	TRAW L	*BRAZI L	CURTA L	*FRIJO L
NIVA L	SHIE L	TRIA L	BRIDA L	*CYMBA L	FRIVO L
NODA L	SHI L L	TRI L L	BRUMA L	DACTY L	FRUGA L
NONY L	SHOA L	TRIO L	BRUTA L	DAEDA L	FU L FI L
NOPA L	SHOO L	TRO L L	BUCCA L	DAMSE L	FUNGA L
NOTA L	SHOR L	TRU L L	BU L BE L	DARNT L	FUNNE L
NOVE L	SIBY L	TUBA L	BU L BI L	DEASI L	GAMBO L
PANE L	SIGI L	TWI L L	BU L BU L	DECKE L	GAVIA L
PAPA L	SISA L	TWIR L	BURIA L	DENIA L	GENIA L
PARO L	SKI L L	TYPA L	BUSHE L	DENTA L	GENTI L
PEAR L	SKIR L	VAGA L	CAMAI L	DENTI L	GERBI L
PEDA L	SKOA L	VAKI L	CANCE L	DETAI L	GIMBA L
PENA L	SKU L L	VENA L	CANFU L	DEWOO L	GIMMA L
PERI L	SMA L L	*VEXI L	CANNE L	DIOBO L	GINGA L
PETA L	SME L L	VIGI L	CAPFU L	DIRND L	G L OBA L
PHIA L	SNAI L	VINA L	CARCE L	DISMA L	G L YCO L
PIBA L	SNAR L	VINY L	CARFU L	DISPE L	*G L YCY L
PICA L	SNE L L	VIRA L	CARNA L	DISTA L	GOOGO L
PICU L	SNOO L	VITA L	CARPA L	DISTI L	GOORA L
PIPA L	SOKO L	VOCA L	CARPE L	*DJEBE L	GOSPE L
PIXE L	SORE L	VOWE L	CARRT L	*DONZE L	GRAVE L
PRI L L	SOTO L	WEDE L	CARTE L	DORSA L	GROVE L
PROW L	SPAI L	WHEA L	CARVE L	DORSE L	GUNNE L
PUPI L	SPA L L	WHEE L	CASUA L	DOSSA L	GUNSE L
QUAI L	SPEE L	WHIR L	CAUDA L	DOSSE L	HAEMA L
QUE L L	SPEI L	WHOR L	CAUSA L	DOSSI L	HA L L E L
QUI L L	SPE L L	WOFU L	CENTA L	DOTTE L	HAMMA L
RATA L	SPIE L	*XY L O L	CEREA L	DREID L	HANGU L
RATE L	SPI L L	*XY L Y L	CHAPE L	DRIVE L	HANSE L
RAVE L	SPOI L	YODE L	CHIRA L	DUCTA L	HASSE L
REBE L	SPOO L	YOKE L	CHISE L	DUFFE L	HATFU L
REFE L	STA L L	ZONA L	CHITA L	FACIA L	HERBA L
REGA L	STEA L	ZORI L	CHORA L	FAL LA L	HIEMA L
RENA L	STEE L	BABOO L	CINEO L	FARDE L	HIRSE L
REOI L	STI L L	BAGFU L	CITRA I.	FARFA L	HOSTE L
REPE L	STOO L	BARBA L	C L INA L	FARFE L	HOUSE L
REVE L	STU L L	BARBE L	*COAXA L	FAUCA L	HYETA L
RIVA L	SURA L	BARRF L	COCCA L	FECIA L	HYMNA L
RIYA L	SWAI L	BEDE L	COEVA L	FENNE L	*JACKA L
ROWE L	SWE L L	BEFA L L	COMPE L	FERRE L	*JARFU L
ROYA L	SWI L L	BEFOO L	CONSO L	FESTA L	*JEZAI L
RURA L	SWIR L	BEFOU L	CONSU L	FETIA L	JINGA L
SALA L	TAMA L	BEGA L L	CORBE L	FEUDA L	*JOVIA L
SALO L	TEPA L	BEHOW L	CORME L	FIBRI L	*JOYFU L
SCA L L	THI L L	*BENZA L	CORNE L	FI L IA L	*JUGFU L
SCHU L	THIO L	*BENZO L	CORRA L	FINIA L	*JUMBA L
SCOW L	THIR L	*BENZY L	CREDA L	FISCA L	KENNE L
SCU L L	THUR L	BETHE L	CRENE L	FITFU L	KERNE L
SEPA L	TICA L	BEWAI L	CRESO L	FODGE L	KITTE L
SERA L	TIDA L	*BIAXA L	CRESY L	FOETA L	KNAWE L
SHA L L	TO L Y L	BOATE L	CREWE L	FORMA L	KUMME L
SHAU L	TONA L	BORDE L	CRURA L	FORMO L	L ABIA L
SHAW L	TOTA L	BOREA L	CUDGE L	FORMY L	LAPFU L
SHEA L	TOWE L	*BOXFU L	CUNEA L	FOSSI L	L AURE L

LAWFU L	PEEPU L	REMAI L	SPINA L	VA L VA L	BRIMFU L
L ENTI L	PENCE L	RENAI L	SPINE L	VANDA L	BRISTO L
L ETHA L	PENCI L	RENTA L	SPIRA L	VASSA L	**BROTHE L**
L IENA L	PENSI L	REPEA L	SPITA L	VATFU L	BUTANO L
L INEA L	**PENTY L**	REPO L L	SPORA L	VEINA L	BUTYRA L
L INTE L	PETRE L	RERO L L	**SPRAW L**	VENIA L	*BUTYRY L
L INTO L	PETRO L	RESAI L	*SQUA L L	**VERBA L**	*CACODY L
L ISTE L	PEYOT L	RESEA L	*SQUEA L	VERNA L	CAGEFU L
L OREA L	PHENO L	RESE L L	*SQUI L L	VERSA L	CA L OME L
L UTEA L	PHENY L	RETAI L	STATA L	VESTA L	CAMBIA L
MA L TO L	PHONA L	RETE L L	STERO L	VINEA L	*CAMPHO L
MAMMA L	PINEA L	RETIA L	STIPE L	VISUA L	CANSFU L
MANFU L	PINNA L	RETOO L	STOMA L	WADMA L	CAPITA L
MANGE L	PISTI L	RETRA L	STRO L L	WADMO L	CAPITO L
MANTE L	PISTI L	REVEA L	STROM L	WADNE L	CAPORA L
MANUA L	PISTO L	RHINA L	**SWIVE L**	**WAEFU L**	CARACA L
MARCE L	P LAGA L	RIDGE L	**SYMBO L**	WEASE L	CARACO L
MARVE L	*P L EXA L	RIDGI L	TAHSI L	**WEEVI L**	CARACU L
MEDIA L	*P L EXA L	RITUA L	TA L LO L	WI L FU L	CARAME L
MENIA L	P L URA L	RONDE L	TARNA L	**WITHA L**	CARAVE L
MENSA L	PODSO L	RONNE L	TARSA L	WITTO L	CAREFU L
MENTA L	*PODZO L	RUEFU L	TASSE L	**WOEFU L**	CARPOO L
MESCA L	POMME L	RUNNE L	TEASE L	**WORMI L**	CARRE L L
MESIA L	PONTI L	SACRA L	*TEAZE L	*WURZE L	CATCA L L
METHY L	PORTA L	SAFRO L	TECTA L	BABBOO L	CATTAI L
*MEZCA L	POSTA L	SAMIE L	TE L IA L	BAGSFU L	CENSUA L
MICE L L	**POTFU L**	SANDA L	TENAI L	BA L EFU L	CENTRA L
MISKA L	**PRIMA L**	SANTO L	TERCE L	BA L NEA L	CERAMA L
MISSA L	**PROPE L**	SAURE L	TERGA L	BANEFU L	CHANCE L
MISSE L	**PROPY L**	**SCHOO L**	TETRY L	BARBE L L	CHANNE L
MITRA L	**PROTY L**	**SCHOR L**	THENA L	*BASHFU L	CHARNE L
MONGO L	PU L PA L	**SCRAW L**	THRA L L	*BATFOW L	CHATTE L
MORSE L	**PUMME L**	SCRO L L	THRI L L	*BATHYA L	*CHERVI L
MORTA L	**PYRRO L**	SEIDE L	**THYMO L**	BECRAW L	CH L ORA L
MUGFU L	*QUEZA L	SENDA L	**TIMBA L**	BEDEVI L	CHORDA L
MUSSE L	*QUINO L	SEPTA L	TINCA L	BEDRAI L	CHORIA L
MUTUA L	RACIA L	*SEQUE L	TINFU L	BEDRO L L	*CHROMY L
MUTUE L	RADIA L	SERAI L	TINSE L	*BEJEWE L	CITADE L
NARWA L	RAMTI L	SERIA L	TO L UO L	BENOMY L	COAEVA L
NEURA L	**RAPPE L**	SERVA L	TO L UY L	BENTHA L	COASTA L
NICKE L	RASCA L	**SEXUA L**	TOMDA L	*BENZOY L	*COAXIA L
NITRI L	REBI L L	**SHEKE L**	TONSI L	BESTIA L	CODICI L
NORMA L	REBOI L	*SHEQE L	**TOPFU L**	*BIAXIA L	*COEQUA L
NUCHA L	RECA L L	**SHOVE L**	TRAME L	BIFOCA L	CO L ONE L
PA L PA L	RECOA L	SHRI L L	TRAVE L	BIMETA L	CO L UME L
PANFU L	RECOI L	SHTET L	TRIBA L	BIMODA L	COMICA L
PARCE L	RECTA L	SIGNA L	TRINA L	*BIVINY L	CONCEA L
PARRA L	REDIA L	SIMNE L	TROTY L	**BOATFU L**	CONGEA L
PARRE L	REFA L L	SINFU L	TROWE L	**BOBTAI L**	CONICA L
PASCA L	REFEE L	**SKATO L**	**TUBFU L**	*BOOKFU L	CONTRO L
PASSE L	REFE L L	SNIVE L	TUNNE L	BORNEO L	**CORBEI L**
PASTE L	REFI L L	**SOBFU L**	TUSSA L	BORSTA L	CORDIA L
PASTI L	REFUE L	SOCIA L	**TWIBI L**	*BOW L FU L	CORONA L
PATRO L	REGNA L	SO L GE L	**TYMBA L**	*BOXHAU L	CORONE L
PAUSA L	REHEE L	SORRE L	VAKEE L	BRADAW L	COSTRE L

COTIDAL	FINICAL	HUMERAL	MISDEAL	POITREL	SAWMILL
COUNCIL	FISTFUL	HUMORAL	MISDIAL	POTBOIL	SCALPEL
COUNSEL	FLANNEL	HURTFUL	MISTRAL	POUNDAL	SCANDAL
COWBELL	FLOATEL	*HUSHFUL	MOANFUL	POUTFUL	SCRIBAL
COWGIRL	FLUVIAL	*JARSFUL	MONGREL	PREANAL	SCURRIL
CRANIAL	*FORKFUL	*JEJUNAL	MONOFIL	PREBILL	SEAFOWL
CREOSOL	*FORMFUL	*JESTFUL	MUDSILL	PREBOIL	SEAGULL
CRESTAL	*FOXTAIL	*JEZEBEL	MUSEPUL	PRECOOL	SEAWALL
CRUCIAL	FRACTAL	*JONQUIL	MUSICAL	PREDIAL	SEGETAL
CRUSTAL	FRESNEL	JOURNAL	NAPHTOL	PREMEAL	SEMINAL
CRYSTAL	FRETFUL	*JUGSFUL	NARWHAL	PREPILL	SENSUAL
CUBICAL	FRONTAL	*JUVENAL	NATURAL	*PREQUEL	SEVERAL
CUPSFUL	FULFILL	*KARAKUL	NEEDFUL	PRESELL	SHRIVEL
CURTAIL	FUNERAL	KESTREL	NEUTRAL	*PRETZEL	SHTETEL
CYNICAL	GADWALL	KISTFUL	NITINOL	PREVAIL	SKILFUL
DAMOSEL	GAINFUL	LACTEAL	NODICAL	*PUSHFUL	SKINFUL
*DAMOZEL	GAMBREL	LANGREL	NOMBRIL	*QUANTAL	SKYSAIL
DAREFUL	GANGREL	LANITAL	NOMINAL	*QUARREL	SNORKEL
DECANAL	GARBOIL	LATOSOL	NONFUEL	*QUETZAL	SONGFUL
DECIBEL	GASOHOL	LATPRAL	NOSTRIL	*RACKFUL	SORORAL
DECRIAL	GASTRAL	*LEXICAL	NUCLEAL	RADICAL	SOULFUL
DECTMAL	GEMINAL	LIBERAL	NUMERAL	RADICEL	SPACIAL
DEPOSAL	GENERAL	LIFEFUL	NUPTIAL	RATTAIL	SPANCEL
DESPOIL	GENITAL	LIMINAL	NUTGALL	REAVAIL	SPANIEL
DEVISAL	GENTEEL	LINALOL	PAGINAL	RECITAL	SPATIAL
DEWFALL	GHARIAL	LINGUAL	PAILFUL	REDPOLL	SPECIAL
*DEXTRAL	GINGALL	LITERAL	PAINFUL	REDRILL	SPHERAL
DIALLEL	GIRASOL	LITORAL	PALATAL	REDTAIL	SPIEGEL
DICOTYL	GIROSOL	LOGICAL	PALLIAL	REFUTAL	SPONSAL
DIGITAL	GLACIAL	LOGROLL	PALUDAL	REFUSAL	SPOUSAL
DIREFUL	GLEEPUL	LOWBALL	PARASOL	REGOSOL	STAMMEL
DISHFUL	GLUTEAL	LUGSAIL	PARBOIL	RELABEL	STENCIL
DISTILL	GNATHAL	LUNGFUL	PARTIAL	REMODEL	STERNAL
DITHIOL	GOMERAL	LUSTFUL	PASCHAL	REMOVAL	STIBIAL
DIURNAL	GOMEREL	LUSTRAL	*PASQUIL	RENEWAL	STRATAL
DOGGREL	GOMERIL	LYRICAL	PAYROLL	REPANEL	STRIGIL
DOLEFUL	GRADUAL	MAGICAL	*PEAFOWL	REPOSAL	STRUDEL
DOMICAL	GRAPNEL	MANDREL	PEDICEL	RESPELL	SUBCELL
DOMICIL	GRAUPEL	MANDRIL	PEDOCAL	RESTFUL	SUBCOOL
DOOMFUL	GREMIAL	MARITAL	PENICIL	RETINAL	SUBDUAL
DOTTREL	GUMBOIL	MARSHAL	PERORAL	RETINOL	SUBGOAL
DREIDEL	HANDFUL	MARTIAL	PERUSAL	RETRIAL	SUBORAL
DRYWALL	HANDSEL	MATINAL	PEYTRAL	REVISAL	SUBOVAL
DUTIFUL	*HARMFUL	*MAXIMAL	PEYTREL	REVIVAL	SUBSOIL
FACTUAL	*HATCHEL	*MAXWELL	PHRASAL	ROOMFUL	SUNDIAL
FALAFEL	HATEFUL	MEDICAL	PINBALL	*RORQUAL	SURREAL
FANTAIL	HATSFUL	MENTHOL	PINITOL	ROSINOL	SURVEIL
FATEFUL	HAVEREL	METICAL	PINTAIL	ROSTRAL	SUTURAL
FAUCIAL	HEEDFUL	MILFOIL	PIPEFUL	ROUNDEL	*SWAYFUL
FAUTEIL	HELICAL	MIMICAL	PITFALL	RUDERAL	SYNFUEL
FEARFUL	*HELPFUL	MINDFUL	PITIFUL	RUTHFUL	TACTFUL
FEDERAL	HEMATAL	MINERAL	PIVOTAL	*SACKFUL	TACTUAL
FELAFEL	HOBNAIL	MINIMAL	*PLAYFUL	SAHIWAL	TANKFUL
FEMORAL	HOLDALL	MISBILL	PLIMSOL	SATCHEL	TEABOWL
FIGURAL	*HOPEFUL	MISCALL	PLUVIAL	SAWBILL	TEARFUL

TEENFU L	*WAMEFU L	B LUEBE L L	CONEPAT L	DREADFU L	G LYCERO L
TENDRI L	WASSAI L	B LUEBI L L	*CONFOCA L	DREAMFU L	*G LYCERY L
TERTIA L	WASTRE L	B LUEGI L L	*CONJUGA L	DRUMRO L L	*G LYCOSY L
TETANA L	*WAXBI L L	*B L USHFU L	CONTRAI L	*DUCKBI L L	GNOMICA L
TEXTUA L	*WAYBI L L	BOASTFU L	CORNBA L L	*DUCKTAI L	GOODWI L L
THEE L O L	WI L L FU L	BOATBI L L	CORNMEA L	*DUMBBE L L	GOOFBA L L
THERMA L	*WISHFU L	BONEMEA L	CORPORA L	*FAITHFU L	GOSSYPO L
THERME L	WISTFU L	BONSPE L L	CORRIVA L	FA L DERA L	GRACEFU L
*THIAZO L	*XY L ITO L	BONSPIE L	CORTISO L	FA L DERO L	GRATEFU L
THIONY L	*ZESTFU L	*BRACHIA L	COSMICA L	FAMI L IA L	GRAYMAI L
TIERCE L	*BACKFI L L	BRANTAI L	COVERA L L	*FANCIFU L	GROMWE L L
TIMBRE L	*BACKHAU L	*BRIMFU L L	*CRACKNE L	*FARCICA L	GUAIACO L
TINFOI L	BA L MORA L	BROCATE L	CRIMINA L	FAREWE L L	GUI L EFU L
TISSUA L	BANDERO L	*BUCKTAI L	CU L TURA L	FARNESO L	GUMBOTI L
TOENAI L	BANGTAI L	*CACOMIX L	CUSPIDA L	FASTBA L L	GUNMETA L
TOI L FU L	BANKRO L L	CA L ENDA L	*CYC L ICA L	FEASTFU L	GUTTURA L
TOMFOO L	BANNERO L	*CA LYCEA L	*CYC L ITO L	FESTIVA L	GYROIDA L
TOPFU L L	BARBICE L	CANNIBA L	*DAFFODI L	FIDUCIA L	HABITUA L
TOPSAI L	BARBITA L	CANTONA L	DEADFA L L	FIREBA L L	HAEMATA L
TOPSOI L	BARONIA L	*CARBARY L	*DEATHFU L	FIREHA L L	HAIRBA L L
*TOXICA L	BARSTOO L	CARBINO L	DECRETA L	*FISHBOW L	HANDBA L L
TRAME L L	BASEBA L L	*CARBONY L	DEFERRA L	*FISHMEA L	HANDBE L L
TRAMME L	BASINFU L	*CARBOXY L	DEIFICA L	FISHTAI L	HANDBI L L
TRAVAI L	*BASOPHI L	CARDINA L	DEMERSA L	F LAVONO L	HANDRAI L
TRAYFU L	BEADRO L L	CARNIVA L	DEMURRA L	*F LYWHEE L	*HANDSFU L
TREFOI L	BEANBA L L	CAROUSA L	DEPRIVA L	FO L DERO L	HANGNAI L
TRENAI L	*BECHAME L	CAROUSE L	DETASSE L	FONTANE L	*HAPTICA L
TRESSE L	BECUDGE L	CARRYA L L	DEVERBA L	FOOTBA L L	HARDBA L L
TRIVIA L	BEDRIVE L	CASCABE L	DIACETY L	FOOTFA L L	HAREBE L L
TROCHA L	BE L L PU L L	*CATCHA L L	DIACONA L	FOOTHI L L	HASTEFU L
TROCHI L	*BE L LYFU L	*CATECHO L	DIAGONA L	FOOTWA L L	*HAWKBI L L
TROMME L	BERASCA L	CEREBRA L	DICROTA L	FORBIDA L	HEADSAI L
TRUNNE L	BESTOWA L	*CERVICA L	*DIDACTY L	*FORCEFU L	*HECTICA L
TRYSAI L	BETRAYA L	CESSPOO L	DIHEDRA L	FOREFEE L	HEE L BA L L
TUMBRE L	*BIACETY L	*CHARCOA L	DI L UVIA L	FORESAI L	HE L IACA L
TUMBRI L	BIANNUA L	*CHEEKFU L	*DIMETHY L	FORESTA L	HEMOCOE L
TUNEFU L	BICAUDA L	*CHEERFU L	DIPTERA L	FORETE L L	HEROICA L
TURMOI L	BIDENTA L	*CHEMICA L	DISANNU L	*FORKBA L L	HIBERNA L
TWIBI L L	BIENNIA L	*CHESTFU L	DISHEVE L	*FORKSFU L	*HIGHBA L L
TYPICA L	*BIFACIA L	*CHOCKFU L	DIS LOYA L	FREEWI L L	*HIGHTAI L
VANPOO L	BI L ABIA L	*CINNAMY L	DISPOSA L	FRUITFU L	*HONEYFU L
VATICA L	BIMANUA L	C LERICA L	DIVIDUA L	FUNEREA L	HORNBI L L
VEGETA L	BIMENSA L	C LODPO L L	DOCTORA L	FURFURA L	HORNTAI L
VENTAI L	*BIMETHY L	*C L UBHAU L	DOGGERE L	GA L ANGA L	HOSPITA L
VENTRA L	BINAURA L	COATTAI L	DOORBE L L	GANG L IA L	HOUSEFU L
VERMEI L	BINOMIA L	*COCKBI L L	DOORNAI L	GERANIA L	*HUMORFU L
VICINA L	BIOTICA L	*COCKERE L	DOORSI L L	GERANIO L	*HYDROGE L
VICTUA L	*BIPHENY L	*COCKTAI L	DOTTERE L	GERMINA L	*HYDROME L
VIRTUA L	BIRACIA L	*COGWHEE L	DOUBTFU L	GESTICA L	*HYDROSO L
VITRIO L	BIRADIA L	COISTRE L	DOVETAI L	GESTURA L	*HYDROXY L
WADMAA L	BIRDCA L L	COISTRI L	*DOWNFA L L	*GHASTFU L	*HYMENEA L
WADMO L L	*BISEXUA L	CO L ONIA L	*DOWNHAU L	GI L DHA L L	*HYPERGO L
WAGTAI L	*B LAMEFU L	CO L ORFU L	*DOWNHI L L	G LASSFU L	*HYPOGEA L
WAI L FU L	*B LOWBA L L	CO L OSSA L	DOWSABE L	G LOOMFU L	*JACKRO L L
*WAKEFU L	B LUEBA L L	COMMUNA L			*JARGONE L

*JUDICIA L	MOONSAI L	PEDESTA L	RAINFA L L	SI L VICA L	SURROYA L
*KEE L HAU L	*MOORFOW L	PE L L ETA L	*RAKEHE L L	SIPHONA L	SURVIVA L
*KICKBA L L	*MOTHBA L L	PE L LME L L	RASORIA L	*SKI L L FU L	TAB L EFU L
L ACRIMA L	MOTIONA L	PENONCE L	RATIONA L	S L OTHFU L	TAFFARE L
L AD L EFU L	MOURNFU L	PENTANO L	REASSAI L	SNEERFU L	TAFFERE L
*L AMBKI L L	*MOUTHFU L	PERONEA L	REBURIA L	SNOWBA L L	TAFFRAI L
L ANDFA L L	MUSCADE L	PERSONA L	REBUTTA L	SNOWBE L L	TAFFRAI L
L ANDFI L L	MUSCATE L	PETRONE L	REENRO L L	SNOWFA L L	TASTEFU L
L ENTICE L	*MYSTICA L	PETROSA L	REFERRA L	SOFTBA L L	TEETOTA L
*L IGHTFU L	*MYTHICA L	PHENETO L	REMEDIA L	SOMEDEA L	TEGMINA L
L INA L OO L	*NAPHTHO L	*PHI L OME L	REMITTA L	SORBITO L	TEMPORA L
L ITHOSO L	*NAPHTHY L	*PHYSICA L	REPRISA L	SOURBA L L	TERMINA L
L ITTORA L	NATIONA L	*PICKADI L	REPROVA L	SPADEFU L	TERPINO L
L OATHFU L	NAUTICA L	*PICKERE L	*REQUITA L	SPANDRE L	*TEXTURA L
L UBRICA L	NEWSREE L	*PINWHEE L	RESCHOO L	SPANDRI L	*THANKFU L
*MACKERE L	NITROSY L	P LANOSO L	RESIDUA L	SPECTRA L	THETICA L
MACRURA L	*NONEQUA L	P LATEFU L	RESTORA L	SPITBA L L	TRAGICA L
MADRIGA L	NONFINA L	*P LAYBI L L	REVERSA L	SPITEFU L	TRAINFU L
MAINSAI L	NONFOCA L	P LAYGIR L	REVIEWA L	SP L ENIA L	*TRANQUI L
MANDRI L L	NONGATA L	P L IMSO L L	REGIONA L	SPOONFU L	TRAPBA L L
MANGONE L	NONIDEA L	POETICA L	*RHEOPHI L	SPORTFU L	TREENAI L
MANNITO L	NON L EGA L	PONYTAI L	*RIGHTFU L	SPRINGA L	*TRIAXIA L
MANURIA L	NON L OCA L	POO L HA L L	RINGTAI L	SPURGA L L	TRIBUNA L
MARGINA L	NONMETA L	POSTANA L	ROADKI L L	*SQUIRRE L	TRIETHY L
MARSHA L L	NONMODA L	POSTOPA L	*ROCKFA L L	STAGEFU L	TRIFOCA L
MATERIA L	NONMORA L	POSTURA L	ROTOTI L L	STAUNRE L	TRIGONA L
MATERIE L	NONNAVA L	*POWERFU L	RUSTICA L	STAYSAI L	TRI L OBA L
MATERNA L	NONNOVE L	PRAEDIA L	*SACKSFU L	STERICA L	TRINODA L
MEATBA L L	NONPAPA L	PRANDIA L	SAGITTA L	*STICKFU L	TRIPEDA L
MEDIEVA L	NONRIVA L	PRATFA L L	SANTA L O L	STOMATA L	TRISTFU L
MEGADEA L	NONROYA L	*PREAXIA L	SAPROPE L	STREUSE L	TROOPIA L
MEMORIA L	NONRURA L	PREBASA L	SCENICA L	STRONGY L	TROUPIA L
MENSEFU L	NONTIDA L	*PRECHI L L	SCEPTRA L	STUNSAI L	*TRUCKFU L
MENSURA L	NONTONA L	PREDRI L L	*SCOOPFU L	*SUBAXIA L	*TRUNKFU L
*MERCIFU L	NONVIRA L	*PREFIXA L	SCORNFU L	SUBDURA L	TRUSTFU L
*MESOPHY L	NONVOCA L	PRE L EGA L	SCRANNE L	SUB L EVE L	TRUTHFU L
METHANO L	NOTARIA L	PREMORA L	SEASHE L L	SUBNASA L	TURBINA L
*METHOXY L	NOVERCA L	PRENATA L	SEASONA L	SUBNODA L	TURNHA L L
*METHY LA L	NUDICAU L	PRERENA L	SECTORA L	SUBPANE L	TURRICA L
METRICA L	NUMSKU L L	PRETRIA L	SE L FHEA L	SUBSHE L L	TUTORIA L
MI L L IGA L	NURTURA L	PRIDEFU L	SENSEFU L	SUBSKI L L	*TYMPANA L
MINSTRE L	NUTSHE L L	PRIMATA L	SENTINE L	SUBTOTA L	VARIETA L
MISENRO L	PA L ATIA L	*PRIMEVA L	SESSPOO L	SUBVIRA L	VAUNTFU L
MIS LABE L	PA L EOSO L	PROCURA L	*SHAMEFU L	*SUBVOCA L	VENEREA L
MISSPE L L	PANBROI L	PRODIGA L	SHEENFU L	*SUCCINY L	*VENGEFU L
MISTRIA L	PARA L L E L	PROPENO L	*SHE L FFU L	*SUFFIXA L	VERTICA L
MOISTFU L	PARENTA L	*PROPENY L	SH L EMIE L	SUICIDA L	VERTICI L
MO L EHI L L	*PARFOCA L	PROPOSA L	SHOEBI L L	SU L FINY L	VESPERA L
*MONACHA L	PARIETA L	PROTOCO L	SHOPGIR L	SU L FONA L	VESTURA L
MONAURA L	PASTORA L	PROUDFU L	*SHOWGIR L	SU L FONY L	VIATICA L
*MONAXIA L	PASTURA L	*PROXIMA L	SHRAPNE L	SU L FURY L	VICARIA L
MONOFUE L	PATAGIA L	*PUFFBA L L	SHRIEVA L	SUMMITA L	VIRGINA L
MONOHU L L	PATERNA L	PUNCTUA L	SIDEHI L L	SUPERNA L	VISCERA L
MONOMIA L	*PEACEFU L	*PUSHBA L L	SIDEREA L	SUPPOSA L	VISIONA L
MONORAI L	PECTORA L	*QUINIRA L	SIDEWA L L	SURGICA L	*VOICEFU L

WARRAGA L   *WATCHFU L   *WI LDFOW L   WOO LFEL L   *WRECKFU L
WARRIGA L   WEARIFU L   *WINDFA L L   *WORTHFU L   *WRONGFU L
*WASHBOW L   *WHIMBRE L   WINDGA L L   *WRACKFU L   *WROTHFU L
WASTEFU L   *WHIPTAI L   WINDMI L L   *WRATHFU L   *YOUTHFU L

M

MAAR	MEAL	MINK	MORN	MADRE	MARSH
MABE	MEAN	MINT	MORT	MAFIA	MARVY
MACE	MEAT	MINX	MOSK	MAFIC	MASER
MACH	MEED	MIRE	MOSS	MAGIC	MASHY
MACK	MEEK	MIRI	MOST	MAGMA	MASON
MADE	MEET	MIRK	MOTE	MAGOT	MASSA
MAGE	MELD	MIRY	MOTH	MAGUS	MASSE
MAGI	MELL	MISE	MOTT	MAHOE	MASSY
MAID	MELT	MISO	MOUE	MAILE	MATCH
MAIL	MEMO	MISS	MOVE	MAILL	MATER
MAIM	MEND	MIST	MOXA	MAIST	MATEY
MAIN	MENO	MITE	*MOZO	*MAIZE	MATIN
MAIR	MENU	MITT	MUCH	MAJOR	MATTE
MAKE	MEOW	MITY	MUCK	MAKAR	*MATZA
MAKO	MERE	MIXT	MUFF	MAKER	*MATZO
MALE	MERK	MOAN	MUGG	MALAR	MAUND
MALL	MERL	MOAT	MULE	MALIC	MAUVE
MALM	MESA	MOCK	MULL	MALMY	MAVEN
MALT	MESH	MODE	MUMM	MALTY	MAVIE
MAMA	MESS	MODI	MUMP	MAMBA	MAVIN
MANA	META	MOIL	MUMU	MAMBO	MAVIS
MANE	METE	MOJO	MUNI	MAMEY	*MAXIM
MANO	METH	MOKE	MUON	MAMIE	MAYBE
MANY	MEWL	MOLA	MURA	MAMMA	MAYOR
MARC	*MEZE	MOLD	MURE	MAMMY	MAYST
MARE	MICA	MOLE	MURK	MANGE	*MAZER
MARK	MICE	MOLL	MURR	MANGO	MBIRA
MARL	MICK	MOLT	MUSE	MANGY	MEALY
MART	MIDI	MOLY	MUSH	MANIA	MEANT
MASH	MIEN	MOME	MUSK	MANIC	MEANY
MASK	MIFF	MOMI	MUSS	MANLY	MEATY
MASS	MIGG	MONK	MUST	MANNA	MECCA
MAST	MIKE	MONO	MUTE	MANOR	MEDAL
MATE	MILD	MONS	MUTT	MANSE	MEDIA
MATH	MILE	MONY	MYNA	MANTA	MEDIC
MATT	MILK	MOOD	MYTH	MANUS	MEDII
MAUL	MILL	MOOL	MACAW	MAPLE	MEINY
MAUN	MILO	MOON	MACER	*MAQUI	MELEE
MAUT	MILT	MOOR	MACHO	MARCH	MELIC
MAXI	MIME	MOOT	MACLE	MARGE	MELON
MAYA	MINA	MOPE	MACON	MARIA	MENAD
*MAZE	MIND	MOPY	MACRO	MARLY	MENSA
*MAZY	MINE	MORA	MADAM	MARRY	MENSE
MEAD	MINI	MORE	MADLY	MARSE	MENTA

MERCY	MISSY	MOSSY	MUSSY	MALICE	MARGAY
MERGE	MISTY	MOSTE	MUSTH	MALIGN	MARGIN
MERIT	MITER	MOTEL	MUSTY	MALINE	MARINA
MERLE	MITIS	MOTET	MUTCH	MALKIN	MARINE
MERRY	MITRE	MOTEY	MUTER	MALLEE	MARISH
MESHY	MIXER	MOTHY	MUTON	MALLEI	MARKER
MESIC	*MIXUP	MOTIF	*MUZZY	MALLET	MARKET
MESNE	*MIZEN	MOTOR	MYNAH	MALLOW	*MARKKA
MESON	MOCHA	MOTTE	MYOID	MALOTI	MARKUP
MESSY	MODAL	MOTTO	MYOMA	MALTED	MARLIN
METAL	MODEL	MOUCH	MYOPE	MALTHA	MARMOT
METER	MODEM	MOULD	*MYOPY	MALTOL	MAROON
METIS	MODUS	MOULT	MYRRH	MAMLUK	*MARQUE
METRE	MOGGY	MOUND	MYSID	MAMMAL	MARRAM
METRO	MOGUL	MOUNT	*MYTHY	MAMMEE	MARRED
*MEZZO	MOHEL	MOURN	MACACO	MAMMER	MARRER
MIAOU	MOHUR	MOUSE	MACING	MAMMET	MARRON
MIAOW	MOIRA	MOUSY	MACKLE	*MAMMEY	MARROW
MIASM	MOIRE	MOUTH	MACRON	MAMMIE	MARSHY
MIAUL	MOIST	MOVED	MACULA	MAMMON	MARTEN
MICHE	MOLAL	MOVER	MACULE	MANAGE	MARTIN
MICRA	MOLAR	MOVIE	MADAME	MANANA	MARTYR
MICRO	MOLDY	MOWER	MADCAP	MANCHE	MARVEL
MIDDY	MOLLY	MOXIE	MADDED	MANEGE	MASCON
MIDGE	MOLTO	MUCID	MADDEN	MANFUL	MASCOT
MIDST	MOMMA	MUCIN	MADDER	MANGEL	MASHER
*MIFFY	MOMMY	*MUCKY	MADMAN	MANGER	MASHIE
MIGHT	MOMUS	MUCOR	MADRAS	MANGEY	*MASJID
MILCH	MONAD	MUCRO	MADURO	MANGLE	MASKEG
MILER	MONAS	MUCUS	MAENAD	MANIAC	MASKER
MILIA	MONDE	MUDDY	MAFFIA	MANILA	*MASQUE
MILKY	MONDO	MUDRA	MAFTIR	MANIOC	MASSIF
MILLE	MONEY	MUFTI	MAGGOT	MANITO	MASTER
MILPA	MONGO	MUGGY	MAGIAN	MANITU	MASTIC
MILTY	MONIE	MUHLY	MAGILP	MANNAN	*MASTIX
MIMEO	MONTE	*MUJIK	MAGLEV	MANNED	MATING
MIMER	MONTH	MULCH	MAGNET	MANNER	MATRES
MIMIC	MOOCH	MULCT	MAGNUM	*MANQUE	*MATRIX
MINAE	MOODY	MULEY	MAGPIE	MANTEL	MATRON
MINCE	MOOLA	MULLA	MAGUEY	MANTES	MATSAH
MINCY	MOONY	MUMMY	MAHOUT	MANTIC	MATTED
MINER	MOORY	MUNCH	*MAHZOR	MANTIS	MATTER
MINGY	MOOSE	MUNGO	MAIDEN	MANTLE	MATTIN
MINIM	MOPED	MURAL	MAIGRE	MANTRA	MATURE
MINKE	MOPER	MUREX	MAIHEM	MANTUA	*MATZAH
MINNY	MOPEY	MURID	MAILER	MANUAL	*MATZOH
MINOR	MORAL	MURKY	MAIMER	MANURE	*MATZOT
MINTY	MORAY	MURRA	MAINLY	MAPPED	MAUGER
MINUS	MOREL	MURRE	MAKEUP	MAPPER	MAUGRE
MIREX	MORON	MURRY	MAKING	*MAQUIS	MAULER
MIRKY	MORPH	MUSCA	MAKUTA	MARACA	MAUMET
MIRTH	MORRO	MUSER	MALADY	MARAUD	MAUNDY
*MIRZA	MORSE	MUSHY	MALATE	MARBLE	*MAXIMA
MISDO	MOSEY	MUSIC	MALFED	MARBLY	*MAXIXE
MISER	MOSSO	MUSKY	MALGRE	MARCEL	*MAYDAY

MAYEST	MENHIR	*MIKVAH	MISSAL	MONODY	MUCOSA
*MAYFLY	MENIAL	*MIKVEH	MISSAY	MONTES	MUCOSE
*MAYHAP	*MENINX	MILADI	MISSEL	MOOLAH	MUCOUS
*MAYHEM	MENSAL	MILADY	MISSET	MOOLEY	MUDCAP
MAYING	MENSCH	MILAGE	MISSIS	MOOTER	MUDCAT
*MAYPOP	MENTAL	MILDEN	MISSUS	MOPERY	MUDDER
MAYVIN	MENTOR	MILDEW	MISTER	MOPIER	MUDDLE
*MAZARD	MENTUM	MILIEU	MISUSE	MOPING	MUESLI
*MAZIER	MERCER	MILIUM	MITHER	MOPISH	MUFFIN
*MAZILY	MERGER	MILKER	MITIER	MOPOKE	MUFFLE
*MAZING	MERINO	MILLER	MITRAL	MOPPED	MUGFUL
*MAZUMA	MERLIN	MILLET	MITTEN	MOPPER	MUGGAR
MEADOW	MERLON	MILNEB	*MIZZEN	MOPPET	MUGGED
MEAGER	MERLOT	MILORD	*MIZZLE	MORALE	MUGGEE
MEAGRE	MERMAN	MILTER	*MIZZLY	MORALS	MUGGER
MEALIE	MESCAL	MIMBAR	MOANER	MORASS	MUGGUR
MEANER	MESIAL	MIMING	MOBBER	MORBID	*MUKLUK
MEANIE	MESIAN	MIMOSA	MOBCAP	MOREEN	*MUKTUK
MEANLY	MESSAN	MINCER	MOBILE	MORGAN	MULETA
MEASLE	MESTEE	MINDER	MOBLED	MORGEN	MULING
MEASLY	METAGE	MINGLE	MOCKER	MORGUE	MULISH
MEATUS	METATE	MINIFY	*MOCKUP	MORION	MULLAH
MEDAKA	METEOR	MINIMA	MODERN	MOROSE	MULLEN
MEDDLE	METEPA	MINING	MODEST	MORPHO	MULLER
*MEDFLY	METHOD	MINION	*MODIFY	MORRIS	MULLET
MEDIAD	METHYL	MINISH	MODISH	MORROW	MULLEY
MEDIAL	METIER	MINIUM	MODIST	MORSEL	MUMBLE
MEDIAN	METING	MINNOW	MODULE	MORTAL	*MUMBLY
*MEDICK	METOPE	MINTER	MODULO	MORTAR	MUMMED
MEDICO	METRIC	MINUET	MOGGIE	MORULA	MUMMER
MEDINA	METTLE	MINUTE	MOHAIR	MOSAIC	MUMPER
MEDIUM	METUMP	MINYAN	MOIETY	MOSHAV	MUNTIN
MEDLAR	MEWLER	MIOLER	MOLDER	*MOSQUE	MURDER
MEDLEY	*MEZCAL	MIOSIS	MOLEST	MOSSER	MUREIN
MEDUSA	*MEZUZA	MIOTIC	MOLIES	MOSTLY	MURINE
MEETER	MIASMA	MIRAGE	MOLINE	MOTHER	MURING
MEETLY	MICELL	MIRIER	MOI LAH	MOTILE	MURMUR
MEGASS	*MICKEY	MIRING	MOLLIE	MOTION	*MURPHY
MEGILP	MICKLE	MIRROR	MOLOCH	MOTIVE	MURREY
MEGOHM	MICRON	MISACT	MOLTEN	MOTLEY	MURRHA
MEGRIM	MIDAIR	MISADD	MOLTER	MOTMOT	MUSCAT
MEIKLE	MIDDAY	MISAIM	MOMENT	MOTTLE	MUSCID
MEINIE	MIDDEN	MISATE	MOMISM	*MOUJIK	MUSCLE
MELDER	MIDDLE	MISCUE	MOMSER	MOULDY	MUSCLY
MELLOW	MIDGET	MISCUT	*MOMZER	MOULIN	MUSEUM
MELODY	MIDGUT	MISEAT	MONGER	MOUSER	MUSHER
MELOID	MIDLEG	MISERY	MONGOE	MOUSEY	MUSING
MELTER	MIDRIB	MISFIT	MONGOL	MOUSSE	*MUSJID
MELTON	*MIDWAY	MISHAP	MONGST	MOUTHY	MUSKEG
MEMBER	MIGGLE	MISHIT	MONIED	MOUTON	MUSKET
MEMOIR	*MIGHTY	MISKAL	MONIES	MOVING	MUSKIE
MEMORY	MIGNON	MISLAY	MONISH	MUCKER	MUSKIT
MENACE	MIHRAB	MISLIE	MONISM	MUCKLE	MUSLIN
MENAGE	MIKADO	MISLIT	MONIST	MUCLUC	MUSSEL
MENDER	MIKRON	MISPEN	*MONKEY	MUCOID	MUSTEE

MUSTER	MADWORT	MANGIER	MARMITE	*MAYWEED	MESALLY
MUTANT	*MADZOON	MANGILY	MARPLOT	*MAZIEST	MESARCH
MUTASE	MAESTRO	MANGLER	*MARQUEE	*MAZURKA	MESEEMS
MUTATE	*MAFFICK	MANGOLD	*MARQUIS	*MAZZARD	MESHIER
MUTEST	MAFIOSO	MANHOLE	MARRANO	MEALIER	MESHUGA
MUTINE	MAGENTA	MANHOOD	MARRIED	MEANDER	*MESQUIT
MUTING	MAGICAL	MANHUNT	MARRIER	MEANIES	MESSAGE
MUTINY	MAGNATE	MANIHOT	MARRIES	MEANING	MESSIAH
MUTISM	MAGNETO	MANIKIN	MARRING	MEASURE	MESSIER
MUTTER	*MAGNIFY	MANILLA	*MARROWY	MEATIER	MESSILY
MUTTON	MAHATMA	MANILLE	MARSALA	MEATLY	MESSMAN
MUTUAL	*MAHJONG	MANIOCA	MARSHAL	MEATMAN	MESTESO
MUTUEL	MAHONIA	MANIPLE	MARTIAL	MEDDLER	MESTINO
MUTULE	MAHUANG	MANITOU	MARTIAN	*MEDEVAC	*MESTIZA
MUUMUU	MAILBAG	MANKIND	MARTINI	*MEDIACY	*MESTIZO
*MUZHIK	*MAILBOX	MANLESS	MARTLET	MEDIANT	METAMER
*MUZJIK	MAILING	MANLIKE	*MARTYRY	MEDIATE	METHANE
*MUZZLE	MAILLOT	MANMADE	MASCARA	MEDICAL	*METHOXY
MYASIS	MAILMAN	MANNING	MASKING	MEDULLA	METICAL
MYCELE	MAINTOP	MANNISH	MASONIC	MEDUSAN	METISSE
MYELIN	*MAJAGUA	MANNITE	MASONRY	MEERKAT	METONYM
MYOPIA	*MAJESTY	MANNOSE	*MASQUER	MEETING	METOPIC
MYOSIN	*MAJORAM	*MANPACK	MASSAGE	MEGABAR	METOPON
MYOSIS	*MAJORLY	MANROPE	MASSEUR	MEGABIT	*METRIFY
MYOTIC	MALACCA	MANSARD	MASSIER	MEGAHIT	METRING
MYRIAD	MALAISE	MANSION	MASSIVE	MEGAPOD	METRIST
MYRICA	MALANGA	MANTEAU	MASTABA	MEGASSE	*MEZQUIT
MYRTLE	MALARIA	MANTLET	MASTERY	MEGATON	*MEZUZAH
MYSELF	*MALARKY	MANTRAP	*MASTIFF	*MEGILPH	MICELLA
MYSOST	MALEATE	MANUARY	MASTOID	MEIOSIS	MICELLE
MYSTIC	MALEFIC	MANUMIT	MATADOR	MELAMED	*MICRIFY
*MYTHIC	MALISON	MANURER	MATCHER	MELANGE	MICROBE
MYTHOS	MALLARD	MANWARD	*MATCHUP	MELANIC	*MICROHM
*MYXOID	MALLEUS	MANWISE	MATELOT	MELANIN	MIDCULT
*MYXOMA	MALMSEY	*MAPLIKE	MATILDA	MELILOT	MIDDIES
MACABER	MALODOR	MAPPING	MATINAL	MELISMA	MIDDLER
MACABRE	MALTASE	MARABOU	MATINEE	MELODIA	MIDIRON
MACADAM	MALTIER	MARANTA	MATLESS	MELODIC	MIDLAND
*MACAQUE	MALTOSE	MARASCA	MATRASS	MELTAGE	MIDLIFE
*MACCHIA	*MAMMARY	MARBLER	MATTERY	MEMENTO	MIDLINE
MACHETE	MAMMATE	MARCATO	MATTING	MENACER	MIDMOST
MACHINE	MAMMIES	MARCHEN	*MATTOCK	*MENAZON	MIDNOON
MACHREE	*MAMMOCK	MARCHER	MATTOID	MENDIGO	MIDRASH
*MACHZOR	*MAMMOTH	MAREMMA	*MATZOON	MENDING	*MIDRIFF
MACRAME	MANACLE	MARENGO	*MATZOTH	*MENFOLK	*MIDSHIP
*MACUMBA	MANAGER	MARGENT	MAUDLIN	MENORAH	*MIDSIZE
MADDEST	MANAKIN	MARIMBA	MAUNDER	MENTHOL	MIDSOLE
MADDING	MANATEE	MARINER	*MAWKISH	MENTION	MIDTERM
MADDISH	MANCHET	MARITAL	*MAXILLA	MERCERY	MIDTOWN
MADEIRA	MANDALA	*MARKHOR	*MAXIMAL	MERCIES	*MIDWEEK
MADNESS	MANDATE	MARKING	*MAXIMIN	MERCURY	*MIDWIFE
MADONNA	MANDOLA	MARLIER	*MAXIMUM	MERGING	MIDYEAR
MADRONA	MANDREL	MARLINE	*MAXWELL	MERISIS	MIGRANT
MADRONE	MANDRIL	MARLING	*MAYBUSH	MERMAID	MIGRATE
MADRONO	*MANGABY	MARLITE	MAYPOLE	MEROPIA	*MILCHIG

*MILDEWY	MISCODE	MISTAKE	MONITOR	MOUILLE	MUNSTER
MILEAGE	MISCOIN	MISTBOW	*MONKERY	MOULAGE	MUNTING
MILFOIL	*MISCOOK	MISTEND	*MONKISH	MOULDER	*MUNTJAC
MILIARY	*MISCOPY	MISTERM	MONOCLE	MOULTER	*MUNTJAK
MILITIA	MISDATE	MISTEUK	MONOCOT	MOUNTER	MUONIUM
MILKIER	MISDEAL	MISTIER	MONOECY	MOURNER	MURIATE
*MILKILY	MISDEED	MISTILY	MONOFIL	MOUSIER	MURICES
*MILKMAN	MISDEEM	MISTIME	MONOLOG	MOUSILY	MURRAIN
*MILKSOP	MISDIAL	MISTOOK	MONOMER	MOUSING	MURRINE
MILLAGE	MISDOER	MISTRAL	MONSOON	MOUTHER	MURTHER
MILLDAM	MISDONE	MISTUNE	MONSTER	MOVABLE	MUSEFUL
MILLIER	MISDRAW	MISTYPE	MONTAGE	*MOVABLY	MUSETTE
MILLIME	MISEASE	MISUSER	MONTANE	MOVIOLA	MUSICAL
MILLINE	MISEDIT	MISWORD	MONTERO	*MOZETTA	MUSKIER
MILLING	MISERLY	*MISYOKE	*MONTHLY	*MUCKIER	*MUSKILY
MILLION	MISFILE	MITERER	MONURON	*MUCKILY	MUSKRAT
MILLRUN	MISFIRE	MITIEST	MOOCHER	MUDDIED	*MUSPIKE
MILREIS	MISFORM	MITOGEN	MOONBOW	MUDDIER	MUSTANG
MIMESIS	MISGIVE	MITOSIS	MOONEYE	MUDDIES	MUSTARD
MIMICAL	MISGROW	*MITSVAH	MOONIER	MUDDILY	MUTABLE
*MIMICRY	MISHEAR	*MITZVAH	MOONILY	MUDDING	MUTAGEN
MINABLE	*MISJOIN	*MIXTURE	MOONISH	MUDDLER	*MUZZIER
MINARET	*MISKEEP	MOANFUL	MOONLET	*MUDFISH	*MUZZILY
MINDFUL	*MISKICK	*MOBBISH	MOONLIT	MUDFLAT	*MUZZLER
MINDSET	*MISKNOW	MOBSTER	MOONSET	MUDHOLE	MYALGIA
MINERAL	MISLAIN	MOCHILA	MOORAGE	MUDLARK	MYCOSIS
MINGIER	MISLEAD	*MOCKERY	MOORHEN	*MUDPACK	MYELINE
MINGLER	MISLIKE	MODELER	MOORIER	*MUDROCK	MYELIOD
MINIBUS	MISLIVE	MODERNE	MOORING	MUDROOM	MYELOMA
MINICAB	*MISMAKE	MODESTY	MOORISH	MUDSILL	MYIASIS
MINICAR	*MISMARK	MODICUM	MOPIEST	MUEDDIN	*MYNHEER
MINIKIN	MISMATE	MODULAR	MOPPING	*MUEZZIN	*MYOLOGY
MINILAB	MISMEET	MODULUS	MORAINE	*MUFFLER	MYOSOTE
MINIMAL	MISMOVE	MOFETTE	MORCEAU	MUGGIER	MYOTOME
*MINIMAX	MISNAME	MOIDORE	MORDANT	MUGGILY	*MYSTERY
MINIMUM	MISPAGE	MOISTEN	MORDENT	MUGGING	*MYSTIFY
MINISKI	MISPART	MOISTLY	MORELLE	MUGGINS	MACARONI
MINIVAN	MISPLAN	*MOJARRA	MORELLO	MUGWORT	MACAROON
MINIVER	MISPLAY	MOLDIER	MORNING	*MUGWUMP	*MACCABAW
MINORCA	MISRATE	MOLDING	MOROCCO	MULATTO	*MACCABOY
MINSTER	MISREAD	MOLLIES	MORPHIA	MULLEIN	*MACCOBOY
MINTAGE	MISRELY	*MOLLIFY	*MORPHIC	MULLION	MACERATE
MINUEND	MISRULE	MOLLUSC	MORPHIN	MULLITE	*MACHISMO
MINUTIA	MISSEAT	MOMENTA	MORRION	*MULLOCK	*MACKEREL
MIRACLE	MISSEND	MOMENTO	MORTARY	MULLUSK	*MACKINAW
MIRADOR	MISSHOD	MONACID	MORTICE	MULTURE	MACRURAL
MIRIEST	MISSIES	MONADES	*MORTIFY	MUMBLER	MACRURAN
MISALLY	MISSILE	MONARCH	MORTISE	*MUMMERY	MACULATE
MISAVER	MISSION	MONARDA	MOSSIER	MUMMIED	MADHOUSE
MISBIAS	MISSIVE	*MONAXON	MOSTEST	MUMMIES	MADRIGAL
MISBILL	MISSORT	MONERAN	*MOTHERY	*MUMMIFY	*MADWOMAN
MISBIND	MISSOUT	MONEYED	MOTIVIC	MUMMING	MAESTOSO
MISCALL	MISSTEP	MONEYER	MOTORIC	MUNCHER	*MAGAZINE
MISCAST	MISSTOP	MONGREL	MOTTLER	MUNDANE	MAGICIAN
MISCITE	MISSUIT	MONIKER	MOUFLON	MUNNION	*MAGICKED

MAGISTER	MANDATOR	*MARKSMAN	*MAZAEDIA	MELANOUS	METALISE
MAGNESIA	MANDIBLE	MARLIEST	*MAZELIKE	MELILITE	METALIST
MAGNETIC	MANDIOCA	MARMOSET	*MAZINESS	MELINITE	*METALIZE
MAGNETON	MANDOLIN	MAROCAIN	*MAZOURKA	*MELLIFIC	METALLED
*MAGNIFIC	*MANDRAKE	*MARQUESS	MEALIEST	MELODEON	METALLIC
MAGNOLIA	MANDRILL	*MARQUISE	MEALLESS	MELODICA	METAMERE
*MAHARAJA	MANEUVER	MARRIAGE	MEALTIME	MELODIES	*METAPHOR
MAHARANI	*MANGABEY	MARSHALL	*MEALWORM	MELODISE	*METAZOAN
*MAHIMAHI	MANGANIC	MARSUPIA	*MEALYBUG	MELODIST	*METAZOON
*MAHJONGG	MANGIEST	MARTAGON	MEANNESS	*MELODIZE	METERAGE
*MAHOGANY	MANGONEL	MARTINET	MEANTIME	MELTDOWN	METHADON
*MAIDHOOD	MANGROVE	*MARTYRLY	MEASURER	MEMBRANE	METHANOL
MAIEUTIC	MANICURE	*MARYJANE	MEATBALL	MEMORIAL	*METHINKS
MAILLESS	MANIFEST	*MARZIPAN	MEATHEAD	MEMORISE	*METHODIC
MAINLAND	MANIFOLD	MASGACRE	MEATIEST	*MEMORIZE	*METHOXYL
MAINLINE	MANNERLY	*MASKLIKE	MEATLESS	*MEMSAHIB	*METHYLAL
MAINMAST	MANNIKIN	MASSAGER	MEATLOAF	*MENARCHE	METRICAL
MAINSAIL	MANNITOL	MASSCULT	*MECHANIC	*MENFOLKS	METRITIS
MAINSTAY	*MANPOWER	MASSEDLY	MECONIUM	MENHADEN	MEUNIERE
MAINTAIN	MANTELET	MASSETER	MEDALIST	MENIALLY	*MEZEREON
MAIOLICA	MANTILLA	MASSEUSE	MEDALLIC	MENISCUS	*MEZEREUM
*MAJESTIC	MANTISSA	MASSICOT	MEDIALLY	MENOLOGY	*MEZQUITE
*MAJOLICA	MANTLING	MASSIEST	MEDIANLY	MENSEFUL	*MICAWBER
*MAJORITY	MANUALLY	MASSLESS	MEDIATOR	MENSTRUA	MICROBAR
*MAKEBATE	MANUBRIA	*MASTABAH	MEDICAID	MENSURAL	MICROBUS
*MAKEFAST	MANURIAL	MASTERLY	MEDICARE	MENSWEAR	MICRODOT
*MAKEOVER	MANURING	MASTHEAD	MEDICATE	MENTHENE	*MICROLUX
*MAKIMONO	MANWARDS	*MASTICHE	MEDICINE	*MEPHITIS	*MICROMHO
MALAMUTE	*MANYFOLD	MASTITIS	MEDIEVAL	MERCAPTO	*MICRURGY
MALAPERT	*MAPMAKER	MASTLESS	MEDIOCRE	*MERCHANT	MIDBRAIN
MALAPROP	*MAPPABLE	MASTLIKE	MEDITATE	*MERCIFUL	MIDDLING
*MALARKEY	*MAQUETTE	MASTODON	MEDUSOID	MERENGUE	*MIDFIELD
MALAROMA	MARABOUT	MASURIUM	MEEKNESS	MERGENCE	*MIDMONTH
MALEDICT	MARASMUS	*MATCHBOX	MEETNESS	MERIDIAN	*MIDNIGHT
MALEMIUT	MARATHON	MATELESS	*MEGABTYE	MERINGUE	MIDPOINT
MALEMUTE	MARAUDER	MATELOTE	*MEGABUCK	MERISTEM	MIDRANGE
MALENESS	MARAVEDI	MATERIAL	*MEGACITY	MERISTIC	*MIDSHIPS
MALIGNER	MARBLING	MATERIEL	MEGADEAL	MESDAMES	*MIDSIZED
MALIGNLY	*MARCHESA	MATERNAL	MEGADOSE	MESHIEST	*MIDSPACE
MALIHINI	*MARCHESE	*MATESHIP	*MEGADYNE	*MESHUGAH	MIDSTORY
MALINGER	MARGARIC	MATINESS	MEGALITH	*MESHUGGA	*MIDWATCH
MALLEOLI	MARGARIN	MATTEDLY	MEGALOPS	*MESHUGGE	MIGNONNE
MALPOSED	MARGINAL	MATTRASS	MEGAPODE	*MESHWORK	MIGRAINE
MALTIEST	MARGRAVE	MATTRESS	MEGASTAR	MESMERIC	MIGRATOR
MALTREAT	*MARIACHI	MATURATE	MEGAVOLT	MESNALTY	MILDNESS
MALTSTER	MARIGOLD	MATURITY	MEGAWATT	MESOCARP	MILEPOST
MALVASIA	MARINADE	*MAUMETRY	MEGILLAH	MESODERM	MILESIMO
MAMALIGA	MARINARA	MAUSOLEA	MELAMINE	MESOGLEA	MILIARIA
*MAMELUKE	MARINATE	*MAVERICK	MELANIAN	*MESOPHYL	MILITANT
MAMMATUS	MARIPOSA	*MAXICOAT	MELANISM	MESOSOME	MILITARY
MAMMILLA	MARITIME	*MAXIMISE	MELANIST	MESOTRON	MILITATE
MAMMITIS	*MARKDOWN	*MAXIMITE	MELANITE	*MESQUITE	*MILKFISH
MANCIPLE	*MARKEDLY	*MAXIMIZE	*MELANIZE	MESSIEST	MILKIEST
MANDAMUS	MARKETER	*MAYAPPLE	MELANOID	MESSMATE	*MILKMAID
MANDARIN	*MARKHOOR	MAYORESS	MELANOMA	MESSUAGE	*MILKSHED

*MILKWEED	MISCIBLE	MISSENSE	MOISTURE	*MONOPOLY	MORTISER
*MILKWOOD	MISCLAIM	*MISSHAPE	MOLALITY	MONORAIL	MORTMAIN
*MILKWORT	MISCLASS	MISSILRY	MOLARITY	MONOSOME	MORTUARY
*MILLCAKE	MISCOLOR	MISSOUND	MOLASSES	*MONOSOMY	MOSASAUR
MILLEPED	MISCOUNT	MISSPACE	MOLDIEST	MONOTINT	*MOSCHATE
MILLIARD	MISDOING	*MISSPEAK	*MOLDWARP	MONOTONE	*MOSQUITO
MILLIARE	MISDOUBT	MISSPELL	MOLECULE	MONOTONY	*MOSSBACK
MILLIARY	MISDRIVE	MISSPEND	MOLEHILL	*MONOTYPE	MOSSIEST
MILLIBAR	MISENROL	*MISSPOKE	MOLESKIN	*MONOXIDE	MOSSLIKE
MILLIEME	MISENTER	MISSTART	MOLESTER	MONSIEUR	*MOTHBALL
MILLIGAL	MISENTRY	MISSTATE	*MOLYBDIC	MONSTERA	*MOTHERLY
*MILLILUX	MISERERE	MISSTEER	*MOMENTLY	MONTEITH	*MOTHLIKE
*MILLIMHO	MISEVENT	MISSTYLE	MOMENTUM	MONUMENT	MOTILITY
MILLINER	*MISFAITH	MISTAKER	*MONACHAL	MOONBEAM	MOTIONAL
*MILLIOHM	MISFIELD	*MISTEACH	MONADISM	*MOONCALF	MOTIONER
MILLIPED	*MISFOCUS	*MISTHINK	MONANDRY	MOONDUST	MOTIVATE
MILLIREM	*MISFRAME	*MISTHROW	*MONARCHY	*MOONFISH	*MOTIVITY
MILLPOND	MISGAUGE	MISTIEST	MONASTIC	MOONIEST	MOTORBUS
MILLRACE	MISGRADE	MISTITLE	MONAURAL	MOONLESS	MOTORCAR
*MILLWORK	MISGRAFT	*MISTOUCH	*MONAXIAL	MOONLIKE	MOTORDOM
MIMETITE	MISGUESS	MISTRACE	*MONAZITE	MOONPORT	MOTORING
*MIMICKER	MISGUIDE	MISTRAIN	MONECIAN	MOONRISE	MOTORISE
*MINACITY	*MISHMASH	MISTREAT	MONELLIN	MOONSAIL	MOTORIST
MINATORY	*MISHMOSH	MISTRESS	MONETARY	MOONSEED	*MOTORIZE
MINDLESS	MISINFER	MISTRIAL	MONETISE	MOONSHOT	MOTORMAN
MINEABLE	MISINTER	MISTRUST	*MONETIZE	*MOONWALK	*MOTORWAY
MINGIEST	*MISJUDGE	MISTRYST	*MONEYBAG	MOONWARD	*MOUCHOIR
*MINIBIKE	MISLABEL	MISTUTOR	*MONEYMAN	MOONWORT	*MOUFFLON
*MINICAMP	MISLAYER	MISUNION	MONGEESE	*MOORCOCK	MOULDING
MINIMISE	MISLEARN	MISUSAGE	MONGOOSE	*MOORFOWL	MOUNTAIN
*MINIMIZE	MISLIGHT	MISVALUE	*MONICKER	MOORIEST	MOUNTING
*MINIPARK	MISLIKER	MISWRITE	MONITION	MOORLAND	MOURNFUL
MINISTER	MISLODGE	MITICIDE	MONITIVE	MOORWORT	MOURNING
MINISTRY	MISLYING	MITIGATE	MONITORY	*MOPBOARD	MOUSIEST
MINORITY	*MISMATCH	MITTIMUS	*MONKFISH	*MOPINGLY	MOUSSAKA
MINSTREL	MISNOMER	*MIXOLOGY	*MONKHOOD	*MOQUETTE	*MOUTHFUL
MINUTING	*MISOGAMY	MNEMONIC	MONOACID	MORALISE	*MOVEABLE
*MIQUELET	*MISOGYNY	MOATLIKE	MONOCARP	MORALISM	*MOVEABLY
MIRINESS	MISOLOGY	MOBILISE	MONOCRAT	MORALIST	MOVELESS
MIRLITON	MISORDER	*MOBILITY	*MONOCYTE	MORALITY	*MOVEMENT
MISADAPT	MISPAINT	*MOBILIZE	MONODIST	*MORALIZE	*MOVIEDOM
MISAGENT	MISPARSE	MOBOCRAT	MONOFUEL	MORATORY	MOVIEOLA
MISALIGN	*MISPATCH	MOCCASIN	*MONOGAMY	*MORBIFIC	*MOVINGLY
MISALTER	MISPLACE	MODALITY	MONOGENY	MORBILLI	*MOZZETTA
MISANDRY	MISPLANT	MODELING	MONOGERM	*MORDANCY	MRIDANGA
*MISAPPLY	MISPLEAD	MODELIST	MONOGLOT	MOREOVER	*MUCHACHO
MISASSAY	MISPOINT	MODELLED	MONOGRAM	*MORESQUE	*MUCHNESS
MISATONE	MISPOISE	MODELLER	*MONOGYNY	MORIBUND	*MUCIDITY
MISAWARD	MISPRINT	MODERATE	MONOHULL	MORONISM	MUCILAGE
MISBEGIN	*MISPRIZE	MODERATO	MONOLITH	MORONITY	*MUCKIEST
MISBEGOT	*MISQUOTE	MODIFIER	MONOLOGY	MOROSITY	*MUCKLUCK
MISBRAND	MISRAISE	MODIOLUS	MONOMIAL	*MORPHEME	*MUCKRAKE
MISBUILD	MISREFER	MODULATE	MONOPODE	*MORPHINE	*MUCKWORM
*MISCARRY	MISROUTE	*MOFFETTE	*MONOPODY	MORTALLY	*MUCOSITY
*MISCHIEF	MISSABLE	MOISTFUL	MONOPOLE	MORTGAGE	MUDDIEST

MUDGUARD	MUTTERER	S M ARTASS	CO M M IE	FA M ISH	HU M M ER
*MUDPUPPY	*MUZZIEST	S M ECTITE	CO M M IT	FA M OUS	HU M M US
MUDSLIDE	*MYCELIUM	S M ITHERS	*CO M M IX	FE M ALE	HU M OUR
MUDSTONE	*MYCETOMA	TE M P	CO M M ON	FI M BLE	HU M VEE
MUENSTER	*MYCOLOGY	WI M P	CO M OSE	FO M ENT	HY M NAL
MUGGIEST	MYELITIS	BU M PH	CO M OUS	FU M BLE	*JA M M ED
*MULBERRY	MYLONITE	*CO M IX	CO M PEL	FU M IER	*JA M M ER
MULETEER	*MYOBLAST	GA M AY	*CO M PLY	FU M ING	*JI M INY
MULLIGAN	*MYOGENIC	GA M MY	CU M BER	GA M BIA	*JU M BAL
MULTIAGE	*MYOGRAPH	GI M M E	CU M M ER	GA M BIR	*JU M BLE
MULTICAR	*MYOPATHY	*HA M ZA	CU M M IN	GA M BIT	*JU M PER
MULTIFID	*MYOSCOPE	*JA M M Y	CY M DAL	GA M BLE	KA M ALA
*MULTIJET	MYOSITIS	LA M BY	CY M ENE	GA M BOL	KA M SIN
MULTIPED	MYOSOTIS	LI M PA	CY M LIN	GA M ELY	*KI M CHI
MULTIPLE	MYOTONIA	M I M EO	CY M OID	GA M EST	KI M ONO
*MULTIPLY	*MYRIAPOD	RO M EO	CY M OSE	GA M ETE	KU M ISS
MULTITON	*MYRIOPOD	*WI M PY	CY M OUS	GA M IER	KU M M EL
MULTIUSE	*MYRMIDON	BE M ATA	DA M AGE	GA M ILY	LA M BDA
*MUNCHIES	*MYSTAGOG	BE M EAN	DA M ASK	GA M INE	LA M BIE
*MUNCHKIN	*MYSTICAL	BE M IRE	DA M M ED	GA M ING	LA M EDH
MUNDUNGO	*MYSTICLY	BE M IST	DA M M ER	GA M M ED	LA M ELY
MUNGOOSE	*MYSTIQUE	BE M OAN	DA M NER	GA M M ER	LA M ENT
MUNIMENT	*MYTHICAL	*BE M OCK	DA M PEN	GA M M ON	LA M EST
MUNITION	*MYXEDEMA	BE M USE	DA M PER	GE M M ED	LA M INA
MURAENID	*MYXOCYTE	BOMBER	DA M PLY	GE M OTE	LA M ING
MURALIST		*BO M BAX	DA M SEL	GI M BAL	LA M M ED
MURDEREE	S M EW	*BO M BYX	DA M SON	GI M LET	LA M PAD
MURDERER	S M OG	BU M BLE	DE M AND	GI M M AL	LA M PAS
MURIATED	S M UG	BU M KIN	DE M ARK	GI M M IE	LI M BUS
MURICATE	S M UT	BU M M ER	DE M AST	GO M UTI	LI M HER
MURMURER	S M ACK	BU M MED	DE M EAN	GU M M ED	LI M IER
MURRELET	S M ALL	BU M PER	DE M ENT	GU M M ER	LI M INA
MUSCADEL	S M ALT	CA M AIL	DE M IES	HA M ATE	LI M ING
MUSCADET	S M ARM	CA M ASS	DE M ISE	HA M LET	LI M M ER
MUSCATEL	S M ART	CA M BIA	DE M ODE	HA M M AL	LI M M IC
MUSCULAR	S M ASH	CA M DER	DE M OTE	HA M M ED	LI M NER
*MUSHROOM	*S M AZE	CA M ERA	DE M URE	HA M M ER	LI M NIC
MUSICALE	S M EAR	CA M ION	DI M ING	HA M PER	LI M PER
MUSICLAN	S M EEK	CA M ISA	DI M ITY	HE M M ED	LI M PET
MUSINGLY	S M ELL	CA M ISE	DI M M ED	HE M M ER	LI M PID
*MUSKETRY	S M ELT	CA M LET	DI M M ER	HE M PIE	LI M PLY
MUSKIEST	S M ERK	CA M PER	DI M OUT	HO M AGE	LI M PSY
*MUSQUASH	S M ILE	CA M PUS	DI M PLE	HO M BRE	LO M EIN
*MUSTACHE	S M IRK	CE M ENT	DI M PLY	HO M ELY	LO M ENT
MUSTARDY	S M ITE	CO M AKE	DI M WIT	HO M IER	LU M BAR
MUTATION	S M ITH	CO M ATE	DO M AIN	HO M ILY	LU M HER
*MUTCHKIN	S M OCK	CO M BAT	DO M INE	HO M ING	*LU M M OX
MUTENESS	S M OKE	CO M DER	DO M ING	HO M INY	LU M PEN
MUTICOUS	S M OKY	CO M EDO	DO M INO	HU M ANE	LU M PER
MUTILATE	S M OLT	CO M EDY	DU M BLY	HU M ATE	*MA M M EY
MUTINEER	S M OTE	CO M ELY	DU M DU M	HU M BLE	M O M ISM
MUTINIED	S M IDGE	CO M ETH	DU M PER	*HU M BLY	M O M SER
MUTINIES	S M ILEY	CO M FIT	FA M ILY	HU M BUG	*M O M ZER
MUTINING	S M ILO M	CO M ING	FA M ING	HU M M ED	*M U M BLY
MUTINOUS	S M EDDU M	CO M ITY			NA M ELY

NA M ING	RE M OVE	SU M MON	BA M BINO	CO M PERE	FU M IEST
NI M BLE	RE M UDA	SY M BOL	BE M ADAM	CO M PETE	FU M ULUS
NI M BUS	RI M IER	TA M ALE	BI M ETAL	CO M PILE	GA M BADE
NI M MED	RI M ING	TA M ARI	BI M ODAL	*CO M PLEX	GA M BADO
NI M ROD	RI M MED	TA M BAC	BO M BARD	CO M PLIN	GA M BIER
NO M ISM	RI M MER	TA M BAK	BO M BAST	CO M PLOT	GA M BLER
NU M BAT	RI M OSE	TA M BUR	BO M BING	CO M PONE	GA M BOGE
NU M BER	RI M OUS	TA M ELY	BU M BLER	*CO M PONY	GA M BREL
NU M BLY	RI M PLE	TA M EST	BU M BOAT	CO M PORT	GA M ELAN
NU M INA	RO M ANO	TA M ING	BU M MEST	CO M POSE	GA M IEST
*NY M PHA	RO M PER	TA M MIE	BU M MING	CO M POST	GA M MIER
*NY M PHO	RU M AKI	TA M PAN	*BU M PKIN	CO M POTE	GA M MING
PA M PER	RU M BLE	TA M PER	CA M BIAL	CO M PUTE	GE M INAL
PI M PLE	RU M BLY	TA M PON	*CA M BISM	CU M ARIN	GE M LIKE
*PI M PLY	RU M EST	TE M PEH	CA M BIST	*CU M QUAT	GE M MATE
PO M ACE	RU M MER	TE M PER	*CA M BIUM	*CU M SHAW	GE M MIER
PO M ADE	RU M OUR	TE M PLE	*CA M BRIC	CU M ULUS	*GE M MILY
PO M ELO	RU M PLE	TI M BAL	CA M ELIA	*CY M LING	GE M MING
PO M MEE	RU M PLY	TI M BER	CA M ISIA	DA M AGER	GE M MULE
PO M MEL	RU M PUS	TI M BRE	CA M ORRA	DA M MING	*GE M SBOK
PO M POM	SA M ARA	TI M ELY	*CA M PHOL	DA M OSEL	*GI M MICK
PO M PON	SA M BAR	TI M ING	*CA M PHOR	*DA M OZEL	GI M PIER
PU M ELO	SA M BUR	TO M ATO	CA M PIER	DA M PING	GO M ERAL
PU M ICE	SA M ECH	TO M BAC	*CA M PILY	*DA M PISH	GO M EREL
PU M MEL	*SA M EKH	TO M BAK	CA M PING	DE M AGOG	GO M ERIL
PU M PER	SA M IEL	TO M BAL	CA M PION	DE M ERGE	GU M BOIL
RA M ATE	SA M ITE	TO M BOY	CA M PONG	DE M ERIT	GU M BOOT
RA M AUL	SA M LET	TO M CAT	CE M BALO	DE M ESNE	GU M DROP
RA M BLE	SA M OSA	TO M COD	*CO M AKER	DE M ETON	GU M LIKE
RA M IFY	SA M PAN	TO M MED	CO M ATIC	DE M IGOD	GU M MIER
*RA M JET	SA M PLE	TO M TIT	*CO M ATIK	DE M IREP	GU M MING
RA M MED	SA M SHU	TU M BLE	CO M BINE	DE M ONIC	GU M MITE
RA M MER	SE M EME	TU M EFY	CO M BUST	DE M OTIC	GU M MOSE
RA M OSE	SE M INA	TU M OUR	CO M EDIC	DE M OUNT	GU M MOUS
RA M OUS	SE M PLE	TU M ULI	CO M ETIC	DI M ERIC	GU M SHOE
RA M ROD	SE M PRE	TU M ULT	CO M FIER	DI M ETER	GU M TREE
RA M SON	SH M EAR	TY M BAL	CO M FORT	DI M MEST	GU M WEED
RA M TIL	*SH M UCK	TY M PAN	*CO M FREY	DI M NESS	GU M WOOD
RE M AIL	SI M IAN	VA M OSE	CO M ICAL	*DI M ORPH	GY M NAST
RE M AIN	SI M ILE	VA M PER	CO M ITIA	DO M ICAL	*HA M BURG
RE M AKE	SI M LIN	VO M ICA	CO M MAND	DO M ICIL	*HA M MADA
RE M AND	SI M MER	VO M ITO	CO M MEND	DO M INIE	HA M MIER
RE M ARK	SI M NEL	WA M BLE	CO M MENT	DU M PIER	*HA M MILY
RE M ATE	SI M ONY	*WA M BLY	CO M MIES	*DU M PILY	*HA M MING
RE M EDY	SI M OOM	WA M MUS	CO M MODE	DU M PING	*HA M MOCK
RE M EET	SI M OON	*WA M PUM	*CO M MOVE	*DU M PISH	HA M STER
RE M ELT	SI M PER	WA M PUS	CO M MUNE	FA M ULUS	HA M ULUS
RE M END	SI M PLE	WI M BLE	CO M MUTE	FE M INIE	HE M AGOG
RE M IND	SO M BER	WI M PLE	*CO M PACT	FE M ORAL	HE M ATAL
RE M INT	SO M BRE	WO M BAT	*CO M PANY	FI M BRIA	HE M ATIC
RE M ISE	SO M ITE	WO M ERA	CO M PARE	FU M ARIC	HE M ATIN
RE M ISS	SU M ACH	YA M MER	CO M PART	FU M BLER	HE M IOLA
RE M OLD	SU M MED	*ZO M BIE	CO M PASS	FU M BLER	HE M LINE
RE M ORA	SU M MER	*ZY M ASE	CO M PEER	FU M ETTE	*HE M LOCK
RE M OTE	SU M MIT		CO M PEND		

*HE M M ING	LE M URES	RA M PAGE	SO M EDAY	*TY M PANY	GI M PIEST
HE M PIER	LI M ACON	RA M PANT	*SO M EHOW	VA M OOSE	GU M M IEST
*HI M SELF	LI M BATE	RA M PART	SO M EONE	VA M PIRE	GU M M OSIS
HO M AGER	*LI M BECK	*RA M PIKE	*SO M EWAY	*VA M PISH	*HA M MERER
*HO M BURG	LI M BIER	RA M PION	SU M LESS	VO M ITER	*HA M M IEST
*HO M EBOY	LI M EADE	RA M POLE	SU M M AND	VO M IT'US	*HO M EOBOX
HO M IEST	LI M IEST	RE M AKER	SU M M ARY	*WA M EFOU	*HO M EOTIC
HO M INES	LI M INAL	RE M ARRY	SU M M ATE	*WA M EFUL	*HO M EPORT
HO M INID	LI M ITED	RE M ATCH	SU M M ERY	*WA M PISH	*HOMEROOM
*HO M MOCK	LI M ITER	RE M ERGE	SU M M ING	*WI M PISH	*HO M ESTAY
HO M OLOG	LI M ITES	RE M NANT	SU M M ONS	*WO M ANLY	*HO M INIZE
*HO M ONY M	*LI M PKIN	RE M ODEL	SU M PTER	WO M M ERA	*HU M ANIS M
*HO M OSEX	LI M PSEY	RE M ORSE	SY M BION	*YA M ALKA	*HUM MABLE
*HU M ANLY	LI M ULUS	RE M OUNT	SY M BIOT	*YA M ULKA	*HY M ENIU M
HU M BLER	LU M BAGO	RE M OVAL	*SY M PTO M	*ZA M ARRA	*KY M OGRA M
*HU M DRU M	LU M PISH	RE M OVER	TA M ABLE	*ZA M ARRO	LA M BIEST
HU M ERAL	*MAM MARY	RI M FIRE	TA M ANDU	*ZE M STVO	LE M URINE
HU M ERUS	*MAM MOCK	RI M IEST	TA M ARAO	*ZO M BIFY	LO M ENTU M
*HU M IDLY	*MAM MOTH	RI M LAND	TA M ARAU	*ZY M OGEN	MA M ALIGA
HU M IDOR	*M I M ICRY	RI M LESS	TA M ARIN	*ZY M OSAN	MA M MATUS
*HU M M ING	*MUM MERY	*RI M M ING	TA M ASHA	*ZY M OSIS	MA M M ILLA
*HU M MOCK	*MUM MIFY	*RI M ROCK	TA M BALA	*ZY M URGY	MA M M ITIS
HU M ORAL	NA M ETAG	RO M AINE	TA M BOUR	BO M BESIN	M E M BRANE
*HY M NARY	NE M ATIC	RO M ANCE	TA M BURA	CE M ENTU M	M E M ORIAL
*HY M NIST	NE M ESIS	RO M AUNT	TA M PALA	*CI M BALO M	M E M ORISE
*HY M NODY	NI M IETY	RO M PISH	TA M PION	CO M ANAGE	M I M ETITE
*JA M BEAU	NI M M ING	RU M BLER	TE M BLOR	*CO M EMBER	MO M ENTU M
*JA M M IES	NO M ARCH	RU M M AGE	TE M PERA	CO M INGLE	NO M ADIS M
*JA M M IST	NO M BLES	SA M BHAR	TE M PEST	*COM MANDO	NO M OGRA M
*JE M ADAR	NO M BRIL	SA M BHUR	TE M PLAR	*COM MENCE	*NU M ERACY
*JE M IDAR	NO M INAL	SA M BUCA	TE M PLET	*COM MERCE	NU M M ULAR
*JI M JA M S	NO M INEE	*SA M BUKE	TE M PTER	CO M M ONER	*PE M M ICAN
*JI M M INY	NU M ERAL	SA M ISEN	TE M PURA	*COM MONLY	RA M ENTU M
*JU M BLER	NU M ERIC	SA M OVAR	TI M ARAU	CO M M UNAL	*RA M IFOR M
*JU M BUCK	NU M M ARY	SA M PLER	TI M BALE	*CY M ATIU M	RA M M IEST
*JU M POFF	*NY M PHET	SA M SARA	TI M BREL	*CY M BALO M	RE M ARKET
*KA M PONG	PA M PEAN	SA M URAI	TI M EOUS	*CY M BIDIA	RE M ASTER
KA M SEEN	PA M PERO	SE M ATIC	TI M EOUT	DE M ERARA	RI M INESS
*KI M CHEE	PE M BINA	SE M IDRY	TI M OLOL	DE M ERGER	RO M ANISE
*KO M ATIK	PE M ICAN	SE M IFIT	TI M PANO	DE M ERSAL	RU M MAGER
*KU M QUAT	*PE M PHIX	SE M ILOG	*TI M OTHY	DE M ONIS M	SA M ARIU M
LA M BAST	PI M ENTO	SE M I M AT	*TO M BACK	DI M ERIS M	*SA M IZDAT
LA M BENT	PO M ATU M	SE M INAL	TO M BOLO	*DI M MABLE	SA M PLIS M
LA M BERT	PO M FRET	SE M INAR	TO M FOOL	DO M INIU M	*SH M ALTZY
LA M BIER	PO M PANO	SE M IPRO	TO M M ING	*DU M BCANE	SI M PLIST
*LA M BKIN	PO M POUS	SE M IRAW	TO M PION	*DU M BHEAD	SU M MABLE
LA M ELLA	PU M ICER	*SH M ALTZ	TU M BLER	*DU M MKOPF	*SU M M ERIY
LA M M ING	PU M M ELO	*SH M OOZE	TU M BREL	*FA M ILIS M	SU M M ITAL
LA M PERS	*PU M PKIN	SI M ILAR	TU M BRIL	*FE M INIS M	*SU M M ITRY
LA M PION	RA M BLER	SI M IOID	TU M M LER	GA M ESMAN	SU M M ONER
LA M POON	RA M EKIN	SI M IOUS	TU M ULAR	GA M MADIA	*SY M METRY
LA M PREY	RA M ILIE	SI M ITAR	TU M ULUS	GA M M IEST	*SY M PODIA
LA M STER	RA M M IER	*SI M PLEX	TY M PANA	GA M M ONER	*SY M POSIA
LE M M ING	RA M M ING	SI M ULAR	TY M PANI	GE M M IEST	TI M ELINE
LE M PIRA	RA M M ISH	*SI M M PLY	TY M PANO	*GI M M ICKY	TI M PANU M

TOMENTUM	NIMMED	*GIMMICK	SUMMAND	*COMMONLY	FLAMINGO
*TOMMYROT	PELMET	*GOOMBAH	SUMMARY	COMMUNAL	*FLAMMING
TOMOGRAM	POMMEE	*GOOMBAY	SUMMATE	COSMETIC	*FLIMFLAM
*TYMPANIC	POMMEL	GUMMIER	SUMMERY	COSMICAL	*FLUMMERY
*TYMPANUM	PUMMEL	GUMMING	SUMMING	COUMARIN	FOAMIEST
*YAMMERER	RAMMED	GUMMITE	SUMMONS	COUMAROU	FOAMLESS
*ZYMOGRAM	RAMMER	GUMMOSE	TOMMING	*CRAMMING	*FOAMLIKE
DOLMA	RIMMED	GUMMOUS	TUMMLER	*CRAMOISY	FORMALIN
DOOMY	RIMMER	*HAMMADA	WOMMERA	CRAMPOON	*FORMALLY
GAMMY	RUMMER	HAMMIER	*BADMOUTH	CREMAINS	*FORMERLY
GIMME	SHAMOS	*HAMMILY	BALMORAL	CREMATOR	FORMLESS
HALMA	SIMMER	*HAMMING	BEAMIEST	CRIMINAL	*FORMWORK
*JAMMY	SUMMED	*HAMMOCK	BEAMLESS	*CROMLECH	FREMITUS
PROMO	SUMMER	*HEIMISH	*BEAMLIKE	CRUMBIER	*FROMENTY
WHAMO	SUMMIT	*HEMMING	*BEDMAKER	*CRUMHORN	*FRUMENTY
BAYMAN	SUMMON	HOLMIUM	BERMUDAS	DALMATIC	*FULMINIC
BUMMER	TAMMIE	*HOMMOCK	*BESMOOTH	DEEMSTER	*FURMENTY
COMMIE	TOMMED	*HUMMING	BESMUDGE	DIAMANTE	GAMMADIA
COMMIT	WAMMUS	*HUMMOCK	*BIGMOUTH	DIAMETER	GAMMIEST
*COMMIX	*WHAMMO	*JAMMIES	*BIOMETRY	*DIEMAKER	GAMMONER
COMMON	YAMMER	*JAMMING	BLAMABLE	*DIMMABLE	GEMMIEST
CUMMER	BASMATI	*JIMMINY	*BLAMEFUL	DISMOUNT	*GEOMANCY
CUMMIN	*BOOMBOX	LAMMING	BOOMIEST	*DOOMSDAY	GEOMETER
DAMMAR	BROMISM	LEMMING	*BOOMTOWN	DOOMSTER	GEOMETRY
DAMMED	*BROMIZE	*MAMMARY	*BRIMFULL	DORMANCY	GERMANIC
DAMMER	BUMMEST	*MAMMOCK	BRIMLESS	DORMIENT	GERMFREE
DIMMED	BUMMING	*MAMMOTH	*BRIMMING	DORMOUSE	GERMIEST
DIMMER	CADMIUM	*MISMAKE	BROMELIN	DRAMATIC	GERMINAL
FILMER	*CHEMISM	*MUMMERY	*BROMIDIC	DRAMMING	*GIMMICKY
GAMMED	*CHOMPER	*MUMMIFY	CALMNESS	*DRAMMOCK	GLIMPSER
GAMMER	CLAMMER	NIMMING	*CAPMAKER	*DRAMSHOP	GLUMNESS
GAMMON	COMMAND	NONMEAT	*CARMAKER	DRUMBEAT	GNOMICAL
GEMMED	COMMEND	NUMMARY	*CHAMBRAY	DRUMFIRE	GORMLESS
GIMMAL	COMMENT	*PLUMBUM	*CHAMFRON	*DRUMFISH	GRAMARYE
GIMMIE	COMMIES	PREMADE	*CHAMPION	*DRUMHEAD	*GRAMERCY
GUMMED	COMMODE	PREMEAL	*CHEMICAL	DRUMLIER	GRIMACER
GUMMER	*COMMOVE	PREMEET	*CHEMURGY	*DRUMLIKE	GRIMIEST
HAMMAL	COMMUNE	PREMIUM	*CHIMAERA	DRUMMING	GRIMMEST
HAMMED	COMMUTE	PREMOLD	*CHIMBLEY	DRUMROLL	GRIMNESS
HAMMER	CONMATA	PREMOLT	*CHIMERIC	*DUMMKOPF	GROMWELL
HEMMED	COSMISM	PROMINE	*CHUMSHIP	FARMHAND	GRUMBLER
HEMMER	*CRUMBUM	PUMMELO	*CHYMOSIN	FARMLAND	GRUMMEST
HOMMOS	DAMMING	RAMMIER	*CLAMBAKE	*FARMWIFE	*GRUMPHIE
HUMMED	DIMMEST	RAMMING	*CLAMMING	*FARMWORK	*GRUMPISH
HUMMER	DRAMEDY	RAMMISH	CLAMORER	*FARMYARD	GUMMIEST
HUMMUS	FERMIUM	RIMMING	*CLAMWORM	*FILMCARD	GUMMOSIS
*JAMMED	*FILMDOM	RUMMAGE	CLEMATIS	FILMGOER	GUNMETAL
*JAMMER	FRAMING	SCHMEAR	*CLEMENCY	FILMIEST	HAEMATAL
*JASMIN	GAMMIER	SCHMEER	*CLUMPISH	FILMLAND	*HAEMATIC
KUMMEL	GAMMING	SCUMBAG	*COEMBODY	FIRMNESS	HAEMATIN
LAMMED	GEMMATE	SLAMMER	*COEMPLOY	*FIRMWARE	*HAMMERER
LIMMER	GEMMIER	SLUMGUM	*COMMANDO	*FLAMENCO	*HAMMIEST
LIMMIC	*GEMMILY	SLUMISM	*COMMENCE	FLAMEOUT	HARMLESS
*LUMMOX	GEMMING	*SOYMILK	*COMMERCE	FLAMIEST	*HARMONIC
*MAMMEY	GEMMULE	SUBMENU	COMMONER	FLAMINES	*HATMAKER

*HAY MAKER	*PLU M BIS M	*SCH M OOZE	SWI M SUIT	*YAR M ELKE	MU M M
*HEL M INTH	PLU M BOUS	SCI M ETAR	*SWI M WEAR	*YAR M ULKE	NEE M
HEL M LESS	PLU M ELET	SCI M ITAR	*SY M METRY	*YAW M ETER	NEU M
*HELMSMAN	PLU M ERIA	SCI M ITER	*TAG M EMIC	*YEO M ANRY	NOR M
*HER M ETIC	PLU M IEST	*SCU M LIKE	TAL M UDIC	*ZOO M ANIA	PAL M
*HER M ITRY	*PLU M IPED	*SCU M MING	TEA M AKER	*ZOO M ETRY	PER M
*HOG M ANAY	*PLU M LIKE	SEA M LESS	TEA M MATE	*ZOO M ORPH	PLU M
*HOG M ENAY	*PLU M PISH	SEA M LIKE	TEA M STER		POE M
*HUM MABLE	*PRE M EDIC	SEA M LIKE	*TEA MWORK	BAL M	PRA M
*KHA M SEEN	PRE M IERE	SEA M OUNT	TEG M ENTA	BAR M	PRI M
*KRUM HORN	PRE M OLAR	SEA M STER	TEG M INAL	BEA M	PRO M
*LAW MAKER	PRE M ORAL	*SHA M ABLE	TER M INAL	BER M	REA M
LOA M LESS	PRE M ORSE	*SHA M EFUL	TER M INUS	BLA M	ROA M
MAM MATUS	PRI M ATAL	*SHAM MASH	TER M LESS	BOO M	ROO M
MAM M ILLA	*PRI M EVAL	*SHA M MIED	TER M TI M E	BRI M	SCA M
MAM M ITIS	PRI M M EST	*SHA M MIES	*THE M ATIC	CAL M	SCU M
*MAP MAKER	*PRI M MING	*SHA M MING	*THU M BNUT	CHA M	SEA M
*MAU METRY	PRI M NESS	*SHA M OSI M	*THU M HKIN	CHU M	SEE M
*MID MONTH	*PRI M ROSE	*SHAM ROCK	*THY M JEST	CLA M	SHA M
*MIS MATCH	PRO M ISEE	*SHI M MERY	*THY M OSIN	COR M	SHI M
*MYR M IDON	PRO M ISER	*SHI M M ING	TIT M OUSE	CRA M	SKI M
*NAU MACHY	PRO M ISOR	*SKI M M ING	*TOM MYROT	CUL M	SLA M
*NEO M ORPH	PRO M OTER	SLI M IEST	TRA M LESS	DEE M	SLI M
*NEO M YCIN	PRO M PTER	SLI M M EST	TRA M LINE	DER M	SLU M
*NON M AJOR	*PRO M PTLY	SLI M M ING	TRA M M ING	DOO M	STE M
NON M ETAL	PRO M ULGE	SLI M NESS	*TRA M PISH	DOR M	STU M
NON M ETRO	PSA M M ITE	*SLU M BERY	TRA M PLER	DOU M	SWA M
NON M ODAL	PTO M AINE	SLU M LORD	TRA M ROAD	DRA M	SWI M
NON M ONEY	PUL M ONIC	SLU M M ING	TRE M BLER	DRU M	SWU M
NON M ORAL	PUL M OTOR	SPU M IEST	TRI M ARAN	FAR M	TEA M
NON M USIC	*PYG M YIS M	STA M PEDE	TRI M ETER	FIL M	TEE M
*NOR M ALCY	*QIO M TAIN	STE M LESS	TRI M M EST	FIR M	TER M
NOR M ALLY	RA M M IEST	STE M LIKE	TRI M M ING	FLA M	THE M
NOR M ANDE	*REE M BARK	*STE M MERY	TRI M NESS	FOA M	TOO M
NOR M LESS	*REE M BODY	STE M M ING	*TRI M ORPH	FOR M	TRA M
NOU M ENON	REE M ERGE	STE M WARE	TRI M OTOR	FRO M	TRI M
NUM M ULAR	*REE M PLOY	STI M ULUS	TRO M BONE	GAU M	WAR M
PAL M ATED	REI M PORT	*STO M ACHY	*TRU M PERY	GER M	WHA M
PAL M ETTE	REI M POSE	STO M ATAL	TUR M ERIC	GEU M	WHI M
PAL M ETTO	REN M INBI	STO M ATIC	VER M OULU	GLI M	WHO M
PAL M IEST	RES M OOTH	STO M ODEA	*VER M OUTH	GLO M	WOR M
PAL M ITIN	RHA M NOSE	STU M BLER	*VIO M YCIN	GLU M	YLE M
*PAL M LIKE	*RHE M ATIC	STU M M ING	*WAR MAKER	GRA M	*ZOO M
*PAN M IXIA	*RHO M BOID	STU M PAGE	WAR M NESS	GRI M	BEDI M
*PAN M IXIS	ROO M ETTE	SUB M ERGE	*WAR M OUTH	GRU M	BEGU M
*PEM M ICAN	ROO M MATE	SUB M ERSE	*WHI M BREL	HAE M	BESO M
PER M EANT	RUM MAGER	SU M MABLE	*WHO M EVER	HAL M	BLOO M
PER M EASE	SAL M ONID	*SU M MERIY	*WIG MAKER	HAR M	BOSO M
PER M EATE	SAR M ENTA	SU M M ITAL	*WORM HOLE	HEL M	BREA M
*PHI M OSIS	*SCA M MONY	*SU M M ITRY	WOR M IEST	HER M	BROO M
PLI M SOLE	*SCA M PISH	SU M M ONER	*WOR M LIKE	HOL M	*BUXO M
PLI M SOLL	*SCH M ALTZ	SUR M ISER	WOR M ROOT	LOA M	CARO M
*PLU M BAGO	*SCH M ALZY	*SWA M PISH	WOR M SEED	LOO M	CECU M
*PLU M BERY	*SCH M ELZE	*SWI M M ING	*WORMWOOD	M AI M	CELO M
*PLU M BING	*SCH M OOSE	*SWI M M ING	*YAM M ERER	M AL M	CHAS M

CHIR M	SCRA M	CUBIS M	M AGNU M	SCHIS M	BOSSDO M
CLAI M	SCRI M	CUNDU M	M AIHE M	SCREA M	BOSSIS M
CREA M	SCRU M	CUPRU M	M ARRA M	SCUTU M	*BRECHA M
DATU M	SEBU M	CURTU M	*M AYHE M	SELDO M	BRO M IS M
DEGU M	SEDU M	CUSTO M	M EDIU M	SENSU M	BRUTIS M
DEIS M	SEIS M	DEFOA M	M EGOH M	SEPTU M	*BRUXIS M
DENI M	SERU M	DEFOR M	M EGRI M	*SEXIS M	*BUCKRA M
DREA M	SHAW M	DEGER M	M ENTU M	SHOLO M	*BUDWOR M
DUNA M	SKEL M	DEPER M	M INIU M	SI M OO M	CAD M IU M
DURU M	S M AR M	DESEE M	M ISAI M	SITCO M	CAESIU M
FANU M	SODO M	DEWOR M	M O M IS M	SLALO M	CALCIU M
FILU M	SOLU M	DIADE M	M ONIS M	S M ILO M	*CA M BIS M
FLEA M	SPAS M	DIATO M	M USEU M	SODIU M	*CA M BIU M
FORA M	SPER M	DICTU M	M UTIS M	SPIRE M	CENTRU M
FORU M	STEA M	DINKU M	NANIS M	SPUTU M	CHARIS M
GENO M	STOR M	DIRDU M	NAPAL M	*SQUIR M	*CHEFDO M
GLEA M	STRU M	DIRHA M	NO M IS M	STREA M	*CHE M IS M
GLOA M	SWAR M	DISAR M	NONCO M	SUBGU M	CHETRU M
GLOO M	THAR M	DODGE M	NUDIS M	SYNCO M	CHILLU M
GOLE M	THER M	DOGDO M	PABLU M	SYSTE M	CHRISO M
GROO M	THRU M	DORSU M	PAYNI M	TALCU M	CLONIS M
HARE M	TOTE M	DRACH M	PEPLU M	TANDE M	*COCOYA M
HAUL M	VELU M	DU M DU M	PHENO M	TECTU M	CONFIR M
HILU M	VENO M	FANDO M	PHLEG M	TEDIU M	CONFOR M
HOKU M	VROO M	FANTO M	PHLOE M	TELIU M	COS M IS M
JORA M	WHEL M	FATHO M	*PHYLU M	TERGU M	CRANIU M
JORU M	*XYLE M	FAVIS M	PILEU M	THAIR M	CRISSU M
*JUGU M	*ZIRA M	FERBA M	PISSI M	THEIS M	*CRU M BU M
KALA M	BALSA M	FERRU M	PLENU M	THIRA M	CULTIS M
KELI M	BANTA M	FOLIU M	PODIU M	TRUIS M	CUTWOR M
KHOU M	BARIU M	FRENU M	POGRO M	VACUU M	*CZARDO M
KILI M	BECAL M	FULHA M	PO M PO M	VAGRO M	*CZARIS M
LARU M	BEDLA M	FULLA M	PORIS M	VAROO M	DADAIS M
LINU M	BEGRI M	GODDA M	POSSU M	VELLU M	DAYROO M
LOCU M	BELDA M	GONIU M	PREAR M	VICTI M	DECLAI M
M ADA M	BESEE M	GRAHA M	PRELI M	*WA M PU M	DECORU M
*M AXI M	BEWOR M	GRANU M	PURIS M	WHILO M	DEIFOR M
M IAS M	BIFOR M	GYPSU M	*QUORU M	*WIGWA M	DIAGRA M
M INI M	BOTTO M	*HAKEE M	RACIS M	WISDO M	DIASTE M
M ODE M	BUNKU M	HANSO M	RADIU M	BAALIS M	DISHEL M
NOTU M	CAECU M	HAREE M	RANDO M	*BAGWOR M	DODOIS M
*NUZA M	CARRO M	HELIU M	RANSO M	BAPTIS M	DOGEDO M
PLAS M	CENTU M	HOLIS M	RECTU M	BARROO M	DUALIS M
PRAA M	CERIU M	*JETSA M	REDEE M	*BECHAR M	*DUKEDO M
PRIS M	CESIU M	*JETSO M	REFIL M	BEDROO M	FADDIS M
PROE M	CHIAS M	KALIU M	REFOR M	BEGLOO M	FANTAS M
PSAL M	CHRIS M	LABIU M	REGNU M	BE M ADA M	FASCIS M
*QUAL M	CILIU M	LABRU M	RETEA M	BERSEE M	*FAUVIS M
REAL M	CIVIS M	LACTA M	RETRI M	BESWAR M	FER M IU M
REAR M	COELO M	LINGA M	REWAR M	BIOHER M	FIDEIS M
REHE M	CONDO M	LISSO M	*RHYTH M	BLELLU M	*FIEFDO M
RETE M	CONIU M	*LOGJA M	SACHE M	BLOSSO M	*FIL M DO M
RHEU M	COPAL M	LUTEU M	SACRU M	BLUEGU M	FIREAR M
SAGU M	CORIU M	LYCEU M	SADIS M	*BOGYIS M	*FOGYIS M
SATE M	CRINU M	LYRIS M	SALAA M	BOREDO M	FOREAR M

FRAENU M	NOSTRU M	SOLANU M	BASIDIU M	DECIGRA M	*HAIRWOR M
FREEDO M	PABULU M	SOPHIS M	*BATHROO M	*DEKAGRA M	HANDLOO M
FRUSTU M	PALLIU M	SORGHU M	BDELLIU M	DELIRIU M	HEADROO M
FULCRU M	PANICU M	STADIU M	BIENNIU M	DE M ONIS M	HEDONIS M
GALLIU M	PANTOU M	STANNU M	BIOPLAS M	*DIAZEPA M	HEIRLOO M
GINGHA M	PARONY M	STARDO M	*BIRDFAR M	*DIDY M IU M	HELOTIS M
GRANDA M	PEONIS M	STATIS M	*BLACKGU M	DIESTRU M	*HEXAGRA M
GROGRA M	PERFOR M	STERNU M	BLUESTE M	DILUVIU M	HOLOGRA M
GUNROO M	PHANTO M	STEWBU M	*BOLLWOR M	DI M ERIS M	*HOMEROO M
HADARI M	PHELLE M	STIBIU M	*BOOKWOR M	DIOECIS M	*HOOKWOR M
*HAFNIU M	PIANIS M	*STICKU M	*BOTHRIU M	DISBOSO M	*HORNBEA M
HALIDO M	PIETIS M	STRATU M	BOTULIS M	DISCLAI M	*HORNWOR M
HEIRDO M	PILGRI M	SUNBEA M	*BOYARIS M	DITHEIS M	HOTELDO M
HEROIS M	PINETU M	SUNROO M	*BRACHIU M	DO M INIU M	*HU M ANIS M
HOBOIS M	PINWOR M	*SY M PTO M	*BROUGHA M	DRUIDIS M	*HY M ENIU M
HOL M IU M	PLENIS M	*SYNONY M	*BRUNIZE M	DUODENU M	*HYPODER M
*HO M ONY M	*PLU M BU M	TACHIS M	CABALIS M	*DWARFIS M	*HYPOGEU M
HOODLU M	PO M ATU M	TANGRA M	CALADIU M	*DYNA M IS M	*JANIFOR M
*HU M DRU M	POPEDO M	TANTRU M	*CAPSICU M	*FACTOTU M	*JEROBOA M
*JARLDO M	PREBOO M	TAPETU M	*CARDAMO M	*FAIRYIS M	*JINGOIS M
*JEJUNU M	PREFOR M	TAPROO M	*CARDAMU M	*FA M ILIS M	*KILOGRA M
*JIBBOO M	PRE M IU M	TEAROO M	*CASEWOR M	FARADIS M	*KYMOGRAM
*JUGULU M	PRETER M	TERAOH M	CASTEIS M	FATALIS M	LABDANU M
*JUJUIS M	PRETRI M	TERBIU M	CE M ENTU M	*FE M INIS M	LABELLU M
*KINGDO M	PREWAR M	TETOTU M	CENTRIS M	*FILIFOR M	LABURNU M
LABARU M	PROBLE M	THEORE M	CEREBRU M	FINALIS M	LACONIS M
LADANU M	PROGRA M	THORIU M	*CHADARI M	FIREROO M	*LADYPAL M
LAICIS M	PROTIU M	THULIU M	*CHIEFDO M	*FIREWOR M	LANDFOR M
LEFTIS M	*QUANTU M	TONEAR M	*CHRO M IU M	*FISHWOR M	LAUDANU M
LEGROO M	*QUONDA M	TOPONY M	CIBORIU M	*FLATWOR M	*LEAFWOR M
*LEHAYI M	REALIS M	TOURIS M	*CI M BALO M	*FLI M FLA M	*LECHAYI M
LITHIU M	REBLOO M	TRANGA M	CINGULU M	FLUIDRA M	LEGALIS M
LOBWOR M	RECLAT M	TRANSO M	*CIVICIS M	*FOREBOO M	LINOLEU M
*LOCKRA M	REDREA M	TRIDUU M	*CLAMWORM	FOREDOO M	*LIXIVIU M
LOCOIS M	REGROO M	TRIFOR M	CLASSIS M	*FRANCIU M	*LOBBYIS M
LUGWOR M	*REQUIE M	TRIGRA M	*CLERKDO M	*FREEFOR M	LOGOGRA M
LUSTRU M	*RHABDO M	TRITIU M	COAGULU M	FRENULU M	LO M ENTU M
M ACADA M	RHENIU M	TRIVIU M	COATROO M	*FURCULU M	LOYALIS M
*M AJORA M	RHODIU M	TROPIS M	*COLIFOR M	*FUSIFOR M	*LUKEWAR M
*M AXI M U M	ROSTRU M	TSARDO M	COLISEU M	FUTURIS M	LUNGWOR M
M ETONY M	SANCTU M	TSARIS M	COLORIS M	GALBANU M	LUTECIU M
*M ICROH M	SARCAS M	*TZARDO M	CONIDIU M	*GAPEWOR M	LUTETIU M
M IDTER M	SCROTU M	*TZARIS M	COREDEE M	GASIFOR M	*LYRICIS M
M ILLDA M	SEDARI M	*WAXWOR M	CORE M IU M	GERANIU M	*LYRIFOR M
M INI M U M	SELFDO M	*WEBWOR M	CORUNDU M	GIANTIS M	M ASURIU M
M ISDEE M	SERFDO M	*WHOLIS M	*CRONYIS M	*GLOWWORM	*MEALWOR M
M ISFOR M	*SHAHDO M	*WIFEDO M	CROSSAR M	GLUCINU M	M ECONIU M
M ISTER M	SHITTI M	*WOLFRA M	*CUBIFOR M	GONIDIU M	M ELANIS M
M ODICU M	SIDEAR M	YARDAR M	*CUNIFOR M	GRANDDA M	M ERISTE M
M UDROO M	SISTRU M	YTTRIU M	*CY M ATIU M	*GRUBWOR M	M ESODER M
M UONIU M	SKELLU M	*ZOARIU M	*CYMBALO M	GUAIACU M	M EZEREU M
NARCIS M	*SKOOKU M	*ZOECIU M	*CYNICIS M	GUAIOCU M	*M ILLIOH M
NATRIU M	SLU M GU M	*BACKROO M	*DANDYIS M	*GYNECIU M	M ILLIRE M
NIOBIU M	SLU M IS M	BALLROO M	*DARKROO M	*GYPSYDO M	M ISCLAI M
NONFAR M	S M EDDU M	BAROGRA M	*DAYDREA M	*GYPSYIS M	

MOMENTUM	*PASHADOM	PROSAISM	SAINTDOM	SOLECISM	*TYMPANUM
MONADISM	PATAGIUM	*PSYLLIUM	SALEROOM	SONOGRAM	VANADIUM
MONOGERM	PECULIUM	*PTYALISM	SAMARIUM	*SPANWORM	*VARIFORM
MONOGRAM	*PEDIFORM	PUDENDUM	SAMPLISM	SPECTRUM	VARIORUM
MOONBEAM	PENDULUM	PUGILISM	SANDWORM	SPECULUM	*VASCULUM
MORALISM	*PEPONJUM	*PUPPYDOM	*SAPPHISM	*SPHAGNUM	*VASIFORM
MORONISM	PERIBLEM	*PYGIDIUM	SATANISM	SPICULUM	VEGANISM
MOTORDOM	PERIDERM	*PYGMYISM	SAVAGISM	SPLENIUM	VELARIUM
*MOVIEDOM	PERIDIUM	*PYRIFORM	SCANDIUM	STOICISM	VENOGRAM
*MUCKWORM	PERINEUM	*PYXIDIUM	*SCHOLIUM	SUDARIUM	VERATRUM
*MUSHROOM	*PHALLISM	*QUACKISM	SCIOLISM	SUPERMOM	*VERBATIM
*MYCELIUM	*PHANTASM	*QUEENDOM	SECUNDUM	*SYCONIUM	*VEXILLUM
NABOBISM	*PHILTRUM	*QUIETISM	SEDILIUM	TALEYSIM	*VIATICUM
NANOGRAM	*PICIFORM	RACEMISM	SELENIUM	TANTALUM	*VIBURNUM
*NAPIFORM	PICLORAM	RAMENTUM	*SERAPHIM	*TAPEWORM	*VILLADOM
NATIVISM	*PICOGRAM	*RAMIFORM	SERIATIM	TAUTONYM	*VINCULUM
NATURISM	*PILIFORM	*REAFFIRM	SETIFORM	TEETOTUM	VIRILISM
NEOPLASM	PIPESTEM	REBELDOM	SETSMISM	TELEFILM	VITALISM
*NEPHRISM	*PIRIFORM	REFUGIUM	*SHAMOSIM	TELEGRAM	*VIVARIUM
NEPOTISM	*PISIFORM	*REHOBOAM	*SHAMOSTM	THALLIUM	*VOCALISM
NEWSROOM	*PLANFORM	REINFORM	*SHEIKDOM	THRALDOM	VOLTAISM
NGULTRUM	PLASTRUM	RENIFORM	*SHIPWORM	TIMPANUM	WARDROOM
NIHILISM	*PLATFORM	RENOGRAM	*SHKOTZIM	TITANISM	WAREROOM
NOBELIUM	PLATINUM	RESIDUUM	*SHOWROOM	TITANIUM	*WASHROOM
NOMADISM	*PLAYROOM	RESTROOM	*SICKROOM	TOADYISM	*WAVEFORM
NOMOGRAM	PLECTRUM	RETIFORM	*SIEROZEM	TOKENISM	*WHIPWORM
*PACHADOM	PLEONASM	RIGHTISM	SILICIUM	TOMENTUM	*WHOREDOM
*PACIFISM	*PLUMBISM	RIGORISM	*SILKWORM	TOMOGRAM	*WIREWORM
PAEANTSM	POLONIUM	RINGWORM	SINAPISM	TOOLROOM	*WOODWORM
PAGANDOM	POOLROOM	ROBOTISM	*SKIAGRAM	TOTALISM	*WORKROOM
PAGANISM	POPULISM	ROSARIUM	*SLIPFORM	TOTEMISM	YAHOOISM
PALUDISM	*POSTFORM	ROTIFORM	*SLOWWORM	TRIADISM	*ZOMBIISM
PARADIGM	PRIAPISM	*ROWDYISM	SNOBBISM	TRILLIUM	*ZOOSPERM
*PARAFORM	PRIGGISM	ROYALISM	SOLARISM	TRITICUM	*ZYMOGRAM
PARECISM	PROCLAIM	RUBIDIUM	SOLARIUM	TROILISM	
*PAROXYSM	PRONOTUM	RURALISM	SOLATIUM	*TUBIFORM	

N

NAAN	NAVE	NENE	NICE	NODE	NOOK
NADA	NAVY	NEON	NICK	NODI	NOON
NAIF	NAZI	NERD	NIDE	NOEL	NOPE
NAIL	NEAP	NESS	NIDI	NOES	NORI
NAME	NEAR	NEST	NIGH	NOGG	NORM
NANA	NEAT	NETT	NILL	NOIL	NOSE
NAOS	NECK	NEUK	NINE	NOIR	NOSH
NAPE	NEED	NEUM	NIPA	NOLO	NOSY
NARC	NEEM	NEVE	NISI	NOMA	NOTA
NARD	NEEP	NEWS	NITE	NOME	NOTE
NARK	NEIF	NEWT	NIXY	NONA	NOUN
NARY	NEMA	NEXT	NOCK	NONE	NOUS

NOVA	NICAD	*NYMPH	NITRID	NULLAH	NINEPIN
NOWT	NICOL	**NACHAS**	NITRIL	**NUMBAT**	NIOBATE
NUDE	NIDAL	**NACHES**	NITWIT	NUMINA	NITINOL
NUKE	NIDUS	NARROW	NOBLER	NUNCIO	*NITPICK
NULL	NIECE	NARWAL	NOCENT	NUNCLE	NITRATE
NUMB	NIEVE	NASION	NODDED	NURSER	NITRIDE
NURD	NIGHT	NASTIC	NODDER	NUTANT	NITRILE
NURL	NIHIL	NATANT	NODDLE	NUTATE	NITRITE
NABIS	**NINJA**	NATION	NODOSE	NUTLET	NITROSO
NABOB	NINNY	NATIVE	NODOUS	NUTMEG	NITROUS
NACHO	NINON	NATRON	NODULE	NUTRIA	NOBLEST
NACRE	NINTH	NATTER	NOESIS	NUTTED	NOCTULE
NADIR	NISEI	NATURE	NOETIC	NUTTER	NOCTURN
NAGGY	NISUS	NAUSEA	NOGGIN	*NUZZLE	NOCUOUS
NAIAD	NITER	NAVIES	NONAGE	*NYMPHA	NODDIES
NAIRA	NITID	*NAZIFY	NONART	*NYMPHO	NOISOME
NAIVE	NITON	NEARLY	NONEGO	**NAMETAG**	NOMINAL
NAKED	NITRE	NEATEN	NONFAN	NANDINA	NOMINEE
NALED	NITRO	NEATLY	NONFAT	NARCOSE	NONAGON
NAMER	NITTY	NEBULA	**NONGAY**	NARGILE	**NONBODY**
NANCE	NIVAL	NEBULE	NONMAN	NARRATE	NONCOLA
NANNY	NOBLE	**NECKER**	NONPAR	*NARTHEX	NONDRUG
NAPPE	NODAL	NECTAR	NONUSE	NASCENT	**NONFACT**
NAPPY	NODUS	NEEDER	NONWAR	NATRIUM	**NONFUEL**
NARCO	NOISE	NEEDLE	NOODGE	NATURAL	**NONHEME**
NARES	NOISY	NEGATE	NOODLE	NECROSE	**NONHOME**
NARIS	NOMAD	NELLIE	NOOSER	NEEDIER	NONIRON
NARKY	NOMEN	NELSON	NORDIC	NEEDLER	*NONJURY
NASAL	NOMOS	NEREID	NORITE	NEGATON	NONMEAT
NASTY	NONCE	NEREIS	NORMAL	NEGATOR	**NONNEWS**
NATAL	NONET	NEROLI	NORMED	NEGLIGE	**NONOILY**
NATCH	NONYL	NESTER	NOSHER	NEGROID	**NONPAID**
NATES	NOOSE	NESTLE	NOSIER	NEGRONI	NONPAST
NATTY	NOPAL	NESTOR	NOSILY	NEMESIS	**NONPEAK**
NAVAL	NORIA	NETHER	NOSING	NEONATE	**NONPLAY**
NAVAR	NORTH	NETTED	NOSTOC	NERITIC	NONPLUS
NAVEL	NOSED	NETTER	NOTARY	NESTLER	NONPOOR
NEATH	NOSEY	NETTLE	NOTATE	NETLESS	NONPROS
NEEDY	NOTAL	NETTLY	NOTHER	NETTIER	**NONSELF**
NEGRO	NOTED	NEURAL	NOTICE	NETTING	NONSLIP
NEGUS	NOTER	NEURON	NOTING	NETTLER	NONSTOP
NEIGH	NOTUM	NEUTER	NOTION	NEURINE	NONSUIT
NEIST	NOVEL	NEWSIE	NOUGAT	NEUROID	NONUPLE
NELLY	NUBIA	NEWTON	NOVENA	NEUROMA	NONUSER
NERDY	NUDER	NIACIN	NOWISE	NEURONE	**NONWORD**
NEROL	NUDGE	NIDGET	*NOZZLE	NEURULA	**NONWORK**
NERTS	NUDIE	NIDING	NUANCE	NEUSTON	*NONZERO
NERVE	*NUDZH	NIELLO	NUBILE	NEUTRAL	NOONING
NETOP	NUMEN	NIGGLE	NUBLES	NEUTRON	NORLAND
NETTY	NURSE	NILGAI	NUCLEI	*NEWMOWN	NOSIEST
NEUME	NUTSY	NILGAU	NUDEST	*NEWSBOY	NOSTRIL
NEVER	NUTTY	NIMROD	NUDGER	*NIBLICK	NOSTRUM
NEVUS	*NUZAM	NINETY	NUDISM	NICOTIN	NOTABLE
NEWEL	NYALA	NITERY	NUDIST	NICTATE	**NOTEPAD**
NGWEE	NYLON	NITRIC	NUGGET	NIGGLER	NOTICER

NOUVEAU	NEUROSIS	*NONQUOTA	K N OP	S N OOD	*BU N CHY
NOWNESS	NEUTRINO	NONRATED	K N OT	S N OOK	BU N DLE
NUCLEAL	*NEWCOMER	NONRURAL	K N OW	S N OOL	BU N GEE
NUCLEAR	*NEWFOUND	NONSENSE	K N UR	S N OOP	BU N GLE
NUCLEIN	*NEWLYWED	NONSOLAR	S N AG	S N OOT	BU N ION
NUCLEON	*NEWSHAWK	NONSOLID	S N AP	S N ORE	BU N KER
NUCLEUS	*NEWSPEAK	NONSTORY	S N AW	S N ORT	BU N KUM
NUMERAL	*NEXTDOOR	NONSTYLE	S N ED	S N OUT	BU N TER
NUNATAK	NGULTRUM	NONSUGAR	S N IB	S N OWY	BY N AME
NUPTIAL	*NICKELIC	NONTIDAL	S N IP	S N UCK	CA N APE
NURSING	*NICKNACK	NONTITLE	S N IT	S N UFF	CA N ARD
NURTURE	*NICKNAME	NONTONAL	S N OB	BA N ANA	CA N ARY
NUTCASE	NIELLIST	*NONTOXIC	S N OT	BA N DER	CA N CAN
NUTGALL	*NIGHTCAP	NONUNION	S N OW	BA N DIT	CA N CEL
NUTMEAT	*NIGHTJAR	NONUSING	S N UB	BA N DOG	CA N CER
*NUTPICK	NIGROSIN	NONVALID	S N UG	BA N GER	CA N CHA
NUTTING	NINETEEN	*NONWOODY	S N YE	BA N GLE	CA N DID
*NUZZLER	*NITPICKY	NOONTIDE	G N ARL	BA N IAN	CA N DLE
*NYMPHET	NITRATOR	*NORMALCY	G N ARR	BA N ISH	CA N DOR
NARRATER	NITROGEN	NORMANDE	G N ASH	BA N KER	CA N FUL
NARRATOR	*NIZAMATE	NOSEDIVE	G N AWN	BAN N ED	CA N GUE
NASALISE	NOISETTE	NOSELESS	G N OME	BAN N ER	CA N INE
*NASCENCY	*NOMARCHY	NOSINESS	J N ANA	BAN N ET	CA N ING
NATATION	NONACTOR	NOTARIAL	*K N ACK	BAN TAM	CA N KER
NATIONAL	NONADULT	*NOTARIZE	K N AUR	BA N TER	CA N NED
NATURISM	*NONBLACK	NOTATION	K N EAD	BA N YAN	CA N NEL
NATURIST	NONBRAND	NOTELESS	K N EEL	*BA N ZAI	CA N NER
*NAUMACHY	NONCLING	NOTORNIS	K N ELT	BE N AME	CA N NIE
NAUSEANT	NONCOLOR	NOTTURNO	K N IFE	BE N DAY	CA N NON
NAUSEATE	NONCRIME	NOUVELLE	K N ISH	BE N DEE	CA N NOT
NAUSEOUS	NONDANCE	*NOVELIZE	*K N OCK	BE N DER	CA N OLA
NAUTILUS	NONELITE	*NOWADAYS	K N OLL	BE N IGN	CA N OPY
NAYSAYER	*NONEMPTY	NUCLEOID	K N OSP	BE N NET	CA N TER
NEARNESS	*NONEQUAL	NUDENESS	K N OUT	*BE N ZAL	CA N TIC
NEARSIDE	NONFATTY	*NUMBFISH	K N OWN	*BE N ZIN	CA N TLE
NEATNESS	NONFINAL	*NUMERACY	K N URL	*BE N ZOL	CA N TON
*NEBULIZE	NONGATAL	*NUNCHAKU	S N ACK	*BE N ZYL	CA N TOR
*NECKHAND	NONGLARE	NURSLING	S N AFU	BI N ARY	CA N TUS
*NECKLACE	NONGUEST	NURTURAL	S N AIL	BI N ATE	CA N ULA
*NECKLIKE	NONGUILT	NURTURER	S N AKE	BI N DER	CA N VAS
*NECKWEAR	*NONHARDY	NUTATION	S N AKY	BI N DLE	CA N YON
*NECROPSY	NONIDEAL	NUTGRASS	S N ARE	BIN N ED	CE N OTE
NEEDIEST	NONIMAGE	*NUTHATCH	S N ARK	BI N OCS	CE N SER
NEEDLESS	NONISSUE	NUTRIENT	S N ARL	BO N ACI	CE N SOR
NEGATION	*NONJUROR	NYSTATIN	S N ASH	BO N BON	CE N SUS
NEGATRON	NONLABOR		S N ATH	BO N DER	CE N TAL
*NEOMORPH	NONLEAFY	G N AR	S N EAK	BO N DUC	CE N TER
*NEOMYCIN	NONLEGAL	G N AT	S N EAP	BO N IER	CE N TRA
*NEOPHYTE	*NONMAJOR	G N AW	S N ECK	BO N ING	CE N TRE
*NEPHRISM	NONMETRO	K N AP	S N EER	BO N ITA	CE N TUM
NESTABLE	NONMUSIC	K N AR	S N ELL	BO N ITO	CI N DER
NESTLING	NONNOVEL	K N EE	S N ICK	BON N ET	CI N EOL
NETTIEST	*NONOHMIC	K N EW	S N IDE	BON N IE	CI N EMA
*NEURAXON	NONPOINT	K N IT	S N IFF	BO N SAI	*CI N QUE
NEURITIS	NONPRINT	K N OB	S N IPE	*BO N ZER	CO N CHA

*CO N CHY	DI N KLY	GA N GLY	HO N KIE	LI N IER	MI N IO N
CO N CUR	DI N KUM	GA N GUE	HO N OUR	LI N I N G	MI N IO N
CO N DOM	DI N N ED	*GA N JAH	HU N GER	LI N KER	MI N TER
CO N DOR	DI N N ER	GA N N ET	HU N GRY	LI N KUP	MI N UET
CO N FAB	DO N ATE	GA N OID	HU N KER	LI N N ET	MI N UTE
CO N FER	DO N ERD	GA N TRY	HU N TER	LI N SEY	MI N YA N
CO N FIT	DO N ERT	GE N DER	JA N GLE	LI N TEL	MI N GLE
CO N GEE	DO N JO N	GE N ERA	*JA N GLY	LI N TER	MO N GER
CO N GER	DO N KEY	GE N EVA	JE N N ET	LI N TOL	MO N GOE
CO N GOU	DO N N ED	GE N IAL	JI N GAL	LO N ELY	MO N GOL
CO N IES	DO N N EE	GE N IUS	*JI N GKO	LO N GA N	MO N GST
CO N INE	DO N SIE	GE N TES	JI N GLE	LO N GER	MO N IED
CO N ING	*DO N ZEL	GE N TIL	*JI N GLY	LO N GLY	MO N IES
CO N IUM	DU N ITE	GE N TLE	*JI N KER	LU N ACY	MO N IST
CO N KER	DU N LI N	GE N TOO	JI N N EE	LU N ATE	*MO N KEY
CO N N ED	DU N N ED	GE N TRY	JU N GLE	LU N GA N	MO N TES
CO N N ER	DU N N ER	GI N GAL	*JU N GLY	LU N GEE	MU N TI N
CO N OID	DY N AST	GI N GER	JU N IOR	LU N GER	N AN DI N
CO N SOL	DY N ODE	GI N GKO	*JU N KER	LU N GYI	N AN ISM
CO N SUL	FA N DOM	GI N KGO	*JU N KET	LU N IER	N AN KI N
CO N TRA	FA N EGA	GI N N ED	*JU N KIE	LU N IES	N AN N IE
*CO N VEX	FA N IO N	GI N N ER	KA N BA N	LU N KER	N IN ETY
CO N VEY	*FA N JET	GO N IFF	KA N TAR	LU N ULA	N ON AGE
CO N VOY	FA N N ED	GO N ION	KE N N ED	LU N ULE	N ON ART
CU N DUM	FA N N ER	GO N IUM	KE N N EL	MA N AGE	N ON COM
CU N EAL	FA N TOD	GO N OPH	KI N ASE	MA N A N A	N ON EGO
CU N N ER	FA N TOM	GU N DOG	KI N DLE	MA N EGE	N ON FAN
DA N CER	FE N CER	GU N MA N	KI N DLY	MA N GEL	N ON FAT
DA N DER	FE N DER	GU N MA N	KI N EMA	MA N GER	N ON GAY
DA N DLE	FE N N EC	GU N N ED	KI N GLY	MA N GLE	N ON MA N
DA N GER	FE N N EL	GU N N EL	LA N ATE	MA N ILA	N ON PAR
DA N GLE	FI N DER	GU N N EN	LA N CER	MA N ITU	N ON TAX
DA N ISH	FI N ELY	GU N N ER	LA N CET	MA N N A N	N ON USE
DE N ARY	FI N ERY	GU N SEL	LA N DAU	MA N N ED	N ON WAR
DE N GUE	FI N EST	HA N DLE	LA N DER	MA N N ER	N UN CIO
DE N IAL	FI N GER	HA N GAR	LA N ELY	*MA N QUE	N UN CLE
DE N IED	FI N IAL	HA N GER	LA N GUE	MA N TEL	PA N ADA
DE N IER	FI N I N G	HA N GUL	LA N GUR	MA N TES	PA N AMA
DE N IES	FI N ISH	HA N GUP	LA N N ER	MA N TID	PA N DER
DE N ME N	FI N ITE	HA N IWA	LA N OSE	MA N TIS	PA N DIT
DE N N ED	FI N N ED	HA N KER	LA N UGO	MA N TLE	PA N FRY
DE N OTE	FO N DLE	HA N KIE	LE N DER	MA N TRA	PA N FUL
DE N TAL	FO N DLY	HA N SEL	LE N GTH	MA N TUA	PA N GE N
DE N TIL	FO N DUE	HA N SOM	LE N ITY	MA N UAL	PA N IER
DE N TI N	FU N DUS	HA N TLE	LE N TE N	MA N URE	PA N N ED
DE N UDE	FU N GAL	HE N BIT	LE N TIC	ME N AGE	PA N TIE
DI N DLE	FU N GIC	HI N DER	LE N TIL	ME N IAL	PA N TRY
DI N ERO	FU N GUS	HI N GER	LI N AGE	ME N SAL	*PA N ZER
DI N GER	FU N KER	HO N CHO	LI N DE N	ME N TAL	PE N AN G
DI N GEY	FU N KIA	HO N DLE	LI N EAL	ME N TOR	PE N CEL
DI N GHY	FU N N ED	HO N EST	LI N EAR	MI N DER	PE N CIL
DI N GLE	FU N N EL	HO N IED	LI N EUP	MINGLE	PE N MA N
DI N GUS	GA N DER	HO N I N G	LI N GAM	MI N I N G	PE N N ED
DI N I N G	GA N GER	HO N KER	LI N GER		PE N N ER
DI N KEY		*HO N KEY	LI N GUA		PE N NON

PE N SEE	*QI N DAR	SA N TOL	TA N GLE	TU N ICA	WI N NER
PE N SIL	*QI N TAR	SA N TUR	**TA N GLY**	TU N ING	**WI N NOW**
PE N TAD	**RA N CHO**	SE N ARY	TA N IST	TU N NED	WI N TER
PE N TYL	RA N CID	SE N ATE	**TA N KER**	TU N NEL	WI N TLE
PE N ULT	RA N COR	SE N DAL	TA N NED	VA N DAL	WI N TRY
PE N URY	RA N DAN	SE N DER	TA N NER	VA N ISH	WO N DER
PI N ANG	RA N DOM	SE N ECA	TA N NIC	VA N ITY	WO N NED
PI N ATA	RA N GER	SE N EGA	TA N NIN	VA N MAN	WO N NER
PI N CER	**RA N KER**	SE N HOR	TA N REC	VA N NED	WO N TON
PI N DER	**RA N KLE**	SE N ILE	TA N TRA	VA N NER	*YA N QUI
PI N EAL	**RA N KLY**	SE N IOR	**TA N UKI**	VE N DEE	YA N TRA
PI N ENE	RA N SOM	SE N ITI	TE N ACE	**VE N DER**	YO N DER
PI N ERY	RA N TER	SE N NET	TE N AIL	**VE N DOR**	YO N KER
PI N GER	RA N ULA	SE N NIT	TE N ANT	VE N DUE	*ZA N ANA
Pi N IER	RE N AIL	SE N ORA	TE N DER	VE N EER	*ZA N DER
PI N ING	RE N AME	SE N SOR	TE N DON	VE N ERY	*ZA N IER
PI N ION	RE N DER	SE N SUM	TE N IST	VE N IAL	*ZA N IES
PI N ITE	RE N EGE	SE N TRY	TE N NER	VE N INE	*ZE N ANA
PI N KE N	RE N EST	**SE N TRY**	TE N NIS	VE N IRE	*ZE N ITH
PI N KER	RE N NET	**SH N APS**	TE N OUR	VE N OSE	*ZI N CIC
*PI N KEY	RE N NIN	**SH N OOK**	TE N PIN	VE N OUS	*ZI N CKY
PI N KIE	RE N OWN	**SI N EWY**	TE N REC	VE N TER	*ZI N GER
*PI N KLY	RE N TAL	SI N FUL	TE N SOR	VE N ULE	*ZI N NIA
PI N NAE	RE N TER	SI N GER	TE N TER	VI N EAL	*ZO N ARY
PI N NAL	RE N VOI	SI N GLE	TE N TIE	**VI N ERY**	*ZO N ATE
PI N NED	RI N GER	**SI N GLY**	TE N UIS	VI N IER	*ZO N ING
PI N NER	RI N SER	**SI N KER**	TE N URE	*VI N IFY	*ZO N KED
PI N OLE	RO N DEL	SI N NED	TE N UTO	VI N ING	*ZO N ULA
PI N TLE	RO N ION	SI N NER	TI N CAL	VI N OUS	*ZO N ULE
PI N YIN	RO N NEL	SI N TER	TI N DER	WA N DER	BA N DAGE
PI N YON	RO N YON	SO N ANT	TI N FUL	WA N DLE	BA N DANA
PO N CHO	RU N DLE	SO N ATA	TI N GLE	WA N GAN	*BA N DBOX
PO N DER	**RU N KLE**	SO N DER	**TI N GLY**	WA N GLE	BA N DEAU
PONENT	RU N LET	SO N ICS	TI N IER	WA N GUN	BA N DIED
PO N GEE	RU N NEL	SO N NET	TI N ILY	WA N IER	BA N DIES
PO N GID	RU N NER	SO N SIE	TI N ING	WA N ING	BA N DORA
PO N IED	**RU N OFF**	**SU N BOW**	**TI N KER**	WA N ION	BA N DORE
PO N IES	RU N OUT	SU N DAE	**TI N KLE**	WA N NED	BA N EFUL
PO N TIL	**RU N WAY**	SU N DER	**TI N KLY**	WA N NER	*BA N GKOK
PO N TON	SA N CTA	SU N DEW	TI N MAN	WA N TER	BA N KING
*PU N CHY	SA N DAL	**SU N DRY**	TI N NED	WA N TON	BA N KSIA
PU N DIT	SA N DER	**SU N KEN**	TI N NER	WI N CER	BA N NING
PU N GLE	SA N DHI	**SU N KET**	TI N SEL	WI N CEY	*BA N NOCK
PU N IER	SA N EST	SU N LIT	TI N TER	WI N DER	*BA N QUET
PU N ILY	SA N GAR	SU N NED	TO N EME	WI N DLE	BA N SHEE
PU N ISH	SA N GER	SU N SET	TO N GER	WI N DOW	BA N SHIE
*PU N KAH	SA N IES	SU N TAN	TO N GUE	WI N DUP	BE N CHER
PU N KER	SA N ING	SY N COM	TO N IER	WI N ERY	BE N EATH
*PU N KEY	SA N ITY	SY N DET	TO N ISH	WI N GER	BE N EFIC
PU N KIE	*SA N JAK	SY N DIC	TO N LET	WI N IER	BE N EFIT
PU N KIN	SA N NOP	SY N GAS	TO N NER	WI N ING	BE N EMPT
PU N NED	SA N NUP	*SY N TAX	TO N SIL	WI N ISH	BE N ISON
PU N NER	SA N SAR	SY N URA	TU N DRA	WI N KER	BE N LIMB
PU N NET	SA N SEI	TA N DEM	TU N EUP	WI N KLE	BE N OMYL
PU N TER	SA N TIR			WI N NED	BE N THAL

BE N THIC	CE N TARE	CO N N ECT	DI N N I N G	FU N GOID	HA N DOUT
BE N THOS	CE N TAUR	CO N N I N G	DO N ATOR	FU N GOUS	HA N DSAW
*BE N ZE N E	CE N TAVO	CO N N IVE	DO N GOLA	FU N ICLE	HA N DSEL
*BE N ZI N E	CE N TILE	CO N N OTE	DO N N I N G	FU N N EST	HA N DSET
*BE N ZOI N	CE N TIME	*CO N QUER	DO N N ISH	FU N N I N G	HA N GDOG
*BE N ZOLE	CE N TIMO	CO N SE N T	DU N GEO N	GA N ACHE	HA N GI N G
*BE N ZOYL	CE N T N ER	CO N SIG N	DU N N AGE	GA N GLIA	HA N GMA N
BI N DERY	CE N TRAL	CO N SIST	DU N N ESS	GA N GREL	HA N GOUT
BI N DI N G	CE N TRIC	CO N SOLE	DU N N EST	*GA N GWAY	HA N GTAG
BI N NI N G	CE N TRUM	CO N SORT	DU N N I N G	GA N TLET	HA N UMA N
BI N OCLE	CE N TURY	CO N SULT	DU N N ITE	GE N ERAL	HE N BA N E
*BO N A N ZA	CI N DERY	CO N SUME	*DY N AMIC	GE N ERIC	HE N COOP
BO N DAGE	CI N EAST	CO N TACT	DY N ASTY	GE N ESIS	HE N LIKE
BO N DI N G	CI N EOLE	CO N TAI N	FA N ATIC	GE N ETIC	HE N N ERY
BO N DMA N	CI N ERI N	CO N TEM N	FA N CIED	GE N ETTE	*HE N PECK
BO N FIRE	CO N ATUS	CO N TE N D	FA N CIER	GE N IPAP	HI N DGUT
BO N KERS	CO N CAVE	CO N TE N T	FA N CIES	GE N ITAL	HO N ESTY
*BO N NOCK	CO N CEAL	CO N TEST	FA N FARE	GE N ITOR	HO N OREE
BU N DIST	CO N CEDE	*CO N TEXT	FA N FOLD	GE N SE N G	HO N ORER
BU N DLER	CO N CEIT	CO N TORT	FA N LIKE	GE N TEEL	HU N DRED
BU N GLER	CO N CE N T	CO N TOUR	FA N N I N G	GE N TIA N	HU N N ISH
BU N TI N G	CO N CEPT	CO N TROL	FA N TAIL	GE N TILE	HU N TI N G
CA N AKI N	CO N CER N	CO N TUSE	FA N TASM	GE N UI N E	*JA N GLER
CA N ASTA	CO N CERT	CO N VECT	FA N TAST	GI N GALL	JA N ITOR
CA N DELA	CO N CHIE	CO N VE N E	FA N TASY	GI N GERY	*JI N GALL
CA N DE N T	CO N CISE	CO N VE N T	FA N WISE	GI N GERY	*JI N GLER
CA N DIDA	CO N COCT	CO N VERT	FA N WORT	GI N GHAM	*JO N QUIL
CA N DIED	CO N CORD	CO N VICT	*FA N ZI N E	GI N GILI	*JU N IPER
CA N DIES	CO N CUSS	*CO N VOKE	FE N AGLE	GI N GIVA	*JU N KMA N
CA N DLER	CO N DEM N	CU N EATE	FE N CI N G	GI N N I N G	KA N TELE
CA N DOUR	CO N DIG N	CU N N I N G	FE N LAND	GI N SE N G	KE N N I N G
CA N ELLA	CO N DOLE	CY N ICAL	FI N ABLE	GI N GELI	KE N OSIS
CA N IKI N	CO N DO N E	DA N DIER	FI N AGLE	GO N DOLA	KI N DLER
CA N N ERY	CO N DUCE	DA N DIES	FI N ALIS	GU N BOAT	KI N DRED
CA N N IER	CO N DUCT	DA N DILY	FI N ALLY	GU N FIRE	KI N ESIC
CA N N ILY	CO N DUIT	DA N DLER	FI N A N CE	GU N LESS	KI N ESIS
CA N N I N G	CO N DYLE	DA N GLER	*FI N BACK	GU N LOCK	KI N ETIC
CA N N OLI	CO N FECT	DA N SEUR	FI N DI N G	GU N N ERY	KI N ETI N
CA N N ULA	CO N FESS	DE N DRO N	FI N ESSE	GU N N I N G	*KI N FOLK
CA N O N RY	CO N FIDE	*DE N IZE N	*FI N FISH	GU N PLAY	*KI N GCUP
CA N SFUL	CO N FI N E	DE N N I N G	FI N FOOT	GU N ROOM	*KI N GDOM
CA N TALA	CO N FIRM	DE N SIFY	FI N ICAL	GU N SHIP	KI N GLET
CA N TATA	*CO N FLUX	DE N SITY	*FI N ICKY	GU N SHOT	KI N GPI N
CA N TDOG	CO N FORM	DE N TI N E	FI N IKI N	GU N WALE	*KI N SHIP
CA N TEE N	CO N FUSE	DE N TIST	FI N LESS	GY N ECIA	KI N SMA N
CA N TEE N	CO N GEAL	DE N TOID	FI N LIKE	*GY N ECIC	*KU N ZITE
CA N THUS	CO N GEST	DE N TURE	*FI N MARK	HA N APER	LA N ATED
CA N TI N A	CO N GIUS	DE N UDER	FI N N IER	HA N DBAG	LA N CI N G
CA N TRAP	CO N ICAL	DI N ERIC	FI N N I N G	HA N DCAR	LA N DI N G
CA N TRIP	CO N IFER	DI N ETTE	FO N DA N T	HA N DFUL	LA N DLER
CA N VASS	CON II N E	DI N GBAT	FO N DLER	HA N DGU N	LA N DMA N
*CA N ZO N A	CON II N E	DI N GIES	FO N TI N A	HA N DIER	LA N DME N
*CA N ZO N E	*CO N JOI N	DI N GILY	FU N CTOR	HA N DILY	LA N EWAY
CE N ACLE	*CO N JURE	DI N KIER	FU N ERAL	HA N DLER	LA N GREL
CE N SURE	CO N N ATE	DI N KIES	FU N FAIR	*HA N DOFF	LA N GUET

LA N GUID	MA N NITE	N O N LIFE	PE N A N CE	*PO N TIFF	SE N MORA
LA N GUOR	MA N NOSE	N O N MEAT	PE N ATES	PO N TOO N	SE N OPIA
LA N IARD	*MA N PACK	N O N NEWS	PE N DA N T	PU N CHER	SE N SATE
LA N IARY	MA N SIO N	N O N OILY	PE N DE N T	PU N GE N T	SE N SI N G
LA N ITAL	MA N TEAU	N O N PAID	PE N GUI N	PU N IEST	SE N SORY
LA N OLI N	MA N TLET	N O N PAST	PE N ICIL	*PU N KISH	SE N SUAL
LA N TA N A	MA N URER	N O N PEAK	PE N LITE	PU N NI N G	SI N CERE
LA N TER N	MA N WARD	N O N PLAY	PE N NAME	PU N STER	SI N GLET
LA N YARD	*ME N AZO N	N O N PLUS	PE N NA N T	RA N CHER	SI N KAGE
LE N GTHY	*ME N FOLK	N O N POOR	PE N NATE	RA N COUR	SI N LESS
LE N IE N T	ME N TIO N	N O N PROS	PE N N IES	RA N DIER	SI N NI N G
LE N SMA N	MI N ARET	N O N SKED	PE N NI N E	RA N DIES	SI N OPIA
LE N TIGO	MI N DSET	N O N SKID	PE N NI N G	RA N KI N G	SI N SY N E
LE N TISK	MI N ERAL	N O N SLIP	PE N OCHE	RA N KISH	SI N UATE
LE N TOID	MI N ILAB	N O N STOP	PE N SILE	RA N PIKE	SI N UOUS
LI N ABLE	*MI N IMAX	N O N SUCH	PE N STER	RA N SACK	SO N A N CE
LI N ALOL	MI N IVA N	N O N SUIT	PE N TA N E	RE N EGER	SO N GFUL
LI N DA N E	MI N STER	N O N UPLE	PE N TODE	RE N EWAL	SO N HOOD
LI N EAGE	MI N UTIA	N O N USER	PE N UCHE	RE N EWER	SO N LESS
LI N EATE	MO N ITOR	N O N WORD	PE N UCHI	RE N NASE	SO N LIKE
LI N ECUT	*MO N KERY	N O N WORK	PF N TA N E	RE N TIER	*SO N OVOX
LI N EMA N	*MO N KISH	*N O N ZERO	PI N BALL	RI N GE N T	SO N SHIP
LI N GCOD	MO N SOO N	N U N LIKE	PI N BO N E	RI N GLET	*SU N BACK
*LI N KBOY	MO N STER	N U N N ERY	PI N CHER	RI N GTAW	SU N BATH
LI N KMA N	MO N TA N E	N U N N ISH	PI N ESAP	RI N NI N G	SU N BEAM
LI N OCUT	MO N TERO	PA N ACEA	PI N ETUM	RI N SI N G	SU N BELT
LI N SA N G	*MO N THLY	PA N ACHE	*PI N FISH	RO N DEAU	SU N BIRD
LI N SEED	MO N URO N	*PA N CAKE	PI N FOLD	RO N DURE	SU N BUR N
LI N TIER	MU N NIO N	*PA N CHAX	PI N GUID	RO N TGE N	SU N DECK
LI N URO N	MU N STER	PA N DECT	PI N HEAD	RU N AWAY	SU N DIAL
LO N GBOW	*MU N TJAC	PA N DIED	PI N HOLE	*RU N BACK	SU N DOW N
LO N GIES	*MU N TJAK	PA N DIES	PI N IEST	RU N DLET	SU N FAST
LO N GI N G	*MY N HEER	PA N DOOR	*PI N KEYE	RU N DOW N	SU N FISH
LO N GISH	N A N DI N A	PA N DORA	PI N KIES	RU N LESS	SU N GLOW
LU N ATED	N A N KEE N	PA N DORE	PI N KI N G	RU N NI N G	SU N LAMP
LU N ATIC	NI N EPI N	PA N DURA	*PI N KISH	RU N OVER	SU N LA N D
LU N CHER	NI N THLY	*PA N FISH	PI N N ACE	SA N CTUM	SU N LESS
LU N ETTE	N O N ACID	PA N GE N E	PI N N ATE	SA N DBAG	SU N LIKE
LU N GFUL	N O N AGO N	PA N ICLE	PI N N IES	SA N DBAR	SU N NI N G
LU N GI N G	N O N BANK	PA N ICUM	PI N NI N G	*SA N DBOX	SU N RISE
LU N IEST	N O N BODY	PA N N IER	PI N N ULA	SA N DBUR	SU N ROOF
LY N CEA N	N O N BOOK	PA N NI N G	PI N N ULE	SA N DDAB	SU N ROOM
*LY N CHER	N O N CASH	PA N OCHA	PI N OCLE	SA N DFLY	SU N SPOT
MA N AKI N	N O N COLA	PA N OCHE	PI N SIO N	SA N DHOG	SU N SUIT
MA N ATEE	N O N DRUG	PA N OPLY	PI N TADA	SA N DIER	SU N WARD
MA N DRIL	N O N FACT	PA N PIPE	PI N TADO	SA N DLOT	SU N WISE
*MA N GABY	N O N FARM	PA N THER	PI N TAIL	SA N DMA N	SY N AGOG
MA N ILLA	N O N FOOD	PA N TIES	PI N TA N O	SA N DPIT	SY N A N ON
MA N ILLE	N O N FUEL	PA N TILE	PI N WALE	SA N GRIA	SY N APSE
MA N ITOU	N O N GAME	PA N TOUM	PI N WEED	SA N ICLE	SY N CARP
MA N LESS	N O N HEME	PE N ALLY	*PI N WORK	SA N TIMS	*SY N CHRO
	N O N HERO	PE N ALTY	PI N WORM	SA N TOUR	SY N COPE
	N O N HOME		PO N IARD	SE N ATOR	SY N ERGY
	N O N IRO N			SE N DOFF	SY N ESIS
	*N O N JURY			SE N ECIO	SY N FUEL

*SY N GAMY	TO N ETTE	WI N IEST	DO N N ISH	PRO N OU N	BER N ICLE
*SY N O NYM	TO N GMA N	WI N LESS	DRU N KE N	PU N N ING	BEU N CLED
SY N OVIA	TO N IEST	WI N SOME	DU N N AGE	*QUI N ELA	BIA N N UAL
SY N TO N Y	TO N IGHT	WI N TERY	DU N N ESS	*QUI N TA N	BIE N N ALE
TA N AGER	TO N N AGE	WI N DAGE	DU N N EST	*QUI N TI N	BIE N N IAL
TA N BARK	TO N N EAU	WI N DIER	DU N N ING	RE N N ASE	BIE N N IUM
TA N GELO	TO N N ISH	WI N DI N G	DU N N ITE	REU N IO N	BIG N O N IA
TA N GE N T	TO N SURE	WI N DROW	FAN N ING	RI N N ING	BI N N ACLE
TA N GIER	TO N TI N E	WI N ESOP	FI N N IER	RU N N ING	*BLA N CHER
TA N GLER	TU N ABLE	*WI N GBOW	FI N N ING	*SCH N OZZ	BLA N DISH
TA N GRAM	TU N DISH	WI N GMA N	FLA N KE N	SIG N AGE	*BLE N CHER
TA N KAGE	TU N EFUL	WI N N ING	FRO N TO N	SI N N ING	BLI N DAGE
TA N KARD	TU N ICLE	*WI N N OCK	FU N N EST	*SPA N DEX	*BLI N KARD
TA N KFUL	TU N N AGE	WO N N ING	FU N N ING	SPO N GI N	BLO N DISH
TA N N AGE	TU N N ING	*XA N THA N	GI N N ING	SPO N SO N	*BOO N DOCK
TA N N ATE	*VA N DYKE	*XA N THIC	GLA N CER	STA N I N E	BOU N DARY
TA N N ERY	VA N ILLA	*XA N THI N	GLO N IO N	STE N OKY	*BRA N CHIA
TA N N EST	VA N N ING	*ZA N YISH	GRA N ITA	SU N N ING	BRA N DISH
TA N N ING	VA N POOL	*ZI N CATE	GRA N OLA	SWA N PA N	BRA N N ING
TA N N ISH	VA N TAGE	*ZI N CIFY	GRU N IO N	*SWI N GBY	BRA N TAIL
TA N TARA	VA N WARD	*ZI N CITE	GU N N ERY	TA N N AGE	BRI N DLED
TA N TIVY	VE N ATIC	*ZI N COUS	GU N N ING	TA N N ATE	BRI N IEST
TA N TRUM	VE N DACE	*ZI N GA N O	*HAH N IUM	TA N N ERY	*BRO N CHIA
TA N YARD	VE N ISO N	*ZI N GARA	HE N N ERY	TA N N EST	*BRO N CHUS
TE N ABLE	VE N OMER	*ZI N GARO	HOR N IST	TA N N ING	*BRO N ZI N G
TE NA N CY	VE N TAGE	*ZI N KIFY	HU N N ISH	TA N N ISH	BRU N ETTE
TE N DRIL	VE N TAIL	*ZI N CKED	*JOB N AME	TEE N IER	*BRU N IZEM
TE N FOLD	VE N TRAL	*ZI N COID	KE N N ING	TE N N IES	BUR N ABLE
TE N N IES	VE N TURE	*ZO N ATED	MA N N ITE	TER N IO N	BUR N OOSE
TE N O N ER	VE N TURI	BA N N ING	MA N N OSE	TI N N IER	CA N N ABIC
TE N SILE	VI N ASSE	*BA N N OCK	MID N OO N	TI N N ILY	CA N N ABI N
TE N SI N G	VI N EGAR	BI N N ING	MU N N IO N	TI N N ING	CA N N ABIS
TE N SIO N	VI N IEST	*BO N N OCK	N O N N EWS	TO N N AGE	CA N N ELON
TE N SITY	VI N TAGE	BOU N DE N	N OW N ESS	TO N N ISH	CA N N IFST
TE N SIVE	VI N T N ER	BRI N I N G	NU N N ERY	TRA N CHE	CA N N IKI N
TE N TAGE	WA N GLER	CA N N ERY	NU N N ISH	TU N N AGE	CAN N O N RY
TE N THLY	WA N IEST	CA N N IER	PAN N IER	TU N N ING	CAR N AUBA
TE N TIER	WA N IGA N	CA N N ILY	PAN N ING	*TWI N JET	CAR N IVAL
TE N UITY	WA N N ESS	CA N N ING	PE N N AME	TWI N SET	CAT N APER
TE N UOUS	WA N N EST	CA N N OLI	PE N N ANT	VA N N ING	CEI N TURE
TI N AMOU	WA N N ING	CA N N OLA	PE N N ATE	WA N N ESS	CER N UOUS
TI N FOIL	WA N TAGE	CHA N SO N	PE N N IES	WA N N EST	*CHA N CERY
TI N GLER	*WE N CHER	CLA N GER	PE N N INE	WA N N ING	*CHA N CIER
TI N HOR N	WE N DIGO	CLO N I N G	PE N N ING	WE N N ISH	*CHA N CILY
TI N IEST	WE N N ISH	CO N N ATE	PHE N ATE	WI N N ING	*CHA N CI N G
TI N KLER	*WI N CHER	CO N N ECT	*PHE N OXY	*WI N N OCK	CHA N DLER
TI N LIKE	WI N CI N G	CO N N I N G	PHO N IED	WO N N ING	*CHA N FRO N
TI N N IER	WI N DBAG	CO N N IVE	PIG N OLI	BA N N ERET	CHA N TAGE
TI N N ILY	WI N DIGO	CO N N OTE	PI N N ACE	BA N N EROL	CHA N TIES
TI N N ING	WI N DILY	COR N ROW	PI N N ATE	BAR N ACLE	CHE N ILLE
TI N TI N G	*WI N DWAY	CU N N I N G	PI N N IES	BAR N YARD	*CHE N OPOD
TI N TYPE	WI N GIER	DEO N TIC	PI N N ING	BEA N BALL	*CHI N BO N E
TI N WARE	WI N GLET	DE N N ING	PI N N ULA	BEA N LIKE	CHI N LESS
TI N WORK	WI N GMA N	DI N N ING	PI N N ULE	BEA N POLE	CHI N N I N G
TO N EARM	WI N GTIP	DO N N ING	PRE N OO N	*BEK N IGHT	CI N N ABAR

CIN NAMON	DAM N DEST	GAU N TLET	LIO N LIKE	POU N DAGE	REI N DUCE
*CIN NAMYL	DAR N DEST	GIA N TESS	LOA N WORD	PRA N DIAL	REI N DUCT
CLA N GOUR	*DAW N LIKE	GIA N TISM	LOR N N ESS	*PRA N KISH	REI N FECT
CLA N N ISH	DEA N SHIP	GLA N DERS	MAG N ETO N	PRE N ATAL	REI N FORM
CLA N SMA N	DIA N THUS	GLA N DULE	*MAG N IFIC	PRE N OME N	REI N FUSE
*CLE N CHER	DOG N APER	GOW N SMA N	MAI N TAI N	PRE N TICE	*REI N JECT
CLI N ALLY	DO N N ERED	GRA N DAME	MA N N ERLY	*PRI N CELY	*REI N JURE
*CLI N CHER	DO N N IKER	GRA N DDAD	MA N N IKIN	PRI N CESS	*REI N JURY
*COA N CHOR	DOW N BEAT	GRA N DDAM	MA N N ITOL	PRI N CIPE	REI N LESS
COE N AMOR	DOW N CAST	GRA N DEUR	*MID N IGHT	*PRI N COCK	REI N SERT
COE N DURE	*DOW N COME	*GRA N DKID	*MIJ N HEER	PRI N TERY	REI N SMA N
COE N URUS	*DOW N FALL	GRA N DSIR	*MOO N CALF	PRI N TI N G	REI N SURE
*COE N ZYME	*DOW N HAUL	GRA N DSO N	MOO N DUST	PRI N TOUT	REI N VADE
*COG N IZER	*DOW N HILL	GRA N ULAR	*MOO N FISH	PRO N ATOR	REI N VE N T
COG N OME N	DOW N IEST	GRI N DERY	MOO N PORT	PRO N OTOM	REI N VEST
COG N OVIT	DOW N LAND	GRI N N ING	*MOONWALK	PRU N ELLA	REI N VITE
COI N CIDE	*DOW N LINK	GUA N IDI N	MOU N TAI N	PRU N ELLE	*REI N VOKE
COI N HERE	DOW N LOAD	*GU N NYBAG	N AI N SOOK	PRU N ELLO	REU N ITER
COI N MATE	*DOW N PIPE	GYM N ASIA	N O N N AVAL	*PYC N IDIA	RHI N ITIS
COI N SURE	*DOW N PLAY	HER N IATE	N O N N OVEL	*PYC N OSIS	*RHO N CHUS
COI N VE N T	DOW N POUR	*HOR N BEAM	N OO N TIDE	*PYC N OTIC	ROE N TGE N
CO N N IVER	DOW N SIDE	HOR N BILL	N OO N TIME	*PYK N OSIS	ROU N DISH
COO N SKI N	*DOW N SIZE	*HOR N BOOK	PAI N LESS	*PYK N OTIC	ROU N DLET
COR N BALL	*DOW N TICK	HOR N FELS	PAI N TI N G	*QUA N DANG	SAI N FOI N
*COR N CAKE	DOW N TROD	HOR N IEST	PA N N IKI N	*QUA N DARY	SAI N TDOM
COR N CRIB	DOW N TUR N	HOR N LESS	*PAW N SHOP	*QUA N DONG	SA N N YASI
COR N EOUS	*DOW N WARD	*HOR N LIKE	PE N N ATED	*QUA N TIFY	SCA N DE N T
*COR N ETCY	*DOW N WASH	*HOR N PIPE	*PHA N TASM	*QUA N TILE	SCA N DIUM
*COR N HUSK	*DOW N WIND	HOR N POUT	PHA N TAST	*QUA N TITY	SCA N N ING
*COR N ICHE	DRE N CHER	HOR N TAIL	*PHA N TASY	*QUA N TIZE	SCA N SIO N
COR N ICLE	DRU N KARD	*HOR N WORM	*PHE N AZI N	*QUA N TONG	SCA N TIER
COR N IEST	FAI N EA N T	HOR N WORT	*PHE N ETIC	*QUE N CHER	SCA N TIES
COR N MEAL	FAI N TISH	*HYM N BOOK	PHE N ETOL	*QUE N ELLE	SCE N ARIO
COR N PO N E	FAR N ESOL	*HYM N LESS	*PHE N OLIC	*QUI N CUN X	SCE N ICAL
COR N UTED	*FAW N LIKE	*HYM N LIKE	*PHO N ETIC	*QUI N ELLA	*SCH N APPS
COU N TESS	*FIE N DISH	*HYP N OSIS	PHO N IEST	*QUI N IELA	*SCH N ECKE
COU N TIA N	*FI N N ICKY	*HYP N OTIC	*PIC N ICKY	*QUI N OLIN	SCI N COID
CRA N IATE	FI N N IEST	*JAU N DICE	PIG N OLIA	*QUI N TILE	SE N N IGHT
CRA N KIER	FLA N CARD	*JOH N BOAT	PI N N ACLE	RAI N BA N D	SHA N GRAI
*CRA N KILY	FLA N ERIE	*JOI N TURE	PI N N ATED	RAI N BIRD	SHA N TIES
*CRA N KISH	*FLI N CHER	KEE N N ESS	PI N N IPED	RAI N COAT	SHA N TU N G
CRA N KOUS	*FLI N KITE	*KEY N OTER	PLA N ARIA	RAI N DROP	SHI N BO N E
*CRA N KPI N	FOU N TAI N	*KID N APEE	*PLA N CHET	RAI N FALL	SHI N GLER
CRA N N IED	*FRA N CIUM	*KID N APER	*PLA N FORM	RAI N IEST	SHI N LEAF
CRA N N IES	*FRA N KEST	LAG N APPE	PLA N GE N T	RAI N LESS	SHI N N ERY
CRA N N OGE	*FRA N KLI N	LA N N ERET	*PLA N KING	RAI N WASH	SHI N N ING
CRE N ATED	FRE N ETIC	LAU N CHER	PLA N KTER	RAI N WEAR	*SHU N PIKE
CRE N ELLE	FRE N ULUM	LEA N N ESS	PLA N KTO N	REA N OI N T	SIG N ALER
*CRO N YISM	*FRE N ZILY	LEM N ISCI	PLA N LESS	REE N GAGE	SIG N ALLY
*CRU N CHER	FRO N DEUR	LIE N ABLE	PLA N N ING	REE N LIST	SIG N IORY
CTE N IDIA	FRO N TAGE	LIE N TERY	PLA N OSOL	REE N ROLL	SIG N POST
*CYA N AMID	FRO N TIER	LIG N EOUS	PLA N TAI N	REG N A N CY	*SKI N HEAD
CYA N OGE N	FRO N TLET	LIM N ETIC	PLA N TI N G	REI N CITE	SKI N LESS
CYA N OSIS	*FU N NYMAN	LIO N FISH	PLA N TLET	REI N DEER	*SKI N LIKE
DAM N ABLE	GAI N LESS	*LIO N IZER	POI N TMA N	REI N DICT	SKI N N ING

*SOUNDBOX	SWANNERY	TURNSPIT	CONN	LOON	THAN
SOUNDING	*SWANSKIN	TWANGIER	COON	LORN	THEN
SOUNDMAN	SWINDLER	TWANGLER	CORN	LOWN	THIN
SPANDREL	*SWINEPOX	TWINBORN	CURN	MAIN	TOON
SPANDRIL	SWINGIER	TWINIEST	CYAN	MAUN	TORN
*SPANKING	SWINGING	*TWINIGHT	DAIN	MEAN	TOWN
SPANLESS	SWINGMAN	*TWINKLER	DAMN	MIEN	TURN
SPANNING	TANNABLE	TWINNING	DAWN	MOAN	TWIN
*SPANWORM	TEENAGED	*TWINSHIP	DEAN	MOON	VAIN
SPINALLY	TEENAGER	VAINNESS	DOWN	MORN	VEIN
SPINDLER	TEENIEST	*VARNISHY	DURN	MUON	WAIN
SPINELLE	*TEENYBOP	VAUNTFUL	FAUN	NAAN	WARN
*SPINIFEX	THANATOS	VEINIEST	FAWN	NEON	WEAN
SPINLESS	*THANKFUL	VEINLESS	FERN	NOON	WEEN
SPINNERY	THINCLAD	*VEINLIKE	FIRN	NOUN	WHEN
SPINNING	*THINDOWN	VEINULET	FLAN	PAIN	WHIN
SPINSTER	*THINKING	VERNACLE	FOHN	PAWN	WORN
SPONDAIC	THINNESS	VERNICLE	FOIN	PEAN	WREN
SPONGIER	THINNEST	VIGNERON	GAIN	PEEN	WYNN
SPONGILY	THINNING	VIGNETTE	GAUN	PEON	YARN
SPONGING	THINNISH	*VINNMARK	GIRN	PHON	YAWN
SPONSION	*THUNDERY	WAINSCOT	GLEN	PIAN	YEAN
SPONTOON	TINNIEST	WANNIGAN	GOON	PION	YUAN
STANCHER	TINNITUS	WEANLING	GOWN	PIRN	ZEIN
*STANCHLY	*TOPNOTCH	*WHENEVER	GRAN	PLAN	ZOON
STANDARD	TORNILLO	*WHINCHAT	GRIN	POON	BACON
STANDING	*TOWNFOLK	WHINIEST	GUAN	PORN	BAIRN
STANDISH	*TOWNHOME	WINNABLE	HAEN	PYIN	BARON
*STANDOFF	TOWNLESS	WINNOWER	HERN	QUIN	BASIN
STANDOUT	*TOWNSHIP	WORNNESS	HISN	RAIN	BATON
STANDPAT	TOWNSMAN	WRANGLER	HWAN	REIN	BEGAN
STANHOPE	TOWNWEAR	*WRONGFUL	HYMN	ROAN	BEGIN
STANNARY	*TRANQUIL	YEANLING	JEAN	RUIN	BEGUN
STANNITE	TRANSACT	*YOUNGISH	JEON	SAIN	BETON
STANNOUS	TRANSECT	*ZOONOSIS	JINN	SAWN	BISON
STENOSED	TRANSEPT		JOHN	SCAN	BLAIN
STENOSIS	*TRANSFIX	BARN	JOIN	SEEN	BLOWN
STINGIER	TRANSHIP	BEAN	KAIN	SEWN	BOGAN
STINGILY	TRANSMIT	BEEN	KAON	SHIN	BORON
STINGRAY	TRANSUDE	BLIN	KARN	SHUN	BOSON
STINKARD	TRENCHER	BOON	KEEN	SIGN	BOSUN
*STINKBUG	TRINKUMS	BORN	KERN	SKIN	BOURN
STINKIER	TRINODAL	BRAN	KHAN	SOON	BRAIN
STINKPOT	TRUNCATE	BREN	KILN	SORN	BRAWN
STONEFLY	TRUNDLER	BRIN	KIRN	SOWN	BROWN
STONIEST	*TRUNKFUL	BUNN	KOAN	SPAN	BRUIN
STUNNING	TRUNNION	BURN	LAIN	SPIN	BURAN
STUNSAIL	TUNNELER	CAIN	LAWN	SPUN	BURIN
STUNTMAN	TURNCOAT	CARN	LEAN	STUN	CABIN
SUBNASAL	TURNDOWN	CHIN	LIEN	SUNN	CAIRN
*SUBNICHE	TURNHALL	CHON	LIMN	SWAN	CAJON
SUBNODAL	TURNOVER	CLAN	LINN	TAIN	CANON
SURNAMER	TURNPIKE	CLON	LION	TARN	CAPON
*SWANHERD	TURNSOLE	COIN	LOAN	TEEN	CHAIN
*SWANLIKE		CION	LOIN	TERN	CHURN

CLEA N	GREE N	MUTO N	ROUE N	TITA N	**BEACO N**
CLOW N	GROA N	N IN ON	ROVE N	TOKE N	**BECKO N**
CODE N	GROI N	N ITO N	ROWA N	TOLA N	**BEDAM N**
CODO N	**GROW N**	N OME N	**ROWE N**	TOMA N	**BEDPA N**
COGO N	GYRO N	N UME N	RUME N	**TOXI N**	BEDUI N
COIG N	*HAZA N	N YLO N	RUTI N	TOYO N	**BEMEA N**
COLI N	**HEMI N**	PAEA N	SABI N	TRAI N	**BEMOA N**
COLO N	HERO N	PAEO N	SARA N	TREE N	BE N IG N
CO N I N	HOGA N	PAGA N	SARI N	TWAI N	*BE N ZI N
COPE N	HO N A N	PATE N	SASI N	TWEE N	BERLI N
COTA N	HUMA N	PATI N	SATI N	VEGA N	**BICOR N**
COVE N	HYME N	PAVA N	SAVI N	VE N I N	**BICRO N**
COVI N	HYSO N	PAVI N	SCIO N	VIME N	BIDDE N
*COZE N	**JAPA N**	PECA N	SCOR N	*VIXE N	**BIFFI N**
CROO N	*JAWA N	PEIO N	SEDA N	VODU N	**BIGGI N**
CROW N	**JETO N**	**PEKA N**	SEME N	WAGO N	BILLO N
CUMI N	**JUPO N**	**PEKI N**	SERI N	**WAKE N**	BIOGE N
CUTI N	KI N I N	PI N ON	SETO N	WHEE N	BIOTI N
CYTO N	K N OW N	PITO N	SEVE N	WIDE N	BITTE N
DAMA N	KROO N	PLAI N	SEWA N	WIGA N	*BLAZO N
DAVE N	LADE N	**PRAW N**	SHAR N	WITA N	**BOBBI N**
DAWE N	LAGA N	PREE N	**SHAW N**	WITE N	**BODKI N**
DEIG N	LAPI N	PRIO N	SHEE N	WITE N	**BOFFI N**
DEMO N	LATE N	PURI N	SHOO N	*WIZE N	BOLSO N
DEVO N	LAUA N	PUTO N	SHOR N	WOKE N	BO N BO N
DEWA N	LEAR N	**PYLO N**	**SHOW N**	WOMA N	BOREE N
DIVA N	LEBE N	**PYRA N**	SIRE N	WOME N	BOSTO N
DIWA N	LEMA N	**QUEA N**	SKEA N	WOVE N	BOUTO N
*DIZE N	LEMO N	**QUEE N**	SKEE N	XE N O N	**BOWFI N**
DOVE N	LEVI N	**QUER N**	SKEI N	*XYLA N	**BOWMA N**
DOYE N	LIGA N	**QUOI N**	SLAI N	YAME N	*BRAZE N
*DOZE N	LIKE N	RACO N	SOLA N	YAMU N	BROGA N
DRAI N	LIMA N	RADO N	SOLO N	YAPO N	**BROKE N**
DRAW N	LIME N	RATA N	**SOZI N**	YEAR N	**BROMI N**
DROW N	LI N E N	RAVE N	**SPAW N**	YOGI N	**BRUCI N**
FAGI N	LI N I N	RAWI N	SPEA N	YOUR N	**BUMKI N**
FA N O N	LIPI N	RAYO N	SPOO N	YULA N	BU N I O N
FEIG N	LIVE N	RECO N	SPUR N	YUPO N	BURDE N
FELO N	LODE N	REDA N	STAI N	*ZAYI N	**BUSKI N**
FICI N	LOGA N	REDO N	STEI N	*ZAZE N	**BUSMA N**
FLOW N	LORA N	REIG N	STER N	BABOO N	BUTTO N
FOEH N	LUME N	REMA N	SWAI N	**BADMA N**	**CABMA N**
FROW N	LUPI N	RE N I N	SWOO N	**BAGMA N**	**CAFTA N**
FURA N	LYSI N	REPI N	SWOR N	BALEE N	CAIMA N
FUTO N	MACO N	RERA N	SWOU N	BALLO N	**CALKI N**
GAMI N	MASO N	RERU N	SYRE N	BA N IA N	CALLA N
GIPO N	MATI N	RESI N	TABU N	BA N TA N	CAMIO N
GIRO N	**MAVE N**	REWA N	TAKI N	BA N YA N	CA N CA N
GIVE N	**MAVI N**	REWI N	TALO N	**BARMA N**	CA N NO N
GLEA N	MELO N	REWO N	**TAXO N**	BARRE N	CA N TO N
GLUO N	MESO N	RICI N	TE N O N	**BARYO N**	CA N YO N
G N AW N	*MIZE N	RIPE N	THEG N	BASIO N	**CAPLI N**
GOBA N	MORO N	ROBI N	THEI N	**BATMA N**	**CAPTA N**
GOWA N	MOUR N	ROMA N	THOR N	BATTE N	**CARBO N**
GRAI N	MUCI N	ROSI N	TIGO N	**BAYMA N**	CAREE N

CARLI N	**DARKE N**	GABIO N	**HEMPE N**	LIG N I N	MOREE N
CARMA N	DEACO N	GABOO N	HEREI N	LI N DE N	MORGA N
CARTO N	DEADE N	**GAGMA N**	HEREO N	**LIPPE N**	MORGE N
CARVE N	**DEAFE N**	GALLO N	HEROI N	LISTE N	MORIO N
CASEI N	DECER N	**GAMMO N**	**HIDDE N**	LITTE N	MOTIO N
CASER N	DEEPE N	GARCO N	**HODDE N**	**LOCHA N**	MOULI N
CATIO N	**DEEWA N**	GARDE N	**HODDI N**	LOGIO N	MOUTO N
CATKI N	**DEHOR N**	GARRO N	**HOIDE N**	LOMEI N	**MUFFI N**
CATLI N	DEMEA N	GASCO N	**HOLDE N**	LO N GA N	MULLE N
CAVER N	DE N TI N	**GASKI N**	**HOLPE N**	LOOSE N	MU N TI N
CAYMA N	DESIG N	GASMA N	**HOYDE N**	LOTIO N	MUREI N
*CHAZA N	DETAI N	GERMA N	*HYPHE N	LOUDE N	MUSLI N
CHITI N	**DEVEI N**	GERME N	**JARGO N**	LUCER N	MUTTO N
CHITO N	DIAMI N	**GIBBO N**	*JASMI N	**LUMPE N**	**MYELI N**
CHOPI N	*DIAZI N	GIBSO N	*JERKI N	LU N GA N	**MYOSI N**
CHOSE N	DIOXA N	GITTI N	**JETTO N**	LURDA N	NA N DI N
CITRI N	DIOXI N	GLOBI N	**JORDA N**	LUTEI N	NA N KI N
CITRO N	**DISOW N**	GLUCA N	**KAFTA N**	**MACRO N**	N APKI N
*CLAXO N	DIURO N	GLUTE N	**KALIA N**	**MADDE N**	N ASTO N
CLOVE N	**DOBBI N**	**GLYCA N**	**KAMSI N**	**MADMA N**	N ATIO N
COCAI N	DOBLO N	**GLYCI N**	KA N BA N	MAGIA N	N ATRO N
COCHI N	DOLMA N	G N OMO N	**KAOLI N**	MAIDE N	N EATE N
COCOO N	DOLME N	GOBLI N	**KATIO N**	MALIG N	**N EKTO N**
CODEI N	DOMAI N	**GODOW N**	**KELSO N**	**MALKI N**	N ELSO N
CODLI N	DORMI N	GODSO N	**KELVI N**	**MAMMO N**	N EURO N
COFFI N	DO N JO N	GOLDE N	**KEPPE N**	MA N NA N	N EWTO N
*COJOI N	**DRIVE N**	GO N IO N	*KHAZE N	MARGI N	N IACI N
COLUM N	DROMO N	GORGO N	**KIPPE N**	MARLI N	N OGGI N
COMMO N	**DUBBI N**	**GORHE N**	**KITTE N**	MAROO N	N ONFA N
CORBA N	DUDEE N	GOSSA N	*KLAXO N	MARRO N	N ON MA N
CORDO N	DU N LI N	GOTTE N	**KRAKE N**	MARTE N	N OTIO N
CORTI N	DURIA N	**GOVER N**	*KUCHE N	MARTI N	N UBBI N
COSIG N	DURIO N	GRABE N	**KURGA N**	MASCO N	PAESA N
COTTO N	DY N EI N	GRADI N	LAGOO N	MATRO N	PAISA N
COUPO N	**FALCO N**	GRATI N	LALLA N	MATTI N	PA N GE N
COUSI N	FALLE N	**GRAVE N**	LARDO N	**MAYVI N**	**PAPAI N**
COWMA N	FA N IO N	GRISO N	LATEE N	MEDIA N	PARDO N
CRATO N	FASTE N	GUA N I N	LATTE N	MELTO N	PARIA N
CRAVE N	FATTE N	GUE N O N	LATTI N	MERLI N	PARSO N
CRAYO N	**FIBRI N**	GUIDO N	**LAWMA N**	MERLO N	PARTA N
CREPO N	**FIRKI N**	GULDE N	**LAYMA N**	MESIA N	PARTO N
CRETI N	**FIRMA N**	GU N MA N	LEADE N	MESSA N	PATRO N
CROTO N	**FLACO N**	GU N NE N	LEAVE N	**MICRO N**	PATTE N
CUMMI N	**FLAGO N**	**HADRO N**	LECTI N	**MIDDE N**	PAULI N
CURRA N	**FLAME N**	**HAGDO N**	LEGGI N	MIG N O N	**PEAHE N**
CYA N I N	**FLAVI N**	**HAPPE N**	LEGIO N	**MIKRO N**	**PECHA N**
CYMLI N	*FLAXE N	**HAPTE N**	LEGMA N	MILDE N	**PECTE N**
DAEMO N	FLYMA N	**HARDE N**	LE N TE N	MI N IO N	**PECTI N**
DAHOO N	**FOEMA N**	**HARMI N**	LEPTO N	MI N YA N	PE N MA N
DAIKO N	FOISO N	**HARPI N**	LESIO N	**MISPE N**	PE N NO N
DAIME N	**FORBA N**	HASTE N	LESSE N	MITTE N	**PEPSI N**
DAIMO N	*FROZE N	**HATPI N**	LESSO N	*MIZZE N	PEREO N
DALTO N	**FRYPA N**	HAUSE N	LEUCI N	MODER N	PERRO N
DAMPE N	FUSAI N	*HAZZA N	**LEUKO N**	MOLTE N	PERSO N
DAMSO N	FUSIO N	**HEAVE N**	**LICHE N**		PHO N O N

PHOTO N	RATTE N	SEXTA N	TARTA N	WITHI N	BOURBO N
PHYLO N	RATTO N	SEXTO N	*TARZA N	WIVER N	BOURDO N
PHYTI N	REAGI N	SHAIR N	TAUTE N	*WIZZE N	*BRACKE N
PHYTO N	REASO N	SHAMA N	TAVER N	WO N TO N	BRADOO N
PIDGI N	REBOR N	SHOGU N	*TAXMA N	WOODE N	BRECHA N
PIGEO N	RECKO N	SHORA N	TEGME N	WOOLE N	BRIDOO N
PIGGI N	RECOI N	SICCA N	TELSO N	WORSE N	BROADE N
PIGPE N	REDDE N	SICKE N	TE N DO N	*WYVER N	*BUCKEE N
PI N IO N	REDFI N	SILKE N	TE N PI N	YAUPO N	BUDGOW N
PI N KE N	REEAR N	SILVA N	TEOPA N	YEELI N	*BUFFOO N
PI N YI N	REGAI N	SIMIA N	TESTO N	YEOMA N	BULLIO N
PI N YO N	REGIO N	SIMLI N	THORO N	YOUPO N	BULLPE N
PIPKI N	REJOI N	SIMOO N	THRAW N	*ZEATI N	*BUMPKI N
PIPPI N	RELOA N	SIPHO N	TIEPI N	*ZECHI N	BURGEO N
PISTO N	REMAI N	SISKI N	TIFFI N	*ZIRCO N	BURTHE N
PITMA N	RE N N I N	SITTE N	TIGLO N	BALLOO N	BUSHMA N
PLATA N	RE N OW N	*SKYMA N	TI N MA N	BARCHA N	BUTYRI N
PLATE N	REOPE N	SLOGA N	TITIA N	BARGAI N	*CABEZO N
PLUTO N	REPLA N	SLOVE N	TITMA N	BASEMA N	*CAFFEI N
POISO N	REPUG N	SOCMA N	TOCSI N	BASSOO N	CAISSO N
POLEY N	*REQUI N	SODDE N	TOUCA N	BASTIO N	CALDRO N
POLLE N	RESEE N	SOFTE N	TRAPA N	BATSMA N	CAMPIO N
POMPO N	RESIG N	SOLDA N	TREPA N	BEADMA N	CA N AKI N
PO N TO N	RETAI N	SOLEM N	TRIGO N	BECLOW N	CA N IKI N
POPGU N	RETOR N	SOLIO N	TRITO N	BEDEMA N	CA N TEE N
POPLI N	RETUR N	SOUDA N	TROGO N	*BEDIZE N	CAPELA N
POSTI N	RHYTO N	SOVRA N	TROPI N	BEDOUI N	CAPELI N
POTEE N	RIBBO N	SPAVI N	TUCHU N	BEGROA N	CAPSTA N
POTIO N	RICHE N	SPLEE N	TURBA N	BELLMA N	CAPTAI N
POTMA N	RIDDE N	SPOKE N	TURFE N	BE N ISO N	CAPTIO N
PREMA N	ROBBI N	SPRAI N	TYCOO N	*BE N ZOI N	CARABI N
PREME N	RODMA N	STAME N	TYMPA N	BETHOR N	CARAVA N
PRISO N	RO N IO N	STOLE N	TYPHO N	BETOKE N	CARBAR N
PROLA N	RO N YO N	STOLO N	VA N MA N	BETWEE N	CARDOO N
PROTO N	ROTTE N	STRAI N	VERDI N	BIGHOR N	CAROTI N
PTERI N	RURBA N	SUBOR N	VERMI N	BILLIO N	CARRIO N
PTISA N	RURTO N	SUDDE N	VIOLI N	BIOTRO N	CARRYO N
PUFFI N	RYOKA N	SULDA N	VIRGI N	BIRCHE N	CARTOO N
PU N KI N	SADDE N	SULLE N	VIRIO N	BIRDMA N	CATERA N
PURLI N	SALMO N	SULTA N	VISIO N	BITTER N	CAUTIO N
PYTHO N	SALOO N	SUMMO N	VODOU N	BITUME N	CAVEMA N
*QUI N I N	SAMPA N	SU N KE N	WAGGO N	*BLACKE N	CELADO N
RABBI N	SARSE N	SU N TA N	WA N GA N	BLOUSO N	CERTAI N
RACOO N	SATEE N	SWEVE N	WA N GU N	BLOWGU N	CERUME N
RADIA N	SCREE N	SYLVA N	WA N IO N	BLUEFI N	CESSIO N
RAGLA N	SEAMA N	SYLVI N	WA N TO N	BOATMA N	CERATI N
RAGMA N	SEASO N	SYPHO N	WARDE N	BODHRA N	CHAGRI N
RAISI N	SEAWA N	TAIPA N	WARRE N	BOGBEA N	CHA N SO N
RAMSO N	SECER N	TALIO N	WEAKE N	*BOGYMA N	*CHAPMA N
RA N DA N	SEISI N	TAMEI N	WEAPO N	BO N DMA N	CHASTE N
RAPPE N	*SEIZI N	TAMPA N	WEDEL N	*BOOKMA N	*CHAZZA N
RATIO N	SELSY N	TAMPO N	WELKI N	*BOOMKI N	*CHAZZE N
RATLI N	*SEQUI N	TA N N I N	WEASO N	*BORAZO N	CHEAPE N
RATOO N	SEREI N	TARPA N	WHITE N	BOTULI N	*CHEVRO N
RATTA N	SERMO N	TARPO N	WIGEO N	BOU N DE N	*CHICKE N

*CHIFFO N	DASHEE N	*FLUXIO N	GUDGEO N	*KITCHE N	MELA N I N
CHIG N O N	DAUPHI N	FOGHOR N	GUERDO N	KLAVER N	*ME N AZO N
CHITLI N	DAYSMA N	FOLACI N	HABITA N	KREMLI N	ME N TIO N
CHLORI N	DEADPA N	FOOTMA N	*HACKMA N	*KRYPTO N	MESSMA N
CHORIO N	DECROW N	FORAME N	HAGBOR N	LACTEA N	METOPO N
CHRO N O N	DECUMA N	FOREIG N	HAIRPI N	*LADYKI N	MIDIRO N
CI N ERI N	DEMETO N	FOREMA N	*HALCYO N	*LAMBKI N	MID N OO N
CIPOLI N	DE N DRO N	FORERU N	HALOGE N	LAMPIO N	MIDTOW N
CISTER N	*DE N IZE N	FORLOR N	HA N DGU N	LAMPOO N	*MILKMA N
CISTRO N	DERAIG N	FORWOR N	HA N GMA N	LA N DMA N	MILLIO N
CITHER N	DERTAI N	FOURGO N	HA N UMA N	LA N DME N	MILLRU N
CITHRE N	DETRAI N	*FOXSKI N	HARDPA N	LA N OLI N	MI N IKI N
*CITIZE N	*DEXTRA N	FREEMA N	*HARIJA N	LA N TER N	MI N IVA N
CITTER N	*DEXTRI N	FRESHE N	HARPOO N	LARDOO N	MISCOI N
CLACHA N	DICTIO N	FRISSO N	HARSHE N	LEADMA N	*MISJOI N
CLARIO N	*DIGOXI N	FROGMA N	HEADMA N	LECTER N	MISLAI N
CLAYPA N	DIP N OA N	FRO N TO N	HEADPI N	LECTIO N	MISPLA N
CLUBMA N	DISCER N	*FUCHSI N	HEARKE N	LEGHOR N	MISSIO N
COALBI N	DISDAI N	FUSTIA N	HEARTE N	LEGUMI N	MITOGE N
COARSE N	DISHPA N	GADROO N	HEATHE N	LE N SMA N	MOISTE N
COITIO N	*DISJOI N	GAGATO N	HECUME N	LESBIA N	*MO N AXO N
COLICI N	DISLIM N	GALLEI N	HELICO N	LETDOW N	MO N ERA N
COLLEE N	DISTAI N	GALLEO N	HEMATI N	LEVULI N	MO N SOO N
COMPLI N	DOESKI N	GALLOO N	HEPARI N	*LEXICO N	MO N URO N
CO N CER N	DOLPHI N	GAMELA N	HERDMA N	LIAISO N	MOORHE N
CO N DEM N	DOORMA N	GASTRI N	HESSTA N	LIFTMA N	MORPHI N
CO N DIG N	DRAGOO N	GATEMA N	*HEXAGO N	LIGHTE N	MORRIO N
*CO N JOI N	DRAYMA N	GELATI N	*HEXOSA N	LIGROI N	MOUFLO N
CO N SIG N	DRUMLI N	GE N TIA N	HIRUDI N	LIMACO N	MUEDDI N
CO N TAI N	DRU N KE N	*GHERKI N	HOARSE N	*LIMPKI N	*MUEZZI N
CO N TEM N	*DUCKPI N	GIAADI N	*HOATZI N	LI N EMA N	MULLEI N
COO N CA N	DUDGEO N	GITTER N	HOEDOW N	LI N KMA N	MULLIO N
COREIG N	DU N GEO N	GLADDE N	HORDEI N	LI N URO N	MU N N IO N
COTHUR N	DURAME N	GLEEMA N	*HORIZO N	LOBEFI N	MURRAI N
COURLA N	DUSTBI N	GLISTE N	*HYPERO N	LORG N O N	MUTAGE N
*COWSKI N	DUSTMA N	GLO N IO N	*JACOBI N	LOWBOR N	NA N KEE N
CRAMPO N	DUSTPA N	GLUTTO N	*JALAPI N	LOWDOW N	N ARCEI N
CREATI N	DUVETY N	GODDAM N	*JARGOO N	LUPULI N	N EGATO N
CREWMA N	FACTIO N	GODROO N	*JAVELI N	LUTHER N	N EPHRO N
CRIMSO N	FASHIO N	GOLDAR N	*JAZZMA N	LY N CEA N	N EUSTO N
CRISPE N	FE N URO N	GOLDUR N	JILLIO N	LYSOGE N	N EUTRO N
CROCEI N	FERMIO N	GOODMA N	*JU N KMA N	*MADZOO N	N EWBOR N
CROUTO N	FESTOO N	GOSSOO N	*JURYMA N	MAILMA N	*N EWMOW N
CRUCIA N	FIBROI N	GRAPLI N	KAMSEE N	MALISO N	N EWSMA N
CRYOGE N	FICTIO N	GREATE N	KEELSO N	MA N AKI N	N ICOTI N
CULLIO N	FIFTEE N	GREISE N	KERATI N	MA N IKI N	NI N EPI N
CUMARI N	FI N IKI N	GREMLI N	KEROGE N	MA N SIO N	N OCTUR N
CURTAI N	FIREMA N	GREYHE N	*KHAMSI N	MARCHE N	N O N AGO N
CUSHIO N	FIREPA N	GRIFFI N	*KIDSKI N	MARTIA N	N O N IRO N
CUTDOW N	FISSIO N	GRIFFO N	KILOTO N	*MATZOO N	N OVATI N
CYCASI N	FLAGMA N	GRIPMA N	KI N ETI N	MAUDLI N	N UCLEI N
CYPRIA N	FLA N KE N	GRISKI N	KI N GPI N	*MAXIMI N	N UCLEO N
CYSTEI N	FLATTE N	GRU N IO N	KI N SMA N	MEATMA N	*PACKMA N
DALAPO N	*FLEXIO N	GRUTTE N	*KIPSKI N	MEDUSA N	PACTIO N
DARSHA N	FLUORI N	*GRYPHO N	*KIRKMA N	MEGATO N	PALADI N

PAMPEA N	*PUMPKI N	SA N DMA N	STIFFE N	TORSIO N	*ZECCHI N
PAPHIA N	PURITA N	SAPO N I N	STOLLE N	TOUGHE N	*ZILLIO N
PARAGO N	PURLOI N	SAURIA N	STOUTE N	TREASO N	*ZITHER N
PASSIO N	PUSHPI N	SAVARI N	STYGIA N	*TRIAZI N	*ZYMOGE N
PASTER N	PUTAME N	*SAXHOR N	SUASIO N	TRICOR N	*ZYMOSA N
PATROO N	PYROGE N	SCULPI N	SUBCLA N	TRODDE N	*BACKSPI N
PATTER N	*QUARTA N	SECTIO N	SUBDEA N	TRUDGE N	BACTERI N
PEEBEE N	*QUASSI N	SEEDMA N	SUBERI N	TRYPSI N	BAILSMA N
PELICA N	*QUICKE N	SERICI N	*SUBJOI N	TUBULI N	BA N DSMA N
PEMICA N	*QUIETE N	SESSIO N	SUBTEL N	TUITIO N	BARBICA N
PE N GUI N	*QUI N TA N	SEXTAI N	SUCTIO N	TURFMA N	BARTISA N
PEREIO N	*QUI N TI N	SHAITA N	SU N BUR N	TWIGGE N	*BARTIZA N
PERIGO N	RACCOO N	SHARPE N	SU N DOW N	TYLOSI N	BASEBOR N
PERTAI N	RAMEKI N	SHEBEA N	SURGEO N	*TYPHOO N	*BAUDEKI N
PHAETO N	RAMPIO N	SHEBEE N	SUSTAI N	VELAME N	BEADSMA N
PICOLI N	RATTEE N	SHEITA N	SWAGMA N	VE N ISO N	BEARSKI N
PIGSKI N	RATTOO N	SHIPMA N	SWA N PA N	VERMIA N	*BEDARKE N
*PIKEMA N	RAVELI N	SHIPPO N	SWEETE N	VERSIO N	BEDEAFE N
PILLIO N	READOR N	SHODDE N	SWIDDE N	VERVAI N	BEDESMA N
PI N SIO N	REALIG N	SHOPMA N	SWOLLE N	VETERA N	BEGOTTE N
PLASMI N	REBEGI N	SHORTE N	SYMBIO N	VIBRIO N	BEHOLDE N
PLASMO N	RECLEA N	SHOTGU N	SY N A N O N	VIDICO N	BEMADDE N
PLATOO N	RECROW N	SHOTTE N	TABORI N	VILLAI N	*BE N JAMI N
PLAYPE N	REDSKI N	*SHOWMA N	*TACHYO N	VILLEI N	*BE N ZIDI N
PLEURO N	REEDMA N	SIDEMA N	TACTIO N	VITAMI N	BERBERI N
PLOSIO N	REFRAI N	SILICO N	TAILFA N	VITRAI N	BESCREE N
PLOWMA N	REGIME N	SILVER N	TAMARI N	VOLUTI N	BETATRO N
PLUMPE N	REGREE N	SIRLOI N	TAMPIO N	WA N IGA N	BEVATRO N
PLUVIA N	RELAXI N	SIXTEE N	TARDYO N	WARISO N	BIATHLO N
POCOSI N	RELEAR N	SLACKE N	*TAXIMA N	WARWOR N	BIGAROO N
POLARO N	RETRAI N	SLEEKE N	TEGUME N	*WAYWOR N	*BILLYCA N
POLYGO N	REU N IO N	SMARTE N	TELAMO N	WESTER N	BIOCLEA N
PO N TOO N	REWAKE N	SMIDGE N	TELEMA N	WHEATE N	*BIOTOXI N
POPCOR N	REWIDE N	SMIDGI N	TELERA N	WHEREI N	*BLACKFI N
PORTIO N	REWOKE N	SMITTE N	TE N SIO N	WHEREO N	BLOODFI N
POSTEE N	REWOVE N	S N OWMA N	TER N IO N	WIDGEO N	*BLOWDOWN
POSTER N	ROCKOO N	*SOCKMA N	TERRAI N	WI N GMA N	BLUDGEO N
POSTMA N	RODSMA N	SOJOUR N	TERREE N	WIREMA N	BLUESMA N
POTHEE N	RO N TGE N	SOKEMA N	TERTIA N	WOODBI N	BOARDMA N
POTTEE N	ROUGHE N	SOLA N I N	TESTOO N	WOODHE N	BOATSMA N
PREDAW N	RUBDOW N	SOLITO N	THEELI N	WOODMA N	*BODEYMA N
PRE N OO N	RUCTIO N	SOUPCO N	THEREI N	WOOLLE N	*BOHEMIA N
PREPLA N	RUFFIA N	SOYBEA N	THEREO N	WOOLMA N	BOMBESI N
PRETEE N	RU N DOW N	SPARTA N	THIAMI N	*WORKMA N	BO N DSMA N
PREWAR N	SABATO N	SPELEA N	*THIAZI N	WRITHE N	*BOOGYMA N
PRO N OU N	SABAYO N	SPO N GI N	*THICKE N	WRITTE N	*BOOMTOWN
PROPMA N	SACATO N	SPO N SO N	THIO N I N	*XA N THA N	BOUGHTE N
PROTEI N	SADIRO N	SPORRA N	TIGHTE N	*XA N THI N	BOUILLO N
PROTEA N	SAFFRO N	STATIO N	TI N HOR N	*XYLIDI N	BOURGEO N
PSAMMO N	SAGAMA N	STEARI N	TOLIDI N	YARDMA N	*BOXTHOR N
PTOMAI N	SALICI N	STEEPE N	TOLIMA N	YATAGA N	BRAI N PA N
PTYALI N	SALPIA N	STEMSO N	TOMPIO N	YEGGMA N	*BRAKEMA N
PUCCOO N	SALTER N	STEPSO N	TO N GANA N	YESTER N	BRASILI N
PULLMA N	SALTPA N	STETSO N	TOPSPI N	*YOYTHE N	BRAZILI N
PULSIO N	SAMISE N	STEWPA N	TORCHO N	*ZACATO N	BRETHRE N

BRIGHTE N	*COACHMA N	DILATIO N	*FRIGHTE N	HISTAMI N	LOCATIO N
BROMELI N	COACTIO N	DILUTIO N	FRUITIO N	HISTIDI N	*LOCKDOW N
*BRYOZOA N	CODESIG N	DILUVIA N	FUGLEMA N	HISTOGE N	LOCUTIO N
*BUCKBEA N	COERCIO N	DILUVIO N	FU N CTIO N	*HOACTZI N	LOGICIA N
*BUCKSKI N	COG N OME N	DIOBOLO N	*FU N NYMAN	HOLSTEI N	LO N GERO N
BULLETI N	COHESIO N	DIOCESA N	FURFURA N	*HOMESPU N	LO N GHOR N
BULLHOR N	COLISTI N	DIOLEFI N	GAMBESO N	*HOMETOW N	LOVELOR N
BUSULFA N	COLLAGE N	DIPTERA N	GAMESMA N	HOMI N IA N	LU N ARIA N
*CABOCHO N	*COLOPHO N	DIPTERO N	GA N GLIO N	*HO N EYBU N	LU N ATIO N
*CALFSKI N	COLORMA N	DISCROW N	GARRISO N	HOOLIGA N	LU N CHEO N
CALUTRO N	COMEDIA N	DISTRAI N	GELATIO N	HORSEMA N	LUTEOLI N
*CAMPAIG N	*COMEDOW N	DISU N IO N	GLASSMA N	HOTELMA N	*LUXATIO N
CA N NABI N	COMPIAI N	DIVISIO N	GLOBULI N	HOUSEMA N	*LY N CHPI N
CA N NELO N	CO N ATIO N	DOMI N IO N	GLUCAGO N	*HYALOGE N	MACAROO N
CA N N IKI N	*CO N QUIA N	DO N ATIO N	GLUTELI N	*HYDROGE N	MACRURA N
*CAPESKI N	COOLDOW N	DOTATIO N	GLYCERI N	*HYPOGEA N	*MADWOMAN
CAPSICI N	COO N SKI N	DOUBLOO N	*GLYCOGE N	*HYPOPYO N	MAGICIA N
*CAPUCHI N	COOPTIO N	DOW N TUR N	G N ATHIO N	*JERRICA N	MAG N ETO N
CARAGEE N	COPATRO N	*DRAWDOW N	GOATSKI N	*JERRYCA N	MAI N TAI N
CARDAMO N	CORDOVA N	DRIFTPI N	GOMBROO N	*JETTISO N	MA N DARI N
CARDIGA N	CORDWAI N	DURATIO N	GO N FALO N	*JU N CTIO N	MA N DOLI N
CAREWOR N	CORPSMA N	*DUTCHMA N	GO N FAN O N	KAISERI N	MA N N IKI N
CARILLO N	COTILLO N	DY N ATRO N	GORGERI N	*KAKIEMO N	MARATHO N
CARROTI N	*COTQUEA N	*FACEDOW N	GOW N SMA N	KALLIDI N	MARGARI N
CARYOTI N	COUMARI N	*FALCHIO N	GRA N DSO N	*KARYOTI N	*MARKDOWN
*CATECHI N	COU N TIA N	FA N FARO N	GRAVAME N	KE N OTRO N	*MARKSMA N
CAULDRO N	*COXSWAI N	FAVO N IA N	GRAVITO N	*KEPHALI N	MAROCAI N
*CAVICOR N	CRAGSMA N	FE N THIO N	GRIDIRO N	*KHAMSEE N	MARTAGO N
*CEPHALI N	CRAMPOO N	FERRITI N	GROSCHE N	*KLYSTRO N	*MARZIPA N
CERULEA N	*CRA N KPI N	*FERRYMA N	GUA N IDI N	*KRUMHOR N	MASTODO N
CESAREA N	CREATIO N	FETATIO N	GUARDIA N	*LAMBSKI N	MELA N IA N
CESARIA N	*CRUMHOR N	FI N ESPU N	GUERIDO N	LA N DSMA N	MELODEO N
CETACEA N	CULTIGE N	*FI N ICKI N	GUMPTIO N	LA N GSHA N	MELTDOW N
*CHAI N MA N	CULVERI N	*FIXATIO N	GYPSEIA N	LA N THOR N	ME N HADE N
*CHAIRMA N	CYA N OGE N	*FLASHGU N	GYRATIO N	LARRIGA N	MERIDIA N
CHALDRO N	*CYCLAME N	FLATIRO N	HAEMATI N	LARRIKI N	MESOTRO N
*CHAMFRO N	*DAKERHE N	FLECTIO N	HALATIO N	LAVATIO N	*METAZOA N
*CHAMPIO N	DALESMA N	*FLEXAGO N	*HA N DSEW N	*LAXATIO N	*METAZOO N
*CHA N FRO N	DECISIO N	FOILSMA N	*HA N DYMAN	*LAYWOMA N	METHADO N
*CHAPERO N	DECURIO N	FOOTWOR N	HARRIDA N	LEADSMA N	*MEZEREO N
*CHAPLAI N	DEERSKI N	FORE N OO N	*HAWTHOR N	LEATHER N	MIRLITO N
*CHARACI N	DELATIO N	*FORESKI N	*HAZELHE N	LECITHI N	MISALIG N
*CHESSMA N	DELETIO N	FOREWAR N	HEADSMA N	LEGATIO N	MISLEAR N
*CHEVERO N	DELUSIO N	FOREWOR N	*HEIGHTE N	LE N GTHE N	MISU N IO N
CHILDRE N	*DEMIJOH N	FORMALI N	*HELMSMA N	LE N ITIO N	MOCCASI N
CHITOSA N	DEMO N IA N	*FOUGHTE N	HEMATEI N	LEWISSO N	MOLESKI N
CHLORDA N	DEMOTIO N	FOU N TAI N	*HE N CHMA N	LIBATIO N	MO N ECIA N
*CHOREMA N	DERISIO N	FOURTEE N	*HE N EQUE N	LICHE N I N	MO N ELLI N
*CHRISMO N	DEUTERO N	FRACTIO N	*HE N EQUI N	LIEGEMA N	*MO N EYMA N
CHRISTE N	*DEVILKI N	*FRA N KLI N	*HE N IQUE N	LIGATIO N	MO N ITIO N
CI N NAMO N	DEVOTIO N	FRAULEI N	HEPTAGO N	LIMEKIL N	MORTMAI N
*CI N QUAI N	DIAPASO N	FREEBOR N	HERDSMA N	*LI N CHPI N	MOTORMA N
CITATIO N	*DIAZI N O N	FREEDMA N	HEREUPO N	LI N ESMA N	*MOUFFLO N
CIVILIA N	DIELDRI N	*FRESHMA N	*HIGHBOR N	LI N KSMA N	MOU N TAI N
CLA N SMA N	DIHEDRO N	FRICTIO N	HIMATIO N	LOBATIO N	

MULLIGA N	*PHE N AZI N	RAMBUTA N	SECRETI N	STRUCKE N	TRAPPEA N
MULTITO N	*PHOSPHI N	*RAMEQUI N	SEDATIO N	STUBBOR N	TRASHMA N
*MU N CHKI N	*PHTHALI N	RAMSHOR N	SEDITIO N	STU N TMA N	TREELAW N
MU N ITIO N	PICAROO N	*RA N CHMA N	SEEDSMA N	STURGEO N	TRILLIO N
MUSICIA N	*PITCHMA N	RATAPLA N	*SHADCHA N	SUBBASI N	TRIMARA N
MUTATIO N	*PIVOTMA N	REACTIO N	SHAGREE N	*SUBHUMA N	TROPO N I N
*MUTCHKI N	PLACEMA N	REASSIG N	SHALLOO N	*SUBTAXO N	*TRUCKMA N
*MYRMIDO N	PLA N KTO N	REATTAI N	*SHEEPMA N	SUBTILI N	TRUDGEO N
N APOLEO N	PLA N TAI N	*REAWAKE N	SHOEHOR N	SUBURBA N	TRUEBOR N
N ATATIO N	PLASTRO N	REBUTTO N	*SHOPWOR N	SUDATIO N	TRU N N IO N
N EGATIO N	*PLAYDOW N	REDESIG N	*SHOWDOWN	SUPERFA N	TU N GSTE N
N EGATRO N	PLEBEIA N	REFASTE N	*SHRU N KE N	SUPERMA N	TURBOFA N
*N EOMYCI N	PLECTRO N	REHARDE N	*SHUTDOW N	*SUZERAI N	TUR N DOW N
*N EURAXO N	PLEUSTO N	REI N SMA N	*SHWA N PA N	*SWA N SKI N	TWI N BOR N
N IGROSI N	PLIOTRO N	RELATIO N	SIDESPI N	SWI N GMA N	VACATIO N
N I N ETEE N	POI N TMA N	RELIGIO N	SIMOLEO N	SWORDMA N	VALERIA N
N ITROGE N	POLTROO N	REMOTIO N	SIRE N IA N	*SYRPHIA N	VA N ILLI N
N OBLEMA N	*POLYZOA N	REOBTAI N	SKELETO N	TACITUR N	VE N ATIO N
N O N GREE N	POSITIO N	REORDAI N	SLATTER N	TAILSPI N	VE N ETIA N
N O N HUMA N	POSITRO N	REPLEVI N	*SLOWDOW N	*TAKEDOW N	VERATRI N
N O N PAGA N	POSTBUR N	REPLICO N	SMIDGEO N	TALAPOI N	VERBOTE N
N O N U N IO N	POSTTEE N	RESCREE N	SMOOTHE N	TALESMA N	VERSEMA N
N O N URBA N	POTATIO N	RESEASO N	SOLATIO N	TALISMA N	VESUVIA N
N O N WOVE N	*POZZOLA N	RESORCI N	SOLUTIO N	TALLYMA N	*VEXATIO N
N ORTHER N	PRECLEA N	RESPOKE N	*SOMEWHE N	TARLATA N	VIG N ERO N
N OTATIO N	*PREHUMA N	RESTRAI N	SO N ARMA N	TARLETA N	*VIOMYCI N
N OUME N O N	PRE N OME N	REVISIO N	SORPTIO N	TARRAGO N	VIRIDIA N
N UTATIO N	PRESSMA N	RESUMMO N	SOU N DMA N	*TAXATIO N	VITELLI N
N UTBROW N	PRESSRU N	RHODAMI N	SOUTHER N	TEARDOW N	VOCATIO N
N YSTATI N	PRETRAI N	RIFLEMA N	SOUTHRO N	TEASPOO N	VOLITIO N
PAGURIA N	PREU N IO N	RIGADOO N	SPACEMA N	TELETHO N	VOLUTIO N
PALMITI N	PRIAPEA N	RIGAUDO N	SPALPEE N	TERRAPI N	WA N N IGA N
PA N GOLI N	*PROCHAI N	RIPARIA N	SPEARGU N	TETRAGO N	WARFARI N
*PA N HUMA N	*PROCHEI N	ROE N TGE N	SPEARMA N	THEREMI N	*WATCHMA N
PA N N IKI N	PROLAMI N	ROGATIO N	SPECIME N	THERMIO N	WATERMA N
PA N THEO N	*PROPYLO N	ROSARIA N	SPELAEA N	THESPIA N	*WEIGHMA N
PAPILLO N	PROTAMI N	ROTATIO N	SPILIKI N	*THI N DOW N	WELLBOR N
*PARAFFI N	PROU N IO N	ROUTEMA N	SPITTOO N	*THIOPHE N	*WHALEMA N
*PARAZOA N	PSILOCI N	SAFRA N I N	SPO N SIO N	THIRTEE N	*WHEELMA N
PARERGO N	PSORALE N	SAI N FOI N	SPO N TOO N	THOLEPI N	WHORESO N
PARTISA N	PUBLICA N	SALESMA N	*SQUADRO N	THREATE N	WI N DBUR N
PARVOLI N	*PU N CHEO N	SA N CTIO N	*SQUIREE N	*THROMBI N	*WI N ESKI N
PATHOGE N	PU N ITIO N	SA N TO N I N	STALLIO N	*THUMBKI N	WI N GSPA N
*PATTYPA N	PUPATIO N	SAUCEPA N	STASIMO N	*THYMOSI N	WOODSMA N
PAULDRO N	PURPURI N	SCALEPA N	STEAPSI N	*THYROXI N	*WOOLSKI N
PAVILIO N	*PUSHDOW N	SCALLIO N	STEGODO N	TIMEWOR N	*XA N THEI N
PAVILLO N	*QIOMTAI N	SCA N SIO N	STER N SO N	TOBOGGA N	*YACHTMA N
PEARMAI N	*QUADROO N	*SCARFPI N	*STICKMA N	TOILWOR N	*YATAGHA N
*PEMMICA N	*QUARTER N	SCISSIO N	*STICKPI N	TOLUIDI N	YESTREE N
PE N TAGO N	*QUATRAI N	SCORPIO N	STICTIO N	TOW N SMA N	*ZEPPELI N
PE N TOSA N	*QUESTIO N	SCULLIO N	STILLMA N	*TRACKMA N	*ZO N ATIO N
PEREGRI N	*QUI N OLI N	SEALSKI N	*STOCKMA N	TRACTIO N	
PETITIO N	RADIOMA N	SEAROBI N	STRAITE N	TRAGOPA N	
	RAFTSMA N	SEATRAI N	STRICKE N	TRAI N MA N	

P

PACA	PELF	PITY	POUF	PYRE	PASEO
PACE	PELT	*PIXY	POUR	PACER	**PASHA**
PACK	PEND	PLAN	POUT	**PACHA**	PASSE
PACT	PENT	PLAT	PRAM	**PADDY**	PASTA
PADI	PEON	PLAY	PRAO	PADLE	PASTE
PAGE	PEPO	PLEA	PRAT	PADRE	**PASTY**
PAID	PERE	PLEB	PRAU	PAEAN	**PATCH**
PAIK	PERI	PLED	PRAY	PAEON	PATEN
PAIL	**PERK**	PLEW	PREE	PAGAN	PATER
PAIN	PERM	PLIE	PREP	PAGED	PATIN
PAIR	PERT	PLOD	**PREX**	PAGER	PATIO
PALE	PESO	PLOP	PREY	PAGOD	**PATLY**
PALL	PEST	PLOT	*PREZ	PAINT	**PATSY**
PALM	**PFFT**	PLOW	PRIG	PAISA	**PATTY**
PALP	PFUI	PLOY	PRIM	PAISE	PAUSE
PALY	PHAT	PLUG	PROA	PALEA	**PAVAN**
PANE	**PHEW**	PLUM	PROD	PALER	**PAVER**
PANG	*PHIZ	PLUS	PROF	PALET	**PAVID**
PANT	PHON	**POCK**	PROG	**PALLY**	**PAVIN**
PAPA	PHOT	POCO	PROM	**PALMY**	PAVIS
PARA	PHUT	POEM	PROP	**PAMPA**	**PAWER**
PARD	PIAL	POET	PROW	PANDA	*PAWKY
PARE	PIAN	**POGY**	PSST	**PANDY**	PAYEE
PARK	PICA	**POKE**	PUCE	PANEL	**PAYER**
PARR	PICE	**POKY**	**PUCK**	PANGA	**PAYOR**
PART	**PICK**	POLE	**PUFF**	PANIC	PEACE
PASE	PIED	POLL	**PUGH**	PANNE	**PEACH**
PASH	PIER	POLO	**PUJA**	**PANSY**	PEAGE
PASS	**PIKA**	POLY	**PUKE**	PANTO	**PEAKY**
PAST	**PIKE**	POME	PULA	**PANTY**	PEARL
PATE	**PIKI**	**POMP**	PULE	PAPAL	PEART
PATH	PILE	POND	PULI	**PAPAW**	PEASE
PATY	PILI	PONE	PULL	PAPER	**PEATY**
PAVE	PILL	PONG	PULP	**PAPPI**	**PEAVY**
PAWL	PILY	PONS	PUMA	**PAPPY**	PECAN
PAWN	PIMA	PONY	**PUMP**	**PARCH**	*PECKY
PEAG	**PIMP**	POOD	PUNA	PARDI	PEDAL
PEAK	PINA	POOF	PUNG	**PARDY**	PEDES
PEAL	PINE	POOH	**PUNK**	PAREO	PEDRO
PEAN	PING	POOL	PUNT	PARER	**PEERY**
PEAR	**PINK**	POON	PUNY	PAREU	**PEEVE**
PEAT	PINT	POOP	PUPA	PARGE	PEISE
PECH	PINY	POOR	PURE	PARGO	**PEKAN**
PECK	PION	POPE	PURI	PARIS	**PEKIN**
PEEK	PIPE	PORE	PURL	**PARKA**	**PEKOE**
PEEL	**PIPY**	**PORK**	PURR	PARLE	PELON
PEEN	PIRN	PORN	PUSH	PAROL	PENAL
PEEP	PISH	PORT	PUSS	**PARRY**	PENCE
PEER	PISO	POSE	PUTT	PARSE	PENES
PEIN	PISS	POSH	*PUTZ	**PARTY**	PENGO
PEKE	PITA	POST	**PYIC**	**PARVE**	PENIS
PELE	PITH	POSY	PYIN	**PARVO**	PENNA

PENNE	PILUS	**PLUCK**	PRASE	*PSYCH	PAESAN
PENNI	**PINCH**	**PLUMB**	PRATE	PUBES	**PAGING**
PENNY	PINED	PLUME	PREEN	PUBIC	**PAGODA**
PEONY	**PINEY**	**PLUMP**	**PRAWN**	PUBIS	**PAINCH**
PEPPY	PINGO	**PLUMY**	PRESA	PUCKA	**PAINTY**
PERCH	**PINKO**	**PLUNK**	PRESE	PUDGY	PAISAN
PERDU	**PINKY**	**PLUSH**	PRESS	PUDIC	*PAJAMA
PERDY	PINNA	**PLYER**	PREST	*PUFFY	*PAKEHA
PERIL	**PINNY**	**POACH**	*PREXY	PUGGY	**PALACE**
PERKY	PINON	*POCKY	PRICE	*PUJAH	PALAIS
PERRY	PINOT	**PODGY**	**PRICK**	*PUKKA	PALATE
PERSE	PINTA	PODIA	**PRICY**	PULER	**PALELY**
PESKY	PINTO	**POESY**	PRIDE	PULIK	PALEST
PESTO	PINUP	**POGEY**	PRIED	PULPY	PALIER
PESTY	PIOUS	POILU	PRIER	PULSE	PALING
PETAL	PIPAL	POIND	PRIES	**PUNCH**	**PALISH**
PETER	PIPER	POINT	PRILL	PUNKA	PALLED
PETIT	PIPET	POISE	PRIMA	**PUNKY**	PALLET
PETTI	PIPIT	**POKER**	PRIME	**PUNNY**	PALLIA
PETTO	*PIQUE	**POKEY**	PRIMI	PUNTO	PALLID
PETTY	PIROG	POLAR	PRIMO	**PUNTY**	PALLOR
PEWEE	PISCO	POLED	**PRIMP**	PUPIL	**PALMAR**
PEWIT	PISTE	POLER	**PRINK**	**PUPPY**	**PALMER**
PHAGE	**PITCH**	POLIO	PRINT	PURDA	**PALPAL**
PHASE	**PITHY**	POLIS	PRION	PUREE	**PALPUS**
PHIAL	PITON	**POLKA**	PRIOR	PURER	PALTER
*PHLOX	**PIVOT**	**POLYP**	PRISE	PURGE	**PALTRY**
PHONE	**PIXEL**	PONCE	PRISM	PURIN	**PAMPER**
PHONO	**PIXIE**	**POOCH**	PRISS	PURSE	PANADA
PHONY	*PIZZA	POORI	**PRIVY**	**PURSY**	**PANAMA**
PHOTO	PLACE	**POPPA**	*PRIZE	PUSHY	PANDER
*PHPHT	**PLACK**	**POPPY**	PROBE	PUSSY	PANDIT
PHYLA	PLAGE	**POPSY**	PROEM	PUTON	**PANFRY**
PHYLE	PLAID	**PORCH**	PROLE	PUTTI	**PANFUL**
PIANO	PLAIN	**PORGY**	PROMO	PUTTO	PANGEN
PIBAL	PLAIT	**PORKY**	PRONE	**PUTTY**	PANIER
PICAL	PLANE	PORNO	PRONG	*PYGMY	PANNED
*PICKY	**PLANK**	**PORNY**	**PROOF**	PYLON	PANTIE
PICOT	PLANT	POSER	PROSE	**PYOID**	**PANTRY**
PICUL	**PLASH**	POSIT	PROSO	PYRAN	*PANZER
PIECE	PLASM	POSSE	PROSS	PYRIC	*PAPACY
PIETA	PLATE	**POTSY**	PROST	*PYXIE	PAPAIN
PIETY	**PLATY**	POTTO	**PROSY**	*PYXIS	PAPAYA
PIGGY	**PLAYA**	**POTTY**	PROUD	PABLUM	**PAPERY**
PIGMY	*PLAZA	**POUCH**	**PROVE**	*PACIFY	PAPIST
PIING	PLEAD	**POUFF**	**PROWL**	PACING	**PAPPUS**
PIKER	PLEAT	POULT	*PROXY	**PACKER**	**PAPULA**
PILAF	PLEBE	POUND	PRUDE	**PACKET**	**PAPULE**
PILAR	**PLENA**	**POUTY**	PRUNE	*PACKLY	PARADE
PILAU	PLICA	**POWER**	PRUTA	PADAUK	**PARAMO**
PILAW	PLIED	**POYOU**	**PRYER**	**PADDER**	PARANG
PILEA	PLIER	PRAAM	PSALM	**PADDLE**	**PARAPH**
PILED	PLIES	**PRAHU**	PSEUD	**PADNAG**	**PARCEL**
PILEI	**PLINK**	PRANG	**PSHAW**	PADOUK	**PARDAH**
PILOT	**PLONK**	**PRANK**	PSOAS	PAELLA	PARDEE

PARDIE	PATTEN	**PELTRY**	**PHASIS**	PIGNUT	**PIRAYA**
PARDON	PATTER	**PELVIC**	**PHATIC**	PIGOUT	PIROGI
PARENT	PATTIE	**PELVIS**	***PHENIX**	PIGOUT	PISTIL
PAREVE	***PATZER**	PENANG	**PHENOL**	**PIGPEN**	PISTOL
PARGET	PAULIN	**PENCEL**	**PHENOM**	***PIKAKE**	PISTON
PARIAH	**PAUNCH**	**PENCIL**	**PHENYL**	**PIKING**	***PITCHY**
PARIAN	**PAUPER**	**PENMAN**	**PHLEGM**	**PILAFF**	PITIED
PARIES	PAUSAL	PENNED	**PHLOEM**	**PILEUM**	PITIER
PARING	PAUSER	PENNER	**PHOBIA**	**PILEUP**	PITIES
PARISH	**PAVANE**	PENNON	***PHOBIC**	PILEUS	**PITMAN**
PARITY	**PAVEED**	PENSEE	**PHOEBE**	**PILFER**	**PITSAW**
PARKER	**PAVING**	PENSIL	**PHONAL**	PILING	PITTED
PARLAY	**PAVIOR**	PENTAD	**PHONEY**	PILLAR	***PIZAZZ**
PARLEY	**PAVISE**	**PENTYL**	**PHONIC**	**PILLOW**	***PIZZLE**
PARLOR	**PAWNEE**	PENULT	**PHONON**	PILOSE	**PLACER**
PARODY	**PAWNER**	**PENURY**	**PHOOEY**	PILOUS	**PLACET**
PAROLE	**PAWNOR**	**PEOPLE**	**PHOTIC**	PILULE	**PLACID**
PAROUS	***PAWPAW**	**PEPLOS**	**PHOTOG**	**PIMPLE**	PLAGAL
PARRAL	***PAXWAX**	**PEPLUM**	**PHOTON**	***PIMPLY**	PLAGUE
PARRED	***PAYDAY**	**PEPLUS**	**PHRASE**	PINANG	**PLAGUY**
PARREL	**PAYNIM**	**PEPPED**	**PHYLAE**	PINATA	**PLAICE**
PARROT	***PAYOFF**	**PEPPER**	**PHYLAR**	**PINCER**	PLAINT
PARSEC	**PAYOLA**	**PEPSIN**	**PHYLLO**	PINDER	PLANAR
PARSER	**PAYOUT**	**PEPTIC**	**PHYLON**	PINEAL	**PLANCH**
PARSON	***PAZAZZ**	**PEPTID**	***PHYLUM**	PINENE	PLANER
PARTAN	***PEACHY**	PERDIE	***PHYSED**	**PINERY**	PLANET
PARTLY	**PEAHEN**	PERDUE	**PHYSES**	PINGER	***PLAQUE**
PARTON	PEANUT	PEREON	***PHYSIC**	PINIER	**PLASHY**
PARURA	**PEARLY**	PERIOD	**PHYSIS**	PINING	**PLASMA**
PARURE	**PEAVEY**	**PERISH**	**PHYTIN**	PINION	PLATAN
PARVIS	**PEBBLE**	**PERMIT**	**PHYTON**	PINITE	PLATED
PASCAL	***PEBBLY**	***PEROXY**	**PIAFFE**	**PINKEN**	PLATEN
PASSEE	**PECHAN**	PERRON	***PIAZZA**	**PINKER**	PLATER
PASSEL	**PECKER**	PERSON	**PICARA**	***PINKEY**	**PLAYER**
PASSER	**PECTEN**	**PERUKE**	**PICARO**	**PINKIE**	**PLEACH**
PASSIM	**PECTIN**	PERUSE	***PICKAX**	PINKLY	PLEASE
PASSUS	PEDALO	**PESADE**	**PICKER**	PINNAE	**PLEDGE**
PASTEL	PEDANT	PESETA	**PICKET**	PINNAL	PLEIAD
PASTER	PEDATE	**PESEWA**	**PICKLE**	PINNED	**PLENCH**
PASTIE	**PEDDLE**	PESTER	***PICKUP**	PINNER	**PLENTY**
PASTIL	PEDLER	PESTLE	**PICNIC**	PINOLE	**PLENUM**
PASTIS	PEELER	PETARD	**PICRIC**	PINTLE	PLEURA
PASTOR	**PEEPER**	PETITE	**PIDDLE**	**PINYIN**	***PLEXAL**
PASTRY	**PEEPUL**	**PETNAP**	**PIDDLY**	**PINYON**	***PLEXOR**
PATACA	PEERIE	PETREL	**PIDGIN**	PIOLET	***PLEXUS**
***PATCHY**	**PEEWEE**	PETROL	**PIECER**	**PIPAGE**	PLIANT
PATENT	**PEEWIT**	PETSAI	PIEING	**PIPIER**	**PLIGHT**
PATHOS	***PEGBOX**	PETTED	**PIERCE**	**PIPING**	**PLINTH**
PATINA	**PEGGED**	PETTER	**PIFFLE**	**PIPKIN**	***PLISKY**
PATINE	PELAGE	**PETTLE**	PIGEON	**PIPPED**	PLISSE
PATOIS	PELITE	**PEWTER**	**PIGGED**	**PIPPIN**	**PLOIDY**
PATROL	PELLET	**PEYOTE**	**PIGGIE**	***PIQUET**	**PLOTTY**
PATRON	**PELMET**	**PEYOTL**	**PIGGIN**	**PIRACY**	**PLOUGH**
PATTED	PELOTA	**PHALLI**	PIGLET	PIRANA	**PLOVER**
PATTEE	PELTER	**PHAROS**	PIGNUS	PIRATE	**PLOWER**

*PLUCKY	PONTON	PRATER	PROPYL	*PUNKEY	*PACKAGE
*PLUMMY	POODLE	*PRAXIS	PROSER	PUNKIE	*PACKING
PLUNGE	POORLY	PRAYER	PROSIT	PUNKIN	*PACKMAN
PLURAL	POPERY	PREACH	PROTEA	PUNNED	*PACKWAX
PLUSHY	POPGUN	PREACT	PROTEI	PUNNER	PACTION
PLUTON	POPISH	PREAMP	PROTON	PUNNET	PADDIES
PNEUMA	POPLAR	PREARM	PROTYL	PUNTER	PADDING
*POACHY	POPLIN	PRECIS	PROVER	PUPATE	PADDLER
POCKET	POPPED	PRECUT	PROWAR	PUPPED	*PADDOCK
PODITE	POPPER	PREFAB	PRUNER	PUPPET	*PADLOCK
PODIUM	POPPET	PREFER	PRUNUS	PURANA	PADRONE
PODSOL	POPPLE	*PREFIX	PRUTAH	PURDAH	*PADSHAH
*PODZOL	POPSIE	PRELIM	PSEUDO	PURELY	PAESANO
POETIC	PORISM	PREMAN	PSOCID	PUREST	PAGEANT
POETRY	PORKER	PREMED	*PSYCHE	PURFLE	*PAGEBOY
POGIES	POROSE	PREMEN	*PSYCHO	PURGER	PAGINAL
POGROM	POROUS	PREMIE	PSYLLA	PURIFY	PAGURID
POINTE	PORTAL	*PREMIX	PSYWAR	PURINE	*PAHLAVI
POINTY	PORTER	PREPAY	PTERIN	PURISM	PAILFUL
POISER	PORTLY	*PREPPY	PTISAN	PURIST	PAINFUL
POISON	POSADA	PRESET	PTOSIS	PURITY	PAINTER
POKIER	POSEUR	PRESTO	PUBLIC	PURLIN	PAIRING
POKIES	POSIES	*PRETAX	PUCKER	PURPLE	PAISANA
*POKILY	POSING	PRETOR	PUDDLE	PURPLY	PAISANO
POKING	POSSET	PRETTY	PUDDLY	PURRED	PAISLEY
POLDER	POSSUM	PREVUE	PUEBLO	PURSER	PALABRA
*POLEAX	POSTAL	PREWAR	PUFFER	PURSUE	PALADIN
POLEIS	POSTER	PREYER	PUFFIN	PURVEY	PALATAL
POLEYN	POSTIN	PRIAPI	PUGGED	PUSHER	PALAVER
POLICE	POTAGE	PRICER	PUGGRY	PUSHUP	*PALAZZO
POLICY	POTASH	PRICEY	PUGREE	PUSLEY	PALETOT
POLING	POTATO	*PRICKY	PUISNE	PUSSLY	PALETTE
POLISH	POTBOY	PRIEST	PULING	PUTLOG	*PALFREY
POLITE	POTEEN	PRIMAL	PULLER	PUTOFF	PALIEST
POLITY	POTENT	PRIMER	PULLET	PUTOUT	PALIKAR
POLLEE	POTFUL	PRIMLY	PULLEY	PUTRID	PALLIAL
POLLEN	POTHER	PRIMUS	PULLUP	PUTSCH	PALLIER
POLLER	POTION	PRINCE	PULPAL	PUTTEE	PALLING
*POLLEX	POTMAN	PRIORY	PULPER	PUTTER	PALLIUM
POLYPI	POTPIE	PRISON	PULPIT	*PUZZLE	PALMARY
POMACE	POTSIE	PRISSY	*PULQUE	PYEMIA	PALMATE
POMADE	POTTED	PRIVET	PULSAR	*PYKNIC	PALMIER
POMELO	POTTER	*PRIZEA	PULSER	PYOSIS	PALMIST
POMMEE	POTTLE	PROBER	PUMELO	PYRENE	PALMYRA
POMMEL	*POTZER	PROBIT	PUMICE	PYRITE	PALOOKA
POMPOM	*POUCHY	PROFIT	PUMMEL	PYROLA	PALPATE
POMPON	POUFFE	*PROJET	PUMPER	PYRONE	PALSHIP
PONCHO	POUNCE	PROLAN	*PUNCHY	PYROPE	PALUDAL
PONDER	POURER	PROLEG	PUNDIT	PYRROL	PAMPEAN
PONENT	POUTER	*PROLIX	PUNGLE	PYTHON	PAMPERO
PONGEE	POWDER	PROLOG	PUNIER	PYURIA	PANACEA
PONGID	POWTER	PROMPT	PUNILY	PABULUM	PANACHE
PONIED	*POWWOW	PRONTO	PUNISH	PACHISI	*PANCAKE
PONIES	PRAISE	PROPEL	*PUNKAH	*PACHUCO	*PANCHAX
PONTIL	PRANCE	PROPER	PUNKER	*PACIFIC	PANDECT

PANDIED	PARONYM	PAUCITY	*PEMPHIX	PERIGON	PHONATE
PANDIES	PAROTIC	*PAUGHTY	PENALLY	PERILLA	PHONEME
PANDOOR	PAROTID	*PAUNCHY	PENALTY	*PERIQUE	PHONICS
PANDORA	*PARQUET	PAVIOUR	PENANCE	PERIWIG	PHONIED
PANDORE	PARRIED	PAVISER	PENATES	*PERJURE	PHONIER
PANDOUR	PARRIES	*PAVLOVA	PENDANT	*PERJURY	PHONIES
PANDURA	PARRING	PAWNAGE	PENDENT	*PERKISH	*PHONILY
*PANFISH	PARROTY	PAYABLE	PENGUIN	PERLITE	PHONING
PANGENE	PARSING	*PAYBACK	PENICIL	PERMUTE	PHORATE
*PANICKY	PARSLEY	PAYLOAD	PENLITE	PERORAL	PHOTICS
PANICLE	PARSNIP	PAYMENT	PENNAME	*PEROXID	PHRASAL
PANICUM	PARTAKE	PAYROLL	PENNANT	PERPEND	*PHRATRY
PANNIER	PARTIAL	PEACHER	PENNATE	PERPENT	PHRENIC
PANNING	PARTIED	PEACING	PENNIES	*PERPLEX	*PHRENSY
PANOCHA	PARTIER	PEACOAT	PENNINE	PERSALT	*PHYTANE
PANOCHE	PARTIES	*PEACOCK	PENNING	PERSIST	*PHYTOID
PANOPLY	PARTING	*PEAFOWL	PENOCHE	PERSONA	*PIAFFER
PANPIPE	PARTITA	PEAKIER	PENSILE	PERTAIN	PIANISM
PANTHER	PARTITE	*PEAKISH	PENSION	PERTURB	PIANIST
PANTIES	PARTLET	PEALIKE	PENSIVE	PERUSAL	PIASABA
PANTILE	PARTNER	PEARLER	PENSTER	PERUSER	PIASAVA
PANTOUM	PARTOOK	PEASANT	PENTANE	PERVADE	PIASTER
PAPERER	*PARTWAY	PEASCOD	PENTENE	PERVERT	PIASTRE
PAPHIAN	PARTYER	PECCANT	PENTODE	PESSARY	*PIBROCH
PAPILLA	PARVENU	*PECCARY	PENTOSE	PETASOS	*PICACHO
PAPOOSE	PARVISE	*PECCAVI	PENUCHE	PETASUS	PICADOR
PAPPIER	PASCHAL	*PECKISH	PENUCHI	*PETCOCK	PICCOLO
PAPPIES	*PASQUIL	PECTASE	PEONAGE	PETIOLE	PICEOUS
PAPRICA	PASSADE	PECTATE	PEONISM	*PETRIFY	*PICKAXE
*PAPRIKA	PASSADO	*PECTIZE	PEOPLER	PETROUS	*PICKEER
PAPYRUS	PASSAGE	PEDAGOG	*PEPPERY	PETTIER	*PICKIER
PARABLE	PASSANT	PEDDLER	PEPPING	PETTILY	*PICKING
PARADER	PASSING	PEDICAB	PEPSINE	PETTING	*PICKOFF
PARADOR	PASSION	PEDICEL	PEPTIDE	PETTISH	PICOLIN
PARADOS	PASSIVE	PEDICLE	*PEPTIZE	PETUNIA	PICOTEE
*PARADOX	*PASSKEY	PEDLARY	PEPTONE	PEYTRAL	*PICQUET
PARAGON	PASTERN	PEDLERY	PERACID	PEYTREL	PICRATE
PARAPET	PASTEUP	PEDOCAL	PERCALE	PFENNIG	PICRITE
PARASOL	PASTIER	PEEBEEN	PERCENT	PHAETON	PICTURE
PARBOIL	PASTIES	PEELING	PERCEPT	*PHALANX	PIDDLER
PARDINE	PASTIME	PEERAGE	PERCHER	PHALLIC	*PIDDOCK
PARDNER	PASTINA	PEERESS	PERCOID	PHALLUS	PIEBALD
PAREIRA	PASTING	*PEEVISH	PERCUSS	PHANTOM	PIECING
PARESIS	PASTURE	PEGGING	PERDURE	*PHARAOH	PIEFORT
PARETIC	PATAMAR	PEGLESS	PEREION	*PHARYNX	PIERCER
PARFAIT	PATCHER	PEGLIKE	PERFECT	*PHASMID	PIEROGI
PARGING	PATELLA	PELAGIC	*PERFIDY	PHELLEM	PIERROT
PARKING	PATENCY	PELICAN	PERFORM	PHENATE	PIETIES
*PARKWAY	*PATHWAY	PELISSE	PERFUME	*PHENOXY	PIETISM
PARLING	PATIENT	PELORIA	PERFUSE	PHILTER	PIETIST
PARLOUR	PATNESS	PELORUS	PERGOLA	PHILTRE	PIGBOAT
PARLOUS	PATRIOT	PELTAST	PERHAPS	*PHLEGMY	*PIGFISH
PARODIC	PATROON	PELTATE	PERIAPT	PHOCINE	PIGGERY
PARODOS	PATTERN	PEMBINA	PERIDOT	PHOEBUS	PIGGIER
PAROLEE	PATTING	PEMICAN	PERIGEE	*PHOENIX	PIGGIES

PIGGING	PIPIEST	PLATING	PLUNDER	POPOVER	POULTRY
PIGGISH	PIPPING	PLATOON	PLUNGER	POPPIED	POUNCER
PIGLIKE	*PIQUANT	PLATTED	PLUNKER	POPPIES	POUNDAL
PIGMENT	PIRAGUA	PLATTER	PLUSSES	POPPING	POUNDER
PIGNOLI	PIRANHA	PLAUDIT	PLUTEUS	POPULAR	POUSSIE
PIGSKIN	PIRATIC	PLAYACT	PLUVIAL	PORCINE	POUTFUL
PIGSNEY	PIROGUE	*PLAYBOY	PLUVIAN	PORCINO	*POVERTY
PIGWEED	*PIROQUE	*PLAYDAY	*PLYWOOD	PORKIER	*POWDERY
*PIKEMAN	PISCARY	*PLAYFUL	POACHER	PORKIES	PRACTIC
PILEATE	PISCINA	PLAYLET	*POCHARD	PORRECT	PRAETOR
PILEOUS	PISCINE	*PLAYOFF	POCOSIN	PORTAGE	PRAIRIE
PILGRIM	PISHOGE	PLAYPEN	PODAGRA	PORTEND	PRAISER
PILLAGE	PISMIRE	PLEADER	PODESTA	PORTENT	PRALINE
*PILLBOX	PISSANT	PLEASER	PODLIKE	PORTICO	PRANCER
PILLION	PISSOIR	PLEATER	POETESS	PORTION	PRATING
PILLORY	PISTOLE	PLEDGEE	POETICS	PORTRAY	PRATTLE
*PILLOWY	PITAPAT	PLEDGER	*POETIZE	POSSESS	PRAWNER
PILSNER	PITCHER	PLEDGET	POETISE	POSTAGE	*PREACHY
PIMENTO	PITEOUS	PLEDGOR	POGONIA	POSTBAG	PREAGED
PINBALL	PITFALL	PLENARY	POGONIP	*POSTBOX	PREANAL
PINBONE	PITHEAD	PLENISH	POINTER	POSTBOY	PREAVER
PINCHER	PITIFUL	PLENISM	POITREL	POSTDOC	*PREBAKE
PINESAP	PITTING	PLENIST	POKIEST	POSTEEN	PREBEND
PINETUM	PIVOTAL	PLEOPOD	POLARON	POSTERN	PREBILL
*PINFISH	*PIZAZZY	PLESSOR	*POLEAXE	*POSTFIX	PREBIND
PINFOLD	PLACARD	PLEURON	POLECAT	POSTING	PREBOIL
PINGUID	PLACATE	PLIABLE	POLEMIC	POSTMAN	*PREBOOK
PINHEAD	PLACEBO	PLIANCY	POLENTA	*POSTTAX	PREBOOM
PINHOLE	PLACING	PLICATE	POLITIC	POSTURE	PRECAST
PINIEST	*PLACKET	PLIMSOL	*POLLACK	POSTWAR	PRECAVA
PINITOL	PLACOID	PLINKER	POLLARD	POTABLE	PRECEDE
*PINKEYE	PLAFOND	PLISKIE	POLLIST	POTAMIC	PRECENT
PINKIES	PLAGUER	PLODDER	*POLLOCK	POTBOIL	PRECEPT
PINKING	PLAGUEY	PLOSION	POLLUTE	POTENCE	PRECESS
*PINKISH	PLAITER	PLOSIVE	POLOIST	POTENCY	PRECIPE
PINNACE	PLANATE	PLOTTED	POLYCOT	POTHEAD	PRECISE
PINNATE	PLANCHE	PLOTTER	POLYENE	POTHEEN	PRECODE
PINNIES	PLANING	*PLOWBOY	POLYGON	POTHERB	*PRECOOK
PINNING	PLANISH	PLOWMAN	POLYMER	POTHOLE	PRECOOL
PINNULA	PLANNED	*PLUCKER	*POLYNYA	*POTHOOK	PRECOUP
PINNULE	PLANNER	PLUGGER	POLYOMA	POTICHE	PRECURE
PINOCLE	PLANTAR	PLUGOLA	*POLYPOD	POTLACH	PREDATE
PINTADA	PLANULA	PLUMAGE	POLYPUS	POTLIKE	PREDAWN
PINTADO	PLASHER	PLUMATE	POMATUM	POTLIKE	PREDIAL
PINTAIL	PLASMID	PLUMBER	POMFRET	POTLINE	PREDICT
PINTANO	PLASMIN	*PLUMBIC	POMPANO	*POTLUCK	PREDIVE
PINWALE	PLASMON	*PLUMBUM	POMPOUS	POTSHOT	PREDUSK
PINWEED	PLASTER	PLUMIER	PONIARD	POTTAGE	PREEDIT
*PINWORK	PLASTIC	PLUMING	*PONTIFF	POTTEFN	PREEMIE
PINWORM	PLASTID	PLUMMET	PONTINE	POTTERY	PREEMPT
PIONEER	PLATANE	PLUMOSE	PONTOON	POTTIER	PREENER
PIOSITY	PLATEAU	PLUMPEN	POORISH	POTTIES	PREFACE
PIPEAGE	PLATIER	PLUMPER	POPCORN	POTTING	PREFADE
PIPEFUL	PLATIES	*PLUMPLY	POPEDOM	POULARD	PREFECT
PIPETTE	PLATINA	PLUMULE	*POPEYED	POULTER	PREFILE

PREFIRE	PRETRIM	PRODUCT	*PROVOKE	PUNNING	*PACKAGER
PREFORM	PRETYPE	PROETTE	PROVOST	PUNSTER	*PACKNESS
PREGAME	*PRETZEL	PROFANE	PROWESS	*PUPFISH	*PACKSACK
PREHEAT	PREVAIL	PROFESS	PROWLER	PUPILAR	PADDLING
PRELACY	PREVENT	*PROFFER	*PROXIES	PUPPING	*PADISHAH
PRELATE	*PREVIEW	PROFILE	*PROXIMO	PURGING	PADUASOY
PRELECT	PREVISE	PROFUSE	PRUDENT	PURITAN	PAEANISM
PRELIFE	PREWARM	PROGENY	PRUDERY	PURLIEU	PAGANDOM
PRELUDE	PREWARN	PROGGER	PRUDISH	PURLINE	PAGANISE
PREMADE	*PREWASH	PROGRAM	PRUNING	PURLOIN	PAGANISH
PREMEAL	*PREWORK	*PROJECT	PRURIGO	PURPORT	PAGANISM
PREMEET	PREWRAP	PROLATE	PRUSSIC	PURPOSE	PAGANIST
PREMIER	PRIAPIC	PROLINE	*PRYTHEE	PURPURA	*PAGANIZE
PREMISE	PRICIER	PROLONG	PSALMIC	PURPURE	PAGINATE
PREMISS	PRICING	PROMINE	PSALTER	PURRING	PAGURIAN
PREMIUM	*PRICKER	PROMISE	PSALTRY	PURSIER	*PAHOEHOE
PREMOLD	*PRICKET	PROMOTE	PSAMMON	PURSILY	PAILLARD
PREMOLT	*PRICKLE	PRONATE	PSCHENT	PURSING	PAINLESS
PREMUNE	*PRICKLY	PRONOUN	*PSYCHIC	PURSUER	PAINTING
PRENAME	*PRIMACY	PROOFER	PSYLLID	PURSUIT	*PAJAMAED
PRENOON	PRIMAGE	PROPEND	PTERYLA	*PURVIEW	PALATIAL
*PREPACK	PRIMARY	PROPENE	PTOMAIN	*PUSHFUL	PALATINE
PREPAID	PRIMATE	PROPHET	PTYALIN	PUSHIER	*PALAZZOS
PREPARE	PRIMELY	PROPINE	PUBERTY	*PUSHILY	*PALEFACE
PREPILL	PRIMERO	*PROPJET	PUBLISH	PUSHPIN	PALENESS
PREPLAN	PRIMINE	PROPMAN	PUCCOON	PUSSIER	PALEOSOL
PREPPED	PRIMING	PROPONE	*PUCKERY	PUSSIES	PALESTRA
PREPPIE	PRIMMED	PROPOSE	*PUCKISH	PUSSLEY	*PALEWAYS
PREPREG	PRIMMER	PROPPED	PUDDING	PUSSLEY	PALEWISE
PREPUCE	PRIMSIE	PRORATE	PUDDLER	PUSTULE	*PALIMONY
*PREQUEL	PRIMULA	PROSAIC	*PUDENCY	PUTAMEN	PALINODE
PRERACE	*PRINCOX	PROSECT	PUERILE	*PUTREFY	PALISADE
PRERIOT	PRINKER	PROSIER	*PUFFERY	PUTTIED	PALLADIA
*PREROCK	PRINTER	PROSILY	PUGAREE	PUTTIER	PALLADIC
PRESAGE	PRIORLY	PROSING	PUGGIER	PUTTING	PALLETTE
PRESALE	PRISERE	PROSODY	PUGGING	*PUZZLER	PALLIATE
PRESELL	PRITHEE	PROSOMA	PUGGISH	PYAEMIA	PALLIEST
PRESENT	*PRIVACY	PROSPER	PUGGREE	*PYJAMAS	PALMATED
PRESHOW	PRIVATE	PROSSIE	*PUGMARK	PYLORUS	PALMETTE
PRESIDE	PRIVIER	PROSTIE	PULLMAN	PYRALID	PALMETTO
PRESIFT	PRIVIES	PROTEAN	PULLOUT	*PYRAMID	PALMIEST
PRESOAK	*PRIVITY	PROTECT	PULPIER	PYRETIC	PALMITIN
PRESOLD	PROBAND	PROTÉGÉ	PULPILY	*PYREXIA	*PALMLIKE
PRESONG	PROBANG	PROTEID	PULPOUS	PRYOGEN	PALOMINO
PRESORT	PROBATE	PROTEIN	PULSANT	PYROSIS	PALPABLE
PRESSER	PROBITY	PROTEND	PULSATE	*PYRRHIC	PALPATOR
PRESSOR	PROBLEM	PROTEST	PULSING	PYRROLE	PALPEBRA
PRESTER	PROCARP	PROTEUS	PULSION	*PACHADOM	PALTERER
PRESUME	PROCEED	PROTIST	PUMICER	*PACHALIC	PALUDISM
PRETAPE	PROCESS	PROTIUM	PUMMELO	*PACHINKO	PAMPERER
PRETEEN	PROCTOR	PROTYLE	*PUMPKIN	*PACHOULI	*PAMPHLET
PRETEND	PROCURE	PROVERB	PUNCHER	*PACIFIED	PANATELA
PRETERM	PRODDER	PROVIDE	PUNGENT	*PACIFIER	PANBROIL
PRETEST	PRODIGY	PROVING	PUNIEST	*PACIFIES	PANCETTA
PRETEXT	PRODUCE	PROVISO	*PUNKISH	*PACIFISM	PANCREAS
				*PACIFIST	

PANDANUS	*PARCHISI	PASTURAL	PEDIGREE	*PERFECTO	*PHANTASM
*PANDEMIC	PARDONER	PASTURER	PEDIMENT	*PERFORCE	PHANTAST
PANDERER	PARECISM	PATAGIAL	*PEDIPALP	*PERFUMER	*PHANTASY
*PANDOWDY	PARENTAL	PATAGIUM	*PEDOLOGY	PERIANTH	PHARISEE
PANELING	PARERGON	PATENTEE	PEDUNCLE	PERIBLEM	*PHARMACY
PANELIST	PARFLESH	PATENTLY	*PEEKABOO	PERICARP	PHASEOUT
PANELLED	*PARFOCAL	PATENTOR	*PEEPHOLE	PERICOPE	PHEASANT
PANETELA	PARHELIA	PATERNAL	*PEEPSHOW	PERIDERM	PHELONIA
PANGOLIN	*PARHELIC	*PATHETIC	PEERLESS	PERIDIUM	*PHENAZIN
*PANHUMAN	PARIETAL	PATHLESS	*PEESWEEP	*PERIGYNY	*PHENETIC
*PANMIXIA	*PARKLAND	PATHOGEN	PEETWEET	PERILOUS	PHENETOL
*PANMIXIS	*PARKLIKE	PATIENCE	PEGBOARD	PERILUNE	*PHENOLIC
PANNIKIN	PARLANCE	PATINATE	PEIGNOIR	PERINEUM	*PHILABEC,
PANOPTIC	PARLANDO	*PATINIZE	PELERINE	PERIODIC	*PHILIBEG
PANORAMA	PARLANTE	PATTAMAR	PELLAGRA	PERIODID	*PHILOMEL
*PANSOPHY	PARLEYER	PATTERER	PELLETAL	PERIOTIC	*PHILTRUM
PANTHEON	PARODIED	*PATTYPAN	PELLICLE	*PERIPETY	*PHIMOSIS
PANTOFLE	PARODIES	PATULENT	PELLMELL	PERIPTER	*PHONETIC
PANTSUIT	PARODIST	PATULOUS	PELLUCID	PERISARC	PHONIEST
*PAPERBOY	*PAROQUET	PAULDRON	*PEMMICAN	*PERJURER	PHORONID
PAPILLON	PAROTOID	*PAVEMENT	PEMOLINE	PERLUDER	PHOSGENE
*PAPISTRY	*PAROXYSM	PAVILLON	PENALISE	PERMEANT	*PHOSPHID
PAPPIES	PARRIDGE	PAVONINE	PENALITY	PERMEASE	*PHOSPHIN
PAPPOOSE	*PARRITCH	*PAWNSHOP	PENALIZE	PERMEATE	*PHOSPHOR
PARABOLA	PARROKET	*PAYABLES	*PENCHANT	PERONEAL	*PHOTOMAP
*PARACHOR	PARROTER	*PAYCHECK	PENCILER	PERORATE	*PHOTOPIA
PARADIGM	PARTAKER	*PAYGRADE	*PENDENCY	*PEROXIDE	PHOTOSET
PARADING	PARTERRE	*PEACEFUL	PENDULUM	PERSONAL	PHRASING
PARADISE	PARTIBLE	*PEACENIK	PENITENT	PERSPIRE	*PHREATIC
PARADROP	PARTICLE	*PEACOCKY	*PENKNIFE	PERSUADE	*PHTHALIC
*PARAFFIN	PARTISAN	PEAKIEST	PENLIGHT	PERTNESS	*PHTHALIN
*PARAFORM	*PARTIZAN	PEAKLESS	PENNATED	PERVADER	*PHTHISIC
PARAGOGE	PARVENUE	*PEAKLIKE	PENOLOGY	PERVERSE	*PHTHISIS
PARAKEET	PARVOLIN	PEARLASH	PENONCEL	PERVIOUS	*PHYLAXIS
PARAKITE	*PASHADOM	PEARLITE	PENPOINT	PESTERER	*PHYLESIS
*PARALLAX	*PASHALIC	PEARMAIN	PENSIONE	PESTHOLE	*PHYLLARY
PARALLEL	*PASHALIK	PEASECOD	*PENSTOCK	PETALINE	*PHYLLITE
PARALYSE	PASSABLE	*PECCABLE	PENTACLE	PETALODY	*PHYLLODE
*PARALYZE	PASSBAND	*PECCANCY	PENTAGON	PETALOID	*PHYLLOID
PARAMENT	*PASSBOOK	PECORINO	PENTANOL	PETALOUS	*PHYLLOME
PARAMOUR	*PASSERBY	PECTORAL	*PENTARCH	*PETECHIA	*PHYSICAL
PARANOEA	PASSIBLE	PECULATE	PENTOMIC	PETIOLAR	*PHYSIQUE
PARANOIA	PASSLESS	PECULIAR	PENTOSAN	PETITION	PIACULAR
PARANOIC	PASSOVER	PECULIUM	*PENUCHLE	PETROLIC	PIASSABA
PARANOID	PASSPORT	*PEDAGOGY	*PENUCKLE	PETRONEL	PIASSAVA
*PARAQUAT	PASSWORD	PEDALFEIR	PENUMBRA	PETROSAL	PICAROON
*PAREQUET	PASTICCI	PEDALIER	PEPERONI	PETTEDLY	*PICAYUNE
PARASANG	*PASTICHE	PEDALLED	PEPONIDA	PETTIEST	*PICIFORM
*PARASHAH	PASTIEST	PEDANTRY	PEPONIUM	PETTIFOG	*PICKADIL
PARASITE	PASTILLE	*PEDDLERY	PEPPERER	PETULANT	*PICKEREL
PARAVANE	PASTLESS	PEDDLING	*PEPTIZER	PETUNTSE	*PICKETER
PARAWING	PASTNESS	PEDERAST	*PERCEIVE	PEWTERER	*PICKIEST
*PARAZOAN	PASTORAL	PEDESTAL	PEREGRIN	PHALANGE	*PICKLOCK
PARCENER	PASTRAMI	PEDICURE	PEREOPOD	*PHALLISM	*PICKWICK
*PARCHESI	PASTROMI	*PEDIFORM	*PERFECTA	PHALLIST	PICLORAM

*PICNICKY	PIRARUCU	*PLAYBILL	PLUVIOSE	*POLYSEMY	POSTCOUP
*PICOGRAM	*PIRIFORM	*PLAYBOOK	PLUVIOUS	*POLYSOME	POSTDATE
PICOLINE	*PIROZHOK	*PLAYDOWN	POACEOUS	POLYTENE	POSTDIVE
PICOMOLE	PISCATOR	PLAYGIRL	*POCKETER	*POLYTENY	POSTDRUG
PIECRUST	PISHOGUE	PLAYGOER	*POCKMARK	*POLYTYPE	POSTFACE
PIEDFORT	*PISIFORM	PLAYLAND	PODIATRY	POLYURIA	POSTFIRE
PIEDMONT	PISOLITE	PLAYLESS	*PODOCARP	*POLYZOAN	POSTFORM
PIEPLANT	*PISTACHE	*PLAYLIKE	PODOMERE	*POLYZOIC	POSTGAME
PIGGIEST	*PITCHIER	*PLAYMATE	*POECHORE	POMANDER	POSTHEAT
PIGNOLIA	*PITCHILY	*PLAYROOM	POETICAL	*POMOLOGY	POSTHOLE
PIGSTICK	*PITCHMAN	PLAYSUIT	POETISER	PONDERER	*POSTICHE
PILASTER	*PITCHOUT	*PLAYTIME	*POETIZER	*PONDWEED	*POSTIQUE
*PILCHARD	PITHLESS	*PLAYWEAR	POETLESS	*PONTIFEX	POSTLUDE
PILEATED	PITIABLE	PLEADING	POETLIKE	*PONTIFIC	*POSTMARK
PILELESS	PITILESS	PLEASANT	POIGNANT	PONYTAIL	POSTORAL
PILEWORT	PITTANCE	PLEASURE	POINTMAN	POOLHALL	POSTPAID
PILFERER	*PIVOTMAN	PLEBEIAN	POISONER	POOLROOM	POSTPONE
*PILIFORM	*PIXINESS	PLECTRON	POKERGOT	POOLSIDE	POSTRACE
PILLAGER	*PIZZERIA	PLECTRUM	*POKEWEED	POORNESS	POSTRIOT
PILOSITY	PLACABLE	PLEDGEOR	POKINESS	POORTITH	*POSTSHOW
PILOTAGE	PLACATER	PLEDGING	POLARISE	*POPINJAY	*POSTSYNC
PILOTING	PLACEMAN	PLEONASM	POLARITY	POPLITIC	POSTTEEN
PILSENER	PLACENTA	PLETHORA	*POLARIZE	POPULACE	POSTTEST
PIMIENTO	PLAGIARY	PLEURISY	POLELESS	POPULATE	POSTURAL
PINAFORE	PLAGUING	PLEUSTON	POLEMIST	POPULISM	POSTURER
PINASTER	PLAISTER	PLICATED	*POLEMIZE	POPULIST	POTASSIC
*PINCHBUG	PLAITING	PLIGHTER	POLESTAR	POPULOUS	POTATION
*PINCHECK	PLANARIA	PLIMSOLE	POLEWARD	PORKIEST	POTATORY
PINDLING	*PLANCHET	PLIMSOLL	POLISHER	*PORKWOOD	*POTBELLY
PINECONE	*PLANFORM	PLIOTRON	*POLITICK	POROSITY	POTHOUSE
PINELAND	PLANGENT	PLOTLESS	POLITICO	*PORPHYRY	*POTLACHE
PINELIKE	*PLANKING	PLOTLINE	POLITICS	PORPOISE	*POTLATCH
PINEWOOD	PLANKTER	PLOTTAGE	POLLINIA	PORRIDGE	POTSTHARD
PINGRASS	PLANKTON	PLOTTIER	POLLINIC	PORTABLE	POTSHERD
PINKNESS	PLANLESS	PLOTTIES	POLLIWOG	*PORTABLY	POTSTONE
PINKROOT	PLANNING	PLOTTING	POLLSTER	PORTANCE	POTTERER
PINNACLE	PLANOSOL	PLOUGHER	*PORTAPAK		
PINNACLE	PLANOSOL	PLOUGHER	*POLLYWOG	*PORTAPAK	POTTIEST
PINNATED	PLANTAIN	*PLOWBACK	POLONIUM	PORTHOLE	POULARDE
PINNIPED	PLANTING	*PLOWHEAD	POLTROON	PORTIERE	POULTICE
*PINOCHLE	PLANTLET	PLOWLAND	*POLYBIRD	PORTLESS	POUNDAGE
PINPOINT	PLASMOID	PLUGLESS	POLYGALA	PORTRAIT	POWDERER
*PINPRICK	PLASTERY	*PLUGUGLY	*POLYGAMY	PORTRESS	*POWERFUL
*PINSCHER	PLASTRON	*PLUMBAGO	POLYGENE	POSHNESS	*POXVIRUS
*PINTSIZE	PLASTRUM	*PLUMBERY	POLYGLOT	POSINGLY	*POZZOLAN
*PINWHEEL	PLATEFUL	*PLUMBING	*POLYGONY	POSITION	PRACTICE
*PIPEFISH	PLATELET	*PLUMBISM	*POLYGYNY	POSITIVE	PRACTISE
PIPELESS	*PLATFORM	PLUMBOUS	*POLYMATH	POSITRON	PRAECIPE
*PIPELIKE	PLATIEST	PLUMELET	*POLYPARY	POSOLOGY	PRAEDIAL
PIPELINE	PLATINIC	PLUMERIA	*POLYPIDE	POSSIBLE	*PRAEFECT
PIPERINE	PLATINUM	PLUMIEST	*POLYPNEA	POSTALLY	PRAELECT
PIPESTEM	PLATONIC	*PLUMIPED	*POLYPODY	POSTANAL	PRANDIAL
PIPINESS	PLATTING	*PLUMLIKE	*POLYPOID	POSTBURN	*PRANKISH
*PIPINGLY	*PLATYPUS	*PLUMPISH	*POLYPORE	POSTCARD	PRATFALL
*PIQUANCE	PLAUSIVE	PLURALLY	*POLYPOUS	POSTCAVA	*PRATIQUE
*PIQUANCY	*PLAYBACK	PLUSSAGE		POSTCODE	PRATTLER

*PREACHER	*PREPPING	*PRIMMING	PROPIENSE	PSILOSIS	*PURCHASE
PREADAPT	PREPRICE	PRIMNESS	*PROPENYL	PSORALEA	PUREBRED
PREADMIT	PREPRINT	PRIMROSE	*PROPERTY	PSORALEN	PURENESS
PREADOPT	*PREPUNCH	*PRINCELY	*PROPHAGE	*PSYLLIUM	PURFLING
PREADULT	PREPUPAL	PRINCESS	*PROPHASE	PTEROPOD	PURIFIER
PREALLOT	PRERENAL	PRINCIPE	*PROPHECY	PTERYGIA	*PURPLISH
PREAMBLE	PRERINSE	PRINCIPE	*PROPHESY	PTOMAINE	PURPURIC
PREAUDIT	PRESAGER	PRINTERY	PROPOLIS	*PTYALISM	PURPURIN
*PREAXIAL	PRESCIND	PRINTING	PROPOSAL	PUBLICAN	PURSIEST
PREBASAL	PRESCORE	PRINTOUT	PROPOSER	*PUBLICLY	PURSLANE
PREBLESS	PRESENCE	PRIORATE	PROPOUND	*PUCKERER	PURSUANT
PREBOUND	PRESERVE	PRIORESS	*PROPPING	PUDDLING	PURSLENT
*PRECHECK	*PRESHAPE	PRIORIES	*PROPYLON	PUDENDUM	*PURVEYOR
*PRECHILL	PRESIDER	PRIORITY	PROROGUE	*PUFFBALL	*PUSHBALL
*PRECIEUX	PRESIDIA	PRISMOID	PROSAISM	PUGGAREE	*PUSHCART
PRECINCT	PRESIDIO	PRISONER	PROSAIST	PUGGIEST	*PUSHDOWN
PRECIOUS	PRESLEEP	PRISTANE	PROSIEST	PUGILISM	PUSHIEST
PRECITED	PRESLICE	PRISTINE	PROSPECT	PUGILIST	*PUSHOVER
PRECLEAN	PRESPLIT	PROBABLE	PROSTATE	PUISSANT	PUSSIEST
PRECLEAR	PRESSING	*PROBABLY	PROSTYLE	PULICENE	PUSSLIKE
PRECLUDE	PRESSMAN	PROCAINE	PROTAMIN	PULICIDE	*PUSSYCAT
*PRECRASH	PRESSRUN	*PROCHAIN	PROTASIS	PULINGLY	PUTATIVE
PREDATOR	PRESSURE	*PROCHEIN	PROTEASE	*PULLBACK	PUTTERER
PREDRILL	PRESTAMP	PROCLAIM	PROTEGEE	PULLOVER	*PYCNIDIA
PREELECT	PRESTIGE	PROCURAL	PROTEIDE	PULMONIC	*PYCNOSIS
PREENACT	PRESUMER	PROCURER	PROTEOSE	PULMOTOR	*PYCNOTIC
PREERECT	PRETASTE	PRODIGAL	PROTOCOL	PULPIEST	PYELITIS
*PREEXIST	PRETENCE	PRODROME	PROTOPOD	PULPLESS	*PYGIDIUM
*PREFACER	PRETENSE	PRODUCER	*PROTOXID	*PULPWOOD	*PYGMYISM
*PREFIGHT	PRETERIT	PROFANER	*PROTOZOA	PULSATOR	*PYKNOSIS
*PREFIXAL	PRETRAIN	PROFILER	PROTRACT	*PULSEJETR	*PYKNOTIC
*PREFLAME	PRETREAT	PROFITER	PROTRUDE	*PULSOJET	*PYODERMA
*PREFOCUS	PRETRIAL	PROFOUND	PROUDFUL	PULVILLI	*PYOGENIC
*PREFRANK	PRETTIED	PROGERIA	PROUNION	PULVINUS	*PYORRHEA
PREGGERS	PRETTIER	PROGGING	*PROVENLY	PUMICITE	PYRANOSE
PREGNANT	PRETTIES	PROGNOSE	PROVIDER	PUMPLESS	PYRENOID
*PREHUMAN	*PRETTIFY	PROGRADE	*PROVINCE	*PUMPLIKE	PYRIDINE
*PREJUDGE	PREUNION	PROGRESS	PROVIRUS	*PUNCHEON	*PYRIFORM
PRELEGAL	PREUNITE	*PROHIBIT	*PROVOKER	PUNCTATE	*PYROLOGY
PRELIMIT	PREVIOUS	PROLABOR	*PROXEMIC	PUNCTUAL	*PYROLYZE
*PRELUNCH	PREVISOR	PROIAMIN	*PROXIMAL	PUNCTURE	PYRONINE
*PREMEDIC	PRIAPEAN	PROLAPSE	*PRTUNTZE	PUNDITRY	PYROSTAT
PREMIERE	PRIAPISM	*PROLIFIC	PRUDENCE	*PUNGENCY	*PYROXENE
PREMOLAR	PRICIEST	PROLOGUE	PRUINOSE	PUNINESS	*PYRUVATE
PREMORAL	*PRICKIER	PROLONGE	PRUNELLA	PUNISHER	*PYXIDIUM
PREMORSE	*PRICKING	PROMISEE	PRUNELLE	PUNITION	
PRENATAL	PRIDEFUL	PROMISER	PRUNELLO	PUNITIVE	S PAE
PRENOMEN	PRIEDIEU	PROMISOR	PRURIENT	PUNITORY	S PAN
PRENTICE	PRIESTLY	PROMOTER	PRURITUS	PUPARIUM	S PAR
PREORDER	*PRIGGERY	PROMPTER	PSALMIST	PUPATION	S PAT
PREPARER	*PRIGGISH	*PROMPTLY	*PSALMODY	PUPILAGE	S PAY
PREPASTE	PRIGGISM	PROMULGE	PSALTERY	*PUPILARY	*S PAZ
PREPENSE	PRIMATAL	PRONATOR	PSAMMITE	*PUPPETRY	S PEC
PREPLACE	*PRIMEVAL	PRONOTUM	*PSEPHITE	*PUPPYDOM	S PED
PREPLANT	PRIMMEST	PROPENOL	PSILOCIN	PURBLIND	S PEW

S P IC	S P ILL	S P OTLIT	CO P IES	GY P SUM	*PA P ACY
S P IK	S P ILT	*S P AETZLE	CO P ING	HA P PED	PA P AIN
S P IN	S P INE	S P EARGUN	CO P LOT	HA P PEN	PA P AYA
S P IT	S P INY	S P EARMAN	CO P PED	HA P TEN	PA P ERY
S P IV	S P IRE	S P IRIEST	CO P PER	HA P TIC	PA P IST
S P OT	S P IRT	S P LURGER	CO P PRA	HE P CAT	PA P PUS
S P RY	S P IRY	*S P OOFERY	CO P RAH	HE P TAD	PA P ULA
S P UD	S P ITE	*S P OOKERY	CO P TER	HI P PED	PA P ULE
S P UE	*S P ITZ	S P OOLING	CO P ULA	HI P PER	PE P LOS
S P UN	S P LAT	*S P OROZOA	CU P FUL	HI P PIE	PE P LUM
S P UR	S P LAY	*S P RITZER	CU P OLA	HO P ING	PE P LUS
S P ACE	S P LIT	*S P OONSFUL	CU P PED	HO P PLE	PE P PED
S P ACY	S P ODE	CE P E	CU P PER	*HY P HEN	PE P PER
S P ADE	S P OIL	LE P T	CU P RIC	*HY P ING	PE P SIN
S P ADO	S P OKE	MO P Y	CU P RUM	*HY P NIC	PE P TIC
S P AHI	S P OOF	RE P O	CU P ULA	*JA P ERY	PE P TID
S P AIL	S P OOK	RE P P	CU P ULE	*JA P ING	PI P AGE
S P AIT	S P OOL	SY P H	*CY P HER	KA P UTT	PI P IER
S P AKE	S P OON	TY P P	CY P RES	*KE P PED	PI P ING
S P ALE	S P OOR	DI P SO	CY P RUS	KE P PEN	PI P KIN
S P ALL	S P ORE	*HO P PY	DA P HNE	KI P PEN	PI P PED
S P ANG	S P ORT	HY P ER	DA P PED	KI P PER	PI P PIN
S P ANK	S P OUT	MO P EY	DA P PER	*KO P ECK	PO P ERY
S P ARE	S P RAG	PO P SY	DA P PLE	KO P PIE	PO P GUN
S P ARK	S P RAT	RE P EG	DE P ART	LA P DOG	PO P ISH
S P ASM	S P RAY	RE P OT	DE P END	LA P FUL	PO P LAR
S P ATE	S P REE	RO P EY	DE P ERM	LA P PED	PO P LIN
S P AWN	S P RIG	TE P OY	DE P ICT	LA P PER	POP P ED
S P EAK	S P RIT	*ZA P PY	DE P LOY	LA P PET	POP P ER
S P EAN	S P RUE	*BI P ACK	DE P ONE	LA P SER	POP P ET
S P EAR	S P RUG	BO P EE P	DE P ORT	LA P SUS	POP P PLE
S P ECK	S P UMY	BO P P ER	DE P OSE	LA P TO P	PO P SIE
S P ECS	S P URN	BU P PIE	DE P UTE	LE P TON	PU P ATE
S P EED	S P URT	BY P ASS	DE P UTY	LI P ASE	PUP P ED
S P EEL	S P UTA	BY P AST	*DI P LEX	LI P IDE	PUP P ET
S P EER	S P ACEY	*BY P ATH	DI P LOE	LI P OID	RA P HIA
S P EIL	S P EEDO	*BY P LAY	DI P NET	LI P OMA	RA P HIS
S P EIR	S P ENSE	CA P FUL	DI P ODY	LI P PED	RA P IER
S P ELL	*S P IKEY	CA P IAS	DI P OLE	LI P PEN	RA P INE
S P ELT	S P INTO	CA P ITA	DI P PED	LI P PER	RA P ING
S P END	S P LIME	CA P LET	DI P PER	LO P PED	RA P INI
S P ENT	S P LINE	CA P LIN	DI P SAS	LO P PER	RA P IST
S P ERM	S P LINK	CA P OTE	DO P ANT	LU P INE	RA P PED
S P ICA	S P OOFY	CA P PER	DO P IER	LU P OUS	RA P PEE
S P ICE	*S P RITZ	CA P RIC	DO P ING	MO P ERY	RA P PEL
S P ICK	*S P ACKLE	CA P RIS	DU P ERY	MO P IER	RA P PEN
S P ICY	*S P ANDEX	CA P SID	DU P ING	NA P ALM	RA P PER
S P IED	*S P ARKLY	CA P TAN	*DU P LEX	NA P ERY	RA P TOR
S P IEL	S P ARTAN	CA P TOR	DU P PED	NA P KIN	RE P ACK
S P IER	*S P ATZLE	CI P HER	FI P PLE	NA P PED	RE P AID
S P IES	S P EEDU P	CO P ALM	GA P ING	NA P PER	RE P AIR
S P IFF	S P IRIER	CO P IED	GA P PED	NA P PIE	RE P AND
S P IKE	S P LODGE	*CO P ECK	GI P PER	NE P HEW	RE P ARK
S P IKY	S P OOFER	CO P IED	GO P HER	NI P PER	RE P ASS
S P ILE	S P ORTIF	CO P IER	GY P P ER	NI P PLE	RE P AST

RE P AVE	SY P HER	CA P ITOL	DI P LOMA	LE P ROSY	RA P TURE
RE P EAL	SY P HON	CA P LESS	DI P NOAN	LE P ROUS	RE P ANEL
RE P EAT	TA P ALO	CA P ORAL	DI P PING	LI P LESS	RE P A P ER
RE P ENT	TA P PED	*CA P OUCH	DI P TERA	LI P LIKE	RE P ATCH
RE P ERK	TA P PER	CA P PING	*DI P TYCA	LI P PING	RE P INER
RE P INE	TA P PET	CA P RICE	DO P IEST	LO P PING	RE P LACE
RE P LAN	TE P EFY	CA P RINE	DU P PING	LU P ANAR	RE P LANT
RE P LAY	TE P HRA	*CA P ROCK	DU P TRAG	LU P ULIN	RE P LATE
RE P LOT	TI P CAT	*CA P SIZE	*FO P PERY	*MA P LIKE	RE P LEAD
RE P OLL	TI P OFF	CA P STAN	*FO P PISH	MO P IEST	RE P LETE
RE P ORT	TI P PED	CA P SULE	GA P OSIS	*NA P HTHA	*RE P LEVY
RE P OSE	TI P PER	CA P TAIN	GA P PING	NA P HTOL	RE P LICA
RE P OUR	TI P PET	CA P TION	GI P PING	NA P LESS	RE P LIER
RE P PED	TI P PLE	CA P TIVE	GY P LURE	NA P PING	RE P LUMB
RE P UGN	TI P TOE	CA P TURE	GY P STER	NE P HRIC	RE P OSAL
RE P UM P	TI P TO P	*CA P UCHE	HA P LESS	NE P HRON	RE P OSER
RE P UTE	TO P FUL	*CI P HONY	HA P LITE	NI P P IER	RE P OSIT
RI P EST	TO P HUS	CI P OLIN	HA P LOID	NI P P ILY	RE P OWER
RI P ING	TO P ING	CO P AIBA	HA P LONT	NI P P ING	RE P RESS
RI P OFF	TO P PED	CO P EPOD	*HA P PING	NU P TIAL	RE P RICE
RI P OST	TO P PER	CO P IHUE	HA P TENE	PA P ERER	RE P RINT
RI P PED	TO P PLE	CO P ILOT	HE P ARIN	PA P HIAN	RE P RISE
RI P PER	TU P ELO	CO P IOUS	HE P ATIC	PA P ILLA	RE P ROBE
RI P PLE	TU P PED	*CO P PERY	HE P TANE	PA P OOSE	RE P ROOF
RI P PLY	TY P HON	*CO P PICE	HE P TOSE	PAP P IER	RE P ROVE
RI P RA P	TY P HUS	CO P PING	HI P BONE	PAP P IES	RE P TANT
RI P SAW	TY P IER	*CO P YBOY	HI P LESS	PA P RICA	RE P TILE
RO P ERY	*TY P IFY	*CO P YCAT	*HI P LIKE	*PA P RIKA	RE P ULSE
RO P IER	TY P ING	CO P YIST	HI P LINE	PA P YRUS	RI P CORD
RO P ILY	TY P IST	*CU P CAKE	HI P NESS	*PE P PERY	RI P ENER
RO P ING	VA P ORY	CU P ELER	HI P PEST	PE P PING	RI P IENO
RU P IAH	VA P OUR	CU P PING	HI P PIER	PE P SINE	RI P OSTE
SA P OTA	WI P ING	CU P RITE	*HI P PING	PE P TIDE	RI P PING
SA P OTE	*YA P OCK	CU P ROUS	*HI P PISH	*PE P TIZE	RI P PLER
SA P OUR	YA P PED	CU P SFUL	*HI P SHOT	PE P TONE	RI P PLET
SA P PED	YA P PER	CU P ULAR	HI P STER	PI P EAGE	RI P STO P
SA P PER	YI P PED	CY P RESS	*HO P EFUL	PI P EFUL	RI P TIDE
SE P SIS	YI P PEE	CY P RIAN	*HO P HEAD	PI P ETTE	*RO P EWAY
SE P TAL	YI P PIE	CY P SELA	HO P LITE	PI P IEST	RO P IEST
SE P TET	YU P PIE	DA P HNIA	*HO P PING	PI P PING	RU P TURE
SE P TIC	*ZA P PER	DA P PING	*HO P SACK	PO P CORN	*SA P AJOU
SE P TUM	*ZE P HYR	DA P SONE	HO P TOAD	PO P EDOM	SA P HEAD
SI P HON	*ZI P PER	DE P LANE	*HY P ERON	*PO P EYED	SA P HENA
SI P ING	BA P TISE	DE P LETE	*HY P NOID	PO P OVER	SA P IENS
SI P PED	BA P TISM	DE P LORE	*HY P OGEA	PO P PIED	SA P IENT
SI P PER	BA P TIST	DE P LUME	*HY P ONEA	PO P PIES	SA P LESS
SI P PET	*BA P TIZE	DE P OSAL	*HY P OXIA	PO P PING	SA P LING
SO P ITE	BI P ARTY	DE P OSER	*KE P PING	PO P ULAR	SA P ONIN
SO P PED	BI P LANE	DE P OSIT	*KI P PING	*PU P FISH	*SA P PHIC
SU P ERB	BI P OLAR	DE P RAVE	*KI P SKIN	PU P ILAR	SA P PING
SU P INE	CA P ABLE	DE P RESS	LA P IDES	PU P PING	SA P ROBE
SU P PED	CA P ELAN	DE P RIVE	LA P PING	RA P HIDE	SA P SAGO
SU P PER	CA P ELET	DE P SIDE	LA P WING	RA P PING	SA P WOOD
SU P PLE	CA P ERER	DI P HASE	LE P ORID	RA P PINI	*SE P PUKU
SU P PLY	CA P ITAL	DI P LOID	LE P ROSE	RA P PORT	SE P TATE

SE P TIME	WI P EOUT	PAP P IER	BES P READ	*CRO P P ING	*FLY P A PER
SI P P ING	*XI P HOID	PAP P IES	BES P RENT	CUL P ABLE	*FRI P P ERY
SO P HIES	*YA P P ING	*PE P P ERY	BIO P LASM	CUS P IDAL	*GAZ P ACHO
SO P HISM	*YI P P ING	PE P P ING	*CAM P AGNA	CUS P IDOR	GEE P OUND
SO P HIST	*ZA P ATEO	PI P P ING	*CAM P AIGN	CUT P URSE	*GEO P HAGY
SO P P ING	*ZA P TIAH	PO P P IED	*CAM P FIRE	DAM P ENER	GEO P HONE
SO P RANO	*ZA P TIEH	PO P P IES	*CAM P HENE	DAM P NESS	*GEO P HYTE
SU P P ING	*ZI P LESS	PO P P ING	*CAM P HINE	DAU P HINE	GEO P ONIC
SU P PORT	*ZI P P ING	P RE P ILL	CAM P IEST	DEE P ENER	GEO P ROBE
SU P POSE	BIO P SIC	P RE P REG	CAM P OREE	DEE P NESS	GIM P IEST
SU P REME	BIO P TIC	PU P P ING	CAM P SITE	DEM P STER	GOS P ELER
SU P REMO	CA P P ING	*QUI P P ER	*CHA P BOOK	DES P ISER	*GRA P HEME
TA P ERER	CAR P OOL	RA P P ING	*CHA P ERON	DIA P ASON	GRA P HITE
TA P ETUM	*CO P P ERY	RA P P INI	*CHA P ITER	DIA P AUSE	GRA P LINE
TA P HOLE	*CO P P ICE	RA P P ORT	*CHA P LAIN	DIA P HONE	GRA P P LER
TA P IOCA	CO P P ING	RES P ACE	*CHA P PATI	*DIA P HONY	GRA P TEST
TA P P ING	*COW P LOP	RES P ADE	*CHA P P ING	DIO P SIDE	GRI P P IER
TA P ROOM	CRO P PIE	RES P EAK	*CHI P MUCK	DIO P TASE	GRI P P ING
TA P ROOT	CU P P ING	RES P LIT	*CHI P MUNK	DIO P TRIC	*GRI P SACK
TA P STER	DAM P ING	RES P OKE	*CHI P P ING	*DI P P ABLE	GRI P TEST
TI P CART	DA P P ING	RES P RAY	*CHO P P ING	*DIS P ATCH	GUM P TION
TI P LESS	*DEL P HIC	RI P P ING	CIO P P INO	DIS P ENSE	GUN P A PER
TI P PIER	DI P P ING	RI P P LER	CLA P TRA P	DIS P ERSE	GUN P OINT
TI P P ING	DU P P ING	RI P P LET	*CLI P P ING	DIS P IRIT	*HAM P ERER
TI P P LER	*FO P P ERY	*SA P P EOID	CLU P EOID	DIS P LACE	HEL P LESS
TI P SIER	*FO P P ISH	SA P P ING	COA P P EAR	DIS P LANT	*HEL P MATE
TI P SILY	GA P P ING	*SCY P HUS	*COD P IECE	DIS P LODE	*HEL P MEET
TI P STER	GIM P IER	*SE P P UKU	COL P ITIS	DIS P OSAL	*HEM P IEST
TO P COAT	GI P P ING	SHA P EUP	*COM P ADRE	DIS P OSER	*HEM P WEED
TO P FULL	GRI P MAN	SHI P LAP	COM P ARER	DIS P READ	*HI P P ARCH
TO P IARY	*HA P P ING	SI P P ING	COM P ILER	*DIS P RIZE	*HI P P IEST
*TO P KICK	HI P P EST	SO P P ING	COM P LAIN	DIS P ROOF	HOO P LESS
TO P KNOT	HI P P IER	STO P GAP	COM P LEAT	DIS P ROVE	*HOO P LIKE
TO P LESS	*HI P P ING	SU P P ING	*COM P LECT	DIS P UTER	HOO P STER
TO P LINE	*HI P P ISH	SU P PORT	COM P LETE	DRI P LESS	HOS P ITAL
TO P MAST	*HO P P ING	SU P POSE	*COM P LICE	DRI P P ING	HOS P ITIA
TO P MOST	*JEE P NEY	*SYM P HON	*COM P LIED	*DRO P HEAD	HOS P ODAR
TO P ONYM	*KE P P ING	*SYM P TOM	COM P LIER	*DRO P KICK	HOT P RESS
TO P P ING	*KI P P ING	TA P P ING	COM P LIES	DRO P P ING	*HUM P BACK
TO P SAIL	*KOU P REY	TEL P HER	COM P LINE	DRO P WORT	*HUM P LESS
TO P SIDE	LA P P ING	TI P P IER	COM P OSER	DRU P ELET	*JEO P ARDY
TO P SOIL	LIM P SEY	TI P P ING	*COM P OUND	DRY P OINT	*KEE P SAKE
TO P SPIN	LI P P ING	TI P P LER	COM P RESS	*DUM P CART	*KER P LUNK
*TO P WORK	LO P P ING	TO P P ING	COM P RISE	DUM P IEST	*KEY P UNCH
TU P P ING	MIS P LAN	TU P P ING	*COM P RIZE	DUM P LING	*KI P P ERER
TY P EBAR	*MUD P ACK	TYM P ANO	COO P TION	DUO P SONY	*KNA P SACK
TY P ESET	NA P P ING	VAN P OOL	*CO P P ERAH	*DYS P EPSY	*KNA P WEED
*TY P HOID	NI P P IER	WA P P ITI	CO P P ERAS	DYS P NOEA	*KRE P LACH
*TY P HOON	NI P P ILY	*WIM P ISH	COR P ORAL	*FLA P JACK	LAM P P OST
*TY P HOSE	NI P P ING	*YA P P ING	COR P SMAN	FLA P LESS	*LAM P YRID
TY P ICAL	NON P AID	*YI P P ING	COU P LING	*FLA P P ING	LEA P FROG
TY P IEST	NON P AST	*ZI P P ING	*CRA P P ING	*FLI P P ANT	LIM P NESS
VA P ORER	NON P EAK	*BAG PI P ER	CRI P P LER	FLA P LESS	LOO P HOLE
*VA P OURY	NON P LAY	BED P LATE	CRO P LAND	*FLA P P ING	*LUM P FISH
WA P P ITI	NON P OOR	BES P OUSE	CRO P LESS	*FLI P P ANT	*LYM P HOMA

*LYO P HILE	P RO P OSER	*SHI P YARD	*STO P BANK	TRA P LINE	BUR P
*MAN POWER	P RO P OUND	SHO P GIRL	*STO P COCK	TRA P NEST	CAM P
*MA P ABLE	*P RO P PING	*SHO P LIFT	STO P OVER	TRA P P EAN	CAR P
*MIS P ATCH	*P RO P YLON	*SHO P P ING	STO P P AGE	TRA P P ING	CHA P
*MIS P RIZE	*P SE P HITE	*SHO P TALK	STO P P ING	TRA P P OSE	CHI P
*MOR P HEME	P UL P IEST	*SHO P WORN	SUB P ANEL	*TRA P ROCK	CHO P
*MOR P HINE	P UL P LESS	SIM P ERER	*SUB P HASE	TRA P UNTO	CLA P
*MYO P ATHY	*P UL P WOOD	*SIM P LIFY	*SUB P HYLA	TRE P HINE	CLI P
NAU P LIUS	P UM P LESS	SIM P LISM	SUB P OENA	TRI P EDAL	CLO P
*NEO P HYTE	*P UM P LIKE	SIM P LIST	SUB P OLAR	TRI P HASE	COM P
NEO P LASM	*P U P P ETRY	*SIX P ENCE	*SUB P UBIC	TRI P LANE	COO P
NEO P RENE	*P U P PYDOM	*SIX P ENNY	SUL P HATE	TRI P LING	COU P
NI P IEST	*P UR P LISH	SKI P LANE	SUL P HIDE	TRI P LITE	CRA P
*NIT P ICKY	P UR P URIC	*SKI P P ING	SUL P HITE	TRI P LOID	CRO P
NON PAGAN	P UR P URIN	SLA P DASH	SUL P HONE	TRI P P ING	CUS P
NON P A PAL	*QUI P P ISH	*SLA P JACK	*SUL P HURY	TRI P TANE	DAM P
NON P ARTY	*QUI P STER	SLA P P ING	*SUM P WEED	*TRI P TYCA	DEE P
NON P OINT	RAM P AGER	SLI P CASE	*SUN P ORCH	*TRI P TYCH	DRI P
NON P OLAR	*RAM P ANCY	*SLI P FORM	SUN P ROOF	TRI P WIRE	DRO P
NON P RINT	RA P P AREE	SLI P KNOT	SU P P LANT	TRO P ONIN	DUM P
PAL P ABLE	*REA P P EAR	SLI P LESS	SU P P LIER	TUM P LINE	FLA P
PAL P ATOR	REA P P EAR	SLI P OVER	SU P P OSAL	TU P P ENCE	FLI P
PAL P EBRA	REO P P OSE	SLI P P AGE	SU P P OSER	*TU P P ENNY	FRA P
PAM P ERER	RES P LICE	*SLI P P ERY	SU P P RESS	*TWO P ENCE	GAM P
*PAM P HLET	RES P OKEN	SLI P P ING	SUR P LICE	*TWO P ENNY	GAS P
PAP P IEST	RES P ONSA	SLI P SHOD	SUR P RINT	*TYM P ANAL	GAW P
PAP P OOSE	RES P ONSE	SLI P SLO P	SUR P RISE	*TYM P ANIC	GIM P
*P EE P HOLE	RES P RANG	SLI P SOLE	*SUR P RIZE	*TYM P ANUM	GLO P
*P EE P SHOW	RES P READ	SLI P WARE	SUS P ENSE	VES P ERAL	GOO P
P EN P OINT	RES P ROUT	SLO P P ING	*SYM P ATHY	*VES P IARY	GOR P
P EP P ERER	RHA P SODE	*SLO P WORK	*SYM P ATRY	VOL P LANE	GRI P
P IE P LANT	*RHA P SODY	*SNA P BACK	*SYM P ODIA	WAR P LANE	GUL P
P IN P OINT	RI P P ABLE	SNA P LESS	*SYM P OSIA	*WAR POWER	HAS P
*P IN P RICK	RI P P LING	*SNA P P IER	*SYR P HIAN	*WAR P WISE	HEA P
*P OR P HYRY	*SAM P HIRE	*SNA P P ILY	TAM P ERER	*WAX P LANT	HEL P
P OR P OISE	SAM P LING	SNA P P ING	TAR P A P ER	*WEA P ONRY	HEM P
P RE P ARER	*SA P P HIRE	*SNA P P ISH	*TAX P AYER	*WET P ROOF	HOL P
P RE P ASTE	*SA P P HISM	SNA P SHOT	TEM P ERER	*WHI P CORD	HUM P
P RE P ENSE	*SA P P HIST	SNA P WEED	TEM P LATE	*WHI P LASH	JAU P
P RE P LACE	*SCA P HOID	*SNI P P ETY	TEM P ORAL	*WHI P LIKE	JEE P
P RE P LANT	SCA P ULAR	SNI P P ING	TEN P ENCE	*WHI P P IER	*JIM P
*P RE P PING	SCE P TRAL	*SOA P BARK	TEN P ENNY	*WHI P P ING	*JUM P
P RE P RICE	*SCU P P AUG	SOA P IEST	TEN P P ING	*WHI P TAIL	KEE P
P RE P RINT	*SCY P HATE	SOA P LESS	TER P INOL	*WHI P WORM	KEL P
*P RE P UNCH	SEA P IECE	SOA P SUDS	TIM P ANUM	WIS P IEST	KEM P
P RO P ENOL	SEA P LANE	SOA P WORT	TIN P LATE	*WIS P LIKE	KNA P
P RO P ENSE	SEM P LICE	SOR P TION	TI P P ABLE	*WRA P P ING	KNO P
*P RO P ENYL	*SHE P HERD	STA P EDES	TI P P IEST	*ZE P P ELIN	LAM P
*P RO P ERTY	SHI P LOAD	STA P ELIA	*TI P P YTOE	*ZOO P HILI	LEA P
*P RO P HAGE	*SHI P MATE	STE P DAME	TOE P IECE	*ZOO P HILY	LIM P
*P RO P HASE	*SHI P MENT	STE P LIKE	TOE P LATE	*ZOO P HOBE	LIS P
*P RO P HECY	*SHI P P ING	STE P P ING	TOR P IDLY	*ZOO P HYTE	LOO P
*P RO P HESY	SHI P SIDE	STE P WISE	TRA P BALL	BEE P	LOU P
P RO P OLIS	SHI P SIDE	STI P P LER	*TRA P DOOR	BLI P	LUM P
P RO P OSAL	*SHI P WORM		TRA P LIKE	BUM P	MAR P

MOO P	WAS P	P RIM P	TWIR P	*MAYHA P	BEDLAM P
MUM P	WEE P	REBO P	WATA P	*MAY PO P	BELLHO P
NEA P	WHA P	RECA P	WHAU P	MEGIL P	*BETHUM P
NEE P	WHI P	REDI P	WHEE P	METUM P	*BIOCHI P
P AL P	WHO P	REMA P	WHEL P	MISHA P	BLUECA P
P EE P	WIM P	SALE P	*WHOM P	MOBCA P	*BREAKU P
P IM P	WIS P	SCAL P	WHOO P	*MOCKU P	BRUSHU P
P LO P	WRA P	SCAM P	*WHUM P	MUDCA P	BUILDU P
P OM P	YAU P	SCAR P	*BACKU P	P ETNA P	CALTRA P
P OO P	YAW P	SCAU P	BARHO P	*P ICKU P	CALTRO P
P RE P	YEL P	SCOO P	BELEA P	P ILEU P	CANTRA P
P RO P	BEBO P	SCRA P	BEWEE P	P REAM P	CANTRI P
PUL P	BECA P	SCRI P	BEWRA P	P ULLU P	*CATCHU P
P UM P	BLEE P	SCUL P	BISHO P	P USHU P	*CHECKU P
*QUI P	BLIM P	SETU P	BLOWU P	RAGTO P	CHIRRU P
RAM P	BLOO P	SHAR P	BO P EE P	RECOU P	CLEANU P
RAS P	CHEA P	SHEE P	BURLA P	REDCA P	*COOKTO P
REA P	CHEE P	SHLE P	CARHO P	REDTO P	COVERU P
RE P P	CHIM P	SIRU P	CARTO P	RE P UM P	*COWFLA P
ROM P	CHIR P	SITU P	CATNA P	RESHI P	*COWFLO P
ROU P	CHOM P	SKEL P	CATNI P	REVAM P	*COW P LO P
RUM P	CHUM P	SKIM P	CATSU P	REWRA P	COWSLI P
SAL P	CLAM P	SLEE P	*COCKU P	RI P RA P	*CRACKU P
SAM P	CLAS P	SLOO P	COLLO P	SALOO P	DEMIRE P
SCO P	CLOM P	SLUM P	DECAM P	SANNO P	DEVELO P
SCU P	CLUM P	SLUR P	DEWLA P	SANNU P	DEWDRO P
SEE P	CRAM P	SNEA P	DOGNA P	SATRA P	FLATCA P
SHI P	CREE P	SNOO P	DOLLO P	SCHLE P	FLATTO P
SHO P	CRIM P	STAM P	DUSTU P	SCRIM P	*FLYTRA P
SIM P	CRIS P	STEE P	FACEU P	SCROO P	FORETO P
SKE P	CROU P	STIR P	FILLI P	SENDU P	GENI P A P
SKI P	CRUM P	STOM P	GALLO P	SHLE P P	*GIDDYA P
SLA P	CUTU P	STOO P	*GAZUM P	SHLUM P	*GIDDYU P
SLI P	DROO P	STOU P	GIDDA P	SHRIM P	GODSHI P
SLO P	FLUM P	STOW P	GOSSI P	*SKYCA P	GROWNU P
SNA P	FRUM P	STRA P	HANGU P	SLI P U P	GUMDRO P
SNI P	GALO P	STRE P	*HICCU P	TAKEU P	GUNSHI P
SOA P	GENI P	STRI P	HOLDU P	TEACU P	HAIRCA P
SOU P	GETU P	STRO P	*HOOKU P	THREA P	HARDTO P
STE P	GRAM P	STUM P	*HUBCA P	THREE P	HARELI P
STO P	GRAS P	SUNU P	HYSSO P	TI P TO P	HENCOO P
SUM P	GROU P	SWAM P	*JOY PO P	TITTU P	HILLTO P
SWA P	GRUM P	SWEE P	*KICKU P	TOECA P	*KETCHU P
SWO P	JALA P	SWOO P	KIDNA P	TOSSU P	*KINGCU P
TAM P	JALO P	SYRU P	LA P TO P	TUNEU P	*KINSHI P
TAR P	JULE P	SYSO P	LARRU P	TURNI P	*KNEECA P
TEM P	KELE P	THRI P	LINEU P	TURNU P	MAINTO P
TRA P	KNOS P	THRO P	LINKU P	*WALKU P	MANTRA P
TRI P	KREE P	THUM P	LOCKU P	WALLO P	*MATCHU P
TRO P	LETU P	TRAM P	LOLLO P	WARMU P	*MIDSHI P
TUM P	*MIXU P	TROM P	LOOKU P	*WIKIU P	*MILKSO P
TY P P	NETO P	TROO P	MADCA P	WINDU P	*MISKEE P
VAM P	P INU P	TRUM P	MAGIL P	*WORKU P	MISSTE P
VEE P	P LUM P	TULI P	MAKEU P	*BARKEE P	MISSTO P
WAR P	P OLY P	TWER P	MARKU P	BECLAS P	*MUGWUM P

NONSLI P	*SHAKEU P	WINESO P	*DRAMSHO P	*LOLLY P O P	*SKULLCA P
NONSTO P	SHALLO P	WINGTI P	DUSTHEA P	LONGSHI P	SLI P SLO P
P ALSHI P	SHA P EU P	WIRETA P	*FIREDAM P	LORDSHI P	SNOWDRO P
P ARSNI P	SHI P LA P	*WORSHI P	FIRETRA P	MALA P RO P	STARSHI P
P ASTEU P	SMASHU P	*BAASKAA P	*FLAGSHI P .	*MATESHI P	SUBGROU P
P INESA P	SNOWCA P	*BACKDRO P	*FOOLSCA P	MESOCAR P	SU P ERCO P
P OGONI P	SONSHI P	*BACKSLA P	FOOTSTE P	*MINICAM P	SWEETSO P
P RECOU P	SOURSO P	*BACKSTO P	*GROGSHO P	MONOCAR P	TABLETO P
P REWRA P	S P EEDU P	*BACKWRA P	GURUSHI P	*NIGHTCA P	TAILLAM P
P ROCAR P	*STACKU P	*BAKESHO P	*HANDGRI P	NONTRUM P	*TANKSHI P
RATTRA P	STANDU P	BEAUCOU P	*HANDICA P	P ARADRO P	TEARDRO P
RECLAS P	STARTU P	*BLACKCA P	*HARDSHI P	*P AWNSHO P	*TEENYBO P
*REEQUI P	*STICKU P	*BLACKTO P	*HEADLAM P	*P EDI P AL P	TIECLAS P
REGROU P	STIRRU P	*BOOKSHO P	*HEADSHI P	*P EESWEE P	*TOWNSHI P
RESTAM P	STO P GA P	*BULLWHI P	*HEDGEHO P	P ERICAR P	TRANSHI P
RI P STO P	SUNLAM P	*CALTHRO P	*HEIRSHI P	*P HOTOMA P	*TUCKSHO P
ROLLMO P	SYNCAR P	CANTRAI P	HELISTO P	*P ODOCAR P	*TWINSHI P
ROLLTO P	TEASHO P	*CHUMSHI P	*HOCKSHO P	P OSTCOU P	*WARDSHI P
ROOFTO P	TIDERI P	CLA P TRA P	HOUSETO P	P RESLEE P	*WHITECA P
ROUNDU P	TOUCHU P	*COOKSHO P	*KINGSHI P	P RESTAM P	*WINESHO P
SCALEU P	*TOYSHO P	*CROWSTE P	*LADYSHI P	RAINDRO P	*WORKSHO P
SCALLO P	TREETO P	DEANSHI P	*LANDSKI P	SAND P EE P	*XYLOCAR P
*SCHLE P P	TROLLO P	*DEATHCU P	LANDSLI P	SANDSOA P	
*SCHLUM P	*WARSHI P	*DOGESHI P	LIVETRA P	SIDESLI P	
SCOLLO P	*WICKIU P	DOORSTE P	*LOCKSTE P	SIDESTE P	
SCREWU P	*WICKYU P	DOORSTO P	LOLLI P O P		

Q

QAID	*QUARK	QUIRT	*QUARTO	*QUOKKA	*QUASSIN
*QOPH	QUART	QUITE	*QUARTZ	*QUORUM	*QUAVERY
QUAD	*QUASH	QUOIN	*QUASAR	*QUOTER	*QUAYAGE
QUAG	QUASI	QUOIT	*QUATRE	*QUOTHA	*QUEENLY
QUAI	QUASS	QUOTA	*QUAVER	*QURUSH	*QUEERLY
*QUAY	QUATE	QUOTE	*QUEASY	*QWERTY	*QUELLER
*QUEY	QUEAN	*QUOTH	*QUEAZY	*QUADRAT	*QUERIDA
QUID	QUEEN	*QURSH	*QUENCH	*QUADRIC	*QUERIED
QUIN	QUEER	*QINDAR	*QUEUER	*QUAFFER	*QUERIER
*QUIP	QUELL	*QINTAR	*QUEZAL	*QUAHAUG	*QUERIES
QUIT	QUERN	*QIVIUT	*QUICHE	*QUALIFY	*QUERIST
*QUIZ	*QUERY	*QUAERE	*QUINCE	*QUALITY	*QUESTER
QUOD	QUEST	*QUAGGA	*QUINIC	*QUAMASH	*QUESTOR
QANAT	QUEUE	*QUAGGY	*QUININ	*QUANTAL	*QUETZAL
*QUACK	*QUICK	*QUAHOG	*QUINOA	*QUANTIC	*QUIBBLE
*QUAFF	QUIET	*QUAICH	*QUINOL	*QUANTUM	*QUICKEN
QUAIL	*QUIFF	*QUAIGH	*QUINSY	*QUARREL	*QUICKIE
*QUAKE	QUILL	*QUAINT	*QUINTE	*QUARTAN	*QUICKLY
*QUAKY	QUILT	*QUAKER	*QUIPPU	*QUARTER	*QUIETEN
QUALE	QUINT	*QUALMY	*QUIRKY	*QUARTET	*QUIETER
*QUALM	*QUIPU	*QUANTA	*QUITCH	*QUARTIC	*QUIETLY
QUANT	QUIRE	*QUARRY	*QUIVER	*QUASHER	*QUIETUS
QUARE	*QUIRK	*QUARTE	*QUOHOG	*QUASSIA	*QUILLAI

*QUILLET	*QIOMTAIN	*QUATRAIN	*QUIPSTER	*PI Q UET	*PRE Q UEL
*QUILTER	*QUAALUDE	*QUAVERER	*QUIRKISH	*RE Q UIN	*BED Q UILT
*QUINARY	*QUACKERY	*QUAYSIDE	*QUISLING	*RO Q UET	*CHA Q UETA
*QUINATE	*QUACKISH	*QUEENDOM	*QUITRENT	*SE Q UEL	*CIN Q UAIN
*QUINELA	*QUACKISM	*QUEERISH	*QUITTING	*SE Q UIN	*CLI Q UISH
*QUININA	*QUADPLEX	*QUENCHER	*QUIVERER	*TO Q UET	*COE Q UATE
*QUININE	*QUADRANS	*QUENELLE	*QUIXOTIC	*BE Q UEST	*CON Q UEST
*QUINNAT	*QUADRANT	*QUERCINE	*QUIXOTRY	*CO Q UINA	*CON Q UIAN
*QUINOID	*QUADRATE	*QUESTION	*QUOTIENT	*CO Q UITO	*COT Q UEAN
*QUINONE	*QUADRIGA	*QUIBBLER		*LI Q UATE	*DAI Q UIRI
*QUINTAL	*QUADROON	*QUICKSET	*S Q UAB	*LI Q UEFY	*DIS Q UIET
*QUINTAN	*QUAGMIRE	*QUIDDITY	*S Q UAD	*LI Q UEUR	*FRE Q UENT
*QUINTAR	*QUAGMIRY	*QUIDNUNC	S Q UAT	*LI Q UIFY	*JAC Q UARD
*QUINTET	*QUALMISH	*QUIETISM	*S Q UAW	*PI Q UANT	*MAR Q UESS
*QUINTIC	*QUANDANG	*QUIETIST	*S Q UEG	*RE Q UEST	*MAR Q UISE
*QUINTIN	*QUANDARY	*QUIETUDE	*S Q UIB	*RE Q UIEM	*MES Q UITE
*QUIPPER	*QUANDONG	*QUILLAIA	*S Q UID	*RE Q UIRE	*MEZ Q UITE
*QUITTED	*QUANTIFY	*QUILLAJA	*S Q UOOSHY	*RE Q UITE	*MIS Q UOTE
*QUITTER	*QUANTILE	*QUILLING	*BU Q SHA	*SE Q UELA	*MOS Q UITO
*QUITTOR	*QUANTITY	*QUILTING	*CO Q UET	*SE Q UENT	*MUS Q UASH
*QUIVERY	*QUANTIZE	*QUINCUNX	*DI Q UAT	*SE Q UOIA	*NON Q UOTA
*QUIXOTE	*QUANTONG	*QUINELLA	*FA Q UIR	*TE Q UILA	*SEA Q UAKE
*QUIZZER	*QUARRIER	*QUINIELA	*LI Q UID	*VA Q UERO	*TOR Q UATE
*QUOMODO	*QUARTERN	*QUINOLIN	*LI Q UOR	*PI Q UANCE	*TOR Q UING
*QUONDAM	*QUARTILE	*QUINTILE	*LO Q UAT	*CLO Q UE	*TUR Q UOIS
*QUOTING	*QUATORZE	*QUIPPISH	*MA Q UIS	*SHE Q EL	*VAN Q UISH

R

RACE	RAPE	REEF	RIFE	RODE	**ROUX**
RACK	RAPT	REEK	**RIFF**	ROIL	ROVE
RACY	RARE	REEL	RIFT	ROLE	RUBE
RAFF	RASE	REFT	RILE	ROLF	RUBY
RAFT	RASH	REIF	RILL	ROLL	**RUCK**
RAGA	RASP	REIN	RIME	ROMP	RUDD
RAGE	RATE	REIS	RIMY	ROOD	RUDE
RAGI	RATH	RELY	RIND	ROOF	RUER
RAIA	RATO	REND	RING	ROOK	**RUFF**
RAID	RAVE	RENT	RINK	ROOM	RUGA
RAIL	RAYA	REPO	RIOT	ROOT	RUIN
RAIN	**RAZE**	REPP	RIPE	ROPE	RULE
RAJA	*RAZZ	RESH	RISE	ROPY	RULY
RAKE	READ	REST	RISK	ROSE	RUMP
RAKI	REAL	RETE	RITE	ROSY	RUNE
RALE	REAM	RHEA	**RITZ**	ROTA	RUNG
RAMI	REAP	RHUS	RIVE	ROTE	RUNT
RAMP	REAR	RIAL	ROAD	ROTI	RUSE
RAND	**RECK**	RICE	ROAM	ROTL	RUSH
RANG	REDD	RICH	ROAN	ROTO	RUSK
RANI	REDE	**RICK**	ROAR	ROUE	RUST
RANK	REDO	RIDE	ROBE	ROUP	RUTH
RANT	REED	RIEL	**ROCK**	ROUT	**RYKE**

RYND	RAYON	**REHAB**	REWAN	**ROOMY**	**RABBIT**
RYOT	**RAZEE**	**REHEM**	*REWAX	ROOSE	**RABBLE**
RABAT	**RAZER**	**REIFY**	REWED	ROOST	**RABBLE**
RABBI	**RAZOR**	**REIGN**	REWET	ROOTY	RABIES
RABIC	**REACH**	REINK	REWIN	ROPER	**RACEME**
RABID	REACT	REIVE	REWON	**ROPEY**	**RACHET**
RACER	READD	**REKEY**	**RHEUM**	**ROQUE**	**RACHIS**
RACON	READY	**RELAX**	RHINO	ROSED	RACIAL
RADAR	REALM	RELAY	**RHOMB**	ROSET	RACIER
RADII	REARM	RELET	**RHUMB**	ROSIN	RACILY
RADIO	REATA	RELIC	**RHYME**	**ROTCH**	RACING
RADIX	REAVE	RELIT	**RHYTA**	ROTOR	**RACISM**
RADON	REBAR	REMAN	RIANT	ROUEN	RACIST
RAGEE	REBBE	REMAP	RIATA	ROUGE	**RACKER**
RAGGY	REBEC	REMET	**RIBBY**	ROUGH	**RACKET**
RAINY	REBEL	**REMEX**	RIBES	ROUND	**RACKLE**
RAISE	REBID	REMIT	RICER	**ROUPY**	RACOON
*RAJAH	REBOP	**REMIX**	RICIN	ROUSE	**RADDLE**
RAKEE	REBUS	RENAL	RIDER	ROUST	RADIAL
RAKER	REBUT	RENEW	RIDGE	ROUTE	RADIAN
RALLY	**REBUY**	RENIG	**RIDGY**	ROUTH	**RADISH**
RALPH	RECAP	RENIN	RIFLE	ROVEN	RADIUM
RAMEE	RECCE	RENTE	RIGHT	ROVER	RADIUS
RAMET	RECON	REOIL	RIGID	ROWAN	RADOME
RAMIE	RECTA	**REPAY**	RIGOR	**ROWDY**	RADULA
RAMMY	RECTI	REPEG	RILEY	ROWEL	**RAFFIA**
RAMUS	RECTO	REPEL	RILLE	ROWEN	**RAFFLE**
RANCE	RECUR	REPIN	RIMER	ROWER	RAFTER
RANCH	RECUT	**REPLY**	RINSE	**ROWTH**	**RAGBAG**
RANDY	REDAN	REPOT	**RIOJA**	ROYAL	RAGGED
RANEE	REDIA	REPRO	RIPEN	RUANA	RAGGEE
RANGE	REDID	RERAN	RIPER	RUBLE	RAGGLE
RANGY	REDIP	RERIG	RISER	RUBUS	RAGING
RANID	REDLY	RERUN	RISHI	**RUCHE**	RAGLAN
RAPER	REDON	RESAW	**RISKY**	**RUDDY**	RAGMAN
RAPHE	**REDOX**	RESAY	RISUS	**RUFFE**	RAGOUT
RAPID	REDRY	RESEE	*RITZY	**RUGBY**	RAGTAG
RARER	REDUB	RESET	RIVAL	**RUGBY**	RAGTOP
RASER	REDYE	RESEW	RIVER	RUING	RAIDER
RASPY	**REDUX**	RESID	RIVET	RULER	RAILER
RATAL	REEDY	RESIN	RIYAL	RUMBA	RAISER
RATAN	**REEFY**	RESOD	**ROACH**	RUMEN	RAISIN
RATCH	**REEKY**	RESOW	ROAST	**RUMMY**	**RAKING**
RATEL	REEST	RETAG	ROBIN	RUMOR	**RAKISH**
RATER	REEVE	**RETAX**	ROBLE	RUNIC	RALLYE
RATHE	REFEL	**RETCH**	ROBOT	RUNNY	RAMATE
RATIO	REFER	RETEM	**ROCKY**	RUNTY	**RAMBLE**
RATTY	REFIT	RETIA	RODEO	RUPEE	**RAMIFY**
RAVEL	*REFIX	RETIE	ROGER	RURAL	RAMOSE
RAVEN	**REFLY**	RETRO	ROGUE	**RUSHY**	*RAMJET
RAVER	**REFRY**	RETRY	ROILY	RUSTY	**RAMMED**
RAVIN	REGAL	REUSE	ROMAN	RUTIN	**RAMMER**
RAWIN	REGES	REVEL	ROMEO	RUTTY	RAMOSE
RAWLY	REGMA	REVET	RONDO	RABATO	RAMOUS
RAYAH	REGNA	REVUE	**ROOKY**	**RABBET**	RAMROD
				RABBIN	RAMSON

RAMTIL	RATTLY	**RECOOK**	REFINE	RELINE	**REPLAY**
RANCHO	RATTON	**RECOPY**	REFIRE	**RELINK**	REPLOT
RANCID	**RAUNCH**	RECORD	REFLET	RELISH	REPOLL
RANCOR	**RAVAGE**	**RECORK**	**REFLEW**	RELIST	REPORT
RANDAN	RAVINE	**RECOUP**	*REFLEX	RELIVE	REPOSE
RANDOM	**RAVING**	RECTAL	**REFLOW**	RELOAD	REPOUR
RANGER	**RAVISH**	RECTOR	*REFLUX	RELOAN	**REPPED**
RANKER	**RAWISH**	**RECTUM**	**REFORM**	**RELOOK**	REPUGN
RANKLE	*RAZING	RECTUS	REFUEL	RELUCT	**REPUMP**
RANKLY	READER	RECUSE	**REFUGE**	RELUME	REPUTE
RANSOM	REAGIN	REDACT	**REFUND**	REMAIL	*REQUIN
RANTER	REALIA	REDATE	REFUSE	REMAIN	**RERACK**
RANULA	REALLY	**REDBAY**	REFUTE	REMAND	REREAD
RAPHIA	REALTY	**REDBUD**	REGAIN	REMAND	RERISE
RAPHIS	REAMER	**REDBUG**	REGALE	**REMARK**	REROLL
RAPIER	REAPER	**REDCAP**	REGARD	REMATE	REROOF
RAPINE	REARER	REDDED	**REGAVE**	**REMEDY**	REROSE
RAPING	REASON	REDDEN	REGEAR	REMEET	RESAID
RAPINI	REAVER	REDDER	REGENT	REMELT	RESAIL
RAPIST	**REAVOW**	REDDLE	REGGAE	REMEND	RESALE
RAPPED	REBAIT	REDEAR	REGILD	REMIND	RESCUE
RAPPEE	REBATE	REDEEM	REGIME	REMINT	RESEAL
RAPPEL	REBATO	**REDEFY**	REGINA	REMISE	RESEAT
RAPPEN	**REBECK**	**REDENY**	REGION	REMISS	RESEAU
RAPPER	REBILL	**REDEYE**	REGIUS	REMOLD	RESECT
RAPTOR	REBIND	**REDFIN**	**REGIVE**	REMORA	RESEDA
RAREFY	**REBODY**	REDIAL	REGLET	REMOTE	RESEED
RARELY	REBOIL	REDING	**REGLOW**	**REMOVE**	**RESEEK**
RAREST	**REBOOK**	REDLEG	REGLUE	REMUDA	RESEEN
RARIFY	REBOOT	**REDOCK**	REGNAL	RENAIL	RESELL
RARING	REBORE	REDONE	REGNUM	RENAME	RESEND
RARITY	REBORN	REDOUT	REGRET	RENDER	RESENT
RASCAL	*REBOZO	**REDOWA**	**REGREW**	RENEGE	**RESHIP**
RASHER	**REBUFF**	**REDRAW**	**REGROW**	RENEST	RESHOE
RASHLY	**REBUKE**	REDTOP	**REHANG**	RENNET	**RESHOW**
RASING	**REBURY**	REDUCE	**REHASH**	RENNIN	RESIDE
RASPER	RECALL	REEARN	REHEAR	RENOWN	RESIFT
RASSLE	RECANE	**REECHO**	REHEAT	RENTAL	RESIGN
RASTER	RECANT	**REECHY**	REHEEL	RENTER	RESILE
RASURE	RECAST	REEDIT	REHIRE	RENVOI	RESINY
RATANY	RECEDE	REEFER	**REHUNG**	REOPEN	RESIST
RATBAG	RECENT	**REEKER**	REIVER	**REPACK**	RESITE
RATHER	**RECEPT**	REELER	*REJECT	REPAID	*RESIZE
RATIFY	RECESS	REEMIT	**REJOIN**	REPAIR	**RESOAK**
RATINE	**RECHEW**	**REFACE**	**REKNIT**	REPAND	RESOLD
RATING	**RECIPE**	REFALL	RELACE	**REPARK**	RESOLE
RATION	RECITE	**REFECT**	RELATE	REPASS	RESORB
RATITE	**RECKON**	**REFEED**	RELEND	REPAST	RESORT
RATLIN	RECLAD	REFEEL	RELENT	**REPAVE**	RESPOT
RATOON	RECOAL	REFELL	RELEVE	REPEAL	RESTER
RATTAN	**RECOCK**	**REFFED**	RELICT	REPEAT	RESULT
RATTED	RECODE	REFILE	RELIED	REPENT	RESUME
RATTEN	RECOIL	REFILL	RELIEF	**REPERK**	**RETACK**
RATTER	RECOIN	**REFILM**	RELIER	REPINE	RETAIL
RATTLE	**RECOMB**	**REFIND**	RELIES	REPLAN	RETAIN

RETAKE	REWRAP	RIMPLE	*ROQUET	RUINER	RAILCAR
RETAPE	*REZONE	RINGER	ROSARY	RULING	RAILING
RETARD	RHAPHE	RINSER	ROSCOE	RUMAKI	RAILWAY
RETEAM	*RHEBOK	RIOTER	ROSERY	RUMBLE	RAIMENT
RETEAR	RHESUS	RIPEST	ROSIER	RUMBLY	RAINBOW
RETELL	RHETOR	RIPING	ROSILY	RUMMER	RAINIER
RETENE	RHEUMY	RIPOFF	ROSING	RUMOUR	RAINILY
RETEST	RHINAL	RIPOST	ROSINY	RUMPLE	RAINOUT
RETIAL	RHOMBI	RIPPED	ROSTER	RUMPLY	RAISING
RETILE	RHUMBA	RIPPER	ROSTRA	RUMPUS	*RAKEOFF
RETIME	RHYMER	RIPPLE	ROTARY	RUNDLE	RALLIED
RETINA	*RHYTHM	RIPPLY	ROTATE	RUNKLE	RALLIER
RETINE	RHYTON	RIPRAP	ROTCHE	RUNLET	RALLINE
RETINT	RIALTO	RIPSAW	ROTGUT	RUNNEL	RAMBLER
RETIRE	RIBALD	RISING	ROTTED	RUNNER	RAMEKIN
RETOLD	RIBAND	RISKER	ROTTEN	RUNOFF	RAMILIE
RETOOK	RIBBED	*RISQUE	ROTTER	RUNOUT	RAMMIER
RETOOL	RIBBER	RITARD	ROTUND	RUNWAY	RAMMING
RETORE	RIBBON	RITTER	ROUBLE	RUPIAH	RAMMISH
RETORN	RIBIER	RITUAL	ROUCHE	RURBAN	RAMPAGE
RETORT	RIBLET	RIVAGE	ROUPET	RUSHEE	RAMPANT
RETRAL	RIBOSE	RIVING	ROUSER	RUSHER	RAMPART
RETRIM	RICHEN	ROADEO	ROUTER	RUSINE	*RAMPIKE
RETTED	RICHES	ROADIE	ROVING	RUSSET	RAMPION
RETUNE	RICHLY	ROAMER	ROWING	RUSTIC	RAMPOLE
RETURN	RICING	ROARER	*ROZZER	RUSTLE	RANCHER
RETUSE	*RICKEY	ROBALO	RUBACE	RUTILE	RANCOUR
RETYPE	RICRAC	ROBAND	RUBATO	RUTTED	RANDIER
REVAMP	RICTUS	ROBBED	RUBBED	RYOKAN	RANDIES
REVEAL	RIDDED	ROBBER	RUBBER	RABBLER	RANKING
REVERB	RIDDEN	ROBBIN	RUBBLE	RABBITY	RANKISH
REVERE	RIDDER	ROBUST	RUBBLY	RABBONI	RANPIKE
REVERS	RIDDLE	ROCHET	RUBIED	RACCOON	RANSACK
REVERT	RIDENT	ROCKER	RUBIER	RACEMIC	RAPHIDE
REVERY	RIDGEL	ROCKET	RUBIES	*RACEWAY	RAPPING
REVEST	RIDGIL	ROCOCO	RUBIGO	RACIEST	RAPPINI
REVIEW	RIDING	RODENT	RUBOFF	*RACKETY	RAPPORT
REVILE	RIDLEY	RODMAN	RUBOUT	*RACKFUL	RAPTURE
REVISE	RIEVER	ROLFER	RUBRIC	*RACQUET	RAREBIT
REVIVE	RIFFED	ROLLER	RUCHED	RADIALE	RASBORA
REVOKE	RIFFLE	ROMANO	RUCKLE	RADIANT	RASPISH
REVOLT	RIFLER	ROMPER	RUCKUS	RADIATE	RATABLE
REVOTE	RIGGED	RONDEL	RUDDER	RADICAL	RATAFEE
REVVED	RIGGER	RONION	RUDDLE	RADICEL	RATAFIA
REWAKE	RIGHTO	RONNEL	RUDEST	RADICES	RATATAT
REWARD	RIGHTY	RONYON	RUEFUL	RADICLE	RATCHET
REWARM	RIGOUR	ROOFER	RUFFLE	*RAFFISH	RATFINK
REWASH	RILING	ROOKIE	*RUFFLY	RAFFLER	RATFISH
REWELD	RILLET	ROOMER	RUFOUS	RAGGEDY	RATHOLE
REWIND	RIMIER	ROOSER	RUGGED	RAGGIES	RATLIKE
REWIRE	RIMING	ROOTER	RUGGER	RAGGING	RATLINE
REWOKE	RIMMED	ROPERY	RUGOLA	RAGTIME	RATTAIL
REWORD	RIMMER	ROPIER	RUGOSA	RAGWEED	RATTEEN
REWORK	RIMOSE	ROPILY	RUGOSE	RAGWORT	RATTIER
REWOVE	RIMOUS	ROPING	RUGOUS	RAILBUS	RATTING

RATTISH	REBUKER	REDUCER	REGRADE	REPANEL	RESPADE
RATTLER	RECARRY	REDWARE	REGRAFT	REPAPER	RESPEAK
RATTOON	RECEIPT	REDWING	REGRANT	REPATCH	RESPECT
RATTRAP	RECEIVE	REDWOOD	REGRATE	REPINER	RESPELL
RAUCITY	RECENCY	REEDIER	REGREEN	REPLACE	RESPIRE
RAUCOUS	RECHART	REEDIFY	REGREET	REPLANT	RESPITE
*RAUNCHY	RECHEAT	REEDILY	REGRESS	REPLATE	RESPLIT
RAVAGER	*RECHECK	REEDING	REGRIND	REPLEAD	RESPOKE
RAVELER	RECITAL	REEDMAN	REGROOM	REPLETE	RESPOND
RAVELIN	RECITER	*REEJECT	REGROUP	*REPLEVY	RESPRAY
RAVELLY	RECLAIM	REELECT	REGULAR	REPLICA	RESTACK
RAVENER	RECLAME	REENACT	REGULUS	REPLIER	RESTAFF
RAVIOLI	RECLASP	REENDOW	REHINGE	REPLUMB	RESTAGE
RAWHIDE	RECLEAN	*REENJOY	REHOUSE	REPOSAL	RESTAMP
RAWNESS	RECLINE	REENTER	REIFIER	REPOSER	RESTART
RAYLESS	RECLUSE	REENTRY	REIMAGE	REPOSIT	RESTATE
RAYLIKE	RECOLOR	*REEQUIP	REINCUR	REPOWER	RESTFUL
REACHER	RECOUNT	REERECT	*REINDEX	REPRESS	RESTIVE
REACTOR	RECOUPE	REEVOKE	REINTER	REPRICE	RESTOCK
READAPT	RECOVER	*REEXPEL	REISSUE	REPRINT	RESTOKE
READIED	RECRATE	REFENCE	*REITBOX	REPRISE	RESTORE
READIER	RECROSS	REFEREE	*REJOICE	REPROBE	RESTUDY
READIES	RECROWN	REFFING	*REJUDGE	REPROOF	RESTUFF
READILY	RECRUIT	REFIGHT	RELABEL	REPROVE	RESTYLE
READING	*RECTIFY	REFINER	RELAPSE	REPTANT	RESUMER
READMIT	RECTORY	REFLATE	RELATER	REPTILE	RESURGE
READOPT	*RECTRIX	REFLECT	RELATOR	REPULSE	RETABLE
READORN	RECURVE	REFLIES	RELAXER	*REQUEST	RETAKER
READOUT	RECUSAL	REFLOAT	RELAXIN	*REQUIEM	RETASTE
*REAFFIX	RECYCLE	REFLOOD	RELEARN	*REQUIRE	RETEACH
REAGENT	REDBAIT	REFOCUS	RELEASE	*REQUITE	RETHINK
REALGAR	REDBIRD	REFORGE	RELIANT	RERAISE	RETIARY
REALIGN	REDBONE	REFOUND	RELIEVE	REREDOS	RETICLE
REALISE	REDCOAT	REFRACT	RELIEVO	REROUTE	RETINAL
REALISM	REDDEST	REFRAIN	RELIGHT	RESCALE	RETINOL
REALIST	REDDING	REFRAME	*RELIQUE	RESCIND	RETINUE
REALITY	REDDISH	REFRESH	REMAKER	RESCORE	RETIREE
*REALIZE	REDFISH	REFRONT	REMARRY	RESCUER	RETIRER
REALLOT	REDHEAD	REFUGEE	REMATCH	*RESEIZE	RETITLE
REALTER	REDLINE	REFUSAL	REMERGE	RESERVE	RETOUCH
REANNEX	REDNECK	REFUSER	REMNANT	RESHAPE	RETRACE
REAPPLY	REDNESS	REFUTAL	REMODEL	RESHAVE	RETRACT
REARGUE	REDOUBT	REFUTER	REMORSE	RESHINE	RETRAIN
REAVAIL	REDOUND	REGALER	REMOUNT	RESHONE	RETREAD
REAWAKE	REDPOLL	REGALIA	REMOVAL	RESHOOT	RETREAT
REBATER	REDRAFT	REGALLY	REMOVER	RESIDER	RETRIAL
REBEGIN	REDREAM	REGATTA	RENEGER	RESIDUA	RETSINA
REBIRTH	REDRESS	REGAUGE	RENEWAL	RESIDUE	RETTING
REBLEND	REDRIED	REGENCY	RENEWER	RESIGHT	RETWIST
REBLOOM	REDRIES	REGIMEN	RENNASE	RESLATE	RETYING
REBOANT	REDRILL	*REGLAZE	RENTIER	RESMELT	REUNIFY
REBOARD	REDRIVE	REGLOSS	REOCCUR	RESOJET	REUNION
REBOUND	REDROOT	REGNANT	REOFFER	RESOLVE	REUNITE
REBREED	REDSKIN	REGORGE	REORDER	RESOUND	REUTTER
REBUILD	REDTAIL	REGOSOL	REPAINT	RESPACE	REVALUE

REVELER	RIDDING	*ROCKERY	ROULADE	RUSTLER	RAMOSITY
REVELRY	RIDDLER	ROCKIER	ROULEAU	RUTHFUL	RAMPAGER
REVENGE	RIDGIER	ROCKOON	ROUNDEL	RUTTIER	*RAMPANCY
REVENUE	RIDGING	RODLESS	ROUNDER	RUTTILY	RAMSHORN
REVERER	RIDOTTO	RODLIKE	ROUNDLY	RUTTING	RAMULOSE
REVERIE	RIFFING	RODSMAN	ROUNDUP	RUTTISH	RAMULOUS
REVERSE	RIFFLER	*ROEBUCK	ROUSTER	RABBITER	RANCHERO
REVERSO	RIFLERY	ROGUERY	ROUTINE	*RABBITRY	*RANCHMAN
REVILER	RIFLING	ROGUISH	ROUTING	RABIDITY	RANDIEST
REVISAL	RIGGING	ROISTER	ROWBOAT	RACEMATE	RANDOMLY
REVISER	RIGHTER	ROLLICK	*ROWLOCK	RACEMISM	RANKNESS
REVISIT	RIGHTLY	ROLLING	ROYALLY	*RACEMIZE	RANSOMER
REVISOR	RIGIDLY	ROLLMOP	ROYALTY	RACEMOID	*RAPACITY
REVIVAL	RIKISHA	ROLLOUT	ROYSTER	RACEMOSE	RAPESEED
REVIVER	*RIKSHAW	ROLLTOP	RUBABOO	RACEMOUS	RAPIDITY
REVOICE	RILIEVO	ROLLWAY	RUBASSE	RACHILLA	RAPPAREE
REVOKER	RIMFIRE	ROMAINE	RUBBERY	RACHITIS	RAPTNESS
REVOLVE	RIMIEST	ROMANCE	RUBBING	RACINESS	RAREFIER
REVUIST	RIMLAND	ROMAUNT	RUBBISH	*RACKWORK	RARENESS
REVVING	RIMLESS	ROMPISH	RUBDOWN	RACLETTE	RARERIPE
REWAKEN	RIMMING	RONDEAU	RUBELLA	RADIABLE	RASCALLY
REWEAVE	*RIMROCK	RONDURE	RUBEOLA	RADIALLY	RASHNESS
REWEIGH	RINGENT	RONTGEN	RUBIEST	RADIANCE	RASORIAL
REWIDEN	RINGGIT	ROOFING	RUBIOUS	RADIANCY	RATAPLAN
REWOKEN	RINGLET	ROOFTOP	RUCHING	RADIATOR	RATEABLE
REWOUND	RINGTAW	ROOKERY	RUCTION	RADICAND	RATICIDE
REWOVEN	RINNING	ROOMFUL	RUDDIER	RADICATE	RATIFIER
REWRITE	RINSING	ROOSTER	RUDDILY	RADIOMAN	RATIONAL
REYNARD	RIOTOUS	ROOTAGE	*RUDDOCK	RADWASTE	RATOONER
*RHABDOM	RIPCORD	ROOTIER	RUDERAL	RAFTERED	RATSBANE
*RHACHIS	RIPENER	ROOTLET	RUDESBY	RAFTSMAN	RATTENER
RHAMNUS	RIPIENO	*ROPEWAY	RUFFIAN	RAGINGLY	RATTIEST
RHATANY	RIPOSTE	ROPIEST	RUFFLER	RAILBIRD	RATTLING
RHENIUM	RIPPING	*RORQUAL	RUFIYAA	RAILHEAD	RAVELING
*RHIZOID	RIPPLER	ROSARIA	RUGGING	RAILLERY	RAVELLED
*RHIZOMA	RIPPLET	ROSEATE	RUGLIKE	RAILROAD	RAVELLER
*RHIZOME	RIPSTOP	ROSEBAY	RUINATE	RAINBAND	RAVENING
RHODIUM	RIPTIDE	ROSEBUD	RUINOUS	RAINBIRD	RAVENOUS
RHODORA	RISIBLE	ROSELLE	RUMBLER	RAINCOAT	RAVIGOTE
*RHOMBIC	RISOTTO	ROSEOLA	RUMMAGE	RAINDROP	*RAVINGLY
RHOMBUS	RISSOLE	ROSETTE	RUMMEST	RAINFALL	RAVISHER
RHUBARB	RIVALRY	ROSIEST	RUNAWAY	RAINIEST	RAWBONED
RIBBAND	RIVETER	ROSINOL	*RUNBACK	RAINLESS	RAYGRASS
RIBBIER	RIVIERA	ROSOLIO	RUNDLET	RAINWASH	REABSORB
RIBBING	RIVIERE	ROSTRAL	RUNDOWN	RAINWEAR	REACCEDE
RIBBONY	RIVULET	ROSTRUM	RUNLESS	RAISONNE	REACCENT
RIBLESS	ROADBED	ROTATOR	RUNNING	*RAKEHELL	REACCEPT
RIBLIKE	ROADWAY	ROTIFER	RUNOVER	RALLYING	REACCUSE
RIBWORT	ROARING	ROTTING	RUPTURE	RALLYIST	REACTANT
RICINUS	ROASTER	ROTUNDA	RURALLY	RAMBUTAN	REACTION
RICKETS	ROBBERY	ROUGHEN	RUSHIER	RAMENTUM	REACTIVE
*RICKETY	ROBBING	ROUGHER	RUSHING	*RAMEQUIN	READDICT
*RICKSHA	ROBOTRY	ROUGHLY	RUSSIFY	*RAMIFORM	*READERLY
RICOTTA	ROBUSTA	ROUGING	RUSTIER	RAMILLIE	READIEST
RIDABLE	*ROCKABY	ROUILLE	RUSTILY	RAMMIEST	*READJUST

*REAFFIRM	*RECOVERY	REFLOWER	*REJACKET	*REOBJECT	RESELLER
REALISER	RECREANT	REFLUENT	*REJECTEE	REOBTAIN	RESEMBLE
*REALIZER	RECREATE	REFOREST	*REJECTER	*REOCCUPY	RESERVER
REALNESS	RECUSANT	REFORMAT	*REJECTOR	REOPPOSE	RESETTER
REANOINT	*RECYCLER	REFORMER	*REJIGGER	REORDAIN	RESETTLE
*REAPHOOK	REDACTOR	*REFOUGHT	*REJOICER	REORIENT	RESHAPER
REAPPEAR	REDAMAGE	*REFREEZE	*REJUGGLE	REOUTFIT	RESIDENT
REARMICE	REDARGUE	REFUGIUM	REKINDLE	REOVIRUS	RESIDUAL
REARMOST	*REDBRICK	REFUNDER	RELAPSER	*REPACIFY	RESIDUUM
REAROUSE	REDECIDE	*REFUSNIK	RELATION	REPAIRER	RESIGNER
REARREST	REDEEMER	REGAINER	RELATIVE	REPARTEE	RESILVER
REARWARD	REDEFEAT	REGALITY	RELAUNCH	REPEALER	RESINATE
REASCEND	REDEFECT	REGATHER	*RELAXANT	REPEATER	RESINIFY
REASCENT	REDEFINE	REGELATE	RELEASER	REPELLER	RESINOID
REASONER	REDEMAND	REGICIDE	RELEGATE	REPENTER	RESINOUS
REASSAIL	REDEPLOY	REGIMENT	RELETTER	REPEOPLE	RESISTER
REASSERT	REDESIGN	REGIONAL	RELEVANT	REPETEND	RESISTOR
REASSESS	REDHORSE	REGISTER	RELIABLE	REPHRASE	*RESKETCH
REASSIGN	REDIGEST	REGISTRY	RELIABLY	REPLACER	RESMOOTH
REASSORT	REDIRECT	REGNANCY	RELIANCE	REPLEDGE	RESOLDER
REASSUME	REDIVIDE	REGOLITH	RELIEVER	REPLEVIN	RESOLUTE
REASSURE	REDOLENT	REGROOVE	RELIGION	REPLICON	RESOLVER
REATTACH	REDOUBLE	*REGROWTH	RELOADER	REPLUNGE	RESONANT
REATTACK	REDRAWER	REGULATE	RELOCATE	REPOLISH	RESONATE
REATTAIN	*REDSHANK	*REHABBER	RELUCENT	REPORTER	RESORCIN
*REAWAKEN	*REDSHIFT	*REHAMMER	RELUMINE	REPOUSSE	RESORTER
REBELDOM	REDSHIRT	REHANDLE	REMANENT	REPRIEVE	RESOUGHT
REBOTTLE	REDSTART	REHARDEN	REMANNED	REPRISAL	RESOURCE
REBOUGHT	REDUCTOR	REHEARSE	REMARKER	*REPROACH	RESPLICE
*REBRANCH	REDUVIID	REHEATER	REMARKET	REPROVAL	RESPOKEN
REBURIAL	REEDBIRD	*REHOBOAM	*REMARQUE	REPROVER	RESPONSA
REBUTTAL	*REEDBUCK	REIGNITE	REMASTER	REPUBLIC	RESPONSE
REBUTTER	REEDIEST	REIMPORT	REMEDIAL	REPULSER	RESPRANG
REBUTTON	REEDLIKE	REIMPOSE	REMEMBER	*REPURIFY	RESPREAD
RECALLER	REEDLING	REINCITE	REMINDER	REPURSUE	RESPRING
RECAMIER	*REEMBARK	REINDEER	REMITTAL	*REQUIRER	RESPROUT
RECANTER	*REEMBODY	REINDICT	REMITTER	*REQUITAL	RESTITCH
RECEIVER	REEMERGE	REINDUCE	REMITTOR	*REQUITER	RESTLESS
RECEPTOR	*REEMPLOY	REINDUCT	*REMODIFY	RERECORD	RESTORAL
RECHANGE	REENGAGE	REINFECT	REMOLADE	REREMICE	RESTORER
RECHARGE	REENLIST	REINFORM	REMOTION	REREMIND	RESTRAIN
RECHOOSE	REENROLL	REINFUSE	RENATURE	REREPEAT	RESTRESS
RECIRCLE	*REEXPORT	*REINJECT	RENDERER	REREVIEW	RESTRICT
RECISION	*REEXPOSE	*REINJURE	RENDIBLE	REREWARD	RESTRIKE
RECKLESS	REFASTEN	*REINJURY	*RENDZINA	REROLLER	RESTRING
RECKONER	REFERENT	REINLESS	RENEGADE	RESADDLE	RESTRIVE
RECLINER	REFERRAL	REINSERT	RENEGADO	RESALUTE	RESTROOM
RECLOTHE	REFERRED	REINSMAN	RENIFORM	RESAMPLE	RESTRUCK
*RECODIFY	REFERRER	REINSURE	RENITENT	RESCHOOL	RESTRUNG
RECOILER	REFIGURE	REINVADE	RENMINBI	RESCREEN	RESUBMIT
RECOMMIT	REFILTER	REINVENT	RENOGRAM	RESCRIPT	RESUMMON
*RECONVEY	REFINERY	REINVEST	RENOTIFY	RESCULPT	RESUPINE
RECORDER	REFINING	REINVITE	RENOUNCE	RESEARCH	*RESUPPLY
RECOUPLE	REFINISH	*REINVOKE	RENOVATE	RESEASON	RESURVEY
RECOURSE	*REFLEXLY	REISSUER	RENUMBER	RESECURE	RETACKLE

RETAILER	REWARDER	RIGORISM	ROLLAWAY	*ROVINGLY		B R ED
RETAILOR	REWINDER	RIGORIST	*ROLLBACK	*ROWDYISH		B R EE
RETAINER	REWRITER	RIGOROUS	*ROLLICKY	*ROWDYISM		B R EN
RETARDER	*RHABDOME	RIMESTER	ROLLOVER	ROYALISM		B R EW
RETARGET	RHAMNOSE	RIMINESS	ROMANCER	ROYALIST		B R IE
RETEMPER	RHAPSODE	RIMOSITY	ROMANISE	RUBAIYAT		B R IG
RETHREAD	*RHAPSODY	*RINGBARK	*ROMANIZE	RUBBABOO		B R IM
RETIARII	*RHBOBASE	RINGBOLT	ROMANTIC	RUBICUND		B R IN
RETICENT	*RHEMATIC	RINGBONE	RONDELET	RUBIDIUM		B R IO
RETICULA	RHEOBASE	RINGDOVE	RONDELLE	*RUBYLIKE		B R IT
RETICULE	*RHEOLOGY	RINGHALS	ROOFLESS	*RUCKSACK		B R OO
RETIFORM	*RHEOPHIL	RINGLIKE	*ROOFLIKE	RUCTIOUS		B R OS
RETINENE	RHEOSTAT	*RINGNECK	ROOFLINE	RUDDIEST		B R OW
RETINITE	RHETORIC	RINGSIDE	ROOFTREE	RUDENESS		B R R R
RETINOID	RHINITIS	RINGTAIL	ROOMETTE	RUDIMENT		B R UT
RETINULA	*RHIZOBIA	RINGTOSS	ROOMMATE	RUFFLIER		C R AB
RETIRANT	*RHIZOPOD	RINGWORM	*ROORBACK	*RUFFLIKE		C R AG
RETIRING	*RHIZOPUS	RIPARIAN	ROOTHOLD	*RUFFLING		C R AM
RETORTER	RHODAMIN	RIPENESS	ROOTIEST	RUGOSITY		C R AP
RETRENCH	*RHOMBOID	RIPPABLE	ROOTLESS	RUGULOSE		C R AW
RETRIEVE	*RHONCHUS	RIPPLING	ROOTLIKE	RULELESS		C R EW
RETROACT	RHYOLITE	RISIBLES	ROPELIKE	RUMBLING		C R IB
RETROFIT	*RHYTHMIC	RISKLESS	*ROPEWALK	RUMINANT		C R IS
RETRORSE	RIBALDLY	RITUALLY	ROPINESS	RUMINATE		C R OC
RETURNEE	RIBALDRY	RIVERBED	ROSARIAN	RUMMAGER		C R OP
RETURNER	RIBBIEST	RIVERINE	ROSARIUM	RUNABOUT		C R OW
REUNITER	RIBGRASS	RIVULOSE	ROSEBUSH	RUNAGATE		C R UD
REUSABLE	RIBOSOME	ROADKILL	ROSEFISH	RUNROUND		C R US
*REVAMPER	RICEBIRD	ROADLESS	ROSELIKE	RURALISE		C R UX
*REVANCHE	RICERCAR	*ROADSHOW	ROSEMARY	RURALISM		D R AB
REVEALER	RICHNESS	ROADSIDE	ROSEROOT	RURALIST		D R AG
REVEHENT	*RICHWEED	ROADSTER	ROSESLUG	RURALITE		D R AM
REVEILLE	*RICKRACK	*ROADWORK	ROSINESS	RURALITY		D R AT
REVELLER	*RICKSHAW	ROBORANT	ROSINOUS	*RURALIZE		D R AW
REVENANT	*RICOCHET	ROBOTICS	ROSTELLA	RUSHIEST		D R AY
REVENGER	RIDDANCE	ROBOTISM	ROSTRATE	*RUSHLIKE		D R EE
REVENUER	RIDEABLE	*ROBOTIZE	ROSULATE	RUSTICAL		D R EG
REVEREND	RIDGIEST	ROCAILLE	ROTATION	RUSTICLY		D R EK
REVERENT	RIDGLING	*ROCKABYE	ROTATORY	RUSTIEST		D R EW
REVERIES	RIDICULE	*ROCKAWAY	ROTENONE	RUSTLESS		D R IB
*REVERIFY	RIESLING	ROCKETER	ROTIFORM	RUSTLING		D R IP
REVERING	*RIFAMPIN	*ROCKETRY	ROTOTILL	RUTABAGA		D R OP
REVERSAL	RIFENESS	*ROCKFALL	ROTURIER	RUTHENIC		D R UB
REVERSER	*RIFFRAFF	*ROCKFISH	ROUGHAGE	RUTHLESS		D R UM
REVERTER	RIFLEMAN	ROCKIEST	*ROUGHDRY	RUTILANT		F R AB
REVIEWAL	RIFTLESS	ROCKLESS	*ROUGHHEW	RUTTIEST		F R AG
REVIEWER	RIGADOON	*ROCKLIKE	*ROUGHISH	RYEGRASS		F R AP
REVISION	RIGATONI	*ROCKLING	ROUGHLEG		B R AD	F R AT
REVISORY	RIGAUDON	ROCKROSE	ROULETTE		B R AE	F R AY
*REVIVIFY	*RIGHTFUL	*ROCKWEED	ROUNDISH		B R AG	F R EE
*REVIVING	RIGHTIES	*ROCKWORK	ROUNDLET		B R AN	F R ET
REVOLTER	RIGHTISM	ROENTGEN	ROUSSEAU		B R AT	F R IG
REVOLUTE	RIGHTIST	ROGATION	ROUTEMAN		B R AW	F R IT
REVOLVER	*RIGIDIFY	ROGATORY	ROUTEWAY		B R AY	*F R IZ
REVULSED	RIGIDITY	ROLAMITE				F R OE

FR OG	TR IM	BR OAD	CR IPE	DR OOP	GR AIN
FR OM	TR IO	**BR OCK**	CR ISP	DR OPT	GR AMA
FR OW	TR IP	BR OIL	**CR OAK**	DR OSS	**GR AMP**
FR UG	TR OD	**BR OKE**	CR OCI	**DR OUK**	GR ANA
GR AB	TR OP	BR OME	**CR OCK**	DR OVE	GR AND
GR AD	TR OT	BR OMO	**CR OFT**	DR OWN	GR ANT
GR AM	TR OW	BR ONC	CR ONE	DR UID	GR APE
GR AN	TR OY	BR OOD	**CR ONY**	**DR UNK**	**GR APH**
GR AT	TR UE	**BR OOK**	**CR OOK**	DR UPE	**GR APY**
GR AY	**VR OW**	BR OOM	CR OON	DR USE	GR ASP
GR EE	WR AP	BR OSE	CR OSS	**DR YAD**	GR ASS
GR EW	WR EN	**BR OSY**	CR OUP	DR YER	GR ATE
GR EY	WR IT	**BR OTH**	**CR OWD**	**DR YLY**	**GR AVY**
GR ID	BR ACE	**BR OWN**	**CR OWN**	FR AIL	***GR AZE**
GR IG	**BR ACH**	BR UGH	***CR OZE**	**FR AME**	GR EAT
GR IM	**BR ACT**	BR UIN	**CR UCK**	FR ANC	GR EBE
GR IN	BR AID	BR UIT	CR UDE	**FR ANK**	GR EED
GR IP	BR AIL	BR UME	CR UEL	FR ASS	**GR EEK**
GR IT	BR AIN	BR UNT	CR UET	FR AUD	GR EEN
GR OG	**BR AKE**	**BR USH**	**CR UMB**	**FR EAK**	GR EET
GR OT	**BR AKY**	**BR USK**	**CR UMP**	FR EED	GR EGO
GR OW	BR AND	BR UTE	CR UOR	FR EER	GR IDE
GR UB	BR ANK	CR AAL	CR USE	**FR EMD**	GR IEF
GR UE	BR ANT	**CR ACK**	**CR USH**	FR ENA	**GR IFF**
GR UM	**BR ASH**	**CR AFT**	CR UST	FR ERE	GR IFT
KR IS	BR ASS	CR AKE	**CR YPT**	**FR ESH**	GR ILL
PR AM	**BR AVA**	**CR AMP**	DR AFF	FR IAR	GR IME
PR AO	**BR AVI**	CR ANE	**DR AFT**	FR IED	**GR IMY**
PR AT	**BR AVO**	**CR ANK**	DR AIL	FR IER	GR IND
PR AU	**BR AWL**	CR APE	**DR AIN**	FR IES	GR IOT
PR AY	**BR AWN**	**CR ASH**	**DR AKE**	FR ILL	GR IPE
PR EE	**BR AWS**	CR ASS	DR AMA	FR ISE	GR IPT
PR EP	***BR AXY**	CR ATE	**DR ANK**	**FR ISK**	**GR IPY**
PR EX	***BR AZA**	CR AWL	DR APE	FR ITH	GR IST
PR EY	***BR AZE**	***CR AZE**	DR AVE	FR ITT	GR ITH
***PR EZ**	BR EAD	***CR AZY**	DR AWL	***FR ITZ**	GR OAN
PR IG	**BR EAK**	**CR EAK**	DR AWN	***FR IZZ**	GR OIN
PR IM	BR EAM	CR EAM	DR EAD	**FR OCK**	GR OOM
PR OA	BR EDE	CR EDO	DR EAM	FR OND	GR OPE
PR OD	BR EED	CR EED	DR EAR	FR ONS	GR OSS
PR OF	BR ENT	**CR EEK**	DR ESS	FR ONT	***GR OSZ**
PR OG	**BR EVE**	CR EEL	DR EST	FR ORE	GR OUP
PR OM	BR IAR	CR EEP	DR IED	**FR OSH**	GR OUT
PR OP	BR IBE	CR EME	DR IER	FR OST	GR OVE
PR OW	**BR ICK**	CR EPE	DR IES	**FR OTH**	GR OWL
TR AD	BR IDE	CR EPT	DR ILL	**FR OWN**	GR OWN
TR AM	**BR IEF**	**CR EPY**	DR ILY	***FR OZE**	GR UEL
TR AP	BR IER	CR ESS	**DR INK**	FR UIT	**GR UFF**
TR AY	BR ILL	CR EST	DR IPT	FR UMP	GR UME
TR EE	BR INE	**CR ICK**	DR IVE	**FR YER**	**GR UMP**
TR EF	BR ING	CR IED	DR OIT	GR AAL	GR UNT
TR EK	**BR INK**	CR IER	DR OLL	GR ACE	KR AAL
TR ET	**BR INY**	CR IES	DR ONE	GR ADE	**KR AFT**
TR EY	**BR ISK**	CR IME	DR OOL	GR AFT	KR AIT
TR IG	BR ITT	**CR IMP**		GR AIL	KR AUT

K REEP	*PR OXY	TR UCK	BAR REN	BU RROW	CE RMET
K RILL	PR UDE	TR UED	BAR RET	BU RSAR	CE ROUS
K RONA	PR UNE	TR UER	BAR RIO	BU RTON	CE RTES
K RONE	PR UTA	TR ULL	BAR ROW	BY RLAW	CE RUSE
K ROON	PR YER	TR ULY	BAR TER	BY RNIE	*CE RVIX
K RUBI	TR ACE	TR UMP	BA RYON	BY ROAD	CH RISM
PR AAM	TR ACK	TR UNK	BA RYTA	CA RACK	CH ROMA
PR AHU	TR ACT	TR USS	BA RYTE	CA RAFE	CH ROME
PR ANG	TR ADE	TR UST	BE RAKE	CA RATE	CH ROMO
PR ANK	TR AGI	TR UTH	BE RATE	CA RBON	CI RCLE
PR ASE	TR AIK	TR YMA	BE RIME	CA RBOY	CI RCUS
PR ATE	TR AIL	TR YST	BE RLIN	CA RCEL	*CI RQUE
PR AWN	TR AIN	VR OOM	BE RTHA	CA RDER	CIR RUS
PR EEN	TR AIT	VR OUW	BI RDER	CA RDIA	CO RBAN
PR ESA	TR AMP	WR ACK	BI RDIE	CA REEN	CO RBEL
PR ESE	TR ANS	WR ANG	BI REME	CA REER	CO RBIE
PR ESS	TR APT	WR APT	BI RKIE	CA RESS	CO RDER
PR EST	TR ASH	WR ATH	BI RLER	CA RFUL	CO RDON
*PR EXY	TR ASS	WR EAK	BO RAGE	CA RIBE	CO RING
PR ICE	TR AWL	WR ECK	BO RANE	CA RIES	CO RIUM
PR ICK	TR EAD	WR EST	BO RATE	CA RINA	CO RKER
PR ICY	TR EAT	WR IED	BO RDEL	CA RING	CO RMEL
PR IDE	TR END	WR IER	BO RDER	CA RLIN	CO RNEA
PR IED	TR ESS	WR IES	BO REAL	CA RMAN	CO RNEL
PR IER	TR EWS	WR ING	BO REEN	CA RNAL	CO RNER
PR IES	TR IAD	WR IST	BO RIDE	CA RNET	CO RNET
PR ILL	TR IAL	WR ITE	BO RING	CA RNEY	CO RNUS
PR IMA	TR IBE	WR ONG	BO RROW	CA RNIE	CO RONA
PR IME	TR ICE	WR OTE	BO RSCH	CA ROCH	CO RPSE
PR IMI	TR ICK	WR OTH	BO RSHT	CA ROLI	CO RPUS
PR IMO	TR IED	WR UNG	*BO RZOI	CA RPAL	CO RRAL
PR IMP	TR IER	BA RBAL	BU RBLE	CA RPEL	CO RRIE
PR INK	TR IES	BA RBEL	BU RBLY	CA RPER	CO RSAC
PR INT	TR IGO	BA RBER	BU RBOT	CA RPET	CO RSET
PR IOR	TR IKE	BA RBET	BU RDEN	CA RPUS	*CO RTEX
PR ISE	TR ILL	BA RBUT	BU RDIE	CAR REL	CO RTIN
PR ISM	TR INE	BA RDIC	BU REAU	CAR ROM	CO RVEE
PR ISS	TR IOL	BA REGE	BU RGEE	CAR ROT	CO RVES
PR IVY	TR IPE	BA RELY	BU RGER	CA RTEL	CO RVET
*PR IZE	TR ITE	BA REST	BU RGLE	CA RTER	*CO RYMB
PR OBE	TR OAK	BA RFLY	BU RGOO	CA RTON	*CO RYZA
PR OEM	TR OCK	BA RHOP	BU RIAL	CA RTOP	CU RAGH
PR OLE	TR ODE	BA RING	BU RIED	CA RVEL	CU RARA
PR OMO	TR OKE	BA RITE	BU RIER	CA RVEN	CU RARE
PR ONE	TR OLL	BA RIUM	BU RIES	CA RVER	CU RARI
PR ONG	TR OMP	BA RKER	BU RING	CE RATE	CU RATE
PR OOF	TR ONA	BA RLEY	BU RKER	CE RCIS	CU RBER
PR OSE	TR ONE	BA RLOW	BU RLAP	CE RCUS	CU RDLE
PR OSO	TR OOP	BA RMAN	BU RLER	CE REAL	CU RFEW
PR OSS	TR OOZ	BA RMIE	BU RLEY	CE REUS	CU RING
PR OST	TR OPE	BA RONG	BU RNER	CE RING	CU RITE
PR OSY	TR OTH	BA RONY	BU RNET	CE RIPH	CU RIUM
PR OUD	TR OUT	*BA RQUE	BU RNIE	CE RISE	CU RLER
PR OVE	TR OVE	BAR RED	BU RRED	CE RITE	CU RLEW
PR OWL	TR UCE	BAR REL	BU RRER	CE RIUM	CUR RAN

CU R R IE	FA R ME R	GA R GET	HE R EOF	LA R DON	MU R DE R
CU R SED	FA R R OW	GA R GLE	HE R EON	LA R IAT	MU R EIN
CU R SE R	FE R HAM	GA R ISH	HE R ESY	LA R INE	MU R INE
CU R SO R	FE R INE	GA R LIC	HE R ETO	LA R KE R	MU R ING
CU R TAL	FE R ITY	GA R NE R	HE R IOT	LA R R UP	MU R MU R
CU R TLY	FE R LIE	GA R NET	HE R MIT	*LA R YNX	*MU R PHY
CU R TSY	FE R R EL	GA R OTE	HE R NIA	LO R DLY	NAR R OW
CU R ULE	FE R R ET	GA R R ED	HE R OIC	LO R EAL	NA R WAL
CU R VEY	FE R R IC	GA R R ET	HE R OIN	LO R ICA	NE R EID
DA R KEN	FE R R UM	GA R R ON	HE R PES	LO R IES	NE R EIS
DA R KEY	FE R ULE	GA R TE R	HI R ING	LU R DAN	NE R OLI
DA R KIE	FE R VID	GA R VEY	HI R PLE	LU R ING	NO R DIC
DA R KLE	FE R VO R	GE R BIL	HI R SEL	LU R KE R	NO R ITE
DA R KLY	FI R ING	GE R ENT	HI R SLE	LY R ATE	NO R MAL
DA R NED	FI R KIN	GE R MAN	HO R A R Y	LY R ISM	NO R MED
DA R NEL	FI R MAN	GE R MEN	HO R NET	LY R IST	NU R SE R
DA R NE R	FI R ME R	GE R UND	HO R R ID	MA R AUD	PA R ADE
DA R TE R	FI R MLY	GI R DE R	HO R R OR	MA R GIN	PA R AMO
DA R TLE	FO R AGE	GI R DLE	HO R SEY	MA R INA	PA R ANG
DE R ATE	FO R BAD	GI R LIE	HO R STE	MA R INE	PA R APH
DE R IDE	FO R BID	GO R GE R	HU R DLE	MA R KE R	PA R CEL
DE R IVE	FO R BYE	GO R GET	HU R LE R	*MA R KKA	PA R DAH
DE R MIS	FO R CE R	GO R GON	HU R LEY	MA R LIN	PA R DEE
DE R R IS	FO R EBY	GO R HEN	HU R R AH	MA R OON	PA R DIE
DI R DUM	FO R EDO	GO R IE R	HU R R AY	*MA R QUE	PA R DON
DI R ECT	FO R EGO	GO R ILY	HU R TE R	MA R R ED	PA R ENT
DI R ELY	FO R EST	GO R ING	HU R TLE	MA R R E R	PA R EVE
DI R EST	FO R GAT	GU R GLE	*JA R FUL	MA R R ON	PA R GET
DI R HAM	FO R GE R	GU R NET	JA R GON	MA R TEN	PA R IAH
DI R NDJ.	FO R GET	GU R NEY	JA R INA	MA R TIN	PA R IAN
DO R ADO	FO R GOT	GY R ASE	*JA R R AH	MA R TY R	PA R ING
DO R BUG	FO R INT	GY R ATE	JA R R ED	ME R CE R	PA R ISH
DO R IES	FO R KE R	GY R ENE	*JA R VEY	ME R INO	PA R ITY
DO R ME R	FO R MAL	GY R ING	*JE R BOA	ME R LIN	PA R KE R
DO R MIE	FO R MAT	GY R OSE	*JE R KE R	ME R LON	PA R LAY
DO R MIN	FO R ME R	HA R ASS	*JE R KIN	ME R LOR	PA R LEY
DO R PE R	FO R MIC	HA R BO R	JE R R ID	ME R LON	PA R LO R
DO R SAD	FO R MOL	HA R DEN	*JE R SEY	MI R AGE	PA R ODY
DO R SAL	FO R MYL	HA R DLY	JO R DAN	MI R IE R	PA R OLE
DO R SEL	*FO R NIX	HA R EEM	JU R ANT	MI R ING	PA R OUS
DO R SE R	FO R R IT	HA R KE R	JU R IES	MI R R OR	PA R R AL
DO R SUM	FO R TES	HA R LOT	JU R IST	MO R ALE	PA R R ED
DU R BA R	FO R TIS	HA R ME R	KA R ATE	MO R ALS	PA R R EL
DU R ESS	*FO R WHY	HA R MIN	KA R OSS	MO R ASS	PA R R OT
DU R IAN	FU R ANE	HA R PE R	KA R R OO	MO R EEN	PA R SEC
DU R ING	FU R FU R	HA R PIN	KE R MES	MO R GAN	PA R SE R
DU R ION	FU R IES	HA R R OW	KE R MIS	MO R GEN	PA R SON
DU R NED	FU R LE R	HA R TAL	KE R NEL	MO R GUE	PA R TAN
FA R CE R	FU R ORE	HE R ALD	KE R R IA	MO R ION	PA R TLY
FA R CIE	FU R R ED	HE R BAL	KE R SEY	MO R OSE	PA R TON
FA R DEL	FU R R OW	HE R BED	*KI R SCH	MO R R IS	PA R U R A
FA R FAL	GA R AGE	HE R DE R	KI R TLE	MO R SEL	PA R U R E
FA R FEL	GA R BLE	HE R DIC	KO R UNA	MO R TAL	PA R VIS
FA R INA	GA R CON	HE R EAT	KU R GAN	MO R TA R	PE R DIE
FA R ING	GA R DEN	HE R EIN	LA R DE R	MO R ULA	PE R DUE

PE R EON	R E R OOF	**SH R UNK**	**ST R IPT**	TE R ROR	VE R DIN
PE R IOD	R E R OSE	SI R DA R	**ST R IPY**	TH R ALL	**VE R GE R**
PE R ISH	R U R BAN	SI R ING	ST R IVE	**TH R ASH**	***VE R IFY**
PE R MIT	SA R APE	SI R R AH	ST R OBE	**TH R AVE**	**VE R ILY**
*PE R OXY	SA R DA R	SI R R EE	ST R ODE	TH R AWN	**VE R ISM**
PE R R ON	SA R ODE	SO R BET	**ST R OKE**	**TH R EAD**	VE R IST
PE R SON	SA R ONG	**SO R BIC**	ST R OLL	**TH R EAP**	VE R ITE
PE R UKE	SA R SA R	SO R DID	ST R OMA	**TH R EEP**	**VE R ITY**
PE R USE	SA R SEN	SO R DO R	ST R ONG	**TH R ESH**	VE R MES
PH R ASE	SA R TO R	SO R ELY	**ST R OOK**	**TH R ICE**	**VE R MIN**
PI R ACY	**SC R APE**	SO R EST	ST R OPE	**TH R IFT**	**VE R MIS**
PI R ANA	**SC R AWL**	**SO R GHO**	ST R OUD	TH R ILL	VE R NAL
PI R ATE	**SC R EAK**	SO R ING	ST R OVE	**TH R IVE**	VE R SAL
PI R AYA	**SC R EAM**	SO R NE R	**ST R UCK**	TH R OAT	**VE R SE R**
PI R OGI	**SC R EED**	SO R R EL	ST R UMA	TH R ONE	VE R SET
PO R ISM	**SC R EEN**	SO R R OW	ST R UNG	**TH R ONG**	**VE R STE**
PO R KE R	**SC R EWY**	SO R TE R	ST R UNT	**TH R OVE**	VE R SUS
PO R OSE	**SC R IBE**	SO R TIE	SU R ELY	**TH R USH**	***VE R TEX**
PO R OUS	**SC R IED**	SP R AIN	SU R EST	TH R UST	**VE R UCA**
PO R TAL	**SC R IES**	SP R ANG	SU R ETY	TI R ADE	**VE R VET**
PO R TE R	**SC R IMP**	SP R AWL	SU R FE R	TI R ING	**VI R AGO**
PO R TLY	**SC R IPT**	SP R EAD	SU R GE R	**TO R ERO**	**VI R GIN**
PU R DAH	**SC R IVE**	SP R ENT	SU R R EY	TO R IES	VI R ILE
PU R ELY	**SC R OLL**	SP R IER	**SU R TAX**	TO R OID	VI R ION
PU R EST	**SC R OOP**	SP R ING	**SU R VEY**	TO R OSE	**VI R OID**
PU R FLE	**SC R UFF**	SP R INT	***SY R INX**	TO R OTH	VI R TUE
PU R GE R	SE R AIL	SP R ITE	TA R GET	TO R OUS	***VO R TEX**
PU R IFY	SE R APE	***SP R ITZ**	**TA R IFF**	TO R PID	**WA R BLE**
PU R INE	**SE R APH**	SP R OUT	TA R ING	TO R PO R	**WA R DEN**
PU R ISM	SE R ATE	**SP R UCE**	**TA R MAC**	***TO R QUE**	**WA R DE R**
PU R IST	SE R DAB	**SP R UCY**	TA R NAL	TO R R ID	WA R IE R
PU R ITY	SE R EIN	SP R UNG	TA R PAN	TO R ULA	**WA R ILY**
PU R LIN	SE R ENE	ST R AFE	TA R PON	TU R ACO	**WA R ING**
PU R PLE	SE R EST	ST R AIN	TA R R ED	TU R BAN	**WA R ME R**
PU R PLY	SE R IAL	ST R AIT	TA R SAL	TU R BID	**WA R MLY**
PU R R ED	SE R IES	**ST R AKE**	TA R SIA	TU R BIT	**WA R MTH**
PU R SE R	SE R INE	ST R AND	TA R SUS	TU R BOT	**WA R MUP**
PU R SUE	SE R MON	ST R ANG	TA R TAN	TU R EEN	WA R NE R
PU R VEY	SE R OSA	ST R ASS	TA R TA R	TU R GID	**WA R PE R**
PY R ENE	SE R OUS	ST R ATA	TA R TLY	TU R GO R	**WA R R ED**
PY R OLA	SE R VAL	ST R ATA	***TA R ZAN**	**TU R KEY**	**WA R R EN**
PY R ONE	SE R VE R	ST R ATH	TE R APH	TU R NE R	**WA R SAW**
PY R OPE	**SH R ANK**	ST R ATI	TE R BIA	TU R NIP	WA R SLE
PY R R OL	**SH R EWD**	**ST R AWY**	TE R CEL	TU R NUP	WI R IE R
*QU R USH	**SH R IEK**	**ST R EAK**	TE R CET	**TU R R ET**	**WO R KE R**
R A R EFY	**SH R IFT**	ST R EAM	TE R EDO	TU R TLE	***WO R KUP**
R A R ELY	**SH R IKE**	**ST R EEK**	TE R ETE	TU R VES	**WO R ME R**
R A R EST	**SH R ILL**	ST R EET	TE R GAL	TY R ANT	**WO R MIL**
R A R IFY	**SH R IMP**	ST R ESS	TE R GUM	VA R IED	WO R R IT
R A R ING	SH R INE	**ST R ICK**	TE R MER	VA R IE R	WO R SEN
R A R ITY	**SH R INK**	ST R ICT	**TE R MLY**	VA R IES	WO R SE R
R E R ACK	**SH R IVE**	ST R IDE	TE R MO R	VA R LET	WO R SET
R E R EAD	***SH R OFF**	ST R IFE	TE R RAS	VA R OOM	***WO R THY**
R E R ISE	**SH R OUD**	ST R ING	TE R R ET	**VE R BAL**	***WU R ZEL**
R E R OLL	**SH R OVE**	ST R IPE	TE R R IT	**VE R BID**	YA R NE R

YA R R OW	BU R GHE R	CA R OACH	CO R EIGN	CU R TESY	FE R VENT
*ZA R EBA	BU R GLA R	CA R OCHE	CO R KAGE	CU R TSEY	FE R VOU R
*ZA R IBA	BU R GOUT	CA R OLE R	CO R KIE R	DA R BIES	FI R EA R M
*ZE R OTH	BU R KITE	CA R OLUS	CO R NCOB	DA R EFUL	*FI R EBOX
*ZI R CON	BU R LESK	CA R OTID	CO R NFED	DA R ESAY	FI R EBUG
BA R BATE	BU R NING	CA R OTIN	CO R NICE	DA R IOLE	FI R EDOG
BA R BELL	BU R NISH	CA R OUSE	CO R NIE R	DA R KIES	*FI R EFLY
BA R BULE	BU R NOUS	CA R PALE	CO R NILY	*DA R KISH	FI R ELIT
BA R CHAN	BU R NOUT	CA R PING	CO R N R OW	DA R NING	FI R EMAN
BA R EFIT	BU R R IE R	CA R POOL	CO R NUTE	DA R R ING	FI R EPAN
BA R GAIN	BU R R ITO	CA R PO R T	CO R NUTO	DA R SHAN	FI R EPOT
BA R GING	BU R SARY	CA R R ELL	CO R OLLA	DE R AIGN	FI R STLY
BA R ILLA	BU R SATE	CA R R IED	CO R ONAL	DE R IDE R	FO R AGE R
*BA R KEEP	BU R SEED	CA R R IER	CO R ONEL	DE R IVE R	FO R AMEN
BA R LESS	BU R STE R	CA R R IES	CO R ONE R	DE R MOID	FO R AYE R
BA R MAID	BU R THEN	CA R R ION	CO R ONET	DE R NIE R	FO R BADE
BA R ONET	BU R WEED	CA R R OCH	CO R PO R A	DE R R ICK	FO R BEA R
BA R ONNE	CA R ABAO	CA R R OTY	CO R RADE	DE R VISH	FO R BODE
*BA R OQUE	CA R ABID	CA R R YON	CO R RECT	DI R EFUL	FO R BO R E
*BA R RACK	CA R ABIN	*CA R SICK	CO R RIDA	DI R TBAG	FO R CEPS
BA R RAGE	CA R ACAL	CA R TAGE	CO R R ODE	*DO R HAWK	FO R CING
BA R R IER	CA R ACOL	CA R TOON	CO R R ODY	DO R MANT	FO R EA R M
BA R R ING	CA R ACUL	CA R VING	CO R R UPT	DO R MICE	*FO R EBAY
BA R R OOM	CA R AMBA	*CA R WASH	CO R SAGE	DO R NECK	*FO R EBYE
BA R TEND	CA R AMEL	CE R AMAL	CO R SAI R	DO R NICK	FO R EGUT
BA R WARE	*CA R APAX	CE R AMIC	CO R SLET	DU R ABLE	FO R EIGN
BE R EAVE	CA R AVAN	CE R ATED	CO R TEGE	DU R AMEN	FO R ELEG
BE R ETTA	CA R AVEL	CE R ATIN	CO R ULE R	DU R ANCE	FO R EMAN
BE R GE R E	*CA R AWAY	CE R OTIC	CO R VINA	DU R MAST	*FO R EPAW
*BE R HYME	CA R BA R N	CE R TAIN	CO R VINE	FA R ADAY	FO R E R UN
BE R LINE	CA R BIDE	*CE R TIFY	CU R ABLE	FA R ADIC	FO R ESEE
BE R OBED	CA R BINE	CE R UMEN	CU R ACAO	*FA R AWAY	FO R ETOP
BE R SEEM	CA R BO R A	CE R VINE	CU R ACOA	FA R CEU R	FO R EVE R
BE R SE R K	CA R CASE	CH R ISOM	CU R ATO R	FA R CING	FO R FEIT
BI R CHEN	CA R CASS	*CH R ISTY	CU R BING	FA R INHA	FO R FEND
BI R DING	CA R DIAC	*CH R OMIC	CU R CUMA	FA R MING	FO R GAVE
BI R DMAN	CA R DING	*CH R OMYL	CU R DIE R	FA R NESS	FO R GE R Y
BI R ETTA	CA R DOON	CH R ONIC	CU R DLE R	FA R RAGO	FO R GING
BI R LING	CA R EFUL	CH R ONON	CU R ETTE	FA R R IER	FO R GIVE
BO R ACES	CA R FA R E	CI R CLE R	CU R IOSA	FA R SIDE	FO R GOE R
BO R ACIC	CA R IBOU	CI R CLET	CU R IOUS	FA R THE R	*FO R KFUL
*BO R AZON	CA R ICES	CI R CUIT	CU R LING	FE R MATA	FO R KIE R
BO R DU R E	CA R IOCA	CI R R ATE	CU R RACH	FE R MENT	FO R LO R N
BO R EDOM	CA R IOLE	CI R R OSE	CU R RACY	FE R MION	FO R MANT
BO R NEOL	CA R IOUS	CI R R OUS	CU R R ANT	FE R MIUM	FO R MATE
BO R NITE	CA R ITAS	CI R SOID	CU R R ENT	FE R NE R Y	*FO R MFUL
BO R OUGH	CA R LESS	CO R ACLE	CU R R IED	FE R RATE	FO R MULA
BO R SCHT	CA R LINE	CO R ANTO	CU R R IER	FE R R ETY	FO R SAKE
BO R STAL	CA R LING	CO R BEIL	CU R R ISH	FE R R IED	FO R TIES
BU R BLE R	CA R LISH	CO R BINA	CU R SING	FE R R IES	*FO R TIFY
*BU R DOCK	CA R LOAD	CO R DAGE	CU R SIVE	FE R R ITE	FO R TUNE
BU R ETTE	CA R MINE	CO R DATE	CU R SO R Y	FE R R OUS	FO R WA R D
BU R GAGE	CA R NAGE	CO R DIAL	CU R TAIL	FE R R ULA	FO R WENT
BU R GEON	CA R NIES	CO R DING	CU R TAIN	FE R R ULE	FO R WO R N
BU R GESS	*CA R NIFY	CO R DOBA	CU R TATE	FE R TILE	*FU R BISH

FU R CATE	HA R ELIP	*JA R LDOM	MA R SUPI	PA R DNE R	PE R IGEE
FU R CULA	HA R IANA	*JA R RING	MA R TAGO	PA R EI R A	PE R IGON
FU R IOSO	HA R ICOT	*JA R SFUL	MA R TIAL	PA R ESIS	PE R ILLA
FU R IOUS	*HA R IJAN	*JE R KIES	MA R TIAN	PA R ETIC	*PE R IQUE
FU R LESS	*HA R MFUL	*JE R R EED	MA R TINE	PA R FAIT	PE R IWIG
FU R LONG	HA R MINE	*JU R IDIC	MA R TINI	PA R GING	*PE R JU R E
*FU R METY	*HA R MONY	*JU R YMAN	MA R TLET	PA R KING	*PE R JU R Y
*FU R MITY	HA R NESS	*KA R AKUL	*MA R TY R Y	*PA R KWAY	*PE R KISH
FU R NACE	HA R PIES	*KA R AOKE	ME R ISIS	PA R LING	PE R LITE
FU R NISH	HA R PING	KA R TING	MI R ADO R	PA R LOU R	PE R MUTE
FU R RIE R	HA R PIST	KE R ATIN	MI R IEST	PA R LOUS	PE R O R AL
FU R RILY	HA R POON	*KE R CHOO	MI R INES	PA R ODIC	*PE R OXID
FU R RING	HA R RIED	KE R MESS	MO R AINE	PA R OLEE	PE R PEND
*FU R ROWY	HA R RIE R	KE R NITE	MO R ELLE	PA R ONYM	PE R PENT
FU R THE R	HA R RIES	KE R OGEN	MO R ELLO	PA R OTIC	*PE R PLEX
FU R TIVE	HA R RING	*KE R YGMA	MO R ION	PA R OTID	PE R SALT
GA R BAGE	HA R SHEN	*KI R KMAN	*MO R PHIC	*PA R QUET	PE R SIST
GA R BLE R	*HA R SHLY	KI R MESS	*MO R TIFY	PA R RIED	PE R SONA
GA R BOIL	HA R SLET	*KU R BASH	MO R TISE	PA R RIES	PE R TAIN
GA R DANT	*HA R UMPH	LA R CENY	MU R IATE	PA R RING	PE R TU R B
GA R FISH	HA R VEST	LA R DIE R	MU R RAIN	PA R ROTY	PE R USAL
GA R GLE R	HE R BAGE	LA R DOON	MU R RINE	PA R SING	PE R USE R
GA R LAND	HE R BIE R	LA R GESS	MU R THE R	PA R SLEY	PE R VADE
GA R MENT	HE R DMAN	LA R GEST	NA R CEIN	PA R SNIP	PE R VE R T
GA R NISH	HE R EDES	LA R GISH	NA R CISM	PA R TAKE	PH R ASAL
GA R OTTE	HE R ETIC	LA R KIE R	NA R CIST	PA R TIAL	*PH R AT R Y
GA R PIKE	HE R ITO R	LA R KISH	NA R COSE	PA R TIED	PH R ENIC
GA R RING	HE R OINE	LO R DING	NA R GILE	PA R TIE R	*PH R ENSY
GA R ROTE	HE R OISM	LO R DOMA	NA R RATE	PA R TIES	PI R AGUA
GE R BERA	*HE R OIZE	LO R GNON	*NA R THEX	PA R TING	PI R ANHA
GE R ENUK	HE R ON R Y	LO R IME R	NE R ITIC	PA R TITA	PI R ATIC
GE R MANE	HE R RING	LO R INE R	NE R VATE	PA R TITE	PI R OGUE
GE R MIE R	HE R SELF	LU R CHE R	NE R VIE R	PA R TLET	*PI R OQUE
GE R MINA	HI R ABLE	LY R ATED	NE R VILY	PA R TNE R	PO R CINE
GI R AFFE	HI R CINE	LY R ICAL	NE R VINE	PA R TOOK	PO R CINO
GI R ASOL	HI R SUTE	MA R ABOU	NE R VING	*PA R TWAY	PO R KIE R
GI R DLE R	HI R UDIN	MA R ANTA	NE R VOUS	PA R TYE R	PO R KIES
GI R LISH	HO R DEIN	MA R BLE R	NE R VULE	PA R VENU	*PO R KPIE
GI R OSOL	*HO R IZON	MA R CATO	NE R VU RE	PA R VISE	PO R RECT
*GO R COCK	HO R NIE R	MA R CHE R	NI R VANA	PE R ACID	PO R TAGE
GO R GING	HO R NILY	MA R ENGO	NO R LAND	PE R CALE	PO R TEND
GO R IEST	HO R NIST	MA R INE R	NO R THE R	PE R CENT	PO R TENT
GO R ILLA	HO R NITO	MA R ITAL	NU R SE R Y	PE R CEPT	PO R TICO
GO R MAND	HO R RENT	*MA R KHO R	NU R SING	PE R CHE R	PO R TION
GU R GLET	*HO R RIFY	MA R LIE R	NU R TURE	PE R COID	PO R T RAY
GU R NARD	HO R SIE R	MA R LINE	PA R ABLE	PE R CUSS	PU R GING
GY R ATO R	HO R SILY	MA R LITE	PA R ADE R	PE R FECT	PU R ITAN
HA R BOU R	HO R SING	*MA R QUEE	PA R ADO R	*PE R FIDY	PU R LIEU
HA R DHAT	HU R DIES	?MA R QUIS	*PA R ADOX	PE R FO R M	PU R LINE
HA R DIE R	HU R DLE R	MA R RANO	PA R AGON	PE R FUME	PU R LOIN
HA R DIES	HU R LING	MA R RIE R	PA R APET	PE R FUSE	PU R PO R T
HA R DILY	HU R RIE R	MA R RIES	PA R ASOL	PE R GOLA	PU R POSE
HA R DPAN	HU R TFUL	*MA R ROWY	PA R BOIL	PE R HAPS	PU R PU R A
HA R DSET	*JA R GOON	MA R SALA	PA R CEU R	PE R IAPT	PU R PU R E
HA R DTOP	*JA R HEAD	MA R SHAL	PA R DINE	PE R IDOT	PU R RANA

PU R RING	SE R FAGE	ST R ETTA	TE R EBIC	TU R ISTA	WA R BLE R
PU R SIE R	SE R FDOM	ST R ETTO	TE R EFAH	TU R KOIS	WA R FA R E
PU R SILY	SE R FISH	ST R EWE R	TE R GITE	TU R MOIL	WA R HEAD
PU R SING	SE R GING	ST R IATE	TE R MITE	TU R NE R Y	WA R IEST
PU R SUE R	SE R IATE	ST R IDE R	TE R NA R Y	TU R NING	WA R ISON
PU R SUIT	SE R ICIN	ST R IDO R	TE R NATE	TU R NKEY	WA R LESS
*PU R VIEW	SE R IEMA	ST R IGIL	TE R NION	TU R NOFF	WA R LIKE
PY R ALID	SE R INGA	ST R IKE R	TE R PENE	TU R NOUT	*WA R LOCK
*PY R AMID	SE R IOUS	ST R INGY	TE R R ACE	TU R PETH	WA R LO R D
PY R ETIC	SE R PENT	ST R IPE R	TE R R AIN	TU R TLE R	*WA R MISH
*PY R EXIA	SE R PIGO	ST R IVE R	TE R R ANE	TY R ANNY	WA R NING
PY R OGEN	SE R R ANO	ST R OBIC	TE R R EEN	VA R IANT	WA R PAGE
PY R OSIS	SE R VANT	ST R OBIL	TE R R ENE	VA R IATE	*WA R PATH
*PY R R HIC	SE R VICE	ST R OKE R	TE R R IE R	VA R ICES	WA R R ANT
PY R R ITE	SE R VILE	ST R OPHE	TE R R IES	VA R IETY	WA R R ING
PY R R OLE	SE R VING	ST R OPPY	TE R R IFY	VA R IOLA	WA R R IO R
R A R E R IT	*SH R IEKY	ST R OYE R	TE R R INE	VA R IOLE	*WA R SHIP
R E R AISE	*SH R IMPY	ST R UDEL	TE R TIAL	VA R IOUS	WA R SLE R
R E R EDOS	SH R IVEL	SU R BASE	TE R TIAN	VA R MENT	WA R STLE
R E R OUTE	SH R IVE R	SU R COAT	TH R EADY	VA R MINT	WA R THOG
*R O R QUAL	SH R LINK	SU R FACE	*TH R IFTY	VA R NISH	WA R TIE R
R U R ALLY	*SH R UBBY	SU R FEIT	TH R IVE R	VA R SITY	WA R TIME
SA R CASM	SI R COIN	SU R FIE R	TH R OATY	VE R ANDA	*WA R WO R K
SA R COID	SI R OCCO	SU R GEON	TH R OUGH	VE R BENA	WA R WO R N
SA R COMA	*SK R EEGH	SU R GE R Y	TH R OWE R	*VE R BIFY	WE R GELD
SA R COUS	*SK R EIGH	SU R GING	TH R R EAT	VE R BILE	WE R GELT
SA R DANA	SO R BATE	SU R MISE	*TH R UMMY	VE R DANT	WE R GILD
SA R DINE	SO R BENT	SU R NAME	TH R UPUT	VE R DICT	*WE R WOLF
SA R DIUS	SO R BOSE	SU R PASS	*TH R UWAY	VE R DU R E	WI R EMAN
SA R MENT	SO R CE R Y	SU R PING	TO R CHON	VE R GING	WI R ETAP
SC R AGGY	SO R DINE	SU R PLUS	TO R MENT	VE R GLAS	*WI R EWAY
SC R AIGH	SO R DINO	SU R R EAL	TO R NADO	VE R IDIC	WI R IEST
SC R APE R	SO R GHUM	SU R TOUT	TO R PEDO	VE R IEST	WI R R IE R
SC R APIE	SO R ITES	SU R VEIL	*TO R QUE R	VE R ISMO	WI R R ILY
*SC R APPY	SO R OCHE	SU R VIVE	*TO R QUES	VE R ITAS	WI R R ING
SC R ATCH	SO R OSIS	SY R INGA	TO R R EFY	VE R MEIL	WO R DAGE
*SC R AWLY	SO R OR AL	SY R INGE	TO R R ENT	VE R MIAN	WO R DIE R
*SC R AWNY	SO R R IER	*SY R PHID	TO R R IFY	*VE R MUTH	WO R DILY
*SC R EAKY	SO R R ILY	TA R BUSH	TO R SADE	VE R NIE R	WO R DING
SC R EECH	*SP R AWLY	TA R DIE R	TO R SION	VE R R IE R	*WO R KBAG
SC R EWE R	SP R AYE R	TA R DIES	TO R TILE	VE R SANT	*WO R KBOX
SC R EWUP	SP R IEST	TA R DYON	TO R TONI	*VE R SIFY	*WO R KDAY
SC R IBAL	SP R IGGY	TA R NISH	TO R T R IX	VE R SINE	*WO R KING
SC R IBE R	SP R IGHT	TA R R IED	TO R TU R E	VE R SING	*WO R KMAN
SC R IEVE	SP R INGE	TA R R IE R	TU R ACOU	VE R SION	WO R KOUT
*SC R IMPY	SP R INGY	TA R R IES	TU R BA R Y	VE R TIGO	WO R LDLY
SC R OGGY	ST R AFE R	TA R R ING	TU R BETH	VE R VAIN	WO R MIE R
SC R OOCH	ST R ANGE	TA R SIE R	TU R BINE	VI R ELAI	*WO R MISH
SC R OOGE	ST R ATAL	TA R TANA	TU R BITH	VI R ELAY	WO R R IED
SC R OTUM	ST R ATUM	TA R TISH	TU R DINE	VI R EMIA	WO R R IE R
SC R OUGE	ST R ATUS	TA R TLET	TU R FIE R	VI R GATE	*WO R SHIP
*SC R UBBY	ST R AYE R	TA R TUFE	TU R FMAN	VI R GULE	WO R STED
*SC R UFFY	ST R EAKY	TA R WEED	TU R FSKI	VI R OSIS	*XE R A R CH
SC R UNCH	ST R EAMY	TE R AOHM	TU R GENT	VI R TUAL	XE R OSIS
SC R UPLE	ST R ETCH	TE R BIUM	TU R GITE	VO R LAGE	YA R DAGE

YA R DA R M	*CHA R ISMA	*DEF R AYE R	GA R R OTE R	LAB R USCA	MO R IBUND
YA R DMAN	*CHA R LADY	DEG R ADE R	GA R R OTTE	LAC R IMAL	MO R ONISM
*ZA R SEBA	*CHA R LOCK	DEG R EASE	GEA R CASE	LAC R OSSE	MO R ONITY
*ZO R ILLA	*CHA R MING	DEP R AVE R	GEA R LESS	LA R R IGAN	MO R OSITY
*ZO R ILLE	CHA R R IE R	DEP R IVAL	GLO R IOLE	LA R R IKIN	MO R TALLY
*ZO R ILLO	CHA R R ING	DEP R IVE R	GLO R IOUS	LA R R UPE R	MO R TGAGE
BA R RABLE	CHA R TEST	DE R R IE R E	GNA R R ING	LAU R EATE	MO R TISER
BA R RANCA	CHA R TIST	DET R ITUS	GOU R MAND	LEA R IEST	MO R TMAIN
BA R RANCO	CHO R AGUS	DIA R R HEA	GUA R ANTY	LEA R NING	MO R TUARY
BA R RATE R	*CHO R ALLY	DIC R OTAL	GUA R DANT	LEP R OTIC	MU R AENID
BA R RATO R	CHO R DATE	DIC R OTIC	GUA R DIAN	LIB R ETTO	MU R ALIST
BA R RATRY	CHO R EGUS	DIE R ESIS	GUE R IDON	LIG R OINE	MU R DEREE
BA R RETO R	*CHO R EMAN	DIS R OBE R	GUE R ILLA	LOW R IDE R	MU R DERER
BA R RETRY	CHO R EOID	DIU R ESIS	GUE R NSEY	LUB R ICAL	MU R IATED
BA R RETTE	CHO R IOID	DIU R ETIC	HAI R BALL	MA R ASMUS	MU R ICATE
BA R ROWER	*CHO R IAMB	*DOO R KNOB	HAI R BAND	MA R ATHON	MU R MURER
BEA R LIKE	CHO R TLE R	DOO R POST	HAI R IEST	MA R AUDE R	MU R R ELET
BEA R SKIN	*CHU R CHLY	DOO R BELL	HAI R LESS	MA R AVEDE	NA R RATE R
*BED R ENCH	CHU R NING	*DOO R JAMB	*HAI R LIKE	MA R BLING	NA R RATO R
BED R IVEL	CI R R IPED	DOO R LESS	HAI R LINE	MA R GARIN	NEA R NESS
BEF R IEND	CIT R EOUS	DOO R NAIL	*HAI R LOCK	MA R GARIO	NEA R SIDE
BEF R INGE	CLA R ENCE	DOO R SILL	*HAIRWORK	MA R GINAL	*NEC R OPSY
BEG R UDGE	CLA R INET	DOO R STEP	*HAIRWORM	MA R GRAVE	NEC R OSIS
BE R RETTA	CLE R ICAL	DOO R STOP	HAR R OWER	MA R IGOLD	*NEU RAXON
BET R AYAL	*CLE R KDOM	DOO R YA R D	*HAR RUMPH	MA R INADE	NEU R ITIC
BET R AYE R	*CLE R KISH	DOU R NESS	*HEB R AIZE	MA R INARA	NEU R ITIS
*BEW R AYE R	*CLE R IHEW	*DWA R FISH	HEI R LESS	MA R INATE	NEU R OSIS
BI R RETTA	COC R EATE	*DWA R FISM	HEI R LOOM	MA R IPOSA	NEU R OTIC
BOA R DING	COD R IVE R	FAI R LEAD	*HEI R SHIP	MA R ITIME	NIG R OSIN
BOA R DMAN	COE R CION	FAI R NESS	HID R OSIS	MA R KETER	NIT R ATO R
*BOA R FISH	*COE R CIVE	*FAI R YISM	HID R OTIC	MA R LIEST	NIT R OGEN
BO R ROWER	COP R EMIA	FA R R IE R Y	HOA R DING	MA R MOSET	NIT R OLIC
BOT R YOID	CO R R IDO R	FEA R LESS	HO R R IBLE	MA R R IAGE	NIT R OSYL
BOT R YOSE	CO R R IVAL	FEA R SOME	*HO R R IBLY	ME R CAPTO	NON R ATED
BOU R GEON	COU R ANTE	FE R R EOUS	*HO R R IFIC	ME R ENGUE	NON R IGID
BOU R T R EE	COU R ANTO	FE R R ETER	*HUA R ACHE	ME R GENCE	NON R IVAL
BU R R IEST	COU R SING	FE R R IAGE	*HUA R ACHO	ME R IDIAN	NON R OYAL
BU R ROWER	COU R TESY	FE R R ITIN	*HYD R ACID	ME R INGUE	NON R U R AL
CAB R ESTA	COU R TIE R	*FER R YMAN	*HYD RAGOG	ME R ISTEM	NUT R IENT
CAB R ESTO	CUP R EOUS	FIB R ANNE	*HYD R ANTH	ME R ISTIC	PA R R IDGE
CAB R ETTA	*CU R R ENCY	FIB R ILLA	*HYD R ATO R	MIC R OBAR	*PA R R ITCH
CAB R ILLA	CU R R ICLE	FIB R OSIS	*HYD R OGEL	MIC R ODOT	PA R R OKET
CAB R IOLE	CU R R IE R Y	FLO R ALLY	*HYD R OMEL	*MIC R OLUX	PA R R OTE R
*CAP R ICCI	CU R R YING	FO R R ADER	*HYD R ONIC	*MIC R OMHO	PEA R LASH
*CAP R IFIG	*CYP R INID	*FOU R CHEE	*HYD R OPIC	*MIC R URGY	PEA R LITE
CAP R IOLE	*CZA R EVNA	*FOU R FOLD	*HYD R OPSY	MIG R ATOR	PEA R MAIN
CA R R IAGE	*CZA R ITZA	*FOU R PLEX	*HYD R OSKI	MIS R EFER	PEE R LESS
CA R R IOLE	DEA R NESS	FOU R SOME	*HYD R OSOL	MIS R OUTE	PET R OLIC
*CA R R ITCH	DEB R UISE	FOU R TEEN	*HYD R OXYL	*MOO R COCK	PET R ONEL
CA R R OTIN	DEC R EASE	*FOU R THLY	*JE R R ICAN	*MOORFOWL	PET R OSAL
CA R R YALL	DEC R EPIT	FU R R IE R Y	*JE R R YCAN	MO R ALISM	PHA R ISEE
CA R R YOUT	DEC R ETAL	FU R R IEST	*JOY R IDE R	MO R ALIST	*PHA R MACY
*CHA R ACID	DEE R SKIN	FU R R INE R	LAB R ADO R	MO R ALITY	PHO R ONID
*CHA R ACIN	DEE R WEED	FU R ROWER		MO R ATORY	PLU R ALLY
*CHA R COAL	DEE R YA R D	GA R R ISON		MO R BILLI	POO R NESS
CHA R IEST	*DEF R AYAL			MO R EOVER	POO R TITH

PO R R IDGE	SCA R R ING	SPI R ALLY	THE R IACA	CA R R	PU R R
P RE R ENAL	*SCH R IEVE	SPI R ELLA	THE R MION	CHA R	R EA R
P RE R INSE	SCI R OCCO	SPI R IEST	THE R MITE	COI R	R OA R
P RO R OGUE	SCI R R HUS	*SPO R OZOA	THE R OPOD	CU R R	R UE R
P R U R IENT	*SCO R CHE R	SPO R TFUL	THI R LAGE	*CZA R	SCA R
P R U R ITUS	SCO R EPAD	SPO R TIVE	THI R STE R	DEA R	SEA R
PSO R ALEA	SCO R NFUL	SPU R GALL	THI R TEEN	DEE R	SEE R
PSO R ALEN	SCO R PION	SPU R IOUS	*THO R OUGH	DOE R	SLU R
PTE R OPOD	SCU R R IED	SPU R R IE R	THU R IBLE	DOO R	SOA R
PTE R YGIA	SCU R R IES	SPU R R ING	THU R IFE R	DO R R	SOU R
*PYO R RHEA	SCU R R ILE	STA R DUST	*THY R EOID	DOU R	SPA R
*QUA R RIER	SEA R CHE R	STA R FISH	*THY R OXIN	DU R R	SPU R
*QUA R TERN	SEA R OBIN	*STA R GAZE	TIT R ABLE	DYE R	STA R
*QUA R TILE	SEC R ETIN	STA R KE R S	TIT R ATO R	FAI R	STI R
*QUE R CINE	SEC R ETLY	STA R LESS	TSA R EVNA	FEA R	SUE R
*QUI R KISH	SEC R ETO R	STA R LIKE	*TSA R ITZA	FIA R	TAH R
R EA R MICE	SE R R ANID	STA R LING	TU R R ICAL	FOU R	TEA R
R EA R MOST	SHE R BE R T	STA R NOSE	*TZA R EVNA	GAU R	THI R
R EA R OUSE	*SHE R LOCK	STA R R ING	*TZA R ITZA	GEA R	TIE R
R EA R R EST	SHE R TING	STA R SHIP	*VAG R ANCY	GNA R	TO R R
R EAR WARD	SHI R R ING	STA R TLE R	*VIB R ANCE	GOE R	TOU R
*R EB R ANCH	SHO R TAGE	STA R WO R T	*VIB R ANCY	GUA R	TSA R
R EC R EANT	SHO R TCUT	STE R ICAL	VIB R ATO R	HAA R	TYE R
R EC R EATE	SHO R TIES	STE R IGMA	VIB R ISSA	HAI R	**TZA R**
R ED R AWE R	SHO R TISH	STE R LING	*VIB R ONIC	HEA R	VAI R
*R EF R EEZE	*SIE R OZEM	STE R NITE	VIT R EOUS	HEI R	VEE R
R EG R OOVE	*SKI R IESH	STE R NSON	WA R R AGAL	HOA R	VIE R
*REG ROWTH	SKI R TING	STE R NWAY	WA R R ANTY	HOE R	WAI R
R EO R DAIN	SLU R R ING	STE R R ING	WA R R ENER	HOU R	WAU R
R EO R IENT	SMA R AGDE	STO R ABLE	WA R R IGAL	JEE R	WEA R
R EP R IEVE	SMA R TASS	STU R GEON	WEA R ABLE	KBA R	WEE R
R EP R ISAL	SOB R IETY	SU R R OUND	WEA R IEST	KEI R	WEI R
*R EP R OACH	SO R R IEST	SU R R OYAL	WEA R IFUL	KIE R	**WHI R**
R EP R OVAL	SO R ROWER	SWO R DMAN	WEI R DIES	KNA R	**WHO R**
R EP R OVE R	SOU R BALL	TA R R AGON	*WHA R FAGE	KNU R	YEA R
R ET R ENCH	SOU R DINE	TA R R ARIA	*WHE R EVER	KYA R	YI R R
R ET R IEVE	SOU R NESS	TEA R AWAY	*WHI R R ING	LAI R	YOU R
R ET R OACT	SOU R PUSS	TEA R DOWN	*WHO R EDOM	LEA R	**BAKE R**
R ET R OFIT	SOU R WOOD	TEA R D R OP	WHO R ESON	LEE R	**BALE R**
R ET R OR SE	SOV R ANLY	TEA R IEST	*YEA R BOOK	LEH R	**BA R E R**
R EW R ITER	SOV R ANTY	TEA R LESS	YEA R LIES	LIA R	**BASE R**
R OA R IEST	SPA R ABLE	TE R R APIN	YEA R LING	LIE R	***BAZA R**
*R OO R BACK	SPA R E R IB	TE R R ARIA	YEA R LONG	LOU R	**BEVO R**
R UN R OUND	*SPA R KILY	*TE R RAZZO	YEA R NING	MAA R	**BIDE R**
SAC R A R IA	*SPA R KISH	TE R R BILE	YOU R SELF	MAI R	**BIKE R**
SAC R ISTY	SPA R KLE R	TE R R ELLA		MOO R	**BITE R**
SAF R ANIN	SPA R LIKE	TE R R IFIC	BEA R	MU R R	**BLEA R**
SAP R OPEL	SPA R LING	TET R ACID	BEE R	NEA R	**BLUE R**
SAU R OPOD	SPA R R IE R	TET R AGON	BIE R	NOI R	**BOLA R**
*SCA R CELY	SPA R R ING	TET R AME R	BI R R	PAI R	**BONE R**
*SCA R CITY	SPA R SITY	TET R APOD	BLU R	PA R R	**BO R E R**
*SCA R FPIN	*SPE R MARY	TET R A R CH	BOA R	PEA R	**BOWE R**
SCA R IEST	SPE R MINE	THE R EFO R	BOO R	PEE R	**BOXE R**
SCA R IOSE	SPE R MOUS	THE R EMIN	B R R R	PIE R	**BOYA R**
SCA R IOUS	SPI R ACLE		BUH R	POO R	B R IA R
SCA R LESS			BU R R	POU R	B R IE R

BUYE R	D REA R	**HEWE R**	LUGE R	**POWE R**	SHEE R
CABE R	D RIE R	***HEXE R**	LUNA R	P RIE R	SHIE R
CAGE R	D RYE R	HIDE R	LU RE R	P RIO R	SHI R R
CANE R	DUPE R	**HIKE R**	MACE R	**P RYE R**	SHOE R
CAPE R	**FACE R**	HILA R	**MAJO R**	PULE R	**SHYE R**
CA RE R	FADE R	HI R E R	**MAKE R**	PU RE R	SIEU R
CATE R	**FAKE R**	**HOME R**	MALA R	**QUEE R**	SIKE R
CAVE R	**FAKI R**	HONE R	MANO R	R ACE R	SIMA R
CEDA R	***FAQI R**	HONO R	MASE R	R ADA R	SITA R
CEDE R	FA RE R	**HOPE R**	MATE R	R AKE R	SIVE R
CHAI R	**FAVO R**	**HOVE R**	**MAYO R**	R APE R	SIZA R
CHEE R	**FEMU R**	HUGE R	***MAZE R**	R ARE R	**SIZE R**
CHI R R	FETO R	HUMO R	METE R	R ASE R	SKIE R
CHOI R	FEUA R	**HYPE R**	MILE R	R ATE R	SKI R R
CHU R R	**FEVE R**	**JAGE R**	MIME R	R AVE R	SLIE R
CIDE R	**FIBE R**	**JAPE R**	MINE R	**R AZE R**	SMEA R
CIGA R	**FIFE R**	**JIBE R**	MINO R	**R AZO R**	SNEE R
CITE R	FILA R	***JIVE R**	MISE R	R EBA R	SOBE R
CLEA R	FILE R	***JOKE R**	MITE R	R ECU R	SOFA R
CLOU R	FINE R	**JU RO R**	**MIXE R**	R EFE R	SOLA R
CODE R	FI R E R	**KABA R**	MOLA R	R ICE R	SONA R
COLO R	**FIVE R**	**KAFI R**	MOPE R	R IDE R	SOPO R
COME R	***FIXE R**	**KEBA R**	MOTO R	R IGO R	SOWA R
COOE R	**FLAI R**	**KEFI R**	**MOVE R**	R IME R	SOWE R
COPE R	**FLEE R**	**KITE R**	**MOWE R**	R IPE R	SPEA R
CO RE R	FLIE R	KNAU R	MUCO R	R ISE R	SPEE R
COVE R	FLOU R	LABO R	MUSE R	R IVE R	SPEI R
COWE R	FLUO R	LACE R	MUTE R	R OGE R	SPIE R
C RIE R	**FLYE R**	LADE R	NADI R	R OPE R	SPOO R
C RUO R	**FOYE R**	LAGE R	NAME R	R OTO R	STAI R
CUBE R	F REE R	LAKE R	NAVA R	R OVE R	STEE R
CU RE R	F RIA R	LAME R	NEVE R	R OWE R	STOU R
CYDE R	F RIE R	LASE R	NITE R	R ULE R	SUBE R
CYMA R	**F RYE R**	LATE R	NOTE R	R UMO R	SUDO R
DAMA R	**FUME R**	LAVE R	NUDE R	SABE R	SUGA R
DA RE R	FU RO R	LAYE R	PACE R	SABI R	SUPE R
DATE R	GAGE R	**LAZA R**	PAGE R	SAFE R	SU RE R
DEAI R	GAME R	LEGE R	PALE R	SAGE R	SWEA R
DEBA R	GAPE R	LEMU R	PAPE R	SAKE R	SWEE R
DEFE R	GATO R	LEPE R	PA R E R	SANE R	TABE R
DEMU R	***GAZA R**	LEVE R	PATE R	SAPO R	TABO R
DETE R	***GAZE R**	LIBE R	**PAVE R**	SATY R	TAKE R
DEWA R	GIBE R	LIDA R	**PAWE R**	SAVE R	TALA R
DICE R	GIVE R	LIFE R	**PAYE R**	SAVO R	TALE R
DIKE R	GLAI R	LIGE R	**PAYO R**	SAWE R	TAME R
DIME R	GLUE R	LIKE R	PETE R	SAYE R	TAPE R
DINA R	**GNA R R**	LINE R	**PIKE R**	SCAU R	TAPI R
DINE R	GOFE R	LITE R	PILA R	SCOU R	TATA R
DI R E R	GONE R	LIVE R	PIPE R	SEDE R	TATE R
DONO R	GULA R	LOBA R	PLIE R	SENO R	TAWE R
DOPE R	HALE R	LONE R	**PLYE R**	SE R E R	**TAXE R**
DOSE R	HATE R	LOPE R	**POKE R**	SEVE R	TENO R
DOTE R	**HAYE R**	LOSE R	POLA R	SEWA R	THEI R
DOWE R	***HAZE R**	LOVE R	POLE R	SEWE R	TIGE R
*DOZE R	HEDE R	LOWE R	POSE R	SHEA R	TILE R

TIME R	BAITE R	**BOOKE R**	CANDO R	COLLA R	**DAMPE R**
TITE R	**BALKE R**	**BOOME R**	**CANKE R**	COLOU R	DANCE R
TOKE R	BALLE R	*BOOZE R	CANNE R	COLTE R	DANDE R
TONE R	BANDE R	**BOPPE R**	CANTE R	**COMBE R**	DANGE R
TOPE R	BANGE R	BO R DE R	CANTO R	**CONCU R**	**DAPPE R**
TOTE R	**BANKE R**	**BOSKE R**	**CAPPE R**	CONDO R	DA R NE R
TOWE R	BANNE R	**BOTHE R**	**CAPTO R**	**CONFE R**	DA R TE R
TOYE R	**BA R BE R**	**BOWLE R**	CA R DE R	CONGE R	**DASHE R**
T R IE R	**BA R KE R**	**BOWYE R**	CA REE R	**CONKE R**	DAUBE R
T R UE R	BA R TE R	*BOXCA R	CA R PE R	CONNE R	DEBTO R
TUBE R	**BASHE R**	*BOXIE R	CA R TE R	**COOKE R**	**DECKE R**
TUMO R	BASTE R	**B RACE R**	**CA R VE R**	COOLE R	**DEFIE R**
TUNE R	**BATHE R**	**B RAVE R**	CASTE R	**COOPE R**	DEICE R
TUTO R	BATTE R	**B RAYE R**	CASTO R	COOTE R	**DELVE R**
TUYE R	**BAWLE R**	*B RAZE R	CAUSE R	**COPIE R**	DENIE R
TWIE R	*BAZAA R	**B REWE R**	CAVIA R	**COPPE R**	DETOU R
TWYE R	**BEAKE R**	**B RIBE R**	CEILE R	**COPTE R**	**DEVOI R**
VALO R	BEA R E R	B RINE R	CELLA R	CO R DE R	**DEWIE R**
VAPO R	BEATE R	**B ROKE R**	CENSE R	**CO R KE R**	**DEXTE R**
VELA R	**BEAVE R**	**BUCKE R**	CENSO R	CO R NE R	DIALE R
*VEXE R	**BEDDE R**	**BUDDE R**	CENTE R	**COSHE R**	DIAPE R
VICA R	**BEEPE R**	**BUDGE R**	**CHADA R**	COSIE R	DIAPI R
VIGO R	*BEEZE R	**BUFFE R**	**CHADO R**	COSTA R	**DIBBE R**
VIPE R	**BEGGA R**	**BUGGE R**	**CHAFE R**	COSTE R	DICIE R
VISO R	BELIE R	BUGLE R	**CHASE R**	COTTA R	**DICKE R**
*VIZI R	BELTE R	BULGE R	**CHAWE R**	COTTE R	DIETE R
*VIZO R	BENDE R	BULGU R	**CHEDE R**	COUGA R	**DIFFE R**
VOLA R	BESTI R	**BUMME R**	**CHEWE R**	COUTE R	DIGGE R
VOME R	BETTE R	**BUMPE R**	**CHIDE R**	**COWIE R**	**DIMME R**
VOTE R	BETTO R	**BUNKE R**	**CHIMA R**	*COZIE R	DINGE R
VOWE R	*BEZOA R	BUNTE R	**CHIME R**	C R ATE R	DINNE R
WADE R	**BIBBE R**	BU R GE R	*CHOKE R	**C R AVE R**	**DIPPE R**
WAFE R	**BICKE R**	BU R IE R	CHOLE R	**C R OWE R**	DISBA R
WAGE R	**BIDDE R**	**BU R KE R**	*CHUKA R	CULLE R	**DITHE R**
WAKE R	**BIGGE R**	BU R LE R	CINDE R	**CULVE R**	**DOBBE R**
WALE R	**BILKE R**	BU R NE R	**CIPHE R**	**CUMBE R**	**DOCKE R**
WATE R	BILLE R	BU R R E R	**CITHE R**	**CUMME R**	DOCTO R
WAVE R	BINDE R	BU R SA R	**CLAMO R**	CUNNE R	DODDE R
*WAXE R	BINGE R	**BUSHE R**	**CLAVE R**	**CUPPE R**	DODGE R
WEBE R	BI R DE R	BUSIE R	**CLAWE R**	**CU R BE R**	**DOFFE R**
WHI R R	BI R LE R	**BUSKE R**	**CLEVE R**	CU R LE R	DOGEA R
WIDE R	BISTE R	BUSTE R	CLONE R	CU R SE R	DOGGE R
WIPE R	BITTE R	BUTLE R	CLOSE R	CU R SO R	DOLLA R
WI R E R	**BLAME R**	BUTTE R	**CLOVE R**	CUSSE R	DOLOU R
WISE R	*BLAZE R	*BUZZE R	COALE R	CUTLE R	*DOOZE R
WIVE R	**BLOWE R**	**CADGE R**	COATE R	CUTTE R	DOPIE R
WOOE R	BOATE R	CAESA R	*COAXE R	**CYCLE R**	DO R ME R
W R IE R	**BOBBE R**	CAGIE R	**COBBE R**	*CYPHE R	DO R PE R
YAGE R	BOILE R	**CAHIE R**	**COCKE R**	**DABBE R**	DO R SE R
ZONE R	BOLTE R	**CALCA R**	**CODDE R**	**DACKE R**	DOSSE R
BACKE R	**BOMBE R**	**CALKE R**	**CODGE R**	**DAGGE R**	DOTIE R
BADGE R	BONDE R	CALLE R	**COFFE R**	**DAIKE R**	DOTTE R
BAGGE R	BONIE R	**CAMBE R**	**COHEI R**	**DAMMA R**	DOUSE R
BAILE R	*BONZE R	**CAMPE R**	COILE R	**DAMME R**	**DOWNE R**
BAILO R	BOOGE R	**CANCE R**	COINE R	DAMNE R	**DOWSE R**

*DOZIE R	FOAME R	GILDE R	HEALE R	*JAZZE R	LAPPE R
D RAPE R	FODDE R	GILLE R	HEA R E R	JEE R E R	LAPSE R
D RAWE R	FOETE R	GINGE R	HEAVE R	*JE R KE R	LA R DE R
D RIVE R	FOGGE R	GINNE R	HECTO R	JESTE R	LA R KE R
D R ONE R	FOLDE R	GIPPE R	HEDGE R	*JIBBE R	LASCA R
D R OVE R	FOLIA R	GI R DE R	HEEDE R	*JIGGE R	LASHE R
DUBBE R	FOOTE R	GLAMO R	HEELE R	JILTE R	LASTE R
DUCKE R	FO R CE R	*GLAZE R	HEFTE R	*JINKE R	LATHE R
DUELE R	FO R GE R	GLIDE R	HEIFE R	JITTE R	LATTE R
DUFFE R	FO R KE R	GLOVE R	HELLE R	*JOBBE R	LAUDE R
DUIKE R	FO R ME R	GLOWE R	HELPE R	*JOGGE R	LAVEE R
DUMPE R	FOSTE R	GNAWE R	HEMME R	JOINE R	LAWYE R
DUNNE R	FOWLE R	GOBBE R	HE R DE R	*JOKIE R	*LAZIE R
DU R BA R	*FOXIE R	GOFFE R	HILLE R	JOLTE R	LEADE R
DUSTE R	F RAME R	GOITE R	HINDE R	*JOSHE R	LEAKE R
DYVOU R	F RATE R	GOLFE R	HINGE R	*JUDDE R	LEANE R
FABLE R	F R ILE R	GOOIE R	HIPPE R	*JUDGE R	LEAPE R
FACTO R	*F R IZE R	GOPHE R	HISSE R	*JUICE R	LEASE R
FAKEE R	FUELE R	GO R GE R	HITHE R	*JUMPE R	LEAVE R
FALLE R	FUH R E R	GO R IE R	*HOAXE R	JUNIO R	LECHE R
FALTE R	FULLE R	GOUGE R	HOMIE R	*JUNKE R	LECTO R
FANNE R	FULMA R	HOGGE R	HONKE R	JUSTE R	LEDGE R
*FAQUI R	FUMIE R	G RATE R	HOLDE R	*KAFFI R	LEKVA R
FA R CE R	FUNKE R	*G RAZE R	HOLIE R	KAISE R	LENDE R
FA R ME R	FUNNE R	G R IME R	HOMIE R	KANTA R	LESSE R
FATHE R	FU R FU R	G ROCE R	HONKE R	KASHE R	LETTE R
FATTE R	FU R LE R	G ROPE R	HONOU R	KEENE R	LEVIE R
FAVOU R	FUSSE R	G ROWE R	HOOFE R	KEEPE R	LIBBE R
FAWNE R	GABBE R	GUIDE R	HOOPE R	KEGLE R	LICKE R
FEA R E R	GADDE R	GUITA R	HOO R O R	KELTE R	LICTO R
FEEDE R	GAFFE R	GULPE R	HOOTE R	*KICKE R	LIFTE R
FEELE R	GAGGE R	GUMME R	HO R R O R	KIDDE R	LIMBE R
FELLE R	GAINE R	GUNNE R	HOSIE R	KILLE R	LIMIE R
FENCE R	GAITE R	GUSHE R	HOTTE R	KILTE R	LIMME R
FENDE R	GAMBI R	GUTTE R	HOUSE R	KIPPE R	LIMNE R
FE R VO R	GAMME R	GYPPE R	HOWLE R	KISSE R	LIMPE R
FESTE R	GANDE R	*HACKE R	HUGGE R	KNIFE R	LINEA R
FETTE R	GANGE R	HAFTE R	HULLE R	KNOWE R	LINGE R
FIBBE R	GAOLE R	HAILE R	HUMME R	KOSHE R	LINIE R
FILLE R	GA R NE R	HALTE R	HUMOU R	K RATE R	LINKE R
FILME R	GA R TE R	HAMME R	HUNGE R	K R ONO R	LINTE R
FILTE R	GASPE R	HAMPE R	HUNKE R	K R ONU R	LIPPE R
FINDE R	GASSE R	HANGA R	HUNTE R	KULTU R	*LIQUO R
FINGE R	GASTE R	HANGE R	HU R LE R	LAAGE R	LISPE R
FI R ME R	GATHE R	HANKE R	HU R TE R	LABOU R	LISTE R
FISHE R	GAUGE R	HA R BO R	HUSKE R	LACIE R	LITTE R
FITTE R	GAWKE R	HA R KE R	HUSSA R	LACKE R	LIVIE R
*FIZZE R	GAWPE R	HA R ME R	*JABBE R	LADDE R	LIVYE R
FLAKE R	*GEEZE R	HA R PE R	*JACKE R	LADLE R	LOADE R
FLAME R	GELDE R	HATTE R	JAEGE R	LAGGE R	LOAFE R
FLAVO R	GENDE R	HAULE R	*JAGGE R	LAMBE R	LOANE R
FLAYE R	GETTE R	HAVIO R	JAGUA R	LANCE R	LOBBE R
*FLEXO R	GEYSE R	*HAWKE R	JAILE R	LANDE R	LOCKE R
FLOWE R	GIAOU R	HAWSE R	JAILO R	LANGU R	LODGE R
FLUTE R	GIBBE R	HEADE R	*JAMME R	LANNE R	LOGGE R

LOGIE R	MIDAI R	**NICKE R**	**PILFE R**	PULSE R	R EPOU R
LOITE R	**MILKE R**	**NIFFE R**	PINDE R	**PUMPE R**	R ESTE R
LOLLE R	MILLE R	**NIPPE R**	PINGE R	PUNIE R	R ETEA R
LONGE R	MILTE R	NOBLE R	PINIE R	**PUNKE R**	R HETO R
LOOKE R	**MIMBA R**	NODDE R	**PINKE R**	PUNNE R	**R HYME R**
LOOPE R	**MINCE R**	NONPA R	PINNE R	PUNTE R	**R IBBE R**
LOOSE R	MINDE R	NONWA R	**PIPIE R**	PU R GE R	R IBIE R
LOOTE R	MINTE R	NOOSE R	PITIE R	PU R SE R	R IDDE R
LOPPE R	MIOLE R	NOSHE R	**PLACE R**	**PUSHE R**	R IEVE R
LOPTE R	MI R IE R	NOSIE R	PLANA R	PUTTE R	R IFLE R
LOUVE R	MI R RO R	NOTHE R	PLANE R	*QINDA R	R IGGE R
LUBBE R	MISTE R	NUDGE R	PLATE R	*QINTA R	R IGOU R
LUGGE R	**MITHE R**	**NUMBE R**	**PLAYE R**	*QUAKE R	R IMIE R
LUMBA R	MITIE R	NU R SE R	*PLEXO R	*QUASA R	**R IMME R**
LUMBE R	MOANE R	NUTTE R	**PLOVE R**	*QUAVE R	R INGE R
LUMPE R	**MOBBE R**	**PACKE R**	**PLOWE R**	*QUEUE R	R INSE R
LUNGE R	**MOCKE R**	**PADDE R**	POISE R	*QUIVE R	R IOTE R
LUNIE R	**MOHAI R**	PALIE R	**POKIE R**	*QUOTE R	**R IPPE R**
LUNKE R	MOLDE R	PALLO R	POLDE R	R ACIE R	**R ISKE R**
LU R KE R	MOLTE R	**PALMA R**	POLLE R	**R ACKE R**	R ITTE R
LUSTE R	**MOMSE R**	**PALME R**	PONDE R	R AFTE R	R OAME R
MAFTI R	*MOMZE R	PALTE R	**POPLA R**	R AIDE R	R OARE R
*MAHZO R	MONGE R	**PAMPE R**	**POPPE R**	R AILE R	**R OBBE R**
MAILE R	MOOTE R	PANDE R	PO R KE R	R AISE R	**R OCKE R**
MAIME R	**MOPIE R**	PANIE R	PO R TE R	**R AMME R**	R OLFE R
MAMME R	**MOPPE R**	*PANZE R	POSEU R	R ANCO R	R OLLE R
MANGE R	MO R TA R	**PA R KE R**	POSTE R	R ANGE R	**R OMPE R**
MANNE R	MOSSE R	PA R LO R	POTHE R	**R ANKE R**	R OOFE R
MAPPE R	**MOTHE R**	PA R SE R	POTTE R	R ANTE R	R OOME R
MA R KE R	MOUSE R	PASSE R	*POTZE R	R APIE R	R OOSE R
MA R RE R	**MUCKE R**	PASTE R	POU R E R	**R APPE R**	R OOTE R
MA R TY R	**MUDDE R**	PASTO R	POUTE R	R APTO R	R OPIE R
MASHE R	**MUGGA R**	PATTE R	**POWDE R**	R ASHE R	R OSIE R
MASKE R	**MUGGE R**	*PATZE R	**POWTE R**	R ASPE R	R OSTE R
MASTE R	**MUGGU R**	**PAUPE R**	P R ATE R	R ASTE R	R OTTE R
MATTE R	MULLE R	PAUSE R	**P R AYE R**	R ATHE R	R OUSE R
MAUGE R	**MUMME R**	**PAVIO R**	P R EFE R	R ATTE R	R OUTE R
MAULE R	**MUMPE R**	**PAWNE R**	P R ETO R	R EADE R	**R UBBE R**
*MAZIE R	MU R DE R	**PAWNO R**	P R EWA R	R EAME R	R UBIE R
MEAGE R	**MU R MU R**	**PECKE R**	P R EYE R	R EAPE R	R UDDE R
MEANE R	**MUSHE R**	PEDLA R	P R ICE R	R EARE R	R UGGE R
MEDLA R	MUSTE R	PEDLE R	P R IME R	R EAVE R	R UINE R
MEETE R	MUTTE R	PEELE R	*P R IZE R	R ECTO R	**R UMME R**
MELDE R	NAGGE R	**PEEPE R**	P R OBE R	R EDDE R	R UMOU R
MELTE R	NAILE R	PELLA R	P R OPE R	R EDEA R	R UNNE R
MEMBE R	**NAPPE R**	PELTE R	P R OSE R	R EEFE R	R USHE R
MEMOI R	NATTE R	**PENCE R**	P R OVE R	**R EEKE R**	**SACKE R**
MENDE R	**NECKE R**	PENNE R	P R OWA R	R EELE R	SAGGA R
MENHI R	NECTA R	**PEPPE R**	P R UNE R	R EGEA R	SAGGE R
MENTO R	NEEDE R	PESTE R	**PSYWA R**	R EHEA R	SAGIE R
ME R CE R	NESTE R	PETTE R	**PUCKE R**	R EIVE R	SAILE R
ME R GE R	NESTO R	**PEWTE R**	**PUFFE R**	R ELIE R	SAILO R
METEO R	NETHE R	**PHYLA R**	PULLE R	R ENDE R	SALTE R
METIE R	NETTE R	**PICKE R**	**PULPE R**	R ENTE R	SALVE R
MEWLE R	NEUTE R	**PIECE R**	PULSA R	R EPAI R	SALVO R

SAMBA R	**SHMEA R**	**SOWCA R**	TEASE R	T R OVE R	**WANDE R**		
SAMBU R	**SHOFA R**	**SPACE R**	TEDDE R	**TUBBE R**	WANIE R		
SANDE R	**SHOVE R**	**SPADE R**	TEEME R	**TUCKE R**	WANNE R		
SANGA R	**SHOWE R**	SPA R E R	TEENE R	TUFTE R	WANTE R		
SANGE R	SIDDU R	**SPEWE R**	TEETE R	TUGGE R	**WA R DE R**		
SANSA R	SIDLE R	**SPICE R**	TELFE R	TUMOU R	WA R IE R		
SANTI R	SIFTE R	SPIDE R	TELLE R	TU R GO R	**WA R ME R**		
SANTU R	**SIGHE R**	**SPIKE R**	**TEMPE R**	TU R NE R	WA R NE R		
SAPOU R	SIGNE R	SPINO R	TENDE R	**TUSKE R**	**WA R PE R**		
SAPPE R	SIGNO R	SP R IE R	TENNE R	TUSSA R	**WASHE R**		
SA R DA R	SILLE R	STAGE R	TENOU R	TUSSE R	WASTE R		
SA R SA R	SILVE R	STA R E R	TENSO R	TUSSO R	WATTE R		
SA R TO R	**SIMME R**	STATE R	TENTE R	TUSSU R	**WAVIE R**		
SAUCE R	**SIMPE R**	STATO R	TE R ME R	TWINE R	***WAXIE R**		
SAUGE R	SINGE R	STAYE R	TE R MO R	**TWOFE R**	WEANE R		
SAVIO R	**SINKE R**	STIVE R	TE R RO R	**TYPIE R**	WEA R E R		
SAVOU R	SINNE R	**STOKE R**	TESTE R	***VALKY R**	**WEAVE R**		
SAWYE R	SINTE R	STONE R	TETHE R	VALOU R	**WEDDE R**		
SCALA R	**SIPPE R**	STOPE R	TETTE R	VALUE R	**WEEDE R**		
SCALE R	SI R DA R	STOVE R	THALE R	**VALVA R**	**WEEPE R**		
SCA R E R	SISTE R	STUPO R	**THAWE R**	**VAMPE R**	**WEEVE R**		
SCO R E R	SITTE R	STYLA R	THENA R	VANNE R	WEINE R		
SCOTE R	***SIZIE R**	STYLE R	**TICKE R**	**VAPOU R**	**WELDE R**		
SEALE R	**SKATE R**	**SUBPA R**	TIDIE R	VA R IE R	**WELDO R**		
SEAME R	**SKEWE R**	**SUCCO R**	TILLE R	VEALE R	WELTE R		
SEA R E R	**SKIVE R**	**SUCKE R**	TILTE R	**VECTO R**	WESTE R		
SEATE R	**SLAKE R**	SUDSE R	**TIMBE R**	VEILE R	**WETHE R**		
SECPA R	SLATE R	**SUFFE R**	TINDE R	VEINE R	WETTE R		
SECTO R	SLAVE R	SUITE R	TINIE R	VELOU R	**WHALE R**		
SEEDE R	SLAYE R	SUITO R	**TINKE R**	**VENDE R**	**WHINE R**		
SEEKE R	SLICE R	SULFU R	TINNE R	**VENDO R**	**WHITE R**		
SEEME R	SLIDE R	**SULKE R**	TINTE R	VENEE R	***WICKE R**		
SEGGA R	SLIVE R	**SUMME R**	**TIPPE R**	VENTE R	**WIDDE R**		
SEINE R	SLOPE R	**SUPPE R**	TITFE R	**VE R GE R**	WIENE R		
SEISE R	SMILE R	SU R FE R	TITHE R	VE R IE R	**WILDE R**		
SEISO R	SMITE R	SU R GE R	TITTE R	VE R SE R	WILIE R		
*SEIZE R	SMOKE R	SUTLE R	**TOCHE R**	VESPE R	WILLE R		
*SEIZO R	SNA R E R	**SWAGE R**	TOILE R	VETOE R	**WINCE R**		
SELLE R	SNIPE R	**SWAYE R**	TOLLE R	VIATO R	**WINDE R**		
SENDE R	SNO R E R	**SYPHE R**	TONGE R	**VICTO R**	**WINGE R**		
SENHO R	**SOAKE R**	TABOU R	TONNE R	VIEWE R	WINIE R		
SENIO R	SOA R E R	**TACKE R**	TOOLE R	VIGOU R	**WINKE R**		
SENSO R	**SOBBE R**	TAGGE R	TOOTE R	VINIE R	WINNE R		
SE R VE R	**SOCCE R**	TAILE R	**TOPPE R**	***VIZIE R**	WINTE R		
SETTE R	SOEVE R	TAILO R	TO R PO R	**VOICE R**	WI R IE R		
SEXIE R	SOLDE R	**TALKE R**	TOSSE R	**VOIDE R**	WISHE R		
SHADE R	SOLVE R	**TAMBU R**	TOTHE R	**VOYEU R**	WITHE R		
SHAKE R	**SOMBE R**	**TAMPE R**	TOTTE R	**VULGA R**	WOLFE R		
SHAPE R	SONDE R	**TANKE R**	TOU R E R	**WADDE R**	**WOLVE R**		
SHA R E R	SOONE R	TANNE R	TOUTE R	**WAFTE R**	**WONDE R**		
SHAVE R	SO R DO R	**TAPPE R**	T R ACE R	**WAGGE R**	WONNE R		
SHEWE R	SO R NE R	TA R TA R	T R ADE R	WAILE R	**WOOFE R**		
SHIKA R	SO R TE R	TASTE R	T R EMO R	WAITE R	WOOLE R		
SHINE R	SOUCA R	TATTE R	T R IME R	**WAIVE R**	**WO R KE R**		
SHIVE R	SOUTE R	TEA R E R	T R OCA R	WALKE R	**WO R ME R**		

WO R SE R	BILAYE R	*B R AZIE R	CAULKE R	CLAVIE R	COU R TE R
WOWSE R	BIPOLA R	B R EAKE R	CAVILE R	CLEANE R	COVE R E R
W R ITE R	BITTIE R	B R EEDE R	CENTAU R	CLEA R E R	COVETE R
WUTHE R	BLABBE R	B R EVIE R	CENTNE R	CLEAVE R	*COZENE R
*XYSTE R	BLADDE R	B R IDLE R	*CHAFFE R	*CLICKE R	C R ABBE R
YABBE R	BLASTE R	B R IEFE R	*CHAMBE R	CLIMBE R	*C R ACKE R
*YAKKE R	BLATHE R	B R IMME R	*CHAMFE R	CLINGE R	C R ADLE R
YAMME R	BLATTE R	B R INGE R	*CHAMPE R	CLINKE R	C R AMME R
YAPPE R	BLEATE R	B R INIE R	CHANGE R	CLIPPE R	C R APPE R
YA R NE R	BLEEDE R	B R OIDE R	CHANTE R	CLOBBE R	C R ASHE R
YATTE R	BLENDE R	B R OILE R	CHANTO R	*CLOCKE R	C R AWLE R
YAUPE R	BLESSE R	*B R ONZE R	CHAPTE R	CLOGGE R	C R EAME R
YAWNE R	BLETHE R	B R OODE R	CHA R GE R	CLOUTE R	C R EASE R
YAWPE R	BLINDE R	B R OTHE R	CHA R IE R	CLOWDE R	C R EATO R
YELLE R	BLINKE R	B R OWSE R	CHA R ME R	CLUBBE R	C R EEPE R
YELPE R	BLISTE R	B R UISE R	CHA R TE R	CLUMBE R	C R IBBE R
YESTE R	BLITHE R	B R UITE R	CHATTE R	CLUNKE R	C R IMME R
YODLE R	BLOATE R	B R USHE R	*CHAUFE R	CLUSTE R	C R IMPE R
YONDE R	*BLOCKE R	BUBBLE R	CHEATE R	CLUTTE R	C R INGE R
YONKE R	BLOOME R	*BUCKLE R	*CHECKE R	CLYSTE R	C R ISPE R
YOWLE R	BLOOPE R	*BUFFIE R	CHEDDA R	COACHE R	C R ITTE R
*ZAFFA R	BLOTTE R	BUGBEA R	CHEE R E R	COACTO R	C R ITTU R
*ZAFFE R	BLOWIE R	BUILDE R	CHEQUE R	COALIE R	C R OAKE R
*ZAFFI R	BLUBBE R	BULLIE R	CHIGGE R	COASTE R	C R OFTE R
*ZANDE R	BLUCHE R	BUMBLE R	CHILLE R	COBBIE R	C R OONE R
*ZANIE R	BLUDGE R	BUNDLE R	*CHIPPE R	COBBLE R	C R OPPE R
*ZAPPE R	*BLUFFE R	BUNGLE R	CHI R PE R	COCHAI R	C R OSIE R
*ZEPHY R	BLUNDE R	BU R BLE R	CHITTE R	*COCKIE R	C R OSSE R
*ZESTE R	BLUNGE R	BU R GHE R	*CHOMPE R	CODDLE R	C R OWBA R
*ZINGE R	BLU R TE R	BU R GLA R	CHOOSE R	COE R CE R	C R OWDE R
*ZIPPE R	BLUSHE R	BU R R IE R	*CHOPPE R	COHE R E R	C R OWNE R
*ZITHE R	BLUSTE R	BU R STE R	CHOUSE R	COINFE R	*C R OZIE R
*ZOSTE R	BOA R DE R	BUSHIE R	*CHOWDE R	COINTE R	C R UISE R
BABBLE R	BOASTE R	BUSTIE R	CHUDDA R	COLLIE R	C R ULLE R
*BAFFLE R	BOGGIE R	BUTCHE R	CHUDDE R	COLO R E R	C R UMBE R
BAHADU R	BOGGLE R	BYLINE R	CHUGGE R	*COMAKE R	C R UPPE R
BA R R IE R	BOLIVA R	*CACKLE R	*CHUKKA R	COMPEE R	C R USHE R
BASILA R	BOLSTE R	*CAJOLE R	CHUNTE R	CONIFE R	CUDBEA R
BATCHE R	BOODLE R	CALAMA R	CHU R NE R	CONINE R	CUDDLE R
BATTIE R	BOOKIE R	CALIBE R	CI R CLE R	*CONQUE R	CUPELE R
BATTLE R	BOOMIE R	CALIPE R	CITATO R	CONTOU R	CUPULA R
BAWDIE R	BOOSTE R	CALOYE R	CLABBE R	CO R KIE R	CU R ATO R
BEADIE R	BOSSIE R	*CAMPHO R	*CLACKE R	CO R NIE R	CU R DIE R
BEAMIE R	BOTCHE R	CAMPIE R	CLAIME R	CO R ONE R	CU R DLE R
BEEFIE R	BOTTLE R	CANDLE R	CLAMBE R	CO R SAI R	CU R R IE R
BEETLE R	BOUDOI R	CANDOU R	CLAMME R	CO R ULE R	CUSHIE R
*BEHAVE R	BOULDE R	CANNIE R	CLAMOU R	COTTIE R	CUTOVE R
BELABO R	BOUNCE R	CAPE R E R	CLAMPE R	COUCHE R	DABBLE R
BELCHE R	BOUNDE R	CA R OLE R	CLANGE R	COUGHE R	DABSTE R
BENCHE R	BOWLDE R	CA R R IE R	CLAPPE R	COULOI R	DALLIE R
BESCOU R	B R AGGE R	CASHIE R	*CLAQUE R	COULTE R	DAMAGE R
BESMEA R	B R ANDE R	CATCHE R	CLASHE R	COUNTE R	DANDIE R
BEVELE R	B R ANNE R	CATE R E R	CLASPE R	COUPLE R	DANDLE R
BICOLO R	B R ASIE R	CATTIE R	CLASSE R	COU R IE R	DANGLE R
BIFILA R	B R AWLE R		CLATTE R	COU R SE R	DANSEU R

DASHIE R	DOUCEU R	FLANGE R	GAMBIE R	G ROUPE R	HOODIE R
DAUNDE R	DOWAGE R	FLANKE R	GAMBLE R	G ROUSE R	HO RNIE R
DAUNTE R	DOWNIE R	FLAPPE R	GAMMIE R	G ROUTE R	HO R SIE R
DAYSTA R	D RAFTE R	FLASHE R	GA R BLE R	G ROWLE R	HOSTLE R
*DAZZLE R	D RAGGE R	FLATCA R	GA R GLE R	G RUBBE R	HOTSPU R
DEBATE R	D RAINE R	FLATTE R	GA R OTE R	G RUDGE R	HOUNDE R
DEBONE R	D RAWBA R	FLAVOU R	GAUFFE R	G RUELE R	HOVE R ER
DECAYE R	D RAWLE R	FLEECE R	*GAWKIE R	G RUMME R	*HOWEVE R
DECIDE R	D REAME R	FLENSE R	GEMMIE R	G RUNTE R	HUDDLE R
DECODE R	D REDGE R	FLESHE R	GENITO R	GUA R DE R	HUMBLE R
DECOLO R	D RESSE R	*FLICKE R	GE R MIE R	GUILDE R	HUMIDO R
DECOYE R	D RIFTE R	FLINDE R	GIGGLE R	GULFIE R	HU R DLE R
DEC R EE R	D RILLE R	FLINGE R	GIMPIE R	GUMMIE R	HU R RIE R
DEC R IE R	D RINKE R	FLIPPE R	GI R DLE R	GUSTIE R	HUSKIE R
DEFACE R	D RIPPE R	FLOUTE R	GLACIE R	GUTTIE R	HUSTLE R
DEFAME R	D ROPPE R	FLUBBE R	GLADDE R	GUTTLE R	*JACAMA R
DEFILE R	D ROWNE R	FLUNKE R	GLADIE R	*GUZZLE R	*JANGLE R
DEFINE R	D RUBBE R	FLUSHE R	GLAMOU R	GYPSTE R	JANITO R
DEIFIE R	D RUDGE R	FLUSTE R	GLANCE R	GY RATO R	*JEMADA R
DELAYE R	D RUMME R	FLUTIE R	*GLAZIE R	*HACKLE R	*JEMIDA R
DELIVE R	DUCKIE R	FLUTTE R	GLEAME R	HAGGLE R	JETTIE R
DELUDE R	DUELLE R	*FLYOVE R	GLEANE R	HAI R IE R	*JEWELE R
DENUDE R	DUMPIE R	FLYTIE R	GLIMME R	HAMMIE R	*JINGLE R
DEPOSE R	DUSTIE R	FOAMIE R	GLISTE R	HAMSTE R	*JOCULA R
DE R IDE R	DWELLE R	FOCUSE R	GLITTE R	HANAPE R	*JODHPU R
DE R IVE R	FABULA R	FONDLE R	GLOATE R	HANDCA R	*JOGGLE R
DE R NIE R	FADDIE R	FOOTIE R	GLOSSE R	HANDIE R	*JOINDE R
DESI R E R	FAGOTE R	FOOTLE R	GOBBLE R	HANDLE R	JOINTE R
DESPAI R	FAINTE R	*FOOZLE R	GODLIE R	HA R BOU R	JOLLIE R
DESUGA R	FAITOU R	FO RAGE R	GOGGLE R	HA R DIE R	JOSTLE R
DEVISE R	FANCIE R	FO RAYE R	G RABBE R	HA R RIE R	JOUSTE R
DEVISO R	FA R CEU R	FO R BEA R	G RAFTE R	*HATCHE R	*JUGGLE R
DEWATE R	FA R RIE R	FO R EVE R	G RAINE R	HAULIE R	*JUGULA R
DIASTE R	FA R THE R	FO R GOE R	G RAMMA R	HAUNTE R	*JUMBLE R
DIBBLE R	FATTIE R	FO R KIE R	G RANGE R	HAUTEU R	*JUNIPE R
DICTIE R	FAVO R E R	FOUNDE R	G RANTE R	HAVIOU R	*KASHMI R
DIDDLE R	FEASTE R	F RACTU R	G RANTO R	HEADIE R	*KAYAKE R
DIESTE R	FEATHE R	F RANKE R	G RAPIE R	HEATHE R	KEESTE R
DIETHE R	FEIGNE R	*F REEZE R	G RASPE R	HEAVIE R	KEGELE R
DILATE R	FELSPA R	F RETTE R	*G RAZIE R	*HECKLE R	KEISTE R
DILATO R	*FEOFFE R	F RISEU R	G REASE R	HEISTE R	KEYSTE R
DILUTE R	*FEOFFO R	F RISKE R	G REETE R	HEMPIE R	*KHADDA R
DILUTO R	FE R VOU R	F RITTE R	G RIDDE R	HE R BIE R	*KICKIE R
DIMETE R	*FETCHE R	*F RIZZE R	G RIEVE R	HE R ITO R	KIESTE R
DINKIE R	FIDDLE R	F ROWNE R	G RIFTE R	HILLIE R	KILOBA R
DIOPTE R	FIELDE R	F RUITE R	G RILLE R	HIPPIE R	KINDLE R
DISHIE R	FIGHTE R	FUEH R E R	G RIMIE R	HIPSTE R	*KLEZME R
DITCHE R	FIGU R E R	FUMBLE R	G RIMME R	*HITCHE R	KLISTE R
DIVIDE R	*FILCHE R	FUNCTO R	G RINDE R	HOA R DE R	*KNACKE R
DIVINE R	FILMIE R	FUNFAI R	G RINNE R	HOA R IE R	*KNAPPE R
DIVISO R	FINNIE R	FU R RIE R	G RIPPE R	HOBBLE R	KNEADE R
DONATO R	FISHIE R	FU R THE R	G ROANE R	HOISTE R	KNEELE R
DOSSIE R	FLAGGE R	GABBIE R	G ROOME R	HOLSTE R	KNITTE R
DOTTIE R	FLAMIE R	GABBLE R	G ROOVE R	HOMAGE R	*KNOCKE R
DOUBLE R	FLANEU R	GAGSTE R	G ROSSE R	HONO R E R	KNOLLE R

KNOTTE R	*LYNCHE R	MONSTE R	PAPE R E R	*PLUCKE R	*PUZZLE R
KOTOWE R	MACABE R	MOOCHE R	PAPPIE R	PLUGGE R	*QUAFFE R
*K R EUZE R	*MACHZO R	MOONIE R	PA R ADE R	PLUMBE R	*QUA R TE R
*K R IMME R	MADDIE R	MOO R IE R	PA R ADO R	PLUMIE R	*QUASHE R
K R ULLE R	MALODO R	MOSSIE R	PA R CEU R	PLUMPE R	*QUELLE R
LABELE R	MALSTE R	MOTTLE R	PA R DNE R	PLUNDE R	*QUE R IE R
LABO R E R	MANAGE R	MOULDE R	PA R LOU R	PLUNGE R	*QUESTE R
LACUNA R	MANGIE R	MOULTE R	PA R TIE R	PLUNKE R	*QUESTO R
LAMBIE R	MANGLE R	MOUNTE R	PA R TNE R	POACHE R	*QUIETE R
LAMSTE R	MANU R E R	MOU R NE R	PA R TYE R	POINTE R	*QUILTE R
LANDLE R	MA R BLE R	MOUSIE R	PASTIE R	POLYME R	*QUINTA R
LANGUO R	MA R CHE R	MOUTHE R	PATAMA R	POPOVE R	*QUIPPE R
LA R DIE R	MA R INE R	*MUCKIE R	PATCHE R	POPULA R	*QUITTE R
LA R KIE R	*MA R KHO R	MUDDIE R	PAVIOU R	PO R KIE R	*QUITTO R
LASHKA R	MA R LIE R	MUDDLE R	PAVISE R	POSTWA R	*QUIZZE R
LASSOE R	MA R R IE R	*MUFFLE R	PEACHE R	POTTIE R	R ABBLE R
LATHIE R	*MASQUE R	MUGGIE R	PEAKIE R	POULTE R	R AFFLE R
LAUGHE R	MASSEU R	MUMBLE R	PEA R LE R	POUNCE R	R AILCA R
LAUNDE R	MASSIE R	MUNSTE R	PEDDLE R	POUNDE R	R AINIE R
LAYOVE R	MATADO R	MU R THE R	PENSTE R	P R AETO R	R ALLIE R
LEACHE R	MATCHE R	MUSKIE R	PEOPLE R	P R AISE R	R AMBLE R
LEADIE R	MAUNDE R	*MUZZIE R	PE R CHE R	P R ANCE R	R AMMIE R
LEAFIE R	MEALIE R	*MUZZLE R	PE R USE R	P R AWNE R	R ANCHE R
LEAGUE R	MEANDE R	*MYNHEE R	PETTIE R	P R EAVE R	R ANCOU R
LEA R IE R	MEATIE R	NEEDIE R	PHILTE R	P R EENE R	R ANDIE R
LEA R NE R	MEDDLE R	NEEDLE R	PHONIE R	P R EMIE R	R ATTIE R
LEATHE R	MEGABA R	NEGATO R	*PIAFFE R	P R ESSO R	R ATTLE R
LEGATO R	MENACE R	NEITHE R	PIASTE R	P R ESTE R	R AVAGE R
LEGGIE R	MESHIE R	NE R VIE R	PICADO R	P R ICIE R	R AVELE R
LEISTE R	MESSIE R	NESTLE R	*PICKEE R	*P R ICKE R	R AVENE R
LEVATO R	METAME R	NETTIE R	*PICKIE R	P R IMME R	R EACHE R
LEVELE R	MIDDLE R	NETTLE R	PIDDLE R	P R INKE R	R EACTO R
LIBELE R	MIDYEA R	NEWSIE R	PIE R CE R	P R INTE R	R EADIE R
LIGHTE R	MILKIE R	NIBBLE R	PIGGIE R	P R IVIE R	R EALGA R
LIMBIE R	MILLIE R	NIPPIE R	PILSNE R	P R OCTO R	R EALTE R
LIMITE R	MINGIE R	NOBBIE R	PINCHE R	P R ODDE R	R EBATE R
LINGIE R	MINGLE R	NOBBLE R	PIONEE R	*P R OFFE R	R EBUKE R
LINTIE R	MINICA R	NONPOO R	PISSOI R	P R OGGE R	R ECITE R
*LIQUEU R	MINIVE R	NONUSE R	PITCHE R	P R OOFE R	R ECOLO R
LIVENE R	MINSTE R	NO R THE R	PLAGUE R	P R OSIE R	R ECOVE R
LOATHE R	MI R ADO R	NOTCHE R	PLAITE R	P R OSPE R	R EDUCE R
LOBBYE R	MISAVE R	NOTICE R	PLANNE R	P R OWLE R	R EEDIE R
LOBSTE R	MISDOE R	NUBBIE R	PLANTA R	PSALTE R	R EENTE R
LOCATE R	MISHEA R	NUCLEA R	PLASHE R	PUDDLE R	R EFINE R
LOCATO R	MISTIE R	*NUZZLE R	PLASTE R	PUELLE R	R EFUSE R
LOCULA R	MISUSE R	PADDLE R	PLATTE R	PUGGIE R	R EFUTE R
LOFTIE R	MITE R E R	PAINTE R	PLEADE R	PUMICE R	R EGALE R
LO R IME R	MOBSTE R	PALAVE R	PLEASE R	PUNCHE R	R EGULA R
LO R INE R	MODELE R	PALIKA R	PLEATE R	PUNSTE R	R EIFIE R
LUCIFE R	MODULA R	PALLIE R	PLEDGE R	PUPILA R	R EINCU R
LUNCHE R	MOLDIE R	PALMIE R	PLEDGO R	PU R SIE R	R EINTE R
LUPANA R	MONEYE R	PANDOO R	PLESSO R	PU R SUE R	R ELATE R
LU R CHE R	MONIKE R	PANDOU R	PLINKE R	PUSHIE R	R ELATO R
LUSTIE R	MONITO R	PANNIE R	PLODDE R	PUSSIE R	R ELAXE R
LUTHIE R	MONOME R	PANTHE R	PLOTTE R	PUTTIE R	R ELAXO R

R EMAKE R	SAMBHA R	SETTLO R	SLACKE R	SPANNE R	STEPPE R
R EMOVE R	SAMBHU R	SHADIE R	SLAMME R	SPA R GE R	STE R TO R
R ENEWE R	SAMOVA R	SHAKIE R	SLANDE R	SPA R KE R	STICKE R
R ENTIE R	SAMPLE R	SHALIE R	SLAPPE R	SPATTE R	STIFLE R
R EOCCU R	SANDBA R	SHAMME R	SLATIE R	SPAWNE R	STINGE R
R EOFFE R	SANDBU R	SHA R KE R	SLEDDE R	SPEAKE R	STINKE R
R EO R DE R	SANDIE R	SHA R PE R	SLEEPE R	SPEA R E R	STINTE R
R EPAPE R	SANTOU R	SHATTE R	SLENDE R	SPECTE R	STI R R E R
R EPINE R	SASSIE R	SHEA R E R	SLICKE R	SPEEDE R	STOCKE R
R EPLIE R	SAUNTE R	SHEDDE R	SLIMIE R	SPELLE R	STOMPE R
R EPOSE R	SAUTOI R	SHEETE R	SLIMME R	SPELTE R	STONIE R
R EPOWE R	SAVIOU R	SHELLE R	SLINGE R	SPENCE R	STOOKE R
R ESCUE R	SAVO R E R	SHELTE R	SLIPPE R	SPENDE R	STOOPE R
R ESIDE R	SCALIE R	SHELVE R	SLITHE R	SPICIE R	STOPPE R
R ESUME R	SCALPE R	*SHICKE R	SLOBBE R	SPIELE R	ST R AFE R
R ETAKE R	SCAMPE R	SHIFTE R	SLOGGE R	SPILLE R	ST R AYE R
R ETI R E R	SCANNE R	*SHIKKE R	SLUBBE R	SPINIE R	ST R EWE R
R EUTTE R	SCA R IE R	SHIMME R	SLUGGE R	SPINNE R	ST R IDE R
R EVELE R	SCA R PE R	SHINIE R	SLUMBE R	SPI R IE R	ST R IDO R
R EVE R E R	SCATTE R	SHIPPE R	SLUMME R	SPITTE R	ST R IKE R
R EVILE R	SCAUPE R	SHI R KE R	*SMACKE R	SPLICE R	ST R IPE R
R EVISE R	SCEPTE R	*SHOCKE R	SMASHE R	SPOILE R	ST R IVE R
R EVISO R	SCHEME R	SHOOTE R	SMATTE R	SPONGE R	ST R OKE R
R EVIVE R	SCHMEA R	*SHOPHA R	SMEA R E R	SPOOFE R	ST R OYE R
R EVOKE R	SCHMEE R	SHOPPE R	SMELLE R	SPO R TE R	STUDIE R
R IBBIE R	SCHOLA R	SHOUTE R	SMELTE R	SPOTTE R	STUFFE R
R IDDLE R	SCISSO R	SHOWIE R	SMI R KE R	SPOUTE R	STUIVE R
R IDGIE R	*SCOFFE R	SH R IVE R	SMOLDE R	SP R AYE R	STUMPE R
R IFFLE R	SCOLDE R	*SHUCKE R	SMOTHE R	SPUDDE R	STUNNE R
R IGHTE R	SCOOPE R	SHUDDE R	SNAPPE R	SPUMIE R	STUTTE R
R IPPLE R	SCOOTE R	SHUNNE R	SNA R LE R	SPU R NE R	SUBADA R
R IVETE R	SCO R NE R	SHUNTE R	SNEAKE R	SPUTTE R	SUBALA R
R OASTE R	SCOU R E R	SHUTTE R	SNEE R E R	*SQUALO R	SUBDUE R
R OCKIE R	SCOUTE R	SHYSTE R	SNIGGE R	*SQUA R E R	SUCCOU R
R OISTE R	SCOWDE R	SIDEBA R	SNIPPE R	STABBE R	SUCKLE R
R OOSTE R	SCOWLE R	SIDECA R	SNOOKE R	STABLE R	SULPHU R
R OOTIE R	SC R APE R	SIGHTE R	SNOOPE R	STACKE R	SUMPTE R
R OTATO R	SC R EWE R	SIGNIO R	*SNOOZE R	STAFFE R	SU R FIE R
R OTIFE R	SC R IBE R	SILKIE R	SNO R TE R	STAGGE R	SWABBE R
R OUGHE R	SCULKE R	SIMILA R	SNOWIE R	STAGIE R	SWAGGE R
R OUNDE R	SCULLE R	SIMITA R	SOAPIE R	STAINE R	SWAMPE R
R OUSTE R	SCUMME R	SIMULA R	SOCAGE R	STALKE R	SWAPPE R
R OYSTE R	SCUNNE R	*SIZZLE R	SOLACE R	STAMME R	SWA R ME R
R UDDIE R	SCUPPE R	SKEETE R	SOLDIE R	STAMPE R	SWASHE R
R UFFLE R	SCUTTE R	SKELTE R	SNUFFE R	STANDE R	SWATHE R
R UMBLE R	SEAMIE R	SKIDDE R	SOAPIE R	STAPLE R	SWATTE R
R UNOVE R	SECEDE R	*SKIMME R	SOCAGE R	STA R TE R	SWEA R E R
R USHIE R	SECULA R	*SKINKE R	SOLACE R	STA R VE R	SWEATE R
R USTIE R	SECU R E R	SKINNE R	SOLDIE R	STEALE R	SWEEPE R
R USTLE R	SEDUCE R	*SKIPPE R	SOOTHE R	STEAME R	SWELTE R
R UTTIE R	SEEDIE R	SKI R TE R	SO R R IE R	STEEPE R	SWE R VE R
SADDLE R	*SELTZE R	SKITTE R	SOUNDE R	STEE R E R	SWIFTE R
SALLIE R	SEMINA R	SKIWEA R	SOUTHE R	STELLA R	SWIGGE R
SALTIE R	SENATO R	*SKULKE R	SPALLE R	STEMME R	SWILLE R
SALUTE R	SETTLE R	SLABBE R	SPANKE R	STENTO R	SWIMME R

SWINGE R	TIPSTE R	VAPO R E R	*WHIPPE R	BA R RATO R	BO R DE R E R
SWISHE R	TITULA R	VASTIE R	WHI R LE R	BA R RETO R	BO R ROWE R
SWITHE R	TOASTE R	VAULTE R	*WHISKE R	BA R ROWE R	BOTTOME R
SWOBBE R	TODDLE R	VAUNTE R	*WHISPE R	BA R TE R E R	B R ABBLE R
SWOONE R	TOGGLE R	VAVASO R	*WHITHE R	BASIFIE R	B R AINIE R
SWOOPE R	TOLLBA R	VEINIE R	WHITTE R	BATTENE R	*B R EACHE R
SWOTTE R	TOOTLE R	VENOME R	*WHIZZE R	BAYADEE R	B R EATHE R
TABO R E R	*TO R QUE R	VE R NIE R	*WHOEVE R	*BEBOPPE R	*B R OACHE R
TABULA R	TOUCHE R	VE R R IE R	*WHOOPE R	*BECKONE R	B R OWNIE R
TACKIE R	T R ACKE R	VETIVE R	*WHOPPE R	*BECLAMO R	B R USHIE R
TACKLE R	T R ACTO R	VIEWIE R	WIDENE R	*BEDCHAI R	BUDGETE R
TALLIE R	T R AILE R	VILIGE R	WIDOWE R	*BEDCOVE R	*BUFFETE R
TAMBOU R	T R AINE R	VINEGA R	WIELDE R	BEDIAPE R	BU R DENE R
TANAGE R	T R AITO R	VINTNE R	WIGGIE R	*BEDMAKE R	BU R ROWE R
TANGIE R	T R AMCA R	VISITE R	WIGGLE R	BEFINGE R	BUSHELE R
TANGLE R	T R AMPE R	VISITO R	*WINCHE R	BEFLOWE R	BUTTONE R
TAPE R E R	T R APPE R	VITAME R	WINDIE R	BEFOULE R	CADASTE R
TAPSTE R	T R AWLE R	VOCODE R	WINGIE R	BEGETTE R	CALCSPA R
TA R DIE R	T R EADE R	VOMITE R	WI R R IE R	BEGINNE R	CALENDA R
TA R R IE R	T R EATE R	*VOUCHE R	WISPIE R	BEGLAMO R	CALLIPE R
TA R SIE R	*T R EKKE R	VOYAGE R	WITHIE R	BEGUILE R	*CALYPTE R
TATTIE R	T R ICKE R	WABBLE R	WITTIE R	*BEHAVIO R	CAMELEE R
TATTLE R	T R IFLE R	WADDLE R	WOBBLE R	BEHOLDE R	CANALLE R
TAUNTE R	T R IGGE R	*WAFFLE R	WOODIE R	BELABOU R	CANCELE R
TEACHE R	T R ILLE R	WAGE R E R	WOOLIE R	BELIEVE R	*CANEPHO R
TEA R IE R	T R IMME R	WAGONE R	WO R DIE R	*BELIQUO R	CANISTE R
TEENIE R	T R IPPE R	WAISTE R	WO R MIE R	BELLOWE R	CANVASE R
TEETHE R	T R OCHA R	WAKENE R	WO R R IE R	BEMU R MU R	*CAPMAKE R
TEGULA R	T R OFFE R	*WALTZE R	W R APPE R	BE R EAVE R	CAPONIE R
TELPHE R	T R OLLE R	WANGLE R	W R EAKE R	BESETTE R	CAPSOME R
TEMBLO R	T R OOPE R	WA R BLE R	*W R ECKE R	*BESHIVE R	CAPSULA R
TEMPLA R	T R OTTE R	WA R R IO R	W R ESTE R	BESIEGE R	CAPTU R E R
TEMPTE R	T R OUPE R	WA R SLE R	W R INGE R	BETATTE R	CA R EENE R
TENONE R	T R OUSE R	WA R TIE R	W R ITHE R	BET R AYE R	CA R EE R E R
TENTIE R	T R UCKE R	WASHIE R	W R ONGE R	BEVELLE R	CA R ESSE R
TE R R IE R	T R UDGE R	*WATCHE R	*YACHTE R	BEWAILE R	*CA R MAKE R
TESTIE R	T R USSE R	WATE R E R	YEA R NE R	BEWILDE R	CA R OUSE R
THANKE R	T R USTE R	WEA R IE R	YIELDE R	*BEW R AYE R	CATB R IE R
THEATE R	T R USTO R	WEATHE R	YODELE R	*BICKE R E R	CATHETE R
THINKE R	T R YSTE R	WEBSTE R	YOUNGE R	BICOLOU R	CATNAPE R
THINNE R	TUBULA R	WEEDIE R	YOUNKE R	*BICYCLE R	CAVALIE R
THITHE R	TUMBLE R	WEIGHE R	*BACHELO R	BILANDE R	CAVEATO R
TH R IVE R	TUMMLE R	*WELCHE R	BACILLA R	BILINEA R	CAVILLE R
TH R OWE R	TUMULA R	WELSHE R	*BACKDOO R	BILLETE R	CAVO R TE R
THUMPE R	TU R FIE R	*WENCHE R	*BAGPIPE R	BIMESTE R	CELLA R E R
THUNDE R	TU R TLE R	*WHACKE R	BALANCE R	BIOVULA R	CELLULA R
*THYMIE R	TUTELA R	*WHAPPE R	BALISAU R	BISECTO R	CEMENTE R
TICKLE R	TUTOYE R	*WHECKE R	BALLOTE R	*BLANCHE R	CENSU R E R
TIDDLE R	TWEETE R	WHEELE R	BALUSTE R	BLASTIE R	*CHANCIE R
TINGLE R	*TWEEZE R	*WHEEZE R	BANDAGE R	*BLAZONE R	CHANDLE R
TINKLE R	TWINIE R	*WHETHE R	BANISHE R	*BLEACHE R	*CHAPITE R
TINNIE R	TWI R LE R	WHETTE R	BANISTE R	*BLENCHE R	CHA R R IE R
TIPPIE R	TWISTE R	*WHIFFE R	BANTE R E R	BLOODIE R	CHASSEU R
TIPPLE R	TWITTE R	*WHIMPE R	*BAPTIZE R	BLOTTIE R	*CHAUFFE R
TIPSIE R	TYPEBA R	WHINIE R	BA R RATE R	*BOB R OWER	CHAUNTE R

CHEE R IE R	*CONJURER	DEEPENE R	*DIFFUSE R	FINAGLE R	GLASSIE R
*CHICANE R	*CONJUROR	DEFECTO R	*DIFFUSO R	FINISHE R	GLIMPSE R
CHISELE R	CONNIVE R	DEFENDE R	DIGESTE R	FLAUNTE R	GLOBULA R
CHO R TLE R	CONSIDE R	DEFE R R E R	DIGESTO R	FLAVO R E R	GLOSSIE R
*CHUCKLE R	CONSOLE R	DEFLATE R	DINOSAU R	FLESHIE R	GOSSAME R
CINNABA R	CONSUME R	DEFLATO R	*DIPLEXE R	*FLETCHE R	GOSSIPE R
CI R CULA R	CONVENE R	*DEFLOWER	DI R ECTO R	*FLICHTE R	GOVE R NO R
CISLUNA R	CONVENO R	DEFOAME R	DISA R ME R	*FLINCHE R	G R ABBLE R
CLAMO R E R	*CONVEYE R	DEFOGGE R	DISASTE R	FLOWE R E R	G R ANDEU R
CLANGOU R	*CONVOKE R	DEFO R ME R	DISCOLO R	*FLYPAPE R	G R ANDSI R
CLASSIE R	COPASTO R	*DEF R AYE R	DISCOVE R	FOLLOWE R	G R ANULA R
CLEANSE R	COPLANA R	DEGASSE R	*DISFAVO R	FOMENTE R	G R APPLE R
*CLENCHE R	CO R R IDO R	DEG R ADE R	DISHONO R	FOOTGEA·R	G R EENIE R
*CLINCHE R	COSIGNE R	DEHO R NE R	DISINTE R	FOOTWEA R	G R IMACE R
CLOISTE R	COSTUME R	*DEJEUNE R	DISLIKE R	FO R EBEA R	G R IPPIE R
CLOTHIE R	COTTAGE R	DELOUSE R	DISO R DE R	FO R EGOE R	*G R IZZLE R
*COANCHO R	COU R TIE R	DELUSTE R	DISPOSE R	FO R ESEE R	G R OUNDE R
COAPPEA R	COWINNE R	DEMANDE R	DISPUTE R	FO R ESTE R	G R OVELE R
COAUTHO R	*COWORKER	DEMEANO R	DIS R OBE R	*FO R GIVE R	G R UELLE R
*COCKSPU R	C R ANKIE R	DEME R GE R	DITHE R E R	FO R RADE R	*G R UFFIE R
CODEBTO R	C R EDITO R	DEMPSTE R	DIVE R TE R	*FO R SAKE R	G R UMBLE R
CODIFIE R	C R EMATO R	DEMUR R E R	DIVO R CE R	FO R SWEA R	GUNPAPE R
COD R IVE R	C R IPPLE R	DEPICTE R	DIVULGE R	FOSTE R E R	HALLOWE R
COEDITO R	C R OSSBA R	DEPICTO R	DODDE R E R	*F R EAKIE R	*HAMME R E R
COENAMO R	C R OUPIE R	DEPLO R E R	DOGNAPE R	F R ESCOE R	*HAMPE R E R
*COFACTO R	*C R UICFE R	DEP R AVE R	DOMINEE R	*F R IBBLE R	*HANDOVE R
*COGNIZE R	C R UMBIE R	DEP R IVE R	DONNIKE R	F R IVOLE R	*HANKE R E R
COHOLDE R	*C R UNCHE R	DE R INGE R	DOOMSTE R	*F R IZZIE R	HA R ASSE R
*COIFFEU R	C R USADE R	DESALTE R	DOPESTE R	*F R IZZLE R	HA R BO R E R
COLANDE R	*CUCUMBE R	DESC R IE R	DOUGHIE R	F R ONDEU R	HA R DENE R
COLEADE R	CUDGELE R	DESE R TE R	*DOUZEPE R	F R ONTIE R	*HA R KENE R
COLESSO R	CULTIVA R	DESE R VE R	DOWNPOU R	F R OTTEU R	HAR ROWER
COLINEA R	CUMBE R E R	DESIGNE R	D R AGGIE R	FU R R INE R	HASTENE R
COLLATO R	CUPELLE R	DESILVE R	D R ENCHE R	FU R R OWE R	*HATMAKE R
COLLEGE R	CUSPIDO R	DESPISE R	D R IBBLE R	FUSILEE R	*HAVOCKE R
COLLIDE R	CUSTOME R	DEST R IE R	D R IVELE R	FUSILIE R	*HAYMAKE R
COLLUDE R	CUTWATE R	DESULFU R	D R UMLIE R	GALLOPE R	HEADGEA R
COLOU R E R	*CYCLECA R	DETACHE R	DULCIME R	GAMESTE R	*HEMIPTE R
COMBATE R	CYLINDE R	DETAILE R	*DUPLEXE R	GAMMONE R	*HIJACKE R
COMBINE R	*CYMBALE R	DETAINE R	FALCONE R	GANGLIA R	HINDE R E R
*COMEMBE R	DAMPENE R	DETECTE R	FALTE R E R	GANGLIE R	*HIZZONE R
*COMETHE R	DA R KENE R	DETECTO R	FAMILIA R	GANGSTE R	*HOLDOVE R
COMMONE R	DAUGHTE R	DETE R GE R	FASTENE R	GANISTE R	HONOU R E R
COMMUTE R	DEADENE R	DETE R R E R	FATTENE R	GA R DENE R	HOOPSTE R
COMPA R E R	DEADLIE R	DETESTE R	FAVOU R E R	GA R OTTE R	HO R SECA R
COMPILE R	DEBONAI R	*DETICKE R	*FELDSHE R	GA R R OTE R	HOSPODA R
COMPOSE R	DEBUGGE R	DEVIATO R	FELDSPA R	GASALIE R	HOTELIE R
COMPUTE R	DECANTE R	DEVOU R E R	FELLATO R	GASELIE R	*HOWITZE R
CONCEDE R	DECEIVE R	DIALOGE R	FE R R ETE R	GASIFIE R	*HUCKSTE R
CONDOLE R	DECENTE R	DIALYSE R	FETTE R E R	GASOLIE R	*HUNGOVE R
CONDUCE R	DECLA R E R	*DIALYZE R	FIDGETE R	GATHE R E R	*HYD R ATO R
CONFIDE R	DECLINE R	DIAMETE R	FIGEATE R	*GAZUMPE R	*JABBE R E R
CONFINE R	DEEMSTE R	DICTATO R	FILISTE R	GEOLOGE R	*JAPPANE R
CONFUTE R		DIDAPPE R	FILMGOE R	GEOMETE R	*JAWBONE R
CONGENE R		*DIEMAKE R	FILTE R E R		

*JETLINE R	LOW R IDE R	MUTINEE R	PE R VADE R	P R OFITE R	REFER RER
*JEWELLE R	LUMBE R E R	MUTTE R E R	PESTE R E R	P R OLABO R	R EFILTE R
*JOKESTE R	MAGISTE R	NA R R ATE R	PETIOLA R	P R OMISE R	R EFLOWE R
*JONGLEU R	*MAKEOVE R	NAR R ATO R	PEWTE R E R	P R OMISO R	R EFO R ME R
*JOY R IDE R	MALINGE R	NAYSAYE R	*PHOSPHO R	P R OMOTE R	R EFUNDE R
*JUNKETE R	MANDATO R	*NECKWEA R	PIACULA R	P R OMPTE R	R EGAINE R
*KEYNOTE R	MANEUVE R	NEIGHBO R	*PICKETE R	P R ONATO R	R EGATHE R
*KIBITZE R	*MANPOWE R	*NEWCOME R	PILASTE R	P R OPOSE R	R EGISTE R
*KIDNAPE R	*MAPMAKE R	*NEXTDOO R	PILFE R E R	P R OVIDE R	*R EHABBE R
KILLDEE R	MA R AUDE R	*NIGHTJA R	PILLAGE R	*P R OVOKE R	*R EHAMME R
*KIPPE R E R	MA R KETE R	NIT R ATO R	PILSENE R	*PUCKE R E R	R EHEATE R
*KNITWEA R	*MA RKHOO R	NONACTO R	PINASTE R	PULLOVE R	R EISSUE R
*KOMONDO R	MASSAGE R	NONCOLO R	*PINSCHE R	PULMOTO R	*R EJECTO R
*KOWTOWER	MASSETE R	*NONJU R O R	PISCATO R	PULSATO R	*R EJIGGE R
*K REUTZE R	MEASU R E R	NONLABO R	*PITCHIE R	PUNISHE R	*R EJOICE R
LABELLE R	MEDIATO R	*NONMAJO R	PLACATE R	PU R IFIE R	R ELAPSE R
LABOU R E R	MEGASTA R	NONOWNE R	PLANKTE R	*PU R VEYO R	R ELEASE R
LAB R ADO R	MENSWEA R	NONPOLA R	PLAYGOE R	*PUSHOVE R	R ELETTE R
LAMENTE R	*METAPHO R	NONSKIE R	*PLAYWEA R	PUTTE R E R	R ELIEVE R
LAMISTE R	*MICAWBE R	NONSOLA R	PLEDGEO R	*QUA R RIE R	R ELOADE R
LA R CENE R	MIC R OBA R	NONSUGA R	PLIGHTE R	*QUAVE R E R	R EMA R KE R
LA R KSPU R	MIG R ATO R	NONVOTE R	PLOTTIE R	*QUENCHE R	R EMASTE R
LA R R UPE R	MILLIBA R	NOTIFIE R	PLOUGHE R	*QUIBBLE R	R EMEMBE R
LATEENE R	MILLINE R	NUMBE R E R	*POCKETE R	*QUIPSTE R	R EMINDE R
LATHE R E R	*MIMICKE R	NUMMULA R	POETISE R	*QUIVE R E R	R EMITTE R
LAUDATO R	MINISTE R	NU R TU R E R	*POETIZE R	R ABBITE R	R EMITTO R
LAUGHTE R	MISALTE R	*PACIFIE R	POISONE R	R ADIATO R	R ENDE R E R
LAUNCHE R	MISCOLO R	*PACKAGE R	POLESTA R	R AINWEA R	R ENUMBE R
LAVALIE R	MISENTE R	PALPATO R	POLISHE R	R AMPAGE R	R EPAI R E R
LAVENDE R	MISINFE R	PALTE R E R	POLLSTE R	R ANSOME R	R EPEALE R
LAVISHE R	MISINTE R	PAMPE R E R	POLLUTE R	R A R EFIE R	R EPEATE R
*LAWGIVE R	MISLAYE R	PANDE R E R	POMANDE R	R ATIFIE R	R EPELLE R
*LAWMAKE R	MISLIKE R	*PA R ACHO R	PONDE R E R	R ATOONE R	R EPENTE R
LECTU R E R	MISNOME R	PA R AMOU R	POSTU R E R	R ATTENE R	R EPLACE R
LEFTOVE R	MISO R DE R	PA R CENE R	POTTE R E R	R AVELLE R	R EPO R TE R
LETTE R E R	MIS R EFE R	PA R DONE R	POWDE R E R	R AVISHE R	R EP R OVE R
LEVANTE R	MISSTEE R	PA R LEYE R	P R ATTLE R	R EALISE R	R EPULSE R
LEVELLE R	MISTAKE R	PA R ROTE R	*P R EACHE R	*R EALIZE R	*R EQUI R E R
LICENCE R	MISTUTO R	PA R TAKE R	P R ECLEA R	R EAPPEA R	*R EQUITE R
LICENSO R	MODELLE R	PASSOVE R	P R EDATO R	R EASONE R	R E R OLLE R
LINGE R E R	MODIFIE R	PASTU R E R	*P R EFACE R	R EBUTTE R	R ESELLE R
LIONISE R	MOLESTE R	PATENTO R	P R EMOLA R	R ECALLE R	R ESE R VE R
*LIONIZE R	*MONICKE R	PATTAMA R	P R EOR DE R	R ECAMIE R	R ESETTE R
LISTENE R	MONSIEU R	PATTE R E R	P R EPA R E R	R ECANTE R	R ESHAPE R
LITTE R E R	MO R EOVE R	PECULIA R	P R ESAGE R	R ECEIVE R	R ESIGNE R
LOADSTA R	MO R TISE R	PEDALFE R	P R ESIDE R	R ECEPTO R	R ESILVE R
LODESTA R	MOTIONE R	PEDALIE R	P R ESUME R	R ECKONE R	R ESISTE R
LOITE R E R	MOTO R CA R	PEIGNOI R	P R ETTIE R	R ECLINE R	R ESISTO R
LONGHAI R	*MOUCHOI R	PENCILE R	P R EVISO R	R ECOILE R	R ESOLDE R
LONGSPU R	MUENSTE R	PEPPE R E R	*P R ICKIE R	R ECO R DE R	R ESOLVE R
LONGUEU R	MULETEE R	*PEPTIZE R	P R ISONE R	*R ECYCLE R	R ESO R TE R
LOOSENE R	MULTICA R	*PE R FUME R	P R OCU R E R	R EDACTO R	R ESTO R E R
LO R DLIE R	MU RDERE R	PE R IPTE R	P R ODUCE R	R EDEEME R	R ETAILE R
LOVELIE R	MU R MURE R	*PE R JU R E R	P R OFANE R	R ED R AWE R	R ETAILO R
LOWLIFE R	MUSCULA R	PE R LUDE R	P R OFILE R	R EDUCTO R	R ETAINE R

R ETA R DE R	SCULPTO R	SNITCHE R	STITCHE R	TAILLEU R	T R IMOTO R
R ETEMPE R	*SCUTCHE R	SNIVELE R	*STOCKCA R	*TAKEOVE R	T R IUMVI R
R ETO R TE R	SEAFLOO R	SNOBBIE R	STOCKIE R	TAMPE R E R	T R OUBLE R
R ETU R NE R	SEAMSTE R	SNUBBIE R	STOPOVE R	TA R PAPE R	T R OUNCE R
R EUNITE R	SEAFA R E R	SNUFFIE R	ST R AINE R	TATTOOE R	T R OUVEU R
*R EVAMPE R	SEA R CHE R	SNUFFLE R	ST R ANDE R	TAUTOME R	T R OWELE R
REVEALE R	SEASONE R	SOFTENE R	ST R ANGE R	TAVE R NE R	T R UCKLE R
R EVELLE R	SEAWATE R	SOLANDE R	ST R APPE R	*TAXPAYE R	T R UNDLE R
R EVENGE R	SECATEU R	SOLDE R E R	ST R EAKE R	TEAMAKE R	TUNNELE R
R EVENUE R	SECONDE R	SONGSTE R	ST R EAME R	TEAMSTE R	TU R BOCA R
R EVE R SE R	SEC R ETO R	SO R CE R E R	ST R EEKE R	TEASELE R	TU R NOVE R
R EVER TE R	SEIGNEU R	SO R ROWE R	ST R ESSO R	TEENAGE R	TWADDLE R
R EVIEWE R	SEIGNIO R	SOUVENI R	ST R INGE R	TEMPE R E R	TWANGIE R
R EVOLTE R	SELECTO R	SPA R KIE R	ST R IPIE R	TENDE R E R	TWANGLE R
R EVOLVE R	SEMESTE R	SPA R KLE R	ST R IPPE R	TESTATO R	TWIDDLE R
R EWA R DE R	*SEQUITU R	SPA R R IE R	ST R OLLE R	TET R AME R	*TWINKLE R
R EWINDE R	SE R VICE R	SPEEDIE R	ST R OPPE R	*THATCHE R	*TWITCHE R
R EW R ITE R	SE R VITO R	SPHE R IE R	ST R UMME R	THE R EFO R	*TYPIFIE R
R ICE R CA R	*SHACKLE R	SPINDLE R	ST R UTTE R	THI R STE R	VALUATO R
R IMESTE R	*SHADOWE R	SPINSTE R	STUBBIE R	TH R ASHE R	VALVULA R
R OADSTE R	SHEATHE R	SPLASHE R	STUCCOE R	TH R EADE R	VANISHE R
R OCKETE R	SHIELDE R	SPLATTE R	STUMBLE R	TH R EAPE R	VAPOU R E R
R OLLOVE R	SHINGLE R	SPLENDO R	STYLISE R	TH R ESHE R	VA R ACTO R
R OMANCE R	SHIVE R E R	SPLINTE R	*STYLIZE R	TH R ILLE R	VA R ISTO R
R OTU R IE R	SHOULDE R	SPLITTE R	SUBAHDA R	*TH R OBBE R	VASCULA R
R UFFLIE R	SHOVELE R	SPLU R GE R	SUBFLOO R	*TH R UMME R	VAVASOU R
R UMMAGE R	SHOWE R E R	SPLUTTE R	SUBLIME R	TH R USTE R	VAVASSO R
SABOTEU R	SH R EDDE R	SPONGIE R	SUBLUNA R	TH R USTO R	VENEE R E R
SACCULA R	*SH R IMPE R	SPOONIE R	SUBO R DE R	THU R IFE R	VENTU R E R
SALVAGE R	*SH R INKE R	SP R AWLE R	SUBO R NE R	THWA R TE R	VE R DE R E R
SANDBU R R	*SHUFFLE R	SP R EADE R	SUBPOLA R	TINKE R E R	VE R DE R O R
SANDSPU R	SICKENE R	SP R IGGE R	SUBSIDE R	TISSULA R	VE R DITE R
SAVO R IE R	SIFFLEU R	SP R INGE R	SUBSOLA R	TIT R ATO R	VE R IFIE R
SAVOU R E R	SIGNALE R	SP R INTE R	*SUBVICA R	TITTE R E R	VIB R ATO R
SCANTIE R	SILENCE R	*SP R ITZE R	SUCCO R E R	TOGETHE R	VILIFIE R
SCAPULA R	SILVE R E R	SPU R R IE R	SUFFE R E R	TOPSIDE R	VILLAGE R
*SCHEMEE R	SIMPE R E R	*SQUALLE R	*SUFFICE R	TO R CHIE R	VINTAGE R
SCHILLE R	SINGULA R	*SQUANDE R	SUMMONE R	TO R EADO R	VIOLATE R
*SCHIZIE R	SINISTE R	*SQUASHE R	SUNDE R E R	TO R TU R E R	VITIATO R
SCHOONE R	*SKETCHE R	*SQUATTE R	SUPE R CA R	TOTTE R E R	*VIVIFIE R
SCHUSSE R	*SKYDIVE R	*SQUAWKE R	SUPE R IO R	TOWNWEA R	VOLLEYE R
SCIMETA R	SLAVE R E R	*SQUEAKE R	SUPPLIE R	T R ADITO R	VOUSSOI R
SCIMITA R	SLEEKIE R	*SQUEALE R	SUPPOSE R	T R ADUCE R	*VOYAGEU R
SCIMITE R	SLEIGHE R	*SQUEEZE R	SU R FACE R	T R AMPLE R	WAGGONE R
*SCLAFFE R	SLIPOVE R	*SQUINTE R	SU R MISE R	T R ANSFE R	*WALKOVE R
*SCO R CHE R	SLIVE R E R	*SQUI R ME R	SU R NAME R	T R APDOO R	WALLOPE R
SCOU R GE R	SLOUCHE R	*SQUI R TE R	SU R VEYO R	T R AVELE R	WALLOWE R
SCOUTHE R	SMOOTHE R	STANCHE R	SU R VIVE R	T R EADLE R	WANDE R E R
SC R APPE R	SMOULDE R	STA R TLE R	SU R VIVO R	T R EMBLE R	WANTONE R
SC R AWLE R	SMUGGLE R	STEADIE R	*SWIMWEA R	T R ENCHE R	*WA R MAKE R
SC R EAME R	SNAPPIE R	STICKIE R	SWINDLE R	T R ESSIE R	*WA R POWE R
SC R EENE R	SNATCHE R	STICKLE R	SWINGIE R	T R ESSOU R	WA R R ENE R
SC R IMPE R	SNIFFIE R	STINGIE R	*SWITCHE R	T R ICKIE R	WA R STLE R
SC R UBBE R	SNIFFLE R	STINKIE R	*SWIZZLE R	T R ICOLO R	WATE R IE R
*SCUFFLE R	SNIGGLE R	STIPPLE R	TABOU R E R	T R IMETE R	WATTHOU R

*WAYFA R E R	WHEATEA R	WHITENE R	WINNOWE R	W R ESTLE R	*ZEMINDA R
*WAYLAYE R	*WHEEDLE R	WHITTLE R	WINTE R E R	W R IGGLE R	*ZOOLATE R
*WEAKENE R	*WHENEVE R	*WHOMEVE R	WI R EHAI R	*YAMMERE R	
*WEIGHTE R	*WHEREVER	*WHOSEVE R	WITHE R E R	*YAWMETE R	
*WELCOME R	*WHIFFLE R	*WIGMAKE R	WONDERE R	YEASAYE R	
WELLDOE R	*WHIPPIE R	WILLOWE R	WOOLLIE R	YODELLE R	
*WHATEVE R	WHISTLE R	*WINGOVE R	W R ANGLE R	*ZAMINDA R	

S

SABE	SCOP	SHAT	SINK	SLUR	SOPH
SACK	SCOT	SHAW	SIPE	SLUT	SORA
SADE	SCOW	SHAY	SIRE	SMEW	SORB
SADI	SCRY	SHEA	SITE	SMOG	SORD
SAFE	SCUD	SHED	SITH	SMUG	SORE
SAGA	SCUM	SHEW	SITI	SMUT	SORI
SAGE	SCUP	SHIM	SIZE	SNAG	SORN
SAGO	SCUT	SHIN	*SIZY	SNAP	SORT
SAGY	SEAL	SHIP	SKAG	SNAW	SOTH
SAID	SEAM	SHIT	SKAT	SNED	SOUK
SAIL	SEAR	SHIV	SKEE	SNIB	SOUL
SAIN	SEAT	SHMO	SKEG	SNIP	SOUP
SAKE	SECT	SHOD	SKEP	SNIT	SOUR
SAKI	SEED	SHOE	SKEW	SNOB	SOWN
SALE	SEEK	SHOG	SKID	SNOG	SOYA
SALL	SEEL	SHOO	SKIM	SNOT	SPAE
SALP	SEEM	SHOP	SKIN	SNOW	SPAN
SALT	SEEN	SHOT	SKIP	SNUB	SPAR
SAME	SEEP	SHOW	SKIT	SNUG	SPAT
SAMP	SEER	SHRI	SKUA	SNYE	SPAY
SAND	SEGO	SHUL	SLAB	SOAK	*SPAZ
SANE	SEIF	SHUN	SLAG	SOAP	SPEC
SANG	SELF	SHUT	SLAM	SOAR	SPED
SANK	SELL	SIAL	SLAP	SOCK	SPEW
SANS	SEME	SIBB	SLAT	SODA	SPIC
SARD	SEMI	SICE	SLAW	SOFA	SPIK
SARI	SEND	SICK	SLAY	SOFT	SPIN
SARK	SENE	SIDE	SLED	SOIL	SPIT
SASH	SENT	SIFT	SLEW	SOJA	SPIV
SASS	SEPT	SIGH	SLIM	SOKE	SPOT
SATE	SERA	SIGN	SLIP	SOLA	SPRY
SATI	SERE	SIKE	SLIT	SOLD	SPUD
SAUL	SERF	SILD	SLOB	SOLE	SPUE
SAVE	SETA	SILK	SLOE	SOLI	SPUN
SAWN	SETT	SILL	SLOG	SOLO	SPUR
SCAB	SEWN	SILO	SLOP	SOMA	STAB
SCAD	SEXT	SILT	SLOT	SOME	STAG
SCAG	SEXY	SIMA	SLOW	SONE	STAT
SCAM	SHAD	SIMP	SLUB	SONG	STAW
SCAN	SHAG	SINE	SLUE	SOOK	STAY
SCAR	SHAH	SING	SLUG	SOON	STEM
SCAT	SHAM	SINH	SLUM	SOOT	STEP

STET	SABER	SATAY	SCOUT	SERAI	SHERD
STEW	SABIN	SATEM	**SCOWL**	SERAL	SHIED
STEY	SABIR	SATIN	SCRAG	SERER	SHIEL
STIR	SABLE	SATYR	SCRAM	SERGE	SHIER
STOA	SABOT	SAUCE	SCRAP	SERIF	SHIES
STOB	SABRA	**SAUCH**	SCREE	SERIN	**SHIFT**
STOP	SABRE	**SAUCY**	**SCREW**	SEROW	SHILL
STOW	SACRA	SAUGH	SCRIM	SERRY	**SHILY**
STUB	SADHE	SAULT	SCRIP	SERUM	SHINE
STUD	SADHU	SAUNA	SCROD	SERVE	**SHINY**
STUM	SADLY	SAURY	SCRUB	SERVO	SHIRE
STUN	SAFER	SAUTE	SCRUM	SETON	**SHIRK**
STYE	SAGER	SAVER	SCUBA	SETUP	SHIRR
SUBA	**SAGGY**	SAVIN	SCUDO	SEVEN	SHIRT
SUCH	SAGUM	SAVOR	**SCUFF**	SEVER	SHIST
SUCK	**SAHIB**	**SAVOY**	SCULK	SEWAN	**SHIVA**
SUDD	SAICE	**SAVVY**	SCULL	SEWAR	**SHIVE**
SUDS	SAIGA	SAWER	SCULP	SEWER	**SHLEP**
SUER	SAINT	SAYER	**SCURF**	**SEXTO**	SHOAL
SUET	SAITH	SAYID	SCUTA	**SHACK**	SHOAT
SUGH	**SAJOU**	SAYST	SCUTE	SHADE	**SHOCK**
SUIT	SAKER	SCALD	**SEAMY**	**SHADY**	SHOER
SULK	SALAD	SCALE	SEBUM	**SHAFT**	*SHOJI
SULU	SALAL	SCALL	SECCO	**SHAKE**	SHONE
SUMO	SALEP	SCALP	SEDAN	**SHAKO**	**SHOOK**
SUMP	SALIC	**SCALY**	SEDER	*SHAKY	SHOOL
SUNG	SALLY	**SCAMP**	SEDGE	SHALE	SHOON
SUNK	SALMI	SCANT	**SEDGY**	SHALL	SHOOT
SUNN	SALOL	SCAPE	SEDUM	SHALT	SHORE
SUPE	SALON	SCARE	SEEDY	**SHALY**	SHORL
SURA	SALPA	**SCARF**	SEELY	**SHAME**	SHORN
SURD	SALSA	SCARP	**SEEPY**	SHANK	SHORT
SURE	SALTY	SCART	SEGNO	**SHAPE**	SHOTE
SURF	SALVE	**SCARY**	SEGUE	SHARD	SHOUT
SUSS	SALVO	SCATT	SEINE	SHARE	**SHOVE**
SWAB	SAMBA	SCAUP	SEISE	**SHARK**	**SHOWN**
SWAG	SAMBO	SCAUR	SEISM	SHARN	**SHOWY**
SWAM	**SAMEK**	SCENA	**SEIZE**	**SHARP**	**SHOYU**
SWAN	SANDY	SCEND	SELAH	SHAUL	SHRED
SWAP	SANER	SCENE	SELLE	**SHAVE**	**SHREW**
SWAT	SANGA	SCENT	SELVA	**SHAWL**	**SHRUB**
SWAY	SANGH	**SCHAV**	SEMEN	**SHAWM**	SHRUG
SWIG	SANTO	**SCHMO**	SEMIS	**SHAWN**	**SHUCK**
SWIM	SAPID	**SCHUL**	SENGI	**SHEAF**	SHUNT
SWOB	SAPOR	**SCHWA**	SENNA	SHEAL	**SHUSH**
SWOP	**SAPPY**	SCION	SENOR	SHEAR	SHUTE
SWOT	SARAN	**SCOFF**	SENSA	SHEEN	SHUTT
SWUM	SAREE	SCOLD	SENSE	**SHEEP**	**SHYER**
SYBO	SARGE	SCONE	SENTE	SHEER	**SHYLY**
SYCE	SARIN	SCOOP	SENTI	SHEET	**SIBYL**
SYKE	**SARKY**	SCOOT	SEPAL	**SHEIK**	**SICKO**
SYLI	SAROD	SCOPE	SEPIA	**SHELF**	SIDED
SYNC	SAROS	SCORE	**SEPOY**	SHELL	SIDLE
SYNE	SASIN	SCORN	SEPTA	SHEND	SIEGE
SYPH	SASSY	SCOUR	SERAC	SHEOL	SIEUR

SIEVE	SKOAL	SMELL	SOLAR	SPEAN	SPRUE
SIGHT	**SKOSH**	SMELT	SOLDI	SPEAR	SPRUG
SIGIL	**SKULK**	**SMERK**	SOLDO	**SPECK**	SPUME
SIGMA	SKULL	SMILE	SOLED	SPECS	**SPUMY**
SIKER	**SKUNK**	**SMIRK**	SOLEI	SPEED	**SPUNK**
SILEX	*****SKYEY**	SMITE	SOLID	SPEEL	SPURN
SILKY	**SLACK**	**SMITH**	SOLON	SPEER	SPURT
SILLY	SLAIN	**SMOCK**	SOLUM	SPEIL	SPUTA
SILTY	SLAKE	**SMOKE**	SOLUS	SPEIR	*****SQUAB**
SILVA	SLANG	**SMOKY**	SOLVE	SPELL	*****SQUAD**
SIMAR	SLANK	SMOLT	SONAR	SPELT	*****SQUAM**
SINCE	SLANT	SMOTE	SONDE	SPEND	**SQUAT**
SINEW	SLASH	**SNACK**	SONIC	SPENT	*****SQUAW**
SINGE	SLATE	SNAFU	SONLY	SPERM	*****SQUEG**
SINUS	SLATY	SNAIL	SONNY	SPICA	*****SQUIB**
SIREE	SLAVE	SNAKE	SONSY	SPICE	*****SQUID**
SIREN	SLEEK	**SNAKY**	SOOEY	**SPICK**	**STACK**
SIRRA	SLEEP	SNARE	SOOTH	**SPICY**	STADE
SIRUP	SLEET	SNARK	SOOTY	SPIED	**STAFF**
SISAL	SLEPT	SNARL	**SOPHY**	SPIEL	STAGE
SISSY	SLICE	SNASH	SOPOR	SPIER	STAGY
SITAR	**SLICK**	SNATH	**SOPPY**	SPIES	STAID
SITUP	SLIDE	SNEAK	SOREL	**SPIFF**	STAIG
SITUS	SLIER	SNEAP	SORER	**SPIKE**	STAIN
SIVER	SLILY	**SNECK**	SORGO	**SPIKY**	STAIR
SIXMO	SLIME	SNEER	SORRY	SPILE	STAKE
SIXTE	**SLIMY**	SNELL	SORUS	SPILL	STALE
*****SIXTH**	SLING	**SNICK**	SOTOL	SPILT	STALK
*****SIXTY**	SLINK	SNIDE	SOUGH	SPINE	STALL
SIZAR	SLIPE	**SNIFF**	SOUND	**SPINY**	STAMP
SIZER	SLIPT	SNIPE	SOUPY	SPIRE	STAND
SKALD	SLOID	SNOOD	SOUSE	SPIRT	STANE
SKATE	**SLOJD**	SNOOK	SOUTH	**SPIRY**	STANG
SKEAN	SLOOP	SNOOL	SOWAR	SPITE	STANK
SKEEN	SLOPE	SNOOP	SOWER	*****SPITZ**	**STAPH**
SKEET	SLOSH	SNOOT	*****SOYUZ**	SPLAT	STARE
SKEIN	SLOTH	SNORE	**SOZIN**	**SPLAY**	STARK
SKELM	SLOYD	SNORT	SPACE	SPLIT	START
SKELP	**SLUFF**	SNOUT	**SPACY**	SPODE	STASH
SKENE	SLUMP	**SNOWY**	SPADE	SPOIL	STATE
SKIED	SLUNG	**SNUCK**	SPADO	**SPOKE**	STAVE
SKIER	SLUNK	**SNUFF**	**SPAHI**	**SPOOF**	STEAD
SKIES	SLURB	**SOAPY**	SPAIL	**SPOOK**	STEAK
SKIEY	SLURP	SOAVE	SPAIT	SPOOL	STEAL
*****SKIFF**	SLUSH	SOBER	**SPAKE**	SPOON	STEAM
SKILL	**SLYPE**	**SOCKO**	SPALE	SPOOR	STEED
SKIMO	**SMACK**	SOCLE	SPALL	SPORE	STEEK
SKIMP	SMALL	**SODDY**	SPANG	SPORT	STEEL
SKINK	SMALT	SODOM	**SPANK**	SPOUT	STEEP
SKINT	SMARM	SOFAR	SPARE	SPRAG	STEER
SKIRL	SMART	SOFTA	**SPARK**	SPRAT	STEIN
SKIRR	**SMASH**	**SOFTY**	SPASM	**SPRAY**	STELA
SKIRT	*****SMAZE**	**SOGGY**	SPATE	SPREE	STELE
SKITE	SMEAR	SOKOL	**SPAWN**	SPRIG	STENO
SKIVE	**SMEEK**	SOLAN	**SPEAK**	SPRIT	STERE

STERN	**STUCK**	**SWANK**	**SADDHU**	SANEST	SCALER
STICH	STUDY	SWARD	SADDLE	SANGAR	**SCAMPI**
STICK	**STUFF**	SWARE	SADISM	SANGER	**SCANTY**
STIED	STULL	**SWARF**	SADIST	SANIES	**SCARAB**
STIES	STUMP	**SWARM**	SAFARI	SANING	**SCARCE**
STIFF	STUNG	SWART	SAFEST	SANITY	SCARER
STILE	STUNK	**SWASH**	**SAFETY**	*SANJAK	SCAREY
STILL	STUNT	**SWATH**	SAFROL	SANNOP	SCARPH
STILT	STUPA	SWEAR	SAGBUT	SANNUP	**SCARRY**
STIME	STUPE	SWEAT	SAGEST	SANSAR	**SCATHE**
STIMY	STURT	SWEDE	SAGGAR	SANSEI	**SCATTY**
STING	STYLE	**SWEEP**	SAGGED	SANTIR	**SCENIC**
STINK	STYLI	**SWEER**	**SAGGER**	SANTOL	**SCHEMA**
STINT	**STYMY**	SWEET	SAGIER	SANTUR	**SCHEME**
STIPE	SUAVE	SWELL	SAILER	SAPOTA	**SCHISM**
STIRK	**SUBAH**	**SWEPT**	SAILOR	SAPOTE	**SCHIST**
STIRP	SUBER	**SWIFT**	SAIMIN	SAPOUR	*SCHIZO
STOAT	SUCRE	SWILL	SAITHE	**SAPPED**	*SCHIZY
STOCK	SUDOR	SWINE	**SAIYID**	**SAPPER**	**SCHLEP**
STOGY	SUDSY	SWING	SALAAM	SARAPE	**SCHMOE**
STOIC	SUEDE	**SWINK**	SALAMI	SARDAR	*SCHNOZ
STOKE	SUGAR	**SWIPE**	SALARY	SARODE	**SCHOOL**
STOLE	SUING	SWIRL	**SALIFY**	SARONG	**SCHORL**
STOMA	SUINT	**SWISH**	SALINA	SARSAR	*SCHRIK
STOMP	SUITE	SWISS	SALINE	SARSEN	**SCHROD**
STONE	SULFA	**SWITH**	SALIVA	SARTOR	*SCHTIK
STONY	SULFO	**SWIVE**	SALLET	**SASHAY**	**SCHUIT**
STOOD	**SULKY**	**SWOON**	SALLOW	SATANG	**SCHUSS**
STOOK	SULLY	**SWOOP**	SALMON	SATARA	SCILLA
STOOL	SUMAC	SWORD	SALOON	SATEEN	**SCLAFF**
STOOP	SUMMA	SWORE	SALOOP	SATING	**SCLERA**
STOPE	SUNNA	SWORN	SALPID	SATINY	*SCOLEX
STOPT	SUNNY	SWOUN	SALTER	SATIRE	**SCONCE**
STORE	SUNUP	SWUNG	SALTIE	SATORI	**SCORCH**
STORK	SUPER	**SYCEE**	**SALUKI**	SATRAP	SCORER
STORM	SUPRA	**SYLPH**	SALUTE	SAUCER	SCORIA
STORY	SURAH	**SYLVA**	SALVER	SAUGER	**SCOTCH**
STOSS	SURAL	**SYNCH**	SALVIA	SAUREL	SCOTER
STOUP	SURER	SYNOD	SALVOR	**SAVAGE**	SCOTIA
STOUR	**SURFY**	**SYNTH**	SAMARA	SAVANT	SCOUSE
STOUT	SURGE	SYREN	**SAMBAR**	SAVATE	**SCOUTH**
STOVE	SURGY	**SYRUP**	**SAMBUR**	SAVINE	**SCRAPE**
STOWP	SURLY	**SYSOP**	SAMECH	**SAVING**	**SCRAWL**
STRAP	SURRA	**SABBAT**	*SAMEKH	SAVIOR	**SCREAK**
STRAW	SUSHI	**SABBED**	SAMIEL	**SAVORY**	**SCREAM**
STRAY	SUTRA	**SABINE**	SAMITE	SAVOUR	**SCREED**
STREP	SUTTA	**SACBUT**	SAMLET	*SAWFLY	**SCREEN**
STREW	SWAGE	**SACHEM**	SAMOSA	SAWLOG	**SCREWY**
STRIA	SWAIL	**SACHET**	SAMPAN	SAWNEY	**SCRIBE**
STRIP	SWAIN	**SACKER**	**SAMPLE**	SAWYER	SCRIED
STROP	SWALE	*SACQUE	**SAMSHU**	*SAXONY	SCRIES
STROW	SWAMI	SACRAL	SANCTA	**SAYING**	**SCRIMP**
STROY	**SWAMP**	SACRED	SANDAL	**SAYYID**	**SCRIPT**
STRUM	**SWAMY**	**SACRUM**	SANDER	*SCABBY	**SCRIVE**
STRUT	SWANG	SADDEN	**SANDHI**	SCALAR	**SCROLL**

SCROOP	SELECT	SETTEE	*SHELVY	*SHTICK	SIPPED
SCRUFF	SELLER	SETTER	*SHEQEL	SIALID	SIPPER
SCULPT	SELSYN	SETTLE	SHERIF	SICCAN	SIPPET
*SCUMMY	SELVES	SEVERE	SHERPA	SICKEE	SIRDAR
SCURPY	SEMEME	SEWAGE	SHERRY	SICKEN	SIRING
SCURRY	SEMINA	SEWING	SHEUCH	SICKIE	SIRRAH
SCURVY	SEMPLE	SEXIER	SHEUGH	SICKLE	SIRREE
SCUTCH	SEMPRE	*SEXILY	SHEWER	*SICKLY	SISKIN
SCUTUM	SENARY	*SEXISM	SHIBAH	SIDDUR	SISTER
*SCUZZY	SENATE	SEXIST	SHIELD	SIDING	SISTRA
SCYTHE	SENDAL	*SEXPOT	SHIEST	SIDLER	SITCOM
SEABAG	SENDER	SEXTAN	*SHIFTY	SIENNA	SITING
SEABED	SENDUP	SEXTET	SHIKAR	SIERRA	SITTEN
SEADOG	SENECA	SEXTON	SHIKSA	SIESTA	SITTER
SEALER	SENEGA	SEXUAL	SHIKSE	SIFAKA	*SIZIER
SEAMAN	SENHOR	*SHABBY	*SHIMMY	SIFTER	*SIZING
SEAMER	SENILE	*SHACKO	SHINDY	SIGHER	*SIZZLE
SEANCE	SENIOR	SHADER	SHINER	SIGLOS	SKATER
SEARCH	SENITI	SHADOW	SHINNY	SIGNAL	SKATOL
SEARER	SENNET	SHADUF	SHIRTY	SIGNEE	SKEANE
SEASON	SENNIT	SHAGGY	*SHIVAH	SIGNER	SKEIGH
SEATER	SENORA	SHAIRD	SHIVER	SIGNET	SKERRY
SEAWAN	SENRYU	SHAIRN	SHLEPP	SIGNOR	*SKETCH
SEAWAY	SENSOR	SHAKER	*SHLOCK	SILAGE	SKEWER
SECANT	SENSUM	SHALED	SHLUMP	SILANE	SKIBOB
SECEDE	SENTRY	SHALEY	SHMEAR	SILENI	*SKIDDY
SECERN	SEPSIS	SHALOM	*SHMUCK	SILENT	SKIDOO
SECOND	SEPTAL	SHAMAN	SHNAPS	SILICA	SKIING
SECPAR	SEPTET	SHAMES	SHNOOK	SILKEN	*SKIMPY
SECRET	SEPTIC	*SHAMMY	SHOALY	SILLER	SKINNY
SECTOR	SEPTUM	SHAMOS	SHODDY	SILVAN	SKIVER
SECUND	*SEQUEL	SHAMOY	SHOFAR	SILVER	*SKIVVY
SECURE	*SEQUIN	SHAMUS	SHOGUN	*SILVEX	SKLENT
SEDATE	SERAIL	SHANDY	SHOLOM	SIMIAN	*SKYBOX
SEDILE	SERAPE	SHANNY	SHOPPE	SIMILE	*SKYCAP
SEDUCE	SERAPH	SHANTI	SHORAN	SIMILIN	SKYLIT
SEEDER	SERDAB	SHANTY	SHORTY	SIMMER	*SKYMAN
SEEING	SEREIN	SHAPER	SHOULD	SIMNEL	*SKYWAY
SEEKER	SERENE	SHARER	SHOVEL	SIMONY	SLAGGY
SEEMER	SEREST	SHARIF	SHOVER	SIMOOM	SLAKER
SEEMLY	SERIAL	SHARPY	SHOWER	SIMOON	SLALOM
SEESAW	SERIES	SHAUGH	SHRANK	SIMPER	SLANGY
SEETHE	SERINE	SHAVER	SHREWD	SIMPLE	SLANTY
SEGGAR	SERING	SHAVIE	SHRIEK	SIMPLY	SLATCH
SEICHE	SERMON	SHEATH	SHRIFT	SINEWY	SLATER
SEIDEL	SEROSA	SHEAVE	SHRIKE	SINFUL	SLATEY
SEINER	SEROUS	SHEENY	SHRILL	SINGER	SLAVER
SEISER	SERVAL	SHEEVE	SHRIMP	SINGLE	SLAVEY
SEISIN	SERVER	*SHEIKH	SHRINE	SINGLY	SLAYER
SEISOR	SESAME	SHEILA	SHRINK	SINKER	SLEAVE
*SEIZER	SESTET	SHEKEL	SHRIVE	SINNED	*SLEAZE
*SEIZIN	SETOFF	SHELLY	*SHROFF	SINNER	*SLEAZO
*SEIZOR	SETOSE	SHELTA	SHROUD	SINTER	*SLEAZY
SEJANT	SETOUS	SHELTY	SHROVE	SIPHON	SLEDGE
SELDOM	SETOUT	SHELVE	SHRUNK	SIPING	SLEEKY

SLEEPY	SMUGLY	SOLANO	SPADER	SPOKEN	*STANZA
SLEETY	SMUTCH	SOLATE	*SPADIX	SPONGE	STARCH
SLEEVE	SMUTTY	SOLDAN	SPAHEE	SPONGY	STARER
SLEIGH	SNAGGY	SOLDER	SPARER	SPOOFY	STARRY
SLEUTH	SNAPPY	SOLELY	SPARGE	*SPOOKY	STARVE
SLICER	SNARER	SOLEMN	SPARID	SPOONY	STASES
SLIDER	SNARKY	SOLEUS	*SPARKY	SPORAL	STASIS
SLIEST	SNARLY	SOLGEL	SPARRY	SPORTY	STATAL
SLIGHT	SNATCH	SOLIDI	SPARSE	SPOTTY	STATER
SLIMLY	SNATHE	SOLING	SPATHE	SPOUSE	STATIC
SLIMSY	*SNAZZY	SOLION	SPAVIE	SPRAIN	STATOR
SLINKY	SNEAKY	SOLUTE	SPAVIN	SPRANG	STATUE
SLIPPY	SNEESH	SOLVER	SPECIE	SPRAWL	STATUS
SLIPUP	*SNEEZE	SOMBER	SPEECH	SPREAD	STAYER
SLIVER	*SNEEZY	SOMBRE	SPEEDO	SPRENT	STEADY
SLOBBY	*SNIFFY	SOMITE	SPEEDY	SPRIER	STEAMY
SLOGAN	SNIPER	SONANT	SPEISE	SPRING	STEELY
SLOPER	SNIPPY	SONATA	SPEISS	SPRINT	STEEVE
SLOPPY	SNITCH	SONDER	*SPELTZ	SPRITE	STELLA
SLOSHY	SNIVEL	SONICS	SPENCE	*SPRITZ	STEMMA
SLOUCH	SNOBBY	SONNET	SPENSE	SPROUT	STEMMY
SLOUGH	SNOOPY	SONSIE	SPEWER	SPRUCE	STENCH
SLOVEN	SNOOTY	SOONER	SPHENE	SPRUCY	STEPPE
SLOWLY	*SNOOZE	SOOTHE	SPHERE	SPRUNG	STEREO
SLUDGE	*SNOOZY	SOPITE	SPHERY	*SPUNKY	STERIC
SLUDGY	SNORER	SOPPED	*SPHINX	SPURGE	STERNA
SLUICE	SNOTTY	SORBET	SPICER	SPURRY	STEROL
SLUICY	SNOUTY	SORBIC	SPICEY	SPUTUM	*STICKY
SLUING	SNUBBY	SORDID	SPIDER	*SQUALL	STIFLE
SLUMMY	*SNUFFY	SORDOR	*SPIFFY	*SQUAMA	STIGMA
SLURRY	SNUGLY	SORELY	SPIGOT	*SQUARE	STILLY
SLUSHY	SOAKER	SOREST	SPIKER	*SQUASH	STINGO
SLUTTY	SOARER	SORGHO	*SPIKEY	*SQUAWK	STINGY
SMALTI	SOBBER	SORING	SPILTH	*SQUEAK	STINKO
SMALTO	SOBEIT	SORNER	SPINAL	*SQUEAL	STINKY
SMARMY	SOBFUL	SORREL	SPINEL	*SQUILL	STIPEL
SMARTY	SOCAGE	SORROW	SPINET	*SQUINT	STIPES
SMEARY	SOCCER	SORTER	SPINNY	*SQUIRE	STIRPS
SMEGMA	SOCIAL	SORTIE	SPINOR	*SQUIRM	STITCH
SMELLY	SOCKET	SOTTED	SPINTO	*SQUIRT	STITHY
SMIDGE	SOCMAN	SOUARI	SPIRAL	*SQUISH	STIVER
*SMILAX	SODDED	SOUCAR	SPIREA	*SQUUSH	*STOCKY
SMILER	SODDEN	SOUDAN	SPIREM	SRADHA	STODGE
SMILEY	SODIUM	SOUGHT	SPIRIT	STABLE	STODGY
SMIRCH	SODOMY	SOURCE	SPITAL	STABLY	STOGEY
*SMIRKY	SOEVER	SOURLY	SPLAKE	STACTE	STOGIE
SMITER	SOFFIT	SOUTER	SPLASH	STADIA	STOKER
SMITHY	SOFTEN	SOVIET	SPLEEN	STAGER	STOLEN
SMOGGY	SOFTIE	SOVRAN	SPLENT	STAGEY	STOLID
SMOKER	SOFTLY	SOWANS	SPLICE	STAGGY	STOLON
*SMOKEY	SOGGED	SOWCAR	SPLINE	STALAG	STOMAL
SMOOCH	SOIGNE	SOWENS	SPLINT	STALKY	STONER
SMOOTH	SOIREE	*SOZINE	SPLORE	STAMEN	STONEY
SMUDGE	SOLACE	SPACER	SPLOSH	STANCE	STOOGE
SMUDGY	SOLAND	SPACEY	SPOILT	STANCH	STOPER

STORAX	STYLAR	SUNDOG	**SWOOSH**	SALTANT	SARDANA
STOREY	STYLER	**SUNDRY**	**SWOUND**	*SALTBOX	SARDINE
STORMY	STYLET	**SUNKEN**	**SYLVAN**	SALTERN	SARDIUS
STOUND	STYLUS	**SUNKET**	**SYLVIN**	SALTIER	SARMENT
STOURE	**STYMIE**	SUNLIT	**SYMBOL**	**SALTILY**	**SASHIMI**
STOURY	*STYRAX	SUNNAH	**SYNCOM**	SALTINE	**SASSABY**
STOVER	SUABLE	SUNNED	**SYNDET**	SALTING	SASSIER
STRAFE	**SUBBED**	SUNSET	**SYNDIC**	SALTIRE	SASSIES
STRAIN	**SUBDEB**	SUNTAN	**SYNGAS**	**SALTISH**	**SASSILY**
STRAIT	SUBDUE	**SUPERB**	*SYNTAX	SALTPAN	SATANIC
STRAKE	*SUBFIX	SUPINE	SYNURA	SALUTER	**SATCHEL**
STRAND	**SUBGUM**	**SUPPED**	**SYPHER**	**SALVAGE**	SATIATE
STRANG	SUBITO	**SUPPER**	**SYPHON**	SALVING	**SATIETY**
STRASS	SUBLET	**SUPPLE**	*SYRINX	**SAMBHUR**	SATINET
STRATA	SUBLOT	**SUPPLY**	**SYSTEM**	**SAMBUAR**	**SATISFY**
STRATH	**SUBMIT**	SURELY	*SYZYGY	**SAMBUCA**	**SATRAPY**
STRATI	SUBNET	SUREST	SABATON	*SAMBUKE	SATSUMA
STRAWY	SUBORN	SURETY	**SABAYON**	SAMISEN	**SATYRID**
STREAK	**SUBPAR**	SURFER	**SABBATH**	SAMOVAR	**SAUCING**
STREAM	SUBSEA	SURGER	**SABBING**	**SAMPLER**	SAUNTER
STREEK	SUBSET	SURIMI	SACATON	SAMSARA	SAURIAN
STREET	SUBTLE	SURREY	**SACCADE**	SAMURAI	SAUSAGE
STRESS	**SUBURB**	**SURTAX**	**SACCATE**	**SANCTUM**	SAUTOIR
STRICK	**SUBWAY**	**SURVEY**	**SACCULE**	**SANDBAG**	**SÁVABLE**
STRICT	**SUCCAH**	**SUSLIK**	*SACKBUT	**SANDBAR**	**SAVANNA**
STRIDE	**SUCCOR**	SUTLER	*SACKFUL	*SANDBOX	**SAVARIN**
STRIFE	**SUCKER**	SUTTEE	**SACKING**	**SANDBUR**	**SAVELOY**
STRIKE	**SUCKLE**	SUTURE	**SACLIKE**	**SANDDAB**	**SAVIOUR**
STRING	**SUDARY**	*SVARAJ	**SACRING**	**SANDFLY**	**SAVORER**
STRIPE	SUDDEN	SVELTE	SACRIST	**SANDHOG**	**SAVOURY**
STRIPT	SUDSER	*SWABBY	SADDLER	SANDIER	**SAWBILL**
STRIPY	**SUFFER**	**SWAGER**	SADIRON	SANDLOT	*SAWBUCK
STRIVE	*SUFFIX	*SWAMPY	SADNESS	SANDMAN	**SAWDUST**
STROBE	**SUGARY**	*SWANKY	**SAFFRON**	**SANDPIT**	*SAWFISH
STRODE	SUITER	*SWARAJ	**SAFROLE**	SANGRIA	**SAWLIKE**
STROKE	SUITOR	**SWARTH**	**SAGAMAN**	SANICLE	**SAWMILL**
STROLL	*SUKKAH	**SWARTY**	**SAGGARD**	SANTIMS	*SAXHORN
STROMA	SULCUS	**SWATCH**	**SAGGING**	SANTOUR	*SAXTUBA
STRONG	SULDAN	**SWATHE**	SAGIEST	*SAPAJOU	**SCABBLE**
STROOK	**SULFID**	**SWAYER**	SAGUARO	SAPHEAD	**SCABIES**
STROUD	**SULFUR**	**SWEATY**	**SAHIWAL**	**SAPHENA**	**SCALADE**
STROVE	**SULKER**	**SWEENY**	**SAHUARO**	SAPIENS	**SCALADO**
STRUCK	SULLEN	**SWEEPY**	SAILING	SAPIENT	**SCALAGE**
STRUMA	**SULPHA**	**SWERVE**	**SAINTLY**	SAPLESS	SCALARE
STRUNG	SULTAN	**SWEVEN**	SALABLE	**SAPLING**	**SCALDIC**
STRUNT	**SULTRY**	*SWIMMY	*SALCHOW	SAPONIN	SCALENE
STUBBY	**SUMACH**	**SWINGE**	SALICIN	*SAPPHIC	**SCALEUP**
STUCCO	**SUMMED**	**SWINGY**	SALIENT	**SAPPING**	SCALIER
STUDIO	**SUMMER**	**SWIPLE**	SALLIED	**SAPROBE**	**SCALING**
STUDLY	**SUMMIT**	**SWIRLY**	SALLIER	**SAPSAGO**	**SCALLOP**
*STUFFY	**SUMMON**	*SWISHY	SALLIES	**SAPWOOD**	**SCALPEL**
STUMPY	**SUNBOW**	**SWITCH**	**SALLOWY**	**SARCASM**	**SCALPER**
STUPID	SUNDAE	**SWITHE**	SALPIAN	**SARCOID**	**SCAMPER**
STUPOR	SUNDER	**SWIVEL**	*SALPINX	**SARCOMA**	**SCANDAL**
STURDY	**SUNDEW**	**SWIVET**	**SALSIFY**	SARCOUS	**SCANDIA**

SCANNED	SCOWDER	SEAPORT	SENATOR	SHADIER	SHERBET
SCANNER	SCOWLER	SEAREST	**SENDOFF**	SHADILY	SHEREEF
SCANTLY	SCRAGGY	**SEASICK**	SENECIO	SHADING	*SHERIFF
SCAPOSE	SCRAICH	SEASIDE	SENHORA	SHADOOF	SHEROOT
SCAPULA	SCRAIGH	SEATING	SENOPIA	*SHADOWY	SHERRIS
SCARIER	SCRAPER	SEAWALL	SENSATE	*SHAHDOM	SHIATSU
*SCARIFY	SCRAPIE	SEAWANT	SENSING	SHAITAN	*SHIATZU
SCARILY	*SCRAPPY	SEAWARD	**SENSORY**	*SHAKEUP	*SHICKER
SCARING	SCRATCH	SEAWARE	SENSUAL	SHAKIER	*SHICKSA
SCARLET	*SCRAWLY	SEAWEED	SENTIMO	*SHAKILY	SHIFTER
SCARPER	*SCRAWNY	SEBACIC	*SEPPUKU	*SHAKING	SHIKARI
SCARRED	*SCREAKY	SEBASIC	SEPTATE	SHALIER	*SHIKKER
SCARVES	SCREECH	SECEDER	SEPTIME	SHALLOP	SHILPIT
SCATTED	SCREWER	SECLUDE	*SEQUELA	SHALLOT	SHIMMER
SCATTER	SCREWUP	SECONDE	*SEQUENT	SHALLOW	SHINDIG
SCAUPER	SCRIBAL	SECONDO	*SEQUOIA	SHAMBLE	SHINGLE
SCENERY	SCRIBER	SECRECY	SERFAGE	SHAMING	SHINGLY
SCEPTER	SCRIEVE	SECRETE	**SERFDOM**	SHAMMAS	SHINIER
SCEPTIC	*SCRIMPY	SECTARY	SERFISH	*SHAMMED	SHINILY
SCEPTRE	SCROGGY	SECTILE	SERGING	SHAMMER	SHINING
*SCHAPPE	SCROOCH	SECTION	SERIATE	SHAMMES	SHINNED
SCHEMER	SCROOGE	SECULAR	SERICIN	SHAMMOS	SHINNEY
*SCHERZO	SCROTUM	SECURER	SERIEMA	SHAMOIS	SHIPLAP
*SCHIZZY	SCROUGE	SEDARIM	SERINGA	SHAMPOO	SHIPMAN
*SCHLEPP	*SCRUBBY	SEDUCER	SERIOUS	SHANTEY	*SHIPPED
*SCHLOCK	*SCRUFFY	SEEDBED	SERPENT	SHANTIH	SHIPPEN
*SCHLUMP	SCRUNCH	SEEDIER	**SERPIGO**	*SHAPELY	SHIPPER
*SCHMALZ	SCRUPLE	SEEDILY	SERRANO	SHAPEUP	SHIPPON
SCHMEAR	*SCUFFLE	SEEDMAN	SERRATE	SHAPING	*SHIPWAY
SCHMEER	SCULKER	SEEDPOD	SERVANT	SHARING	SHIRKER
SCHMOOS	SCULLER	SEEMING	**SERVICE**	SHARKER	SHITAKE
*SCHMUCK	SCULPIN	SEEPAGE	SERVILE	SHARPEN	SHITTAH
SCHNAPS	SCUMBAG	SEERESS	**SERVING**	SHARPER	SHITTIM
*SCHNOOK	SCUMBLE	SEGETAL	SESSILE	SHARPIE	*SHIVERY
*SCHNOZZ	SCUMMED	SEGMENT	SESSION	*SHARPLY	*SHLUMPY
SCHOLAR	SCUMMER	SEISING	SESTINA	SHASLIK	*SHMALTZ
*SCHTICK	SCUNNER	SEISURE	SESTINE	SHATTER	*SHMOOZE
SCIATIC	SCUPPER	*SEIZING	*SETBACK	SHAVING	*SHOCKER
SCIENCE	SCURRIL	*SEIZURE	SETLINE	SHEARER	SHODDEN
SCISSOR	SCUTAGE	SEJEANT	SETTING	SHEATHE	SHOEPAC
SCIURID	SCUTATE	SELENIC	SETTLER	SHEBANG	*SHOOFLY
*SCOFFER	SCUTTER	SELFDOM	SETTLOR	SHEBEAN	SHOOTER
SCOLDER	SCUTTLE	SELFISH	SEVENTH	SHEBEEN	*SHOPBOY
SCOLLOP	*SCYPHUS	SELLOUT	SEVENTY	SHEDDER	*SHOPHAR
SCOOPER	SEABIRD	*SELTZER	SEVERAL	SHEENEY	SHOPMAN
SCOOTER	SEABOOT	SELVAGE	*SEVICHE	SHEENIE	*SHOPPED
SCOPULA	*SEACOCK	SEMATIC	SEXIEST	SHEETER	SHOPPER
*SCORIFY	SEAFOOD	SEMIDRY	SEXLESS	*SHEGETZ	SHORING
SCORING	SEAFOWL	SEMIFIT	SEXTAIN	SHEITAN	SHORTEN
SCORNER	SEAGIRT	SEMILOG	SEXTANT	SHELLAC	SHORTIA
SCOTOMA	SEAGULL	SEMIMAT	SEXTILE	SHELLER	SHORTIE
SCOTTIE	SEALANT	SEMINAL	SFERICS	SHELTER	SHORTLY
SCOURER	SEALERY	SEMINAR	SFUMATO	SHELTIE	SHOTGUN
SCOURGE	SEAMARK	SEMIPRO	*SHACKLE	SHELVER	SHOTTED
SCOUTER	SEAMIER	SEMIRAW	*SHADFLY	SHELVES	SHOTTEN

SHOUTER	SILENTS	*SKIFFLE	SLIDING	SMUTTED	SOLARIA
SHOVING	SILENUS	SKILFUL	SLIMIER	SNAFFLE	SOLATIA
*SHOWBIZ	SILESIA	SKILLET	SLIMILY	SNAPPED	SOLDIER
*SHOWERY	SILICIC	*SKIMMER	SLIMING	SNAPPER	SOLERET
SHOWIER	SILICLE	SKINFUL	SLIMMED	SNARLER	SOLFEGE
*SHOWILY	SILICON	*SKINKER	SLIMMER	*SNATCHY	SOLICIT
SHOWING	*SILIQUA	SKINNED	SLIMPSY	SNEAKER	SOLIDLY
*SHOWMAN	*SILIQUE	SKINNER	SLINGER	SNEERER	SOLIDUS
*SHOWOFF	SILKIER	*SKIPPED	SLIPOUT	*SNEEZER	SOLITON
*SHRIEKY	SILKILY	*SKIPPER	SLIPPED	SNICKER	SOLOIST
*SHRIMPY	SILURID	*SKIPPET	SLIPPER	SNIFFER	SOLUBLE
SHRIVEL	SILVERN	SKIRRET	*SLIPWAY	SNIFFLE	SOLUBLY
SHRIVER	SILVERY	SKIRTER	SLITHER	SNIFTER	SOLVATE
*SHRUBBY	SILVICS	SKITTER	SLITTED	SNIGGER	SOLVENT
SHTETEL	SIMILAR	SKITTLE	SLOBBER	SNIGGLE	SOLVING
*SHUCKER	SIMIOID	SKIWEAR	SLOGGER	SNIPPED	SOMEDAY
SHUDDER	SIMIOUS	*SKOOKUM	*SLOPPED	SNIPPER	*SOMEHOW
*SHUFFLE	SIMITAR	*SKREEGH	SLOTTED	SNIPPET	SOMEONE
SHUNNER	*SIMPLEX	*SKREIGH	*SLOUCHY	SNOOKER	*SOMEWAY
SHUNTER	SIMULAR	*SKULKER	SLOUGHY	SNOOPER	SONANCE
SHUTEYE	SINCERE	*SKYDIVE	SLOWISH	*SNOOZER	SONGFUL
*SHUTOFF	SINGLET	*SKYHOOK	SLUBBER	*SNOOZLE	SONHOOD
SHUTOUT	SINKAGE	*SKYJACK	SLUGGED	SNORKEL	SONLESS
SHUTTER	SINLESS	*SKYLARK	SLUGGER	SNORTER	SONLIKE
SHUTTLE	SINNING	SKYLINE	SLUMBER	SNOWCAP	*SONOVOX
*SHYLOCK	SINOPIA	*SKYPHOS	SLUMISM	SNOWIER	SONSHIP
SHYNESS	SINSYNE	SKYSAIL	SLUMMED	SNOWILY	SOOTHER
SHYSTER	SINUATE	*SKYWALK	SLUMMER	SNOWMAN	SOOTHLY
SIALOID	SINUOUS	*SKYWARD	SLUMGUM	SNUBBER	SOPHIES
SIAMANG	SIPPING	SLABBER	SLURRED	SNUFFER	SOPHISM
SIAMESE	SIRLOIN	SLACKEN	SLYNESS	SNUFFLE	SOPHIST
SIBLING	SIROCCO	SLACKER	*SMACKER	*SNUFFLY	SOPPING
*SICKBAY	SISTRUM	*SLACKLY	SMARTEN	SNUGGLE	SOPRANO
*SICKBED	SITHENS	SLAINTE	SMARTIE	SOAKAGE	SORBATE
*SICKISH	SITTING	SLAMMER	SMARTLY	*SOAPBOX	SORBENT
SICKOUT	SITUATE	SLANDER	SMASHER	SOAPIER	SORBOSE
SIDEARM	*SIXFOLD	*SLAPPED	SMASHUP	SOAPILY	SORCERY
SIDEBAR	SIXTEEN	SLAPPER	SMATTER	SOARING	SORDINE
SIDECAR	*SIXTHLY	SLASHER	SMEARER	SOBERLY	SORDINO
SIDEMAN	*SIZABLE	SLATHER	SMECTIC	SOCAGER	SORGHUM
SIDEWAY	*SIZIEST	SLATIER	SMEDDUM	SOCCAGE	SORITES
SIEMENS	*SIZZLER	SLATING	SMELLER	SOCIETY	SOROCHE
SIENITE	*SJAMBOK	SLATTED	SMELTER	*SOCKEYE	SORORAL
SIFTING	SKATING	SLAVERY	SMIDGEN	*SOCKMAN	SOROSIS
SIGANID	SKATOLE	SLAVING	SMIDGIN	SODDING	SORRIER
SIGHTER	SKEETER	SLAVISH	SMIRKER	SOFTIES	SORRILY
SIGHTLY	SKELLUM	SLEDDER	SMITING	SOFTISH	SOTTISH
SIGMOID	SKELTER	SLEEKEN	SMITTEN	SOIGNEE	SOUBISE
SIGNAGE	SKEPSIS	SLEEKIT	SMOKING	SOILAGE	SOUFFLE
SIGNIFY	*SKEPTIC	SLEEKLY	SMOLDER	SOILURE	SOULFUL
SIGNIOR	*SKETCHY	SLEEPER	*SMOOCHY	SOJOURN	SOUNDER
SIGNORA	SKIABLE	SLEIGHT	*SMOOTHY	SOKEMAN	SOUNDLY
SIGNORE	SKIDDER	SLENDER	SMOTHER	SOLACER	SOUPCON
SIGNORY	SKIDDOO	SLICKER	SMUGGLE	SOLANIN	SOURISH
SILENCE	*SKIDWAY	*SLICKLY	*SMUTCHY	SOLANUM	SOURSOP

SOUTANE	SPHERAL	SPONSOR	STABILE	STEELIE	STOMATE
SOUTHER	SPHERIC	SPOOFER	STABLER	STEEPEN	STOMPER
*SOVKHOZ	SPICERY	SPOONEY	STACKER	STEEPER	STONIER
SOYBEAN	SPICIER	SPOROID	*STACKUP	STEEPLE	STONILY
*SOYMILK	SPICILY	SPORRAN	STADDLE	STEEPLY	STONING
*SOZZLED	SPICING	SPORTER	STADIUM	STEERER	STONISH
SPACIAL	SPICULA	SPORTIF	STAFFER	STELLAR	STOOKER
SPACING	SPICULE	SPORULE	STAGGED	STEMMED	STOOLIE
*SPACKLE	SPIDERY	SPOTLIT	STAGGER	STEMMER	STOOPER
SPADING	SPIEGEL	SPOTTER	STAGGIE	STEMSON	STOPGAP
SPAEING	SPIELER	SPOUSAL	STAGIER	*STENCHY	STOPING
SPALLER	SPIKING	SPOUTER	STAGILY	STENCIL	STOPPED
SPANCEL	SPILING	*SPRAWLY	STAGING	STENGAH	STOPPER
*SPANDEX	SPILLER	SPRAYER	STAINER	STENOKY	STOPPLE
SPANGLE	SPINACH	SPRIEST	STAITHE	STENTOR	STORAGE
SPANGLY	SPINAGE	SPRIGGY	STALKER	STEPPED	STORIED
SPANIEL	SPINATE	SPRIGHT	STAMINA	STEPPER	STORIES
SPANKER	SPINDLE	SPRINGE	STAMMEL	STEPSON	STORING
SPANNED	SPINDLY	SPRINGY	STAMMER	STERILE	STOURIE
SPANNER	SPINIER	SPUDDER	STAMPER	STERLET	STOUTEN
SPAREST	SPINIES	SPUMIER	STANDBY	STERNAL	STOUTLY
SPARGER	SPINNER	SPUMING	STANDEE	STERNLY	STOWAGE
SPARING	SPINNEY	SPUMONE	STANDER	STERNUM	STRAFER
SPARKER	*SPINOFF	SPUMONI	STANDUP	STEROID	STRANGE
SPARKLE	SPINOSE	SPUMOUS	STANINE	STERTOR	STRATAL
*SPARKLY	SPINOUS	SPUNKIE	STANING	STETSON	STRATUM
SPAROID	SPINOUT	SPURNER	STANNIC	STEWARD	STRATUS
SPARRED	SPINULA	SPURRED	STANNUM	STEWBUM	STRAYER
SPARROW	SPINULE	SPURRER	STARDOM	STEWPAN	STREAKY
SPARTAN	SPIRAEA	SPURREY	STARETS	STHENIA	STREAMY
SPASTIC	SPIRANT	SPURTLE	STARING	STIBIAL	STRETCH
SPATHIC	SPIREME	SPUTNIK	STARLET	STIBINE	STRETTA
SPATIAL	SPIRIER	SPUTTER	STARLIT	STIBIUM	STRETTO
SPATTED	SPIRING	*SQUABBY	STARRED	STICKER	STREWER
SPATTER	SPIROID	*SQUALID	STARTER	STICKIT	STRIATE
SPATULA	SPIRULA	*SQUALLY	STARTLE	STICKLE	STRIDER
*SPATZLE	SPITING	*SQUALOR	STARTSY	*STICKUM	STRIDOR
SPAWNER	SPITTED	*SQUARER	STARTUP	*STICKUP	STRIGIL
SPEAKER	SPITTER	'SQUASHY	STARVER	STIFFEN	STRIKER
SPEARER	SPITTLE	*SQUATTE	STATANT	*STIFFLY	STRINGY
SPECIAL	*SPLASHY	*SQUATTY	STATELY	STIFLER	STRIPER
*SPECIFY	SPLEENY	*SQUAWKE	STATICE	STINGER	STRIVER
*SPECKLE	SPLENIA	*SQUEAKY	STATING	STINKER	STROBIC
SPECTER	SPLENIC	*SQUEEZE	STATION	STINTER	STROBIL
SPECTRA	SPLICER	*SQUELCH	STATISM	STIPEND	STROKER
SPECTRE	SPLODGE	*SQUIFFY	STATIST	STIPPLE	STROPHE
SPEEDER	SPLOTCH	*SQUILLA	STATIVE	STIPULE	STROPPY
SPEEDUP	SPLURGE	*SQUINCH	STATURE	STIRRED	STROYER
SPELEAN	SPLURGY	*SQUINNY	STATUSY	STIRRER	STRUDEL
SPELLER	SPOILER	*SQUINTY	STATUTE	STIRRUP	STUBBLE
SPELTER	SPONDEE	*SQUIRMY	STAUNCH	STOCKER	STUBBLY
SPELUNK	SPONGER	*SQUISHY	STEALER	STOKING	STUDDIE
SPENCER	SPONGIN	*SQUOOSH	STEALTH	STOLLEN	STUDENT
SPENDER	SPONSAL	SRADDHA	STEAMER	STOMACH	STUDIED
SPHENIC	SPONSON	STABBER	STEARIN	STOMATA	STUDIER

STUDIES	SUBLATE	**SULFATE**	SURMISE	**SWIPPLE**	SAGENESS
STUFFER	**SUBLIME**	**SULFIDE**	SURNAME	**SWISHER**	SAGITTAL
STUIVER	SUBLINE	**SULFITE**	SURPASS	**SWITHER**	**SAILBOAT**
STUMBLE	**SUBMENU**	**SULFONE**	SURPLUS	*SWITHLY	**SAILFISH**
STUMMED	**SUBMISS**	**SULFURY**	SURREAL	SWIVING	SAINFOIN
STUMPER	SUBORAL	SULLAGE	SURTOUT	*SWIZZLE	SAINTDOM
STUNNED	SUBOVAL	**SULPHID**	SURVEIL	SWOBBER	**SALACITY**
STUNNER	**SUBPART**	**SULPHUR**	SURVIVE	SWOLLEN	SALADANG
*STUPEFY	SUBPENA	SULTANA	SUSPECT	SWOONER	**SALARIAT**
STUTTER	**SUBPLOT**	SUMLESS	SUSPEND	SWOOPER	**SALEABLE**
STYGIAN	SUBRACE	**SUMMAND**	SUSPIRE	SWOTTER	**SALEROOM**
STYLATE	SUBRENT	**SUMMARY**	SUSTAIN	SYCOSIS	**SALESMAN**
STYLING	**SUBRING**	**SUMMATE**	SUTURAL	**SYENITE**	**SALICINE**
STYLISE	SUBRULE	**SUMMERY**	SWABBER	**SYLLABI**	**SALIENCE**
STYLISH	SUBSALE	**SUMMING**	SWABBIE	*SYLPHID	**SALIENCY**
STYLIST	**SUBSECT**	**SUMMONS**	SWADDLE	SYLVINE	**SALINITY**
STYLITE	SUBSERE	**SUMPTER**	SWAGGED	SYLVITE	*SALINIZE
*STYLIZE	**SUBSIDE**	*SUNBACK	**SWAGGER**	**SYMBION**	**SALIVATE**
STYLOID	**SUBSIDY**	**SUNBATH**	SWAGGIE	**SYMBIOT**	**SALMONID**
STYPSIS	SUBSIST	**SUNBEAM**	SWAGING	*SYMPTOM	SALSILLA
STYPTIC	SUBSITE	SUNBELT	SWAGMAN	SYNAGOG	**SALTBUSH**
STYRENE	SUBSOIL	**SUNBIRD**	SWALLOW	SYNANON	**SALTIEST**
SUASION	**SUBSUME**	**SUNBURN**	SWAMIES	**SYNAPSE**	**SALTLESS**
SUAVITY	**SUBTASK**	**SUNDECK**	SWAMPER	SYNCARP	**SALTLIKE**
SUBACID	SUBTEEN	SUNDIAL	SWANNED	*SYNCHRO	**SALTNESS**
SUBADAR	**SUBTEND**	**SUNDOWN**	SWANPAN	SYNCOPE	*SALTWORK
SUBALAR	SUBTEST	**SUNFAST**	SWAPPER	**SYNERGY**	**SALTWORT**
SUBAREA	*SUBTEXT	**SUNFISH**	SWARMER	**SYNESIS**	**SALUTARY**
SUBARID	SUBTILE	**SUNGLOW**	*SWARTHY	SYNFUEL	**SALVABLE**
SUBATOM	SUBTONE	**SUNLAMP**	SWASHER	*SYNGAMY	**SALVAGEE**
SUBBASE	**SUBTYPE**	SUNLAND	SWATHER	*SYNONYM	**SALVAGER**
SUBBASS	SUBUNIT	SUNLESS	SWATTED	SYNOVIA	*SALVIFIC
SUBBING	**SUBVENE**	**SUNLIKE**	SWATTER	SYNTONY	**SAMARIUM**
SUBCELL	**SUBVERT**	SUNNING	*SWAYFUL	SYRINGA	**SAMENESS**
SUBCLAN	*SUBZERO	SUNRISE	**SWEARER**	SYRINGE	*SAMIZDAT
SUBCODE	*SUBZONE	**SUNROOF**	**SWEATER**	*SYRPHID	*SAMPHIRE
SUBCOOL	**SUCCEED**	**SUNROOM**	**SWEEPER**	**SYSTOLE**	**SAMPLING**
SUBCULT	**SUCCESS**	SUNSPOT	**SWEETEN**	SABBATIC	**SANATIVE**
SUBDEAN	**SUCCORY**	SUNSUIT	**SWEETIE**	SABOTAGE	*SANCTIFY
SUBDUAL	**SUCCOTH**	**SUNWARD**	**SWEETLY**	SABOTEUR	**SANCTION**
SUBDUCE	**SUCCOUR**	**SUNWISE**	**SWELTER**	SABULOSE	**SANCTITY**
SUBDUCT	**SUCCUBA**	**SUPPING**	**SWELTRY**	SABULOUS	SANDARAC
SUBDUER	*SUCCUMB	**SUPPORT**	SWERVER	SACCULAR	*SANDBANK
SUBECHO	**SUCCUSS**	**SUPPOSE**	SWIDDEN	SACCULUS	**SANDBURR**
SUBEDIT	**SUCKLER**	**SUPREME**	SWIFTER	*SACKLIKE	*SANDFISH
SUBERIC	**SUCRASE**	**SUPREMO**	*SWIFTLY	*SACKSFUL	**SANDIEST**
SUBERIN	**SUCROSE**	SURBASE	SWIGGER	SACRARIA	**SANDLIKE**
SUBFILE	**SUCTION**	SURCOAT	SWILLER	SACRISTY	**SANDLING**
SUBFUSC	**SUFFARI**	**SURFACE**	SWIMMER	SADDLERY	**SANDPEEP**
SUBGOAL	*SUFFICE	**SURFEIT**	SWINDLE	**SADDLING**	**SANDPILE**
SUBHEAD	**SUFFUSE**	**SURFIER**	*SWINGBY	SAFENESS	**SANDSHOE**
SUBIDEA	**SUGGEST**	**SURFING**	**SWINGER**	SAFRANIN	**SANDSOAP**
SUBITEM	**SUICIDE**	SURGEON	**SWINGLE**	**SAGACITY**	**SANDSPUR**
*SUBJECT	**SUITING**	**SURGERY**	SWINISH	SAGAMORE	*SANDWICH
*SUBJOIN	SULCATE	**SURGING**	SWINNEY	SAGANASH	**SANDWORM**

SANDWORT	SAVAGISM	*SCHLOCKY	*SCRAPPED	SEASHELL	*SELFHOOD
SANENESS	SAVANNAH	*SCHMALTZ	SCRAPPER	SEASHORE	SELFLESS
SANGAREE	*SAVINGLY	*SCHMALZY	SCRAPPLE	SEASONAL	SELFNESS
SANGUINE	SAVORIER	*SCHMELZE	*SCRATCHY	SEASONER	SELFSAME
SANITARY	SAVORIES	*SCHMOOSE	SCRAWLER	SEATLESS	*SELFWARD
SANITATE	SAVOROUS	*SCHMOOZE	SCREAMER	SEATMATE	SELVEDGE
SANITIES	SAVOURER	*SCHNAPPS	*SCREECHY	SEATRAIN	SEMANTIC
SANITISE	SAWBONES	*SCHNECKE	SCREENER	*SEATWORK	SEMESTER
*SANITIZE	SAWHORSE	*SCHOLIUM	SCRIBBLE	SEAWATER	SEMIARID
SANNYASI	SAWTOOTH	SCHOONER	SCRIMPER	SECALOSE	SEMIBALD
SANSERIF	*SAXATILE	*SCHRIEVE	SCRIMPIT	SECANTLY	SEMICOMA
SANTALIC	SAYONARA	SCHUSSER	*SCRIPTER	SECATEUR	SEMIDEAF
SANTALOL	*SCABBARD	SCIAENID	SCROFULA	SECONDER	SEMIDOME
SANTONIN	SCABIOSA	SCIATICA	*SCROOTCH	SECONDLY	SEMIGALA
SAPIDITY	SCABIOUS	SCILICET	SCROUNGE	SECRETIN	SEMIHARD
SAPIENCE	SCABLAND	SCIMETAR	SCROUNGY	SECRETLY	*SEMIHIGH
*SAPIENCY	*SCABLIKE	SCIMITAR	SCRUBBER	SECRETOR	*SEMIHOBO
*SAPONIFY	SCABROUS	SCIMITER	SCRUTINY	SECTORAL	SEMIMATT
SAPONINE	*SCAFFOLD	SCINCOID	*SCUFFLER	SECUNDUM	SEMIMUTE
SAPONITE	SCALABLE	SCIOLISM	SCULLERY	SECUREST	SEMINARY
*SAPPHIRE	SCALAWAG	SCIOLIST	SCULLION	SECURING	SEMINUDE
*SAPPHISM	SCALENUS	SCIROCCO	SCULPTOR	SECURITY	SEMIOSTS
*SAPPHIST	SCALEPAN	SCIRRHUS	*SCUMLIKE	SEDATION	SEMIOTIC
SAPREMIA	SCALIEST	SCISSILE	*SCUMMING	SEDATIVE	SEMISOFT
SAPROPEL	SCALLION	SCISSION	*SCUPPAUG	SEDERUNT	SEMITIST
SARABAND	*SCAMMONY	SCISSURE	SCURRIED	SEDILIUM	SEMITONE
SARCENET	*SCAMPISH	SCIURINE	SCURRIES	SEDIMENT	SEMIWILD
SARDONIC	SCANDENT	SCIUROID	SCURRILE	SEDITION	SEMOLINA
*SARDONYX	SCANDIUM	*SCLAFFER	*SCUTCHER	SEDULITY	SEMPLICE
SARGASSO	SCANNING	SCLEREID	SCUTELLA	SEDULOUS	SENARIUS
SARMENTA	SCANSION	SCLERITE	*SCYPHATE	*SEECATCH	SENILELY
SARODIST	SCANTIER	SCLEROID	*SEABEACH	*SEEDCAKE	SENILITY
SARSENET	SCANTIES	SCLEROMA	SEABOARD	SEEDCASE	SENNIGHT
SARTORII	*SCAPHOID	SCLEROSE	SEABORNE	SEEDIEST	SENORITA
SASSIEST	SCAPULAR	SCLEROUS	SEACOAST	SEEDLESS	SENSEFUL
SASSWOOD	*SCARCELY	*SCOFFLAW	SEACRAFT	SEEDLIKE	SENSIBLE
SASTRUGA	*SCARCITY	SCOLDING	SEADROME	SEEDLING	SENSILLA
SATANISM	*SCARFPIN	SCOLIOMA	SEAFARER	SEEDSMAN	SENSORIA
SATANIST	SCARIEST	*SCOOPFUL	SEAFLOOR	SEEDTIME	SENSUOUS
SATIABLE	SCARIOSE	*SCORCHER	SEAFRONT	SEICENTO	SENTENCE
SATINPOD	SCARIOUS	SCOREPAD	SEAGOING	SEIGNEUR	SENTIENT
SATIRISE	SCARLESS	SCORNFUL	SEALLIKE	SEIGNIOR	SENTINEL
SATIRIST	SCARRING	SCORPION	SEALSKIN	SEIGNORY	SEPARATE
*SATIRIZE	*SCATBACK	SCOTOPIA	SEAMIEST	SEISMISM	SEPTARIA
SATIRTSE	SCATTING	SCOURGER	SEAMLESS	SELADANG	SEPTETTE
SATURANT	SCAVENGE	SCOURING	SEAMLIKE	SELAMLIK	SEPTUPLE
SATURATE	SCENARIO	SCOUTHER	SEAMOUNT	SELCOUTH	*SEQUENCE
*SAUCEBOX	SCENICAL	SCOUTING	SEAMSTER	SELECTEE	*SEQUENCY
SAUCEPAN	SCEPTRAL	SCRABBLE	SEAPIECE	SELECTLY	*SEQUITUR
SAUROPOD	SCHEDULE	*SCRABBLY	SEAPLANE	SELECTOR	SERAGLIO
SAUTERNE	SCHILLER	*SCRAGGLY	*SEAQUAKE	SELENATE	*SERAPHIM
SAUTOIRE	*SCHIZIER	SCRAMBLE	SEARCHER	SELENIDE	SERENADE
*SAVAGERY	*SCHIZOID	*SCRAMJET	SEAROBIN	SELENITE	SERENATA
SAVAGEST	*SCHIZONT	SCRANNEL	SEASCAPE	SELENIUM	SERENITY
SAVAGING	SCHLIERE	SCRAPING	SEASCOUT	SELFHEAL	*SERFHOOD

*SERFLIKE	SHANTIES	*SHMALTZY	SIDEHILL	SIMULANT	*SKYDIVER
SERGEANT	SHANTUNG	SHOEBILL	*SIDEKICK	SIMULATE	*SKYLIGHT
SERIALLY	*SHASHLIK	SHOEHORN	SIDELINE	SINAPISM	*SKYWARDS
SERIATIM	SHEALING	SHOELACE	SIDELING	SINCIPUT	*SKYWRITE
*SERJEANT	SHEARING	SHOELESS	SIDELONG	SINECURE	*SLABBERY
SEROLOGY	SHEATHER	*SHOEPACK	SIDEREAL	SINFONIA	SLABBING
SEROSITY	SHEDABLE	SHOETREE	SIDERITE	SINGSONG	SLABLIKE
SEROTINE	SHEDDING	SHOOTING	*SIDESHOW	SINGULAR	SLAPDASH
SEROTYPE	*SHEDLIKE	SHOOTOUT	SIDESLIP	*SINICIZE	*SLAPJACK
SERRANID	SHEENFUL	SHOPGIRL	SIDESPIN	SINISTER	SLAPPING
SERVABLE	*SHEEPCOT	*SHOPLIFT	SIDESTEP	*SINKHOLE	SLASHING
SERVICER	*SHEEPDOG	*SHOPPING	*SIDEWALK	SINOLOGY	SLATIEST
SERVITOR	*SHEEPISH	*SHOPTALK	SIDEWALL	SINUSOID	SLATTERN
SESAMOID	*SHEEPMAN	*SHOPWORN	SIDEWARD	SIPHONAL	SLATTING
SESSPOOL	*SHEETFED	SHORTAGE	*SIDEWAYS	*SIPHONIC	SLAVERER
SESTERCE	SHEETING	SHORTCUT	SIDEWISE	SIRENIAN	SLEDDING
SETENANT	*SHEIKDOM	SHORTIES	*SIEROZEM	SIRVENTE	SLEEKIER
SETIFORM	*SHELDUCK	SHORTISH	SIFFLEUR	SISSYISH	SLEEPING
SETSCREW	*SHELFFUL	SHOTTING	SIGHLESS	SISTERLY	SLEIGHER
SETTLING	*SHELLACK	SHOULDER	*SIGHLIKE	SISTROID	*SLIDEWAY
SETULOSE	*SHELVING	SHOULDST	SIGHTING	SITARIST	SLIMIEST
SETULOUS	*SHEPHERD	SHOVELER	SIGHTSEE	SITHENCE	SLIMMEST
SEVERITY	SHERBERT	*SHOWBOAT	SIGNALER	SITOLOGY	SLIMMING
SEWERAGE	*SHERLOCK	*SHOWCASE	SIGNALLY	*SITZMARK	SLIMNESS
*SEXINESS	SHETLAND	*SHOWDOWN	SIGNIORY	*SIXPENCE	SLIPCASE
*SEXOLOGY	SHIELDER	SHOWERER	SIGNPOST	*SIXPENNY	*SLIPFORM
*SEXTARII	SHIELING	*SHOWGIRL	SILENCER	*SIXTIETH	SLIPKNOT
*SEXTETTE	SHIGELLA	SHOWIEST	SILICATE	*SIXTYISH	SLIPLESS
*SEXTUPLE	*SHIITAKE	*SHOWRING	SILICIDE	*SIZEABLE	SLIPOVER
*SEXTUPLY	*SHIKAREE	*SHOWROOM	*SILICIFY	*SIZINESS	SLIPPAGE
*SFORZATO	SHILINGI	SHRAPNEL	SILICIUM	SKELETON	*SLIPPERY
*SHACKLER	SHILLALA	SHREDDER	SILICONE	*SKETCHER	SLIPPING
*SHADBLOW	SHILLING	*SHREWDIE	SILICULA	*SKEWBACK	SLIPSHOD
*SHADBUSH	*SHIMMERY	*SHREWISH	SILKIEST	*SKEWBALD	SLIPSLOP
*SHADCHAN	*SHIMMING	*SHRIEKER	*SILKLIKE	*SKEWNESS	SLIPSOLE
*SHADDOCK	SHINBONE	SHRIEVAL	*SILKWEED	*SKIAGRAM	SLIPWARE
SHADIEST	SHINGLER	*SHRIMPER	*SILKWORM	*SKIJORER	SLITHERY
*SHADOWER	SHINIEST	*SHRINKER	SILLABUB	SKILLESS	SLITLESS
*SHADRACH	SHINLEAF	*SHRIVING	SILLIBUB	*SKILLFUL	SLITTING
*SHAFTING	SHINNERY	*SHRUNKEN	*SILOXANE	SKILLING	SLIVERER
*SHAGBARK	SHINNING	*SHUCKING	SILUROID	*SKIMMING	*SLIVOVIC
SHAGREEN	SHIPLOAD	*SHUDDERY	SILVERER	*SKINHEAD	*SLOBBERY
*SHAKEOUT	*SHIPMATE	*SHUFFLER	SILVERLY	SKINLESS	*SLOBBISH
*SHAKIEST	*SHIPMENT	*SHUNPIKE	SILVICAL	*SKINLIKE	SLOGGING
SHALIEST	*SHIPPING	*SHUTDOWN	SIMARUBA	SKINNING	SLOPPING
SHALLOON	SHIPSIDE	SHUTTING	*SIMAZINE	SKIORING	*SLOPWORK
*SHAMABLE	*SHIPWORM	*SHWANPAN	SIMOLEON	*SKIPJACK	*SLOTBACK
*SHAMEFUL	*SHIPYARD	SIALIDAN	SIMONIAC	SKIPLANE	SLOTHFUL
*SHAMMASH	SHIRRING	SIBILANT	SIMONIES	*SKIPPING	SLOTTING
*SHAMMIED	SHIRTING	SIBILATE	SIMONIST	*SKIRMISH	SLOUCHER
*SHAMMIES	SHITTING	SICKENER	*SIMONIZE	SKIRTING	SLOVENLY
*SHAMMING	SHIVAREE	*SICKERLY	SIMPERER	*SKITTERY	*SLOWDOWN
*SHAMOSIM	SHIVERER	SICKNESS	*SIMPLIFY	*SKITTISH	SLOWNESS
*SHAMROCK	*SHKOTZIM	*SICKROOM	SIMPLISM	*SKULLCAP	*SLOWPOKE
*SHANGHAI	SHLEMIEL	SIDEBAND	SIMPLIST	*SKYBORNE	*SLOWWORM

SLUBBING	SNITCHER	*SODOMIZE	SONGFEST	*SPANKING	SPINALLY
SLUGABED	SNIVELER	*SOFTBACK	SONGLESS	SPANLESS	SPINDLER
SLUGFEST	*SNOBBERY	SOFTBALL	SONGLIKE	SPANNING	SPINELLE
SLUGGARD	SNOBBIER	SOFTENER	SONGSTER	*SPANWORM	*SPINIFEX
SLUGGING	*SNOBBILY	*SOFTHEAD	SONICATE	SPARABLE	SPINLESS
SLUGGISH	*SNOBBISH	SOFTNESS	SONOBUOY	SPARERIB	SPINNERY
SLUGPEST	SNOBBISM	SOFTWARE	SONOGRAM	SPARKIER	SPINNING
*SLUMBERY	SNOUTISH	*SOFTWOOD	SONORANT	*SPARKILY	SPINSTER
SLUMLORD	SNOWBALL	SOILLESS	SONORITY	*SPARKISH	SPIRACLE
SLUMMING	*SNOWBANK	SOLANDER	SONOROUS	SPARKLER	SPIRALLY
SLURRING	SNOWBELL	SOLANINE	SOOCHONG	SPARLIKE	SPIRIEST
SLYBOOTS	SNOWBELT	SOLARISE	SOOTHEST	SPARLING	SPIRILLA
SMALLAGE	SNOWBIRD	SOLARISM	SOOTHING	SPARRIER	SPITBALL
SMALLISH	*SNOWBUSH	SOLARIUM	SOOTHSAY	SPARRING	SPITEFUL
*SMALLPOX	SNOWDROP	*SOLARIZE	SORBITOL	SPARSITY	SPITFIRE
SMALTINE	SNOWFALL	SOLATION	SORCERER	SPATTING	SPITTING
SMALTITE	SNOWIEST	SOLATIUM	SOREHEAD	*SPEAKING	SPITTOON
SMARAGDE	SNOWLAND	SOLDERER	SORENESS	SPEARGUN	SPLASHER
SMARTASS	SNOWLESS	SOLDIERY	SORICINE	SPEARMAN	SPLATTER
SMECTITE	*SNOWLIKE	SOLECISE	SORORATE	SPECIATE	SPLENDID
SMELTERY	SNOWMELT	SOLECISM	SORORITY	*SPECIFIC	SPLENDOR
SMIDGEON	SNOWMOLD	SOLECIST	SORPTION	SPECIMEN	SPLENIAL
SMITHERS	*SNOWPACK	*SOLECIZE	SORRIEST	SPECIOUS	SPLENIUM
*SMITHERY	*SNOWPLOW	SOLELESS	SORROWER	SPECTATE	SPLENIUS
*SMOCKING	*SNOWSHED	SOLENESS	SOUCHONG	SPECTRAL	SPLINTER
*SMOKEPOT	SNOWSHOE	SOLENOID	*SOUFFLED	SPECTRUM	SPLITTER
SMOOTHEN	SNOWSUIT	SOLFEGGI	*SOUNDBOX	SPECULUM	*SPLOTCHY
SMOOTHER	SNUBNESS	SOLIDAGO	SOUNDING	SPEEDIER	SPLURGER
SMOOTHIE	*SNUFFBOX	SOLIDARY	SOUNDMAN	SPEEDILY	SPLUTTER
*SMOOTHLY	SNUFFIER	*SOLIDIFY	SOURBALL	SPEEDING	SPOILAGE
*SMOTHERY	*SNUFFILY	SOLIDITY	SOURDINE	*SPEEDWAY	SPOLIATE
SMOULDER	SNUFFLER	*SOLIQUID	SOURNESS	SPEERING	SPONDAIC
SMUGGLER	SNUGGERY	SOLITARY	SOURPUSS	SPELAEAN	SPONGIER
SMUGNESS	SNUGGEST	SOLITUDE	SOURWOOD	SPELLING	SPONGILY
SMUTTING	SNUGGIES	SOLLERET	SOUTACHE	*SPERMARY	SPONGING
SNAGLIKE	SNUGGING	SOLONETS	SOUTHERN	SPERMINE	SPONSION
SNAKEBIT	SNUGNESS	*SOLONETZ	SOUTHING	SPERMOUS	SPONTOON
*SNAPBACK	*SOAPBARK	SOLSTICE	*SOUTHPAW	*SPHAGNUM	*SPOOFERY
SNAPLESS	SOAPIEST	SOLUTION	SOUTHRON	SPHENOID	*SPOOKERY
SNAPPIER	SOAPLESS	SOLVABLE	SOUVENIR	*SPHERICS	*SPOOKISH
*SNAPPILY	SOAPSUDS	*SOLVENCY	*SOUVLAKI	SPHERIER	SPOOLING
SNAPPING	SOAPWORT	SOMBRERO	SOVRANLY	SPHERING	SPOONFUL
*SNAPPISH	*SOBERIZE	SOMBROUS	SOVRANTY	SPHEROID	SPOONIER
SNAPSHOT	SOBRIETY	*SOMEBODY	*SOWBELLY	SPHERULE	SPOONIES
SNAPWEED	SOCIABLE	SOMEDEAL	SOWBREAD	SPHINGES	SPOONING
SNATCHER	*SOCIABLY	SOMERSET	SPACEMAN	*SPHINGID	SPORADIC
SNEERFUL	SOCIALLY	SOMETIME	SPACIOUS	*SPHYGMUS	*SPOROZOA
*SNICKERY	SOCKLESS	*SOMEWAYS	SPADEFUL	SPICCATO	SPORTFUL
SNIFFIER	SODALIST	*SOMEWHAT	SPADICES	SPICIEST	SPORTIVE
*SNIFFILY	SODALITE	*SOMEWHEN	SPADILLE	SPICULUM	SPOTLESS
*SNIFFISH	SODALITY	SOMEWISE	*SPAETZLE	*SPIFFING	SPOTTING
SNIFFLER	SODAMIDE	SONARMAN	*SPAGYRIC	SPIKELET	SPRADDLE
SNIGGLER	SODDENLY	SONATINA	SPALPEEN	SPILIKIN	SPRATTLE
*SNIPPETY	SODOMIST	SONGBIRD	SPANDREL	SPILLAGE	SPRAWLER
SNIPPING	SODOMITE	*SONGBOOK	SPANDRIL	*SPILLWAY	SPREADER

SPRIGGER	STAKEOUT	STELLIFY	STOKESIA	STROLLER	*SUBERIZE
SPRINGAL	STALLION	STEMLESS	STOLPORT	STRONGYL	SUBEROSE
SPRINGER	STALWART	STEMLIKE	*STOMACHY	STRONTIA	SUBEROUS
SPRINKLE	STAMPEDE	*STEMMERY	STOMATAL	STROPPER	SUBFIELD
SPRINTER	STANCHER	STEMMING	STOMATIC	STRUCKEN	SUBFLOOR
*SPRITZER	*STANCHLY	STEMWARE	STOMODEA	STRUGGLE	SUBFLUID
*SPROCKET	STANDARD	STENOSED	STONEFLY	STRUMMER	*SUBFRAME
SPRYNESS	STANDING	STENOSIS	STONIEST	STRUMOSE	SUBGENRE
SPUMIEST	STANDISH	STEPDAME	*STOPBANK	STRUMOUS	SUBGENUS
SPURGALL	*STANDOFF	STEPLIKE	*STOPCOCK	STRUMPET	SUBGRADE
SPURIOUS	STANDOUT	STEPPING	STOPOVER	STRUTTER	*SUBGRAPH
SPURRIER	STANDPAT	STEPWISE	STOPPAGE	STUBBIER	SUBGROUP
SPURRING	STANHOPE	STERICAL	STOPPING	*STUBBILY	*SUBHUMAN
SPYGLASS	STANNARY	STERIGMA	STORABLE	STUBBING	*SUBHUMID
*SQUABBLE	STANNITE	STERLING	STOTINKA	STUBBORN	*SUBINDEX
*SQUADRON	STANNOUS	STERNITE	STOUTISH	STUCCOER	SUBLEASE
*SQUALENE	STAPEDES	STERNSON	*STOWAWAY	*STUDBOOK	SUBLEVEL
*SQUALLER	STAPELIA	STERNWAY	STRADDLE	STUDDING	SUBLIMER
*SQUANDER	STARFISH	STIBNITE	STRAGGLE	*STUDFISH	SUBLUNAR
*SQUARELY	*STARGAZE	*STICKFUL	STRAGGLY	STUDIOUS	SUBMERGE
*SQUAREST	STARKERS	STICKIER	STRAIGHT	*STUDWORK	SUBMERSE
*SQUARING	STARLESS	*STICKILY	STRAINER	STUFFIER	SUBNASAL
*SQUARISH	STARLIKE	STICKLER	STRAITEN	*STUFFING	*SUBNICHE
*SQUASHER	STARLING	*STICKMAN	STRAMASH	STULTIFY	SUBNODAL
*SQUATTER	STARNOSE	STICKOUT	STRAMONY	STUMBLER	SUBOPTIC
*SQUAWKER	STARRING	*STICKPIN	STRANDER	STUMMING	SUBORDER
*SQUEAKER	STARSHIP	STICTION	STRANGER	STUMPAGE	SUBORNER
*SQUEALER	STARTLER	*STIFFISH	STRANGLE	STUNNING	SUBOVATE
*SQUEEGEE	STARWORT	STILBENE	STRAPPER	STUNSAIL	*SUBOXIDE
*SQUEEZER	STASIMON	STILBITE	STRATEGY	STUNTMAN	SUBPANEL
*SQUELCHY	STATABLE	STILETTO	STRATIFY	STURGEON	*SUBPHASE
*SQUIFFED	STATEDLY	STILLMAN	STRATOUS	STYLISER	*SUBPHYLA
*SQUIGGLE	*STATICKY	STIMULUS	STRAVAGE	*STYLIZER	SUBPOENA
*SQUIGGLY	STATUARY	STINGIER	STRAVAIG	SUBABBOT	SUBPOLAR
*SQUILGEE	STAUMREL	STINGILY	STRAWHAT	SUBACRID	*SUBPUBIC
*SQUINTER	STAYSAIL	STINGRAY	STREAKER	SUBACUTE	SUBSCALE
*SQUIREEN	STEADIED	STINKARD	STREAMER	SUBADULT	SUBSENSE
*SQUIRISH	STEADIER	*STINKBUG	STREEKER	SUBAGENT	SUBSERVE
*SQUIRMER	STEADIES	STINKIER	STRENGTH	SUBANHAR	*SUBSHAFT
*SQUIRREL	STEADING	STINKPOT	STRESSOR	*SUBAXIAL	SUBSHELL
*SQUIRTER	STEALAGE	STIPPLER	*STRETCHY	SUBBASIN	*SUBSHRUB
*SQUOOSHY	STEALING	STIRRING	STREUSEL	*SUBBLOCK	SUBSIDER
STABLEST	STEALTHY	STITCHER	STRICKEN	SUBBREED	SUBSKILL
STABLING	STEAPSIN	STOCCADO	STRICKLE	SUBCASTE	SUBSOLAR
STABLISH	STEARATE	STOCCATA	STRIDENT	SUBCAUSE	SUBSONIC
STACCATO	STEARINE	*STOCKADE	STRIDING	*SUBCHIEF	SUBSPACE
STAGEFUL	STEATITE	*STOCKCAR	STRIGOSE	SUBCLASS	SUBSTAGE
STAGGARD	STEDFAST	STOCKIER	STRINGER	*SUBCLERK	SUBSTATE
STAGGART	STEENBOK	*STOCKILY	STRIPIER	SUBCUTIS	*SUBTAXON
STAGGERY	STEEPISH	*STOCKING	STRIPING	SUBDEPOT	*SUBTHEME
STAGGING	STEERAGE	*STOCKISH	STRIPPED	SUBDURAL	SUBTILIN
STAGIEST	STEEVING	STOCKIST	STRIPPER	SUBENTRY	SUBTILTY
STAGNANT	STEGODON	*STOCKMAN	STROBILA	*SUBEPOCH	SUBTITLE
STAGNATE	STEINBOK	*STOCKPOT	STROBILE	SUBERECT	SUBTLETY
STAIRWAY	STELLATE	STOICISM	STROBILI	SUBERISE	SUBTONIC

SUBTOPIA	SUMMONER	SURGICAL	SYLLABLE	PE S TO	BU S TIC
SUBTOPIC	*SUMPWEED	SURICATE	*SYLLABUB	PE S TY	BU S TLE
SUBTOTAL	*SUNBAKED	SURMISER	SYLLABUS	PI S CO	BY S SU S
SUBTRACT	SUNBATHE	SURMOUNT	*SYLVATIC	PI S TE	CA S ABA
SUBTREND	*SUNBLOCK	SURNAMER	*SYMBIONT	RE S OD	CA S AVA
SUBTRIBE	SUNBURST	SURPLICE	*SYMBIOTE	RI S U S	CA S BAH
SUBTUNIC	*SUNCHOKE	SURPRINT	*SYMBOLIC	S U S HI	CA S EFY
SUBULATE	SUNDERER	SURPRISE	*SYMMETRY	S Y S OP	CA S EIN
SUBURBAN	SUNDRESS	*SURPRIZE	*SYMPATHY	WA S HY	CA S ERN
SUBURBIA	SUNDRIES	SURROUND	*SYMPATRY	WU S S Y	CA S HEW
*SUBVICAR	SUNDROPS	SURROYAL	*SYMPHONY	BA S ALT	CA S ING
SUBVIRAL	SUNGLASS	SURVEYOR	*SYMPODIA	BA S ELY	CA S INO
*SUBVOCAL	SUNLIGHT	SURVIVAL	*SYMPOSIA	BA S E S T	CA S ITA
SUBWORLD	*SUNPORCH	SURVIVER	SYNAPSID	BA S HAW	CA S KET
SUCCINCT	SUNPROOF	SURVIVOR	SYNAPSIS	BA S HER	*CA S QUE
SUCCINIC	SUNSCALD	SUSPENSE	*SYNCARPY	BA S IFY	CA S RAW
*SUCCINYL	SUNSHADE	SUSURRUS	SYNCLINE	BA S ING	CA S ROD
SUCCORER	SUNSHINE	*SUZERAIN	*SYNCYTIA	BA S ION	CA S SIA
SUCCUBUS	SUNSTONE	*SVEDBERG	SYNDESIS	BA S KET	CA S SIS
*SUCHLIKE	SUNWARDS	*SWABBING	SYNDETIC	*BA S QUE	CA S TER
SUCHNESS	SUPERADD	SWAGGING	SYNDROME	BA S SET	CA S TLE
*SUCKFISH	SUPERBAD	*SWAMPISH	*SYNECTIC	BA S SLY	CA S TOR
SUCKLESS	SUPERCAR	*SWANHERD	SYNERGIA	BA S TER	CA S UAL
*SUCKLING	SUPERCOP	*SWANLIKE	SYNERGID	BE S EEM	CE S IUM
SUDARIUM	SUPEREGO	SWANNERY	*SYNONYME	BE S IDE	CE S SU S
SUDATION	SUPERFAN	SWANNING	*SYNONYMY	BE S MUT	CE S TO S
SUDATORY	*SUPERFIX	*SWANSKIN	SYNOPSIS	BE S NOW	CE S TU S
SUDSLESS	SUPERHIT	SWASTICA	SYNTAGMA	BE S TIR	CE S URA
SUFFERER	SUPERHOT	*SWASTIKA	*SYPHILIS	BE S TOW	CI S TU S
*SUFFICER	SUPERIOR	SWATTING	*SYRPHIAN	BE S TUD	CO S HER
*SUFFIXAL	*SUPERJET	*SWAYBACK	*SYSTEMIC	BI S ECT	CO S IED
SUFFLATE	SUPERLIE	*SWEATBOX		BI S HOP	CO S IER
*SUFFRAGE	SUPERMAN	SWEEPING	PS ST	*BI S QUE	CO S IE S
SUICIDAL	SUPERMOM	SWEETING	T S AR	BI S TER	CO S ILY
SUITABLE	SUPERNAL	SWEETISH	P S ALM	BI S TRE	CO S INE
SUITCASE	SUPERPRO	SWEETSOP	P S EUD	BI S TRO	CO S MIC
SUITLIKE	*SUPERSEX	SWELLING	P S HAW	BO S KER	CO S MO S
*SUKIYAKI	*SUPERSPY	SWIFTLET	P S OA S	BO S KET	CO S SET
SULCATED	*SUPERTAX	*SWIMMING	*P S YCH	BO S OMY	CO S TAR
SULFINYL	SUPINATE	SWIMSUIT	T S ADE	*BO S QUE	CO S TER
SULFONAL	SUPINELY	*SWIMWEAR	T S ADI	BO S TON	CO S TLY
SULFONIC	SUPPLANT	SWINDLER	T S UBA	BU S BOY	CU S CU S
SULFONYL	SUPPLIER	*SWINEPOX	BA S E S	BU S HEL	CU S HAT
SULFURET	SUPPOSAL	SWINGIER	BA S I S	BU S HER	CU S HAW
SULFURIC	SUPPOSER	SWINGING	CA S U S	BU S HWA	CU S PID
SULFURYL	SUPPRESS	SWINGMAN	CI S S Y	BU S IER	CU S PI S
SULPHATE	SURCEASE	*SWITCHER	DA S HI	BU S IE S	CU S SER
SULPHIDE	SUREFIRE	*SWIZZLER	GU S S Y	BU S ILY	CU S TOM
SULPHITE	SURENESS	SWORDMAN	HI S S Y	BU S ING	CU S TO S
*SULPHONE	SURFACER	SYBARITE	HO S TA	BU S KER	CY S TIC
*SULPHURY	SURFBIRD	*SYCAMINE	KI S S Y	BU S KIN	DA S HER
SUMMABLE	SURFBOAT	*SYCAMORE	LU S U S	BU S MAN	DA S SIE
*SUMMERLY	*SURFFISH	*SYCOMORE	LY S I S	BU S SED	DE S ALT
SUMMITAL	SURFIEST	*SYCONIUM	MY S ID	BU S SE S	DE S AND
*SUMMITRY	*SURFLIKE	*SYLLABIC	NI S U S	BU S TER	DE S CRY

DE S ERT	GA S TER	LI S TEL	PA S TI S	RE S IST	TU S SEH
DE S IRE	GE S TIC	LI S TEN	PA S TOR	RE S ITE	TU S S ER
DE S IST	GO S PEL	LI S TER	**PA S TRY**	RE S ITE	TU S SIS
DE S MID	GO S S AN	LO S ING	PE S ADE	*RE S IZE	TU S S LE
DE S ORB	GO S S IP	LU S TER	PE S ETA	**RE S OAK**	TU S S OR
*DE S OXY	**GU S HER**	LU S TRA	**PE S EWA**	RE S OLD	TU S S UR
DE S POT	GU S S ET	LU S TRE	PE S TER	RE S OLE	VA S S AL
DI S ARM	GU S S IE	LY S ATE	PE S TLE	RE S ORB	**VA S TLY**
DI S BAR	HA S LET	LY S INE	PI S TIL	RE S ORT	VE S ICA
DI S BUD	HA S S EL	**LY S ING**	PI S TOL	RE S POT	**VE S PER**
DI S CU S	HA S S LE	*MA S JID	PI S TON	RE S TER	**VE S PID**
DI S MAL	HA S TEN	*MA S QUE	PO S ADA	RE S ULT	VE S S EL
DI S MAY	**HI S PID**	MA S TER	PO S EE S	RE S UME	VE S TAL
DI S OWN	HI S S ER	*MA S TIX	PO S EUR	RI S ING	VE S TEE
DI S PEL	HO S IER	ME S IAL	PO S IE S	RI S KER	VE S TRY
DI S S ED	**HO S ING**	ME S IAN	PO S ING	*RI S QUE	VI S AGE
DI S SES	HO S TEL	ME S S AN	PO S S ET	RO S ARY	VI S ARD
DI S TAL	**HO S TLY**	ME S TEE	**PO S S UM**	RO S COE	VI S CID
DI S TIL	**HU S KER**	MI S EAT	PO S TAL	RO S ERY	**VI S CU S**
DI S USE	HU S S AR	MI S LIE	PO S TER	RO S IER	**VI S ING**
DO S AGE	HU S TLE	MI S LIT	PO S TIN	RO S ILY	VI S ION
DO S S AL	**HY S S OP**	MI S S EL	**PU S HER**	RO S ING	VI S IVE
DO S S EL	*JA S MIN	MI S S ET	PU S HUP	RO S INY	VI S UAL
DO S S ER	*JA S PER	MI S SIS	PU S LEY	RO S TER	**WA S ABI**
DO S S IL	JA S SID	MI S SUS	**PU S SLY**	RO S TRA	**WA S HER**
DU S TER	**JE S TER**	MI S USE	RA S CAL	RU S HEE	WA S TER
DU S TUP	**JE S UIT**	MI S TER	RA S HER	RU S HER	**WA S TRY**
FA S CE S	*JO S EPH	*MO S QUE	**RA S HLY**	RU S INE	WE S KIT
FA S CIA	*JO S HER	MO S S ER	RA S ING	RU S S ET	WE S TER
FA S TEN	JO S TLE	*MU S JID	RA S PER	RU S TIC	WI S DOM
FE S CUE	JU S TER	MU S LIN	RA S S LE	RU S TLE	WI S ELY
FE S TAL	**JU S TLE**	MU S S EL	RA S TER	S A S HAY	WI S ENT
FE S TER	*JU S TLY	MU S TEE	RA S URE	S E S AME	WI S EST
FI S CAL	*KA S BAH	MU S TER	RE S AID	S E S TET	WI S HER
*FI S HLY	KA S HER	**MY S TER**	RE S ALE	S I S KIN	*XY S TER
FI S TIC	*KI S HKA	NA S ION	RE S CUE	S I S TER	*XY S TO S
FI S HER	*KI S HKE	NA S TIC	RE S EAL	S I S TRA	*XY S TU S
FO S S IL	KI S MAT	NE S TER	RE S EAT	S U S LIK	*YA S MAK
FO S TER	KI S MET	NE S TLE	RE S EAU	S Y S TEM	YE S S ED
FU S AIN	KI S S ER	NE S TOR	RE S ECT	TA S S EL	YE S SES
FU S ILE	KO S HER	NO S HER	RE S EDA	TA S S ET	YE S TER
FU S ION	LA S CAR	NO S IER	RE S EED	TA S SIE	*ZE S TER
FU S S ER	LA S HER	NO S ILY	**RE S EEK**	TA S TER	*ZO S TER
FU S TIC	LA S ING	NO S ING	RE S EEN	TE S TEE	**BA S CULE**
GA S BAG	LA S SIE	NO S TOC	RE S ELL	TE S TER	**BA S EMAN**
GA S CON	LA S TER	PA S CAL	RE S END	TE S TE S	*BA S ENJI
GA S IFY	LA S TLY	PA S S EL	RE S ENT	TE S TI S	*BA S HFUL
GA S KET	LE S ION	PA S S ER	**RE S HIP**	TE S TON	*BA S HLYK
GA S KIN	LE S S EE	PA S S IN	RE S HOE	TI S ANE	**BA S ILAR**
GA S LIT	LE S S EN	PA S SUS	**RE S HOW**	TI S SUE	**BA S ILIC**
GA S MAN	LE S S ON	PA S TEL	RE S IDE	TO S S ER	**BA S INET**
GA S PER	LI S PER	PA S TER	RE S IFT	TO S S UP	**BA S MATI**
GA S S ED	LI S S OM	PA S TIE	RE S IGN	TU S KER	BA S SIST
GA S S ER	LI S TEE	PA S TIL	RE S ILE	TU S S AH	BA S SOON
GA S SES			RE S INY	TU S S AL	**BA S TARD**

BA S TILE	CA S S ATA	DI S ABLE	DO S S IER	GO S S OON	LU S TILY
BA S TING	CA S S AVA	DI S AVOW	*DU S KI S H	GU S TIER	LU S TRAL
BA S TION	CA S S INO	DI S BAND	DU S THIN	GU S TILY	LU S TRUM
BE S COUR	*CA S S OCK	DI S CANT	DU S TIER	*HA S HI S H	LY S OGEN
BE S EECH	CA S TING	DI S CARD	DU S TILY	*HA S S OCK	*MA S QUER
BE S HAME	*CA S TOFF	DI S CA S E	DU S TMAN	HA S TATE	MA S S AGE
*BE S HREW	CA S UI S T	DI S CEPT	DU S TOFF	HE S S IAN	MA S S EUR
BE S IDE S	CE S S ION	DI S CERN	DU S TPAN	HE S S ITE	MA S S IER
BE S IEGE	CE S S PIT	DI S COID	DY S PNEA	HI S S ELF	*MA S TIFF
BE S LIME	CE S TODE	DI S CORD	DY S URIA	HI S S ING	ME S EEM S
BE S MEAR	CE S TOID	DI S CU S S	FA S CINE	HI S TOID	ME S HIER
BE S MILE	CI S S OID	DI S DAIN	FA S CI S M	HI S TONE	ME S HUGA
*BE S MOKE	CI S TERN	DI S EA S E	FA S CI S T	HI S TORY	ME S TE S O
*BE S PEAK	CI S TRON	DI S EU S E	FA S HION	HO S ANNA	ME S TINO
BE S TEAD	CO S IE S T	DI S GU S T	FA S TING	HO S IERY	*ME S TIZA
BE S TIAL	CO S MI S M	DI S HELM	FE S TIVE	HO S PICE	*ME S TIZO
BE S TREW	CO S MI S T	DI S HFUL	FE S TOON	HO S TAGE	MI S BIA S
BE S TROW	*CO S S ACK	DI S HIER	*FI S HERY	HO S TE S S	MI S CODE
BE S WARM	CO S TARD	DI S HPAN	*FI S HEYE	HO S TILE	*MI S COOK
BI S CUIT	CO S TATE	DI S HRAG	*FI S HGIG	HO S TLER	*MI S COPY
BI S MUTH	CO S TIVE	*DI S JECT	FI S HING	HU S BAND	MI S DIAL
BI S NAGA	CO S TREL	*DI S JOIN	FI S HNET	*HU S HABY	MI S EA S E
BI S TORT	CO S TUME	DI S LIKE	*FI S HWAY	*HU S HFUL	*MI S JOIN
BI S TATE	CU S HIER	DI S LIMN	FI S S ATE	HU S KIER	*MI S KEEP
BO S CAGE	*CU S HILY	DI S MA S T	FI S S ILE	HU S KIE S	*MI S KICK
BO S KAGE	CU S HION	DI S MI S S	FI S S ION	*HU S KILY	*MI S KNOW
*BO S QUET	CU S S CU S	DI S OBEY	FI S S URE	*HU S KING	MI S LAIN
BO S S DOM	CU S TARD	DI S OMIC	FI S TFUL	HU S RIE S	MI S LIKE
BO S S IER	CU S TODY	DI S PART	FI S TULA	HU S TLER	*MI S MAKE
BO S S IE S	CY S TEIN	DI S PEND	*FO S S ICK	*JA S MINE	*MI S MARK
BO S S I S M	CY S TINE	DI S PLAY	FU S COU S	JE S S ANT	MI S PLAN
BU S HIDO	CY S TOID	DI S PORT	FU S IBLE	*JE S TFUL	MI S RATE
BU S HIER	DA S HEEN	DI S PO S E	FU S ILLI	*JE S TING	MI S RULE
*BU S HILY	DA S HIER	DI S PUTE	FU S S ING	JO S TLER	MI S S EAT
BU S HING	*DA S HIKI	DI S RATE	FU S S POT	*JU S S IVE	MI S S IE S
BU S HMAN	DA S HPOT	DI S ROBE	FU S TIAN	*JU S TICE	MI S S ILE
*BU S HPIG	DA S TARD	DI S ROOT	GA S EOU S	*JU S TIFY	MI S S ION
BU S HTIT	DA S YURE	DI S RUPT	GA S KING	*KA S HMIR	MI S S ORT
*BU S HWAH	DE S CANT	DI S S AVE	GA S LE S S	KA S HRUT	MI S S OUT
BU S IE S T	DE S CEND	DI S S EAT	GA S OHOL	KE S TREL	MI S S UIT
BU S LOAD	DE S CENT	DI S S ECT	GA S S ING	KI S TFUL	MI S TAKE
BU S S ING	DE S ERVE	DI S S ENT	GA S TRAL	LA S AGNA	MI S TIER
BU S TARD	DE S IRER	DI S S ERT	GA S TREA	LA S AGNE	MI S TIE S
BU S TIER	DE S MOID	DI S S ING	GA S TRIC	LA S HING	MI S TRAL
CA S CADE	DE S PAIR	DI S TAFF	GE S TALT	LA S HIN S	MI S TUNE
CA S CARA	DE S PI S E	DI S TAIN	GE S TAPO	LA S HKAR	MI S U S ER
CA S EA S E	DE S PITE	DI S TANT	GE S TATE	LA S S OER	*MI S YOKE
CA S EATE	DE S POIL	DI S TEND	GE S TURE	LA S TING	MO S S IER
CA S EO S E	DE S POND	DI S TENT	GI S ARME	LE S BIAN	MO S TE S T
CA S EOU S	DE S S ERT	DI S TICH	*GO S HAWK	LI S ENTE	MU S ETTE
CA S ERNE	DE S TAIN	DI S TILL	GO S LING	LI S S OME	MU S ICAL
CA S ETTE	DE S TINE	DI S TOME	GO S PORT	LI S TING	*MU S KILY
*CA S HBOX	DE S TINY	DI S TORT	GO S S IPY	LU S TFUL	*MU S PIKE
CA S HIER	DE S TROY	DI S TURB		LU S TIER	MU S S ING
CA S S ABA	DE S UGAR	*DI S YOKE			

*MY S TIFY	PU S S IE S	RO S ARIA	VE S TIGE	BLA S TEMA	CLA S S ILY
NA S ALLY	PU S S LEY	RO S EATE	VE S TING	BLA S TIER	CLA S S ISM
NA S CENT	PU S TULE	RO S EBAY	VE S TUBE	BLA S TING	CLA S S IST
NE S TLER	RA S BORA	RO S EBUD	VI S CERA	*BLA S TOFF	CLO S EOUT
NO S EBAG	RA S PI S H	RO S ELLE	VI S COID	BLA S TOMA	CLU S TERY
NO S EGAY	RE S CALE	RO S EOLA	VI S CO S E	BLA S TULA	COA S SIST
NO S IE S T	RE S CIND	RO S ETTE	VI S COU S	*BLE S BUCK	COA S S UME
NO S TRIL	RE S CORE	RO S IE S T	VI S IBLE	BLE S S ING	COA S TING
NO S TRUM	RE S CUER	RO S INOL	VI S ITER	BLI S TERN	COI S TREL
PA S CHAL	*RE S EIZE	RO S OLIO	VI S ITOR	BLO S S ONY	COI S TRIL
*PA S QUIL	RE S ERVE	RO S TRAL	*WA S HDAY	*BLU S HFUL	CON S ERVE
PA S S ADE	RE S HAPE	RO S TRUM	WA S HIER	BLU S TERY	CON S IDER
PA S S ADO	RE S HAVE	RU S HIER	WA S HING	BOA S TFUL	CON S OLER
PA S S AGE	RE S HINE	RU S HING	WA S HOUT	BOI S ERIE	CON S OMME
PA S S ANT	RE S HONE	RU S S IFY	*WA S HTUB	BON S PELL	CON S PIRE
PA S S ING	RE S HOOT	RU S TIER	WA S HRAG	BON S PIEL	CON S TANT
PA S S ION	RE S IDER	RU S TILY	WA S S AIL	BOU S OUKI	CON S TRUE
PA S S IVE	RE S IDUA	RU S TLER	WA S TAGE	*BOW S PRIT	CON S UMER
*PA S S KEY	RE S IDUE	SA S HIMI	WA S TERY	BRA S ILIN	COR S ELET
PA S TERN	RE S IGHT	SA S S ABY	WA S TING	BRA S S AGE	COR S ETRY
PA S TEUP	RE S LATE	SA S S IER	WA S TREL	BRA S S ARD	COU S COU S
PA S TIER	RE S MELT	SA S S IE S	WA S TRUE	BRA S S ART	COU S INRY
PA S TIE S	RE S OJET	SA S S ILY	WE S S AND	BRA S S ICA	*COX S WAIN
PA S TIME	RE S OLVE	SE S S ILE	WE S TERN	BRA S S I S H	CRE S CENT
PA S TINA	RE S OUND	SE S S ION	WE S TING	BRI S ANCE	*CRE S CIVE
PA S TING	RE S PACE	SE S TINA	WI S EAS S	BRI S LING	CRE S TING
PA S TURE	RE S PADE	SE S TINE	*WI S HFUL	BRU S HIER	*CRE S YLIC
PE S S ARY	RE S PEAK	SI S TRUM	WI S PIER	*BRU S HOFF	CRI S PATE
PI S CARY	RE S PECT	SU S PECT	*WI S PILY	BUR S ITI S	CRI S TATE
PI S CINA	RE S PELL	SU S PEND	*WI S PI S H	BUR S TONE	CRO S S ARM
PI S CINE	RE S PIRE	SU S TAIN	WI S S ING	CAB S TAND	CRO S S BAR
PI S HOGE	RE S PITE	SY S TOLE	WI S TFUL	*CAN S HAFT	*CRO S S BOW
PI S MIRE	RE S PLIT	TA S TING	*YA S HMAC	CAP S ICIN	CRO S S CUT
PI S S ANT	RE S POKE	TE S S ERA	*YA S HMAL	*CAP S ICUM	CRO S S ING
PI S S OIR	RE S POND	TE S TACY	*YE S HIVA	CAP S OMER	CRO S S LET
PI S TOLE	RE S PRAY	TE S TATE	YE S S ING	CAP S TONE	CRO S S TIE
PO S SES S	RE S TACK	TE S TIER	YE S TERN	CAP S ULAR	*CRO S S WAY
PO S TAGE	RE S TAFF	TE S TIFY	*ZE S TFUL	CA S S ETTE	CRU S ADER
PO S TBAG	RE S TAGE	TE S TILY	*BAA S KAAP	CAU S ABLE	CRU S TOSE
*PO S TBOX	RE S TAMP	TE S TING	*BAK S HI S H	CAU S ALLY	CU S S EDLY
PO S TBOY	RE S TART	TE S TOON	BAL S AMIC	CAU S ERIE	CU S S WORD
PO S TDOC	RE S TATE	TE S TUDY	BAR S TOOL	*CAU S EWAY	*DAI S HIKI
PO S TEEN	RE S TFUL	TI S S UAL	BA S S INET	CEN S URER	DAN S EU S E
PO S TERN	RE S TIVE	TI S S UEY	BA S S NES S	CE S S POOL	DIA S PORA
*PO S TFIX	RE S TOCK	TO S S POT	BA S S WOOD	CHA S S EUR	DIA S PORE
PO S TING	RE S TOKE	TO S TADA	BED S HEET	CHA S TI S E	DIA S TA S E
PO S TMAN	RE S TORE	TO S TADO	BED S ONIA	*CHA S TITY	DIA S TEMA
*PO S TTAX	RE S TUDY	TU S S CHE	BED S TAND	*CHA S UBLE	DIA S TOLE
PO S TURE	RE S TUFF	TU S S OCK	BED S TEAD	*CHE S SMAN	*DIE S TOCK
PO S TWAR	RE S TYLE	TU S S ORE	BED S TRAW	*CHE S TFUL	DIE S TRUM
*PU S HFUL	RE S UMER	TU S S UCK	BEE S WING	CHE S TNUT	DIE S TRU S
PU S HIER	RE S URGE	VA S TIER	BIA S NES S	CHI S ELER	*DIP S TICK
PU S HILT	RI S IBLE	VA S TITY	BIO S COPE	CLA S S IFY	DI S S EI S E
PU S HPIN	RI S OTTO	VE S ICLE	*BIO S COPY	CLA S S ICO	*DI S S EIZE
PU S S IER	RI S S OLE	VE S PINE	*BIT S TOCK	CLA S S IER	DI S S ERVE

DIS SUADE	GRIS EOUS	MIS SILRY	*PEES WEEP	PROS TATE	SENS UOUS
*DOGS BODY	GRIS ETTE	MIS SOUND	PENS IONE	PROS TYLE	SESS POOL
DORS ALLY	*GROS BEAK	MIS SPACE	*PENS TOCK	PUIS SANT	SETS CREW
DOS SERET	GROS CHEN	*MIS SPEAK	PERS ONAL	PULS ATOR	*SHAS HLIK
DOWS ABEL	GUNS MITH	MIS SPELL	PERS PIRE	*PULS EJET	SIS SYISH
DRES SAGE	*GUNS TOCK	MIS SPEND	PERS UADE	*PULS OJET	SLAS HING
DRES SING	GYPS EOUS	*MIS SPOKE	PHAS EOUT	PURS IEST	SOLS TICE
DRYS TONE	*GYPS YDOM	MIS START	PHOS GENE	PURS LANE	STAS IMON
*DYES TUFF	*GYPS YISH	MIS STATE	*PHOS PHID	PURS UANT	SUBS CALE
FALS ETTO	*GYPS YISM	MIS STEER	*PHOS PHIN	PUS SIEST	SUBS ENSE
*FATS TOCK	HAUS FRAU	MIS STYLE	*PHOS PHOR	PUS SLIKE	SUBS ERVE
FEAS ANCE	*HAYS TACK	MONS TERA	*PHYS ICAL	*PUS SYCAT	*SUBS HAFT
FEAS IBLE	HERS TORY	*MOSS BACK	*PHYS IQUE	*QUES TION	SUBS HELL
FEAS TFUL	*HOGS HEAD	MOS SIEST	PIAS ABA	*QUIS LING	*SUBS HRUB
FELS TONE	*HOOSEGOW	MOS SLIKE	PIAS AVA	RAIS ONNE	SUBS IDER
FES SWISE	HORS ECAR	MUDS LIDE	*PIGS TICK	RAMS HORN	SUBS KILL
FIS SIPED	*HORS EFLY	*MYOS COPE	PILS ENER	RANS OMER	SUBS OLAR
*FLAS HGUN	HORS EMAN	MYOS ITIS	*PINS CHER	RATS BANE	SUBS ONIC
*FLAS HING	HORS IEST	MYOS OTIS	PLAS MOID	REAS CEND	SUBS PACE
FLES HIER	*HOUS EBOY	NAUS EANT	PLAS TERY	REAS CENT	SUBS TAGE
*FLES HING	*HOUS EFLY	NAUS EATE	PLAS TRON	REAS ONER	SUBS TATE
*FLES HPOT	HOUS EFUL	NAUS EOUS	PLAS TRUM	REAS SAIL	SUDS LESS
*FLYS PECK	HOUS EMAN	NAYS AYER	PLUS SAGE	REAS SERT	SUNS CALD
*FORS AKER	HOUS ETOP	NEWS CAST	POIS ONER	REAS SESS	SUNS HADE
FORS OOTH	*HYOS CINE	*NEWS HAWK	POSS IBLE	REAS SORT	SUNS TONE
FORS PENT	*JOYS TICK	NEWS IEST	POTS HARD	REAS SUME	SWAS TICA
FORS WEAR	KAIS ERIN	NEWS LESS	POTS HERD	REAS SURE	*SWAS TIKA
FOS SETTE	*KEES HOND	*NEWS PEAK	POTS TONE	*REDS HANK	TEAS ELER
FRES COER	*KEYS TONE	NEWS REEL	PRES AGER	*REDS HIFT	TEAS POON
*FRES HMAN	*KINS FOLK	NEWS ROOM	PRES CIND	REDS HIRT	TENS IBLE
FRIS ETTE	*KLYS TRON	NOIS ETTE	PRES CORE	RED START	TEOS INTE
FROS TBIT	LINS TOCK	NON SENSE	PRES ENCE	REIS SUER	THES AURI
FROS TING	*LIPS TICK	NONS KIER	PRES ERVE	REUS ABLE	THES PIAN
FRUS TULE	*LOBS TICK	NON SOLAR	PRES IDER	RIES LING	TINS ELLY
GEL SEMIA	LOOS ENER	NON SOLID	PRES IDIA	ROLS TEIN	TINS MITH
*GEMS BUCK	LOPS IDED	NONS TICK	PRES IDIO	ROUS SEAU	TINS TONE
GEM STONE	*LOPS TICK	NON STORY	PRES LEEP	SALS ILLA	TIPS IEST
*GHAS TFUL	MAS SACRE	NON STYLE	PRES LICE	SANS ERIF	*TIPS TAFF
GHOS TING	MAS SCULT	NON SUGAR	PRES PLIT	SARS ENET	*TIPS TOCK
GLAS NOST	MAS SEDLY	NUIS ANCE	PRES RAPE	SAS SIEST	TIS SULAR
GLAS SFUL	MAS SETER	NUMS KULL	PRES SING	SAS SWOOD	TOPS IDER
GLAS SIER	MAS SEUSE	NURS LING	PRES SMAN	SCIS SILE	TOPS TONE
GLAS SILY	MAS SICOT	NUTS EDGE	PRES SRUN	SCIS SION	TRAS HMAN
GLAS SINE	MAS SIEST	NUTS HELL	PRES SURE	SCIS SURE	TRES PASS
GLAS SMAN	MAS SLESS	*PANS OPHY	PRES TAMP	SEAS CAPE	TRES SIER
GLIS SADE	*MEMS AHIB	PAS SBAND	PRES TIGE	SEAS COUT	TRES SOUR
GLOS SARY	MES SIEST	PAS SBAND	PRES UMER	SEAS DORE	TRES SURE
GLOS SEME	MES SMATE	*PAS SBOOK	PRIS MOID	SEAS HELL	TRIS CELE
GLOS SIER	MES SUAGE	*PAS SERBY	PRIS ONER	SEAS ONAL	TRIS KELE
GLOS SIES	*MIDS HIPS	PAS SIBLE	PRIS TANE	SEAS ONER	TRIS OMIC
GLOS SINA	*MIDS IZED	PAS SLESS	PRIS TINE	SEIS MISM	TRIS TATE
GOS SAMER	*MIDS PACE	PAS SOVER	PROS AISM	SENS EFUL	*TRIS TEZA
GOS SIPER	MIS SABLE	PAS SPORT	PROS AIST	SENS IDLE	TRIS TFUL
GOS SIPRY	MIS SENSE	PAS SWORD	PROS IEST	SENS ILLA	TRIS TICH
GOS SYPOL	*MIS SHAPE	PEAS ECOD	PROS PECT	SENS ORIA	

TRU S S ING	MI S S	DEMO S	LUPU S	**S OLU S**	**BU S S E S**
TRU S TFUL	MON S	DRE S S	LU S U S	**S ORU S**	**BYPA S S**
TWI S TING	MO S S	DRIE S	LY S I S	S PEC S	**BY S S U S**
VER S EMAN	MU S S	DRO S S	MABI S	S PIE S	**CACTU S**
VER S ICLE	NAO S	**FAVU S**	MAGU S	S TO S S	**CADDI S**
VOU S S OIR	NE S S	**FECE S**	MANU S	S WI S S	CALCE S
*WAE S UCK S	NEW S	FETU S	MAVI S	TABE S	CALLU S
WAI S TING	NOE S	**FICU S**	**MAVI S**	TALU S	**CALVE S**
WAR S TLER	NOU S	FINI S	METI S	TALU S	**CAMA S S**
WEA S ELLY	PA S S	FLIE S	MINU S	TAMI S	**CAMPU S**
*WHI S PERY	PI S S	**FOCU S**	MITI S	TAPI S	CANTU S
WHI S TLER	PLU S	FRA S S	MODU S	**TAXU S**	**CANVA S**
*WHO S EVER	PON S	FRIE S	MOMU S	TELO S	**CAPIA S**
WRE S TLER	PU S S	FRON S	MONA S	**TEXA S**	**CAPRI S**
WRI S TLET	REI S	**FUCU S**	MUCU S	TONU S	CARE S S
YEA S AYER	RHU S	GAU S S	NARE S	TOOT S	CARIE S
*ZOO S PERM	S AN S	GENU S	NARI S	TOPO S	**CARPU S**
*ZOO S PORE	S A S S	GIGA S	NATE S	TORU S	CA S S I S
	S UD S	GLAN S	NEGU S	TRAN S	**CAUCU S**
BAA S	S U S S	GLA S S	NERT S	TRA S S	CAULE S
BA S S	TA S S	GLO S S	NEVU S	TRE S S	CAULI S
BIA S	THI S	GRA S S	**NEXU S**	TREW S	**CAVIE S**
BO S S	THU S	GRO S S	NIDU S	TRIE S	CEN S U S
BRO S	TO S S	GUE S S	NI S U S	TROI S	**CERCI S**
BU S S	WI S S	GULE S	NODU S	TRU S S	**CERCU S**
CE S S	WU S S	GYRU S	NOMO S	TURP S	CEREU S
CRI S	**YWI S**	HARD S	PARI S	VAGU S	CEROU S
CRU S	BALA S	HERE S	PAVI S	VARU S	CERTE S
CU S S	BANN S	HILU S	**PAVI S**	VIBE S	CE S S U S
DAI S	BA S E S	**HOCU S**	PEDE S	**VIBE S**	CE S TO S
DIE S	BA S I S	**HUMU S**	PENE S	VIRE S	CE S TU S
DI S S	BLE S S	HURD S	PENI S	VIRU S	**CHARA S**
DOE S	BLI S S	*JAKE S	PILU S	**VOCE S**	CHIAU S
DO S S	BOGU S	**JONE S**	PIOU S	**WAMU S**	CHINT S
FE S S	BOLA S	**JUDA S**	PLIE S	WIVE S	CHORU S
FO S S	BOLU S	**KUMY S**	POLI S	WOOP S	CIRCU S
FU S S	BONU S	**KVA S S**	PRE S S	**XERU S**	CIRRU S
GEN S	BRA S S	LAPI S	PRIE S	**YIKE S**	CI S TU S
HER S	**BRAW S**	LARE S	PRI S S	**YIPE S**	CITIE S
HI S S	BURB S	LEGE S	PRO S S	YOUR S	CITRU S
HOL S	CAMA S	LENE S	P S OA S	*ZOOK S	CIVIC S
JE S S	CA S U S	LENI S	PUBE S	**BABIE S**	**CLAVU S**
JO S S	CHAO S	LEWI S	PUBI S	BAGA S S	**CLEVI S**
KAA S	**CHE S S**	**LEXI S**	*PYXI S	**BATHO S**	CLONU S
KI S S	CLA S S	LIME S	QUA S S	**BEEVE S**	**COCCU S**
KO S S	CONU S	LITA S	RAMU S	**BEKI S S**	COITU S
KRI S	CORP S	LIVE S	REBU S	**BEVIE S**	COLEU S
KVA S	CRA S S	LOCU S	REGE S	**BICEP S**	COLIE S
LA S S	CRE S S	LOE S S	RIBE S	**BINOC S**	**COMOU S**
LEN S	CRIE S	LOGO S	RI S U S	BLINI S	CONIE S
LE S S	CRO S S	LORI S	RUBU S	BODIE S	**COPIE S**
LO S S	CUTE S	LOTO S	S ARO S	BOGIE S	CORNU S
LUE S	CUTI S	LOTU S	S EMI S	**BREEK S**	**CORPU S**
MA S S	**CYCA S**	LOUI S	S HIE S	**BREWI S**	**CORVE S**
ME S S	DEGA S	LUCE S	S INU S	BURIE S	CO S IE S
			S ITU S	BU S IE S	
			S KIE S		

CO S MO S	FUNGU S	MATRE S	*PRAXI S	TABER S	*ZOUND S
*COZIE S	FURIE S	MEATU S	PRECI S	TALLI S	BADNE S S
*COZZE S	GABIE S	MEGA S S	PRIMU S	TAR S U S	*BAFFIE S
CRA S E S	GALLU S	MIO S L S	PRUNU S	TENNI S	BALDIE S
CRA S I S	GA S S E S	MI S S I S	PTO S I S	TENUI S	BALLIE S
CRIPE S	GENIU S	MI S S U S	PYO S I S	TERRA S	BANDIE S
CRI S I S	GENTE S	MOLIE S	RABIE S	TE S TE S	BARLE S S
CROCU S	GLACI S	MONIE S	RACHI S	TE S TI S	BAWDIE S
CRUCE S	GLOMU S	MONTE S	RADIU S	THEIR S	BEDLE S S
CULLI S	GNEI S S	MORAL S	RAMOU S	THE S I S	*BEJE S U S
CULTU S	GNO S I S	MORA S S	RAPHI S	THOLO S	BELLIE S
CU S CU S	GOBIE S	MORRI S	RECE S S	THYMU S	BENTHO S
CU S PI S	GRADU S	MUCOU S	RECTU S	TIDIE S	BE S IDE S
CU S TO S	GRATI S	MYA S I S	REGIU S	TIGHT S	BETIME S
CUTLA S	HAERE S	MYO S I S	RELIE S	TME S I S	BIBLE S S
CYE S I S	HAGGI S	MYTHO S	REMI S S	TOPHU S	BIGNE S S
CYMOU S	HALVE S	NACHA S	REPA S S	TORIE S	BILIOU S
CYPRE S	HARA S S	NACHE S	REVER S	TOROU S	BILLIE S
CYPRU S	HERPE S	NAEVU S	RHE S U S	TRAGU S	BIOMA S S
DALLE S	HIATU S	NAVIE S	RICUE S	TRAPE S	BIONIC S
DEBRI S	HOLIE S	NEREI S	RIMOU S	TRIEN S	BIOTIC S
DEDAN S	HOMMO S	NIMBU S	RUBIE S	TRIPO S	BOBBIE S
DEFIE S	HOOVE S	NODOU S	RUCKU S	T S ORE S	BOLETU S
DEIXI S	HUBRI S	NOE S I S	RUFOU S	T S ORI S	BONKER S
DEMIE S	HUMMU S	NOWAY S	RUGOU S	T S URI S	BOONIE S
DENIE S	HYBRI S	NUBLE S	RUMPU S	TURVE S	BOOTIE S
DERMI S	*JOYOU S	PALAI S	S ANIE S	TU S S I S	BORACE S
DERRI S	JURIE S	PALPU S	S CHU S S	TYPHO S	BO S S IE S
DEXIE S	KARO S S	PAPPU S	S CRIE S	*TZURI S	BOWLE S S
DIDIE S	KAVA S S	PARIE S	S ELVE S	VALGU S	BRALE S S
DINGU S	KAYLE S	PAROU S	S EP S I S	VARIE S	BRINIE S
DIP S A S	KERME S	PARVI S	S ERIE S	VENOU S	BRI S S E S
DI S CU S	KERMI S	PA S S U S	S EROU S	VERME S	BUBALI S
DI S S E S	KNIVE S	PA S TI S	S ETOU S	VERMI S	BUBBIE S
DOBIE S	KOUMI S	PATHO S	S HAME S	VER S U S	BUDDIE S
DOGIE S	*KOUMY S	PATOI S	S HAMO S	VILLU S	BUDLE S S
DOOFU S	KOURO S	PELVI S	S HAMU S	VINOU S	BUGLO S S
DORIE S	KUMI S S	PEPLO S	S HNAP S	VI S CU S	BULBOU S
DURE S S	LACHE S	PEPLU S	S IGLO S	VITAL S	BULLIE S
FACIE S	LADIE S	PHARO S	S OLEU S	VIVER S	BULLOU S
FAECE S	LAMPA S	PHA S I S	S ONIC S	VULGU S	BURGE S S
FALCE S	LAP S U S	PHY S E S	S OWAN S	WADIE S	BURNOU S
FAMOU S	*LAZIE S	PHY S I S	S OWEN S	WALIE S	BUTTAL S
FA S CE S	LEAVE S	PIGNU S	S PEI S S	WALRU S	BUTTIE S
FAUCE S	LEVIE S	PILEU S	S TAPE S	WAMMU S	CABROU S
*FIZZE S	LIMBU S	PILOU S	S TA S E S	WAMPU S	CAE S TU S
FLATU S	LITMU S	PITIE S	S TA S I S	WAVIE S	CALAMU S
FOETU S	LOAVE S	*PLEXU S	S TATU S	WHENA S	CALEND S
FOLLE S	LORIE S	POGIE S	S TIPE S	WHO S I S	CALICE S
FOLLI S	LUNIE S	POKIE S	S TIRP S	WOLVE S	CALLOU S
FORTE S	LUPOU S	POLEI S	S TRA S S	*XY S TO S	CALYCE S
FORTI S	MADRA S	PONIE S	S TRE S S	*XY S TU S	CANDIE S
FRACA S	MANTE S	PORCU S	S TYLU S	YE S S E S	CANTHU S
FUCOU S	MANTI S	PO S EE S	S ULCU S	*YOICK S	CANVA S S
FUNDU S	*MAQUI S	PO S IE S	S YNGA S	*ZANIE S	CAPLE S S

CARCA S S	DEARIE S	FORTRE S	HIPNE S S	LIMULU S	NONPRO S
CARICE S	DECLA S S	FOULNE S	HITLE S S	LIONE S S	NOWNE S S
CARIOU S	DEFOCU S	*FOXINE S	HOBBIE S	LIPLE S S	NOXIOU S
CARITA S	DEGAU S S	*FOZINE S	HOLLIE S	LITOTE S	NUCLEU S
CARLE S S	DEPRE S S	FRACTU S	HOMINE S	LOCULU S	PADDIE S
CARNIE S	DEVIOU S	FREENE S	HOOKIE S	LOGGAT S	PANDIE S
CAROLU S	DEWLE S S	FRONTE S	HO S TE S S	LOGGET S	PANTIE S
CARRIE S	DIARIE S	FULNE S S	HOTNE S S	LOLLIE S	PAPPIE S
CA S EOU S	DICKEN S	FULVOU S	HUGEOU S	LONGIE S	PAPYRU S
CHABLI S	DIGRE S S	FUMULU S	HUMERU S	LOWNE S S	PARADO S
CHALLI S	DIMNE S S	FUNGOU S	HURDIE S	LUTEOU S	PARE S I S
CHAMOI S	DINGIE S	FURIOU S	HU S KIE S	*LYCHNI S	PARLOU S
CHA S SIS	DINKIE S	FURLE S S	HU S RIE S	MADNE S S	PARODO S
*CHEVIE S	DI S CU S S	FU S COU S	*HYDROP S	MALLEU S	PARRIE S
*CHLAMY S	DI S MI S S	GALLOU S	HYDROU S	MAMMIE S	PARTIE S
*CHYMOU S	DOGGIE S	GALLOW S	*JACKA S S	MANLE S S	PA S TIE S
CIRROU S	DOLLIE S	GAPO S I S	*JACKIE S	*MARQUI S	PATNE S S
CITROU S	DRYNE S S	GA S EOU S	*JACOBU S	MARRIE S	PEERE S S
CLARIE S	DUBIOU S	GA S LE S S	*JAGLE S S	MATLE S S	PEGLE S S
CLA S SE S	DUCHE S S	*GAWKIE S	*JAMMIE S	MATRA S S	PELORU S
CLA S SIS	DUCKIE S	GAYNE S S	JEALOU S	MEANIE S	PENATE S
CLIVER S	DUENE S S	GENE S I S	*JEEPER S	MEIO S I S	PENNIE S
CLYPEU S	DULNE S S	GIBBOU S	*JERKIE S	MERCIE S	PERCU S S
CODICE S	DUNNE S S	GLOBOU S	JETTIE S	MERI S I S	PERHAP S
COLITI S	DUTEOU S	GLORIE S	*JIMJAM S	ME S EEM S	PETA S O S
COLLIE S	DWARVE S	GLOTTI S	*JIVEA S S	MIDDIE S	PETA S U S
COLLIN S	FAIRIE S	GLUTEU S	JOANNE S	MILREI S	PETROU S
COLOBU S	FAMULU S	GODDE S S	*JOBLE S S	MIME S I S	PHALLU S
COLONU S	FANCIE S	GODLE S S	JOLLIE S	MINIBU S	PHOEBU S
COMMIE S	FARNE S S	GOODIE S	*JOYLE S S	MI S BIA S	PHONIC S
COMPA S S	FATLE S S	GRAMPU S	KALEND S	MI S SIE S	PHONIE S
CONATU S	FATNE S S	GRAVIE S	KENO S I S	MI S TIE S	PHOTIC S
CONCU S S	FATTIE S	GRUMOU S	KERME S S	MITO S I S	PICEOU S
CONFE S S	FATUOU S	GUMLE S S	KETO S I S	MODULU S	PIETIE S
CONGIU S	FEELE S S	GUMMOU S	KEYLE S S	MOLLIE S	PIGGIE S
COOKIE S	FELLIE S	GUNLE S S	KIDDIE S	MONADE S	PILEOU S
COOLIE S	FERRIE S	GUTLE S S	KINE S I S	MUDDIE S	PINKIE S
COPIOU S	FERROU S	HABITU S	KIRME S S	MUGGIN S	PINNIE S
COYNE S S	FEWNE S S	HALITU S	KITTIE S	MUMMIE S	PITEOU S
*CROQUI S	FEYNE S S	HALVER S	*KOLKHO S	MURICE S	PLATIE S
CUDDIE S	FIBROU S	HAMULU S	KOUMI S S	MYCO S I S	PLU S SE S
CUIRA S S	FILLIE S	HAPLE S S	*KOUMY S S	MYIA S I S	PLUTEU S
CULLIE S	FINALI S	HARDIE S	LAMPER S	NAPLE S S	POETE S S
CUMULU S	FINLE S S	HARNE S S	LAPIDE S	NEME S I S	POETIC S
CUPROU S	FITNE S S	HARPIE S	LARGE S S	NERVOU S	POLYPU S
CURIOU S	*FIXING S	HARRIE S	LA S HIN S	NETLE S S	POMPOU S
CU S S CU S	FLYLE S S	HATLE S S	LATICE S	NEWNE S S	POPPIE S
CUTLA S S	FOGLE S S	HEAVIE S	LAWLE S S	NEW S IE S	PORKIE S
CUTTIE S	FOLIOU S	HEINOU S	LAXNE S S	NITROU S	PO S SE S S
*CYCLOP S	FOLLIE S	HEIRE S S	LEFTIE S	NIVEOU S	POTTIE S
CYPRE S S	FORCEP S	HELICE S	LEGLE S S	NOCUOU S	PRECE S S
*CZARDA S	FORDLE S	HEREDE S	LEMURE S	NODDIE S	PREMI S S
DANDIE S	FORKLE S	HIDEOU S	LEPROU S	NOMBLE S	PRIAPU S
DARBIE S	FORMLE S	*HIJINK S	LIDLE S S	NONNEW S	PRIVIE S
DARKIE S	FORTIE S	HIPLE S S	LIMITE S	NONPLU S	PROCE S S

PROFE S S	*S CYPHU S	TEARGA S	WEARIE S	BIMANOU S	*CHROMOU S
PROTEU S	S EERE S S	TEDIOU S	WEBLE S S	BLOODIE S	*CHUCKIE S
PROWE S S	S ERIOU S	TELE S I S	WELLIE S	BLOTLE S S	CITREOU S
*PROXIE S	S EXLE S S	TELLIE S	WETNE S S	BLUENE S S	CLAWLE S S
PULPOU S	S FERIC S	TENNIE S	WHAT S I S	BODILE S S	CLEMATI S
PU S S IE S	S HAMMA S	TENUOU S	WHEREA S	BOLDNE S S	CLITORI S
*PYJAMA S	S HAMME S	TERRIE S	WHITIE S	*BOLLOCK S	CLUELE S S
PYLORU S	S HAMMO S	TETANU S	*WHIZZE S	BONELE S S	COALLE S S
PYRO S I S	S HAMOI S	THALLU S	WHOO S I S	BONINE S S	COATLE S S
*PYXIDE S	S HELVE S	THERMO S	WIGLE S S	BOOTLE S S	CODELE S S
*QUERIE S	S HERRI S	THIEVE S	WILLIE S	BOTANIE S	COENURU S
*QUIETU S	S HYNE S S	THYR S U S	WINLE S S	BOTRYTI S	COLDNE S S
RADICE S	S IEMEN S	TIELE S S	WI S EA S S	*BOXINE S S	COLINIE S
RAGGIE S	S ILENT S	TIGRE S S	WITHIE S	BRIMLE S S	COLO S SU S
RAILBU S	S ILENU S	TIMEOU S	WITLE S S	*BRITCHE S	COLPITI S
RANDIE S	S ILVIC S	TIPLE S S	WITNE S S	*BRONCHU S	*COMBING S
RAUCOU S	S IMLOU S	TITTIE S	WOENE S S	BROWLE S S	COMEDIE S
RAWNE S S	S INLE S S	TOADIE S	WOODIE S	BUR S ITI S	COMPLIE S
RAYLE S S	S INUOU S	TODDIE S	WOOLIE S	BU S HLE S S	COMPRE S S
READIE S	S ITHEN S	TOELE S S	WRYNE S S	BU S INE S S	CONGRAT S
RECRO S S	S KEP S I S	TOPLE S S	XERO S I S	BU S YNE S S	CONGRE S S
REDNE S S	*S KYPHO S	*TORQUE S	*ZEALOU S	BUTTRE S S	COOKLE S S
REDRE S S	S LYNE S S	TOWARD S	*ZEBRA S S	BUTYROU S	COOLNE S S
REDRIE S	S OFTIE S	TOWNIE S	*ZINCOU S	CADUCEU S	COPPERA S
REFLIE S	S OLIDU S	TOYLE S S	*ZIPLE S S	CADUCOU S	CORDLE S S
REFOCU S	S ONLE S S	TRAVOI S	*ZYGO S I S	CAGINE S S	CORELE S S
REGLO S S	S OPHIE S	TRELLI S	*ZYMO S T S	CALATHO S	CORNEOU S
REGRE S S	S ORITE S	TRICEP S	*BACCHIU S	CALATHU S	CO S INE S S
REGULU S	S ORO S I S	TRI S MU S	BACILLU S	CALCULU S	CO S TLE S S
REPRE S S	S PINIE S	TROILU S	*BACKLE S S	CALMNE S S	COUNTE S S
REREDO S	S PINOU S	T S IMME S	BALDNE S S	CALVADO S	COVETOU S
*RHACHI S	S PUMOU S	T S OORI S	BARBLE S S	CANITIE S	*COZINE S S
RHAMNU S	S TARET S	TUGLE S S	BARENE S S	CANNABI S	CRANKOU S
RHOMBU S	S TORIE S	TUMULU S	BARKLE S S	CANONE S S	CRANNIE S
RIBLE S S	S TRATU S	TURKOI S	BARONE S S	CANOROU S	CREMAIN S
RICINU S	S TUDIE S	*TZIMME S	BA S ALTE S	CAPTIOU S	CREWLE S S
RICKET S	S TYP S I S	*TZITZI S	BA S ELE S S	CARDITI S	CRIBROU S
RIMLE S S	S UBBA S S	VACUOU S	BA S ENE S S	CARELE S S	CROPLE S S
RIOTOU S	S UBMI S S	VARICE S	BA S SNE S S	CA S HLE S S	CROUPOU S
RODLE S S	S UCCE S S	VARIOU S	BATHLE S S	CATERE S S	CRUDITE S
RUBIOU S	S UCCU S S	VELITE S	BAUDRON S	*CATHEXI S	*CRYONIC S
RUINOU S	S UMLE S S	VERGLA S	BEAMLE S S	CAUTIOU S	*CUFFLE S S
RUNLE S S	S UMMON S	VERITA S	BEATLE S S	CENTE S I S	CUMBROU S
S ADNE S S	S UNLE S S	VICIOU S	*BEDWARD S	CERA S TE S	CUPREOU S
S ALLIE S	S URPA S S	VIRO S I S	BEEFLE S S	CERNUOU S	CURELE S S
S ANTIM S	S URPLU S	VI S COU S	*BEJABER S	CERVELA S	CURTNE S S
S APIEN S	S WAMIE S	VOMITU S	*BEJEEZU S	CHALLIE S	CU S TODE S
S APLE S S	S YCO S I S	VOTRE S S	BELTLE S S	CHANTIE S	CUTENE S S
S ARCOU S	S YNE S I S	VOWLE S S	*BENDWAY S	CHAU S SE S	CUTGRA S S
S ARDIU S	TABBIE S	WADDIE S	BERBERI S	*CHIA S MU S	CYANO S I S
SAS S IE S	TALIPE S	WAENE S S	BERMUDA S	*CHICNE S S	CY S TITI S
S CABIE S	TALLIE S	WALLIE S	BIA S NE S S	CHINLE S S	DACTYLU S
S CARVE S	TARDIE S	WANNE S S	BIBULOU S	CHLOROU S	DAFTNE S S
S CHMOO S	TARRIE S	WARLE S S	BIGAMOU S	CHORAGU S	DAMPNE S S
S CHNAP S	TAXLE S S	WAYLE S S	*BIJUGOU S	CHOREGU S	

DANKNE S S	FAMELE S S	GLADNE S S	HOLINE S S	LIFELE S S	ME S DAME S
DARKNE S S	FA S HIOU S	GLANDER S	HOMELE S S	LIGNEOU S	*METHINK S
DATELE S S	FA S TNE S S	GLAUCOU S	HOMINE S S	LIKENE S S	METRITI S
DEADNE S S	FA S TUOU S	GLEGNE S S	HOMINIE S	LIMELE S S	MICROBU S
DEAFNE S S	FEARLE S S	GLIBNE S S	HOODLE S S	LIMINE S S	*MID S HIP S
DEARNE S S	*FECKLE S S	GLORIOU S	HOOFLE S S	LIMPNE S S	MILDNE S S
DECOROU S	FELLNE S S	GLO S S IE S	*HOOKLE S S	LINELE S S	MINDLE S S
DECURIE S	FERREOU S	GLUMNE S S	HOOPLE S S	LINTLE S S	MIRINE S S
DEEDLE S S	FETIALI S	GOALLE S S	HOPELE S S	LI S TLE S S	MI S CLA S S
DEEPNE S S	FEVEROU S	GONENE S S	HORNFEL S	LIVENE S S	*MI S FOCU S
DEFTNE S S	FIBRO S I S	GOODNE S S	HORNLE S S	LOAMLE S S	MI S GUE S S
DEMONE S S	FINENE S S	GORGEOU S	HOTPRE S S	LOFTLE S S	MI S TRE S S
DEMOTIC S	FIRELE S S	GORINE S S	HUGENE S S	LOGINE S S	MITTIMU S
DENARIU S	FIRMNE S S	GORMLE S S	HUMOROU S	LONENE S S	MODIOLU S
DE S IROU S	FI S HLE S S	GRACILI S	*HUMPLE S S	LONGNE S S	MOLA S S E S
DETRITU S	*FIVEPIN S	GRACIOU S	HURTLE S S	*LONGWAY S	MOONLE S S
*DEXTROU S	FLAGLE S S	GRAVITA S	HU S TING S	LORDLE S S	MOTORBU S
DIABETE S	FLAMINE S	*GRAVLAK S	*HYMNLE S S	LORDO S I S	MOVELE S S
DIALY S I S	FLAPLE S S	GRAYNE S S	*HYPNO S I S	LORNNE S S	*MUCHNE S S
DIANTHU S	FLATNE S S	GREYNE S S	*JOHANNE S	LO S TNE S S	*MUNCHIE S
*DIDYMOU S	*FLATWAY S	GRIEVOU S	*JOKINE S S	LOUDNE S S	MUTENE S S
DIECIOU S	FLAWLE S S	GRIMNE S S	*JU S TNE S S	LOVELE S S	MUTICOU S
DIERE S I S	*FLEXUOU S	GRI S EOU S	KEELLE S S	LOVELIE S	MUTINIE S
DIE S TRU S	FLUERIC S	GUMMO S I S	KEENNE S S	LUCKLE S S	MUTINOU S
DIGAMIE S	FLUIDIC S	GU S TLE S S	KINDLE S S	LUMINOU S	MYELITI S
DIGGING S	FOAMLE S S	GYP S EOU S	KINDNE S S	LU S CIOU S	MYO S ITI S
DIMEROU S	FONDNE S S	HAIRLE S S	KINE S IC S	LU S HNE S S	MYO S OTI S
DIOICOU S	*FOODWAY S	HALENE S S	KINETIC S	LU S TROU S	NABOBE S S
DIPLO S I S	FOOTLE S S	HALFNE S S	*KINFOLK S	MAILLE S S	NAMELE S S
DIRENE S S	*FORCIPE S	HARDNE S S	KINGLE S S	MALENE S S	NARCO S I S
DI S TAVE S	*FRABJOU S	HARMLE S S	*KNICKER S	MAMMATU S	NATHLE S S
DI S TRE S S	FREMITU S	HAUTBOI S	KNOTLE S S	MAMMITI S	NAUPLIU S
DIURE S I S	FRETLE S S	*HAZINE S S	KURTO S I S	MANDAMU S	NAU S EOU S
*DIZYGOU S	FULLNE S S	HEADLE S S	*KYPHO S I S	MANWARD S	NAUTILU S
DOLDRUM S	FUMELE S S	HEATLE S S	LACELE S S	MARA S MU S	NEARNE S S
DOLOROU S	FU S ELE S S	HEDONIC S	LACINE S S	*MARQUE S S	NEATNE S S
DONENE S S	*GADZOOK S	HEEDLE S S	LACTEOU S	MA S S LE S S	NEBULOU S
DOORLE S S	GAINLE S S	HEELLE S S	LAMENE S S	MA S TITI S	NECKLE S S
DOPINE S S	GALLEA S S	HEIRLE S S	LAMINOU S	MA S TLE S S	NECRO S I S
DOURNE S S	GAMA S HE S	HELMLE S S	LANCIER S	MATELE S S	NEEDLE S S
*DOZINE S S	GAMENE S S	HELPLE S S	LANDLE S S	MATINE S S	NEURITI S
DRABNE S S	GAMINE S S	HERBLE S S	LANDMA S S	MATTRA S S	NEURO S I S
DRIPLE S S	GARBLE S S	HERCULE S	LANKNE S S	MATTRE S S	NEW S LE S S
DRUIDE S S	GA S TNE S S	*HIBI S CU S	LAPILLU S	MAYORE S S	NICENE S S
DRUTHER S	*GA S WORK S	HIDELE S S	LATENE S S	*MAZINE S S	NIGHNE S S
DUCTLE S S	GATELE S S	HIDRO S I S	*LAZINE S S	MEANNE S S	NIGHTIE S
DULLNE S S	*GAYWING S	HIGAMIE S	LEADLE S S	MEATLE S S	NORMLE S S
DUMBNE S S	GEARLE S S	*HIGHNE S S	LEAFLE S S	MEEKNE S S	NO S ELE S S
DURABLE S	GENEROU S	HILTLE S S	LEAKLE S S	MEETNE S S	NO S INE S S
DU S TLE S S	GENETIC S	HIOLY S I S	LEANNE S S	MEGALOP S	NOTELE S S
FABULOU S	GENITAL S	HIPAROU S	*LECYTHI S	MELANOU S	NOTORNI S
FACELE S S	*GEOTAXI S	HIRAMOU S	*LECYTHU S	MELODIE S	*NOWADAY S
FACTIOU S	GIANTE S S	HIVELE S S	*LEKYTHO S	*MENFOLK S	NUBILOU S
FADELE S S	GIFTLE S S	*HOKINE S S	*LEKYTHU S	MENI S CU S	NUCELLU S
FAIRNE S S	GLABROU S	HOLELE S S	LIBELOU S	*MEPHITI S	NUDENE S S

NUMBNESS	PORTRESS	RIGOROUS	SIGHLESS	STEMLESS	TIDELESS
NUMEROUS	POSHNESS	RIMINESS	SIMONIES	STENOSIS	TIDINESS
NUMINOUS	*POXVIRUS	RINGHALS	*SIZINESS	STIMULUS	TIDYTIPS
NUTGRASS	PREBLESS	RINGTOSS	*SKEWNESS	STRATOUS	TIMELESS
*PACIFIES	PRECIOUS	RIPENESS	SKILLESS	STRUMOUS	TIMOROUS
*PACKNESS	*PREFOCUS	RISIBLES	SKINLESS	STUDIOUS	TININESS
PAINLESS	PREGGERS	RISKLESS	*SKYWARDS	SUBCLASS	TINNITUS
*PALAZZOS	PRETTIES	ROADLESS	SLIMNESS	SUBCUTIS	TINTLESS
PALENESS	PREVIOUS	ROBOTICS	SLIPLESS	SUBEROUS	TIRELESS
*PALEWAYS	PRIMNESS	ROCKLESS	SLITLESS	SUBGENUS	TITANESS
PANCREAS	PRINCESS	ROOFLESS	SLOWNESS	SUCCUBUS	TITANOUS
PANDANUS	PRIORESS	ROOTLESS	SLYBOOTS	SUCHNESS	TOADLESS
*PANMIXIS	PRIORIES	ROPINESS	SMARTASS	SUCKLESS	TOMBLESS
PARODIES	PROGRESS	ROSINESS	SMITHERS	SUDSLESS	TONELESS
PASSLESS	PROPOLIS	ROSINOUS	SMUGNESS	SUNDRESS	TONETICS
PASTLESS	PROTASIS	RUCTIOUS	SNAPLESS	SUNDRIES	TOOLLESS
PASTNESS	PROVIRUS	RUDENESS	SNOWLESS	SUNDROPS	TOPCROSS
PATHLESS	PRURITUS	RULELESS	SNUBNESS	SUNGLASS	TORTIOUS
PATULOUS	PSILOSIS	RUSTLESS	SNUGGIES	SUNWARDS	TORTUOUS
*PAYABLES	PULPLESS	RUTHLESS	SNUGNESS	SUPPRESS	TOUGHIES
PEAKLESS	PULVINUS	RYEGRASS	SOAPLESS	SURENESS	TOWNLESS
PEERLESS	PUMPLESS	SABULOUS	SOAPSUDS	SUSURRUS	TRAMLESS
PERILOUS	PUNINESS	SACCULUS	SOCKLESS	SYLLABUS	TRAPPOUS
PERTNESS	PURENESS	SAFENESS	SOFTNESS	SYNAPSIS	TREELESS
PERVIOUS	*PYCNOSIS	SAGENESS	SOILLESS	SYNDESIS	TRESPASS
PETALOUS	PYELITIS	SALTLESS	SOLELESS	SYNOPSIS	TRIGNESS
*PHIMOSIS	*PYKNOSIS	SALTNESS	SOLENESS	*SYPHILIS	TRIMNESS
*PHTHISIS	*QUADRANS	SAMENESS	SOLONETS	TACKLESS	TRINKUMS
*PHYLAXIS	RACEMOUS	SANENESS	SOMBROUS	TACTLESS	TROLLIES
*PHYLESIS	RACHITIS	SCABIOUS	*SOMEWAYS	TAILLESS	TROUSERS
PILELESS	RACINESS	SCALENUS	SONGLESS	TALLNESS	TROWSERS
PINGRASS	RAINLESS	SCANTIES	SONOROUS	TAMELESS	TRUENESS
PINKNESS	RAMULOUS	SCARIOUS	SORENESS	TAMENESS	*TRYWORKS
PIPELESS	RANKNESS	SCARLESS	SOURNESS	TANTALUS	TSORRISS
PIPINESS	RAPTNESS	*SCHNAPPS	SOURPUSS	TAPELESS	TUBELESS
PITHLESS	RARENESS	SCIRRHUS	SPACIOUS	TARANTAS	TUBEROUS
PITILESS	RASHNESS	SCLEROUS	SPADICES	TARTNESS	TUBULOUS
*PIXINESS	RAVENOUS	SCURRIES	SPANLESS	TAUTNESS	TUMULOUS
PLANLESS	RAYGRASS	SEAMLESS	SPECIOUS	TEARLESS	TUNELESS
*PLATYPUS	REALNESS	SEATLESS	SPERMOUS	TENESMUS	TURFLESS
PLAYLESS	REASSESS	SEDULOUS	*SPHERICS	TENIASIS	*TURQUOIS
PLOTLESS	RECKLESS	SEEDLESS	SPHINGES	TENTLESS	TUSKLESS
PLOTTIES	REINLESS	SELFLESS	*SPHYGMUS	TERMINUS	TUTORESS
PLUGLESS	RESINOUS	SELFNESS	SPINLESS	TERMLESS	TWIGLESS
PLUMBOUS	RESTLESS	SEMIOSIS	SPLENIUS	TETANIES	VAINNESS
PLUVIOUS	RESTRESS	SENARIUS	SPOONIES	*TEXTLESS	VALOROUS
POACEOUS	REVERIES	SENSUOUS	SPOTLESS	THALAMUS	VAPOROUS
POETLESS	RHINITIS	SETULOUS	SPRYNESS	THANATOS	VASTNESS
POKINESS	*RHIZOPUS	*SEXINESS	SPURIOUS	THAWLESS	VEINLESS
POLELESS	*RHONCHUS	*SHAMMIES	SPYGLASS	THELITIS	VENOMOUS
POLITICS	RIBGRASS	SHANTIES	STANNOUS	THEORIES	VENTLESS
*POLYPOUS	RICHNESS	SHOELESS	STAPEDES	THEWLESS	VERBLESS
POORNESS	RIFENESS	SHORTIES	STARKERS	THINNESS	VESTLESS
POPULOUS	RIFTLESS	SICKNESS	STARLESS	THOWLESS	VICELESS
PORTLESS	RIGHTIES	*SIDEWAYS	STEADIES	*THROMBUS	VICTRESS

VIEWLESS	VOTELESS	WATTLESS	WIDENESS	WISENESS	*YOKELESS
VIGOROUS	VULVITIS	WAVELESS	WIFELESS	WISHLESS	*ZANINESS
VILENESS	*WAESUCKS	WAVINESS	WILDNESS	WONDROUS	*ZESTLESS
VIRTUOUS	WAGELESS	*WAXINESS	WILINESS	WOODLESS	*ZONELESS
VITELLUS	WAITRESS	*WEAKNESS	WINDLASS	WOOLLIES	*ZOONOSIS
VITREOUS	*WAKELESS	WEEDLESS	WINDLESS	WORDLESS	
VOIDNESS	WARDRESS	WEIRDIES	WINELESS	*WORKLESS	
VOLVULUS	WARINESS	WELDLESS	WINGLESS	WORNNESS	
VOMITOUS	WARMNESS	WELLNESS	WIRELESS	*XANTHOUS	
VOTARESS	WARTLESS	WHATNESS	WIRINESS	YEARLIES	

T

TABU	TEAT	TIDY	TONG	TRIO	TYPP
TACE	TEEL	TIED	TONY	TRIP	TYPY
TACH	TEEM	TIER	TOOK	TROD	TYRE
TACK	TEEN	TIFF	TOOL	TROP	TYRO
TACO	TEFF	TIKE	TOOM	TROT	TZAR
TACT	TELA	TIKI	TOON	TROW	TABBY
TAEL	TELE	TILE	TOOT	TROY	TABER
TAHR	TELL	TILL	TOPE	TRUE	TABES
TAIL	TEMP	TILT	TOPH	TSAR	TABID
TAIN	TEND	TIME	TOPI	TUBA	TABLA
TAKA	TENT	TINE	TORA	TUBE	TABLE
TAKE	TEPA	TING	TORC	TUCK	TABOO
TALA	TEPF	TINT	TORE	TUFA	TABOR
TALC	TERM	TINY	TORI	TUFF	TABUN
TALE	TERN	TIPI	TORN	TUFT	TACET
TALI	TEST	TIRE	TORO	TULE	TACHE
TALK	TETH	TIRL	TORR	TUMP	TACIT
TALL	TEXT	TIRO	TORT	TUNA	TACKY
TAME	THAE	TITI	TORY	TUNE	TAFFY
TAMP	THAN	TIVY	TOSH	TUNG	TAFIA
TANG	THAT	TOAD	TOSS	TURD	TAIGA
TANK	THAW	TOBY	TOST	TURF	TAINT
TAPA	THEE	TODY	TOTE	TURK	TAKER
TAPE	THEM	TOEA	TOUR	TURN	TAKIN
TARE	THEN	TOFF	TOUT	TUSH	TALAR
TARN	THEW	TOFT	TOWN	TUSK	TALER
TARO	THEY	TOFU	TOWY	TUTU	TALKY
TARP	THIN	TOGA	TOYO	TWAE	TALLY
TART	THIO	TOIL	TRAD	TWAT	TALON
TASK	THIR	TOIT	TRAM	TWEE	TALUK
TASS	THIS	TOKE	TRAP	TWIG	TALUS
TATE	THOU	TOLA	TRAY	TWIN	TAMAL
TAUT	THRO	TOLD	TREE	TWIT	TAMER
TAXA	THRU	TOLE	TREF	TYEE	TAMIS
TAXI	THUD	TOLL	TREK	TYER	TAMMY
TEAK	THUG	TOLU	TRET	TYKE	TANGO
TEAL	THUS	TOMB	TREY	TYNE	TANGY
TEAM	TICK	TOME	TRIG	TYPE	TANKA
TEAR	TIDE	TONE	TRIM	TYPO	TANSY

TANTO	TENTH	**THRIP**	TONDO	TRAPT	TSADE
TAPER	TENTY	**THROB**	TONER	TRASH	TSADI
TAPIR	TEPAL	THROE	TONEY	TRASS	TSUBA
TAPIS	TEPEE	**THROW**	TONGA	TRAVE	TUBAL
TARDO	TEPID	**THRUM**	TONIC	TRAWL	**TUBBY**
TARDY	**TEPOY**	*THUJA	TONNE	TREAD	TUBER
TARGE	TERAI	**THUMB**	TONUS	TREAT	**TUFTY**
TAROC	TERCE	THUMP	TOOTH	TREEN	TULIP
TAROK	TERGA	**THUNK**	TOOTS	TREND	TULLE
TAROT	TERNE	THURL	*TOPAZ	TRESS	TUMID
TARRE	TERRA	**THUYA**	TOPEE	TREWS	**TUMMY**
TARRY	**TERRY**	**THYME**	TOPER	TRIAC	TUMOR
TARSI	TERSE	**THYMI**	**TOPHE**	TRIAD	TUNER
TARTY	TESLA	TIARA	TOPIC	TRIAL	TUNIC
TASSE	TESTA	TIBIA	TOPOI	TRIBE	TUNNY
TASTE	**TESTY**	TICAL	TOPOS	TRICE	**TUPIK**
TASTY	TETRA	TIDAL	**TOQUE**	**TRICK**	**TUQUE**
TATAR	**TEUCH**	TIGER	TORAH	TRIED	TURBO
TATER	TEUGH	TIGHT	**TORCH**	TRIER	**TURFY**
TATTY	**TEXAS**	TIGON	TORIC	TRIES	TURPS
TAUNT	**THACK**	TILAK	TORII	TRIGO	TUTEE
TAUPE	THANE	TILDE	TOROT	TRIKE	TUTOR
TAWER	**THANK**	TILER	TORSE	TRILL	TUTTI
TAWIE	**THARM**	TILTH	TORSI	TRINE	TUTTY
TAWNY	**THEBE**	TIMER	TORSK	TRIOL	TUYER
TAWSE	**THECA**	TIMID	TORSO	TRIPE	TWAIN
TAXER	**THEFT**	TINCT	TORTE	TRITE	TWANG
TAXON	THEGN	TINEA	TORUS	TROAK	**TWEAK**
TAXUS	THEIN	TINGE	TOTAL	**TROCK**	TWEED
*TAZZA	THEIR	TINNY	TOTEM	TRODE	TWEEN
TEACH	**THEME**	**TIPPY**	TOTER	TROIS	TWEET
TEARY	THERE	**TIPSY**	**TOUCH**	TROKE	**TWERP**
TEASE	**THERM**	TIRED	TOUGH	TROLL	**TWICE**
TECHY	THESE	TITAN	TOUSE	TROMP	TWIER
TECTA	THETA	TITER	TOWEL	TRONA	TWILL
TEDDY	**THEWY**	TITHE	TOWER	TRONE	TWINE
TEENY	**THICK**	TITLE	TOWIE	TROOP	**TWINY**
TEETH	**THIEF**	TITRE	**TOWNY**	**TROOZ**	TWIRL
TEGUA	**THIGH**	TITTY	**TOXIC**	TROPE	**TWIRP**
TEIID	THILL	*TIZZY	**TOXIN**	TROTH	TWIST
TEIND	THINE	TOADY	TOYER	TROUT	*TWIXT
TELEX	THING	TOAST	TOYON	TROVE	**TWYER**
TELIA	**THINK**	TODAY	TRACE	TRUCE	TYING
TELIC	THIOL	**TODDY**	**TRACK**	**TRUCK**	**TYPAL**
TELLY	THIRD	**TOFFY**	TRACT	TRUED	**TYPED**
TELOS	THIRL	TOGUE	TRADE	TRUER	**TYPEY**
TEMPI	THOLE	TOILE	TRAGI	TRULL	**TYPIC**
TEMPO	THONG	**TOKAY**	TRAIK	TRULY	**TYTHE**
TEMPT	THORN	TOKEN	TRAIL	**TRUMP**	TABARD
TENCH	THORO	TOKER	TRAIN	TRUNK	**TABBED**
TENET	**THORP**	TOLAN	TRAIT	TRUSS	**TABBIS**
TENIA	THOSE	TOLYL	TRAMP	TRUST	TABLET
TENON	**THRAW**	TOMAN	TRANK	TRUTH	TABOUR
TENOR	THREE	**TOMMY**	**TRANQ**	**TRYMA**	TABULI
TENSE	**THREW**	TONAL	TRANS	TRYST	**TACKER**

TACKET	TAPPED	TEEMER	TESTIS	THRUST	TIPPER
*TACKEY	TAPPER	TEENER	TESTON	THULIA	TIPPET
TACKLE	TAPPET	TEENSY	TETANY	THUSLY	TIPPLE
TACTIC	TARAMA	TEEPEE	TETCHY	*THWACK	TIPTOE
TAENIA	TARGET	TEETER	TETHER	THWART	TIPTOP
TAFFIA	TARIFF	TEETHE	TETRAD	*THYMEY	TIRADE
TAGGED	TARING	TEGMEN	TETRYL	*THYMIC	TIRING
TAGGER	TARMAC	TELEDU	TETTER	THYMOL	TISANE
TAGRAG	TARNAL	TELEGA	THAIRM	THYMUS	TISSUE
TAHINI	TARPAN	TELFER	THALER	THYRSE	TITBIT
TAHSIL	TARPON	TELIAL	THATCH	TICKER	TITFER
TAILER	TARRED	TELIUM	THAWER	TICKET	TITIAN
TAILLE	TARSAL	TELLER	THEINE	TICKLE	TITMAN
TAILOR	TARSIA	TELOME	THEIRS	TICTAC	TITTER
TAIPAN	TARSUS	TELSON	THEISM	TICTOC	TITTIE
TAKAHE	TARTAN	TEMPEH	THEIST	TIDBIT	TITTLE
TAKEUP	TARTAR	TEMPER	THENAL	TIDDLY	TITTUP
TAKING	TARTLY	TEMPLE	THENAR	TIDIED	TMESIS
TALCUM	*TARZAN	TENACE	THENCE	TIDIER	TOASTY
TALENT	TASSEL	TENAIL	THEORY	TIDIES	TOCHER
TALION	TASSET	TENANT	THERBY	TIDILY	TOCSIN
TALKER	TASSIE	TENDER	THERME	TIDING	TODDLE
TALKIE	TASTER	TENDON	THESIS	TIEPIN	TOECAP
TALLIS	TATAMI	TENNER	THETIC	TIERCE	TOFFEE
TALLIT	TATTED	TENNIS	THIEVE	TIFFIN	TOGATE
TALLOL	TATTER	TENOUR	THINLY	TIGHTS	TOGGED
TALLOW	TATTIE	TENPIN	THIRAM	TIGLON	TOGGLE
TALUKA	TATTLE	TENREC	THIRST	TILING	TOILER
TAMALE	TATTOO	TENSOR	THIRTY	TILLER	TOILET
TAMARI	TAUGHT	TENTER	THOLOS	TILTER	TOKING
TAMBAC	TAUTEN	TENTIE	*THORAX	TIMBAL	TOLANE
TAMBAK	TAUTLY	TENUIS	THORIA	TIMBER	TOLEDO
TAMBUR	TAUTOG	TENURE	THORIC	TIMBRE	TOLING
TAMEIN	TAVERN	TENUTO	THORNY	TIMELY	TOLLER
TAMELY	TAWDRY	TEOPAN	THORON	TIMING	TOLUIC
TAMEST	TAWNEY	TEPEFY	THORPE	TINCAL	TOLUID
TAMING	TAWPIE	TEPHRA	THOUGH	TINDER	TOLUOL
TAMMIE	*TAXEME	TERAPH	THRALL	TINEID	TOLUYL
TAMPAN	TAXITE	TERBIA	THRASH	TINFUL	TOMATO
TAMPER	*TAXMAN	TERCEL	THRAVE	TINGLE	TOMBAC
TAMPON	*TEABOX	TERCET	THRAWN	TINGLY	TOMBAK
TANDEM	TEACUP	TEREDO	THREAD	TINIER	TOMBAL
TANGLE	TEAPOT	TERETE	THREAP	TINILY	TOMBOY
TANGLY	TEAPOY	TERGAL	THREAT	TINING	TOMCAT
TANIST	TEARER	TERGUM	THREEP	TINKER	TOMCOD
TANKER	TEASEL	TERMER	THRESH	TINKLE	TOMMED
TANNED	TEASER	TERMLY	THRICE	TINKLY	TOMTIT
TANNER	*TEAZEL	TERMOR	THRIFT	TINMAN	TONEME
TANNIC	*TEAZLE	TERRAS	THRILL	TINNED	TONGER
TANNIN	TECHED	TERRET	THRIVE	TINNER	TONGUE
TANREC	TECHIE	TERRIT	THROAT	TINSEL	TONIER
TANTRA	TECTAL	TERROR	THRONE	TINTER	TONING
TANUKI	TECTUM	TESTEE	THRONG	TIPCAT	TONISH
TAPALO	TEDDER	TESTER	THROVE	TIPOFF	TONLET
TAPING	TEDIUM	TESTES	THRUSH	TIPPED	TONNER

TONSIL	TRAPES	TROVER	**TURKEY**	**TABETIC**	TANAGER
TOOLER	**TRASHY**	TROWEL	TURNER	TABLEAU	**TANBARK**
TOOTER	TRAUMA	**TROWTH**	TURNIP	**TABLING**	TANGELO
TOOTHY	TRAVEL	TRUANT	TURNUP	**TABLOID**	TANGENT
TOOTLE	TREATY	TRUDGE	TURRET	TABORER	TANGIER
TOOTSY	TREBLE	TRUEST	TURTLE	TABORET	TANGLER
TOPFUL	**TREBLY**	**TRUFFE**	TURVES	TABORIN	**TANGRAM**
TOPHUS	**TREFAH**	TRUING	**TUSCHE**	TABOULI	**TANKAGE**
TOPING	TREMOR	TRUISM	**TUSKER**	TABULAR	**TANKARD**
TOPPED	**TRENCH**	TRUSTY	TUSSAH	**TACHISM**	TANKFUL
TOPPER	**TRENDY**	TRYOUT	TUSSAL	**TACHIST**	TANNAGE
TOPPLE	TREPAN	TRYSTE	TUSSAR	*TACHYON	TANNATE
*TOQUET	TREPID	TSETSE	TUSSEH	**TACKIER**	**TANNERY**
TORERO	TRESSY	**TSKTSK**	**TUSSER**	*TACKIFY	TANNEST
TORIES	TREVET	TSORES	TUSSIS	*TACKILY	TANNING
TOROID	TRIAGE	TSORIS	TUSSLE	**TACKLER**	**TANNISH**
TOROSE	TRIBAL	TSURIS	TUSSOR	TACNODE	TANTARA
TOROTH	*TRICKY	TUBATE	TUSSUR	**TACTFUL**	**TANTIVY**
TOROUS	TRICOT	**TUBBED**	TUTTED	TACTILE	TANTRUM
TORPID	TRIENE	**TUBBER**	**TUXEDO**	TACTION	**TANYARD**
TORPOR	TRIENS	**TUBFUL**	TUYERE	**TADPOLE**	TAPERER
*TORQUE	**TRIFID**	TUBING	**TWANGY**	**TAFFETA**	**TAPETUM**
TORRID	TRIFLE	TUBIST	*TWANKY	**TAGGING**	**TAPHOLE**
TORULA	**TRIGLY**	TUBULE	*TWEAKY	**TAGLIKE**	**TAPIOCA**
TOSSER	TRIGON	**TUCHUN**	**TWEEDY**	**TAGMEME**	**TAPPING**
TOSSUP	**TRIJET**	**TUCKER**	**TWEENY**	**TAILFAN**	**TAPROOM**
TOTHER	**TRILBY**	**TUCKET**	*TWEEZE	TAILING	TAPROOT
TOTING	TRIMER	**TUFFET**	**TWELVE**	*TAKEOFF	TAPSTER
TOTTED	**TRIMLY**	TUFOLI	**TWENTY**	**TAKEOUT**	**TARBUSH**
TOTTER	TRINAL	TUFTER	**TWIBIL**	TALARIA	TARDIER
TOUCAN	TRIODE	TUGGER	**TWIGGY**	**TALIPED**	TARDIES
TOUCHE	TRIOSE	**TUGRIK**	TWILIT	TALIPES	**TARDYON**
TOUCHY	TRIPLE	TUILLE	TWINER	TALIPOT	**TARNISH**
TOUGHY	**TRIPLY**	TULADI	**TWINGE**	**TALKING**	TARRIED
TOUPEE	TRIPOD	**TUMBLE**	**TWIRLY**	TALLAGE	TARRIER
TOURER	TRIPOS	**TUMEFY**	**TWISTY**	**TALLBOY**	TARRIES
TOUSLE	**TRIPPY**	**TUMOUR**	**TWITCH**	TALLIED	TARRING
TOUTER	TRISTE	TUMULI	**TWOFER**	TALLIER	TARSIER
*TOUZLE	TRITON	TUMULT	**TYCOON**	TALLIES	TARTANA
TOWAGE	TRIUNE	TUNDRA	**TYMBAL**	**TALLISH**	**TARTISH**
TOWARD	TRIVET	TUNEUP	**TYMPAN**	TALLITH	TARTLET
TOWERY	TRIVIA	TUNICA	**TYPHON**	TALLOWY	**TARTUFE**
TOWHEE	TROCAR	TUNING	**TYPHUS**	TALLYHO	**TARWEED**
TOWNEE	**TROCHE**	TUNNED	**TYPIER**	TALOOKA	TASTING
TOWNIE	TROGON	TUNNEL	*TYPIFY	TAMABLE	**TATOUAY**
TOXINE	**TROIKA**	TUPELO	**TYPING**	**TAMANDU**	TATTIER
TOXOID	TROLLY	**TUPPED**	**TYPIST**	TAMARAO	**TATTILY**
TOYISH	**TROMPE**	TURACO	TYRANT	TAMARAU	TATTING
TRACER	**TROPHY**	TURBAN	*TZETZE	TAMARIN	TATTLER
TRADER	**TROPIC**	TURBID	*TZURIS	TAMASHA	TAUNTER
TRAGIC	TROPIN	TURBIT	**TABANID**	TAMBALA	TAURINE
TRAGUS	TROTYL	TURBOT	TABARET	**TAMBOUR**	TAUTAUG
TRAMEL	**TROUGH**	TUREEN	**TABBIED**	**TAMBURA**	**TAVERNA**
TRANCE	TROUPE	TURGID	TABBIES	**TAMPALA**	*TAXABLE
TRAPAN	TROUTY	TURGOR	**TABBING**	**TAMPION**	*TAXICAB

*TAXIMAN	TENSING	**THEELIN**	**THUNDER**	**TISSUEY**	TOOLING
*TAXIWAY	TENSION	**THEELOL**	*THYMIER	TITANIA	TOOTLER
TAXLESS	TENSITY	**THENAGE**	*THYMINE	TITANIC	TOOTSIE
*TAXPAID	TENSIVE	**THEOLOG**	THYROID	TITHING	TOPCOAT
*TAXWISE	TENTAGE	**THEORBO**	THYRSUS	TITLARK	TOPFULL
*TAXYING	TENTHLY	**THEOREM**	*THYSELF	TITLIST	TOPIARY
TEABOWL	TENTIER	*THERAPY	TICKING	TITRANT	*TOPKICK
TEACAKE	TENUITY	**THEREAT**	TICKLER	TITRATE	TOPKNOT
TEACART	TENUOUS	**THEREIN**	TIDDLER	TITTIES	TOPLESS
TEACHER	*TEQUILA	**THEREOF**	TIDERIP	TITULAR	TOPLINE
TEALIKE	TERAOHM	**THEREON**	TIDEWAY	TOADIED	TOPMAST
TEARFUL	TERBIUM	**THERETO**	TIDIEST	TOADIES	TOPMOST
TEARGAS	TEREBIC	**THERIAC**	*TIEBACK	TOADISH	TOPONYM
TEARIER	TEREFAH	**THERMAE**	TIELESS	TOASTER	TOPPING
TEARILY	TERGITE	**THERMAL**	**TIERCED**	TOBACCO	TOPSAIL
TEAROOM	TERMITE	**THERMEL**	TIERCEL	TOCCATA	TOPSIDE
TEASHOP	TERNARY	.THERMIC	*TIFFANY	TODDIES	TOPSOIL
TEASING	TERNATE	**THERMIT**	TIGHTEN	TODDLER	TOPSPIN
TEATIME	TERNION	**THERMOS**	TIGRESS	TOEHOLD	*TOPWORK
TEAWARE	TERPENE	**THEROID**	TIGRISH	TOELESS	TORCHON
TECHNIC	TERRACE	**THEURGY**	TILAPIA	**TOELIKE**	TORMENT
TECTITE	TERRAIN	**THIAMIN**	TILBURY	TOENAIL	TORNADO
*TECTRIX	TERRANE	*THIAZIN	TILLAGE	TOESHOE	TORPEDO
TEDIOUS	TERREEN	*THIAZOL	TILLITE	TOGATED	*TORQUER
TEENAGE	TERRENE	*THICKEN	TIMARAU	**TOGGERY**	*TORQUES
TEENFUL	TERRIER	*THICKET	**TIMBALE**	TOGGING	TORREFY
TEENIER	TERRIES	*THICKLY	TIMBREL	TOGGLER	TORRENT
TEENTSY	TERRIFY	**THIEVES**	TIMEOUS	TOILFUL	TORRIFY
TEETHER	TERRINE	**THIMBLE**	TIMEOUT	*TOKAMAK	TORSADE
TEGULAR	TERTIAL	**THINKER**	TIMOLOL	*TOKOMAK	TORSION
TEGUMEN	TERTIAN	**THINNED**	*TIMOTHY	TOLIDIN	TORTILE
TEKTITE	TESSERA	**THINNER**	TIMPANO	TOLLAGE	TORTONI
TELAMON	TESTACY	**THIONIC**	TINAMOU	TOLLBAR	TORTRIX
TELEMAN	TESTATE	**THIONIN**	TINFOIL	TOLLMAN	TORTURE
TELEOST	TESTIER	**THIONYL**	TINGLER	TOLLWAY	TOSSPOT
TELERAN	TESTIFY	**THIRDLY**	TINHORN	TOLUATE	TOSTADA
TELESIS	TESTILY	**THIRSTY**	TINIEST	TOLUENE	TOSTADO
TELFORD	TESTING	**THISTLE**	TINKLER	TOLUIDE	TOTABLE
TELLIES	TESTOON	**THISTLY**	TINLIKE	TOLUOLE	TOTALLY
TELPHER	TESTUDO	**THITHER**	TINNIER	*TOMBACK	TOTTERY
TEMBLOR	TETANAL	**THORITE**	TINNILY	TOMBOLO	TOTTING
TEMPERA	TETANIC	**THORIUM**	TINNING	TOMFOOL	TOUCHER
TEMPEST	TETANUS	**THOUGHT**	TINTING	TOMMING	TOUCHUP
TEMPLAR	TETCHED	**THREADY**	TINTYPE	TOMPION	TOUGHEN
TEMPLET	TETOTUM	*THRIFTY	TINWARE	TONEARM	TOUGHIE
TEMPTER	TETRODE	**THRIVER**	TINWORK	TONETTE	TOUGHLY
TEMPURA	TEXTILE	**THROATY**	TIPCART	TONGMAN	TOURACO
TENABLE	TEXTUAL	**THROUGH**	TIPLESS	TONIEST	TOURING
TENANCY	TEXTURE	**THROWER**	TIPPIER	TONIGHT	TOURISM
TENDRIL	THALLUS	*THRUMMY	TIPPING	TONNAGE	TOURIST
TENFOLD	THANAGE	**THRUPUT**	TIPPLER	TONNEAU	TOURNEY
TENNIES	THANKER	*THRUWAY	TIPSIER	TONNISH	TOWARDS
TENNIST	*THATCHY	**THUGGEE**	TIPSILY	TONSURE	*TOWAWAY
TENONER	THEATER	**THULIUM**	TIPSTER	TONTINE	TOWBOAT
TENSILE	THEATRE	**THUMPER**	TISSUAL	*TOOLBOX	TOWHEAD

TOWLINE	TREHALA	TRISHAW	TSUNAMI	TWANGLE	*TACHISME
TOWMOND	*TREKKER	TRISMUS	TUATARA	TWASOME	TACHISTE
TOWMONT	TRELLIS	TRISOME	TUATERA	TWATTLE	TACITURN
TOWNIES	TREMBLE	TRISOMY	TUBAIST	TWEEDLE	TACKIEST
TOWNISH	TREMBLY	TRITIUM	TUBBING	TWEETER	TACKLESS
TOWNLET	TREMOLO	TRITOMA	*TUBIFEX	*TWEEZER	*TACKLING
*TOWPATH	TRENAIL	TRITONE	TUBLIKE	*TWELFTH	TACONITE
TOWROPE	TREPANG	TRIUMPH	TUBULAR	TWIBILL	TACTLESS
*TOXEMIA	TRESSEL	TRIVIAL	TUBULIN	TWIDDLE	TAFFAREL
*TOXICAL	TRESTLE	TRIVIUM	TUGBOAT	*TWIDDLY	TAFFEREL
TOYLESS	TRIABLE	TROCHAL	TUGGING	TWIGGEN	TAFFRAIL
TOYLIKE	TRIACID	TROCHAR	*TUGHRIK	TWINIER	TAFFRAIL
*TOYSHOP	TRIADIC	TROCHEE	TUGLESS	TWINING	TAGALONG
TRACERY	*TRIAZIN	TROCHIL	TUITION	*TWINJET	TAGBOARD
TRACHEA	TRIBADE	TRODDEN	TUMBLER	TWINKLE	*TAGMEMIC
TRACHLE	TRIBUNE	TROFFER	TUMBREL	*TWINKLY	TAIGLACH
TRACING	TRIBUTE	TROILUS	TUMBRIL	TWINNED	*TAILBACK
TRACKER	TRICEPS	TROLAND	TUMMLER	TWINSET	TAILBONE
TRACTOR	TRICING	TROLLER	TUMULAR	TWIRLER	TAILCOAT
TRADUCE	TRICKER	TROLLEY	TUMULUS	TWISTER	TAILGATE
*TRAFFIC	TRICKIE	TROLLOP	TUNABLE	*TWITCHY	TAILLAMP
TRAGEDY	TRICKLE	TROMMEL	TUNDISH	TWITTED	TAILLESS
TRAILER	*TRICKLY	TROOPER	TUNEFUL	TWITTER	TAILLEUR
TRAINEE	*TRICKSY	TROPHIC	TUNICLE	TWOFOLD	TAILLIKE
TRAINER	TRICLAD	TROPINE	TUNNAGE	TWOSOME	TAILPIPE
TRAIPSE	TRICORN	TROPISM	TUNNING	TYLOSIN	TAILRACE
TRAITOR	TRIDENT	TROTTED	TUPPING	TYMPANA	TAILSKID
*TRAJECT	TRIDUUM	TROTTER	TURACOU	TYMPANI	TAILSPIN
TRAMCAR	TRIFLER	TROUBLE	TURBARY	TYMPANO	TAILWIND
TRAMELL	TRIFOLD	TROUNCE	TURBETH	*TYMPANY	*TAKEAWAY
TRAMMED	TRIFORM	TROUPER	TURBINE	TYPEBAR	*TAKEDOWN
TRAMMEL	TRIGGER	TROUSER	TURBITH	TYPESET	*TAKEOVER
TRAMPER	TRIGRAM	TRUANCY	TURDINE	*TYPHOID	*TAKINGLY
TRAMPLE	TRILLER	TRUCKER	TURFIER	*TYPHOON	TALAPOIN
*TRAMWAY	TRILOGY	TRUCKLE	TURFMAN	*TYPHOSE	TALESMAN
TRANCHE	TRIMMED	TRUDGEN	TURFSKI	TYPICAL	TALEYSIM
TRANGAM	TRIMMER	TRUDGER	TURGENT	TYPIEST	TALISMAN
TRANSIT	TRINARY	TRUFFLE	TURGITE	TYRANNY	TALKABLE
TRANSOM	TRINDLE	TRUMEAU	TURISTA	*TZADDIK	TALLNESS
*TRAPEZE	TRINITY	TRUMPET	TURKOIS	*TZARDOM	TALLYMAN
TRAPPED	TRINKET	TRUNDLE	TURMOIL	*TZARINA	TALMUDIC
TRAPPER	TRIOLET	TRUNNEL	TURNERY	*TZARISM	TAMANDUA
TRAVAIL	*TRIOXID	TRUSSER	TURNING	*TZARIST	*TAMARACK
TRAVOIS	*TRIPACK	TRUSTEE	TURNKEY	*TZIGANE	TAMARIND
TRAWLER	TRIPART	TRUSTER	TURNOFF	*TZIMMES	TAMARISK
TRAWLEY	TRIPLET	TRUSTOR	TURNOUT	*TZITZIS	TAMBOURA
TRAYFUL	*TRIPLEX	TRYPSIN	TURPETH	*TZITZIT	TAMEABLE
TREACLE	TRIPODY	TRYSAIL	TURTLER	TABLEFUL	TAMELESS
TREADER	TRIPOLI	TRYSTER	TUSSOCK	TABLETOP	TAMENESS
TREADLE	TRIPPED	TSARDOM	TUSSORE	TABOOLEY	TAMPERER
TREASON	TRIPPER	TSARINA	TUSSUCK	TABORINE	TANGENCE
TREATER	TRIPPET	TSARISM	TUTELAR	TABOURER	TANGENCY
TREDDLE	TRIREME	TSARIST	TUTOYER	TABOURET	TANGIBLE
TREETOP	TRISECT	TSIMMES	TUTTING	TABULATE	TANGIBLY
TREFOIL	TRISEME	TSOORIS	TWADDLE	TACHINID	TANGIEST

TANISTRY	TEENIEST	TEPIDITY	THEREFOR	THRUSTOR	*TIPSTAFF
*TANKLIKE	*TEENYBOP	TERATISM	THEREMIN	*THUGGERY	*TIPSTOCK
*TANKSHIP	TEETHING	TERATOMA	THERIACA	*THUGGISH	TIRAMISU
TANNABLE	TEETOTAL	TERAWATT	THERMION	*THUMBKIN	TIRELESS
TANTALUM	TEETOTUM	TERCELET	THERMITE	*THUMBNUT	TIRESOME
TANTALUS	TEFILLIN	TEREBENE	THEROPOD	*THUNDERY	TIRRIVEE
TAPADERA	TEGMENTA	*TERIYAKI	THESAURI	THURIBLE	TISSULAR
TAPADERO	TEGMINAL	TERMINAL	THESPIAN	THURIFER	TITANATE
TAPELESS	TEGUMENT	TERMINUS	THETICAL	*THWACKER	TITANESS
TAPELIKE	TEIGLACH	TERMLESS	THEWLESS	THWARTER	TITANISM
TAPELINE	TELECAST	TERMTIME	THIAMINE	*THWARTLY	TITANITE
TAPESTRY	TELEFILM	TERPINOL	*THIAZIDE	*THYMIEST	TITANIUM
*TAPEWORM	TELEGONY	TERRAPIN	*THIAZINE	*THYMOSIN	TITANOUS
TAPHOUSE	TELEGRAM	TERRARIA	*THIAZOLE	*THYREOID	TITHABLE
TARANTAS	TELEMARK	*TERRAZZO	*THICKISH	*THYROXIN	TITHONIA
TARBOOSH	TELEPATH	TERRELLA	*THICKSET	*TICKLISH	TITIVATE
TARLATAN	TELEPLAY	TERRIBLE	*THIEVERY	*TICKSEED	TITMOUSE
TARLETAN	TELEPORT	TERRIFIC	*THIEVING	*TICKTACK	TITRABLE
TARPAPER	TELESTIC	TERTIARY	*THIEVISH	*TICKTOCK	TITRATOR
TARRAGON	*TELETEXT	TESTATOR	THINCLAD	TIDELAND	TITTERER
TARRIEST	TELETHON	TESTICLE	*THINDOWN	TIDELESS	*TITTUPPY
TARTNESS	TELEVIEW	TESTIEST	*THINKING	TIDELIKE	TITULARY
TARTRATE	TELEVISE	TETANIES	THINNESS	*TIDEMARK	*TOADFLAX
TARTUFFE	TELLTALE	TETANISE	THINNEST	TIDINESS	*TOADFISH
*TASKWORK	TELLURIC	*TETANIZE	THINNING	TIDYTIPS	TOADLESS
TASTEFUL	TELOMERE	TETRACID	THINNISH	TIECLASP	TOADLIKE
TATTIEST	TEMERITY	TETRAGON	THIONATE	TIGEREYE	*TOADYISH
TATTOOER	TEMPERER	TETRAMER	THIONINE	TIGERISH	TOADYISM
TAUTNESS	TEMPLATE	TETRAPOD	*THIOPHEN	*TIGHTWAD	TOBOGGAN
TAUTOMER	TEMPORAL	TETRARCH	THIOTEPA	TILEFISH	TOCOLOGY
TAUTONYM	TENACITY	*TETROXID	THIOUREA	TILELIKE	TOEPIECE
TAVERNER	TENACULA	*TEXTBOOK	THIRLAGE	TILTYARD	TOEPLATE
*TAXATION	TENAILLE	*TEXTLESS	THIRSTER	TIMECARD	TOGETHER
*TAXINGLY	TENANTRY	*TEXTUARY	THIRTEEN	TIMELESS	TOILETRY
*TAXONOMY	TENDANCE	*TEXTURAL	THOLEPIN	TIMELINE	TOILETTE
*TAXPAYER	TENDENCE	THALAMUS	*THOROUGH	*TIMEWORK	TOILSOME
TEABERRY	TENDENCY	THALLIUM	THOUSAND	TIMEWORN	TOILWORN
TEABOARD	TENDERER	THANATOS	THOWLESS	TIMIDITY	TOKENISM
TEACHING	TENDERLY	*THANKFUL	THRALDOM	TIMOROUS	*TOKOLOGY
TEAHOUSE	TENEBRAE	*THATAWAY	THRASHER	TIMPANUM	TOKONOMA
*TEAKWOOD	TENEMENT	*THATCHER	THRAWART	TINCTURE	TOLBOOTH
TEAMAKER	TENESMUS	THAWLESS	THREADER	TININESS	TOLERANT
TEAMMATE	TENIASIS	*THEARCHY	THREAPER	TINKERER	TOLERATE
TEAMSTER	TENORITE	THEBAINE	THREATEN	TINKLING	TOLIDINE
*TEAMWORK	TENOTOMY	THELITIS	THRENODE	TINNIEST	TOLLGATE
TEARAWAY	TENPENCE	*THEMATIC	*THRENODY	TINNITUS	TOLUIDIN
TEARDOWN	TENPENNY	THEOCRAT	THRESHER	TINPLATE	*TOMAHAWK
TEARDROP	TENSIBLE	*THEODICY	THRILLER	TINSELLY	TOMALLEY
TEARIEST	TENTACLE	*THEOGONY	*THROBBER	TINSMITH	TOMBLESS
TEARLESS	TENTIEST	*THEOLOGY	*THROMBIN	TINSTONE	*TOMBLIKE
TEASELER	TENTLESS	*THEONOMY	*THROMBUS	TINTLESS	TOMENTUM
TEASPOON	TENTLIKE	THEORIES	THROSTLE	TIPPABLE	*TOMMYROT
TECTONIC	TEOCALLI	THEORISE	THROTTLE	TIPPIEST	TOMOGRAM
TEENAGED	TEOSINTE	THEORIST	*THRUMMER	*TIPPYTOE	TOMORROW
TEENAGER	TEPHRITE	*THEORIZE	THRUSTER	TIPSIEST	TONALITY

TONELESS	TRABEATE	TREADLER	TRIMETER	TRUANTRY	TURBINAL
TONETICS	TRACHEID	TREASURE	TRIMMEST	*TRUCKAGE	TURBOCAR
TONGUING	*TRACHOMA	TREASURY	TRIMMING	*TRUCKFUL	TURBOFAN
TONICITY	*TRACHYTE	TREATISE	TRIMNESS	*TRUCKING	*TURBOJET
TOOLHEAD	*TRACKAGE	TRECENTO	*TRIMORPH	TRUCKLER	TURFIEST
TOOLLESS	*TRACKING	TREELAWN	TRIMOTOR	*TRUCKMAN	TURFLESS
TOOLROOM	*TRACKMAN	TREELESS	TRINKUMS	TRUDGEON	*TURFLIKE
TOOLSHED	*TRACKWAY	TREELIKE	TRINODAL	TRUDGING	TURGENCY
TOPCROSS	TRACTATE	TREENAIL	*TRIOXIDE	TRUEBLUE	TURMERIC
*TOPLOFTY	TRACTILE	TREMBLER	TRIPEDAL	TRUEBORN	TURNCOAT
*TOPNOTCH	TRACTION	TRENCHER	TRIPHASE	TRUEBRED	TURNDOWN
TOPOLOGY	*TRADEOFF	TREPHINE	TRIPLANE	TRUELOVE	TURNHALL
*TOPONYMY	TRADITOR	TRESPASS	TRIPLING	TRUENESS	TURNOVER
*TOPOTYPE	TRADUCER	TRESSIER	TRIPLITE	*TRUMPERY	TURNPIKE
TOPSIDER	TRAGICAL	TRESSOUR	TRIPLOID	TRUNCATE	TURNSOLE
TOPSTONE	TRAGOPAN	TRESSURE	TRIPPING	TRUNDLER	TURNSPIT
TORCHERE	TRAINFUL	TRIADISM	TRIPTANE	*TRUNKFUL	*TURQUOIS
TORCHIER	TRAINING	TRIANGLE	TRISCELE	TRUNNION	TURRICAL
TOREADOR	TRAINMAN	*TRIARCHY	*TRIPTYCH	TRUSSING	TURTLING
TOREUTIC	TRAINWAY	*TRIAXIAL	TRIPWIRE	TRUSTFUL	TUSKLESS
TORNILLO	TRAMLESS	*TRIAZINE	TRISCELE	TRUTHFUL	*TUSKLIKE
TOROSITY	TRAMLINE	*TRIAZOLE	TRISKELE	*TRYINGLY	TUTELAGE
TORPIDLY	TRAMMING	TRIBASIC	TRISOMIC	*TRYWORKS	TUTELARY
*TORQUATE	*TRAMPISH	*TRIBRACH	TRISTATE	TSAREVNA	TUTORAGE
*TORQUING	TRAMPLER	TRIBUNAL	*TRISTEZA	*TSARITZA	TUTORESS
TORTILLA	TRAMROAD	TRICHINA	TRISTFUL	TSORRISS	TUTORIAL
TORTIOUS	*TRANQUIL	TRICHITE	TRISTICH	TUBBABLE	TWADDLER
TORTOISE	TRANSACT	TRICHOID	TRITHING	TUBELESS	TWANGIER
TORTUOUS	TRANSECT	*TRICHOME	TRITICUM	TUBELIKE	TWANGLER
TORTURER	TRANSEPT	*TRICKERY	TRIUMVIR	TUBENOSE	*TWELVEMO
TOTALISE	TRANSFER	TRICKIER	TRIUNITY	TUBERCLE	TWIDDLER
TOTALISM	*TRANSFIX	*TRICKILY	TRIVALVE	TUBEROID	TWIGLESS
TOTALIST	TRANSHIP	*TRICKISH	*TROCHAIC	TUBEROSE	*TWIGLIKE
TOTALITY	TRANSMIT	TRICOLOR	TROCHILI	TUBEROUS	*TWILIGHT
*TOTALIZE	TRANSUDE	TRICORNE	TROCHLEA	*TUBEWORK	TWILLING
TOTALLED	TRAPBALL	TRICTRAC	TROCHOID	*TUBIFORM	TWINBORN
TOTEMISM	TRAPDOOR	*TRICYCLE	TROILISM	TUBULATE	TWINIEST
TOTEMIST	*TRAPEZIA	TRIENNIA	TROILITE	TUBULOSE	*TWINIGHT
TOTEMITE	TRAPLIKE	TRIETHYL	TRIUMVIR	TUBULOUS	*TWINKLER
TOTTERER	TRAPLINE	TRIFECTA	TROLLIED	TUBULURE	TWINNING
TOUGHIES	TRAPNEST	TRIFLING	TROLLIES	*TUCKAHOE	*TWINSHIP
*TOUGHISH	TRAPPEAN	TRIFOCAL	TROLLING	*TUCKSHOP	TWISTING
*TOVARICH	TRAPPING	TRIFORIA	TROOPIAL	TULLIBEE	*TWITCHER
TOVARISH	TRAPPOSE	TRIGGEST	TROPONIN	TUMBLING	TWITTERY
*TOWARDLY	TRAPPOUS	TRIGGING	TROTLINE	TUMIDITY	TWITTING
TOWELING	*TRAPROCK	*TRIGLYPH	TROTTING	TUMPLINE	*TWOPENCE
*TOWNFOLK	TRAPUNTO	TRIGNESS	TROUBLER	TUMULOSE	TWOPENNY
*TOWNHOME	TRASHMAN	TRIGONAL	TROUNCER	TUMULOUS	*TYMPANAL
TOWNLESS	TRAUCHLE	TRIGRAPH	TROUPIAL	TUNEABLE	*TYMPANIC
*TOWNSHIP	TRAVELER	TRIHEDRA	TROUPING	TUNELESS	*TYMPANUM
TOWNSMAN	TRAVELOG	TRILLION	TROUSERS	TUNGSTEN	*TYPECASE
TOWNWEAR	TRAVERSE	TRILLIUM	TROUVERE	TUNICATE	*TYPECAST
*TOXAEMIA	TRAVESTY	TRILOBAL	TROUVEUR	TUNNELER	*TYPEFACE
*TOXICANT	TRAVOISE	TRILOBED	TROWELER	TUPPENCE	*TYPIFIER
*TOXICITY	TRAWLNET	TRIMARAN	TROWSERS	*TUPPENNY	*TYPOLOGY

TYRAMINE	S T EAK	S T OWP	BO T T OM	DE T AIN	HO T T ED
TYRANNIC	S T EAL	S T RAP	BU T ANE	DE T ECT	HO T T ER
TYROSINE	S T EAM	S T RAW	BU T ENE	DE T EN T	HU T T ED
*TZAREVNA	S T EED	S T RAY	BU T LER	DE T ES T	*HU T ZPA
*TZARITZA	S T EEK	S T REP	BU T T ER	DE T ICK	*JE T SAM
*TZITZITH	S T EEL	S T REW	BU T T ON	DE T OUR	*JE T SOM
	S T EEP	S T RIA	*BY T ALK	DI T HER	JE T T ED
S T AB	S T EER	S T RIP	*CA T CHY	DO T AGE	JE T T ON
S T AG	S T EIN	S T ROP	CA T ENA	DO T ARD	*JI T NEY
S T AR	S T ELA	S T ROW	CA T GU T	DO T IER	JI T T ER
S T AT	S T ELE	S T ROY	CA T ION	DO T ING	KA T ION
S T AW	S T ENO	S T RUM	CA T ISH	DO T T ED	KE T ENE
S T AY	S T ERE	S T RUT	CA T KIN	DO T T EL	KE T ONE
S T EL	S T ERN	S T UDY	CA T LIN	DO T T ER	KE T OSE
S T EM	S T ICH	S T UFF	CA T NAP	DO T T LE	KE T T LE
S T EP	S T ICK	S T ULL	CA T NIP	FA T HER	KI T IES
S T ET	S T IED	S T UNT	CA T SUP	FA T HOM	KI T ING
S T EW	S T IES	S T UPA	CA T T ED	FA T ING	*KI T SCH
S T EY	S T IFF	S T UPE	CA T T IE	FA T T ED	KI T T ED
S T IR	S T ILE	S T URT	CA T T LE	FA T T EN	KI T T EL
S T OA	S T ILL	S T YLE	CE T ANE	FA T T ER	KI T T EN
S T OB	S T IL T	S T YLI	CI T RIN	FE T ICH	KI T T LE
S T OP	S T IME	S T YMY	CI T HER	FE T ING	LA T EEN
S T OW	S T IMY	BA T BOY	CI T IED	FE T ISH	LA T ELY
S T UB	S T ING	BA T EAU	CI T IES	FE T T ED	LA T EN T
S T UD	S T INK	BA T HER	CI T IFY	FE T T ER	LA T ES T
S T UM	S T IN T	BA T HOS	CI T ING	FE T T LE	LA T HER
S T UN	S T IPE	BA T ING	CI T OLA	*FI T CHY	LA T IGO
S T YE	S T IRK	BA T MAN	CI T OLE	FI T FUL	LA T INO
S T ACK	S T IRP	BAT T ED	CI T RAL	FI T T ED	LA T ISH
S T ADE	S T OA T	BAT T EN	CI T RIC	FI T T ER	LA T RIA
S T AFF	S T OCK	BAT T ER	CI T RON	FU T ILE	LA T T EN
S T AGE	S T OGY	BA T T IK	CI T RUS	FU T URE	LA T T ER
S T AGY	S T OIC	BAT T LE	CO T EAU	GA T EAU	LA T T IN
S T AID	S T OKE	BAT T UE	CO T ING	GA T HER	LE T HAL
S T AIG	S T OLE	BE T AKE	CO T T AR	GA T ING	LE T T ED
S T AIN	S T OMA	BE T HEL	CO T T ER	GE T T ER	LE T T ER
S T AIR	S T OMP	BE T IDE	CO T T ON	GI T ANO	LI T ANY
S T AKE	S T ONE	BE T IME	CO T YPE	GO T T EN	LI T CHI
S T ALE	S T ONY	BE T ISE	CU T ES T	GU T T ED	LI T ERY
S T ALK	S T QOD	BE T ONY	CU T ESY	GU T T ER	LI T HIA
S T ALL	S T OOK	BE T OOK	CU T LAS	GU T T LE	LI T HIC
S T AMP	S T OOL	BE T RAY	CU T LER	*HA T BOX	LI T MUS
S T AND	S T OOP	BE T TED	CU T LE T	HA T FUL	LI T T EN
S T ANE	S T OPE	BE T T ER	CU T OFF	HA T ING	LI T T ER
S T ANG	S T OPT	BE T T OR	CU T OU T	HA T PIN	LI T T LE
S T ANK	S T ORE	*BI T CHY	CU T T ER	HA T RED	LO T ION
S T APH	S T ORK	BI T T ED	CU T T LE	HA T T ED	LO T T ED
S T ARE	S T ORM	BI T T EN	DA T ARY	HA T T ER	LU T EAL
S T ARK	S T ORY	BI T T ER	DA T CHA	HE T ERO	LU T EIN
S T AR T	S T OSS	BO T ANY	DA T ING	HI T HER	LU T ES T
S T ASH	S T OUP	*BO T CHY	DA T IVE	HO T BED	LU T EUM
STATE	S T OUR	BO T FLY	DA T URA	*HO T BOX	LU T ING
S T AVE	S T OU T	BO T HER	DE T ACH	HO T DOG	LU T IS T
S T EAD	S T OVE	BO T T LE	DE T AIL	HO T ROD	MA T RES

*MATRIX	NOTING	PUTLOG	RETYPE	TITTER	*BETHINK
MATRON	NOTION	PUTOFF	RITARD	TITTIE	BETHORN
MATSAH	NUTANT	PUTOUT	RITTER	TITTLE	*BETHUMP
MATTED	NUTATE	PUTRID	RITUAL	TITTUP	BETIMES
MATTER	NUTING	PUTSCH	ROTARY	TOTHER	BETOKEN
MATTIN	NUTLET	PUTTEE	ROTATE	TOTING	BETROTH
MATURE	NUTMEG	PUTTER	ROTCHE	TOTTED	BETTING
*MATZAH	NUTRIA	PYTHON	ROTGUT	TOTTER	BETWEEN
*MATZOH	NUTTED	RATANY	ROTTED	TUTTED	*BETWIXT
*MATZOT	NUTTER	RATBAG	ROTTEN	VATFUL	BITABLE
METAGE	PATACA	RATHER	ROTTER	VATTED	BITTERN
METATE	*PATCHY	RATIFY	ROTUND	VETOER	BITTIER
METEOR	PATENT	RATINE	RUTILE	VITALS	BITTING
METIER	PATHOS	RATING	RUTTED	VITRIC	*BITTOCK
METING	PATINA	RATION	SATANG	VITTLE	BITUMEN
METTLE	PATINE	RATITE	SATARA	VOTARY	BOTANIC
MITIER	PATOIS	RATLIN	SATEEN	VOTING	BOTCHER
MITRAL	PATROL	RATOON	SATING	VOTIVE	BOTONEE
MITTEN	PATRON	RATTAN	SATINY	WATAPE	BOTTLER
MOTILE	PATTED	RATTED	SATORI	WATERY	BOTULIN
MOTION	PATTEE	RATTEN	SATRAP	WATSIT	BUTANOL
MOTTLE	PATTEN	RATTER	SETOFF	WATTER	BUTCHER
MUTANT	PATTER	RATTLE	SETOSE	WATTLE	BUTLERY
MUTASE	PATTIE	RATTLY	SETOUS	WETHER	BUTTALS
MUTATE	PETARD	RATTON	SETOUT	WETTED	BUTTERY
MUTEST	PETITE	RETACK	SETTEE	WETTER	BUTTIES
MUTINE	PETNAP	RETAIL	SETTER	*WITCHY	*BUTTOCK
MUTING	PETREL	RETAIN	SETTLE	WITHAL	BUTTONY
MUTTER	PETROL	RETAKE	SHTETL	WITHER	BUTYRAL
MUTTON	PETTED	RETAPE	*SHTICK	WITHIN	BUTYRIC
MUTUAL	PETTER	RETARD	SITCOM	WITING	BUTYRIN
MUTUEL	PETTLE	RETEAM	SITING	WITTED	*BUTYRYL
MUTULE	PITIED	RETEAR	SITTEN	WUTHER	CATALOG
*MYTHIC	PITIER	RETELL	SITTER	YATTER	CATALPA
NATANT	PITIES	RETENE	SOTTED	YTTRIA	CATARRH
NATION	PITMAN	RETEST	SUTLER	*ZITHER	CATAWBA
NATIVE	PITSAW	RETIAL	SUTTEE	BATCHER	CATBIRD
NATRON	PITTED	RETILE	SUTURE	*BATFISH	CATBOAT
NATTER	POTAGE	RETIME	TATAMI	*BATFOWL	CATCALL
NATURE	POTASH	RETINA	TATTED	BATHING	CATCHER
NETHER	POTATO	RETINE	TATTER	BATHMAT	*CATCHUP
NETTED	POTBOY	RETINT	TATTIE	BATHTUB	CATCLAW
NETTER	POTEEN	RETIRE	TATTLE	*BATHYAL	CATECHU
NETTLE	POTENT	RETOLD	TATTOO	BATISTE	CATERAN
NETTLY	POTFUL	RETOOK	TETANY	BATLIKE	CATERER
NITERY	POTHER	RETOOL	TETCHY	BATSMAN	CATFACE
NITRIC	POTION	RETORE	TETHER	BATTEAU	CATFALL
NITRID	POTMAN	RETORN	TETRAD	BATTERY	*CATFISH
NITRIL	POTPIE	RETORT	TETRYL	BATTIER	CATHEAD
NITWIT	POTSIE	RETRAL	TETTER	BATTING	CATHECT
NOTARY	POTTED	RETRIM	TITBIT	BATTLER	CATHODE
NOTATE	POTTER	RETTED	TITFER	BATWING	CATLIKE
NOTHER	POTTLE	RETUNE	TITHER	BETAINE	CATLING
NOTICE	*POTZER	RETURN	TITIAN	*BETAXED	CATMINT
NOTIFY		RETUSE	TITMAN	*BETHANK	CATSPAW

CA T TAIL	DO T TREL	*HA T CHEL	LA T TICE	NI T ROSO	PO T LIKE
CA T TALO	DU T EOUS	*HA T CHER	LE T DOWN	NI T ROUS	PO T LINE
CA T TERY	DU T IFUL	*HA T CHET	LE T TING	NO T ABLE	*PO T LUCK
CA T TIER	FA T ALLY	HA T EFUL	LE T TUCE	NO T ABLY	PO T SHOT
CA T TILY	*FA T BACK	HA T LESS	LI T ERAL	NO T CHER	PO T TEEN
CA T TING	FA T BIRD	HA T LIKE	*LI T HIFY	NO T EDLY	PO T TENT
*CA T WALK	FA T EFUL	*HA T RACK	LI T HIUM	NO T EPAD	PO T TERY
CI T ABLE	FA T HEAD	HA T SFUL	LI T HOID	NO T HING	PO T TIER
CI T ADEL	FA T IDIC	HE T AERA	LI T ORAL	NO T ICER	PO T TIES
CI T ATOR	FA T IGUE	HE T AIRA	LI T OTES	NU T CASE	PO T TING
CI T HARA	FA T LESS	*HI T CHER	LI T URGY	NU T GALL	PU T AMEN
CI T HERN	FA T LIKE	HI T LESS	LO T TERY	NU T LIKE	*PU T REFY
CI T HREN	FA T LING	*HO T CAKE	LO T TING	NU T MEAT	PU T TIED
*CI T IZEN	FA T NESS	HO T FOOT	LU T EOUS	*NU T PICK	PU T TIER
CI T RATE	FA T TEST	HO T HEAD	LU T HERN	NU T WOOD	PU T TING
CI T RINE	FA T TIER	HO T LINE	LU T HIER	PA T AMAR	RA T ABLE
CI T ROUS	FA T TIES	HO T NESS	*MA T CHUP	PA T CHER	RA T AFEE
CI T TERN	FA T TILY	HO T SHOT	MA T ELOT	PA T ELLA	RA T AFIA
CO T ERIE	FA T TING	HO T SPUR	MA T INAL	PA T ENCY	RA T ATAT
CO T HURN	FA T TISH	HO T TEST	MA T INEE	*PA T HWAY	RA T CHET
CO T IDAL	FA T UITY	HO T TISH	MA T LESS	PA T IENT	RA T FINK
CO T TAGE	FA T UOUS	HU T LIKE	MA T RASS	PA T NESS	RA T FISH
CO T TIER	FA T WOOD	HU T MENT	MA T TING	PA T RIOT	RA T HOLE
CO T TONY	*FE T CHER	HU T TING	*MA T TOCK	PA T ROON	RA T LIKE
*CU T AWAY	*FE T LOCK	*HU T ZPAH	*MA T ZOON	PA T TERN	RA T LINE
*CU T BACK	FE T TING	*JE T BEAD	*MA T ZOTH	PA T TING	RA T TAIL
*CU T BANK	*FI T CHEE	*JE T LIKE	ME T AMER	PE T ASOS	RA T TEEN
CU T DOWN	*FI T CHET	*JE T PORT	*ME T HOXY	PE T ASUS	RA T TIER
CU T ESIE	*FI T CHEW	*JE T TIED	ME T ICAL	*PE T COCK	RA T TING
CU T ICLE	FI T MENT	JE T TIER	ME T ISSE	PE T IOLE	RA T TISH
CU T LASS	FI T NESS	JE T TIES	ME T IOLE	*PE T RIFY	RA T TLER
CU T LERY	FI T TEST	*JE T TING	ME T RIST	PE T ROUS	RA T TOON
CU T LINE	FI T TING	*JI T TERY	MI T ERER	PE T TIER	RA T TRAP
CU T OVER	*FU T HARC	*JI T TERY	MI T ICID	PE T TING	RE T ABLE
CU T TAGE	*FU T HARK	*JO T TING	MI T IEST	PE T TISH	RE T AKER
CU T TIES	*FU T HORC	KA T CINA	*MI T ZVAH	PE T UNIA	RE T ASTE
CU T TING	*FU T HORK	*KA T HODE	*MO T HERY	PI T APAT	RE T EACH
*CU T WORK	*FU T TOCK	*KA T YDID	MO T TLER	PI T CHER	RE T HINK
CU T WORM	GA T EMAN	*KI T CHEN	NA T RIUM	PI T EOUS	RE T IARY
DA T ABLE	GA T EWAY	KI T HARA	NA T URAL	PI T FALL	RE T ICLE
DA T EDLY	GE T AWAY	KI T LING	NE T LESS	PI T HEAD	RE T INAL
DE T ENTE	GE T TING	KI T TING	NE T LIKE	PI T IFUL	RE T INOL
DE T ERGE	GI T TERN	KO T OWER	NE T SUKE	PI T TING	RE T INUE
DE T INUE	GO T HITE	LA T AKIA	NE T TIER	PO T ABLE	RE T IREE
DE T RACT	GO T THIC	LA T CHET	NE T TING	PO T AMIC	RE T IRER
DE T RAIN	GU T LESS	LA T ENCY	NE T TLER	PO T BOIL	RE T ITLE
DE T RUDE	GU T LIKE	LA T ERAD	NE T WORK	PO T ENCE	RE T OUCH
DI T CHER	GU T SILY	LA T ERAL	NI T CHIE	PO T ENCY	RE T RACE
DI T HERY	GU T TATE	LA T HERY	NI T INOL	PO T HEAD	RE T RACK
DI T HIOL	GU T TERY	LA T HIER	*NI T PICK	PO T HEEN	RE T RACT
DI T TANY	GU T TIER	LA T ICES	NI T RATE	PO T HERB	RE T RAIN
DO T IEST	GU T TING	LA T OSOL	NI T RIDE	PO T HOLE	RE T READ
DO T TIER	GU T TLER	LA T RINE	NI T RIFY	PO T ICHE	RE T REAT
DO T TILY	HA T ABLE	LA T RING	NI T RILE	PO T LACH	RE T RIAL
DO T TING	HA T BAND		NI T RITE		RE T SINA

RETTING	TOTTING	BISTORT	FATTIES	PARTIER	RUTTISH
RETWIST	TUTELAR	BITTERN	FATTILY	PARTLET	SALTANT
RETYING	TUTOYER	BITTIER	FATTING	PARTYER	SALTING
ROTATOR	TUTTING	BITTING	FATTISH	PASTEUP	SENTIMO
ROTIFER	VATICAL	*BITTOCK	FETTING	PATTERN	SETTING
ROTTING	VATTING	BLATANT	FITTEST	PATTING	SETTLER
ROTUNDA	VETERAN	BOATFUL	FITTING	PELTAST	SETTLOR
RUTHFUL	VETIVER	BRITTLY	FLATLET	PENTENE	SEXTANT
RUTTIER	VETTING	BUSTIER	FLUTIST	PENTODE	SHITAKE
RUTTILY	VITALLY	BUTTALS	*FOXTROT	PETTIER	SHUTOUT
RUTTING	VITAMER	BUTTERY	FRETTER	PETTING	SITTING
RUTTISH	VITAMIN	BUTTIES	*FUTTOCK	PETTISH	SMOTHER
SATANIC	VITESSE	*BUTTOCK	GANTLET	PIETIST	SOFTBAC
SATCHEL	VITIATE	BUTTONY	GESTALT	PITTING	SOFTISH
SATIATE	VITRAIN	CATTAIL	GETTING	PLUTEUS	SOTTISH
SATIETY	*VITRIFY	CATTALO	GITTERN	PORTENT	SOUTANE
SATINET	VITRINE	CATTERY	*GLITCHY	POSTDOC	*SPATZLE
SATISFY	VITRIOL	CATTIER	GOTHIC	*POSTTAX	SPOTLIT
SATRAPY	VOTABLE	CATTILY	GUTTATE	POTTEEN	STATANT
SATSUMA	VOTRESS	CATTING	GUTTERY	POTTENT	STATIST
SATYRID	WATERER	CHATTED	GUTTIER	POTTERY	STATUSY
*SETBACK	WATTAGE	CHETRUM	GUTTING	POTTIER	SUBTASK
SETLINE	WATTAPE	CHUTIST	GUTTLER	POTTIES	SUBTEST
SETTING	WATTEST	CITTERN	HASTING	POTTING	*SUBTEXT
SETTLER	*WETBACK	CONTACT	HOTTEST	PRETAPE	SURTOUT
SETTLOR	WETLAND	CONTENT	HOTTING	PRETERM	TARTLET
SHTETEL	WETNESS	CONTEST	HOTTISH	PRETEST	TATTIER
SITHENS	WETTEST	*CONTEXT	HUTTING	PRETRIM	TATTILY
SITTING	WETTING	CONTORT	*JETTIED	PRETYPE	TATTING
SITUATE	WITHIER	COTTAGE	JFTTIES	PROTECT	TATTLER
SOTTISH	WITHIES	COTTIER	JETTIES	PROTEST	TECTITE
SUTURAL	WITHING	COTTONY	*JETTING	PROTEUS	TITTIES
TATOUAY	WITHOUT	CULTISH	*JITTERY	PUTTIED	TOSTADA
TATTIER	WITLESS	CULTIST	*JOTTING	PUTTIER	TOSTADO
TATTILY	WITLING	CUTTAGE	KITTING	PUTTING	TOTTERY
TATTING	WITLOOP	CUTTIES	KNOTTED	RATTAIL	TOTTING
TATTLER	WITNESS	CUTTING	*KVETCHY	RATTEEN	TUTTING
TETANAL	WITTIER	DENTIST	LATTICE	RATTIER	TWATTLE
TETANIC	WITTILY	DICTIER	LEFTIES	RATTING	*TZITZIT
TETANUS	WITTING	DIETHER	LEFTISH	RATTISH	VATTING
TETCHED	WOTTETH	DIRTBAG	LEFTIST	RATTLER	VETTING
TETOTUM	YATAGAN	DISTANT	LETTING	RATTOON	WATTAGE
TETRODE	YTTRIUM	DISTENT	LETTUCE	RATTRAP	WATTAPE
TITANIA	*ZITHERN	DISTORT	LOFTIER	REDTAIL	WATTEST
TITANIC	BANTENG	DITTANY	LOTTERY	REPTANT	WETTEST
TITHING	BAPTIST	DOGTROT	LOTTING	RESTART	WETTING
TITLARK	BARTMAN	DOTTIER	MANTLET	RESTOKE	WETTISH
TITLIST	BATTEAU	DOTTILY	MARTLET	RETTING	WHATNOT
TITRANT	BATTERY	DOTTING	MATTING	ROOTLET	WHATSIS
TITRATE	BATTIER	DOTTREL	*MATTOCK	ROTTING	WHITEST
TITTIES	BATTING	DUSTOFF	MOSTEST	RUTTIER	WITTIER
TITULAR	BATTLER	FACTOID	MOTTLER	RUTTILY	WITTILY
TOTABLE	BEETLER	FANTAST	NETTIER	RUTTING	WITTING
TOTALLY	BETTING	FATTEST	NETTING	RUTTILY	*XANTHAN
TOTTERY		FATTIER	NETTLER	RUTTING	BACTERIA

BAC T ERIN	BUS T INGS	CON T RACT	DIS T AS TE	FLA T LAND	GES T ICAL
BAN T ERER	BUS T LINE	CON T RAIL	DIS T AVES	FLA T LING	GES T URAL
BAN T LING	BU T T ONER	CON T RARY	DIS T INC T	FLA T LONG	*GIF T EDLY
*BAP T IZER	BU T T RESS	CON T RAS T	DIS T RACT	FLA T MA T E	GIF T LESS
BAR T ERER	BYS T REE T	CON T RI T E	DIS T RAIN	FLA T NESS	*GIF T WARE
BAR T ISAN	*CAL T HROP	CON T RIVE	DIS T RAI T	FLA T T ERY	GIL T HEAD
BAS T ILLE	CAN T ICLE	COR T ISOL	DIS T RESS	FLA T T ES T	GLI T T ERY
BA T T ALIA	CAN T ONAL	COS T LESS	DIS T RIC T	FLA T T ING	GLU T ELIN
BA T T ENER	CAN T RAIP	*COS T MARY	DIS T RUS T	FLA T T ISH	GLU T T ING
BA T T ERIE	CAP T IOUS	COS T UMER	DOC T ORAL	FLA T WARE	GLU T T ONY
BA T T IES T	CAP T URER	*COS T UMEY	DOC T RINE	*FLA T WASH	GNA T HION
*BEA T IFIC	CAR T LOAD	CO T T AGER	DOG T OO TH	*FLA T WAYS	GNA T HI T E
BEA T LESS	CAR T OONY	CRE T ONNE	DO T T EREL	FLA T WISE	GNA T LIKE
BEE T ROO T	*CAR T OUCH	CRI T ERIA	DO T T IES T	*FLA T WORK	*GOA T FISH
BEL T LESS	CAS T ANE T	*CRI T IQUE	DRU T HERS	*FLA T WORM	GOA T HERD
BEL T LINE	*CAS T AWAY	*CRO T CHE T	DUC T LESS	*FLE T CHER	GOA T LIKE
BEN T WOOD	CAS T EISM	CUL T IGEN	*DUC T WORK	FLU T IES T	GOA T SKIN
BES T IARY	CAS T RA T E	CUL T IVAR	DUE T T IS T	FLU T T ERY	GOE T HI T E
BES T OWAL	CAS T RA T O	CUL T RA T E	DUS T HEAP	*FOO T BALL	GRA T EFUL
BES T RIDE	CA T T IES T	CUL T URAL	DUS T IES T	*FOO T BATH	GRA T INEE
BIA T HLON	CA T T LEYA	*CUR T ALAX	DUS T LESS	*FOO T FALL	GRA T UI T Y
BIO T ICAL	CAU T IOUS	CUR T NESS	DUS T LIKE	*FOO T GEAR	GUS T ABLE
*BIO T OXIN	CEN T AURY	CUS T ODES	*DYS T AXIA	*FOO T HILL	GUS T IES T
*BIR T HDAY	CEN T ESIS	CUS T OMER	DYS T ONIA	*FOO T HOLD	GUS T LESS
BIS T OURY	CEN T IARE	CUS T UMAL	DYS T OPIA	FOO T IES T	GUT T ATED
BI T T IES T	CEN T RING	CU T T ABLE	FAC T IOUS	*FOO T LESS	GU T T IES T
*BLA T ANCY	CEN T RISM	CYS T EINE	*FAC T O TUM	*FOO T LIKE	GU T T URAL
BLA T T ING	CEN T RIS T	CYS T I T IS	*FAI T HFUL	*FOO T MARK	*HAF T ARAH
BLO T LESS	CEN T ROID	*DAC T YLIC	FAL T BOA T	*FOO T NOTE	*HAF T ORAH
BLO T T IER	CEN T UPLE	DAC T YLUS	FAL T ERER	*FOO T PACE	*HAP T ICAL
BLO T T ING	*CHA T CHKA	DAF T NESS	FAN T ASIA	*FOO T PATH	HAS T EFUL
BOA T BILL	*CHA T CHKE	DAL T ONIC	FAN T ASIE	*FOO T RES T	HAS T ENER
*BOA T HOOK	CHA T T ING	*DEA T HBED	FAR T HES T	*FOO T SORE	HA T T ERIA
BOA T LIKE	*CHI T CHA T	*DEA T HCUP	*FAR T HING	*FOO T WEAR	*HAW T HORN
BOA T LOAD	CHI T LING	*DEA T HFUL	*FAS T BACK	*FOO T WORK	*HEA T EDLY
BOA T SMAN	CHI T OSAN	DEF T NESS	FAS T BALL	FOR T BESS	HEA T LESS
BOA T YARD	*CHU T ZPAH	DEN T ALIA	FAS T ENER	FOR T IETH	*HEC T ICAL
BOL T HEAD	CIS T ERNA	DEN T A T ED	FAS T NESS	FOR T UI T Y	HEP T AGON
BOL T HOLE	CLA T T ERY	DEN T ICLE	FAS T UOUS	*FOR T YISH	*HEP T ARCH
BOL T ONIA	CLI T ELLA	DES T RIER	*FEA T HERY	FOS T ERER	HIL T LESS
BOL T ROPE	CLI T ORIS	DES T RUC T	*FEL T LIKE	*FRE T WORK	HIS T AMIN
*BON T EBOK	CLO T HIER	DEU T ERIC	FES T IVAL	FRI T T ING	HIS T IDIN
*BOO T JACK	CLO T HING	*DEX T RINE	FE T T ERER	FRO T T AGE	HIS T OGEN
BOO T LACE	CLO T T ING	*DEX T ROSE	FE T T LING	FRO T T EUR	HIS T ORIC
BOO T LESS	CLU T T ERY	*DEX T ROUS	*FIF T YISH	FUR T HES T	HUR T LESS
*BOO T LICK	COA T LESS	DIA T OMIC	FIL T ERER	GAN T LINE	HYS T ERIA
BO T T OMER	*COA T RACK	DIA T ONIC	FIL T RA T E	GAN T LOPE	*HYS T ERIC
*BO T T OMRY	COA T ROOM	DIC T A T OR	FIS T NO T E	GAS T IGH T	*JE T T IES T
*BOU T IQUE	COA T T AIL	DIC T IES T	FI T T ABLE	GAS T NESS	*JE T T ISON
*BOX T HORN	COA T T END	DIE T E T IC	FLA T BOA T	GAS T RAEA	*JUS T NESS
BRA T T ICE	COA T T ES T	DIP T ERAL	FLA T FOO T	GAS T RULA	KNI T T ING
BRE T HREN	CON T AGIA	DIP T ERAN	*FLA T HEAD	GEN T RICE	*KNI T WEAR
*BRI T CHES	CON T EMP T	DIP T ERON	FLA T IRON	*GEN T RIFY	KNO T LESS
*BRI T ZSKA	CON T INUA	DIS T ANCE		*GEO T AXIS	*KNO T LIKE
BUN T LINE	CON T INUE				KNO T T ING

*KNO T WEED	*MOU T HFUL	PAS T NESS	*POR T ABLY	PRO T AMIN	RUS T LESS
*KOW T OWER	MUL T IAGE	PAS T ORAL	POR T ANCE	PRO T ASIS	RUS T LING
KUR T OSIS	MUL T ICAR	PAS T RAMI	*POR T APAK	PRO T EASE	RU T T IES T
LAC T EOUS	*MUL T IJE T	PAS T ROMI	POR T HOLE	PRO T EGEE	SAL T BUSH
LAE T RILE	*MUL T IPLY	PAS T URAL	POR T IERE	PRO T EIDE	SAL T IES T
LAI T ANCE	MUL T IUSE	PAS T URER	POR T LESS	PRO T EOSE	SAL T LESS
LAN T HORN	MUL T IT ON	PA T T ERER	POR T RAI T	PRO T OCOL	SAL T LIKE
'LA T T ERLY	*MUS T ACHE	PEC T ORAL	POR T RESS	PRO T OPOD	SAL T NESS
LEA T HERN	MUS T ARDY	PEE T WEE T	POS T ALLY	*PRO T OXID	*SAL T WORK
LEA T HERY	MU T T ERER	PEN T ACLE	POS T ANAL	*PRO T OZOA	SAL T WOR T
LEC T URER	*MYS T AGOG	PEN T AGON	POS T BURN	PRO T RAC T	SAN T ALIC
LEF T OVER	*MYS T ICAL	PEN T ANOL	POS T CARD	PRO T RUDE	SAN T ALOL
*LEF T WARD	*MYS T ICLY	*PEN T ARCH	*POS T CAVA	PU T T ERER	SAN T ONIN
*LEF T WING	*MYS T IQUE	PEN T OMIC	POS T CODE	*QUA T ORZE	SAR T ORII
LE T T ERER	NAE T HING	PEN T OSAN	POS T DA T E	*QUA T RAIN	SAS T RUGA
LIF T GA T E	NAU T ICAL	*PEP T IZER	POS T DIVE	*QUI T REN T	SAU T ERNE
LIN T IES T	NAU T ILUS	PER T NESS	POS T DRUG	*QUI T T ING	SAU T OIRE
LIN T LESS	NEA T HERD	PES T ERER	*POS T FACE	*QUO T IEN T	SAW T OO T H
LIS T ENER	NEA T NESS	PES T HOLE	POS T FIRE	RAF T ERED	*SCA T BACK
LIS T LESS	NEO T ERIC	PE T T EDLY	*POS T FORM	RAF T SMAN	SCA T T ING
LI T T ERER	NES T ABLE	PE T T IES T	POS T GAME	RAP T NESS	SCO T OPIA
LI T T LISH	NES T LIKE	PE T T IFOG	POS T HEA T	RA T T ENER	*SCU T CHER
LI T T ORAL	NES T LING	PEW T ERER	POS T HOLE	RA T T IES T	SCU T ELLA
LOA T HFUL	NE T T ABLE	*PHO T OMAP	*POS T ICHE	RA T T LING	SEA T LESS
LOA T HING	NE T T IES T	*PHO T OPIA	*POS T IQUE	REA T T ACH	SEA T MA T E
LOF T IES T	NEU T RINO	PHO T OSE T	POS T LUDE	REA T T ACK	SEA T RAIN
LOF T LESS	*NEX T DOOR	*PIN T SIZE	*POS T MARK	REA T T AIN	*SEA T WORK
LOI T ERER	NOC T URNE	*PIS T ACHE	POS T ORAL	RES T I T CH	SEC T ORAL
LOS T NESS	NON T IDAL	PI T T ANCE	POS T PAID	RES T LESS	SEN T ENCE
LUS T IES T	NON T I T LE	PLA T ELE T	POS T PONE	RES T ORAL	SEN T IEN T
LUS T RA T E	NON T ONAL	PLA T EFUL	POS T RACE	RES T ORER	SEN T INEL
LUS T RING	*NON T OXIC	PLA T IES T	POS T RIO T	RES T RAIN	SEP T ARIA
LUS T ROUS	NON T RUMP	PLA T INIC	*POS T SHOW	RES T RESS	SEP T E T T E
MAL T IES T	NON T RU T H	PLA T INUM	*POS T SYNC	RES T RIC T	SEP T UPLE
MAL T REA T	NOR T HING	PLA T T ING	POS T T EEN	RES T RIKE	SES T ERCE
MAN T ELE T	NOR T HERN	*PLA T YPUS	POS T T ES T	RES T RIVE	SE T T LING
MAR T INE T	NO T T URNO	PLE T HORA	POS T URAL	RES T ROOM	*SEX T ARII
*MAR T YRLY	NUR T URAL	PLO T LESS	POS T URER	RES T RUCK	*SEX T E T T E
*MAS T ABAH	NUR T URER	PLO T LINE	PO T T ERER	RES T RUNG	*SEX T UPLE
*MAS T ICHE	NYS T A T IN	PLO T T AGE	PO T T IES T	RHE T ORIC	*SEX T UPLY
MA T T EDLY	PAL T ERER	PLO T T IER	PRA T FALL	*RHY T HMIC	SHE T LAND
MA T T RASS	PAN T HEON	PLO T T IES	*PRA T IQUE	RIF T LESS	SHI T T ING
MA T T RESS	PAN T OFLE	PLO T T ING	PRA T T LER	ROO T HOLD	SHO T T ING
MEA T IES T	PAN T SUI T	POE T ICAL	PRE T AS T E	ROO T IES T	*SHU T DOWN
MEA T LOAF	PAR T AKER	POE T ISER	PRE T ENCE	ROO T LESS	SHU T T ING
MEL T DOWN	PAR T ERRE	*POE T IZER	PRE T ENSE	ROO T LIKE	SIS T ERLY
*MIS T EACH	PAR T IBLE	POE T LESS	PRE T ERI T	ROS T ELLA	SIS T ROID
*MIS T HROW	PAR T ICLE	POE T LIKE	PRE T REA T	ROS T RA T E	*SIX T IE T H
MIS T IES T	PAR T ISAN	POL T ROON	PRE T RIAL	ROU T EMAN	*SIX T YISH
*MIS T OUCH	*PAR T IZAN	*PON T IFEX	PRE T T IED	ROU T EWAY	*SKE T CHER
MIS T REA T	PAS T ICCI	*PON T IFIC	PRE T T IER	RUC T IOUS	*SKI T T ERY
MIS T HINK	*PAS T ICHE	POR T ABLE	PRE T T IES	RUS T ICAL	*SKI T T ISH
MIS T RUS T	PAS T IES T		*PRE T T IFY	RUS T ICLY	SLA T IES T
MIS T RYS T	PAS T ILLE			RUS T IES T	SLA T T ERN
MON T EDLY	PAS T LESS				SLA T T ING

SLIT HERY	SWAT TING	VAST IEST	WIS TERIA	CLOT	GLUT
SLIT LESS	*SWIT CHER	VAST NESS	WIT TIEST	COAT	GNAT
SLIT TING	SYNT AGMA	VENT LESS	*WORT HFUL	COFT	GOAT
*SLOT BACK	*SYST EMIC	VENT URER	WOST TETH	COLT	GOUT
SLOT HFUL	TACT LESS	VERT EBRA	*WRAT HFUL	COOT	GRAT
SLOT TING	TANT ALUM	VERT ICAL	*WRET CHED	CULT	GRIT
SMIT HERS	TANT ALUS	VERT ICIL	WRIT RING	CURT	GROT
*SMIT HERY	TART NESS	VEST ALLY	*WROT HFUL	CYST	GUST
*SMOT HERY	TART RATE	VEST IARY	*XANT HEIN	DAFT	HAET
SMUT TING	TART UFFE	VEST IGIA	*XANT HENE	DART	HAFT
SNAT CHES	TAST EFUL	VEST LESS	*XANT HINE	DAUT	HALT
SNIT CHER	TAT TIEST	*VEST LIKE	*XANT HOMA	DAWT	HART
SOFT BALL	TAT TOOER	VEST MENT	*XANT HONE	DEBT	HAST
SOFT ENER	TAUT NESS	VEST URAL	*XANT HOUS	DEET	HAUT
*SOFT HEAD	TAUT OMER	VIAT ICAL	YEST REEN	DEFT	HEAT
SOFT NESS	TAUT ONYM	*VIAT ICUM	*YOUT HFUL	DENT	HEFT
SOFT WARE	TECT ONIC	VICT ORIA	*ZAST RUGA	DIET	HENT
*SOFT WOOD	TEET OTAL	VICT RESS	*ZEST LESS	DINT	HEST
SOOT HEST	TEET OTUM	VINT AGER		DIPT	HILT
SOOT HSAY	TEET HING	VIRT UOSA	BAHT	DIRT	HIST
SOUT ACHE	TENT ACLE	VIRT UOSO	BAIT	DOAT	HOLT
SOUT HERN	TENT IEST	VIRT UOUS	BANT	DOIT	HOOT
*SOUT HPAW	TENT LESS	VOLT AISM	BAST	DOLT	HOST
SOUT HRON	TENT LIKE	WAIT RESS	BATT	DOST	HUNT
SOUT RING	TERT IARY	WANT ONER	BEAT	DRAT	HURT
SPAT TING	TEST ATOR	WANT ONLY	BEET	DUCT	JEST
SPIT BALL	TEST ICLE	WART IEST	BELT	DUET	JILT
SPIT EFUL	TEST IEST	WART LESS	BENT	DUIT	JOLT
SPIT FIRE	*TEXT BOOK	*WART LIKE	BEST	DUNT	JUST
SPIT TING	*TEXT LESS	WAST EFUL	BHUT	FACT	KART
SPIT TOON	*TEXT UARY	WAST ELOT	BINT	FART	KEET
SPOT LESS	*TEXT URAL	WAST ERIE	BITT	FAST	KENT
SPOT TING	*THAT AWAY	*WAST EWAY	BLAT	FEAT	KEPT
STAT ABLE	*THAT CHER	WAT THOUR	BLET	FEET	KHAT
STAT EDLY	THET ICAL	WAT TLESS	BLOT	FELT	KHET
*STAT ICKY	TILT YARD	*WEFT WISE	BOAT	FIAT	KILT
STAT UARY	TINT LESS	WEST ERLY	BOLT	FIST	KIST
STIT CHER	TIT TERER	WEST MOST	BOOT	FIXT	KNIT
STOT INKA	*TIT TUPPY	*WEST WARD	BORT	FLAT	KNOT
*SUBT AXON	TORT ILLA	WET TABLE	BOTT	FONT	KYAT
*SUBT HEME	TORT IOUS	*WHAT EVER	BOUT	FOOT	LAST
SUBT ILTY	TORT OISE	WHAT NESS	BRAT	FORT	LEET
SUBT ITLE	TORT UOUS	WHIT ENER	BRIT	FRAT	LEFT
SUBT LETY	TORT URER	WHIT EOUT	BRUT	FRET	LENT
SUBT ONIC	TOT TERER	WHIT IEST	BUNT	FRIT	LEPT
SUBT OPIA	TRIT HING	*WHIT RACK	BUST	GAIT	LEST
SUBT OPIC	TRIT ICUM	WHIT TLER	BUTT	GAST	LIFT
SUBT OTAL	TROT LINE	WHIT TRET	CANT	GELT	LILT
SUBT RACT	TROT TING	*WID THWAY	CART	GENT	LINT
SUBT REND	TRUT HFUL	WINT ERER	CAST	GEST	LIST
SUBT RIBE	TURT LING	WINT ERLY	CELT	GHAT	LOFT
SUBT UNIC	*TWIT CHER	*WID THWAY	CENT	GIFT	LOOT
SUIT ABLE	TWIT TERY	WIN TERER	CHAT	GILT	LOST
SUIT CASE	TWIT TING	WIN TERLY	CHIT	GIRT	LOUT
SUIT LIKE	*TZIT ZITH	WIS TARIA	CIST	GIST	LUNT

LUS T	REF T	TIN T	BIGO T	CRAP T	FROS T
MAL T	REN T	TOF T	BINI T	CREP T	FRUI T
MAR T	RES T	TOI T	BION T	CRES T	**FUME T**
MAS T	RIF T	TOO T	BLAS T	**CROF T**	GAMU T
MAT T	RIO T	TOR T	BLEA T	CRUE T	GAUL T
MAU T	ROO T	TOS T	BLEN T	CRUS T	GAUN T
MEA T	ROU T	TOU T	BLES T	**CRYP T**	GAVO T
MEL T	RUN T	TRE T	BLOA T	CUBI T	GEES T
MIL T	RUS T	TRO T	BLUE T	CULE T	GEMO T
MIN T	RYO T	TUF T	BLUN T	CURE T	GENE T
MIS T	SAL T	TWA T	BLUR T	CURS T	GHAS T
MIT T	SCA T	TWI T	BOAR T	DAUN T	GHAU T
MIX T	SCO T	VAS T	BOAS T	DAVI T	GHOS T
MOA T	SCU T	VEN T	BOOS T	DEAL T	GIAN T
MOL T	SEA T	VER T	BRAC T	DEBI T	GIGO T
MOO T	SEC T	VES T	BRAN T	DEBU T	GLEE T
MOR T	SEN T	**VEX T**	BREN T	DEFA T	GLIN T
MOS T	SEP T	VOL T	BRIT T	DEIS T	GLOA T
MOT T	SET T	**WAF T**	BRUI T	DEMI T	GLOS T
MUS T	**SEX T**	WAI T	BRUN T	DEPO T	GLOU T
MUT T	SHA T	WAN T	BUIL T	DERA T	GODE T
NEA T	SHI T	WAR T	BUND T	DICO T	GRAF T
NES T	SHO T	WAS T	BURE T	DIDS T	GRAN T
NET T	SHU T	WAT T	BURN T	**DIGH T**	GREA T
NEW T	SIF T	WEE T	BURS T	DIGI T	GREE T
NEX T	SIL T	**WEF T**	BUTU T	DIVO T	GRIF T
NOW T	SKA T	WEL T	CADE T	DOES T	GRIO T
PAC T	SKI T	WEN T	CANS T	DONU T	GRIP T
PAN T	SLA T	WEP T	CAPU T	DRAF T	GRIS T
PAR T	SLI T	WER T	CARA T	DRES T	GROU T
PAS T	SLO T	WES T	CARE T	DRIF T	GRUN T
PEA T	SLU T	**WHA T**	**CHAN T**	DRIP T	GUES T
PEL T	SMU T	**WHE T**	**CHAP T**	DROI T	GUIL T
PEN T	SNI T	**WHI T**	**CHEA T**	DROP T	GUYO T
PER T	SNO T	WIL T	**CHER T**	DUVE T	**HABI T**
PES T	SOF T	WIS T	**CHES T**	DWEL T	HADS T
PFF T	SOO T	WON T	**CHOT T**	**FACE T**	HAUN T
PHA T	SOR T	WOR T	**CIVE T**	FAGO T	HEAR T
PHO T	SPA T	WOS T	CLAS T	FAIN T	HEIS T
PHU T	SPI T	WRI T	**CLEA T**	FAUL T	HELO T
PIN T	SPO T	**XYS T**	**CLEF T**	FEAS T	**HIGH T**
PLA T	STAT	YET T	**CLIF T**	FEIN T	HOIS T
PLO T	STET	YUR T	CLIP T	FEIS T	HORS T
POE T	SUE T	**ZES T**	CLOO T	**FIGH T**	HURS T
POR T	SUI T	BEAS T	CLOU T	FILE T	**JABO T**
POS T	SWA T	BEAU T	COAC T	FIRS T	**JAUN T**
POU T	SWO T	**BEFI T**	COAP T	***FIXI T**	**JOIN T**
PRA T	TAC T	BEGE T	COAS T	FLEE T	**JOIS T**
PSS T	TAR T	BEGO T	COME T	FLIN T	**JOUS T**
PUN T	TAU T	BERE T	COMP T	FLOU T	**JURA T**
PUT T	TEA T	BESE T	COOP T	**FLUY T**	**KAPU T**
QUI T	TEN T	BESO T	COSE T	FOIS T	**KARA T**
RAF T	TES T	**BHOO T**	COUN T	FOUN T	**KARS T**
RAN T	**TEX T**	BIDE T	COUR T	FRIT T	**KEMP T**
RAP T	TIL T	**BIGH T**	**COVE T**	FRON T	KNEL T

KNOU T	QUIE T	SLEE T	T RYS T	BOMLE T	CORNE T	
KORA T	QUIL T	SLEP T	T WEE T	BONNE T	CORSE T	
KRAF T	QUIN T	SLIP T	T WIS T	BORSH T	CORVE T	
KRAI T	QUIR T	SMAL T	*T WIX T	BOSKE T	COSSE T	
KRAU T	QUOI T	SMAR T	VALE T	BOUGH T	COVER T	
LEAN T	RABA T	SMEL T	VAUL T	BOWPO T	COWPA T	
LEAP T	RAME T	SMOL T	VAUN T	BREAS T	CRAUN T	
LEAS T	REAC T	SNOO T	VELD T	BREVE T	CRAVA T	
LEGI T	REBU T	SNOR T	VERS T	BRIGH T	CREDI T	
LICH T	RECU T	SNOU T	VISI T	BRULO T	CRUSE T	
LICI T	REES T	SPAI T	VOMI T	BRUNE T	CUBIS T	
LIGH T	REFI T	SPEL T	WAIS T	BUCKE T	CULLE T	
LIMI T	RELE T	SPEN T	WECH T	BUDGE T	CUSRA T	
LUNE T	RELI T	SPIL T	WEES T	BUFFE T	CU T ES T	
LYAR T	REME T	SPIR T	WHEA T	BULLE T	CU T LE T	
MAGO T	REMI T	SPLA T	WHIP T	BURBO T	CU T OU T	
MAIS T	REPO T	SPLI T	WHIS T	BURKE T	CYGNE T	
MAYS T	RESE T	SPOR T	WHOR T	BUYOU T	DACOI T	
MEAN T	REVE T	SPOU T	WIGH T	BYPAS T	DECAN T	
MERI T	REWE T	SPRA T	WORS T	*BYZAN T	DECEI T	
MIDS T	RIAN T	SPRI T	WRAP T	CABLE T	DECEN T	
MIGH T	RIGH T	SPUR T	WRES T	CACHE T	DECOC T	
MOIS T	RIVE T	SQUA T	WRIS T	CADEN T	DEDUC T	
MOTE T	ROAS T	S T ART	WURS T	CAHOO T	DEFEA T	
MOUL T	ROBO T	S T ILT	YACH T	CALLE T	DEFEC T	
MOUN T	ROOS T	S T INT	YEAS T	CAMLE T	DEGUS T	
MULC T	ROSE T	S T OAT	*ZIBE T	CANNO T	DEHOR T	
NEIS T	ROUS T	S T OPT	*ZIZI T	CAPLE T	*DEJEC T	
NIGH T	SABO T	S T OUT	BAGUE T	CARNE T	DELIC T	
NONE T	SAIN T	S T RUT	BALES T	CARPE T	DELIS T	
PAIN T	SAUL T	S T UNT	BALLE T	CARRO T	DEMAS T	
PALE T	SAYS T	S T URT	BALLO T	CASKE T	DEMEN T	
PEAR T	SCAN T	SUIN T	BANDI T	CA T GU T	DEPAR T	
PE T I T	SCAR T	SWAR T	BANNE T	CAUGH T	DEPIC T	
PEWI T	SCA T T	SWEA T	BARBE T	CAVEA T	DEPOR T	
*PHPH T	SCEN T	SWEE T	BARBU T	CAVOR T	DESAL T	
PICO T	SCOO T	SWEP T	BARES T	CEMEN T	DESER T	
PILO T	SCOU T	SWIF T	BARRE T	CERME T	DESIS T	
PINO T	SHAF T	T ACE T	BASAL T	CHALE T	DESPO T	
PIPE T	SHAL T	T ACI T	BASES T	CHALO T	DE T EC T	
PIPI T	SHEE T	T AIN T	BASKE T	CLARE T	DE T EN T	
PIVO T	SHIF T	T ARO T	BASSE T	CLIEN T	DE T ES T	
PLAI T	SHIR T	T AUN T	BECKE T	CLOSE T	DEVES T	
PLAN T	SHIS T	T EMP T	BEDSI T	COBAL T	DEVOU T	
PLEA T	SHOA T	T ENE T	BEFRE T	COBNU T	DICAS T	
POIN T	SHOO T	T HEF T	BEHES T	COEMP T	DIDAC T	
POSI T	SHOR T	T IGH T	BEKNO T	COGEN T	DIGES T	
POUL T	SHO T T	T INC T	BEMIS T	COHOR T	DIGLO T	
PRES T	SHOU T	T OAS T	BENNE T	COHOS T	DIK T A T	
PRIN T	SHUN T	T RAC T	BESMU T	COLLE T	DIMOU T	
PROS T	SIGH T	T RAI T	*BEZAN T	COMBA T	DIMWI T	
QANA T	SKEE T	T RAP T	BILLE T	COMFI T	DIPNE T	
QUAN T	SKIN T	T REA T	BISEC T	COMMI T	*DIQUA T	
QUAR T	SKIR T	T ROU T	BLUES T	COPLO T	DIREC T	
QUES T	SLAN T	T RUS T	BOBCA T	*COQUE T	DIRES T	

DIVER T	GOBBE T	LIMPE T	NONAR T	PUNDI T	RESPO T
DIVES T	GOBLE T	LINNE T	NONFA T	PUNNE T	RESUL T
DOCEN T	GODWI T	LIVES T	NOUGA T	PUPPE T	RET ES T
DOCKE T	GOGLE T	LOCKE T	NOUGH T	PURES T	RET IN T
DOPAN T	GORGE T	LOCUS T	NUDES T	PURIS T	RET OR T
DOUGH T	GRIVE T	LOMEN T	NUDIS T	PU T OU T	REVER T
DREAM T	GUGLE T	*LOQUA T	NUGGE T	*QIVIU T	REVES T
DRIES T	GULLE T	LUCEN T	NUMBA T	*QUAIN T	REVOL T
DRYLO T	GURNE T	LU T ES T	NU TAN T	RABBE T	RIBLE T
DULCE T	GUSSE T	LU T IS T	NU T LE T	RABBI T	RIDEN T
DYNAS T	HAGBU T	LYRIS T	PACKE T	RACHE T	RILLE T
FAGGO T	HALES T	MAGGO T	PALES T	RACIS T	RIPES T
*FANJE T	HALLO T	MAGNE T	PALLE T	RACKE T	RIPOS T
FERRE T	HARLO T	MAHOU T	PANDI T	RAGOU T	ROBUS T
FIDGE T	HASLE T	MALLE T	PAPIS T	*RAMJE T	ROCHE T
FILLE T	HEIGH T	MAMME T	PAREN T	RAPIS T	ROCKE T
FINES T	HELME T	MARKE T	PARGE T	RARES T	RODEN T
FLAUN T	HENBI T	MARMO T	PARRO T	REBAI T	*ROQUE T
FLIES T	HEPCA T	MASCO T	PA TEN T	REBOO T	RO T GU T
FLIGH T	HEREA T	*MA T ZO T	PAYOU T	RECAN T	ROUPE T
FLUEN T	HERIO T	MAUME T	PEANU T	RECAS T	RUBOU T
FOMEN T	HERMI T	MAYES T	PEDAN T	RECEN T	RUDES T
FORES T	HOBBI T	MERLO T	PEEWI T	RECEP T	RUNLE T
FORGA T	HOGNU T	MIDGE T	PELLE T	REDAC T	RUNOU T
FORGE T	HOLIS T	MIDGU T	PELME T	REDOU T	RUSSE T
FORGO T	HONES T	MILLE T	PENUL T	REEDI T	SABBA T
FORIN T	HORNE T	MINUE T	PERMI T	REEMI T	SACBU T
FORMA T	HOWLE T	MISAC T	PICKE T	REFEC T	SACHE T
FORRI T	HUGES T	MISCU T	PIGLE T	REFLE T	SADIS T
FOUGH T	*JACKE T	MISEA T	PIGNU T	REGEN T	SAFES T
FREES T	JENNE T	MISFI T	PIGOU T	REGLE T	SAGBU T
FRIGH T	JESUI T	MISHI T	PIOLE T	REGRE T	SAGES T
FROWS T	*JUNKE T	MISLI T	*PIQUE T	REHEA T	SALLE T
FUNES T	JURAN T	MISSE T	PLACE T	*REJEC T	SAMLE T
FYLPO T	JURIS T	MODES T	PLAIN T	REKNI T	SANES T
GADGE T	KAINI T	MODIS T	PLANE T	RELEN T	SAVAN T
GAINS T	KAPU T	MOLES T	PLIAN T	RELIC T	SCHIS T
GALIO T	KEYSE T	MOMEN T	PLIGH T	RELIS T	SCHUI T
GALLE T	KISMA T	MONGS T	POCKE T	RELUC T	SCRIP T
GALOO T	KISME T	MONIS T	PONEN T	REMEE T	SCULP T
GAMBI T	*KLEPH T	MOPPE T	POPPE T	REMEL T	SECAN T
GAMES T	KNIGH T	MO T MO T	POSSE T	REMIN T	SECRE T
GANNE T	KRUBU T	MUDCA T	PO TEN T	RENES T	SEJAN T
GARGE T	LABRE T	MULLE T	PREAC T	RENNE T	SELEC T
GARNE T	LAMEN T	MUSCA T	PRECU T	REPAS T	SENNE T
GARRE T	LAMES T	MUSKE T	PRESE T	REPEA T	SENNI T
GASKE T	LANCE T	MUSKI T	PRIES T	REPEN T	SEP T E T
GASLI T	LAPPE T	MU TAN T	PRIVE T	REPLO T	SERES T
GELAN T	LARIA T	MU T ES T	PROBI T	REPOR T	SES T E T
GEREN T	LA TEN T	MYSOS T	PROFI T	RESEA T	SET OU T
GIBBE T	LA T ES T	NA TAN T	*PROJE T	RESEC T	SEXIS T
GIBLE T	LEARN T	NAUGH T	PROMP T	RESEN T	*SEXPO T
GIGLE T	LEGIS T	NIDGE T	PROSI T	RESIF T	SEX T E T
GIGLO T	LEVAN T	NI T WI T	PULLE T	RESIS T	SHIES T
GIMLE T	LIKES T	NOCEN T	PULPI T	RESOR T	SHRIF T

SIGNE T	T EAPO T	WEIGH T	BLANKE T	CHU T IS T	COOKOU T
SILEN T	T ENAN T	WESKI T	BLA T AN T	*CHYMIS T	COOLAN T
SIPPE T	T ERCE T	WHILS T	BLOWOU T	CIGARE T	COPILO T
SKLEN T	T ERRE T	*WHISH T	BOMBAS T	CINEAS T	*COPYCA T
SKYLI T	T ERRI T	*WICKE T	BONESE T	CIRCLE T	COPYIS T
SLIES T	T HEIS T	WIDES T	BONIES T	CIRCUI T	CORONE T
SLIGH T	T HIRS T	WIDGE T	BOOKLE T	CLADIS T	CORREC T
SOBEI T	T HREA T	WIGLE T	BORSCH T	CLAMAN T	CORRUP T
SOCKE T	T HRIF T	WILLE T	*BOSQUE T	CLAUCH T	CORSLE T
SOFFI T	T HROA T	WISEN T	*BOUQUE T	CLAUGH T	COSIES T
SONAN T	T HRUS T	WISES T	*BOWKNO T	CLEMEN T	COSMIS T
SONNE T	T HWAR T	WOMBA T	*BOWSHO T	CLOSES T	COULDS T
SORBE T	T ICKE T	WORRI T	*BOXIES T	COADMI T	COUPLE T
SORES T	T IDBI T	WORSE T	BOYCO T T	COAGEN T	COURAN T
SOUGH T	T IPCA T	WRIES T	BRACHE T	COALPI T	COWIES T
SOVIE T	T IPPE T	WRIGH T	*BRACKE T	*COCKPI T	*COZIES T
SPIGO T	T IT BI T	YCLEP T	BRAVES T	COCOMA T	CRAMPI T
SPINE T	T OILE T	YOGUR T	*BRIQUE T	COCONU T	CREDEN T
SPIRI T	T OMCA T	*ZEALO T	BRISKE T	COENAC T	CRESSE T
SPLEN T	T OM T IT	BABBI T T	*BROCKE T	COEREC T	*CRICKE T
SPLIN T	T ONLE T	*BACKFI T	BROUGH T	*COEXER T	CROCHE T
SPOIL T	*T OQUE T	*BACKLI T	BULBLE T	*COEXIS T	*CROCKE T
SPREN T	T REVE T	*BACKOU T	BULLBA T	*COFFRE T	*CROQUE T
SPRIN T	T RICO T	*BACKSE T	BUMBOA T	COHABI T	CROWNE T
SPROU T	T RIJE T	BAILOU T	BUMMES T	COLLEC T	CRUMPE T
*SQUIN T	T RIVE T	BALLAS T	BUNDIS T	COMBUS T	CULPRI T
*SQUIR T	T RUAN T	*BANQUE T	BUOYAN T	COMFOR T	CUL T IS T
S TRAI T	T RUES T	BAP T IS T	BURGOU T	COMMEN T	CULVER T
S TREE T	T RYOU T	BAREFI T	BURNOU T	*COMPAC T	*CUMQUA T
S TRIC T	T UBIS T	BARONE T	BUSH TI T	COMPAR T	CURRAN T
S TRIP T	T UCKE T	BASINE T	BUSIES T	COMPLO T	CURREN T
S TRUN T	T UFFE T	BASSIS T	CABARE T	COMPOR T	CYCLIS T
S TYLE T	T UMUL T	BA T HMA T	CABINE T	COMPOS T	*CZARIS T
SUBLE T	T URBI T	BAWSUN T	CAGIES T	CONCEI T	DADAIS T
SUBLO T	T URBO T	BAYONE T	*CAJAPU T	CONCEN T	DASHPO T
SUBMI T	T URRE T	BEARCA T	*CAJUPU T	CONCEP T	*DECRYP T
SUBNE T	T WILI T	BECRUS T	CALLAN T	CONCER T	DEFAUL T
SUBSE T	T YPIS T	BEDFAS T	CALUME T	CONDUC T	DEFIAN T
SUFLI T	T YRAN T	BEDIGH T	CAMBIS T	CONDUI T	DEFICI T
SUMMI T	VACAN T	BEDPOS T	CANDEN T	CONFEC T	DEFLEC T
SUNKE T	VARLE T	BEIGNE T	CAPELE T	CONGES T	DEFROS T
SUNSE T	VELVE T	BENEFI T	CARPOR T	CONNEC T	DEFUNC T
SURES T	VERIS T	BENEMP T	CASUIS T	CONSEN T	DELIGH T
SWIVE T	VERSE T	BEPAIN T	CA T BOA T	CONSIS T	DELIMI T
SYNDE T	VERVE T	*BEQUES T	CA T.HEC T	CONSOR T	DEMERI T
TABLE T	VIBIS T	BESHOU T	CA T MIN T	CONSUL T	DEMOUN T
TACKE T	VIOLE T	*BE T WIX T	CELLIS T	CON T AC T	DEN T IS T
TALEN T	VOLAN T	BEVOMI T	CESSPI T	CON T EN T	DEORBI T
TALLI T	VOLOS T	*BEZZAN T	CHALLO T	CON T ES T	DEPAIN T
TAMES T	WADSE T	BIBELO T	CHAPLE T	*CON T EX T	DEPOSI T
TANIS T	WALLE T	BIBLIS T	CHARIO T	CON T OR T	DESCAN T
TAPPE T	WALNU T	BIGFOO T	CHEMIS T	CONVEC T	DESCEN T
TARGE T	WA T SI T	BIGGES T	CHEROO T	CONVEN T	DESSER T
TASSE T	WAUCH T	BISCUI T	*CHEVIO T	CONVER T	DE T RAC T
TAUGH T	WAUGH T	BIS T OR T	CHOLEN T	CONVIC T	DEVIAN T

DEWIES T	FERMEN T	GILBER T	HO T SHO T	*MAZIES T	*PARQUE T
DIALEC T	FERVEN T	GILLNE T	HO T TES T	MEANES T	PAR T LE T
DIALIS T	FEUDIS T	*GJE T OS T	*HOWBEI T	MEDIAN T	PASSAN T
DIARIS T	FIDEIS T	GLAIKE T	HU T MEN T	MEERKA T	PA T IEN T
DICIES T	FIGMEN T	GLAIKI T	HYDRAN T	MEGABI T	PA T RIO T
DILUEN T	FIGWOR T	GLUEPO T	HYGEIS T	MEGAHI T	PAYMEN T
DIMMES T	FILBER T	GNOMIS T	*HYMNIS T	MELILO T	PEACOA T
DINGBA T	FILEMO T	GOOIES T	*JACKPO T	*MESQUI T	PEASAN T
DISCAN T	FILMSE T	GORIES T	*JACONE T	ME T RIS T	PECCAN T
DISCEP T	FINFOO T	GOSPOR T	JESSAN T	*MEZQUI T	PEL T AS T
DISGUS T	FIRELI T	GOURME T	*JE T POR T	MIDCUL T	PENDAN T
*DISJEC T	FIREPO T	GRAVES T	*JOKIES T	MIDMOS T	PENDEN T
DISMAS T	FISHNE T	GRAYOU T	*JUDOIS T	MIGRAN T	PENNAN T
DISPAR T	*FI T CHE T	GROMME T	*JUJUIS T	MINARE T	PERCEN T
DISPOR T	FI T MEN T	GRUMME T	*KAJEPU T	MINDSE T	PERCEP T
DISROO T	FI T TES T	GUMBOO T	KASHRU T	MIRIES T	PERFEC T
DISRUP T	FLASKE T	GUNBOA T	KILOBI T	MISCAS T	PERIAP T
DISSEA T	FLA T LE T	GUNSHO T	KINGLE T	MISEDI T	PERIDO T
DISSEC T	FLEAPI T	GURGLE T	KNESSE T	MISMEE T	PERPEN T
DISSEN T	FLU T IS T	GYMNAS T	*KUMQUA T	MISPAR T	PERSAL T
DISSER T	*FLYBEL T	HABI T A T	LACIES T	MISSEA T	PERSIS T
DIS T AN T	*FLYBOA T	*HACKBU T	LAMBAS T	MISSOR T	PERVER T
DIS T EN T	*FLYPAS T	HADDES T	LAMBEN T	MISSOU T	PIANIS T
DIS T OR T	FOLDOU T	HAIRCU T	LAMBER T	MISSUI T	*PICQUE T
DOGCAR T	*FOLKMO T	HAIRNE T	LANGUE T	MI T IES T	PIEFOR T
DOG T RO T	FONDAN T	HALBER T	LARGES T	MONOCO T	PIERRO T
DONNER T	FOREGU T	HALIBU T	LA T CHE T	MOONLE T	PIE T IS T
DOORMA T	FORFEI T	HANDOU T	LAWSUI T	MOONLI T	PIGBOA T
DOPIES T	FORMAN T	HANDSE T	*LAZARE T	MOONSE T	PIGMEN T
DORMAN T	FORWEN T	HANGOU T	*LAZIES T	MOPIES T	PINIES T
DO T IES T	*FOXHUN T	HAPLON T	LEAFLE T	MORDAN T	PIPIES T
DOUBLE T	*FOXIES T	HARDHA T	LEF T IS T	MORDEN T	*PIQUAN T
DOVECO T	*FOX T RO T	HARDSE T	LENIEN T	MOS T ES T	PISSAN T
*DOZIES T	FRAUGH T	HARICO T	LEVERE T	MUDFLA T	PI T APA T
DRABBE T	FREIGH T	HARPIS T	LIMIES T	MUGWOR T	*PLACKE T
DRAGNE T	FRESHE T	HARSLE T	LINECU T	MUSKRA T	PLAUDI T
DRAUGH T	FRISKE T	HARVES T	LINOCU T	NAILSE T	PLAYAC T
DRIBLE T	FUGUIS T	*HA T CHE T	LOCKNU T	NARCIS T	PLAYLE T
DROPLE T	FULGEN T	*HAYLOF T	LOCKOU T	NASCEN T	PLEDGE T
DROPOU T	FUMIES T	*HAZIES T	LOGIES T	NEGLEC T	PLENIS T
DROUGH T	FUNNES T	HEADSE T	LOOKOU T	NOBLES T	PLUMME T
DRUGGE T	FUSSPO T	HELIAS T	LOOSES T	NONFAC T	POKIES T
DUALIS T	GABBAR T	HELLCA T	LUNIES T	NONMEA T	POLECA T
DUELIS T	GABFES T	HIDEOU T	MADDES T	NONPAS T	POLLIS T
DUNNES T	GALIPO T	HINDGU T	MADWOR T	NONSUI T	POLOIS T
DURMAS T	GALLAN T	HIPPES T	MAILLO T	NOSIES T	POLYCO T
FADDIS T	GALLNU T	*HIPSHO T	MANCHE T	NU T MEA T	POMFRE T
FALLOU T	GALLOO T	HOLDOU T	MANHUN T	*NYMPHE T	PORREC T
FAN T AS T	GAMIES T	HOLIBU T	MANIHO T	PAGEAN T	POR T EN T
FANWOR T	GAN T LE T	HOLIES T	MAN T LE T	PALE T O T	PO T SHO T
FASCIS T	GARDAN T	HOMIES T	MANUMI T	PALIES T	PO T TEN T
FA T TES T	GARMEN T	HOOKLE T	MARGEN T	PALMIS T	PRECAS T
FAUVIS T	GELLAN T	HORNIS T	MARPLO T	PANDEC T	PRECEN T
FEEDLO T	GES T AL T	HORREN T	MAR T LE T	PARAPE T	PRECEP T
FELWOR T	GIGABI T	HO T FOO T	MA T ELO T	PARFA T T	PREDIC T

PREEDI T	REALIS T	ROLLOU T	SOLVEN T	T HEREA T	VIADUC T
PREEMP T	REALLO T	ROMAUN T	SOPHIS T	T HERMI T	VIBRAN T
PREFEC T	REBOAN T	ROO T LE T	SORBEN T	*T HICKE T	VILAYE T
PREHEA T	RECEIP T	ROPIES T	SPARES T	T HOUGH T	VINIES T
PRELEC T	RECHAR T	ROSIES T	SPINOU T	T HRUPU T	VIOLEN T
PREMEE T	RECHEA T	ROWBOA T	SPIRAN T	T IDIES T	VIOLIS T
PREMOL T	RECOUN T	RUBIES T	SPO T LI T	T IMEOU T	WALKOU T
PRERIO T	RECRUI T	RUMMES T	SPRIES T	T INIES T	WANIES T
PRESEN T	REDBAI T	RUNDLE T	SPRIGH T	T IPCAR T	WANNES T
PRESIF T	REDCOA T	*SACKBU T	S T ARLE T	T I T LIS T	WARIES T
PRESOR T	REDDES T	SACRIS T	S T ARLI T	T I T RAN T	WARRAN T
PRE T ES T	REDOUB T	SAGIES T	S T A T AN T	T ONIES T	WASHOU T
*PRE T EX T	REDRAF T	SALIEN T	S T A T IS T	T ONIGH T	WA T T ES T
PREVEN T	REDROO T	SAL T AN T	S T ERLE T	T OPCOA T	WAVELE T
*PRICKE T	*REEJEC T	SANDLO T	S T ICKI T	T OPKNO T	WAVIES T
PRODUC T	REELEC T	SANDPI T	S T UDEN T	T OPMAS T	*WAXIES T
*PROJEC T	REENAC T	SAPIEN T	S T YLIS T	T OPMOS T	*WEBFOO T
PROPHE T	REEREC T	SARMEN T	SUBCUL T	T ORMEN T	WERGEL T
*PROPJE T	REFIGH T	SA T INE T	SUBDUC T	T ORREN T	WE T T ES T
PROSEC T	REFLEC T	SAWDUS T	SUBEDI T	T OSSPO T	WHA T NO T
PRO T EC T	REFLOA T	SCARLE T	*SUBJEC T	T OURIS T	WHEREA T
PRO T ES T	REFRAC T	SEABOO T	SUBPAR T	T OWBOA T	*WHIFFE T
PRO T IS T	REFRON T	SEAGIR T	SUBPLO T	T OWMON T	*WHIPPE T
PROVOS T	REGNAN T	SEALAN T	SUBREN T	T OWNLE T	WHI T ES T
PRUDEN T	REGRAF T	SEAPOR T	SUBSEC T	*T RAJEC T	WIDEOU T
PSCHEN T	REGRAN T	SEARES T	SUBSIS T	T RANSI T	WILDCA T
PULLOU T	REGREE T	SEAWAN T	SUB T ES T	T RIDEN T	WILIES T
PULSAN T	RELIAN T	SEGMEN T	*SUB T EX T	T RINKE T	WINGLE T
PUNGEN T	RELIGH T	SEJEAN T	SUBUNI T	T RIOLE T	WINIES T
PUNIES T	REMNAN T	SELLOU T	SUBVER T	T RIPAR T	WIPEOU T
PURPOR T	REMOUN T	SEMIFI T	SUGGES T	T RIPLE T	WIRIES T
PURSUI T	REPAIN T	SEMIMA T	SUNBEL T	T RIPPE T	WI T HOU T
*QUADRA T	REPLAN T	*SEQUEN T	SUNFAS T	T RISEC T	WOODCU T
*QUAR T E T	REPOSI T	SERPEN T	SUNSPO T	T RUMPE T	WOODLO T
*QUERIS T	REPRIN T	SERVAN T	SUNSUI T	T SARIS T	WOOLHA T
*QUILLE T	REP T AN T	SEXIES T	SUPPOR T	T UBAIS T	WORKOU T
*QUINNA T	*REQUES T	SEX T AN T	SURCOA T	T UGBOA T	WOULDS T
*QUIN T E T	RESHOO T	SHALLO T	SURFEI T	T URGEN T	WROUGH T
RACIES T	RESIGH T	SHERBE T	SUR T OU T	T URNOU T	YOGHUR T
*RACQUE T	RESMEL T	SHEROO T	SUSPEC T	*T WINJE T	*ZIKURA T
RADIAN T	RESOJE T	SHILPI T	SYMBIO T	T WINSE T	BACCARA T
RAGWOR T	RESPEC T	SHU T OU T	T ABARE T	T YPESE T	*BACCHAN T
RAIMEN T	RESPLI T	SICKOU T	T ABORE T	T YPIES T	*BACKBEA T
RAINOU T	RES T AR T	SINGLE T	T ACHIS T	*T ZARIS T	*BACKCAS T
RAMPAN T	RE T RAC T	*SIZIES T	T AKEOU T	*T ZI T ZI T	*BACKCHA T
RAMPAR T	RE T REA T	SKILLE T	T ALIPO T	VAGRAN T	*BACKLIS T
RAPPOR T	RE T WIS T	*SKIPPE T	T ANGEN T	VALIAN T	*BACKMOS T
RAREBI T	REVISI T	SKIRRE T	T ANNES T	VARIAN T	*BACKRES T
RA T A T A T	REVUIS T	SLEEKI T	T APROO T	VARMEN T	*BACKSEA T
RA T CHE T	RIBWOR T	SLEIGH T	T AR T LE T	VARMIN T	BAILMEN T
READAP T	RIMIES T	SLIPOU T	T EACAR T	VEINLE T	*BAKEMEA T
READMI T	RINGEN T	SNIPPE T	T ELEOS T	VERDAN T	BALLONE T
READOP T	RINGLE T	SOLERE T	T EMPES T	VERDIC T	*BANJOIS T
READOU T	RIPPLE T	SOLICI T	T EMPLE T	VERIES T	*BANKRUP T
REAGEN T	RIVULE T	SOLOIS T	T ENNIS T	VERSAN T	BANNERE T

BAREBOA T	*BUFFIES T	*COCKIES T	DASHIES T	DOWNBEA T	FOO T RES T
BAREFOO T	BULLIES T	*COCKLOF T	*DAYLIGH T	DOWNCAS T	FORECAS T
BARGHES T	BULLPOU T	*COCKSHU T	DEADBEA T	DOWNIES T	FOREFOO T
BARGUES T	BULLSHI T	CODIREC T	DEADBOL T	DRAGONE T	FOREMAS T
BASEMEN T	BURGONE T	*COEFFEC T	DEADLIF T	DRIBBLE T	FOREMOS T
BASSINE T	BURRIES T	COGNOVI T	DEBU T AN T	DROPSHO T	FOREPAR T
BA T T IES T	BUSHGOA T	COHEREN T	DECADEN T	DROPWOR T	FOREPAS T
BAWDIES T	BUSHIES T	COINVEN T	DECEDEN T	DRUGGIS T	FOREWEN T
BEADIES T	BYS T REE T	COLEWOR T	DECREPI T	DRUMBEA T	*FORKIES T
BEAMIES T	CABALIS T	COLLARE T	DEFEREN T	DRUPELE T	*FORKLIF T
BECARPE T	CABERNE T	COLONIS T	DEFORES T	DRYPOIN T	FORSPEN T
*BEDQUIL T	*CACHALO T	COLORAN T	DEMIVOL T	DUBONNE T	FOVEOLE T
BEDSHEE T	*CACHEPO T	COLORIS T	DEMOCRA T	*DUCKIES T	FRAGMEN T
*BEECHNU T	CALAMIN T	*COMFIES T	DEMONIS T	DUELLIS T	FRAGRAN T
BEEFIES T	CAMPIES T	COMPLEA T	DEMO T IS T	DUE T T IS T	*FRANKES T
BEE T ROO T	CANNIES T	*COMPLEC T	DEPONEN T	*DUMPCAR T	*FREAKOU T
*BEKNIGH T	CANOEIS T	*CONFLIC T	DERELIC T	DUMPIES T	FREEBOO T
BELLWOR T	CANONIS T	CONFRON T	DESELEC T	DUS T IES T	*FREQUEN T
BENEDIC T	*CANZONE T	*CONJUNC T	DESINEN T	DYNAMIS T	FRON T LE T
BERGAMO T	CARBURE T	CONODON T	DES T RUC T	FABULIS T	FROS T BI T
BESOUGH T	CARCANE T	*CONQUES T	DIALLIS T	FADDIES T	FRUI T LE T
BESPREN T	CARRYOU T	CONS T AN T	DIC T IES T	FAINEAN T	FUMIGAN T
BE T ELNU T	CASEMEN T	CON T EMP T	*DIFFRAC T	FALCONE T	FURRIES T
BIGAMIS T	CAS T ANE T	CON T RAC T	DIGAMIS T	FAL T BOA T	FU T URIS T
BIRDSHO T	CA T ALYS T	CON T RAS T	DILA T AN T	*FANLIGH T	GABBIES T
BI T T IES T	CA T APUL T	COPAREN T	DILIGEN T	FAR T HES T	GADABOU T
BIVALEN T	CA T ARAC T	*COPYEDI T	DINKIES T	FA T ALIS T	GALAVAN T
*BLACKOU T	*CA T FIGH T	CORKIES T	DIPLOMA T	FA T T IES T	GALIVAN T
BLOWIES T	CA T T IES T	CORNIES T	DIRIMEN T	FECULEN T	GAMMIES T
BLUECOA T	CELLARE T	CORSELE T	DISCOUN T	FEMINIS T	GASLIGH T
BOBBINE T	CEN T RIS T	*CORYBAN T	DISCREE T	FIGURAN T	GAS T IGH T
BODEMEN T	CERAMIS T	COSCRIP T	DISHERI T	FILAMEN T	GA T EPOS T
BODYSUI T	CEREMEN T	COSECAN T	DISHIES T	FILMIES T	GAUN T LE T
BOGGIES T	CERVELA T	CO T ENAN T	*DISJOIN T	FINALIS T	GEMMIES T
BONGOIS T	CHARIES T	*COUCHAN T	*DISJUNC T	FINNIES T	GERMIES T
BOOKRES T	CHAR T IS T	COULDES T	DISMOUN T	FIREBOA T	GIGAWA T T
BOOMIES T	*CHECKOU T	COVALEN T	DISPIRI T	FIREBRA T	GIMPIES T
BO T ANIS T	CHES T NU T	COVENAN T	DISPLAN T	*FISHBOL T	GLADDES T
*BOUFFAN T	*CHEVALE T	COVERLE T	*DISQUIE T	FISHIES T	GLADIES T
*BOUGHPO T	CHILIAS T	CRABMEA T	DIS T INC T	FLAGRAN T	GLASNOS T
*BOWFRON T	*CHI T CHA T	*CRACKPO T	DIS T RAC T	FLAMEOU T	GOALPOS T
*BOWSPRI T	CLAIMAN T	CREODON T	DIS T RAI T	FLAMIES T	GODLIES T
BRACELE T	CLARINE T	CRESCEN T	DIS T RIC T	FLA T BOA T	GRADIEN T
BRAC T LE T	CLASSIS T	CROSSCU T	DIS T RUS T	FLA T FOO T	GRAPIES T
BRAGGAR T	CLOSEOU T	CROSSLE T	DI T HEIS T	FLA T T ES T	GREENLE T
BRAGGES T	CLOUDLE T	*CRO T CHE T	DIVALEN T	FLEAWOR T	GRIEVAN T
BRASSAR T	*CLUBFOO T	*CROWFOO T	DOCUMEN T	*FLESHPO T	GRIMIES T
BREADNU T	CLUBROO T	CRYOS T A T	*DOGFIGH T	*FLIPPAN T	GRIMMES T
BREAKOU T	COALIES T	CUCURBI T	DOGGIES T	FLOWERE T	GRIPIES T
*BRICKBA T	COASSIS T	CURDIES T	DOMINAN T	FLU T IES T	GRUMMES T
BRINIES T	COA T T ES T	CUSHIES T	DOORPOS T	FOAMIES T	GUARDAN T
BROOKLE T	COBBIES T	DAMEWOR T	DORMIEN T	*FOGFRUI T	*GUI T QUI T
*BROWBEA T	*COCKBOA T	DAMNDES T	DOSSERE T	FOLDBOA T	GULFIES T
BROWNOU T		DANEWOR T	DO T T IES T	*FOLKMOO T	GUMMIES T
*BUCKSHO T		DARNDES T	DOUGHNU T	FOO T IES T	

*GUNFIGH T	*JAILBAI T	LU T ENIS T	MIS T RYS T	NO T ORIS T	PLAYSUI T
GUNFLIN T	*JE T T IES T	LYRICIS T	MI T LIAN T	NOVELIS T	PLEASAN T
GUNPOIN T	*JINGOIS T	MAINMAS T	MOBOCRA T	NUBBIES T	PLUMELE T
GUS T IES T	*JOHNBOA T	*MAKEFAS T	MODELIS T	NU T RIEN T	PLUMIES T
GU T T IES T	*JOLLIES T	MALAPER T	MOLDIES T	*PACIFIS T	POIGNAN T
GYROS T A T	*JUBILAN T	MALEDIC T	MONOCRA T	PAGANIS T	POKEROO T
HABI T AN T	*JUDGMEN T	MALEMIU T	MONODIS T	PALLIES T	POLYGLO T
HAGADIS T	KEELBOA T	MAL T IES T	MONOGLO T	PALMIES T	POO T IES T
HAIRIES T	*KICKIES T	MAL T REA T	MONO T IN T	*PAMPHLE T	POO T RES T
*HALAKIS T	*KILOVOL T	MANGIES T	MONUMEN T	PANELIS T	POPULIS T
*HAMMIES T	*KILOWA T T	MANIFES T	MOONDUS T	PAN T SUI T	PORKIES T
HANDCAR T	*KINGBOL T	MAN T ELE T	MOONIES T	PAPPIES T	POR T RAI T
*HANDFAS T	*KINGPOS T	MARABOU T	MOONPOR T	PARAKEE T	POS T HEA T
HANDIES T	*KNOCKOU T	MARLIES T	MOONSHO T	PARAMEN T	POS T RIO T
HANDLIS T	LAKEPOR T	MARMOSE T	MOONWOR T	*PARAQUA T	POS T T ES T
HANGNES T	LAMBIES T	MAR T INE T	MOORIES T	*PARAQUE T	PO T T IES T
HARDBOO T	LAMPPOS T	MASSCUL T	MOORWOR T	PARODIS T	*PRAEFEC T
HARDIES T	LANCELE T	MASSICO T	MORALIS T	*PAROQUE T	PRAELEC T
*HAZELNU T	LANNERE T	MASSIES T	MOSSIES T	PARROKE T	PREADAP T
HEADIES T	LAPIDIS T	*MAXICOA T	MO T ORIS T	PASSPOR T	PREADMI T
HEADMOS T	LARDIES T	MEALIES T	MOUSIES T	PAS T IES T	PREADOP T
HEADRES T	LARKIES T	MEA T IES T	*MOVEMEN T	PA T ULEN T	PREADUL T
HEDONIS T	LA T HIES T	MEDALIS T	*MUCKIES T	*PAVEMEN T	PREALLO T
*HELICOP T	LAYABOU T	MEGAVOL T	MUDDIES T	PEAKIES T	PREAUDI T
HELILIF T	LEADIES T	MEGAWA T T	MUGGIES T	PEDERAS T	PRECINC T
HELIPOR T	LEADWOR T	MELANIS T	*MUL T IJE T	PEDIMEN T	PREELEC T
HELLBEN T	LEAFIES T	MELODIS T	MUNIMEN T	PEE T WEE T	PREENAC T
*HELPMEE T	LEARIES T	*MERCHAN T	MURALIS T	*PENCHAN T	PREEREC T
HEMOS T A T	LEGALIS T	MESHIES T	MURRELE T	PENI T EN T	*PREEXIS T
*HEMPIES T	LEGGIES T	MESSIES T	MUSCADE T	PENLIGH T	*PREFIGH T
HERBIES T	LIBELAN T	ME T ALIS T	MUSKIES T	PENPOIN T	PREGNAN T
HESI T AN T	LIBELIS T	MICRODO T	*MUZZIES T	PERMEAN T	PRELIMI T
*HIGHSPO T	*LICKSPI T	*MIDNIGH T	*MYOBLAS T	PE T T IES T	PREPLAN T
HILLIES T	LIFEBOA T	MIDPOIN T	NANOWA T T	PE T ULAN T	PREPRIN T
HINDMOS T	LIGAMEN T	MILEPOS T	NA T IVIS T	PHALLIS T	PRESPLI T
*HIPPIES T	LILLIPU T	MILKIES T	NA T URIS T	PHAN T AS T	PRE T ERI T
HOARIES T	LIMBIES T	*MILKWOR T	NAUSEAN T	PHASEOU T	PRE T REA T
*HOBBYIS T	LINGIES T	MINGIES T	NAVICER T	PHEASAN T	PRICIES T
*HOLDFAS T	LINGUIS T	*MIQUELE T	NEEDIES T	PHONIES T	PRIMMES T
*HOMEPOR T	LINIMEN T	MISADAP T	NEPO T IS T	PHO T OSE T	PRIN T OU T
HOMILIS T	LIN T IES T	MISAGEN T	NERVIES T	*PICKIES T	*PROHIBI T
HONEWOR T	LI T IGAN T	MISBEGO T	NESCIEN T	PIECRUS T	PROSAIS T
HOODIES T	*LOBBYIS T	MISCOUN T	NE T T IES T	PIEDFOR T	PROSPEC T
*HOOFBEA T	LOCALIS T	MISDOUB T	NEWSCAS T	PIEDMON T	PROS T ES T
*HOOKIES T	LODGMEN T	MISEVEN T	NEWSIES T	PIEPLAN T	PRO T RAC T
HORNIES T	LOF T IES T	MISGRAF T	NIELLIS T	PIGGIES T	PSALMIS T
HORNPOU T	LONGBOA T	MISLIGH T	NIHILIS T	PILEWOR T	PUGGIES T
HORNWOR T	LORIKEE T	MISPAIN T	NIPPIES T	PINKROO T	PUGILIS T
HORSIES T	*LOWLIGH T	MISPLAN T	NOBBIES T	PINPOIN T	PUISSAN T
*HO T CHPO T	LOYALIS T	MISPOIN T	NONADUL T	*PI T CHOU T	PULPIES T
*HUMBLES T	LUCULEN T	MISPRIN T	NONELEC T	*PLANCHE T	*PULSEJE T
HUMORIS T	LUMINIS T	MISS T AR T	NONEVEN T	PLANGEN T	*PULSOJE T
*HUSKIES T	LUNGWOR T	MIS T IES T	NONGUIL T	PLAN T LE T	PURSIES T
*HYGIEIS T	LUS T IES T	MIS T REA T	NONPOIN T	PLA T ELE T	PURSUAN T
*JACKBOO T	LU T ANIS T	MIS T RUS T	NONPRIN T	PLA T IES T	PURULEN T

*PUSHCAR T	REINVES T	SANDIES T	SIMPLIS T	S T RAWHA T	T O T EMIS T
PUSHIES T	*REJACKE T	SANDWOR T	SIMULAN T	S T RIDEN T	*T OXICAN T
PUSSIES T	*RELAXAN T	*SAPPHIS T	SINCIPU T	S T RUMPE T	T RANSAC T
*PUSSYCA T	RELEVAN T	SARCENE T	SI T ARIS T	SUBABBO T	T RANSEC T
PYROS TA T	RELUCEN T	SARODIS T	*SKYLIGH T	SUBADUL T	T RANSEP T
*QUADRAN T	REMANEN T	SARSENE T	SLA T IES T	SUBAGEN T	T RANSMI T
*QUICKSE T	REMARKE T	SASSIES T	SLIMIES T	SUBDEPO T	T RAPNES T
*QUIE T IS T	RENI T EN T	SA T ANIS T	SLIMMES T	SUBEREC T	T RAWLNE T
*QUI T REN T	*REOBJEC T	SA T IRIS T	SLIPKNO T	*SUBSHAF T	T RIGGES T
*QUO T IEN T	REORIEN T	SA T URAN T	SLUGFES T	SUB T RAC T	T RIMMES T
RAINCOA T	REOU T FI T	SAVAGES T	*SMOKEPO T	SUCCINC T	*T URBOJE T
RAINIES T	REREPEA T	SCALIES T	SNAKEBI T	SULFURE T	T URFIES T
RALLYIS T	RESCRIP T	SCANDEN T	SNAPSHO T	SUNBURS T	T URNCOA T
RAMMIES T	RESCULP T	SCARIES T	SNOWBEL T	SUNLIGH T	T URNSPI T
RANDIES T	RESIDEN T	*SCHIZON T	SNOWIES T	SUPERHI T	*T WILIGH T
RA T T IES T	RESONAN T	SCILICE T	SNOWMEL T	SUPERHO T	T WINIES T
REACCEN T	RESPROU T	SCIOLIS T	SNOWSUI T	*SUPERJE T	*T WINIGH T
REACCEP T	RES T RIC T	*SCRAMJE T	SNUGGES T	SUPPLAN T	*T YPECAS T
REAC T AN T	RESUBMI T	SCRIMPI T	SOAPIES T	SURFBOA T	VALVELE T
READDIC T	RE T ARGE T	SEACOAS T	SOAPWOR T	SURFIES T	VAR T IES T
READIES T	RE T ICEN T	SEACRAF T	SODALIS T	SURMOUN T	VAS T ELO T
*READJUS T	RE T IRAN T	SEAFRON T	SODOMIS T	SURPRIN T	VAS T IES T
REANOIN T	RE T ROAC T	SEAMIES T	SOLECIS T	SWIF T LE T	VEGE T AN T
REARMOS T	RE T ROFI T	SEAMOUN T	SOLLERE T	SWIMSUI T	VEGE T IS T
REARRES T	REVEHEN T	SEASCOU T	SOMERSE T	*SYMBION T	*VEHEMEN T
REASCEN T	REVENAN T	SECURES T	*SOMEWHA T	T ABOURE T	VEINIES T
REASSER T	REVEREN T	SEDERUN T	SONGFES T	T ACKIES T	VEINULE T
REASSOR T	RHEOS TA T	SEDIMEN T	SONORAN T	T AILCOA T	VELVERE T
REBOUGH T	RIBBIES T	SEEDIES T	SOO T HES T	T ANGIES T	VESICAN T
RECOMMI T	*RICOCHE T	SEMIMA T T	SOO T RES T	T ARRIES T	VES T MEN T
RECREAN T	RIDGIES T	SEMISOF T	SORRIES T	TA T T IES T	VE T IVER T
RECUSAN T	RIGH T IS T	SEMI T IS T	SPICIES T	T EARIES T	VIEWIES T
REDEFEA T	RIGORIS T	SENNIGH T	SPIKELE T	T EENIES T	VIGILAN T
REDEFEC T	RINGBOL T	SEN T IEN T	SPIRIES T	T EGUMEN T	VIRULEN T
REDIGES T	ROBORAN T	SERGEAN T	*SPROCKE T	T ELECAS T	VISCOUN T
REDIREC T	ROCKIES T	*SERJEAN T	SPUMIES T	T ELEPOR T	VISI T AN T
REDOLEN T	RONDELE T	SE T ENAN T	*SQUARES T	T ENEMEN T	VI T ALIS T
*REDSHIF T	ROO T IES T	SHADIES T	S T ABLES T	T EN T IES T	*VIVISEC T
REDSHIR T	ROSEROO T	*SHAKEOU T	S T AGGAR T	T ERAWA T T	VOCALIS T
REDS T AR T	ROUNDLE T	*SHAKIES T	S T AGIES T	T ERCELE T	VOLI T AN T
REEDIES T	ROYALIS T	SHALIES T	S T AGNAN T	T ES T IES T	VO T ARIS T
REENLIS T	RUBAIYA T	*SHEEPCO T	S T AKEOU T	T HEOCRA T	WAINSCO T
*REEXPOR T	RUDDIES T	SHERBER T	S T ALWAR T	T HEORIS T	*WARCRAF T
REFEREN T	RUDIMEN T	SHINIES T	S T ANDOU T	*T HICKSE T	WAR T IES T
REFLUEN T	RUMINAN T	*SHIPMEN T	S T ANDPA T	T HINNES T	WASHIES T
REFORES T	RUNABOU T	SHOO T OU T	S T ARDUS T	T HINNES T	WAS T ELO T
REFORMA T	RURALIS T	*SHOPLIF T	S T ARWOR T	T HRAWAR T	*WA T CHOU T
*REFOUGH T	RUSHIES T	SHOR T CU T	S T EDFAS T	*T HUMBNU T	*WAXPLAN T
REGIMEN T	RUS T IES T	SHOULDS T	S T ICKOU T	*T HYMIES T	WEARIES T
REIMPOR T	RU T ILAN T	*SHOWBOA T	S T INKPO T	T INNIES T	WEEDIES T
REINDIC T	RU T T IES T	SHOWIES T	S T OCKIS T	T IPPIES T	WELDMEN T
REINDUC T	SAILBOA T	SIBILAN T	*S T OCKPO T	T IPSIES T	WES T MOS T
REINFEC T	SALARIA T	SIGNPOS T	S T OLPOR T	T OLERAN T	*WHINCHA T
*REINJEC T	SAL T IES T	SILKIES T	S T ONIES T	*TOMMYRO T	WHINIES T
REINSER T	SAL T WOR T	SIMONIS T	S T RAIGH T	T O T ALIS T	WHI T EOU T

WHI T IES T	WILLYAR T	WI T HIES T	WOOLIES T	WORMROO T	*YOGHOUR T
WHI T T RE T	WINDIES T	WI T T IES T	WORDIES T	WOULDES T	*ZIGGURA T
*WHODUNI T	WINGIES T	*WOODCHA T	*WORKBOA T	WRIS T LE T	*ZIKKURA T
WIGGIES T	WISPIES T	WOODIES T	WORMIES T	*YAHRZEI T	

V

VAGI	VIRL	VENAL	*VIXEN	VALOUR	VENDOR
VAIL	VISA	VENGE	*VIZIR	VALUER	VENDUE
VAIN	VISE	VENIN	*VIZOR	VALUTA	VENEER
VAIR	VITA	VENOM	VOCAL	VALVAL	VENERY
VALE	VIVA	VENUE	VOCES	VALVAR	VENIAL
VAMP	VIVE	VERGE	VODKA	VAMOSE	VENINE
VANE	VOID	VERSE	VODUN	VAMPER	VENIRE
VANG	VOLE	VERSO	VOGIE	VANDAL	VENOSE
VARA	VOLT	VERST	VOGUE	VANISH	VENOUS
VARY	VOTE	VERTU	VOICE	VANITY	VENTER
VASE	VROW	VERVE	VOILA	VANMAN	VENULE
VAST	VUGG	VESTA	VOILE	VANNED	VERBAL
VATU	VUGH	VETCH	VOLAR	VANNER	VERBID
VEAL	VACUA	*VEXER	VOLTA	VAPORY	VERDIN
VEEP	VAGAL	*VEXIL	VOLTE	VAPOUR	VERGER
VEER	VAGUE	VIÁND	VOLTI	VARIED	VERIER
VEIL	VAGUS	VIBES	VOLVA	VARIER	*VERIFY
VEIN	VAKIL	VICAR	VOMER	VARIES	VERILY
VELA	VALET	*VICHY	VOMIT	VARLET	VERISM
VELD	VALID	VIDEO	VOTER	VAROOM	VERIST
VENA	VALOR	VIEWY	VOUCH	VASSAL	VERITE
VEND	VALSE	VIGIL	VOWEL	VASTLY	VERITY
VENT	VALUE	VIGOR	VOWER	VATFUL	VERMES
VERA	VALVE	VILLA	VROOK	VATTED	VERMIN
VERB	VANDA	VIMEN	VROUW	VAULTY	VERMIS
VERT	VAPID	VINAL	VUGGY	VAUNTY	VERNAL
VERY	VAPOR	VINCA	VULGO	VAWARD	*VERNIX
VEST	VARIA	VINIC	VULVA	VEALER	VERSAL
VETO	*VARIX	VINYL	VYING	VECTOR	VERSER
VEXT	VARNA	VIOLA	VACANT	*VEEJAY	VERSET
VIAL	VARUS	VIPER	VACATE	VEEPEE	VERSTE
VIBE	VARVE	VIRAL	VACUUM	VEGETE	VERSUS
VICE	VASTY	VIREO	VADOSE	VEGGIE	*VERTEX
VIDE	VATIC	VIRES	VAGARY	VEILER	VERVET
VIER	VAULT	VIRGA	VAGILE	VEINAL	VESICA
VIEW	VAUNT	VIRID	VAGINA	VEINER	VESPER
VIGA	VEALY	VIRTU	VAGROM	VELATE	VESPID
VILE	VEENA	VIRUS	VAHINE	VELLUM	VESSEL
VILL	VEERY	VISIT	VAKEEL	VELOCE	VESTAL
VINA	VEGAN	VISOR	VALGUS	VELOUR	VESTEE
VINE	VEINY	VISTA	VALINE	VELURE	VESTRY
VINO	VELAR	VITAL	VALISE	VELVET	VETOER
VINY	VELDT	VITTA	*VALKYR	VENDEE	VETTED
VIOL	VELUM	VIVID	VALLEY	VENDER	VIABLE

VIATIC	VOMICA	VATTING	VESPINE	VITAMIN	*VALUABLY
VIATOR	VOMITO	VAULTER	VESTIGE	VITESSE	VALUATOR
VIBIST	VOODOO	VAUNTER	VESTING	VITIATE	VALVELET
VIBRIO	*VORTEX	VAUNTIE	VESTURE	VITRAIN	VALVULAR
VICING	VOTARY	VAVASOR	VETERAN	*VITRIFY	*VAMBRACE
VICTIM	VOTING	VAWNTIE	VETIVER	VITRINE	VANADATE
VICTOR	VOTIVE	VEBROSE	VETTING	VITRIOL	VANADIUM
VICUNA	VOYAGE	VEDALIA	*VEXEDLY	*VIVIFIC	VANGUARD
VIEWER	VOYEUR	VEDETTE	VIADUCT	VOCABLE	VANILLIN
VIGOUR	VULGAR	VEGETAL	VIBRANT	*VOCABLY	VANISHER
VIKING	VULGUS	*VEHICLE	VIBRATE	VOCALIC	VANITORY
*VILIFY	*VACANCY	VEILING	VIBRATO	*VOCALLY	*VANQUISH
VILLUS	VACCINA	VEINIER	VIBRION	VOCODER	*VAPIDITY
VINEAL	VACCINE	VEINING	*VICARLY	VOGUISH	VAPORING
VINERY	*VACUITY	VEINLET	*VICEROY	VOICING	VAPORISE
VINIER	VACUOLE	VEINULE	VICINAL	VOLANTE	*VAPORISH
*VINIFY	VACUOUS	VELAMEN	VICIOUS	VOLCANO	*VAPORIZE
VINING	VAGRANT	VELIGER	VICOMTE	VOLTAGE	VAPOROUS
VINOUS	VALANCE	VELITES	*VICTORY	VOLUBLE	VAPOURER
VIOLET	VALENCE	VELOUTE	VICTUAL	VOLUTIN	VARACTOR
VIOLIN	*VALENCY	VENATIC	VICUGNA	VOMITER	VARIABLE
VIRAGO	VALIANT	VENDACE	VIDETTE	VOMITUS	*VARIABLY
VIRGIN	VALIDLY	VENISON	VIDICON	VORLAGE	VARIANCE
VIRILE	VALLATE	VENOMER	VIDUITY	VOTABLE	VARICOSE
VIRION	VALONIA	VENTAGE	VIEWIER	VOTRESS	*VARIEDLY
VIROID	VALUATE	VENTAIL	VIEWING	*VOUCHEE	VARIETAL
VIRTUE	VALVATE	VENTRAL	VILAYET	*VOUCHER	*VARIFORM
VISAGE	VALVULA	VENTURE	VILLAGE	*VOUVRAY	VARIORUM
VISARD	VALVULE	VENTURI	VILLAIN	VOWLESS	VARISTOR
VISCID	VAMOOSE	VERANDA	VILLEIN	VOYAGER	VARLETRY
VISCUS	VAMPIRE	VERBENA	VINASSE	VULGATE	*VARNISHY
VISING	*VAMPISH	*VERBIFY	VINEGAR	VULPINE	VASCULAR
VISION	*VANDYKE	VERBILE	VINIEST	VULTURE	*VASCULUM
VISIVE	VANILLA	VERDANT	VINTAGE	*VYINGLY	*VASIFORM
VISUAL	VANNING	VERDICT	VINTNER	VACATION	*VASOTOMY
VITALS	VANPOOL	VERDURE	VIOLATE	*VACCINEE	VASTIEST
VITRIC	VANTAGE	VERGING	VIOLENT	*VACCINIA	VASTNESS
VITTLE	VANWARD	VERGLAS	VIOLIST	*VAGABOND	VATICIDE
VIVACE	VAPORER	VERIDIC	VIOLONE	*VAGILITY	VAULTING
*VIVARY	*VAPOURY	VERIEST	VIRELAI	VAGINATE	VAUNTFUL
VIVERS	*VAQUERO	VERISMO	VIRELAY	*VAGOTOMY	VAVASOUR
*VIVIFY	VARIANT	VERITAS	VIREMIA	*VAGRANCY	VAVASSOR
*VIZARD	VARIATE	VERMEIL	VIRGATE	VAINNESS	VEGANISM
*VIZIER	VARICES	VERMIAN	VIRGULE	VALENCIA	VEGETANT
*VIZSLA	VARIETY	*VERMUTH	VIROSIS	VALERATE	VEGETATE
VODOUN	VARIOLA	VERNIER	VIRTUAL	VALERIAN	VEGETIST
VOICER	VARIOLE	VERRUCA	VISCERA	VALIANCE	*VEGETIVE
VOIDER	VARIOUS	VERSANT	VISCOID	*VALIANCY	*VEHEMENT
VOLANT	VARMENT	*VERSIFY	VISCOSE	VALIDATE	*VEILEDLY
VOLERY	VARMINT	VERSINE	VISCOUS	*VALIDITY	*VEILLIKE
VOLLEY	VARNISH	VERSING	VISIBLE	*VALKYRIE	VEINIEST
VOLOST	VARSITY	VERSION	VISITER	VALORISE	VEINLESS
VOLUME	VASTIER	VERTIGO	VISITOR	*VALORIZE	*VEINLIKE
VOLUTE	VASTITY	VERVAIN	VITALLY	VALOROUS	VEINULET
*VOLVOX	VATICAL	VESICLE	VITAMER	VALUABLE	VELARIUM

*VELARIZE	VESTIARY	VIOLENCE	VOLITIVE	DY V OUR	REVIVE
VELLEITY	VESTIGIA	*VIOMYCIN	VOLLEYER	FA V ELA	RE V OKE
*VELOCITY	VESTLESS	VIRGINAL	VOLPLANE	FA V ISM	RE V OLT
VELVERET	*VESTLIKE	VIRICIDE	VOLTAISM	FA V OUR	RE V OTE
VENALITY	VESTMENT	VIRIDIAN	VOLUTION	GA V AGE	REV V ED
VENATION	VESTURAL	VIRIDIAN	VOLVULUS	GA V IAL	RI V AGE
VENDETTA	VESUVIAN	VIRILISM	*VOMITIVE	GI V ING	RI V ING
VENDEUSE	VETIVERT	VIRILITY	*VOMITORY	GO V ERN	SA V AGE
VENDIBLE	*VEXATION	*VIROLOGY	VOMITOUS	HA V ING	SA V ANT
*VENDIBLY	*VEXILLUM	VIRTUOSA	*VORACITY	HA V IOR	SA V ATE
VENEERER	'VEXINGLY	VIRTUOSO	VOTARESS	*JO V IAL	SA V INE
VENENATE	VIATICAL	VIRTUOUS	VOTARIST	KA V ASS	SA V ING
VENENOSE	*VIATICUM	VIRUCIDE	VOTEABLE	LA V ABO	SA V IOR
VENERATE	*VIBRANCE	VIRULENT	VOTELESS	LA V AGE	SA V ORY
VENEREAL	*VIBRANCY	*VISCACHA	VOUSSOIR	LA V EER	SA V OUR
VENETIAN	VIBRATOR	VISCERAL	*VOWELIZE	LA V ING	SO V IET
*VENGEFUL	VIBRISSA	VISCOUNT	*VOYAGEUR	LA V ISH	SO V RAN
VENOGRAM	*VIBRONIC	*VISELIKE	*VULCANIC	LE V IED	TA V ERN
VENOMOUS	*VIBURNUM	VISIONAL	VULVITIS	LE V IER	VI V ACE
VENOSITY	VICARAGE	VISITANT		LE V IES	*VI V ARY
VENTLESS	VICARATE	VISUALLY	K V AS	LE V ITY	VI V ERS
VENTURER	VICARIAL	VITALISE	K V ASS	LI V ELY	*VI V IFY
*VERACITY	VICELESS	VITALISM	CO V IN	LI V ERY	*WA V ERY
*VERANDAH	*VICENARY	VITALIST	DU V ET	LI V EST	WA V IER
VERATRIA	VICINAGE	VITALITY	*JI V ER	LI V IER	WA V IES
VERATRIN	*VICINITY	*VITALIZE	*JI V EY	LI V ING	*WA V ILY
VERATRUM	VICTORIA	VITAMINE	SA V VY	LI V YER	WA V ING
*VERBALLY	VICTRESS	VITELLIN	BE V IES	LO V AGE	WI V ERN
*VERBATIM	*VIDEOTEX	VITELLUS	BO V INE	LO V ERY	WI V ING
VERBIAGE	*VIEWDATA	VITIATOR	CA V EAT	LO V ING	*WY V ERN
VERBLESS	VIEWIEST	VITILIGO	CA V ERN	NA V AID	BE V ELER
VERBOTEN	VIEWLESS	VITREOUS	CA V IAR	NO V ENA	BE V OMIT
*VERDANCY	VIGILANT	VITULINE	CA V IES	NO V ICE	*BI V ALV E
VERDERER	VIGNERON	*VIVACITY	CA V ITY	PA V ANE	*BI V INYL
VERDEROR	VIGNETTE	*VIVARIUM	CA V ORT	PA V EED	BI V OUAC
VERDITER	*VIGORISH	*VIVERRID	CI V ICS	PA V ING	CA V ALLA
VERECUND	VIGOROSO	*VIVIFIER	CI V ISM	PA V IOR	*CA V ALLY
VERGENCE	VIGOROUS	*VIVIPARA	CO V ERT	PA V ISE	*CA V ALRY
VERIFIER	VILENESS	*VIVISECT	CO V ING	*QI V IUT	CA V EMAN
*VERJUICE	VILIFIER	*VIZCACHA	DE V EIN	RA V AGE	CA V ETTO
VERMOULU	VILIPEND	*VIZIRATE	DE V EST	RA V INE	CA V ILER
*VERMOUTH	VILLADOM	VOCALISE	DE V ICE	RA V ING	CA V TARE
VERNACLE	VILLAGER	*VOCALISM	DE V ISE	RA V ISH	*CE V ICHE
VERNICLE	VILLAINY	VOCALIST	DE V OID	RE V AMP	*CI V ILLY
VERONICA	VILLATIC	*VOCALITY	DE V OIR	RE V EAL	CO V ERER
VERSEMAN	*VINCIBLE	*VOCALIZE	DE V OTE	RE V ERB	CO V ERUP
VERSICLE	*VINCULUM	VOCATION	DE V OUR	RE V ERE	CO V ETER
VERTEBRA	VINDALOO	*VOCATIVE	DE V OUT	RE V ERS	CU V ETTE
VERTICAL	*VINEYARD	*VOICEFUL	DI V ERT	RE V ERT	DE V ALUE
VESICANT	VINIFERA	VOIDANCE	DI V EST	RE V ERY	DE V ELOP
VESICATE	VINOSITY	VOIDNESS	DI V IDE	RE V EST	DE V IATE
VESICULA	VINTAGER	VOLATILE	DI V INE	RE V IEW	DE V ILRY
VESPERAL	VIOLABLE	*VOLCANIC	DI V ING	RE V ILE	DE V IOUS
*VESPIARY	VIOLATER	VOLITANT	DO V ISH	RE V ISE	DE V ISAL
VESTALLY	VIOLATOR	VOLITION			DE V ISEE

DE V ISER	MO V IOLA	RE V UIST	CLE V EITE	NON V IRAL	SIL V ICAL
DE V ISOR	NA V ETTE	RE V V ING	*COE V ALLY	NON V OCAL	SIR V ENTE
DE V OICE	NA V V IES	RI V ALRY	*COE V OLV E	NON V OTER	SLA V ERER
DE V OLV E	NI V EOUS	RI V ETER	CON V ENER	NOU V ELLE	SLI V ERER
DE V OTEE	NO V ATIN	RI V IERA	CON V ENOR	PAR V ENUE	*SLI V O V IC
DI V ERSE	NO V ELLA	RI V IERE	CON V ERGE	PAR V OLIN	SLO V ENLY
DI V IDER	NO V ELLY	RI V ULET	CON V ERSE	PER V ADER	SNI V ELER
DI V INER	NO V ELTY	RO V V ING	*CON V EXLY	PER V ERSE	SOL V ABLE
DI V ISOR	PA V IOUR	SA V ABLE	*CON V EYER	PER V IOUS	*SOL V ENCY
DI V ORCE	PA V ISER	SA V ANNA	*CON V EYOR	PLU V IOSE	SOU V ENIR
DI V ULGE	*PA V LO V A	SA V ARIN	*CON V INCE	PLU V IOUS	*SOU V LAKI
DO V ECOT	PI V OTAL	SA V ELOY	*CON V OKER	*POX V IRUS	*SUB V ICAR
*DO V EKEY	*PO V ERTY	SA V IOUR	*CON V OLV E	PRE V IOUS	SUB V IRAL
*DO V EKIE	RA V AGER	SA V ORER	CON V ULSE	PRE V ISOR	*SUB V OCAL
DU V ETYN	RA V ELER	SA V OURY	COR V ETTE	*PRO V ENLY	SUR V EYOR
FA V ELLA	RA V ELIN	SE V ENTH	*CRA V ENLY	PRO V IDER	SUR V I V AL
FA V ORER	RA V ELLY	SE V ENTY	CRE V ALLE	PRO V IRUS	SUR V I V OR
FO V EOLA	RA V ENER	SE V ERAL	CRE V ASSE	*PRO V OKER	*SYL V ATIC
FO V EOLE	RA V IOLI	*SE V ICHE	CUL V ERIN	PUL V ILLI	TRA V ELER
GA V OTTE	RE V ALUE	SE V V ERE	DIS V ALUE	PUL V INUS	TRA V ELOG
HA V EREL	RE V ELER	*SO V KHOZ	DRI V ELER	*PUR V EYOR	TRA V ERSE
HA V IOUR	RE V ELRY	TA V ERNA	*DRI V EWAY	*QUA V ERER	TRA V ESTY
HO V ERER	RE V ENGE	V A V ASOR	*FER V ENCY	*QUI V ERER	TRA V OISE
*JA V ELIN	RE V ENUE	*V I V IFIC	FLA V ONOL	REO V IRUS	TRI V AL V E
*JI V EASS	RE V ERER	WA V ELET	FLA V ORER	SAL V ABLE	V AL V ELET
*JU V ENAL	RE V ERIE	*WA V EOFF	*FLA V OURY	SAL V AGEE	V AL V ULAR
*LA V ROCK	RE V ERSE	WA V ERER	FRI V OLER	SAL V AGER	V EL V ERET
LE V ATOR	RE V ERSO	WA V IEST	GAL V ANIC	*SAL V IFIC	V OL V ULUS
LE V ELER	RE V ILER	BIO V ULAR	GRA V AMEN	SCA V ENGE	V UL V ITIS
LE V ELLY	RE V ISAL	BLO V IATE	*GRA V ELLY	SEL V EDGE	
LE V ERET	RE V ISER	*BRE V ETCY	GRA V ITAS	SER V ABLE	SHI V
LE V ULIN	RE V ISIT	*BRE V IARY	GRA V ITON	SER V ICER	SPI V
LI V ABLE	RE V ISOR	CAL V ADOS	*GRA V LAKS	SER V ITOR	GANE V
LI V ENER	RE V I V AL	CAL V ARIA	GRO V ELER	SHI V AREE	SCHA V
LO V ABLE	RE V I V ER	CAN V ASER	*HEA V ENLY	SHI V ERER	MAGLE V
LO V EBUG	RE V OICE	CER V ELAS	*HEA V YSET	SHO V ELER	MOSHA V
*MO V ABLY	RE V OKER	CER V ELAT	NER V IEST	SIL V ERER	
MO V ELES	RE V OLV E	*CHE V ALET	NON V ALID	SIL V ERLY	

W

WACK	WAIT	WARD	WATT	WEAR	WELD
WADE	WAKE	WARE	WAUK	WEED	WELL
WADI	WALE	WARK	WAUL	WEEK	WELT
WADY	WALK	WARM	WAUR	WEEL	WEND
WAFF	WALL	WARN	WAVE	WEEN	WENT
WAFT	WALY	WARP	WAVY	WEEP	WEPT
WAGE	WAME	WART	WAWL	WEER	WERE
WAIF	WAND	WARY	*WAXY	WEET	WERT
WAIL	WANE	WASH	WEAK	WEFT	WEST
WAIN	WANT	WASP	WEAL	WEIR	WHAM
WAIR	WANY	WAST	WEAN	WEKA	WHAP

WHAT	WORE	WEDEL	WIDEN	WOULD	*WALKUP
WHEE	WORK	WEDGE	WIDER	WOUND	WALLAH
WHEN	WORM	WEDGY	WIDOW	WOVEN	WALLET
WHET	WORN	WEEDY	WIDTH	WRACK	WALLIE
WHEW	WORT	WEENY	WIELD	WRANG	WALLOP
WHEY	WOST	WEEPY	WIFTY	WRAPT	WALLOW
WHID	WOVE	WEEST	WIGAN	WRATH	WALNUT
WHIG	WRAP	WEIGH	WIGGY	WREAK	WALRUS
WHIM	WREN	WEIRD	WIGHT	WRECK	WAMBLE
WHIN	WRIT	WELCH	WILCO	WREST	*WAMBLY
WHIP	WUSS	WELLY	WILLY	WRICK	WAMMUS
WHIR	*WYCH	WELSH	*WIMPY	WRIED	*WAMPUM
WHIT	WYLE	WENCH	WINCE	WRIER	WAMPUS
*WHIZ	WYND	WENNY	WINCH	WRIES	WANDER
WHOA	WYNN	WETLY	WINDY	WRING	WANDLE
WHOM	WYTE	*WHACK	WINEY	WRIST	WANGAN
WHOP	WACKE	WHALE	WINGY	WRITE	WANGLE
WICH	WACKO	WHAMO	*WINZE	WRONG	WANGUN
WICK	*WACKY	WHANG	WIPER	WROTE	WANIER
WIDE	WADDY	WHARF	WIRER	WROTH	WANING
WIFE	WADER	WHAUP	WIRRA	WRUNG	WANION
WILD	WAEFU	WHEAL	WISED	WURST	WANNED
WILE	WAFER	WHEAT	WISER	WUSSY	WANNER
WILL	WAGER	WHEEL	WISHA	WABBLE	WANTER
WILT	WAGON	WHEEN	WISPY	*WABBLY	WANTON
WILY	WAHOO	WHEEP	WITAN	WADDER	WAPITI
WIMP	WAIST	*WHELK	WITCH	WADDIE	WARBLE
WIND	WAIVE	WHELM	WITEN	WADDLE	WARDEN
WINE	WAKEN	WHELP	WITHE	WADDLY	WARDER
WING	WAKER	WHERE	WITHY	WADIES	WARIER
WINK	WALER	*WHICH	WITTY	WADING	WARILY
WINO	WALLA	*WHIFF	WIVER	WADMAL	WARING
WINY	WALLY	WHILE	WIVES	WADMEL	WARMER
WIPE	*WALTZ	WHINE	*WIZEN	WADMOL	WARMLY
WIRE	WAMUS	WHINY	WOALD	WADSET	WARMTH
WIRY	WANEY	WHIPT	WODGE	WAEFUL	WARMUP
WISE	WANLY	WHIRL	WOFUL	*WAFERY	WARNER
WISH	WARTY	WHIRR	WOKEN	*WAFFIE	WARPER
WISP	WASHY	WHISH	WOMAN	*WAFFLE	WARRED
WISS	WASPY	*WHISK	*WOMBY	WAFTER	WARREN
WIST	WASTE	WHIST	WOMEN	WAGGED	WARSAW
WITE	WATAP	WHITE	*WONKY	WAGGER	WARSLE
WITH	WATCH	WHITY	WOODY	WAGGLE	WASABI
WIVE	WATER	*WHIZZ	WOOER	WAGGLY	WASHER
WOAD	WAUGH	WHOLE	WOOLY	WAGGON	WASTER
WOKE	WAVER	*WHOMP	WOOPS	WAGING	WASTRY
WOLD	WAVEY	WHOOF	WOOSH	WAHINE	WATAPE
WOLF	*WAXEN	WHOOP	*WOOZY	WAILER	WATERY
WOMB	*WAXER	WHORE	WORDY	WAITER	WATTER
WONK	WEALD	WHORL	WORLD	WAIVER	WATTLE
WONT	WEARY	WHORT	WORMY	*WAKIKI	WAUCHT
WOOD	WEAVE	WHOSE	WORRY	WAKING	WAUGHT
WOOF	*WEBBY	WHOSO	WORSE	WALIES	*WAVERY
WOOL	WEBER	*WHUMP	WORST	WALING	WAVIER
WORD	WECHT	WIDDY	WORTH	WALKER	WAVIES

*WAVILY	WHILOM	WINCEY	WOOFER	WAKENER	WATERER
WAVING	WHILST	WINDER	WOOLED	*WALKING	WATTAGE
*WAXIER	*WHIMSY	WINDLE	WOOLEN	WALKOUT	WATTAPE
*WAXILY	WHINER	WINDOW	WOOLER	*WALKWAY	WATTEST
*WAXING	*WHINEY	WINDUP	WOOLIE	*WALLABY	WAVELET
*WAYLAY	WHINGE	WINERY	WOOLLY	WALLEYE	*WAVEOFF
WEAKEN	*WHINNY	WINGER	WORKER	WALLIES	WAVERER
*WEAKLY	*WHIPPY	WINIER	*WORKUP	*WALTZER	WAVIEST
WEALTH	*WHIRLY	WINING	WORMER	*WAMEFOU	*WAXBILL
WEANER	*WHIRRY	WINISH	WORMIL	*WAMEFUL	*WAXIEST
WEAPON	*WHISHT	WINKER	WORRIT	*WAMPISH	*WAXLIKE
WEARER	*WHISKY	WINKLE	WORSEN	WANGLER	*WAXWEED
WEASEL	WHITEN	WINNED	WORSER	WANIEST	*WAXWING
WEASON	WHITER	WINNER	WORSET	WANIGAN	*WAXWORK
WEAVER	*WHITEY	WINNOW	*WORTHY	WANNESS	*WAXWORM
*WEBFED	*WHOLLY	WINTER	WOWSER	WANNEST	*WAYBILL
WEDDER	WHOMSO	WINTLE	WRAITH	WANNING	WAYLESS
WEDELN	*WHOOSH	WINTRY	WRASSE	WANTAGE	WAYSIDE
WEDGIE	WHOSIS	WIPING	*WRATHY	WARBLER	*WAYWARD
WEEDER	*WHYDAH	WIRIER	WREATH	WARFARE	*WAYWORN
*WEEKLY	*WICKED	WIRILY	WRENCH	WARHEAD	*WEAKISH
WEENIE	*WICKER	WIRING	WRETCH	WARIEST	*WEALTHY
WEENSY	*WICKET	WISDOM	WRIEST	WARISON	WEARIED
WEEPER	*WICOPY	WISELY	WRIGHT	WARLESS	WEARIER
WEEVER	WIDDER	WISENT	WRISTY	WARLIKE	WEARIES
WEEVIL	WIDDIE	WISEST	WRITER	*WARLOCK	WEARISH
WEEWEE	WIDDLE	WISHER	WRITHE	WARLORD	WEASAND
WEIGHT	WIDEST	WISING	*WURZEL	*WARMISH	WEASELY
WEINER	WIDGET	*WITCHY	WUTHER	WARNING	WEATHER
WEIRDO	WIDISH	WITHAL	*WYVERN	WARPAGE	*WEAZAND
WEIRDY	WIELDY	WITHER	WABBLER	*WARPATH	*WEBBING
WELDER	WIENER	WITHIN	WADABLE	WARRANT	*WEBFOOT
WELDOR	WIENIE	WITING	WADDIED	WARRING	WEBLESS
WELKIN	*WIFELY	WITNEY	WADDIES	WARRIOR	*WEBLIKE
WELLIE	WIFING	WITTED	WADDING	*WARSHIP	WEBSTER
WELTER	WIGEON	WITTOL	WADDLER	WARSLER	*WEBWORM
WESKIT	WIGGED	WIVERN	WADMAAL	WARSTLE	WEDDING
WESTER	WIGGLE	WIVING	WADMOLL	WARTHOG	*WEDLOCK
WETHER	WIGGLY	*WIZARD	WAENESS	WARTIER	WEEDIER
WETTED	WIGLET	*WIZZEN	*WAESUCK	WARTIME	WEEDILY
WETTER	WIGWAG	WOBBLE	*WAFFLER	*WARWORK	*WEEKDAY
*WHACKO	*WIGWAM	*WOBBLY	WAFTAGE	WARWORN	*WEEKEND
*WHACKY	*WIKIUP	WOEFUL	WAFTURE	*WASHDAY	WEIGELA
WHALER	WILDER	WOLFER	WAGERER	WASHIER	WEIGHER
*WHAMMO	WILDLY	WOLVER	*WAGGERY	WASHING	*WEIGHTY
*WHAMMY	WILFUL	WOLVES	WAGGING	WASHOUT	WEIRDIE
*WHARVE	WILIER	WOMBAT	*WAGGISH	WASHRAG	WEIRDLY
*WHEEZE	WILILY	WOMERA	WAGONER	*WASHTUB	*WELCHER
*WHEEZY	WILING	WONDER	WAGSOME	WASSAIL	WELCOME
*WHELKY	WILLER	WONNED	WAGTAIL	WASTAGE	WELFARE
WHENAS	WILLET	WONNER	WAILFUL	WASTERY	WELLIES
WHENCE	WILLOW	WONTON	WAISTER	WASTING	WELSHER
*WHERRY	WIMBLE	WOODEN	WAITING	WASTREL	WELTING
*WHERVE	WIMPLE	WOODIE	*WAKANDA	WASTRIE	*WENCHER
*WHIDAH	WINCER	WOODSY	*WAKEFUL	*WATCHER	WENDIGO

WENNISH	WHITEST	WINDROW	WOOLHAT	WAGGONER	*WATCHCRY
WERGELD	*WHITHER	*WINDWAY	WOOLIER	WAGONAGE	*WATCHDOG
WERGELT	WHITIES	WINESOP	WOOLIES	*WAHCONDA	*WATCHEYE
WERGILD	WHITING	*WINGBOW	WOOLLED	*WAIFLIKE	*WATCHFUL
*WERWOLF	*WHITISH	WINGIER	WOOLLEN	WAILSOME	*WATCHMAN
WESSAND	*WHITLOW	WINGLET	WOOLMAN	WAINSCOT	*WATCHOUT
WESTERN	WHITTER	WINGMAN	WOOMERA	WAISTING	WATERAGE
WESTING	WHITTLE	WINGTIP	WOORALI	WAITRESS	WATERBED
*WETBACK	*WHIZZED	WINIEST	WOORARI	*WAKELESS	WATERDOG
WETLAND	*WHIZZER	WINLESS	WORDAGE	*WAKENING	WATERIER
WETNESS	*WHIZZES	WINNING	WORDIER	*WAKERIFE	WATERILY
WETTEST	*WHOEVER	*WINNOCK	WORDILY	*WALKAWAY	WATERING
WETTING	*WHOLISM	WINSOME	WORDING	*WALKOVER	WATERISH
WETTISH	*WHOOPEE	WINTERY	*WORKBAG	*WALKYRIE	WATERLOG
*WHACKER	*WHOOPER	WIPEOUT	*WORKBOX	WALLAROO	WATERLOO
WHALING	*WHOOPLA	WIREMAN	*WORKDAY	WALLOPER	WATERMAN
WHANGEE	WHOOSIS	WIRETAP	*WORKING	WALLOWER	*WATERWAY
*WHAPPER	*WHOPPER	*WIREWAY	*WORKMAN	WANDERER	WATTHOUR
WHATNOT	WHORING	WIRIEST	WORKOUT	WANDEROO	WATTLESS
WHATSIS	*WHORISH	WISEASS	WORLDLY	WANNIGAN	*WAVEBAND
WHEATEN	WHORTLE	WORMIER	WANTONER	WAVEFORM
WHEEDLE	*WICKAPE	WISPIER	*WORMISH	WANTONLY	WAVELESS
WHEELER	*WICKING	*WISPILY	WORRIED	*WARCRAFT	*WAVELIKE
WHEELIE	*WICKIUP	*WISPISH	WORRIER	*WARDENRY	WAVINESS
*WHEEPLE	*WICKYUP	WISTFUL	*WORSHIP	WARDRESS	*WAXBERRY
*WHEEZER	WIDENER	WITHIER	WORSTED	WARDROBE	*WAXINESS
WHEREAS	WIDEOUT	WITHIES	WOTTETH	WARDROOM	*WAXPLANT
WHEREAT	WIDGEON	WITHING	WOULDST	*WARDSHIP	*WAYFARER
*WHEREBY	WIDOWER	WITHOUT	WRANGLE	WAREROOM	*WAYGOING
WHEREIN	WIELDER	WITLESS	WRAPPER	WARFARIN	*WAYLAYER
*WHEREOF	*WIFEDOM	WITLING	WRASSLE	WARHORSE	*WEAKENER
WHEREON	*WIGGERY	WITLOOF	WRASTLE	WARINESS	*WEAKFISH
WHERETO	WIGGIER	WITNESS	WREAKER	*WARMAKER	*WEAKLING
*WHETHER	WIGGING	WITTIER	WREATHE	WARMNESS	*WEAKNESS
WHETTER	WIGGLER	WITTILY	*WRECKER	*WARMOUTH	*WEAKSIDE
*WHICKER	WIGLESS	WITTING	WRESTER	WARPLANE	WEANLING
*WHIFFER	*WIGLIKE	*WOADWAX	WRESTLE	*WARPOWER	*WEAPONRY
*WHIFFET	WILDCAT	WOBBLER	WRIGGLE	*WARPWISE	WEARABLE
*WHIFFLE	WILDING	WOENESS	*WRIGGLY	WARRAGAL	WEARIEST
*WHIMPER	WILDISH	WOESOME	WRINGER	WARRANTY	WEARIFUL
*WHIMSEY	WILIEST	*WOLFISH	WRINKLE	WARRENER	WEASELLY
WHINIER	WILLFUL	*WOLFRAM	*WRINKLY	WARRIGAL	WEEDIEST
WHINING	WILLIED	*WOMANLY	WRITHEN	WARSTLER	WEEDLESS
*WHIPPED	WILLIES	WOMMERA	WRITHER	WARTIEST	*WEEDLIKE
*WHIPPER	WILLING	WONNING	WRITING	WARTLESS	*WEEKLONG
*WHIPPET	*WILLOWY	WOODBIN	WRITTEN	*WARTLIKE	*WEFTWISE
*WHIPRAY	*WIMPISH	*WOODBOX	WRONGER	*WASHABLE	WEIGELIA
*WHIPSAW	*WINCHER	WOODCUT	WRONGLY	*WASHBOWL	*WEIGHMAN
WHIRLER	WINCING	WOODHEN	WROUGHT	WASHIEST	*WEIGHTER
WHIRRED	WINDAGE	WOODIER	*WRYNECK	*WASHROOM	WEIRDIES
*WHISKER	WINDBAG	WOODIES	WRYNESS	WASTABLE	*WELCOMER
*WHISKEY	WINDIER	WOODLOT	WADEABLE	WASTEFUL	WELDLESS
*WHISPER	WINDIGO	WOODMAN	*WAESUCKS	WASTELOT	WELDMENT
WHISTLE	WINDILY	WOODSIA	*WAFFLING	WASTERIE	*WELLADAY
*WHITELY	WINDING	*WOODWAX	WAGELESS	*WASTEWAY	*WELLAWAY

WELLBORN	*WHOSEVER	*WIREWORK	*WOOLWORK	S W OP	S W OUN
*WELLCURB	*WIDEBAND	*WIREWORM	*WORDBOOK	S W OT	S W UNG
WELLDOER	WIDENESS	WIRINESS	WORDIEST	S W UM	T W AIN
*WELLHEAD	*WIDTHWAY	WISEACRE	WORDLESS	T W AE	T W ANG
WELLHOLE	*WIFEHOOD	WISENESS	*WORDPLAY	T W AT	T W EAK
WELLNESS	WIFELESS	*WISHBONE	*WORKABLE	T W EE	T W EED
WELLSITE	*WIFELIKE	WISHLESS	*WORKADAY	T W IG	T W EEN
WEREGILD	WIGGIEST	WISPIEST	*WORKBOAT	T W IN	T W EET
*WEREWOLF	*WIGMAKER	*WISPLIKE	*WORKBOOK	T W IT	T W ERP
WESTERLY	*WILDFIRE	WISTARIA	*WORKFARE	Y W IS	T W ICE
WESTMOST	*WILDFOWL	WISTERIA	*WORKFOLK	B W ANA	T W IER
*WESTWARD	WILDLAND	*WITCHERY	*WORKLESS	D W ARF	T W ILL
*WETPROOF	*WILDLIFE	*WITCHING	*WORKLOAD	D W ELL	T W INE
WETTABLE	WILDLING	*WITHDRAW	*WORKMATE	D W ELT	T W INY
*WHALEMAN	WILDNESS	WITHERER	*WORKROOM	D W INE	T W IRL
*WHARFAGE	*WILDWOOD	*WITHHOLD	*WORKSHOP	S W AGE	T W IRP
*WHATEVER	WILINESS	WITHIEST	*WORKWEEK	S W AIL	T W IST
WHATNESS	WILLIWAU	WITTIEST	*WORMHOLE	S W AIN	*T W IXT
WHEATEAR	*WILLIWAW	*WIZARDRY	WORMIEST	S W ALE	T W YER
*WHEEDLER	WILLOWER	WOBEGONE	*WORMLIKE	S W AMI	*K W ANZA
*WHEELING	*WILLYARD	*WOLFFISH	WORMROOT	S W AMP	*Q W ERTY
*WHEELMAN	WILLYART	*WOLFLIKE	WORMSEED	S W AMY	T W EENY
*WHENEVER	*WILLYWAW	WOMANISE	*WORMWOOD	S W ANG	T W ISTY
*WHEREVER	WINDBURN	*WOMANISH	WORNNESS	S W ANK	S W AGGIE
*WHETTING	*WINDFALL	*WOMANIZE	*WORTHFUL	S W ARD	S W ALLO W
*WHEYFACE	*WINDFLAW	WONDERER	WOSTTETH	S W ARE	S W IDDEN
*WHEYLIKE	WINDGALL	WONDROUS	WOULDEST	S W ARF	*S W INGBY
*WHIFFLER	WINDIEST	*WONTEDLY	*WRACKFUL	S W ARM	T W ATTLE
*WHIMBREL	WINDLASS	*WOODBIND	WRANGLER	S W ART	*T W IDDLY
*WHINCHAT	WINDLESS	WOODBINE	*WRAPPING	S W ASH	*T W INJET
WHINIEST	WINDLING	*WOODCHAT	*WRATHFUL	S W ATH	T W INSET
*WHIPCORD	WINDMILL	*WOODCOCK	*WRECKAGE	S W EAR	S W IFTLET
*WHIPLASH	*WINDPIPE	WOODIEST	*WRECKFUL	S W EAT	*SW IM W EAR
*WHIPLIKE	*WINDSOCK	WOODLAND	*WRECKING	S W EDE	S W INGIER
*WHIPPIER	*WINDSURF	*WOODLARK	WRESTLER	S W EEP	S W INGING
*WHIPPING	*WINDWARD	WOODLESS	*WRETCHED	S W EER	S W INGMAN
*WHIPTAIL	WINELESS	WOODLORE	WRIGGLER	S W EET	*S W INGIES
*WHIPWORM	*WINESHOP	WOODNOTE	WRISTLET	S W ELL	DE W AR
*WHIRRING	*WINESKIN	WOODPILE	*WRITHING	S W EPT	*JO W AR
*WHISPERY	*WINGBACK	*WOODRUFF	*WRONGFUL	S W IFT	RA W IN
WHISTLER	WINGDING	*WOODSHED	*WROTHFUL	S W ILL	RE W ED
*WHITECAP	*WINGEDLY	WOODSMAN	WRITERLY	S W INE	RE W ET
*WHITEFLY	WINGIEST	*WOODWIND		S W ING	BA .W BEE
WHITENER	WINGLESS	*WOODWORK	H W AN	S W INK	*BA W DRY
WHITEOUT	*WINGLIKE	*WOODWORM	L W EI	S W IPE	BA W LER
WHITIEST	*WINGOVER	*WOOINGLY	S W AB	S W IRL	BA W TIE
*WHITRACK	WINGSPAN	WOOLFELL	S W AG	S W ISH	BE W AIL
WHITTLER	WINNABLE	WOOLIEST	S W AM	S W ISS	BE W ARE
WHITTRET	WINNOWER	WOOLLIER	S W AN	S W ITH	BE W EEP
*WHIZBANG	WINTERER	WOOLLIES	S W AP	S W IVE	BE W ORM
*WHIZZING	WINTERLY	*WOOLLIKE	S W AT	S W OON	BE W RAP
*WHODUNIT	*WIREDRAW	*WOOLPACK	S W AY	S W OOP	BE W RAY
*WHOMEVER	WIREHAIR	*WOOLSACK	S W IG	S W ORD	BO W ERY
*WHOREDOM	WIRELESS	*WOOLSHED	S W IM	S W ORE	BO W FIN
WHORESON	*WIRELIKE	*WOOLSKIN	S W OB	S W ORN	BO W ING

BO W LEG	PA W NEE	*BE W ORRY	*JA W LINE	TO W NLET	*DRA W BACK
BO W LER	PA W NER	*BO W HEAD	*JE W ELER	*TO W PATH	DRA W BORE
BO W MAN	PA W NOR	*BO W KNOT	*JE W ELRY	TO W ROPE	*DRAWDOWN
BO W POT	*PA W PA W	BO W LDER	*JE W FISH	VA W NTIE	DRA W TUBE
*BO W WOW	PE W TER	BO W LESS	*LA W BOOK	VO W LESS	FLA W LESS
BO W YER	PO W DER	*BO W LFUL	LA W LESS	*YA W PING	FLO W ERER
*BY W ORD	PO W TER	*BO W LIKE	LA W LIKE	DO W NLAND	FLO W ERET
*BY W ORK	*PO W WO W	BO W LINE	LA W SUIT	*DO W NLINK	*FLY W HEEL
CO W AGE	RA W ISH	BO W LING	LO W BALL	*DO W NLOAD	*GAS W ORKS
CO W ARD	RE W AKE	*BO W SHOT	LO W BORN	*DO W NPIPE	*GAY W INGS
*CO W BOY	RE W ARD	CO W BANE	LO W BRED	DO W NSIDE	*GLOW WORM
CO W IER	RE W ARM	CO W BELL	*LO W BRO W	*DO W NSIZE	GRE W SOME
CO W MAN	RE W ASH	*CO W BIND	LO W DO WN	*DO W NTICK	*LAY W OMAN
CO W PAT	RE W ELD	*CO W BIRD	LO W LAND	*DOWNWASH	*MAD W OMAN
CO W PEA	RE W IND	*CO W EDLY	LO W LIFE	*HA W KEYED	*MID W ATCH
CO W PIE	RE W IRE	*CO W FISH	LO W NESS	*HA WKSHA W	NAR W HALE
*CO W POX	RE W OKE	*CO W FLAP	*MA W KISH	*JA W BONER	NON W HITE
CO W RIE	RE W ORD	*CO W FLOP	NE W BORN	LO W LIFER	*NON W OODY
DA W TIE	RE W ORK	CO W GIRL	*NE W MOWN	*LO W LIGHT	NON W OVEN
DE W IER	RE W OVE	*CO W HERB	NE W NESS	LO W RIDER	*PIN W HEEL
DE W ILY	RE W RAP	*CO W HERD	*NE W SBOY	*NEWSHA WK	*PLO W BACK
DE W LAP	RO W ING	*CO W HIDE	NE W SIER	*TO W NHOME	*PLO W HEAD
DE W OOL	*SA W FLY	CO W IEST	NE W SIES	*BED W ARDS	PLO W LAND
DE W ORM	SA W LOG	*CO W LICK	NE W SMAN	*BLO W BALL	RAD W ASTE
DO W ERY	SA W NEY	CO W LING	NO W HERE	*BLO W DOWN	*REA W AKEN
DO W NER	SA W YER	*CO W PLOP	NO W NESS	*BLO W FISH	SEA W ATER
DO W SER	SE W AGE	*CO W POKE	PA W NAGE	*BLO W HARD	*SHO W BOAT
FA W NER	SE W ING	CO W RAGE	*PO W DERY	*BLO W HOLE	*SHO W CASE
FO W LER	SO W ANS	CO W RAND	RA W HIDE	BLO W IEST	*SHOWDOWN
GA W KER	SO W CAR	CO W RITE	RA W NESS	*BLO W PIPE	SHO W ERER
GA W PER	SO W ENS	*CO W SHED	RE W AKEN	*BLO W TUBE	*SHO W GIRL
GA W SIE	TA W DRY	*CO W SKIN	RE W EAVE	*BOB W HITE	SHO W IEST
GE W GA W	TA W NEY	CO W SLIP	RE W EIGH	*BRO W BAND	*SHO W RING
*HA W KER	TA W PIE	DE W ATER	RE W IDEN	*BRO W BEAT	*SHOW ROOM
*HA W KEY	*TH W ACK	*DE W CLA W	RE W OKEN	BRO W LESS	*SKE W BACK
*HA W KIE	TH W ART	DE W DROP	RE W OUND	BRO W NIER	*SKE W BALD
HA W SER	TO W AGE	DE W FALL	RE W OVEN	*BRO W NISH	*SKE W NESS
HO W LER	TO W ARD	DE W IEST	RE W RITE	BRO W NOUT	*SKY W ARDS
HO W LET	TO W ERY	DE W LESS	RO W BOAT	*CHO W CHOW	*SKY W RITE
*KO W TO W	TO W HEE	DO W ABLE	*RO W LOCK	*CHO W TIME	*SLOWDOWN
LA W FUL	TO W NEE	DO W AGER	SA W BILL	CLA W LESS	SLO W NESS
LA W INE	TO W NIE	DO W NIER	*SA W BUCK	*CLO W NERY	*SLO W POKE
LA W ING	VA W ARD	FE W NESS	SA W DUST	*CLO W NISH	*SLOW WORM
LA W MAN	W O W SER	FO W LING	*SA W FISH	*COB W EBBY	SNO W BALL
LA W YER	YA W NER	*FO W LPOX	SA W LIKE	*COG W HEEL	*SNO W BANK
LO W BOY	YA W PER	*GA W KIER	SA W MILL	*CRA W FISH	SNO W BELL
LO W BRO	YO W LER	*GA W KIES	TO W ARDS	*CRA WLWAY	SNO W BELT
LO W ERY	*BA W COCK	*GA W KISH	*TO W A WAY	CRE W LESS	SNO W BIRD
LO W ING	BA W DIER	*HA W KING	TO W BOAT	*CRE W MATE	*SNO W BUSH
LO W ISH	BA W DIES	*HA W KISH	TO W HEAD	*CRE W NECK	SNO W DROP
NE W ISH	*BA W DILY	*HO W BEIT	TO W LINE	*CRO W FOOT	SNO W FALL
NE W SIE	*BA W DRIC	*HO W EVER	TO W MOND	*CRO W STEP	SNO W IEST
NE W TON	BA W SUNT	*HO W WDAH	TO W MONT	CUT W ATER	SNO W LAND
NO W AYS	*BE W EARY	*JA W BONE	TO W NIES		SNO W LESS
NO W ISE	*BE W ITCH	*JA W LIKE	TO W NISH	*DOG W ATCH	*SNO W LIKE

SNO W MELT	GRO W	SHRE W	MARRO W	*CUMSHA W	*CHECKRO W
SNO W MOLD	KNE W	SINE W	MEADO W	*DAYGLO W	*CHOW CHOW
*SNO W PACK	KNO W	*SQUA W	MELLO W	*DE W CLA W	*CLERIHE W
*SNO W PLO W	MEO W	STRA W	MILDE W	DISAVO W	*COCKCRO W
*SNO W SHED	PHE W	STRE W	MINNO W	*FLYBLO W	COLESLA W
SNO W SHOE	PLE W	STRO W	MORRO W	*FOREPA W	*CROSSBO W
SNO W SUIT	PLO W	THRA W	NARRO W	FRETSA W	CURASSO W
*STO W A WAY	PRO W	THRE W	NEPHE W	*HACKSA W	DISALLO W
SUB W ORLD	SCO W	THRO W	*PA W PA W	HANDSA W	DISENDO W
SUN W ARDS	SHA W	VROU W	PILLO W	HOOSGO W	*FENCERO W
THA W LESS	SHE W	W IDO W	PITSA W	*JACKDA W	*FEVERFE W
THE W LESS	SKE W	BARLO W	*PO W WO W	*LOCKJA W	*FOOFARA W
THO W LESS	SLA W	BARRO W	REAVO W	LONGBO W	*FOREKNO W
TRA W LNET	SLE W	BASHA W	RECHE W	*LO W BRO W	*FORESHO W
TRO W ELER	SLO W	BELLO W	REDRA W	MISDRA W	*FURBELO W
TRO W SERS	SME W	BESNO W	REFLE W	MISGRO W	*GANGPLO W
*TRY W ORKS	SNA W	BESTO W	REFLO W	*MISKNO W	*HA W KSHA W
*VIE W DATA	SNO W	BILLO W	REGLO W	MISTBO W	*HEDGERO W
VIE W IEST	SPE W	BORRO W	REGRE W	MOONBO W	*HIGHBRO W
VIE W LESS	STA W	*BO W WO W	REGRO W	*PRESHO W	*HONEYDE W
*CLA W LIKE	STE W	BURRO W	RESHO W	*PREVIE W	*HOOSEGO W
	STO W	BYELA W	REVIE W	*PURVIE W	*KICKSHA W
BLA W	THA W	CALLO W	RIPSA W	RAINBO W	*LOBBYGO W
BLO W	THE W	CASHA W	SALLO W	REENDO W	*MACCABA W
BRA W	TRO W	CASHE W	SEESA W	*RIKSHA W	*MACKINA W
BRE W	VIE W	CURFE W	SHADO W	RINGTA W	*MISTHRO W
BRO W	VRO W	CURLE W	SORRO W	*SALCHO W	*PEEPSHO W
CHA W	W HE W	CUSHA W	SUNBO W	SEMIRA W	*POSTSHO W
CHE W	BEDE W	FALLO W	SUNDE W	SHALLO W	REREVIE W
CHO W	BELO W	FARRO W	TALLO W	*SOMEHO W	*RICKSHA W
CLA W	BYLA W	FELLO W	W ALLO W	SPARRO W	*ROADSHO W
CLE W	CAHO W	*FOGBO W	W ARSA W	SUNGLO W	*ROUGHHE W
CRA W	KOTO W	FOLLO W	W ILLO W	S W ALLO W	*SCOFFLA W
CRE W	MACA W	FURRO W	W INDO W	TRISHA W	SETSCRE W
CRO W	MIAO W	GEEGA W	W INNO W	*VITCHE W	*SHADBLO W
DHO W	NOHO W	GE W GA W	YARRO W	*W HIPSA W	*SIDESHO W
DRA W	PAPA W	*GUFFA W	YELLO W	*W HITLO W	*SNO W PLO W
DRE W	PILA W	HALLO W	*BACKSA W	W INDRO W	*SOUTHPA W
FLA W	PSHA W	HARRO W	*BESHRE W	*W INGBO W	TELEVIE W
FLE W	RENE W	*HAYMO W	BESTRE W	*BACKFLO W	TOMORRO W
FLO W	RESA W	*HEEHA W	BESTRO W	BEDSTRA W	*W ILLI WA W
FRO W	RESE W	HOLLO W	*BUCKSA W	*BESHADO W	*WILLY WA W
GLO W	RESO W	*JIGSA W	CATCLA W	BUNGALO W	*W INDFLA W
GNA W	SCRE W	*KO W TO W	CATSPA W	CARASSO W	*W IREDRA W
GRE W	SERO W	MALLO W	CORNRO W	*CHAINSA W	*W ITHDRA W

X

XYST	XENON	*XYLAN	*XYLENE	*XYSTOS	*XANTHIN
*XEBEC	XERIC	*XYLEM	*XYLOID	*XYSTUS	*XERARCH
XENIA	*XEROX	*XYLOL	*XYLOSE	*XANTHAN	XEROSIS
XENIC	XERUS	*XYLYL	*XYSTER	*XANTHIC	*XIPHOID

*XYLIDIN	SE X TET	SE X TILE	FAU X	*COCCY X	*COANNE X
*XANTHATE	SE X TON	*SI X FOLD	FLA X	*COMMI X	*COMPLE X
*XANTHEIN	SE X UAL	SI X TEEN	FLE X	*CONVE X	*CONFLU X
*XANTHENE	*TA X EME	*SI X THLY	FLU X	*CORTE X	*FEEDBO X
*XANTHINE	TA X ITE	*TA X ABLE	HOA X	*COWPO X	*FIREBO X
*XANTHOMA	*TA X MAN	*TA X ICAB	*JIN X	*DIPLE X	*FLUMMO X
*XANTHONE	TO X INE	*TA X IMAN	LYN X	*DUPLE X	*FOWLPO X
*XANTHOUS	TO X OID	*TA X IWAY	MIN X	*FORNI X	*GEARBO X
*XENOGAMY	TU X EDO	TA X LESS	PRE X	*HALLU X	*GRAVLA X
*XENOGENY	*WA X IER	*TA X PAID	ROU X	*HATBO X	*HELLBO X
*XENOLITH	*WA X ILY	*TA X WISE	BEAU X	*HOTBO X	*HOMOSE X
*XEROSERB	*WA X ING	TE X TILE	*BEMI X	*LARYN X	*JUKEBO X
*XYLIDINE	*BO X FISH	TE X TUAL	BORA X	*LUMMO X	*LOCKBO X
*XYLOCARP	*BO X HAUL	TE X TURE	CALI X	*MASTI X	*MAILBO X
*XYLOTOMY	*BO X IEST	*TO X EMIA	*CALY X	*MATRI X	*MINIMA X
	*BO X LIKE	*TO X ICAL	CARE X	*MENIN X	*NARTHE X
*DE X Y	*BO X WOOD	*VE X EDLY	*CIME X	NONTA X	*PACKWA X
*PI X Y	*CO X ALGY	*WA X BILL	*CODE X	*PA X WA X	*PANCHA X
DE X IE	*CO X COMB	*WA X IEST	*COMI X	*PEGBO X	*PARADO X
*FI X IT	*DE X TRAL	*WA X LIKE	CULE X	*PHENI X	*PEMPHI X
LE X IS	*DE X TRIN	*WA X WEED	*CYLI X	*PICKA X	*PERPLE X
PI X EL	*DE X TRAN	*WA X WING	DESE X	*POLEA X	*PHALAN X
*BO X CAR	*FI X EDLY	*WA X WORK	DETO X	*POLLE X	*PHARYN X
*BO X FUL	*FI X INGS	*WA X WORM	*DEWA X	*PREFI X	*PHOENI X
*BO X IER	*FI X TUTE	*BO X BOARD	GALA X	*PREMI X	*PILLBO X
*BO X ING	*FO X FIRE	*PI X INESS	*HAPA X	*PRETA X	*POSTBO X
DE X IES	*FO X FISH	*SI X TYISH	*HELI X	*PROLI X	*POSTFI X
DE X TER	*FO X HOLE	*DEO X Y	*HYRA X	*REFLE X	*POSTTA X
DE X TRO	*FO X HUNT	DEI X IS	*KYLI X	*REFLU X	*PRINCO X
*FI X ATE	*FO X IEST	DIO X AN	LATE X	*SCOLE X	*REAFFI X
*FI X ITY	*FO X LIKE	DIO X IN	MIRE X	*SILVE X	REANNE X
*FI X URE	*FO X SKIN	*PLE X AL	MURE X	*SKYBO X	*RECTRI X
*FO X ILY	*FO X TAIL	*COE X TEND	*PHLO X	*SMILA X	*REINDE X
*FO X ING	*FO X TROT	*FLA X SEED	RADI X	*SPADI X	*SALPIN X
*FO X TER	*HE X AGON	*FLE X AGON	REDO X	*SPHIN X	*SALTBO X
*HE X ADE	*HE X APLA	*FLE X IBLE	REDU X	STORA X	*SANDBO X
*HE X ANE	*HE X APOD	*FLE X TIME	*REFI X	*STYRA X	*SIMPLE X
*HE X ONE	*HE X EREI	*FLE X UOSE	RELA X	*SUBFI X	*SOAPBO X
*HE X OSE	*HE X OSAN	*FLE X UOUS	REME X	*SUFFI X	*SONOVO X
*LA X ITY	LA X NESS	*FLU X GATE	REMI X	SURTA X	*SPANDE X
*LE X EME	*LE X ICAL	*GLO X INIA	RETA X	*SYNTA X	*TECTRI X
LU X ATE	*LE X ICON	*PRO X EMIC	*REWA X	*SYRIN X	*TOOLBO X
*LU X URY	*MA X ILLA	*PRO X IMAL	SILE X	*TEABO X	TORTRI X
*MA X IMA	*MA X IMAL	*QUI X OTIC	TELE X	*THORA X	*TRIPLE X
*MA X I X E	*MA X IMUM	*QUI X OTRY	*VARI X	*VERNI X	*TUBIFE X
*MY X OID	*MA X WELL	*REE X PORT	*X ERO X	*VERTE X	*WOADWA X
*MY X OMA	*MI X TURE	*REE X POSE	*BANJA X	*VOLVO X	*WOODBO X
*PA X WA X	NO X IOUS		*BIFLE X	*VORTE X	*WOODWA X
*SA X ONY	*PY X IDES		*BOLLI X	*BANDBO X	*WORKBO X
SE X IER	*SA X HORN	BOA X	*BOLLO X	*BEESWA X	*BICONVE X
*SE X ILY	*SA X TUBA	CAL X	*BOMBA X	*BOOMBO X	*BORDEAU X
*SE X ISM	SE X IEST	COA X	*BOMBY X	*BROADA X	*BREADBO X
SE X IST	SE X LESS	CRU X	*CAUDE X	*CARAPA X	*CICATRI X
*SE X POT	SE X TAIN	DOU X	*CERVI X	*CASHBO X	*CRUCIPI X
SE X TAN	SE X TANT	FAL X	*CLIMA X	*COALBO X	*CURTALA X

*FOURPLE X	*MICROLU X	*QUADPLE X	*SNUFFBO X	*SUPERSE X	*TRANSFI X
*HARUSPE X	*MILLILU X	*QUINCUN X	*SOUNDBO X	*SUPERTA X	*VIDEOTE X
*HERETRI X	*PARALLA X	*SARDONY X	*SPINIFE X	*SWEATBO X	
*HERITRI X	*PONTIFE X	*SAUCEBO X	*SUBINDE X	*SWINEPO X	
*MATCHBO X	*PRECIEU X	*SMALLPO X	*SUPERFI X	*TOADFLA X	

Y

YACK	YOWL	YOWIE	YONKER	*YARMELKE	G Y VE
YAFF	YUAN	YUCCA	YOUPON	*YARMULKE	H Y LA
YAGI	YUCA	*YUCCH	YOWLER	*YATAGHAN	H Y MN
YALD	YUCH	*YUCKY	YTTRIA	*YAWMETER	H Y PO
YANG	YUCK	YULAN	YUPPIE	YEANLING	H Y TE
YANK	YUGA	*YUMMY	*YACHTER	*YEARBOOK	*K Y AK
YARD	YULE	YUPON	*YAMALKA	YEARLIES	K Y AR
YARE	YURT	YABBER	*YAMULKA	YEARLING	K Y AT
YARN	YWIS	*YAKKER	*YAPPING	YEARLONG	K Y TE
YAUD	YACHT	YAMMER	YARDAGE	YEARNING	L Y NX
YAUP	YAGER	*YANQUI	YARDARM	YEASAYER	L Y RE
YAWL	YAHOO	YANTRA	YARDMAN	*YEOMANRY	L Y SE
YAWN	YAIRD	*YAPOCK	*YASHMAC	*YESHIVAH	M Y NA
YAWP	YAMEN	YAPPED	*YASHMAK	YESTREEN	P Y IC
YEAH	YAMUN	YAPPER	YATAGAN	YODELLER	P Y IN
YEAN	YAPOK	YARNER	*YAWPING	*YOGHOURT	P Y RE
YEAR	YAPON	YARROW	*YCLEPED	*YOKELESS	R Y KE
YECH	YAULD	*YASMAK	YEALING	*YOKELISH	R Y ND
YEGG	YEARN	YATTER	YEAREND	*YOKEMATE	R Y OT
YELD	YEAST	YAUPER	YEARNER	*YOKOZUNA	S Y BO
YELK	*YECCH	YAUPON	YEGGMAN	*YOUNGISH	S Y CE
YELL	*YECHY	YAUTIA	*YELLOWY	YOURSELF	S Y KE
YELP	YENTA	YAWNER	*YESHIVA	*YOUTHFUL	S Y LI
YERK	YENTE	YAWPER	YESSING	YTTERBIA	S Y NC
YETI	YERBA	YCLEPT	YESTERN	YULETIDE	S Y NE
YETT	*YEUKY	YEARLY	YIELDER	YODELLING	S Y PH
YEUK	YIELD	YEASTY	*YIPPING		T Y EE
YILL	YIKES	YEELIN	YODELER	B Y RE	T Y ER
YIPE	YINCE	YELLER	YOGHURT	B Y RL	T Y KE
YIRD	YIPES	YELLOW	YOUNGER	B Y TE	T Y NE
YIRR	YIRTH	YELPER	YOUNKER	C Y AN	T Y PE
YLEM	YOBBO	YEOMAN	*YOYTHEN	C Y MA	T Y PO
YOCK	YODEL	YESSED	YPERITE	C Y ME	T Y PP
YODH	YODLE	YESSES	YTTRIUM	C Y ST	T Y PY
YOGA	YOGEE	YESTER	*YACHTING	D Y AD	T Y RE
YOGH	YOGIC	YIPPED	*YACHTMAN	D Y ER	T Y RO
YOGI	YOGIN	YIPPEE	*YAHOOISM	D Y KE	*W Y CH
YOKE	YOKEL	YIPPIE	*YAHRZEIT	D Y NE	W Y LE
YOLK	*YOLKY	YODLER	*YAKITORI	F Y CE	W Y ND
YOND	YOUNG	YOGINI	*YAMMERER	F Y KE	W Y NN
YONI	YOURN	YOGURT	*YARDBIRD	G Y BE	W Y TE
YORE	YOURS	*YOICKS	YARDLAND	G Y RE	X Y ST
YOUR	YOUSE	YOKING	*YARDWAND	G Y RI	*Z Y ME
YOWE	YOUTH	YONDER	*YARDWORK	G Y RO	B Y LAW

*B Y WA Y	P Y RAN	GL Y COL	*SK Y HOO	FE Y NESS	*PH Y TANE
C Y ANO	P Y RTC	*GL Y CY L	SK Y LIT	*FL Y ABLE	*PH Y TOID
C Y CAD	*P Y XIS	HA Y ING	*SK Y MAN	*FL Y AWA Y	*PL Y WOOD
C Y CAS	S Y CEE	*HA Y MOW	*SK Y WA Y	*FL Y BELT	*PR Y THEE
C Y CLE	S Y LPH	*HE Y DA Y	ST Y LAR	*FL Y BLOW	*PS Y CHIC
C Y CLO	S Y LVA	*HE Y DE Y	ST Y LER	*FL Y BOAT	PS Y LLID
C Y DER	S Y NCH	HO Y DEN	ST Y LET	*FL Y LEAF	PT Y ALIN
*C Y LIX	S Y NOD	*JA Y GEE	ST Y LUS	FL Y LESS	*RA Y COCK
C Y MAR	S Y NTH	*JA Y VEE	ST Y MIE	*FL Y OVER	RA Y LESS
C Y MOL	S Y REN	*JO Y FUL	*ST Y RAX	*FL Y PAST	RA Y LIKE
C Y NIC	S Y RUP	*JO Y OUS	*TH Y ME Y	FL Y TIER	RA Y WIRE
C Y TON	S Y SOP	*JO Y POP	*TH Y MIC	FL Y TING	RE Y NARD
D Y ING	T Y PED	KA Y LES	TH Y MOL	*FL Y TRAP	RO Y ALL Y
D Y NEL	T Y ING	KE Y SET	TH Y MUS	GA Y NESS	RO Y ALT Y
F Y TTE	T Y PAL	*KE Y WA Y	TH Y RSE	GL Y CINE	RO Y STER
G Y PS Y	T Y PE Y	LA Y MAN	TO Y ISH	*GL Y PTIC	*SC Y PHUS
G Y RAL	T Y PIC	*LA Y OFF	TR Y OUT	*GR Y PHON	*SH Y LOCK
G Y RON	T Y THE	*MA Y DA Y	TR Y STE	GU Y LINE	SH Y NESS
G Y RUS	V Y ING	*MA Y FL Y	TU Y ERE	*HA Y COCK	SH Y STER
H Y DRA	*X Y LAN	*MA Y HAP	VO Y AGE	*HA Y FORK	*SK Y DIVE
H Y DRO	*X Y LEM	*MA Y HEM	VO Y EUR	HA Y LAGE	*SK Y JACK
H Y ENA	*X Y LOL	*MA Y POP	*WH Y DAH	*HA Y LOFT	*SK Y LARK
H Y ING	*X Y LY L	NO Y ADE	*WA Y LA Y	*HA Y RACK	SK Y LINE
H Y MEN	BA Y AMO	*PA Y DA Y	*ZO Y SIA	*HA Y RICK	*SK Y PHOS
H Y PER	BA Y ARD	PA Y NIM	BA Y ONET	HA Y RIDE	SK Y SAIL
*H Y PHA	BA Y MAN	*PA Y OFF	*BA Y WOOD	HA Y SEED	*SK Y WALK
*H Y RAX	*BE Y LIK	PA Y OLA	*BO Y CHIK	*HA Y WARD	*SK Y WARD
H Y SON	BE Y OND	PA Y OUT	BO Y COTT	*JA Y BIRD	SL Y NESS
*K Y ACK	BO Y ARD	PE Y OTE	*BO Y HOOD	*JA Y WALK	SO Y BEAN
*K Y LIX	BO Y ISH	PE Y OTL	*BU Y BACK	*JO Y ANCE	*SO Y MILK
K Y RIE	BR Y ON Y	PH Y LAE	CA Y ENNE	*JO Y LESS	ST Y GIAN
*K Y THE	BU Y OUT	PH Y LAR	*CH Y MIST	*JO Y RIDE	ST Y LATE
L Y ARD	CA Y MAN	PH Y LLO	*CH Y MOUS	*KA Y AKER	ST Y LING
L Y ART	CA Y USE	PH Y LON	CL Y PEUS	*KE Y CARD	ST Y LISE
L Y ASE	*CH Y MIC	*PH Y LUM	CL Y STER	*KE Y HOLE	ST Y LISH
L Y CEA	CO Y DOG	*PH Y SED	CO Y NESS	KE Y LESS	ST Y LIST
L Y CEE	CO Y ISH	PH Y SES	*CR Y BAB Y	KE Y NOTE	ST Y LITE
L Y ING	CO Y OTE	*PH Y SIC	CR Y OGEN	KE Y STER	*ST Y LIZE
*L Y MPH	CO Y POU	PH Y SIS	CR Y STAL	*KE Y WORD	ST Y LOID
L Y NCH	CR Y PTO	PH Y TIN	*DA Y BOOK	*KR Y PTON	ST Y PSIS
L Y RIC	DA Y BED	PH Y TON	*DA Y GLOW	*LA Y AWA Y	ST Y PTIC
L Y SIN	*DA Y FL Y	PR Y PAN	DA Y LIL Y	LA Y ETTE	ST Y RENE
L Y SIS	DO Y LE Y	*PS Y CHE	DA Y LONG	LA Y OVER	*TH Y MIER
L Y SSA	DR Y ISH	*PS Y CHO	DA Y MARE	LO Y ALL Y	*TH Y MINE
L Y TIC	DR Y LOT	PS Y LLA	DA Y ROOM	LO Y ALT Y	TH Y ROID
L Y TTA	*FL Y BO Y	PS Y WAR	DA Y SIDE	*MA Y BUSH	TH Y RSUS
*M Y OP Y	FL Y ING	RH Y MER	DA Y SMAN	MA Y ORES	*TH Y SELF
M Y SID	*FL Y OFF	*RH Y THM	DA Y STAR	*MA Y WEED	TO Y LESS
*M Y TH Y	*FL Y SCH	RH Y TON	DA Y TIME	PA Y ABLE	TO Y LIKE
N Y ALA	*FL Y WA Y	SA Y ING	*DA Y WORK	*PA Y BACK	*TO Y SHOP
N Y LON	GA Y ET Y	SA Y YID	DO Y ENNE	PA Y LOAD	TR Y PSIN
*N Y MPH	GE Y SER	SC Y THE	DR Y LAND	PA Y MENT	TR Y SAIL
*P Y GM Y	GL Y CAN	*SK Y BOX	DR Y NESS	PA Y ROLL	TR Y STER
P Y LON	GL Y CIN	*SK Y CAP	DR Y WALL	PE Y TRAL	VO Y AGER
P Y OID				PE Y TREL	*WA Y BILL

WA Y LESS	*GAN Y MEDE	POL Y TENE	DUL Y	PLO Y	*ZAN Y
WA Y SIDE	*GRA Y BACK	*POL Y TEN Y	DUT Y	POG Y	BADD Y
*WA Y WARD	*GRA Y FISH	*POL Y TYPE	FLA Y	POK Y	BADL Y
*WA Y WORN	GRA Y LING	POL Y URIA	FLE Y	POL Y	*BAFF Y
*WR Y NECK	GRA Y MAIL	*POL Y ZOAN	FOG Y	PON Y	BAGG Y
WR Y NESS	GRA Y NESS	*POL Y ZOIC	*FOX Y	POS Y	BALD Y
*Y O Y THEN	GRE Y NESS	PON Y TAIL	*FOZ Y	PRA Y	BALK Y
*BAB Y HOOD	*HOK Y POKY	*QUA Y SIDE	FRA Y	PRE Y	BALL Y
BAR Y TONE	*HOL Y TIDE	*REC Y CLER	FUM Y	PUN Y	BALM Y
*BIC Y CLER	*KAL Y PTRA	*RUB Y LIKE	FUR Y	*QUA Y	BAND Y
*BIC Y CLIC	*KAR Y OTIN	*SPH Y GMUS	GAB Y	*QUEY	BANT Y
BOD Y SUIT	*LAD Y BIRD	SPR Y NESS	GAM Y	RACY	BARK Y
*BOD Y SURF	*LAD Y FISH	STA Y SAIL	GAP Y	REL Y	BARM Y
*BOD Y WORK	*LAD Y HOOD	*SWA Y BACK	GLE Y	RIM Y	BARN Y
*BUO Y ANCE	*LAD Y LIKE	TID Y TIPS	GOB Y	ROP Y	BASS Y
*BUO Y ANCY	*LAD Y LOVE	*WHE Y FACE	GOR Y	ROS Y	BATT Y
*BUS Y BOD Y	*LAD Y PALM	*WHE Y LIKE	GRA Y	RUB Y	BAWD Y
BUS Y NESS	*LAD Y SHIP		GRE Y	RUL Y	BAWT Y
*BUS Y WORK	*LEC Y THIS	BAB Y	*HAZ Y	SAG Y	BEAD Y
BUT Y LATE	*LEC Y THUS	BEV Y	HOL Y	SCR Y	BEAK Y
BUT Y LENE	*LEK Y THOS	BOD Y	HOM Y	SEX Y	BEAM Y
BUT Y RATE	*LEK Y THUS	BOG Y	JOE Y	SHA Y	BEEF Y
BUT Y ROUS	*MAN Y FOLD	BON Y	*JOK Y	*SIZ Y	BEER Y
*CAL Y CATE	*MAR Y JANE	*BOX Y	JUR Y	SLA Y	BEIG Y
*CAL Y CINE	*MOL Y BDIC	BRA Y	LAC Y	SPA Y	BELA Y
*CAL Y CULI	*PLA Y TIME	BUO Y	LAD Y	SPR Y	BELL Y
*CAL Y PTER	*PLA Y BACK	BUR Y	LAK Y	STA Y	BEND Y
*CAL Y PTRA	*PLA Y BILL	BUS Y	*LAZ Y	STE Y	BENN Y
*CAP Y BARA	*PLA Y BOOK	CAG Y	LEV Y	SWA Y	BERR Y
*CAR Y ATIC	*PLA Y DOWN	CAK Y	LIL Y	THE Y	BIAL Y
CAR Y ATID	PLA Y GIRL	CAV Y	LIM Y	TID Y	BIDD Y
CAR Y OTIN	PLA Y GOER	CHA Y	LIN Y	TIN Y	*BIFF Y
*CIT Y FIED	PLA Y LAND	CIT Y	LOG Y	TIV Y	BIGL Y
*CIT Y WARD	PLA Y LESS	CLA Y	LOR Y	TOB Y	BILG Y
*CIT Y WIDE	*PLA Y LIKE	CLO Y	LUN Y	TOD Y	BILL Y
*CLA Y BANK	*PLA Y MATE	COL Y	MAN Y	TON Y	BITS Y
*CLA Y LIKE	*PLA Y ROOM	CON Y	*MAZ Y	TOR Y	BITT Y
*CLA Y MORE	PLA Y SUIT	COP Y	MIR Y	TOW Y	BLIM Y
*CLA Y WARE	*PLA Y WEAR	COR Y	MIT Y	TRA Y	BLOW Y
*COP Y BOOK	*POL Y BIRD	COW Y	MOL Y	TRE Y	BLUE Y
*COP Y DESK	POL Y GALA	*COZ Y	MON Y	TRO Y	BOBB Y
*COP Y EDIT	*POL Y GAM Y	DAV Y	MOP Y	TYP Y	BOGE Y
*COP Y HOLD	POL Y GENE	DEF Y	NAN Y	VAR Y	BOGG Y
*COP Y READ	POL Y GLOT	DEM Y	NAR Y	VER Y	BONE Y
*COR Y BANT	*POL Y GON Y	DEN Y	NAV Y	VIN Y	BONN Y
*COR Y PHEE	*POL Y GY N Y	DEW Y	NIX Y	WAD Y	BOOB Y
COT Y LOID	*POL Y MATH	*DEX Y	NOS Y	WAL Y	BOOG Y
*CRA Y FISH	*POL Y PAR Y	DID Y	PAL Y	WAN Y	BOOM Y
*DIC Y CLIC	*POL Y PIDE	DOG Y	PAT Y	WAR Y	BOOT Y
*DID Y MIUM	*POL Y PNEA	DOP Y	PIL Y	WAV Y	*BOOZ Y
*DID Y MOUS	*POL Y POD Y	DOR Y	PIN Y	*WAX Y	BOSK Y
*DID Y NAM Y	*POL Y POID	DOT Y	PIP Y	WHE Y	BOSS Y
*DIH Y BRID	*POL Y PORE	*DOX Y	PIT Y	WIL Y	BOTH Y
*DIH Y DRIC	*POL Y SEM Y	*DOZ Y	*PIX Y	WIN Y	BOUS Y
*DIZ Y GOUS	*POL Y SOME	DRA Y	PLA Y	WIR Y	BRAK Y

*BRAX Y	*COZE Y	DOBB Y	FLAW Y	GOOE Y	HOOL Y
BRIN Y	*CRAZ Y	DOGE Y	*FLAX Y	GOOF Y	*HOPP Y
BROS Y	CREP Y	DOGG Y	*FLUK Y	GOON Y	HORN Y
BUBB Y	CRON Y	DOIL Y	FLUT Y	GOOS Y	HORS Y
BUDD Y	CUBB Y	DOLL Y	*FL Y B Y	GOOP Y	HOTL Y
*BUFF Y	CUDD Y	DONS Y	FOAM Y	GOOS Y	*HUBB Y
BUGG Y	CULL Y	DOOL Y	FOGE Y	GORS Y	*HUFF Y
BULG Y	CUMM Y	DOOM Y	FOGG Y	GOUT Y	*HULK Y
BULL Y	CUPP Y	*DOOZ Y	*FOLK Y	GRAP Y	*HUMP Y
BUMP Y	CURD Y	DOPE Y	FOLL Y	GRAV Y	*HUNK Y
BUNN Y	CURL Y	DORK Y	FOOT Y	GRIM Y	HURL Y
BURL Y	CURR Y	DORM Y	FORA Y	GRIP Y	*HUSK Y
BURR Y	CURV Y	DORT Y	FORB Y	GULF Y	HUSS Y
BUSB Y	CUSH Y	DOTT Y	*FORK Y	GULL Y	*JACK Y
BUSH Y	CUTE Y	DOUG Y	FORT Y	GULP Y	*JAGG Y
BUST Y	CUTT Y	DOWD Y	FUBS Y	GUMM Y	*JAMM Y
BUTT Y	DADD Y	DOWN Y	FUGG Y	GUNN Y	*JANT Y
*B Y WA Y	*DAFF Y	DOWR Y	FULL Y	GUPP Y	*JAZZ Y
CABB Y	DAIL Y	DO Y L Y	*FUNK Y	GURR Y	*JELL Y
CADD Y	DAIR Y	DRIL Y	FUNN Y	GUSH Y	*JEMM Y
CADG Y	DAIS Y	DR Y L Y	FURR Y	GUSS Y	*JENN Y
CAGE Y	DALL Y	DUCH Y	*FURZ Y	GUST Y	*JERK Y
CAKE Y	DAND Y	*DUCK Y	FUSS Y	GUTS Y	*JERR Y
CAMP Y	DARK Y	DUDD Y	FUST Y	GUTT Y	*JETT Y
CAND Y	DASH Y	DULL Y	*FUZZ Y	G Y PS Y	*JIFF Y
CANN Y	DAUB Y	DUMM Y	GABB Y	HAIR Y	*JIMM Y
CANT Y	DEAR Y	DUMP Y	GAIL Y	*HAMM Y	*JIMP Y
CARN Y	DECA Y	DUNG Y	GALL Y	HAND Y	*JIVE Y
CARR Y	DECO Y	DUST Y	GAMA Y	*HANK Y	*JOLL Y
CASK Y	DECR Y	FADD Y	GAME Y	HAPL Y	*JOLT Y
CATT Y	DEED Y	FAER Y	GAMM Y	*HAPP Y	*JOTT Y
*CHEV Y	DEIF Y	FAIR Y	GAPP Y	HARD Y	*JOWL Y
*CHEW Y	DEIT Y	*FAKE Y	GASS Y	HARP Y	*JUIC Y
*CHIV Y	DELA Y	FANC Y	GAUD Y	HARR Y	*JUMP Y
*CHOK Y	DELL Y	FANN Y	*GAUZ Y	HEAV Y	*JUNK Y
CISS Y	*DEOX Y	FARC Y	*GAWK Y	HEDG Y	*JUTT Y
*CIVV Y	DERA Y	FATL Y	GAWS Y	HEFT Y	KAUR Y
CLAR Y	DERB Y	FATT Y	GA Y L Y	*HEMP Y	KELL Y
COAL Y	DERR Y	FAWN Y	GEEK Y	HENR Y	KELP Y
COBB Y	DIAR Y	FELL Y	GEMM Y	HERB Y	KERR Y
*COCK Y	DICE Y	FENN Y	GERM Y	HERR Y	*KICK Y
COLL Y	*DICK Y	FERL Y	GIDD Y	HILL Y	KIDD Y
*COMF Y	DICT Y	FERN Y	GILL Y	HINN Y	KILT Y
CONE Y	DILL Y	FERR Y	GIMP Y	*HIPP Y	*KINK Y
CONK Y	DIML Y	FIER Y	GINN Y	HISS Y	KISS Y
COOE Y	DING Y	FIFT Y	GIPS Y	HOAG Y	KITT Y
COOK Y	DINK Y	FILL Y	GIRL Y	HOAR Y	*KOOK Y
COOL Y	DIPP Y	FILM Y	GLAD Y	*HOBB Y	LACE Y
CORB Y	DIRT Y	FINN Y	GLAR Y	*HOKE Y	LAIT Y
CORK Y	DISH Y	FIRR Y	*GLAZ Y	HOLE Y	LAMB Y
CORN Y	DITS Y	FISH Y	GLOR Y	HOME Y	LANK Y
COSE Y	DITT Y	FITL Y	GLUE Y	HONE Y	LARD Y
COVE Y	*DITZ Y	*FIZZ Y	GODL Y	*HONK Y	LARK Y
COWR Y	*DIVV Y	*FLAK Y	GOLL Y	HOOD Y	LATH Y
CO Y L Y	*DIZZ Y	FLAM Y	GOOD Y	HOOE Y	*LAXL Y

LEAD Y	MIDD Y	NINN Y	*POCK Y	RESA Y	SISS Y
LEAF Y	*MIFF Y	NIPP Y	PODG Y	RETR Y	*SIXT Y
LEAK Y	MILK Y	NITT Y	POES Y	RIBB Y	SKIE Y
LEAR Y	MILT Y	NOBB Y	POGE Y	RIDG Y	*SK Y E Y
LEAV Y	MING Y	NOBL Y	POKE Y	RILE Y	SLAT Y
LEDG Y	MINN Y	NODD Y	POPP Y	RISK Y	SLIL Y
LEER Y	MINT Y	NOIS Y	POPS Y	*RITZ Y	SLIM Y
LEFT Y	MIRK Y	NOOK Y	PORG Y	ROCK Y	SMOK Y
LEGG Y	MISS Y	NOSE Y	PORK Y	ROIL Y	SNAK Y
LIMB Y	MIST Y	NOWA Y	PORN Y	ROOK Y	SNOW Y
LIND Y	MOGG Y	NUBB Y	POTS Y	ROOM Y	SOAP Y
LINE Y	MOLD Y	NUTS Y	POTT Y	ROOT Y	SODD Y
LING Y	MOLL Y	NUTT Y	POUT Y	ROPE Y	SOFT Y
LINK Y	MOMM Y	PADD Y	*PREX Y	ROUP Y	SOGG Y
LINT Y	MONE Y	PALL Y	PRIC Y	ROWD Y	SONL Y
LIPP Y	MOOD Y	PALM Y	PRIV Y	RUDD Y	SONN Y
LOAN Y	MOON Y	PALS Y	PROS Y	RUGB Y	SONS Y
LOBB Y	MOOR Y	PAND Y	*PROX Y	RUMM Y	SOOE Y
LOFT Y	MOPE Y	PANS Y	*PUFF Y	RUNN Y	SOOT Y
LOGG Y	MORA Y	PANT Y	PUGG Y	RUNT Y	SOPH Y
LOLL Y	MOSE Y	PAPP Y	PULP Y	RUSH Y	SOPP Y
LOOB Y	MOSS Y	PARD Y	PUNK Y	RUST Y	SORR Y
LOOE Y	MOTE Y	PARR Y	PUNN Y	RUTT Y	SOUP Y
LOON Y	MOTH Y	PART Y	PUNT Y	SADL Y	SPAC Y
LOOP Y	MOUS Y	PAST Y	PUPP Y	SAGG Y	SPIC Y
LOPP Y	*MUCK Y	PATL Y	PURS Y	SALL Y	SPIK Y
LORR Y	MUDD Y	PATS Y	PUSH Y	SALT Y	SPIN Y
LOSS Y	MUGG Y	PATT Y	PUSS Y	SAND Y	SPIR Y
LOUR Y	MUHL Y	*PAWK Y	PUTT Y	SAPP Y	SPLA Y
LOUS Y	MULE Y	PEAK Y	*P Y GM Y	SARK Y	SPRA Y
LOWL Y	MUMM Y	PEAT Y	*QUAK Y	SASS Y	SPUM Y
LUCK Y	MURK Y	PEAV Y	*QUER Y	SATA Y	STAG Y
LUMP Y	MURR Y	*PECK Y	RAGG Y	SAUC Y	STIM Y
LUST Y	MUSH Y	PEER Y	RAIN Y	SAUR Y	STOG Y
MADL Y	MUSK Y	PENN Y	RALL Y	SAVO Y	STON Y
MALM Y	MUSS Y	PEON Y	RAMM Y	SAVV Y	STOR Y
MALT Y	MUST Y	PEPP Y	RAND Y	SCAL Y	STRA Y
MAME Y	*MUZZ Y	PERD Y	RANG Y	SCAR Y	STRO Y
MAMM Y	*M Y OP Y	PERK Y	RASP Y	SEAM Y	STUD Y
MANG Y	*M Y TH Y	PERR Y	RATT Y	SEDG Y	ST Y M Y
MANL Y	NAGG Y	PESK Y	RAWL Y	SEED Y	SUDS Y
MARL Y	NANN Y	PEST Y	READ Y	SEEL Y	SULK Y
MARR Y	NAPP Y	PETT Y	REBU Y	SEEP Y	SULL Y
MARV Y	NARK Y	PHON Y	REDL Y	SEPO Y	SUNN Y
MASH Y	NAST Y	*PICK Y	REDR Y	SERR Y	SURF Y
MASS Y	NATT Y	PIET Y	REED Y	SHAD Y	SURG Y
MATE Y	NAVV Y	PIGG Y	REEF Y	*SHAK Y	SURL Y
MEAL Y	NEED Y	PIGM Y	REEK Y	SHAL Y	SWAM Y
MEAN Y	NELL Y	PINE Y	REFL Y	SHIL Y	TABB Y
MEAT Y	NERB Y	PINK Y	REFR Y	SHIN Y	TACK Y
MEIN Y	NERD Y	PINN Y	REIF Y	SHOW Y	TAFF Y
MERC Y	NETT Y	PITH Y	REKE Y	SH Y L Y	TALK Y
MERR Y	NEWL Y	PLAT Y	RELA Y	SILK Y	TALL Y
MESH Y	NEWS Y	PLOW Y	REPA Y	SILL Y	TAMM Y
MESS Y	NIFT Y	PLUM Y	REPL Y	SILT Y	TANG Y

TANS Y	*WEBB Y	*BAWDR Y	*BRONZ Y	*CHUNK Y	CRUDD Y
TARD Y	WEDG Y	*BEACH Y	BROOD Y	CICEL Y	*CRUMB Y
TARR Y	WEED Y	BEAUT Y	BROOM Y	CITIF Y	*CRUMM Y
TART Y	WEEN Y	*BEECH Y	BROTH Y	*CLAMM Y	CRUST Y
TAST Y	WEEP Y	BELAD Y	BROWN Y	CLASS Y	CUDDL Y
TATT Y	WELL Y	BELFR Y	*BRUMB Y	CLA Y E Y	CULLA Y
TAWN Y	WENN Y	BENDA Y	BRUSH Y	CLERG Y	CURAC Y
TEAR Y	WETL Y	BETON Y	BR Y ON Y	CLING Y	CURTL Y
TECH Y	WHIN Y	BETRA Y	*BUBBL Y	*CLIQU Y	CURTS Y
TEDD Y	WHIT Y	BEWRA Y	*BUNCH Y	CLODD Y	CURVE Y
TEEN Y	WIDD Y	BIGAM Y	BURBL Y	CLOGG Y	CUTES Y
TELL Y	WIFT Y	BINAR Y	BURLE Y	CLOTT Y	DAINT Y
TENT Y	WIGG Y	BIOPS Y	BUSBO Y	CLOUD Y	DAMPL Y
TERR Y	WILL Y	*BITCH Y	BUSIL Y	*CLUBB Y	DARKE Y
TEST Y	*WIMP Y	*BLABB Y	*B Y PLA Y	*CLUMP Y	DARKL Y
THEW Y	WIND Y	BLAST Y	CAGIL Y	CLUMS Y	DATAR Y
*TH Y M Y	WINE Y	BLEAR Y	CALOR Y	*CLUNK Y	DAUBR Y
TINN Y	WING Y	BLENN Y	CANAR Y	*CODIF Y	*DA Y FL Y
TIPP Y	WISP Y	BLIME Y	CANOP Y	*COGWA Y	DEADL Y
TIPS Y	WITH Y	*BLOCK Y	CARBO Y	COLDL Y	DEAFL Y
TITT Y	WITT Y	BLOOD Y	CARNE Y	COLON Y	DEARL Y
*TIZZ Y	*WOMB Y	BLOOE Y	CASEF Y	COMED Y	DEATH Y
TOAD Y	*WONK Y	BLOOM Y	*CATCH Y	COMEL Y	DECUR Y
TODA Y	WOOD Y	BLOTT Y	CAUSE Y	COMIT Y	*DEEJA Y
TODD Y	WOOL Y	BLOUS Y	CAVIT Y	*COMPL Y	DEEPL Y
TOFF Y	*WOOZ Y	*BLOWB Y	CELER Y	*CONCH Y	DEFRA Y
TOKA Y	WORD Y	BLOWS Y	*CHAFF Y	CONVE Y	DENAR Y
TOMM Y	WORM Y	*BLOWZ Y	*CHALK Y	CONVO Y	DEPLO Y
TONE Y	WORR Y	BLUEL Y	CHALL Y	*COOKE Y	DEPUT Y
TOWN Y	WUSS Y	BLUES Y	*CHAMM Y	COOLL Y	DESCR Y
TRUL Y	*Y ECH Y	BLURR Y	*CHAMP Y	COROD Y	*DESOX Y
TUBB Y	*Y EUK Y	BODIL Y	*CHANC Y	COSIL Y	DHOOL Y
TUFT Y	*Y OLK Y	BOLSH Y	CHANT Y	COSTL Y	*DICKE Y
TUMM Y	*Y UCK Y	BOOGE Y	CHARR Y	COUNT Y	DIDDL Y
TUNN Y	*Y UMM Y	BOSOM Y	CHATT Y	*COWBO Y	DIGAM Y
TURF Y	*ZAPP Y	BOTAN Y	*CHEEK Y	*CRABB Y	DIMIT Y
TUTT Y	*ZEST Y	*BOTCH Y	CHEER Y	*CRACK Y	DIMPL Y
TWIN Y	*ZINC Y	BOTFL Y	CHEES Y	CRAFT Y	DINGE Y
T Y PE Y	*ZING Y	BOUNC Y	CHERR Y	CRAGG Y	DINGH Y
VAST Y	*ZINK Y	BOUNT Y	CHERT Y	*CRANK Y	DINKE Y
VEAL Y	*ZIPP Y	BOWER Y	CHEST Y	CRANN Y	DINKL Y
VEER Y	*ZLOT Y	BRAGG Y	*CHICL Y	*CRAPP Y	DIOEC Y
VEIN Y	*ZOOT Y	BRAIN Y	CHILL Y	CRAWL Y	DIPOD Y
*VICH Y	BAILE Y	BRAND Y	*CHINK Y	*CREAK Y	DIREL Y
VIEW Y	*BAKER Y	BRANN Y	*CHIPP Y	CREAM Y	DISMA Y
*WACK Y	BALDL Y	BRASH Y	*CHIRP Y	CREAS Y	*DJINN Y
WADD Y	BAREL Y	BRASS Y	CHITT Y	CREEP Y	DONKE Y
WALL Y	BARFL Y	BRATT Y	*CHIVV Y	CREPE Y	DOUBL Y
WANE Y	BARLE Y	BRAWL Y	*CHOKE Y	*CRIKE Y	DOUGH Y
WANL Y	BARON Y	BRAWN Y	*CHOPP Y	*CRIMP Y	DOURL Y
WART Y	BASEL Y	BREAD Y	*CHUBB Y	CRISP Y	DOWER Y
WASH Y	BASIF Y	*BREEZ Y	*CHUCK Y	*CROAK Y	DO Y LE Y
WASP Y	BASSL Y	*BRICK Y	*CHUFF Y	CROUP Y	*DOZIL Y
WAVE Y	BATBO Y	BRION Y	*CHUMM Y	*CROWD Y	DRABL Y
WEAR Y	*BAULK Y	BROLL Y			*DRAFF Y

DRAFT Y	*FOLKS Y	GOODL Y	*HUBBL Y	LONGL Y	MUTIN Y
DRAGG Y	FONDL Y	GOOGL Y	*HUMBL Y	LOONE Y	NAMEL Y
DRAPE Y	FOOTS Y	GOONE Y	HUNGR Y	LORDL Y	NAPER Y
DRAWL Y	FOREB Y	GOOSE Y	HURLE Y	LOUDL Y	*NAZIF Y
DREAM Y	*FORWH Y	GORIL Y	HURRA Y	LOUNG Y	NEARB Y
DREGG Y	FOULL Y	GRABB Y	*JALOP Y	LOVEL Y	NEARL Y
DRESS Y	*FOXIL Y	GRAIN Y	*JANGL Y	LOWBO Y	NEATL Y
DRIFT Y	*FREAK Y	GRANN Y	*JAPER Y	LOWER Y	NEBUL Y
DRIPP Y	FREEL Y	GRASS Y	*JARVE Y	LUNAC Y	NETTL Y
DROLL Y	*FRENZ Y	GRA Y L Y	*JAUNT Y	*LUXUR Y	NICET Y
DROOP Y	FRETT Y	GREAS Y	*JERSE Y	MAGUE Y	NIDIF Y
DROPS Y	FRIAR Y	GREED Y	*JIGGL Y	MAINL Y	NIGHT Y
DROSK Y	FRILL Y	GREEN Y	*JIMIN Y	MALAD Y	NINET Y
DROSS Y	FRING Y	GREMM Y	*JINGL Y	MAMME Y	NITER Y
DROWS Y	*FRISK Y	GRE Y L Y	*JITNE Y	MANGE Y	NOBOD Y
DRUGG Y	*FRIZZ Y	GRIPE Y	*JOCKE Y	MARBL Y	NONGA Y
DRUML Y	FROGG Y	GRIPP Y	*JOHNN Y	MARGA Y	NOSIL Y
DUALL Y	FROST Y	GRISL Y	*JOUNC Y	MARSH Y	NOTAR Y
DUMBL Y	*FROTH Y	GRITT Y	*JUNGL Y	MAUND Y	NOTIF Y
DUPER Y	*FROUZ Y	GROGG Y	*JUSTL Y	*MA Y DA Y	NUBBL Y
FAIRL Y	*FROWS Y	GROOV Y	KEENL Y	*MA Y FL Y	NUDIT Y
*FAKER Y	*FROWZ Y	GROUT Y	KERSE Y	*MAZIL Y	NUMBL Y
FEALT Y	FRUIT Y	GROWL Y	*KE Y WA Y	MEANL Y	*PACIF Y
*FECKL Y	*FRUMP Y	GRUBB Y	KIDNE Y	MEASL Y	*PACKL Y
FEIST Y	GADFL Y	*GRUFF Y	KINDL Y	*MEDFL Y	PAINT Y
FELON Y	GAIET Y	GRUMP Y	KINGL Y	MEDLE Y	PALEL Y
FERIT Y	GAINL Y	GRUNG Y	*KLUTZ Y	MEETL Y	PALTR Y
FIDDL Y	*GALAX Y	GUANA Y	*KNOBB Y	MELOD Y	PANFR Y
*FILTH Y	GALLE Y	GUILT Y	KNOLL Y	MEMOR Y	PANTR Y
FIRML Y	GAMEL Y	GULLE Y	KNOTT Y	*MICKE Y	*PAPAC Y
*FISHL Y	GAMIL Y	GURNE Y	KNURL Y	MIDDA Y	PAPER Y
*FITCH Y	GANGL Y	*HACKL Y	LACIL Y	*MIDWA Y	PARIT Y
*FIXIT Y	GANTR Y	HARDL Y	*LACKE Y	*MIGHT Y	PARLA Y
*FLABB Y	GARVE Y	HAULM Y	LAMEL Y	MILAD Y	PARLE Y
FLAGG Y	GASIF Y	*HAWKE Y	LANEL Y	MINIF Y	PAROD Y
*FLAKE Y	GA Y ET Y	*HAZIL Y	LASTL Y	MISER Y	PARTI Y
*FLAPP Y	GENTR Y	HEART Y	LATEL Y	MISLA Y	PASTR Y
*FLASH Y	GHOST Y	*HEATH Y	*LAXIT Y	MISSA Y	*PATCH Y
FLATL Y	GIGGL Y	HERES Y	*LAZIL Y	*MIZZL Y	*PA Y DA Y
*FLECK Y	GLADL Y	*HE Y DA Y	LEACH Y	*MODIF Y	*PEACH Y
FLEDG Y	GLAIR Y	*HE Y DE Y	LEALT Y	MOIET Y	PEARL Y
FLEEC Y	GLASS Y	*HICKE Y	LEEWA Y	*MONKE Y	PEAVE Y
*FLESH Y	GLEAM Y	*HIGHL Y	LEGAC Y	MONOD Y	*PEBBL Y
FLEUR Y	GLEET Y	*HOCKE Y	LENIT Y	MOOLE Y	PELTR Y
FLIMS Y	*GLITZ Y	HOLIL Y	LEVIT Y	MOPER Y	PENUR Y
FLINT Y	GLOBB Y	HOMEL Y	LIKEL Y	MOSTL Y	*PEROX Y
*FLIPP Y	GLOOM Y	HOMIL Y	LIMPL Y	MOTLE Y	PHONE Y
FLOUR Y	GLOPP Y	HOMIN Y	LIMPS Y	MOULD Y	PHOOE Y
*FLUFF Y	GLOSS Y	*HONKE Y	LINSE Y	MOUSE Y	PIDDL Y
*FLUKE Y	GLUMP Y	*HOOKE Y	LITAN Y	MOUTH Y	PIGST Y
*FLUNK Y	GNARL Y	HOORA Y	LIVEL Y	MULLE Y	*PIMPL Y
FLURR Y	GNATT Y	HORAR Y	LIVER Y	*MUMBL Y	PINER Y
FLUTE Y	GOBON Y	HORSE Y	LOGIL Y	*MURPH Y	*PINKE Y
*FL Y BO Y	GOGGL Y	HOSTL Y	LOGWA Y	MURRE Y	*PINKL Y
*FL Y WA Y	GOODB Y	HOURL Y	LONEL Y	MUSCL Y	PIRAC Y

*PITCH Y	RASHL Y	*SCUZZ Y	SLOWL Y	SPORT Y	*TACKE Y
PLAGU Y	RATAN Y	SEAWA Y	SLUDG Y	SPOTT Y	TAMEL Y
PLASH Y	RATIF Y	SEEML Y	SLUIC Y	SPRUC Y	TANGL Y
PLENT Y	RATTL Y	SENAR Y	SLUMM Y	*SPUNK Y	TARTL Y
*PLISK Y	REALL Y	SENTR Y	SLURR Y	SPURR Y	TAUTL Y
PLOID Y	REALT Y	*SEXIL Y	SLUSH Y	STAGE Y	TAWDR Y
*PLUCK Y	REBOD Y	*SHABB Y	SLUTT Y	STAGG Y	TAWNE Y
*PLUMM Y	REBUR Y	SHAGG Y	SMARM Y	STAHL Y	TEAPO Y
PLUSH Y	RECOP Y	SHALE Y	SMART Y	STALK Y	TEENS Y
*POACH Y	REDBA Y	*SHAMM Y	SMEAR Y	STARR Y	TEPEF Y
POETR Y	REDEF Y	SHAMO Y	SMELL Y	STEAD Y	TERML Y
POINT Y	REDEN Y	SHAND Y	SMILE Y	STEAM Y	TETAN Y
*POKIL Y	REECH Y	SHANN Y	*SMIRK Y	STEEL Y	TETCH Y
POLIC Y	REMED Y	SHANT Y	SMITH Y	STEMM Y	THEOR Y
POLIT Y	REPLA Y	SHARP Y	SMOGG Y	*STICK Y	THERB Y
POORL Y	RESIN Y	SHEEN Y	*SMOKE Y	STILL Y	THINL Y
POPER Y	REVER Y	SHELL Y	SMUDG Y	STING Y	THIRT Y
PORTL Y	RHEUM Y	SHELT Y	SMUGL Y	STINK Y	THORN Y
POTBO Y	RICHL Y	*SHELV Y	SMUTT Y	STITH Y	THUSL Y
*POUCH Y	RIDLE Y	SHERR Y	SNAGG Y	*STOCK Y	*TH Y ME Y
PREPA Y	RIGHT Y	*SHIFT Y	SNAPP Y	STODG Y	TIDDL Y
*PREPP Y	RIPPL Y	*SHIMM Y	SNARK Y	STOGE Y	TIDIL Y
PRETT Y	ROPER Y	SHIND Y	SNARL Y	STONE Y	TIMEL Y
PRICE Y	ROPIL Y	SHINN Y	*SNAZZ Y	STORE Y	TINGL Y
*PRICK Y	ROSAR Y	SHIRT Y	SNEAK Y	STORM Y	TINIL Y
PRIML Y	ROSER Y	SHOAL Y	*SNEEZ Y	STOUR Y	TINKL Y
PRIOR Y	ROSIL Y	SHODD Y	*SNIFF Y	STRAW Y	TOAST Y
PRISS Y	ROSIN Y	SHORT Y	SNIPP Y	STRIP Y	TOMBO Y
PUDDL Y	ROTAR Y	*SICKL Y	SNOBB Y	STUBB Y	TOOTH Y
PUGGR Y	RUBBL Y	SIMON Y	SNOOP Y	STUDL Y	TOOTS Y
PULLE Y	*RUFFL Y	SIMPL Y	SNOOT Y	*STUFF Y	TOUCH Y
*PUNCH Y	RUMBL Y	SINEW Y	*SNOOZ Y	STUMP Y	TOUGH Y
PUNIL Y	RUMPL Y	SINGL Y	SNOTT Y	STURD Y	TOWER Y
*PUNKE Y	RUNWA Y	SKERR Y	SNOUT Y	SUBWA Y	TRASH Y
PUREL Y	SAFET Y	*SKIDD Y	SNUBB Y	SUDAR Y	TREAT Y
PURIF Y	SALAR Y	*SKIMP Y	*SNUFF Y	SUGAR Y	TREBL Y
PURIT Y	SALIF Y	SKINN Y	SNUGL Y	SULTR Y	TREND Y
PURPL Y	SANIT Y	*SKIVV Y	SODOM Y	SUNDR Y	TRESS Y
PURVE Y	SASHA Y	*SK Y WA Y	SOFTL Y	SUPPL Y	*TRICK Y
PUSLE Y	SATIN Y	SLAGG Y	SOLEL Y	SUREL Y	TRIGL Y
PUSSL Y	SAVOR Y	SLANG Y	SOREL Y	SURET Y	TRILB Y
*QUAGG Y	*SAWFL Y	SLANT Y	SOURL Y	SURRE Y	TRIML Y
*QUALM Y	SAWNE Y	SLATE Y	SPACE Y	SURVE Y	TRIPL Y
*QUARR Y	*SAXON Y	SLAVE Y	*SPARK Y	*SWABB Y	TRIPP Y
*QUEAS Y	*SCABB Y	*SLEAZ Y	SPARR Y	*SWAMP Y	TROLL Y
*QUEAZ Y	SCANT Y	SLEEK Y	SPEED Y	*SWANK Y	TROPH Y
*QUINS Y	SCARE Y	SLEEP Y	SPHER Y	SWART Y	TROUT Y
*QUIRK Y	SCARR Y	SLEET Y	SPICE Y	SWEAT Y	TRUST Y
RACIL Y	SCATT Y	SLIML Y	*SPIFF Y	SWEEN Y	TUMEF Y
RAMIF Y	*SCHIZ Y	SLIMS Y	*SPIKE Y	SWEEP Y	TURKE Y
RANKL Y	SCREW Y	SLINK Y	SPINN Y	*SWIMM Y	TWANG Y
RAREF Y	*SCUMM Y	SLIPP Y	SPONG Y	SWING Y	*TWANK Y
RAREL Y	SCURF Y	SLOBB Y	SPOOF Y	SWIRL Y	*TWEAK Y
RARIF Y	SCURR Y	SLOPP Y	*SPOOK Y	*SWISH Y	TWEED Y
RARIT Y	SCURV Y	SLOSH Y	SPOON Y	*S Y Z Y G Y	TWEEN Y

TWENT Y	*WHITE Y	*BLACKL Y	*CHANTR Y	*CRUCIF Y	*DRIBBL Y
TWIGG Y	*WHOLL Y	*BLANKL Y	*CHARIL Y	CRUDIT Y	*DRIZZL Y
TWIRL Y	*WICOP Y	BLARNE Y	*CHARIT Y	CRUELT Y	*DROSHK Y
TWIST Y	WIELD Y	*BLEAKL Y	*CHARLE Y	*CRUMBL Y	DROUTH Y
*T Y PIF Y	*WIFEL Y	*BLIGHT Y	*CHARPO Y	*CRUMPL Y	DUALIT Y
VAGAR Y	WIGGL Y	BLINDL Y	*CHEAPL Y	*CRUNCH Y	DUBIET Y
VALLE Y	WILDL Y	*BLOTCH Y	*CHEERL Y	CRUSIL Y	*DULCIF Y
VANIT Y	WILIL Y	*BLOWFL Y	*CHICOR Y	CUTLER Y	*DUMPIL Y
VAPOR Y	WINCE Y	*BLUEJA Y	*CHIEFL Y	*CR Y BAB Y	DUOPOL Y
VASTL Y	WINER Y	*BOBBER Y	*CHILDL Y	*CUBICL Y	DUSTIL Y
VAULT Y	WINTR Y	BOBSTA Y	*CHIMBL Y	CURSOR Y	*D Y ARCH Y
VAUNT Y	WIRIL Y	BOLONE Y	*CHIMLE Y	CURTES Y	D Y NAST Y
*VEEJA Y	WISEL Y	BOOTER Y	*CHIMNE Y	CURTSE Y	*FACTOR Y
VENER Y	*WITCH Y	*BRAMBL Y	*CHINCH Y	*CUSHIL Y	*FACULT Y
*VERIF Y	WITNE Y	*BRANCH Y	*CHINTZ Y	CUSTOD Y	FAINTL Y
VERIL Y	*WOBBL Y	*BRAVER Y	*CHOOSE Y	*CUTAWA Y	*FAIRWA Y
VERIT Y	WOODS Y	*BREATH Y	*CHRIST Y	CUTLER Y	*FALLAC Y
VESTR Y	WOOLL Y	*BREVIT Y	*CHURCH Y	*C Y CLER Y	*FALSIF Y
*VILIF Y	*WORTH Y	*BREWER Y	*CHUTNE Y	DACOIT Y	FALSIT Y
VINER Y	WRIST Y	BRIBER Y	CILIAR Y	*DAKOIT Y	FANTAS Y
*VINIF Y	Y EARL Y	*BRIEFL Y	CINDER Y	*DAMNIF Y	FARADA Y
*VIVAR Y	Y EAST Y	*BRISKL Y	*CIPHON Y	DANDIL Y	*FARAWA Y
*VIVIF Y	*ZINCK Y	BRISTL Y	*CIVILL Y	DARESA Y	FATALL Y
VOLER Y	*ZONAR Y	BRITTL Y	*CLARIF Y	DATEDL Y	FATTIL Y
VOLLE Y	BAIRNL Y	BROADL Y	CLARIT Y	DAUBER Y	FATUIT Y
VOTAR Y	BALCON Y	BRUTEL Y	CLEANL Y	DA Y LIL Y	FELONR Y
*WABBL Y	BALONE Y	*BRUTIF Y	CLEARL Y	DEANER Y	FEODAR Y
WADDL Y	BATTER Y	BUGGER Y	CLERIS Y	DEATHL Y	FERNER Y
*WAFER Y	*BAWDIL Y	BUIRDL Y	*CLERKL Y	*DECENC Y	FERRET Y
WAGGL Y	BEADIL Y	BURSAR Y	*CLIQUE Y	DEERFL Y	FEUDAR Y
*WAMBL Y	BEAMIL Y	*BUSHIL Y	*CLUTCH Y	DENSIF Y	*FIDGET Y
WARIL Y	BEANER Y	BUTLER Y	*COALIF Y	DENSIT Y	*FIFTHL Y
WARML Y	BEASTL Y	BUTTER Y	*COCKIL Y	DESTIN Y	FILMIL Y
WASTR Y	*BEATIF Y	BUTTON Y	*COCKNE Y	DESTRO Y	FINALL Y
WATER Y	BEDIRT Y	*CACHEX Y	*COCKSH Y	DEVILR Y	*FINICK Y
*WAVER Y	*BEEFIL Y	*CADENC Y	*COGENC Y	*DIARCH Y	*FIREFL Y
*WAVIL Y	BEGGAR Y	*CALCIF Y	*COLICK Y	DICLIN Y	FIRSTL Y
*WAXIL Y	BELLBO Y	CALLBO Y	*COMFRE Y	*DIC Y CL Y	*FISHER Y
*WA Y LA Y	*BELTWA Y	CALUMN Y	*COMPAN Y	DIDDLE Y	*FISHWA Y
*WEAKL Y	*BEWEAR Y	*CALVAR Y	*COMPON Y	DIETAR Y	*FIXEDL Y
*WEEKL Y	*BEWORR Y	*CAMPIL Y	*COOKER Y	*DIGNIF Y	FLAUNT Y
WEENS Y	*BHEEST Y	CANNER Y	COOPER Y	DIGNIT Y	*FLAVOR Y
WEIRD Y	*BIBBER Y	CANNIL Y	*COP Y BO Y	DINGIL Y	*FLESHL Y
*WHACK Y	BIGGET Y	CANONR Y	CORNIL Y	DISOBE Y	*FLIGHT Y
*WHAMM Y	BIGGIT Y	*CARAWA Y	CORROD Y	DISPLA Y	*FLOWER Y
*WHEEZ Y	BIGOTR Y	*CARNIF Y	COTTON Y	DITHER Y	*FLUENC Y
*WHELK Y	*BIKEWA Y	CARROT Y	COUNTR Y	DITTAN Y	FLUIDL Y
*WHERR Y	BILIAR Y	CATTER Y	COURTL Y	DODDER Y	*FLUNKE Y
*WHIMS Y	*BILLOW Y	CATTIL Y	*COWEDL Y	DODGER Y	*FL Y AWA Y
*WHINE Y	BINDER Y	CAUTER Y	*COXALG Y	DOGGER Y	*FOAMIL Y
*WHINN Y	BIOGEN Y	*CAVALL Y	*CRANKL Y	DOORWA Y	*FOCALL Y
*WHIPP Y	BIOLOG Y	*CAVALR Y	*CRICKE Y	DOTTIL Y	*FOLKWA Y
*WHIRL Y	BIONOM Y	CENTUR Y	*CRINKL Y	*DOUGHT Y	FOOLER Y
*WHIRR Y	BIPART Y	*CERTIF Y	CRISPL Y	*DOVEKE Y	*FOOTBO Y
*WHISK Y		*CHANTE Y	CROSSL Y	DRAMED Y	*FOOTWA Y
				DRAPER Y	

*FOPPER Y	*GRUMPH Y	*JOBBER Y	*MALARK Y	NAUGHT Y	PETTIL Y
*FOREBA Y	GUNNER Y	*JOINER Y	MALMSE Y	NECTAR Y	*PHENOX Y
FORGER Y	GUNPLA Y	*JOINTL Y	*MAMMAR Y	NEEDIL Y	*PHLEGM Y
*FORTIF Y	GUSTIL Y	*JOLLIF Y	*MANGAB Y	NEOLOG Y	*PHONIL Y
FOUNDR Y	GUTSIL Y	*JOLLIT Y	MANGIL Y	NEOTEN Y	*PHRATR Y
FRAILT Y	GUTTER Y	*JOURNE Y	MANUAR Y	NERVIL Y	*PHRENS Y
*FRANKL Y	*HACKNE Y	*JUSTIF Y	*MARROW Y	*NEWSBO Y	PIGGER Y
*FRECKL Y	*HALFWA Y	*KILLJO Y	*MART Y R Y	NIGHTL Y	PIGSNE Y
*FREEWA Y	*HALLWA Y	*KNAVER Y	MASONR Y	NIGRIF Y	PILLOR Y
*FRESHL Y	*HAMMIL Y	*KNOBBL Y	MASTER Y	NIMIET Y	*PILLOW Y
*FRIZZL Y	HANDIL Y	*KNUCKL Y	MATTER Y	NINTHL Y	PIOSIT Y
*FROWST Y	HARDIL Y	*KOLACK Y	MEATIL Y	NIPPIL Y	PISCAR Y
*FULFIL Y	*HARMON Y	*KOUPRE Y	*MEDIAC Y	NITRIF Y	*PIZAZZ Y
FULLER Y	*HARSHL Y	*KVETCH Y	MERCER Y	NOBBIL Y	PLAGUE Y
*FURMET Y	*HAUGHT Y	*LACQUE Y	MERCUR Y	NONBOD Y	*PLA Y BO Y
*FURMIT Y	*HAUTBO Y	LACTAR Y	MESALL Y	*NONJUR Y	*PLA Y DA Y
FURRIL Y	*HAZELL Y	LAMPRE Y	MESSIL Y	NONOIL Y	PLENAR Y
*FURROW Y	HEADIL Y	LANEWA Y	*METHOX Y	NONPLA Y	PLIANC Y
GAINSA Y	*HEADWA Y	LANIAR Y	*METRIF Y	NOONDA Y	*PLOWBO Y
GALLER Y	*HEALTH Y	LARCEN Y	*MICRIF Y	NOSEGA Y	*PLUMPL Y
GALLFL Y	HEARSA Y	LATENC Y	*MILDEW Y	NOTABL Y	PORTRA Y
*GANGWA Y	HELLER Y	LATHER Y	MILIAR Y	NOTEDL Y	POSTBO Y
GATEWA Y	HELOTR Y	LAUNDR Y	*MILKIL Y	NOVELL Y	POTENC Y
GAUDER Y	HENNER Y	*LA Y AWA Y	*MIMICR Y	NOVELT Y	POTTER Y
GAUNTR Y	HERONR Y	*LECHER Y	MISALL Y	NULLIF Y	POULTR Y
*GEMMIL Y	*HICKOR Y	LEGALL Y	*MISCOP Y	NULLIT Y	*POVERT Y
GEODES Y	*HIGHBO Y	LENGTH Y	MISERL Y	NUMMAR Y	*POWDER Y
GEOLOG Y	*HIGHWA Y	LEPROS Y	MISPLA Y	NUNNER Y	*PREACH Y
GETAWA Y	HISTOR Y	LEVELL Y	MISREL Y	NURSER Y	PRELAC Y
GHASTL Y	HOARIL Y	LIBERT Y	MISTIL Y	*PAGEBO Y	*PRICKL Y
GHOSTL Y	*HODADD Y	LIBRAR Y	*MOCKER Y	PAISLE Y	*PRIMAC Y
GINGEL Y	HOLIDA Y	*LICHTL Y	MODEST Y	*PALFRE Y	PRIMAR Y
GINGER Y	*HOL Y DA Y	*LIFEWA Y	MOISTL Y	PALMAR Y	PRIMEL Y
*GLITCH Y	*HOMEBO Y	LIGHTL Y	*MOLLIF Y	*PANICK Y	PRIORL Y
GLORIF Y	HONEST Y	LIGNIF Y	*MONKER Y	PANOPL Y	*PRIVAC Y
*GLOWFL Y	HOOTER Y	LIMPSE Y	MONOEC Y	PARROT Y	*PRIVIT Y
*GOOMBA Y	HORNIL Y	*LINKBO Y	*MONTHL Y	PARSLE Y	PROBIT Y
GOSSIP Y	*HORRIF Y	*LIQUEF Y	MOONIL Y	*PARTWA Y	PRODIG Y
GRAMAR Y	HORSIL Y	*LIQUIF Y	MORTAR Y	*PASSKE Y	PROGEN Y
GRANAR Y	HOSIER Y	*LITHIF Y	*MORTIF Y	PATENC Y	PROSIL Y
GRANDL Y	*HUMANL Y	LITTER Y	*MOTHER Y	*PATHWA Y	PROSOD Y
GRAPER Y	*HUMIDL Y	LITURG Y	MOUSIL Y	PAUCIT Y	PRUDER Y
GRATIF Y	*HUSHAB Y	LOATHL Y	*MOVABL Y	*PAUGHT Y	PSALTR Y
GRAVEL Y	*HUSKIL Y	LOCALL Y	*MUCKIL Y	*PAUNCH Y	PUBERT Y
GRAVIT Y	*H Y DROX Y	LOFTIL Y	MUDDIL Y	*PECCAR Y	*PUCKER Y
GREATL Y	*H Y MNAR Y	LOTTER Y	MUGGIL Y	PEDIAR Y	*PUDENC Y
GREENL Y	*H Y MNOD Y	LO Y ALL Y	*MUMMER Y	PEDLER Y	*PUFFER Y
*GRIML Y	*JAGGAR Y	LO Y ALT Y	*MUMMIF Y	PENALL Y	PURSIL Y
GRISTL Y	*JAGGER Y	LUCENC Y	*MUSKIL Y	PENALT Y	*PUSHIL Y
*GRIZZL Y	*JALOPP Y	LULLAB Y	*MUZZIL Y	*PEPPER Y	PUSSLE Y
GROCER Y	*JEEPNE Y	LUSTIL Y	*M Y OLOG Y	*PERFID Y	*PUTREF Y
GROSSL Y	*JELLIF Y	L Y INGL Y	*M Y STER Y	*PERJUR Y	*QUALIF Y
*GROUCH Y	*JEWELR Y	*MAGNIF Y	*M Y STIF Y	PESSAR Y	*QUALIT Y
*GROWTH Y	*JIMMIN Y	*MAJEST Y	NAIVET Y	*PETRIF Y	*QUAVER Y
*GRUFFL Y	*JITTER Y	*MAJORL Y	NASALL Y		*QUEENL Y

*QUEERL Y	RUBBER Y	*SHLUMP Y	SPLEEN Y	TANNER Y	TROLLE Y
*QUICKL Y	RUDDIL Y	*SHOOFL Y	SPLURG Y	TANTIV Y	TRUANC Y
*QUIETL Y	RUDESB Y	*SHOPBO Y	SPOONE Y	TATOUA Y	TUGGER Y
*QUINAR Y	RUNAWA Y	SHORTL Y	*SPRAWL Y	TATTIL Y	TURBAR Y
*QUIVER Y	RURALL Y	*SHOWER Y	SPRIGG Y	*TAXIWA Y	TURNER Y
RABBIT Y	RUSSIF Y	*SHOWIL Y	SPRING Y	TEARIL Y	TURNKE Y
*RACEWA Y	RUSTIL Y	*SHRIEK Y	SPURRE Y	TEENTS Y	*TWIDDL Y
*RACKET Y	RUTTIL Y	*SHRIMP Y	*SQUABB Y	TENANC Y	*TWINKL Y
RAGGED Y	SAINTL Y	*SHRUBB Y	*SQUALL Y	TENSIT Y	*TWITCH Y
RAILWA Y	SALLOW Y	*SICKBA Y	*SQUASH Y	TENTHL Y	*TYMPAN Y
RAINIL Y	SALSIF Y	SIDEWA Y	*SQUATT Y	TENUIT Y	TYRANN Y
RAUCIT Y	SALTIL Y	SIGHTL Y	*SQUEAK Y	TERNAR Y	*VACANC Y
*RAUNCH Y	SANDFL Y	SIGNIF Y	*SQUIFF Y	TERRIF Y	*VACUIT Y
RAVELL Y	SASSAB Y	SIGNOR Y	*SQUINN Y	TESTAC Y	*VALENC Y
READIL Y	SASSIL Y	SILKIL Y	*SQUINT Y	TESTIF Y	VALIDL Y
REALIT Y	SATIET Y	SILVER Y	*SQUIRM Y	TESTIL Y	*VAPOUR Y
REAPPL Y	SATISF Y	*SIXTHL Y	*SQUISH Y	*THATCH Y	VARIET Y
RECARR Y	SATRAP Y	*SKETCH Y	STAGIL Y	*THERAP Y	VARSIT Y
RECENC Y	SAVELO Y	*SKIDWA Y	STANDB Y	THEURG Y	VASTIT Y
*RECTIF Y	SAVOUR Y	*SLACKL Y	*STARCH Y	*THICKL Y	*VERBIF Y
RECTOR Y	SCANTL Y	SLAVER Y	STARTS Y	THIRDL Y	*VERSIF Y
REEDIF Y	*SCARIF Y	SLEEKL Y	STATEL Y	THIRST Y	*VEXEDL Y
REEDIL Y	SCARIL Y	*SLICKL Y	STEEPL Y	THISTL Y	*VICARL Y
*REENJO Y	SCENER Y	SLIMIL Y	*STENCH Y	THREAD Y	*VICERO Y
REENTR Y	*SCHIZZ Y	SLIMPS Y	STERNL Y	*THRIFT Y	*VICTOR Y
REGALL Y	*SCORIF Y	*SLIPWA Y	*STIFFL Y	THROAT Y	VIDUIT Y
REGENC Y	SCRAGG Y	*SLOUCH Y	STONIL Y	*THRUMM Y	VIRELA Y
REMARR Y	*SCRAPP Y	SLOUGH Y	STOUTL Y	TIDEWA Y	VITALL Y
*REPLEV Y	*SCRAWL Y	SMARTL Y	STREAK Y	*TIFFAN Y	VITRIF Y
RESPRA Y	*SCRAWN Y	*SMOOCH Y	STREAM Y	TILBUR Y	*VOCABL Y
RESTUD Y	*SCREAK Y	*SMOOTH Y	STRING Y	*TIMOTH Y	*VOCALL Y
RETIAR Y	*SCRIMP Y	*SMUTCH Y	STROPP Y	TINNIL Y	*VOUVRA Y
REUNIF Y	SCROGG Y	*SNATCH Y	STUBBL Y	TIPSIL Y	*WAGGER Y
REVELR Y	*SCRUBB Y	SNOWIL Y	*STUPEF Y	TISSUE Y	*WALKWA Y
RHATAN Y	*SCRUFF Y	*SNUFFL Y	SUAVIT Y	TOLLWA Y	*WALLAB Y
RIBBON Y	SEALER Y	SOAPIL Y	SUBSID Y	TOPIAR Y	*WASHDA Y
*RICKET Y	SECREC Y	SOBERL Y	SUCCOR Y	TORREF Y	WASTER Y
RIFLER Y	SECTAR Y	SOCIET Y	SULFUR Y	TORRIF Y	*WEALTH Y
RIGHTL Y	SEEDIL Y	SOLIDL Y	SUMMAR Y	TOTALL Y	WEASEL Y
RIGIDL Y	SEMIDR Y	SOLUBL Y	SUMMER Y	TOTTER Y	WEEDIL Y
RIVALR Y	SENSOR Y	SOMEDA Y	SURGER Y	TOUGHL Y	*WEEKDA Y
ROADWA Y	SEVENT Y	*SOMEWA Y	*SWARTH Y	TOURNE Y	*WEIGHT Y
ROBBER Y	*SHADFL Y	SOOTHL Y	SWEETL Y	*TOWAWA Y	WEIRDL Y
ROBOTR Y	SHADIL Y	SORCER Y	SWELTR Y	TRACER Y	*WHEREB Y
*ROCKAB Y	*SHADOW Y	SORRIL Y	*SWIFTL Y	TRAGED Y	*WHIMSE Y
*ROCKER Y	*SHAKIL Y	SOUNDL Y	*SWINGB Y	*TRAMWA Y	*WHIPRA Y
ROGUER Y	SHANTE Y	SPANGL Y	SWINNE Y	TRAWLE Y	*WHISKE Y
ROLLWA Y	*SHAPEL Y	*SPARKL Y	*SWITHL Y	TREMBL Y	*WHITEL Y
ROOKER Y	*SHARPL Y	*SPECIF Y	SYNERG Y	*TRICKL Y	*WIGGER Y
*ROPEWA Y	SHEENE Y	SPICER Y	*SYNGAM Y	*TRICKS Y	*WILLOW Y
ROSEBA Y	SHINGL Y	SPICIL Y	SYNTON Y	TRILOG Y	WINDIL Y
ROUGHL Y	SHINIL Y	SPIDER Y	*TACKIF Y	TRINAR Y	*WINDWA Y
ROUNDL Y	SHINNE Y	SPINDL Y	*TACKIL Y	TRINIT Y	WINTER Y
ROYALL Y	*SHIPWA Y	SPINNE Y	TALLBO Y	TRIPOD Y	*WIREWA Y
ROYALT Y	*SHIVER Y	*SPLASH Y	TALLOW Y	TRISOM Y	*WISPIL Y

WITTIL Y	BORINGL Y	*CHICKOR Y	*CUPIDIT Y	*FALLAWA Y	GADGETR Y
*WOMANL Y	*BOTCHER Y	*CHIMBLE Y	*CURRENC Y	FARRIER Y	*GAPINGL Y
WORDIL Y	*BOTTOMR Y	*CHIVALR Y	CURRIER Y	FATALIT Y	GARGANE Y
*WORKDA Y	BOUNDAR Y	*CHOIRBO Y	*CUSHION Y	*FATHERL Y	GELIDIT Y
WORLDL Y	*BOVINEL Y	*CHORALL Y	CUSSEDL Y	*FEATHER Y	*GEMOLOG Y
*WRIGGL Y	*BOVINIT Y	*CHRONAX Y	*CUTCHER Y	*FEDERAC Y	*GENTRIF Y
*WRINKL Y	*BOWINGL Y	*CHURCHL Y	*C Y TOGEN Y	*FELICIT Y	GEOGNOS Y
WRONGL Y	*BOXBERR Y	*CINERAR Y	*C Y TOLOG Y	FELINEL Y	*GEOMANC Y
*Y ELLOW Y	BRAINIL Y	*CIRCUIT Y	DARINGL Y	FELINIT Y	GEOMETR Y
*ZEDOAR Y	*BRAZENL Y	*CIVILIT Y	DEACONR Y	*FELLOWL Y	*GEOPHAG Y
*ZINCIF Y	*BREVETC Y	*CLASSIF Y	DEBILIT Y	*FEMINAC Y	*GIFTEDL Y
*ZINKIF Y	*BREVIAR Y	CLASSIL Y	DECENAR Y	*FEMINIT Y	*GIMMICK Y
*ZOMBIF Y	BRIDALL Y	CLATTER Y	*DELEGAC Y	*FERACIT Y	GINGELE Y
*ZOOLOG Y	BROGUER Y	*CLEMENC Y	*DELICAC Y	FERETOR Y	GINGELL Y
*ZOOTOM Y	BROIDER Y	CLINALL Y	*DELIVER Y	*FEROCIT Y	GINGERL Y
*Z Y MURG Y	*BR Y OLOG Y	*CLOWNER Y	DELUSOR Y	FERVENC Y	*GIVEAWA Y
*BACKSTA Y	*BULL Y BO Y	CLUSTER Y	*DEMAGOG Y	*FETOLOG Y	GLASSIL Y
*BADGERL Y	*BUO Y ANC Y	CLUTTER Y	*DENAZIF Y	*FIDELIT Y	*GLAZIER Y
BANALIT Y	BURGLAR Y	*COAGENC Y	DERISOR Y	FINALIT Y	GLITTER Y
BANDITR Y	*BURGUND Y	*COBWEBB Y	*DETOXIF Y	FINITEL Y	GLOSSAR Y
*BARBERR Y	*BUS Y BOD Y	*COEMBOD Y	*DEVILTR Y	*FINNICK Y	GLUTTON Y
BARRETR Y	*BUTCHER Y	*COEMPLO Y	*DEWBERR Y	*FIRECLA Y	GORBELL Y
*BASICIT Y	*CABLEWA Y	*COEVALL Y	DIABLER Y	*FLACKER Y	*GORBLIM Y
BASILAR Y	*CADUCIT Y	COLLIER Y	*DIAPHON Y	FLATTER Y	GOSSIPR Y
*BASKETR Y	*CAJOLER Y	*COLLOQU Y	*DID Y NAM Y	*FLICKER Y	*GRAMERC Y
BASTARD Y	*CALAMAR Y	*COLOTOM Y	DILATOR Y	FLORALL Y	GRATUIT Y
*BA Y BERR Y	*CALAMIT Y	*COMMONL Y	*DIPLOID Y	*FLUIDIT Y	*GRAVELL Y
*BEACHBO Y	*CANDIDL Y	*CONICIT Y	DISARRA Y	*FLUMMER Y	GREENER Y
*BEAUTIF Y	CANINIT Y	CONTRAR Y	DISUNIT Y	FLUTTER Y	*GREENFL Y
*BEGGARL Y	CANNONR Y	*CONVEXL Y	*DIVINIT Y	*FOLDAWA Y	*GREENWA Y
BESTIAR Y	*CAPACIT Y	COOINGL Y	DOCILIT Y	*FOREBOD Y	GRINDER Y
*BIFIDIT Y	CARTOON Y	*COPURIF Y	*DOGBERR Y	*FORELAD Y	GROGGER Y
*BIGEMIN Y	*CASTAWA Y	*COQUETR Y	*DOGGEDL Y	*FOREPLA Y	*GRUFFIL Y
*BIHOURL Y	CASUALL Y	CORDURO Y	*DOGSBOD Y	FORESTA Y	GUARANT Y
*BILBERR Y	CASUALT Y	*CORNETC Y	*DOMESDA Y	FORESTR Y	GUERNSE Y
BIOASSA Y	*CATCHFL Y	CORONAR Y	*DOOMSDA Y	*FORMALL Y	*GUIDEWA Y
*BIOMETR Y	CATEGOR Y	CORSETR Y	*DORMANC Y	*FORMERL Y	GULOSIT Y
*BIOSCOP Y	CATENAR Y	*COSTMAR Y	DORSALL Y	FORTUIT Y	*G Y NANDR Y
*BIRTHDA Y	CAUSALL Y	*COSTUME Y	DOTINGL Y	*FOURTHL Y	*G Y NARCH Y
BISTOUR Y	*CAUSEWA Y	COURTES Y	*DOUGHBO Y	*FREAKIL Y	*G Y NIATR Y
*BITCHER Y	*CAVITAR Y	COUSINR Y	*DOWNPLA Y	*FRENZIL Y	*G Y RATOR Y
BITINGL Y	CELERIT Y	*COVERTL Y	*DOXOLOG Y	FRIENDL Y	*HAGBERR Y
*BIWEEKL Y	*CELIBAC Y	*COWARDL Y	*DRAUGHT Y	*FRIPPER Y	*HAPLOID Y
*BI Y EARL Y	*CEMETER Y	*COWBERR Y	*DRIVEWA Y	*FRIZZIL Y	HARLOTR Y
*BLACKBO Y	CENTAUR Y	*CRAMOIS Y	DROLLER Y	FROMENT Y	*HATCHER Y
*BLACKFL Y	*CEREMON Y	*CRANKIL Y	*DROUGHT Y	*FRUCTIF Y	*HATCHWA Y
*BLATANC Y	CETOLOG Y	*CRAVENL Y	DRUDGER Y	*FRUMENT Y	*HEADACH Y
*BLAZONR Y	*CHAMBRA Y	*CRAWLWA Y	*DUDISHL Y	*FUGACIT Y	*HEADSTA Y
BLISTER Y	*CHANCER Y	*CREAMER Y	DULCETL Y	*FUMATOR Y	*HEATEDL Y
BLOODIL Y	*CHANCIL Y	*CROCKER Y	DUOPSON Y	*FUMITOR Y	*HEAVENL Y
*BLOOMER Y	*CHARLAD Y	*CROOKER Y	*D Y SPEPS Y	FUNERAR Y	*HEGEMON Y
*BLOSSOM Y	*CHASTIT Y	*CROSSWA Y	*FACIALL Y	*FURMENT Y	*HEGUMEN Y
*BLUBBER Y	*CHEERIL Y	*CR Y OGEN Y	*FACILIT Y	FURRIER Y	*HELICIT Y
BLUSTER Y	*CHEMURG Y	*CUBICIT Y	*FADEAWA Y	FUTILIT Y	*HERALDR Y
*BODINGL Y	*CHICCOR Y	CULINAR Y	*FALCONR Y	FUTURIT Y	*HEREDIT Y

*HERMITR Y	LATENTL Y	MILLIAR Y	*M Y STICL Y	*PHANTAS Y	*QUACKER Y
HERSTOR Y	LATINIT Y	*MINACIT Y	*NABOBER Y	*PHARMAC Y	*QUAGMIR Y
*HEXAPOD Y	LATTERL Y	MINATOR Y	NASALIT Y	*PH Y LLAR Y	*QUANDAR Y
*HEXARCH Y	LAVATOR Y	MINISTR Y	*NASCENC Y	*PICNICK Y	*QUANTIF Y
*HIDEAWA Y	LEATHER Y	MINORIT Y	NATALIT Y	PILOSIT Y	*QUANTIT Y
*HILAPIT Y	LEGALIT Y	MISANDR Y	NATATOR Y	*PIPINGL Y	*QUIDDIT Y
*HOGMANA Y	LEGENDR Y	*MISAPPL Y	NATIVEL Y	*PIQUANC Y	*QUIXOTR Y
*HOGMENA Y	LEGERIT Y	MISASSA Y	NATIVIT Y	*PITCHIL Y	*RABBITR Y
*HOK Y POK Y	LENIENC Y	*MISCARR Y	*NAUMACH Y	PLAGIAR Y	RABIDIT Y
*HOLOGAM Y	LETHALL Y	MISENTR Y	*NECROPS Y	PLASTER Y	RADIALL Y
*HOLOG YN Y	*LETHARG Y	*MISOGAM Y	NIHILIT Y	PLEURIS Y	RADIANC Y
*HOMEBOD Y	LIENTER Y	MISOLOG Y	*NITPICK Y	*PLUGUGL Y	RAGINGL Y
*HOMESTA Y	LIMITAR Y	MISSILR Y	NOBILIT Y	*PLUMBER Y	RAILLER Y
*HOMOGON Y	*LIQUIDL Y	*MIXOLOG Y	NODALIT Y	PLURALL Y	RAMOSIT Y
*HOMOLOG Y	LITERAC Y	*MOBILIT Y	NODOSIT Y	PODIATR Y	*RAMPANC Y
*HOMONYM Y	LITERAR Y	MODALIT Y	NOGATOR Y	POLARIT Y	RANDOML Y
HONORAR Y	*LIVIDIT Y	MOLALIT Y	*NOMARCH Y	*POLY GAM Y	*RAPACIT Y
*HOROLOG Y	*LIVINGL Y	MOLARIT Y	NOMOLOG Y	*POLY GON Y	RAPIDIT Y
*HORRIBL Y	LOBLOLL Y	*MOMENTL Y	NONDAIR Y	*POLY GYN Y	RASCALL Y
*HORSEFL Y	*LOBOTOM Y	MONANDR Y	*NONEMPT Y	*POLY PAR Y	*RAVINGL Y
*HOUSEBO Y	LOCALIT Y	*MONARCH Y	NONENTR Y	*POLY POD Y	*RECONVE Y
*HOUSEFL Y	LOCUTOR Y	MONETAR Y	NONFATT Y	*POLY SEM Y	*RECOVER Y
*HUMIDIF Y	*LOGOT YP Y	MONITOR Y	*NONHARD Y	*POLY TEN Y	REDEPLO Y
*HUMILIT Y	LOSINGL Y	*MONOGAM Y	*NONLEAF Y	POMOLOG Y	*REEMBOD Y
*HUMIVIT Y	LOVELIL Y	MONOGEN Y	NONMONE Y	*POPINJA Y	*REEMPLO Y
*H Y DROPS Y	*LOVINGL Y	*MONOG YN Y	NONPART Y	POROSIT Y	REFINER Y
*HY POG YN Y	LUCIDIT Y	MONOLOG Y	NONSTOR Y	*PORPH Y R Y	*REFLEXL Y
*JACKSTA Y	LUMINAR Y	*MONOPOD Y	*NONWOOD Y	*PORTABL Y	REGALIT Y
*JAGGHER Y	*L Y SOGEN Y	*MONOPOL Y	*NORMALC Y	POSINGL Y	REGISTR Y
*JANISAR Y	*MACCABO Y	*MONOSOM Y	NORMALL Y	POSOLOG Y	REGNANC Y
*JANIZAR Y	*MACCOBO Y	MONOTON Y	NOSOLOG Y	POSTALL Y	*REINJUR Y
*JAPINGL Y	*MAHOGAN Y	*MOPINGL Y	NUBILIT Y	POTATOR Y	*REMODIF Y
*JEALOUS Y	MAINSTA Y	MORALIT Y	*NUMERAC Y	*POTBELL Y	RENOTIF Y
*JEJUNIT Y	*MAJORIT Y	MORATOR Y	NUMERAR Y	*PRETTIF Y	*REOCCUP Y
*JEOPARD Y	*MALARKE Y	*MORDANC Y	PADUASO Y	PRIESTI Y	*REPACIF Y
*JESUITR Y	MALIGNL Y	MORONIT Y	*PALIMON Y	*PRIGGER Y	*REPURIF Y
*JOCOSIT Y	*MANGABE Y	MOROSIT Y	*PANDOWD Y	*PRINCEL Y	RESINIF Y
*JOKINGL Y	MANNERL Y	MORTALL Y	*PANSOPH Y	PRINTER Y	*RESUPPL Y
*JOVIALT Y	MANUALL Y	MORTUAR Y	*PAPERBO Y	PRIORIT Y	RESURVE Y
*JUGGLER Y	*MARKEDL Y	*MOTHERL Y	*PAPISTR Y	*PROBABL Y	*REVERIF Y
*JURATOR Y	*MART Y RL Y	MOTILIT Y	PASSERB Y	*PROMPTL Y	REVISOR Y
*KAZATSK Y	MASSEDL Y	*MOTIVIT Y	PATENTL Y	*PROPERT Y	*REVIVIF Y
*KNACKER Y	MASTERL Y	*MOTORWA Y	*PEACOCK Y	*PROPHEC Y	*RHAPSOD Y
*KNIGHTL Y	MATTEDL Y	*MOVEABL Y	*PECCANC Y	*PROPHES Y	*RHEOLOG Y
*KOLINSK Y	MATURIT Y	*MOVINGL Y	*PEDAGOG Y	*PROVENL Y	RIBALDL Y
LABIALL Y	*MAUMETR Y	*MUCIDIT Y	PEDANTR Y	*PSALMOD Y	RIBALDR Y
LABILIT Y	MEDIALL Y	*MUCOSIT Y	*PEDDLER Y	PSALTER Y	*RIGIDIF Y
*LACKADA Y	*MEGACIT Y	*MUDPUPP Y	*PEDOLOG Y	*PUBLICL Y	RIGIDIT Y
LAMASER Y	MENIALL Y	*MULBERR Y	PENALIT Y	PULINGL Y	RIMOSIT Y
*LAMBENC Y	MENOLOG Y	*MULTIPL Y	*PENDENC Y	PUNDITR Y	RITUALL Y
LANDLAD Y	MESNALT Y	MUSINGI Y	PENOLOG Y	*PUNGENC Y	*ROCKAWA Y
LANOSIT Y	*METON YM Y	*MUSKETR Y	*PERIG YN Y	PUNITOR Y	*ROCKETR Y
LAPIDAR Y	*MICRURG Y	MUSTARD Y	*PERIPET Y	*PUPILAR Y	ROGATOR Y
*LAPIDIF Y	MIDSTOR Y	*MY COLOG Y	PETALOD Y	*PUPPETR Y	ROGATOR Y
*LATCHKE Y	MILITAR Y	*MY OPATH Y	PETTEDL Y	*PY ROLOG Y	ROLLAWA Y

*ROLLICK Y	*SEXOLOG Y	SOVRANL Y	*SUPERSP Y	TONICIT Y	*VEXINGL Y
ROSEMAR Y	*SEXTUPL Y	SOVRANT Y	SUPINEL Y	*TOPLOFT Y	*VIBRANC Y
ROTATOR Y	*SHIMMER Y	*SOWBELL Y	SWANNER Y	TOPOLOG Y	*VICENAR Y
*ROUGHDR Y	SHINNER Y	*SPARKIL Y	*SYMMETR Y	*TOPONYM Y	*VICINIT Y
ROUTEWA Y	*SHMALTZ Y	SPARSIT Y	*SYMPATH Y	TOROSIT Y	VILLAIN Y
*ROVINGL Y	*SHUDDER Y	SPEEDIL Y	*SYMPATR Y	TORPIDL Y	VINOSIT Y
RUGOSIT Y	*SICKERL Y	*SPEEDWA Y	*SYMPHON Y	TOTALIT Y	*VIRIDIT Y
RURALIT Y	SIGNALL Y	*SPERMAR Y	*SYNCARP Y	*TOWARDL Y	VIRILIT Y
RUSTICL Y	SIGNIOR Y	*SPILLWA Y	*SYNONYM Y	*TOXICIT Y	*VIROLOG Y
SACRIST Y	*SILICIF Y	SPINALL Y	TABOOLE Y	*TRACKWA Y	*VISCALL Y
SADDLER Y	SILVERL Y	SPINNER Y	*TAKEAWA Y	TRAINWA Y	VISUALL Y
SAGACIT Y	*SIMPLIF Y	SPIRALL Y	*TAKINGL Y	TRAVEST Y	VITALIT Y
SALACIT Y	SINOLOG Y	*SPLOTCH Y	TANGENC Y	TREASUR Y	*VIVACIT Y
SALIENC Y	SISTERL Y	SPONGIL Y	TANGIBL Y	*TRIARCH Y	*VOCALIT Y
SALINIT Y	SITOLOG Y	*SPOOFER Y	TANISTR Y	*TRICKER Y	*VOMITOR Y
SALUTAR Y	*SIXPENN Y	*SPOOKER Y	TAPESTR Y	*TRICKIL Y	*VORACIT Y
*SANCTIF Y	*SKITTER Y	*SQUAREL Y	*TAXINGL Y	TRIUNIT Y	*WALKAWA Y
SANCTIT Y	*SLABBER Y	*SQUELCH Y	*TAXONOM Y	TRUANTR Y	WANTONL Y
SANITAR Y	*SLIDEWA Y	*SQUIGGL Y	TEABERR Y	*TRUMPER Y	*WARDENR Y
SAPIDIT Y	*SLIPPER Y	*SQUOOSH Y	TEARAWA Y	*TRYINGL Y	WARRANT Y
*SAPIENC Y	SLITHER Y	STAGGER Y	TELEGON Y	TUMIDIT Y	*WASTEWA Y
*SAPONIF Y	*SLOBBER Y	STAIRWA Y	TELEPLA Y	*TUPPENN Y	*WATCHCR Y
*SAVAGER Y	SLOVENL Y	*STANCHL Y	TEMERIT Y	TURGENC Y	WATERIL Y
*SAVINGL Y	*SLUMBER Y	STANNAR Y	TENACIT Y	TUTELAR Y	*WATERWA Y
*SCAMMON Y	SMELTER Y	STATEDL Y	TENANTR Y	TWITTER Y	*WAXBERR Y
*SCARCEL Y	*SMITHER Y	*STATICK Y	TENDENC Y	*TWOPENN Y	*WEAPONR Y
*SCARCIT Y	*SMOOTHL Y	STATUAR Y	TENDERL Y	*TYPOLOG Y	WEASELL Y
*SCHLOCK Y	*SMOTHER Y	STEALTH Y	TENOTOM Y	*VAGILIT Y	*WELLADA Y
*SCHMALZ Y	*SNAPPIL Y	STELLIF Y	TENPENN Y	*VAGOTOM Y	*WELLAWA Y
*SCRABBL Y	*SNICKER Y	*STEMMER Y	TEPIDIT Y	*VAGRANC Y	WESTERL Y
*SCRAGGL Y	*SNIFFIL Y	STERNWA Y	TERTIAR Y	*VALIANC Y	*WHISPER Y
*SCRATCH Y	*SNIPPET Y	*STICKIL Y	*TEXTUAR Y	*VALIDIT Y	*WHITEFL Y
*SCREECH Y	*SNOBBER Y	STINGIL Y	*THATAWA Y	*VALUABL Y	*WIDTHWA Y
SCROUNG Y	*SNOBBIL Y	STINGRA Y	*THEARCH Y	VANITOR Y	*WINGEDL Y
SCRUTIN Y	*SNUFFIL Y	*STOCKIL Y	*THEODIC Y	*VAPIDIT Y	WINTERL Y
SCULLER Y	SNUGGER Y	*STOMACH Y	*THEOGON Y	*VARIABL Y	*WITCHER Y
SECANTL Y	SOBRIET Y	STONEFL Y	*THEOLOG Y	*VARIEDL Y	*WIZARDR Y
SECONDL Y	*SOCIABL Y	*STOWAWA Y	*THEONOM Y	VARLETR Y	*WONTEDL Y
SECRETL Y	SOCIALL Y	STRAGGL Y	*THIEVER Y	*VARNISH Y	*WOOINGL Y
SECURIT Y	SODALIT Y	STRAMON Y	*THRENOD Y	*VASOTOM Y	*WORDPLA Y
SEDULIT Y	SODDENL Y	STRATEG Y	*THUGGER Y	*VEILEDL Y	*WORKADA Y
SEIGNOR Y	SOLDIER Y	STRATIF Y	*THUNDER Y	VELLEIT Y	*XENOGAM Y
SELECTL Y	SOLIDAR Y	*STRETCH Y	*THWARTL Y	*VELOCIT Y	*XENOGEN Y
SEMINAR Y	*SOLIDIF Y	*STUBBIL Y	TIMIDIT Y	VENALIT Y	*XYLOTOM Y
SENILEL Y	SOLIDIT Y	STULTIF Y	TINSELL Y	*VENDIBL Y	*YEOMANR Y
SENILIT Y	SOLITAR Y	SUBENTR Y	*TITTUPP Y	VENOSIT Y	*ZEALOTR Y
*SEQUENC Y	*SOLVENC Y	SUBTILT Y	TITULAR Y	*VERACIT Y	*ZOOLATR Y
SERENIT Y	*SOMEBOD Y	SUBTLET Y	TOCOLOG Y	*VERBALL Y	*ZOOMETR Y
SERIALL Y	SONOBUO Y	SUDATOR Y	TOILETR Y	*VERDANC Y	*ZOOPHIL Y
SEROLOG Y	SONORIT Y	*SULPHUR Y	*TOKOLOG Y	*VESPIAR Y	*ZYGOSIT Y
SEROSIT Y	SOOTHSA Y	*SUMMERL Y	TOMALLE Y	VESTALL Y	*ZYMOLOG Y
SEVERIT Y	SORORIT Y	*SUMMITR Y	TONALIT Y	VESTIAR Y	

Z

*ZANY	*ZAFFRE	*ZAMARRA	*ZAIBATSU		*BA Z OO	*MI Z Z LY
*ZARF	*ZAFTIG	*ZAMARRO	*ZAMINDAR		*GA Z AR	*MU Z HIK
ZEAL	*ZAIKAI	*ZANYISH	*ZANINESS		*Z A Z EN	*MU Z JIK
*ZEBU	*ZANANA	*ZAPATEO	*ZARATITE		*Z I Z IT	*MU Z Z LE
ZEIN	*ZANDER	*ZAPTIAH	*ZARZUELA		*BA Z AAR	*NA Z IFY
*ZERK	*ZANIER	*ZAPTIEH	*ZASTRUGA		*BE Z ANT	*NO Z Z LE
ZERO	*ZANIES	*ZAREEBA	*ZEALOTRY		*BE Z OAR	*PA Z A Z Z
ZEST	*ZAPPER	*ZEALOUS	*ZECCHINO		*BI Z ONE	*PI Z A Z Z
ZETA	*ZAREBA	*ZEBRASS	*ZEMINDAR		*BU Z UKI	*PI Z Z LE
ZILL	*ZARIBA	*ZEBRINE	*ZEPPELIN		*BU Z Z ER	*PU Z LER
*ZINC	*ZEALOT	*ZEBROID	*ZESTLESS		*BY Z ANT	*PU Z Z LE
ZING	*ZEATIN	*ZECCHIN	*ZIBELINE		*CO Z IED	*RE Z ONE
ZITI	*ZEBECK	*ZEDOARY	*ZIGGURAT		*CO Z IER	*RO Z Z ER
ZOEA	*ZECHIN	*ZELKOVA	*ZIKKURAT		*CO Z IES	*SI Z IER
*ZOIC	*ZENANA	*ZEMSTVO	*ZINCKING		*CO Z Z ES	*SI Z ING
ZONE	*ZENITH	*ZENAIDA	*ZIRCONIA		*DA Z Z LE	*SI Z Z LE
*ZONK	*ZEPHYR	*ZEOLITE	*ZIRCONIC		*DE Z INC	*SO Z INE
*ZOOM	*ZEROTH	*ZESTFUL	*ZOMBIISM		*DO Z IER	*SY Z YGY
ZOON	*ZESTER	*ZIKURAT	*ZONATION		*DO Z ILY	*VI Z ARD
ZORI	*ZEUGMA	*ZILLION	*ZONELESS		*DO Z ING	*VI Z IER
*ZYME	*ZIBETH	*ZINCATE	*ZONETIME		*FI Z GIG	*VI Z SLA
ZAIRE	*ZIGZAG	*ZINCIFY	*ZOOCHORE		*FI Z Z ER	*WI Z ARD
*ZAMIA	*ZILLAH	*ZINCITE	*ZOOGENIC		*FI Z Z ES	*WI Z Z EN
*ZANZA	*ZINCIC	*ZINCKED	*ZOOGLOEA		*FI Z Z LE	*Z I Z Z LE
*ZAPPY	*ZINCKY	*ZINCOID	*ZOOLATER		*GA Z ABO	*Z I Z ITH
*ZAYIN	*ZINGER	*ZINCOUS	*ZOOLATRY		*GA Z EBO	*BA Z OOKA
*ZAZEN	*ZINNIA	*ZINGANO	*ZOOMANIA		*GA Z ING	*BE Z IQUE
*ZEBEC	*ZIPPER	*ZINGARA	*ZOOMETRY		*GA Z UMP	*BE Z ANT
*ZEBRA	*ZIRCON	*ZINGARO	*ZOOMORPH		*GU Z Z LE	*BI Z ARRE
*ZESTY	*ZITHER	*ZINKIFY	*ZOONOSIS		*HA Z ARD	*BI Z NAGA
*ZIBET	*ZIZITH	*ZIPLESS	*ZOOPHILE		*HA Z IER	*BU Z ARD
*ZILCH	*ZIZZLE	*ZIPPING	*ZOOPHILY		*HA Z ILY	*BU Z Z WIG
*ZINCY	*ZODIAC	*ZITHERN	*ZOOPHOBE		*HA Z ING	*CA Z IQUE
*ZINEB	*ZOFTIG	*ZOARIUM	*ZOOPHYTE		*HA Z AN	*CO Z ENER
*ZINGY	*ZOMBIE	*ZOECIUM	*ZOOSPERM		*HU Z ZAH	*CO Z IEST
*ZINKY	*ZONARY	*ZOISITE	*ZOOSPORE		*JA Z Z ER	*DA Z LER
*ZIPPY	*ZONATE	*ZOMBIFY	*ZUCCHINI		*JE Z AIL	*DO Z ENTH
*ZIRAM	*ZONING	*ZONATED	*ZWIEBACK		*LA Z IED	*DO Z IEST
*ZIZIT	*ZONKED	*ZOOGLEA	*ZYGOSITY		*LA Z IER	*FA Z ENDA
*ZLOTY	*ZONULA	*ZOOLOGY	*ZYGOTENE		*LA Z IES	*FU Z ING
*ZOMBI	*ZONULE	*ZOOTOMY	*ZYMOGENE		*LA Z ILY	*GA Z ANIA
ZONAL	*ZOSTER	*ZORILLA	*ZYMOGRAM		*LA Z ING	*GA Z ELLE
ZONER	*ZOUAVE	*ZORILLE	*ZYMOLOGY		*LA Z ULI	*GA Z ETTE
*ZOOID	*ZOUNDS	*ZORILLO			*LI Z ARD	*GI Z ARD
*ZOOKS	*ZOYSIA	*ZYGOSIS		*C Z AR	*MA Z ARD	*GU Z LER
*ZOOTY	*ZYDECO	*ZYMOGEN		T Z AR	*MA Z ING	*HA Z ELLY
ZORIL	*ZYGOID	*ZYMOSAN		*T Z IT Z IT	*MA Z UMA	*HA Z IEST
*ZOWIE	*ZYGOMA	*ZYMOSIS		*FI Z Z	*ME Z CAL	*JA Z MAN
*ZADDIK	*ZYGOTE	*ZYMURGY		*FU Z Z	*ME Z UZA	*JE Z EBEL
*ZAFFAR	*ZYMASE	*ZYZZYVA		*JA Z Z	*MI Z Z EN	*LA Z ARET
*ZAFFER	*ZACATON	*ZABAIONE		*ME Z E	*MI Z Z LE	*LA Z IEST
*ZAFFIR	*ZADDICK	*ZABAJONE		*RA Z Z		*LA Z YISH

*LO Z ENGE	*BEN Z OATE	*GRA Z IOSO	DIT Z	*GLIT Z	*QUART Z
*MA Z IEST	*BLA Z ONER	*GRI Z Z LER	*FI Z Z	*GROS Z	*SCHNO Z
*MA Z URKA	*BLA Z ONRY	*HI Z Z ONER	*FRI Z	*HAFI Z	*SPELT Z
*MA Z Z ARD	*BLI Z Z ARD	*JA Z Z LIKE	*FUT Z	*HERT Z	*SPRIT Z
*MA Z Z ILY	*BOU Z OUKI	*MAR Z IPAN	*FU Z Z	*KLUT Z	*CHALUT Z
*ME Z QUIT	*BRA Z ENLY	*MO Z ZETTA	GEE Z	NERT Z	*KIBBIT Z
*ME Z U Z AH	*BRA Z ILIN	*MU Z Z IEST	*JA Z Z	*SPIT Z	*KIBBUT Z
*MO Z ETTA	*BUZ Z WORD	*PI Z Z ERIA	*JEE Z	*TOPA Z	*KOLKHO Z
*MU Z Z IER	*CAN Z ONET	*PO Z ZOLAN	LUT Z	TROO Z	*SCHMAL Z
*MU Z Z ILY	*CRU Z EIRO	*RHI Z OBIA	*PHI Z	*WALT Z	*SCHNO Z Z
*MU Z Z LER	*DIA Z EPAM	*RHI Z OPOD	*PRE Z	*WHI Z Z	*SHEGET Z
*NU Z Z LER	*DIA Z INON	*RHI Z OPUS	*PUT Z	*BLINT Z	*SHMALT Z
*PI Z A Z Z Y	*DOU Z EPER	*SIT Z MARK	*QUI Z	*CHINT Z	*SHOWBI Z
*RA Z Z ING	*FOR Z ANDO	*SWI Z Z LER	*RA Z Z	*HALUT Z	*SOVKHO Z
*SI Z ABLE	*FRI Z ETTE	*WHI Z BANG	RIT Z	*KIBIT Z	*SOLONET Z
*SI Z IEST	*FRI Z Z IER	*WHI Z Z ING	*SPA Z	*KOLHO Z	
*SI Z Z LER	*FRI Z Z ILY	*Z AR Z UELA	*BLIT Z	*KOLKO Z	
*SO Z Z LED	*FRI Z Z LER		*BORT Z	*KUVAS Z	
*Z Y Z Z YVA	*GAD Z OOKS	*BU Z Z	*FRIT Z	*PA Z A Z Z	
*BEN Z IDIN	*GLA Z IERY	*CHE Z	*FRI Z Z	*PI Z A Z Z	

CHAPTER 3

Two-Letter Words

If there's one list in this book that you should memorize, this is it.

AA	BE	ET	LI	OP	TO
AB	BI	FA	LO	OR	UN
AD	BO	GO	MA	OS	UP
AE	BY	HA	ME	OW	US
AH	DA	HE	MI	OX	UT
AI	DE	HI	MY	OY	WE
AM	DO	HO	NA	PA	XI
AN	ED	ID	NO	PE	YA
AR	EF	IF	NU	PI	YE
AS	EH	IN	OD	RE	YO
AT	EL	IS	OE	SH	
AW	EM	IT	OF	SI	
AX	EN	JO	OH	SO	
AY	ER	KA	OM	TA	
BA	ES	LA	ON	TI	

C H A P T E R   4

3-Letter Words Formed from 2-Letter Words

B AA	G AR	T AW	A EF	S ET	S IN
C AD	J AR	W AW	R EF	V ET	T IN
D AD	L AR	Y AW	Y EH	W ET	V IN
F AD	M AR	F AX	B EL	Y ER	W IN
H AD	O AR	L AX	D EL		Y IN
L AD	P AR	P AX	G EL	A GO	B IS
M AD	T AR	R AX	M EL	E GO	S IS
P AD	W AR	S AX	S EL		V IS
R AD	Y AR	T AX	G EM	A HA	W IS
S AD	G AS	W AX	H EM	S EH	A IT
T AD	H AS	Z AX	R EM	T HE	B IT
W AD	P AS	B AY	B EN	C HI	F IT
H AE	V AS	C AY	F EN	G HI	G IT
K AE	W AS	D AY	H EN	K HI	K IT
M AE	B AT	F AY	M EN	P HI	L IT
N AE	C AT	G AY	P EN	M HO	N IT
S AE	E AT	H AY	S EN	O HO	P IT
W AE	F AT	J AY	T EN	R HO	S IT
A AH	G AT	L AY	W EN	T HO	T IT
H AH	H AT	M AY	Y EN		U IT
P AH	L AT	N AY	F ER	D ID	W IT
R AH	M AT	P AY	H ER	F ID	
Y AH	O AT	R AY	P ER	G ID	O KA
B AN	P AT	S AY	S ER	L ID	
C AN	S AT	W AY	P ES	M ID	A LA
F AN	T AR	Y AY	R ES	R ID	
G AN	V AT		Y ES	K IF	A MA
M AN	W AT	A BA	F ET	D IN	E ME
P AN	D AW	O BE	G ET	F IN	A MI
R AN	H AW	O BI	J ET	G IN	
T AN	J AW	O BO	L ET	J IN	A NA
W AN	M AW	A BY	M ET	K IN	
B AR	P AW		N ET	L IN	B OD
E AR	R AW	O DE	P ET	P IN	C OD
F AR	S AW	A DO	R ET	R IN	G OD

265

H OD	C OX	T UT	BA T	EL L	HO B
N OD	F OX	A WE	BA Y	EL M	HO D
P OD	G OX	E WE	BE D	EM E	HO E
R OD	L OX	O WE	BE E	EN D	HO G
S OD	O OX		BE G	EN G	HO P
T OD	S OX	P YA	BE L	EN S	HO T
Y OD	B OY	R YA	BE N	ER A	HO W
H OE	F OY	A YE	BE T	ER E	**HO Y**
J OE	G OY	D YE	BI B	ER G	
R OE	H OY	E YE	BI D	ER N	**IN K**
W OE	S OY	L YE	BI G	ER R	IN N
N OH	T OY	P YE	BI N	ER S	IS M
O OH		R YE	BI O	ES S	IT S
P OH	A PE	T YE	BI S	ET A	
D OM	O PE	W YE	BI T	ET H	JO B
C ON			BO A		JO E
D ON	A RE	AA H	BO B	FA D	
E ON	I RE	AA L	BO D	FA G	JO G
F ON		AD D	BO G	FA N	
I ON	A SH	AD O	BO P	FA R	KA B
M ON	P SI	AD Z	BO T	FA T	KA E
S ON		AH A	BO W	FA X	KA X
T ON	E TA	AI L	BO X	FA Y	KA Y
V ON	U TA	AI M	BO Y		
W ON		AI R		GO A	LA B
Y ON	B UN	AI T	DA B	GO B	LA C
B OP	D UN	AM A	DA D	GO D	LA D
C OP	F UN	AM I	DA G	GO O	LA G
F OP	G UN	AM P	DA K	GO R	LA M
L OP	H UN	AM U	DA M	GO X	LA P
M OP	J UN	AN A	DA W	GO Y	LA R
O OP	M UN	AN D	DA Y		LA T
S OP	N UN	AN E	DE I	HA D	LI B
T OP	P UN	AN I	DE L	HA E	LI D
W OP	S UN	AN T	DE N	HA G	LI E
D OR	T UN	AN Y	DE S	HA H	LI N
G OR	C UP	AR C	DE V	HA J	LI P
M OR	D UP	AS H	DE W	HA M	LI T
N OR	H UP	AS K	DE X	HA P	LO B
T OR	P UP	AS P	DE Y	HA S	LO G
C OS	S UP	AS S	DO C	HA T	LO O
K OS	T UP	AT E	DO E	HA W	LO P
B OW	Y UP	AW A	DO G	HA Y	LO T
C OW	B US	AW E	DO L	HE M	LO W
D OW	J US	AW L	DO M	HE N	LO X
H OW	P US	AW N	DO N	HE P	
L OW	B UT	AX E	DO R	HE R	MA C
M OW	C UT	AY E	DO T	HE X	MA D
N OW	G UT		DO R	HE Y	MA E
O OW	H UT	BA A	DO W	HI C	MA G
S OW	J UT	BA D		HI E	MA N
T OW	M UT	BA G	EF F	HI M	MA P
V OW	N UT	BA H	EF T	HI N	MA R
W OW	O UT	BA L	EL D	HI P	MA T
Y OW	P UT	BA N	EL F	HI S	MA W
B OX	R UT	BA R	EL K	HI T	MA Y
					ME L

ME N	NU B	PA N	RE P	TA D	TO R
ME T	NU N	PA P	RE S	TA E	TO T
ME W	NU T	PA R	RE T	TA G	TO W
MI B		PA S	RE V	TA J	TO Y
MI D	OD D	PA T	RE X	TA M	
MI G	OD E	PA W		TA N	UP O
MI L	OF F	PA X	SH H	TA O	US E
MI M	OF T	PA Y	SH Y	TA P	UT A
MI R	OH M	PE A	SI B	TA R	
MI X	OH O	PE D	SI M	TA T	WE B
	ON E	PE E	SI N	TA U	WE D
NA B	OP T	PE G	SI P	TA V	WE E
NA E	OR A	PE N	SI S	TA W	WE N
NA G	OR B	PE P	SI T	TA X	WE T
NA P	OR C	PE R	SI X	TI C	
NA Y	OR E	PE S	SO L	TI E	YA Y
NO B	OR T	PE T	SO N	TI L	YE A
NO D	OS E	PE W	SO P	TI N	YE H
NO G	OW E		SO T	TI P	YE N
NO H	OW L	RE B	SO U	TI T	YE P
NO M		RE D	SO W	TO D	YE S
NO O	PA D	RE E	SO X	TO G	YE T
NO R	PA H	RE F	SO Y	TO M	
NO T	PA L	RE I		TO N	
NO W	PA M	RE M	TA B	TO P	

CHAPTER 5

Prefixes, Suffixes, and Plurals

PREFIXES

The criteria for an acceptable Scrabble® prefix is:

1. The word cannot contain a hyphen.
2. The root or base word must be able to stand alone.

The following are acceptable prefixes:

A	COL	FORE	ORTHO	SUPER
AB	COM	HAY	OVER	TRANS
ABS	CON	IL	PAR	TRI
AD	DE	IM	PARA	ULTRA
ANTE	DI	IN	POST	UN
ANTI	DIA	INTER	PRE	UNI
AUTO	DIS	MAL	PRO	UP
BE	EM	MICRO	RE	
BI	EN	MIS	SEMI	
CO	EX	NON	SUB	

A-	BIDE	BOUT	AB-	SENT
BASE	BLOOM	BREAST	BE	SOLVE
BASH	BOARD	BRIDGE	BEY	USE
BEAM	BODE	BUT	DUCE	USER
BED	BOIL	BUTTED	NORMAL	VOLT
BET	BOON	BUTTER	OUT	YE
BETTER	BOUGHT	BUZZ	REACT	
BETTING	BOUND			

268

ABS-	AD-	JOIN	MIX	VERSE	ANTE-
TRACT	APT	JOINT	OPTION	VICE	DATE
	AXIAL	JUDGE	RIFT	VISOR	LOPE
	DRESS	JUROR	SCRIPT		TYPE
	DOCT	MAN	VENT		
	HERE	MIRE	VERB		

ANTI-	HERO	NODE	SKID	AUTO-	GYRO
BODY	KING	POLE	SMOG	BUS	MATE
DOTE	LOG	POPE		CADE	SOME
FAT	MASK	RUST		GIRO	TYPE

BE-	DAZZLE	GET	LACED	RATE	STOW
BLOOD	DECK	GIRDLE	LADY	RINGED	STREW
BOP	DELL	GLAD	LAY	ROBED	STRIDE
BOPPER	DEVIL	GLOOM	LEAP	ROUGED	STUD
CALM	DEW	GONE	LIKE	SCORCH	SWARM
CAME	DIAPER	GOT	LIQUOR	SCREEN	TAKE
CAP	DIM	GOTTEN	LITTLE	SEEM	TAXED
CARPET	DOTTED	GRIM	LIVE	SET	THANK
CAUSE	DRAPE	GRIME	LONG	SETTER	THINK
CHALK	DRENCH	GROAN	LOW	SHADOW	THORN
CHANCE	DROLL	GRUDGE'	LYING	SHAME	THUMP
CHARM	DUMB	GUILE	MADAM	SHIVER	TIDE
CLAMOR	DUNCE	GULF	MEAN	SHOUT	TIME
CLASP	FALL	GUM	MINGLE	SHREW	TIMES
CLOAK	FINGER	GUN	MIRE	SHROUD	TOKEN
CLOG	FLAG	HALF	MIST	SIEGE	TOOK
CLOTHE	FLEA	HAVE	MIX	SLIME	TRAY
CLOUD	FLECK	HEAD	MOAN	SMEAR	TROTH
CLOWN	FLOWER	HIND	MOCK	SMIRCH	VOMIT
COME	FOG	HOLD	MUDDLE	SMOKE	WAIL
COMING	FOOL	HOLDER	MURMUR	SMOOTH	WARE
COWARD	FORE	HOOF	MUSE	SMUDGE	WEARY
CRAWL	FOUL	HOWL	MUZZLE	SMUT	WEEP
CRIME	FOULER	JEWEL	NAME	SNOW	WIG
CROWD	FRET	JUMBLE	PAINT	SOOTHE	WINGED
CRUST	FRIEND	KISS	PIMPLE	SOUGHT	WORM
CUDGEL	FRINGE	KNIGHT	QUEST	SPEAK	WORRY
CURSE	GALL	KNOT	RASCAL	SPOUSE	WRAP
DABBLE	GAZE	LABOR	RAKE	SPREAD	

BI-	CONVEX	FOLD	CO-	APPEAR	CHIN
ANNUAL	CORN	FORKED	ACT	ASSIST	COON
AXAL	CUSPID	GOT	ACTION	ASSUME	CREATE
AXIAL	DENTAL	LINEAR	ACTIVE	ATTEND	DEBTOR
CHROME	FACIAL	MANUAL	ADMIRE	ATTEST	DERIVE
COLOR	FOCAL	METAL	ADMIT	AUTHOR	EDITOR
			AGENCY	AXAL	EFFECT
			AGENT	CAIN	EMBODY
			ANNEX	CHAIR	EMPLOY

CO-
ENACT, ENURE, ENZYME, EQUAL, EQUATE, ERECT, EXERT, EXIST, EXTEND, FACTOR, HABIT, HOG, LESSEE, LESSOR, LOCATE, LOG, MAKER, MATE, MEDIAN, MEDIC, MET, NATION, PALM, PARENT, PASTOR, PATRON, PECK, PIED, PIER, PIES, PILOT, PIOUS, PLOT, REDEEM, REIGN, RING, ROTATE, SET, STAR, TENANT, TIDAL, TING, TYPE, UPON, WAGE, WARD, WINNER, WORKER

COL-
DISH, LAPSE, LARD, LATE, LET, LIES, LOP, ON

COM-
ATIC, BAT, BUST, FIT, FORT, MIX, MOVE, MUTE, PACT, PADRE, PARE, PART, PEER, PLAIN, PLIER, PLIES, PLOT, POSE, POST, POUND, PRESS, PRIZE

CON-
CAVE, DENSE, DOLE, DONE, DUCE, DUCT, FINE, FIRM, FLUX, FOCAL, FOUND, FRONT, FUSE, GLOBE, JOIN, JUROR, QUEST, SENT, SERVE, SIGN, SOLE, SORT, TACT, TEMPT, TEND, TENT, TEST, TEXT, TORT, TOUR, TRACT, TRAIL, TRITE, VENT, VERGE, VERSE, VEX

DE-
AIR, ASH, BARK, BASE, BIT, BONE, BRIEF, BRUISE, BUG, BUNK, BUT, BYE, CAMP, CANE, CANTER, CARE, CAY, CEASE, CENT, CIDER, CLAIM, CLASS, CODE, COLOR, COY, LAY, LEAD, LEGACY, LIGHT, LIME, LIST, LOUSE, MARK, MAST, MEAN, MERIT, MOB, MODE, MOUNT, NATURE, NOTE, PAINT, PART, PEND, PLOY, PLUME, POLISH, PORT, POSE, POT, PRESS, RAIL, RANGE, RAT, RAY, RIDE, SALT, SAND, SELECT, SERVE, SEX, SIGN, SILVER, SIRE, SPITE, SPOIL, SUGAR, SULFUR, TAIL, TENT, TEST, TESTER, TICK, TOUR, TRACT, TRAIN, VALUE, VEIN, VEST, VICE, VISE, VISOR, VOICE, VOID, VOTE, WAN, WATER, WAX, WOOL, WORM

DI-
ACID, ARIES, ATOM, BASIC, CAST, COT, DAPPER, OXIDE, PHASE, POLE, REST, VAN, VERSE, VEST, VINE, VISOR

DIA-	LOGIC	MINE	PHONE		
GRAM	METER	PAUSE	SPORE		
LIST					

DIS-	BUD	FAVOR	MISS	PROOF	TRACT
ABLE	CASE	FROCK	MOUNT	PROVE	TRAIN
ABUSE	CLAIM	GORGE	OBEY	QUIET	TRAIT
AGREE	CLOSE	GRACE	ORDER	ROBE	TRUST
ALLOW	COLOR	GUST	OWN	ROOT	UNION
ARM	CORD	HELM	PATCH	SAVE	UNITE
ARRAY	COUNT	JOIN	PLACE	SEIZE	UNITY
AVOW	COVER	LIKE	PLAY	SERVE	USE
BAND	CROWN	LODGE	PLUME	SOLVE	VALUE
BAR	CUSS	LOYAL	PORT	TASTE	YOKE
BOUND	EASE	MAST	POSE	TILL	
BOWEL	ENDOW	MAY	PRIZE	TORT	

EM-	BLAZE	BRACE	PLOY		
BANK	BODY	IRATE	POISON		
BARK	BORDER	MET	POWER		
BARRED	BOSOM	PALE	PRESS		
BATTLE	BOSS	PANEL	PRIZE		
BED	BOW	PLACE			
BITTER	BOWEL	PLANE			

EN-	CORE	GRAFT	NOBLER	SKY	TREAT
ABLE	CRUST	GRAIL	OUNCE	SLAVE	TREATY
ABLER	CRYPT	GRAIN	PLANE	SLAVER	TREE
ACT	CYST	GRAM	RAGE	SNARE	TRENCH
ACTIVE	DAMAGE	GRAVE	RAPT	SNARL	TRIES
ACTOR	DANGER	GRAVER	RAVISH	SOUL	TRUST
AMOUR	DIVE	GROSS	RICH	SPHERE	TRY
ATE	DOWER	GULF	RICHER	SUE	TWINE
CAGE	DUE	HALO	ROBE	SURE	TWIST
CAMP	FETTER	ISLE	ROLL	SURER	VENOM
CASE	FEVER	JAMBED	ROLLER	SWATHE	VIABLE
CASH	FIN	JOIN	ROLLING	TAIL	VISON
CHAIN	FLAME	JOY	ROOT	THRONE	WHEEL
CHANT	FOLD	KINDLE	SAMPLE	TIRE	WIND
CHASER	FOLDER	LACE	SCONCE	TITLE	WOMB
CIPHER	FORCE	LARGE	SCROLL	TOIL	WRAP
CIRCLE	FRAME	LARGER	SERF	TOMB	
CLASP	GENDER	LIST	SHEATH	TOPIC	
CLOSE	GIRDLE	LIVEN	SHRINE	TRAILS	
CLOSER	GLUT	MESH	SHROUD	TRANCE	
CODE	GORGE	NOBLE	SIGN	TRAP	

EX-	AMPLE	PLAIN	PULSE	TORT
ACT	ARCH	PLANT	SECT	TRACT
ACTION	CHANGE	PORT	TEND	
ACTOR	CITE	POSE	TENT	
ALTER	CLAIM	POUND	TOLL	
AMEN	HALE	PRESS	TOLLING	

FORE-	DATE	HAND	MILK	RUN	TIME
ARM	DECK	HEAD	MOST	SAID	TOP
BAY	DO	HOOF	NAME	SAIL	WARN
BEAR	DOOM	KNOW	NOON	SEE	WENT
BODE	FACE	LADY	PART	SEER	WORD
BODY	FEEL	LEG	PAST	SHOW	WORN
BOOM	FEND	LIMB	PAW	SIDE	YARD
BY	FOOT	LOCK	PEAK	SKIN	
BYE	GO	MAN	PLAY	STAY	
CAST	GUT	MAST	RANK	TELL	

HAY-	RACK	IL-
COCK	RIDE	LEGAL
FORK	SEED	LIQUID
LOFT	STACK	LOGIC
MAKER	WARD	
MOW	WIRE	

IM-	BOSOM	MODEST	PLANT	PORTER	PROPER
AGE	BROWN	MORAL	PLEAD	POSE	PROVE
AGING	BRUTE	PACT	PLEDGE	POSTER	PULSE
BALM	MANE	PAIN	PLIED	POTENT	PURE
BARK	MATURE	PAIR	PLIES	POUND	PURITY
BED	MERGE	PALE	PLY	POWER	
BITTER	MESH	PANEL	POLICY	PRESS	
BLAZE	MIX	PARITY	POLITE	PRINT	
BODY	MOBILE	PEACH	PORT	PRISON	

IN-	CAGE	CROSS	DOW	FARE	FORMER
ACTION	CASE	CRUST	DRAFT	FIELD	FRINGE
ACTIVE	CITE	CULT	DRAWN	FIRM'	FRUGAL
ARCH	CIVIL	CUR	DUCE	FIRMLY	FUSE
ARM	CLASP	CURVE	DUCT	FLAME	FUSION
BEING	CLIP	CUS	DUE	FLEXED	GATE
BOARD	CLOSE	DEED	EARTH	FLIGHT	GATHER
BORN	CLOSER	DENT	EDIBLE	FLOW	GOING
BOUND	COG	DEVOUT	EDITED	FLUENT	GOT
BOUNDS	COME	DIRECT	EQUITY	FLUX	GRAFT
BREED	COMING	DOCILE	EXACT	FOLD	GRAIN
BUILT	CORPSE	DOLE	EXPERT	FOLDER	GROUP
BURST	CREASE	DOOR	FAMOUS	FORM	GROWN
BYE	CREATE	DOORS	FANCY	FORMAL	GROWTH

GULF	MESH	SET	STALL	TENSE	VALID
HABIT	MOST	SETTER	STANCE	TENT	VENT
HALE	NERVE	SHEATH	STAR	THRONE	VEST
HAUL	POUR	SHORE	STATE	TIME	VIABLE
HUMAN	PUT	SHRINE	STEAD	TITLE	VITAL
HUMANE	QUEST	SIDE	STEP	TOMB	VOICE
JURY	QUIET	SIGHT	STILL	TONE	WALL
LACE	ROAD	SISTER	STROKE	TONER	WARD
LAID	RUSH	SNARE	SURE	TORT	WARDS
LAND	SANE	SOLE	SWATHE	TOWN	WEAVE
LAY	SANITY	SOLD	TACT	TREAT	WIND
LAYER	SCRIBE	SPAN	TAKE	TRENCH	WRAP
LET	SCROLL	SPHERE	TEND	TRUST	
LIER	SEAM	SPIRIT	TENDED	TWINE	
MATE	SECT	STABLE	TENDER	URBANE	

INTER-	MAL-	MICRO-
ACT	LARD	BAR
CUT	LOW	BUS
LAP	MY	
MIX	ODOR	
RING	POSED	
SEX	TIER	
TIE	TREAT	
WAR		

MIS-	COOK	FIT	LIVE	SAY	THROW
ADD	COPY	FORM	LODGE	SEAT	TIER
AGENT	COUNT	FRAME	LYING	SEND	TIME
AIM	CUE	GAUGE	MARK	SENSE	TITLE
ALLY	CUT	GIVE	MATCH	SHAPE	TOOK
ALTER	DATE	GRAFT	MATE	SHOD	TOUCH
APPLY	DEAL	GROW	MEET	SORT	TRACE
ASSAY	DEED	GUESS	MOVE	SOUND	TREAT
ATE	DEEM	GUIDE	NAME	SPACE	TRIAL
ATONE	DO	HEAR	PAGE	SPEAK	TRUST
AVER	DOER	HIT	PAINT	SPELL	TRYST
AWARD	DOING	INFER	PART	SPEND	TUNE
BEGIN	DONE	JOIN	PATCH	SPOKE	TUTOR
BEGOT	DOUBT	JUDGE	PEN	SPOKEN	TYPE
BIAS	DRAW	KEEP	PLACE	START	UNION
BILL	DRIVE	KNOW	PLEAD	STATE	USAGE
BIND	EASE	LABEL	POINT	STEER	USE
BRAND	EAT	LABOR	POISE	STEP	USER
BUILD	EDIT	LAIN	PRINT	STOP	VALUE
CALL	ENROLL	LAY	PRIZE	STYLE	WORD
CARRY	ENTER	LAYER	QUOTE	SUIT	WRITE
CAST	ENTRY	LEAD	RAISE	TAKE	YOKE
CHIEF	EVENT	LEARN	RATE	TAKER	
CLAIM	FAITH	LIE	READ	TEACH	
CLASS	FIELD	LIGHT	REFER	TEND	
COIN	FILE	LIKE	RELY	TERM	
COLOR	FIRE	LIT	RULE	THINK	

NON-	EQUAL	IDEAL	PAPAL	SLIP	TRUTH
ACID	EVENT	JUROR	PARTY	SOLAR	UNION
ADULT	FARM	LEGAL	PLUS	SOLID	URBAN
AGE	FAT	LIFE	POLAR	STICK	USE
BANK	FATAL	LOCAL	QUOTA	STOP	USER
BASIC	FLUID	MAN	RATED	SUCH	USING
BEING	FOCAL	METAL	RIGID	SUGAR	VIRAL
BOOK	FOOD	MONEY	RIVAL	SUIT	VOCAL
CASH	GAME	MORAL	ROYAL	TAX	VOTER
DAIRY	GREEN	NAVAL	RURAL	TIDAL	WHITE
ELECT	GUILT	OBESE	SENSE	TITLE	WOODY
EMPTY	HERO	OWNER	SKID	TOXIC	WOVEN
ENTRY	HUMAN	PAGAN	SKIER	TRUMP	ZERO

ORTHO-	COOL	HANG	LONG	RUN	TASK
TIC	COY	HARD	LOOK	SAD	TAX
	CRAM	HATE	LORD	SALE	THIN
OVER-	CROP	HAUL	LOUD	SALT	TIME
ABLE	DARE	HEAD	LOVE	SAVE	TIRE
ACT	DEAR	HEAP	LYING	SAW	TOIL
AGE	DECK	HEAR	MAN	SEA	TONE
ALL	DO	HEAT	MANY	SEAS	TOOK
APT	DOER	HIGH	MEEK	SEE	TOP
ARCH	DOSE	HOLD	MELT	SEED	TRIM
ARM	DRAW	HOLY	MEN	SEER	TURN
ATE	DRY	HOPE	MILD	SELL	URGE
AWE	DUE	HOT	MIX	SET	USE
BAKE	DYE	HUNG	MUCH	SEW	VIEW
BEAR	EASY	HUNT	NEAR	SHOE	VOTE
BET	EAT	IDLE	NEAT	SHOT	WARM
BID	FAR	JOY	NEW	SICK	WARY
BIG	FAST	JUST	NICE	SIDE	WEAK
BITE	FAT	KEEN	PASS	SIZE	WEAR
BLOW	FEAR	KILL	PAY	SLIP	WEEN
BOLD	FEED	KIND	PERT	SLOW	WET
BOOK	FILL	LAID	PLAY	SOAK	WIDE
BORE	FISH	LAIN	PLUS	SOFT	WILY
BORN	FLOW	LAND	PLY	SOLD	WIND
BORNE	FLY	LAP	RAN	SOON	WISE
BOUGHT	FOND	LATE	RANK	SOUL	WORD
BRED	FOUL	LAX	RASH	SPIN	WORE
BUSY	FREE	LAY	RATE	STAY	WORK
BUY	FULL	LEAF	RICH	STEP	WORN
CALL	GILD	LEAP	RIDE	STIR	WOUND
CAME	GIRD	LET	RIFE	SUP	WROUGHT
CAST	GLAD	LEWD	RIPE	SURE	ZEAL
COAT	GOAD	LIE	RODE	TAKE	
COLD	GROW	LIVE	RUDE	TAME	
COME	HAND	LOAD	RULE	TART	
COOK					

PAR-	LANCE	TIED	PARA	POST-	FACE
BOIL	LAY	TIES	DROP	AGE	FIX
DINE	RED	TON	FORM	ALLY	FORM
DONER	RIDGE	TOOK	PET	ANAL	HOLE
EVE	SING	VENUE	SANG	BAG	MAN
FLESH	SNIP	VISE	SHAH	BOX	MARK
FOCAL	SON		SITE	BOY	PAID
GET	TAKE		SOL	CARD	PONE
GO	TAKER		VANE	DATE	WAR
KING	TAN				

PRE-	BIND	DUSK	MEDIC	SCORE	TENSE
ACT	BLESS	ELECT	MEN	SELL	TEST
ADAPT	BOIL	ENACT	MIX	SENT	TEXT
ADMIT	BOUND	EXIST	MOLAR	SERVE	TREAT
ADOPT	CAST	FACE	NAME	SET	UNION
ADULT	CENT	FIX	NATAL	SHAPE	UNITE
AGED	CHECK	FOCUS	PACK	SHOW	VENT
ALLOT	CHILL	FORM	PAID	SIDE	VIEW
AMBLE	CITED	FRANK	PARE	SIFT	VISE
AMP	CLEAN	GAME	PAY	SOAK	VISOR
ANAL	COOK	HEAT	PLACE	SOLD	WAR
ARM	COOL	HUMAN	PLAN	STAMP	WARM
AVER	CURE	JUDGE	PLANT	TASTE	WARN
AXIAL	DATE	LEGAL	PRINT	TAX	WASH
BEND	DAWN	LIMIT	PUNCH	TEEN	WRAP
BILL	DIAL	MAN	SAGE	TEND	

PRO-	GRADE	PANE	STYLE
BAND	GRAM	PHASE	TEASE
CARP	JET	PONE	TEND
CLAIM	LABOR	POSE	TEST
CURE	LAPSE	PYLON	TRACT
DUCE	LATE	RATE	UNION
FILE	LEG	ROGUE	VIRUS
FIT	LONG	SECT	WAR
FOUND	MOTE	SING	
FUSE	NOUN	STATE	

RE-	ADORN	ASSAIL	BIRTH	BUTTON	CLASP
ACTIVE	AFFIX	ASSORT	BLOOM	CALL	CLEAN
ACTOR	AGENT	ASSUME	BOIL	CANE	CLOTHE
ABSORB	ALLOT	ATTACH	BOP	CAP	COAL
ACCEDE	ALTER	ATTACK	BRANCH	CARRY	COCK
ACCENT	ANNEX	ATTAIN	BUFF	CAST	CODIFY
ACCEPT	ANOINT	AWAKE	BURIAL	CHANGE	COIL
ACCUSE	ARGUE	AWAKEN	BURY	CHART	COIN
ADAPT	AROUSE	BAIT	BUS	CHOOSE	COLOR
ADD	ASCEND	BID	BUT	CLAD	COMMIT
ADDICT	ASCENT	BIND	BUTTING	CLAIM	CONVEY

RE- *(cont.)*

COOK	EVOKE	GROOVE	LEND	PURIFY	STACK
CORD	EXPEL	GORGE	LETTER	PURSUE	STRIKE
CROWN	EXPORT	HAMMER	LINE	QUITE	STRUCK
CURVE	FALL	HANDLE	LIST	RISE	STRUNG
DATE	FEED	HANG	LIT	ROLL	STUDY
DEAR	FELL	HARDEN	LOAN	ROLLER	STUFF
DEEM	FLEX	HEAR	MAIL	SAID	SUMMON
DEFEAT	FIGHT	HEARSE	MANNED	SAIL	SUPPLY
DEFY	FILTER	HEEL	MAP	SALUTE	TAILOR
DEMAND	FIND	HEM	MARQUE	SAW	TASTE
DIRECT	FIRE	HINGE	MEMBER	SAY	TIME
DIVIDE	FLEW	HOUSE	MEET	SCREEN	TINT
DOCK	FLIES	HUNG	MEND	SCRIPT	TITLE
DRAW	FLOW	IMAGE	MERGE	SEAT	TRIM
DRIED	FLOWER	IMPORT	MET	SEE	TUNE
DRIES	FLY	IMPOSE	MOLD	SEEK	TWIST
DRILL	FORGE	INCITE	MOTION	SEEN	TYING
DRIVE	FOUGHT	INDEX	NATURE	SEIZE	UTTER
DRY	FOUND	INDUCE	OBJECT	SEND	VEST
DYE	FRONT	INFORM	OIL	SEW	VOICE
EARN	FUSE	INJURE	OPPOSE	SHIP	WAKE
ECHO	GAUGE	INSERT	PACIFY	SHOW	WAN
EDIT	GAVE	INTER	PASS	SIFT	WEIGH
EJECT	GEAR	INVENT	PEOPLE	SILVER	WELD
EMBARK	GILD	INVITE	PERK	SIZE	WIN
EMBODY	GIVE	INVOKE	PIN	SMELT	WOKE
EMERGE	GLAZE	JUDGE	PLAN	SMOOTH	WOKEN
EMIT	GLOSS	KEY	PLATE	SOLD	WON
ENDOW	GLOW	KNIT	PLEDGE	SOLDER	WROUGHT
ENJOY	GRADE	LABEL	PLUNGE	SOUGHT	ZONE
EQUIP	GRAFT	LACE	POWER	SPELL	
ERECT	GREW	LAPSE	PRICE	SPREAD	
	GRIND	LEARN	PROBE	SPRING	

SEMI-

ARID	DEAF	HOBO	RAW
BALD	DOME	LOG	SOFT
COMA	GALA	MUTE	TONE
	HIGH	NUDE	WILD

SUB-

ABBOT	BASS	DUCT	GUM	ORDER	SOLAR
ACID	BED	DUE	HEAD	OVAL	SONIC
ACRID	BREED	ECHO	HUMAN	OXIDE	STAGE
ACUTE	CAUSE	EDIT	HUMID	PAR	TEND
ADULT	CELL	ENTRY	IDEA	POLAR	TONIC
AGENT	CLAN	ERECT	INDEX	RACE	TOPIC
AREA	CLASS	FIELD	JOIN	RING	TRIBE
ARID	CLERK	FIX	LEVEL	RULE	TUNIC
ATOM	DEAN	FLOOR	LIME	SECT	URBAN
AXIAL	DEPOT	FLUID	NASAL	SHAFT	VOCAL
BASE	DUAL	GRADE	OPTIC	SHRUB	ZONE
	DUCE	GROUP	ORAL	SOIL	

SUPER-	TRANS-	TRI-	PART	SOME	ULTRA-
ADD	ACT	METER	PHASE	STATE	RED
JET	SECT	MOTOR	PLANE	UNITY	
LIE	FIX	OXIDE	POD	VALVE	
SEX		PACK	SECT		

UN-	BROKE	EARTH	HEROIC	NOISY	ROUGH
ABATED	BUILD	EDIBLE	HEWN	NOTED	ROUND
ABUSED	BUNDLE	ENVIED	HIP	OILED	ROVE
ACTED	BURIED	ERASED	HIRED	ORNATE	ROVEN
AGED	BURNT	EVADED	HOOD	OWNED	RUSHED
AGEING	CAKE	EXOTIC	HOPED	PAGED	SALTED
AGILE	CANDID	EXPERT	HOUSE	PAIRED	SAVED
AGING	CASE	FADED	HUNG	PARTED	SAY
AIMED	CAUGHT	FADING	HUSK	PAYING	SEAM
AIRED	CAUSED	FAITH	IDEAL	PEG	SEIZED
ALLIED	CHANCY	FALLEN	JOYFUL	PEOPLE	SEW
ANCHOR	CHARGE	FANCY	KENNEL	PILE	SEXUAL
ANELED	CHARY	FENCE	KINGLY	PITIED	SHADED
APT	CHASTE	FEARED	KNIT	PLACED	SHARED
APTLY	CHIC	FED	LEAD	PLIANT	SHARP
ARGUED	CHOKE	FELT	LEASED	PLOWED	SHED
ARTFUL	CHURCH	FILIAL	LED	POETIC	SHELL
ATONED	CLENCH	FILMED	LETHAL	POISED	SHIFT
AVOWED	CLINCH	FIRED	LET	POLLED	SHIP
AWARE	CLOAK	FITLY	LETTED	POSED	SHRUNK
AWED	CLOSE	FIX	LEVEL	POSTED	SHUT
BACKED	CLOUD	FLEXED	LEVIED	PRETTY	SICKER
BAKED	CLOYED	FOLDER	LIMBER	PRICED	SIGHT
BAR	COATED	FORCED	LIVE	PRIMED	SILENT
BARBED	COCK	FORGOT	LIVELY	PRIZED	SINFUL
BASED	COFFIN	FORKED	LOBED	PROBED	SLAKED
BATED	COIL	FREE	MAKER	PRUNED	SLING
BEAR	COMELY	FROCK	MAN	PUCKER	SOAKED
BELIEF	COMIC	FUNNY	MAPPED	PURGED	SOBER
BELT	CREATE	FUSED	MARRED	PUZZLE	SOLID
BEND	CROWN	GALLED	MASKER	QUIET	SORTED
BID	CURED	GENIAL	MATED	RAISED	SOUGHT
BIDDEN	CURSED	GIFTED	MATTED	RANKED	SOURED
BIND	DAMPED	GLAZED	MEANT	RAZED	SOWN
BITTED	DARING	GOT	MEET	READY	SPEAK
BLAMED	DECKED	GOTTEN	MELLOW	REASON	SPHERE
BLEST	DENIED	GOWNED	MENDED	REELER	SPOILT
BLOODY	DEVOUT	GRACED	MET	REEVE	SPRUNG
BODIED	DIMMED	GRADED	MEW	RENT	SPUN
BONED	DOCK	GREEDY	MILLED	REPAIR	STABLY
BONNET	DOER	HAILED	MIXT	RESTED	STEEL
BOSOM	DOUBLE	HAIR	MODISH	RHYMED	STEP
BOWED	DREAMT	HALLOW	MOLTEN	RIFLED	STICK
BOX	DRIED	HALVED	MORAL	RIG	STOP
BRACE	DRUNK	HASTY	MOVING	RIMED	STRESS
BRED	DULLED	HEALED	MOWN	RISEN	STUNG
BREECH	DYED	HELM	NEEDED	ROOF	SUBTLE

UN- *(cont.)*	THINK	VEXED	WARMED	WILLED	WORKED
SUNK	TILLED	VIABLE	WARNED	WINDER	WORN
SWATHE	TILTED	VOCAL	WARPED	WISDOM	WRUNG
SWEAR	TRUSTY	VOICE	WEANED	WISH	
SWAYED	TUNE	WALLED	WEIGHT	WIT	
TAGGED	TUFTED	WARIER	WEPT	WON	
TAKEN	VARIED	WARIEST	WETTED	WOODED	
TEACH	VEINED	WARILY	WIFELY	WOOED	

UNI-	FACE	VERSE
AXIAL	FORM	VOCAL
COLOR	SEX	
CORN	SON	
CYCLE	VALVE	

UP-	DIVE	LAND	SEND	THROW
BEAR	DRY	LANDER	SETTER	TILT
BEARER	FIELD	LEAP	SHIFT	TIME
BIND	FLOW	LIGHT	SOAR	TOWNER
BOIL	FOLD	PILE	SPRING	TREND
BORE	GATHER	PITY	STAIR	WAFT
BUILD	GAZE	PROP	STARE	WELL
BYE	GOING	RAISE	STATER	
CAST	GROWTH	RAISER	STEP	
CHUCK	HEAP	ROOTER	STIR	
CLIMB	HEAVER	ROSE	STOOD	
CURL	HOARD	ROUSE	SWEEP	
DATER	HOLDER	RUSH	TEAR	

Suffixes

The criteria for an acceptable Scrabble® suffix is:

1. No letter can be dropped when adding the suffix.

2. The suffix, in most cases, does not have a meaning of its own.

3. The use of the suffix changes the meaning of the base or root word or converts it to another part of speech.

The following are acceptable suffixes:

ABLE	EER	IBLE	KIN	RY
AGE	EN	IE/Y	LER	SHIP
AL	ER	IER	LESS	SOME
AN	ERY	ING	LET	STER
ANCE	ESE	ISH	LIKE	TH
ATION	ESS	ISM	LING	ULE
CLE	ETTE	IST	LY	WARD
CY	FOLD	ITIS	MENT	WAYS
DOM	FUL	ITY	NESS	WISE
ED	GRAPHER	IVE	OCK	Y
EE	HOOD	IZE	OUS	

-ABLE
AGREE
BREAK
DETECT
EAT
EXCHANGE
IMPRESSION
PREFER
READ
TREASON
UNDER-
STAND

-AGE
ACRE
CART
CELLAR
HERMIT
ORPHAN
PACK
PEER
STOP
VICAR

-AL
BESTOW
BETROTH
COAST
EDUCATION
FICTION
MUSIC
OCCASION
PROVISION
RENEW
WITHDRAW

-AN
REPUBLIC

-ANCE
FORBEAR
FURTHER
UTTER

-ATION
BOTHER
FLIRT
SEDIMENT

-CLE
MONO
UN

-CY
BANKRUPT
CAPTAIN
CHAPLAIN
COLONEL
NORMAL

-DOM
BORE
DUKE
EARL
FILM
HEATHEN
MARTYR
OFFICIAL
SAVAGE
VILLA

-ED
BOOT
LAND
MONEY
TALENT
ROOT
UMBRELLA
WOOD

-EE
BIOGRAPH
MURDER
TEST
TOWN
STAND

-EER
AUCTION
PAMPHLET
SLOGAN
SONNET

-EN
BLACK
DARK
DEEP
EARTH
FAST
FRIGHT
GOLD
HARD
LENGTH
MOIST
SHORT
SILK
WOOD

-ER
FOREIGN
HEAD
HUNT
PAINT
TROT

-ERY
BREW
COOK
DEAN
FISH
FOOL
ROOK

-ESE
JOURNAL
TRANSLA-
TION

-ESS
AUTHOR
COUNT
MURDER

-ETTE
CELLAR
FLANNEL
KITCHEN
LEADER
SERMON

-FOLD
TWO
TEN
THOUSAND

-FUL
FORGET
HAND

-GRAPHER
PHOTO
TELE

-HOOD
BACHELOR
FALSE
FATHER
NEIGHBOR
PRIEST

-IBLE	-IER	-ISH		-ISM	-IST
CONVERT	HOTEL	AMATEUR	GIRL	ALCOHOL	BALLOON
DISCERN		BOOK	GREEN	BARBAR	COLON
	-ING	BOY	HELL	DESPOT	COPY
-IE/Y	INN	CHILD	POP	HERO	NOVEL
DEAR	OFF	FEVER	SELF	IMPERIAL	ROYAL
HANK	OUT	DEVIL		PARALLEL	SAD
NIGHT	SACK	FOOL		PATRIOT	VIOLIN
	SHIRT			IMPERIAL	
	SKIRT				

-ITY	-IVE	-IZE	-KIN	-LESS	
COMICAL	ATTRACT	CIVIL	LAMB	CEASE	DOUBT
HISTORIC	POSSESS	FAMILIAR	MUNCH	COUNT	NUMBER
SENTI-	PRODUCT	LEGAL		FEAR	TAME
MENTAL	INSTINCT	MATERIAL	-LER	LIFE	TIRE
		NATIONAL	CUT		
		PATRON			
		SOBER			

-LET	IS	-LIKE	-LING	-LY	KING
ARM	KING	CHILD	CAT	COWARD	LEISURE
BOOK	LEAF	GENTLE-	NURSE	DEAD	LIVE
CAB	NECK	MAN	PRINCE	EARTH	LOVE
EYE	OWE	GOD	SAP	GENTLE-	MAN
FLAT	RING	LADY	SEED	MAN	MASTER
		SPORTS-	UNDER	GREAT	MONTH
		MAN		HEAVEN	SCHOLAR
				KIND	USUAL

-MENT	-NESS	-OCK	-RY	-SHIP	-SOME
ARRANGE	DIVINE	BULL	CHEMIST	AUTHOR	BURDEN
BEWILDER	DRUNKEN	HILL	DRUDGE	CENSOR	FEAR
EMPLOY	GOOD		NURSE	FELLOW	LONE
ENDOW	HARSH	-OUS	PEASANT	FRIEND	QUARREL
EN-	KIND	DANGER	RIVAL	HARD	TIRE
LIGHTEN	PREPARED	MOUNTAIN	YEOMAN	LADY	TROUBLE
REFRESH	SWEET	MURDER		MEMBER	
SHIP	WICKED	THUNDER		SCHOLAR	
TREAT				TOWN	

-STER	-TH	-ULE	-WARD	HOME
GAME	FOUR	NOD	BACK	LAND
PUNT	HUNDRED		DOWN	ON
SPEED	SIX		EAST	UP
SPIN	THIRTEEN		FOR	
TAP	THOUSAND		HEAVEN	
TRICK				

-WAYS	-WISE	-Y
LENGTH	CLOCK	EARTH
NO	LENGTH	CHOOSE
SIDE	CRAB	CRAFT
	LIKE	FISH
	NO	SLANG
	OTHER	WOODS
	POKER	

PLURALS

Pluralization can create some of the most spirited disagreements in a Scrabble® game. Keep in mind that a plural may sound new and unusual to you and may even be omitted from some dictionaries, but if the rules are followed you should have little difficulty claiming the rights to use the plural.

1. Most nouns become plural with the addition of "s" or "es."

2. If pluralization requires the removal of a letter or letters or the addition of an apostrophe, under Scrabble® rules the plural cannot be made.

3. Most exceptions to the rules are listed in the dictionary. Here are a few:

OX-	EN
CHILD-	REN
LARVA-	E
TABLEAU-	X
MORCEAU-	X
CHERUB-	IM
ANTENNA-	E
FORMULA-	E
NEBULA-	E
ALGA-	E
ALUMNA-	E
PLATEAU-	X
BUREAU-	X
ADIEU-	X
KIBBUTZ-	IM

Quick-Check Usage Guide

This section lists all the official Scrabble® words that fall into one of eight major categories of special knowledge:

Animal

Computer

Legal

Medical

Military

Nautical

Performing Arts

Sports

Players using an unusual word in one of these categories need only provide the subject or category (very often a precise definition is not known even by the individual playing the word) and in a very few seconds, using the Quick-Check Usage Guide, the authenticity of the word can be verified. The Quick-Check Usage Guide can also be used to review your knowledge of the specific terms in the specific fields provided.

ANIMALS

AARDVARK	ANT	BASENJI	BLUEFIN	BRIT	CALVES
AARDWOLF	ANTBEAR	BASILISK	BLUEFISH	BROCK	CAMEL
AASVOGEL	ANTEATER	BASS	BLUEGILL	BROCKET	CANARY
ABALONE	ANTELOPE	BASSET	BLUEHEAD	BRONC	CANID
ABOMA	ANTLION	BATFISH	BLUEJAY	BRONCHO	CANINE
ACALEPH	ANURAN	BAUDRONS	BLUETICK	BRONCO	CAPELAN
ACALEPHE	AOUDAD	BAWTIE	BOA	BROOKIE	CAPELIN
ACARID	APHID	BAWTY	BOAR	BRUIN	CAPLIN
ACARIDAN	APHIDIAN	BAY	BOARFISH	BRULOT	CAPON
ACARINE	APHIS	BAYARD	BOATBILL	BRUMBY	CAPUCHIN
ACARUS	APOD	BEAGLE	BOBCAT	BRYOZOAN	CAPYBARA
ACCENTOR	APTERYX	BEARCAT	BOBOLINK	BUBAL	CARABAO
ACRODONT	ARACHNID	BEAST	BOBWHITE	BUBALE	CARABID
ACTINIA	ARANEID	BEASTIE	BOCACCIO	BUCK	CARACAL
ACTINIAN	ARAPAIMA	BEAVER	BOLLWORM	BUDGIE	CARACARA
ADDAX	ARGALA	BEDBUG	BOMBYCID	BUDWORM	CARACUL
ADDER	ARGALI	BEE	BOMBYX	BUFFALO	CARANGID
AEDES	ARGONAUT	BEEF	BONACI	BULBUL	CARASSOW
AGAMA	ARGUS	BEEFALO	BONEFISH	BULL	CARBORA
AGOUTI	ARIEL	BEETLE	BONGO	BULLBAT	CARCAJOU
AGOUTY	ARMYWORM	BEHEMOTH	BONITA	BULLDOG	CARCASE
AI	ASCARID	BELLBIRD	BONITO	BULLFROG	CARCASS
AIVER	ASCARIS	BELUGA	BONTEBOK	BULLHEAD	CARDINAL
ALAN	ASCIDIAN	BENTHOS	BOOBY	BULLOCK	CARIBE
ALAND	ASP	BERNICLE	BOOKLICE	BUNNY	CARIBOU
ALANT	ASPIC	BETTA	BOOKWORM	BUNTING	CARP
ALATE	ASPIS	BEVY	BORZOI	BURBOT	CARRION
ALBACORE	ASS	BHARAL	BOSCHBOK	BURRO	CASEWORM
ALBICORE	AUDAD	BIDDY	BOSHBOK	BUSHBUCK	CATALO
ALCID	AUK	BIGEYE	BOSHVARK	BUSHGOAT	CATBIRD
ALDERFLY	AUKLET	BIGFOOT	BOSSY	BUSHPIG	CATFISH
ALEC	AUROCHS	BIGHORN	BOTFLY	BUSHTIT	CATTALO
ALEVIN	AVADAVAT	BILLBUG	BOUQUET	BUSTARD	CATTLE
ALEWIFE	AVIAN	BILLFISH	BOUVIER	BUT	CAVALLA
ALIPED	AVIFAUNA	BIPAROUS	BOVID	BUTEO	CAVALLY
ALPACA	AVOCET	BIPED	BOVINE	BUZZARD	CAVEFISH
AMADAVAT	AVOSET	BISON	BOWFIN		CAVIES
AMEBA	AXIS	BITTERN	BOWHEAD	CABEZON	CAVY
AMIA	AXOLOTL	BIVALVE	BOXER	CABEZONE	CAYMAN
AMMOCETE		BLACKCAP	BOXFISH	CABRILLA	CAYUSE
AMMONITE	BABIRUSA	BLACKFIN	BRACH	CACHALOT	CAZIQUE
AMPHIBIA	BABOON	BLACKFLY	BRACHET	CACIQUE	CEBID
AMPHIPOD	BACALAO	BLAUBOK	BRACONID	CACOMIXL	CEBOID
ANABAS	BALE	BLEAK	BRAHMA	CADELLE	CERASTES
ANABLEPS	BALISAUR	BLENNY	BRAIZE	CAGELING	CERCARIA
ANACONDA	BANDOG	BLESBOK	BRANT	CAHOW	CERO
ANCHOVY	BANGTAIL	BLESBUCK	BRANTAIL	CAIMAN	CETACEAN
ANHINGA	BANTAM	BLOODFIN	BREAM	CALAMAR	CETE
ANI	BANTENG	BLOWFISH	BRENT	CALAMARI	CETOLOGY
ANNELID	BANTY	BLOWFLY	BRIARD	CALAMARY	CHACMA
ANOA	BARBET	BLUEBILL	BRILL	CALF	CHAFER
ANOLE	BARNACLE	BLUEBIRD	BRISLING	CALICO	CHALCID

CHAMOIS	COCKATOO	CRAWFISH	DESMAN	DUROC	EWE
CHARACID	COCKEREL	CRAYFISH	DESTRIER		EYAS
CHARACIN	COCKLE	CREEPER	DEVON	EAGLE	EYRA
CHARGER	COD	CREODONT	DHOLE	EAGLET	
CHARR	CODFISH	CREVALLE	DIDAPPER	EARWIG	FALCON
CHAT	COHO	CRICETID	DIKDIK	EARWORM	FALCONET
CHEBEC	COHOG	CRICKET	DINGO	EBBET	FALLFISH
CHEETAH	COLIES	CRINITE	DINOSAUR	ECHIDNA	FATBACK
CHEGOE	COLIN	CRINOID	DIPLOPOD	ECHINOID	FATBIRD
CHETAH	COLLIE	CRITTER	DIPNOAN	ECHINUS	FATLING
CHEWINK	COLOBUS	CRITTUR	DIPPER	ECOTYPE	FATSTOCK
CHICK	COLONY	CROAKER	DIPTERA	ECTOZOAN	FAUNA
CHIGETAI	COLT	CROC	DIPTERAN	ECTOZOON	FAWN
CHIGGER	COLUBRID	CROPPIE	DIPTERON	EDENTATE	FEIST
CHIGOE	COLUGO	CROW	DISCUS	EEL	FELID
CHILOPOD	COLY	CRUCIAN	DISTOME	EELPOUT	FELINE
CHIMAERA	COMATULA	CRUMMIE	DOBBIN	EELWORM	FENNEC
CHIMP	CONCH	CUB	DOBSON	EFT	FERRET
CHINCH	CONDOR	CUCKOO	DODO	EGGER	FIGEATER
CHIPMUCK	CONENOSE	CUDDY	DOE	EGRET	FILARIA
CHIPMUNK	CONEPATE	CULCH	DOGEY	EIDER	FILARIID
CHIRO	CONEPATL	CULEX	DOGFISH	ELAND	FILEFISH
CHITAL	CONEY	CULICID	DOGGY	ELAPHINE	FILLIES
CHOOK	CONGER	CULICINE	DOGIE	ELAPID	FILLY
CHORDATE	CONGO	CULVER	DOGIES	ELAPINE	FINBACK
CHOUGH	CONY	CUNNER	DOGY	ELATER	FINCH
CHROMIDE	COON	CUR	DOLPHIN	ELATERID	FINFISH
CHUB	COOT	CURASSOW	DOMINICK	ELATERID	FINFOOT
CHUCKY	COOTER	CURCULIO	DONKEY	ELEPHANT	FIREBIRD
CHUKAR	COOTIE	CURLEW	DOR	ELK	FIREBRAT
CICADA	COPEPOD	CURTAL	DORADO	ELKHOUND	FIREFLY
CICALA	COQUINA	CUSCUS	DORBUG	ELVER	FIREWORM
CICHLID	CORAL	CUSHAT	DORHAWK	EMEU	FISHER
CIMEX	CORBIE	CUSK	DORMICE	EMMET	FISHWORM
CIRRIPED	CORBINA	CUTWORM	DORMOUSE	EMU	FISSIPED
CISCO	CORBY	CYCLOPS	DORPER	EMYD	FITCH
CIVET	CORGI	CYGNET	DOTTEREL	EMYDE	FITCHET
CLAM	CORSAC	CYPRINID	DOTTREL	ENDAMEBA	FITCHEW
CLAMWORM	CORVINA		DOVE	ENTAMEBA	FLAMINGO
CLERID	COUGAR	DABCHICK	DOVEKEY	ENTELLUS	FLATFISH
CLOWDER	COURLAN	DACE	DOVEKIE	EOHIPPUS	FLATHEAD
CLUMBER	COVERT	DAKERHEN	DRAGON	EPIFAUNA	FLATWORM
CLUPEID	COVEY	DAMAN	DRAGONET	EQUID	FLEA
CLUPEOID	COW	DANIO	DRAKE	EQUINE	FLICKER
COALA	COWBIRD	DAPHNIA	DRILL	ERGATE	FLIGHT
COALFISH	COWFISH	DARTER	DRONE	ERMINE	FLOCK
COATI	COYDOG	DASSIE	DRONGO	ERN	FLOUNDER
COB	COYOTE	DASYURE	DROVE	ERNE	FLUKE
COBB	COYPOU	DAYFLY	DRUMFISH	ESCARGOT	FOAL
COBIA	COYPU	DEALATE	DUCK	ESCOLAR	FOOLFISH
COBRA	CRAB	DEALFISH	DUCKBILL	ETHOLOGY	FORAM
COCCID	CRAKE	DECAPOD	DUCKLING	EUGLENA	FOSSA
COCHIN	CRANE	DEER	DUGONG	EULACHAN	FOSSETTE
COCK	CRAPPIE	DEERFLY	DUIKER	EULACHON	FOWL
COCKAPOO	CRAWDAD	DENTALIA	DUNLIN	EURYBATH	FOXFISH

FOXHOUND	GLOWWORM	GUACHARO	HEXAPOD	JABIRU	KITE
FROGFISH	GNAT	GUAN	HIND	JACAMAR	KITLING
FUGU	GNU	GUANACO	HINNY	JACANA	KITTEN
FULMAR	GOA	GUANAY	HIPPO	JACK	KITTY
	GOANNA	GUENON	HIVE	JACKAL	KIWI
GADFLY	GOAT	GUITGUIT	HOATZIN	JACKAROO	KNOT
GADID	GOATFISH	GULL	HOG	JACKASS	KOALA
GADOID	GOBBLER	GUNDOG	HOGFISH	JACKDAW	KOB
GADWALL	GOBIES	GUNNEL	HOGG	JACKEROO	KOEL
GAGGLE	GOBIOID	GUPPY	HOGGET	JACKFISH	KOI
GALAGO	GOBY	GURNARD	HOGNOSE	JACOBIN	KOKANEE
GALAH	GODWIT	GURNET	HOLIBUT	JAEGER	KOLINSKI
GALLFLY	GOLDBUG	GWEDUC	HOLSTEIN	JAGUAR	KOLINSKY
GAM	GOLDEYE	GWEDUCK	HOMINOID	JAVELINA	KOMONDOR
GAMBUSIA	GOLDFISH		HONEYBEE	JAY	KOODOO
GAMECOCK	GOONEY	HABU	HOODIE	JAYBIRD	KORAT
GAMODEME	GOOSE	HACKEE	HOOKWORM	JENNET	KOUPREY
GANDER	GOPHER	HADDOCK	HOOPOE	JENNY	KRAIT
GANG	GORAL	HAGDON	HOPTOAD	JERBOA	KRILL
GANNET	GORCOCK	HAGFISH	HORNBILL	JEWFISH	KUDU
GANOID	GORHEN	HAGGARD	HORNET	JOCKO	KUVASZ
GAPEWORM	GORILLA	HAIRWORM	HORNPOUT	JOEY	
GAR	GOSHAWK	HAKE	HORNTAIL	JUMBUCK	LABRADOR
GARFISH	GOSLING	HALFBEAK	HORNWORM	JUNCO	LABROID
GARGANEY	GOURAMI	HALIBUT	HORSEFLY	JUREL	LACERTID
GARPIKE	GRACKLE	HAMLET	HOST		LACEWING
GARRON	GRAMPUS	HAMSTER	HOTBLOOD	KABELJOU	LADYBIRD
GATOR	GRANDDAM	HANGBIRD	HOUND	KAE	LADYBUG
GAUR	GRAYBACK	HANGNEST	HOUSEFLY	KAGU	LADYFISH
GAVIAL	GRAYFISH	HANUMAN	HOWLER	KAKA	LAKER
GAYAL	GRAYLAG	HARE	HOWLET	KAKAPO	LAMB
GAZELLE	GRAYLING	HARIANA	HUSK	KALONG	LAMBER
GECKO	GREBE	HARRIER	HUSKY	KANGAROO	LAMBIE
GED	GREENBUG	HART	HYDRA	KARAKUL	LAMBKIN
GEESE	GREENFLY	HATTERIA	HYENA	KATYDID	LAMPREY
GELADA	GREENLET	HAUSEN	HYLA	KEA	LAMPYRID
GELDING	GREYHEN	HAWFINCH	HYRACOID	KEESHOND	LANCELET
GEMSBOK	GREYLAG	HAWK	HYRAX	KEET	LANGSHAN
GEMSBUCK	GRIBBLE	HAWKBILL		KEITLOA	LANGUR
GENET	GRIFFIN	HAWKEY	IBEX	KELEP	LANNER
GENTOO	GRIFFON	HAWKIE	IBIS	KELPFISH	LANNERET
GEODUCK	GRILSE	HAWKMOTH	IGUANA	KELPIE	LAPDOG
GERBIL	GRISON	HAZELHEN	IGUANIAN	KENNEL	LAPIN
GERBILLE	GRIVET	HEADFISH	IMAGO	KERRY	LAPWING
GERENUK	GRIZZLY	HEDGEHOG	IMPALA	KESTREL	LARK
GHARIAL	GROSBEAK	HEDGEPIG	INCHWORM	KIANG	LARVA
GIBBON	GROUPER	HEIFER	INCONNU	KID	LAUNCE
GILT	GROUSE	HELLERI	INDRI	KILLDEE	LAVEROCK
GILTHEAD	GRUB	HELMINTH	INFAUNA	KILLDEER	LAVROCK
GIRAFFE	GRUBWORM	HEMIPTER	INFAUNAL	KILLIE	LEAFWORM
GLED	GRUIFORM	HEN	INSECT	KINE	LEAP
GLEDE	GRUMPHIE	HERD	ISOPOD	KINGBIRD	LECHWE
GLIDER	GRUMPHY	HERN	ISOPODAN	KINGFISH	LEECH
GLOSSINA	GRUNION	HERON	IXODID	KINGLET	LEMMING
GLOWFLY	GRUNT	HERRING		KINKAJOU	LEMUR

LEMUROID	MALEMIUT	METAZOON	MUDFISH	NILGHAI	OUSEL
LEOPARD	MALEMUTE	MEW	MUDPUPPY	NILGHAU	OUZEL
LEPORID	MALLARD	MICE	MUGGER	NOCTUID	OVENBIRD
LEVERET	MAMBA	MIDGE	MULE	NOCTULE	OVIBOS
LIGER	MAMMAL	MILKFISH	MULEY	NOTORNIS	OVINE
LIMPET	MAMMOTH	MILLIPED	MULLET	NUMBAT	OVIPARA
LIMPKIN	MANAKIN	MILTER	MULTIPED	NUMBFISH	OWL
LIMULOID	MANATEE	MINK	MUNGOOSE	NUTHATCH	OWLET
LIMULUS	MANDRILL	MINKE	MUNTJAC	NUTRIA	OWSE
LINGCOD	MANGABEY	MINNOW	MUNTJAK	NYALA	OWSEN
LINNET	MANGABY	MINNY	MURAENID	NYLGHAI	OX
LINSANG	MANTA	MINORCA	MUREX	NYLGHAU	OXEN
LION	MANTES	MISSEL	MURICES		OXPECKER
LIONESS	MANTID	MITE	MURID	OARFISH	OYSTER
LIONFISH	MANTIS	MOA	MURINE	OBELIA	
LIZARD	MARABOU	MOGGIE	MURR	OCELOT	PACA
LLAMA	MARABOUT	MOGGY	MURRE	OCELOID	PACER
LOACH	MARE	MOJARRA	MURRELET	OCTOPI	PACK
LOBEFIN	MARGAY	MOKE	MURRY	OCTOPOD	PADNAG
LOBO	MARKHOOR	MOL	MUSCA	OCTOPUS	PAGURIAN
LOBSTER	MARKHOR	MOLA	MUSCOVY	ODONATE	PAGURID
LOCUST	MARLIN	MOLDWARP	MUSKIE	OILBIRD	PALFREY
LONGHORN	MARMOSET	MOLE	MUSKRAT	OKAPI	PALOMINO
LONGSPUR	MARMOT	MOLLIE	MUSPIKE	OLDSQUAW	PANCHAX
LOOKDOWN	MARTEN	MOLLIES	MUSQUASH	OLDWIFE	PANDA
LOON	MARTIN	MOLLUSC	MUSSEL	OLDWIVES	PANFISH
LORICATE	MARTLET	MOLLUSK	MUSTANG	OMNIVORA	PANGOLIN
LORIES	MASTIFF	MOLLY	MUSTER	OMNIVORE	PANTHER
LORIKEET	MASTODON	MOLOCH	MUTT	ONAGER	PAPILLON
LORIS	MAVERICK	MONGEESE	MYNA	ONAGRI	PARAKEET
LORY	MAVIE	MONGOOSE	MYNAH	OOLACHAN	PARAQUET
LOTTE	MAVIS	MONGREL	MYRIAPOD	OPAH	PARAZOAN
LOUSE	MAYFLY	MONITOR	MYRIOPOD	OPHIDIAN	PARD
LOVEBIRD	MEALWORM	MONKFISH	MYSID	OPOSSUM	PARGO
LOVEBUG	MEALYBUG	MONOPODE		OPPOSSUM	PAROQUET
LUCE	MEASLE	MOONEYE	NAG	OQUASSA	PARR
LUGWORM	MEDAKA	MOONFISH	NARWAL	ORANG	PARROKET
LUMPFISH	MEDFLY	MOORCOCK	NARWHAL	ORC	PARROT
LUNGFISH	MEDUSA	MOORFOWL	NARWHALE	ORCA	PARTAN
LUNGWORM	MEDUSAN	MOORHEN	NAUPLIUS	ORIBATID	PEACOCK
LUNKER	MEDUSOID	MOOSE	NAUPLIAL	ORIBI	PEAFOWL
LYNX	MEERKAT	MOPOKE	NAUTILUS	ORIOLE	PEAHEN
LYREBIRD	MEGALOPS	MORAY	NEAT	ORMER	PECCARY
	MEGAPOD	MORPHO	NEKTON	ORNIS	PEEPER
MACACO	MEGAPODE	MOSASAUR	NEKTONIC	ORTOLAN	PEESWEEP
MACAQUE	MELOID	MOSQUITO	NEMA	ORYX	PEETWEET
MACAW	MENDIGO	MOSSBACK	NEMATODE	OSCINE	PEEWIT
MACKEREL	MENHADEN	MOTH	NENE	OSCININE	PEKAN
MACRURAN	MERL	MOTMOT	NEREIS	OSPREY	PEKE
MAGGOT	MERLE	MOUFFLON	NEST	OSTRACOD	PELICAN
MAGOT	MERLIN	MOUFLON	NESTLING	OSTRICH	PEN
MAGPIE	MESSAN	MOUSE	NEWT	OTTER	PENGUIN
MAHIMAHI	METAZOAN	MUCKWORM	NIGHTJAR	OUISTITI	PERCH
MAKO	METAZOAL	MUDCAT	NILGAI	OURANG	PERCOID
MALAMUTE	METAZOIC	MUDDER	NILGAU	OUREBI	PEREGRIN

PERMIT	POLECAT	QUOKKA	RINGHALS	SANDLING	SHEEPDOG
PETRALE	POLLACK		RINGNECK	SANDPEEP	SHELDUCK
PETREL	POLLIWOG	RACCOON	RINGTAIL	SANDWORM	SHELTIE
PEWEE	POLLOCK	RACOON	ROACH	SAPAJOU	SHELTY
PEWIT	POLLYWOG	RAIL	ROADKILL	SARDINE	SHEPHERD
PHASMID	POMFRET	RAINBIRD	ROAN	SASIN	SHIER
PHEASANT	POMPANO	RAM	ROBALO	SASSABY	SHINER
PHILOMEL	PONGID	RAMSHORN	ROBIN	SATYRID	SHIPWORM
PHOEBE	PONY	RANID	ROCKFISH	SAUGER	SHOAL
PHORONID	POOCH	RAPTOR	ROCKLING	SAUREL	SHOAT
PICKEREL	POODLE	RASBORA	RODENT	SAURIAN	SHOEBILL
PIDDOCK	PORGY	RATEL	ROEBUCK	SAUROPOD	SHOTE
PIEBALD	PORKER	RATFISH	RONION	SAURY	SHOVELER
PIG	PORKY	RATITE	RONYON	SAWBILL	SHREW
PIGEON	PORPOISE	RATTAIL	ROOK	SAWFISH	SHRIKE
PIGFISH	POSSUM	RATTER	ROOKERY	SAWFLY	SHRIMP
PIGGY	POTTO	RATTON	ROOSTER	SCAD	SIALID
PIGLET	POULARD	RAVEN	RORQUAL	SCALARE	SIALIDAN
PIKA	POULARDE	REARMICE	ROSEFISH	SCALLOP	SIAMANG
PIKE	POULT	REDBIRD	ROSESLUG	SCARAB	SIFAKA
PILCHARD	POULTRY	REDBONE	ROTCH	SCAT	SIFFLEUR
PINCHBUG	POWTER	REDBUG	ROTCHE	SCAUP	SIGANID
PINFISH	POYOU	REDEAR	ROTIFER	SCHOOL	SILD
PINNIPED	PRAWN	REDFIN	ROUEN	SCHROD	SILKWORM
PINSCHER	PREDATOR	REDFISH	ROUGHLEG	SCIAENID	SILKY
PINTADA	PREY	REDHORSE	RUDD	SCINCOID	SILURID
PINTADO	PRIDE	REDIA	RUDDOCK	SCIURINE	SILUROID
PINTAIL	PRIMATE	REDIAL	RUFFE	SCORPION	SIMIAN
PINTANO	PSOCID	REDLEG	RUMINANT	SCOTER	SIRE
PINTO	PTEROPOD	REDPOLL	RUNT	SCOTTIE	SIRENIAN
PINWORM	PUFFER	REDSHANK		SCROD	SISKIN
PIPEFISH	PUFFIN	REDSTART	SABLE	SCULPIN	SKATE
PIPIT	PUG	REDTAIL	SAHIWAL	SCUP	SKEIN
PIRANA	PULI	REDUVIID	SAIGA	SCUPPAUG	SKEWBALD
PIRANHA	PULLET	REDWING	SAILFISH	SCIURID	SKIMMER
PIRARUCU	PUMA	REE	SAITHE	SEAFOWL	SKINK
PIRAYA	PUNKIE	REEDBIRD	SAJOU	SEAGULL	SKIPJACK
PISMIRE	PUP	REEDBUCK	SAKER	SEAPERCH	SKUA
PLACOID	PUPFISH	REEDLING	SAKI	SEAROBIN	SKUNK
PLAGUE	PUPPY	REINDEER	SALADANG	SEECATCH	SLIDER
PLAICE	PUREBRED	REITBOK	SALMON	SEI	SLOTH
PLANARIA	PUSS	REMORA	SALMONID	SELADANG	SLOWWORM
PLANKTER	PUSSYCAT	REMUDA	SALP	SERIEMA	SLUG
PLANKTON	PYRALID	REPTILE	SALPA	SERIN	SMELT
PLANULA	PYTHON	REQUIN	SALPIAN	SEROTINE	SMEW
PLATY		REREMICE	SALPID	SEROW	SMOLT
PLATYPUS	QUAGGA	REX	SALUKI	SERPENT	SNAIL
PLOVER	QUAHAUG	REYNARD	SAMBAR	SERRANID	SNAKE
PLUMIPED	QUAHOG	RHEA	SAMBHAR	SERVAL	SNAPPER
PLUTEI	QUAIL	RHEBOK	SAMBHUR	SETTER	SNARK
PLUTEUS	QUETZAL	RHESUS	SAMBUR	SHAD	SNIPE
POCHARD	QUEY	RICEBIRD	SAMLET	SHADFLY	SNOOK
POD	QUEZAL	RIDGLING	SANDDAB	SHANNY	SNOWBIRD
POGY	QUINNAT	RIDLEY	SANDFISH	SHARK	SOCKEYE
POINTER	QUOHOG	RINGDOVE	SANDFLY	SHEEP	SOLAN

SOLE	SUNBIRD	TERRIER	TUATERA	VIVIPARA	WIGEON
SONGBIRD	SUNFISH	TETRA	TUBENOSE	VIXEN	WILDCAT
SORA	SURFBIRD	TETRAPOD	TUBIFEX	VIZCACHA	WILDFOWL
SORD	SURFFISH	THEROPOD	TUI	VIZSLA	WILDING
SORICINE	SURICATE	THRASHER	TULADI	VOLE	WILDLIFE
SOW	SUSLIK	THROSTLE	TULLIBEE	VOLVOX	WILDLING
SPANIEL	SWALLOW	THRUSH	TUNA	VULTURE	WILLET
SPANWORM	SWARM	TICK	TUNICATE		WIREHAIR
SPARID	SWIFT	TIDDLER	TUNNY	WAGTAIL	WISENT
SPARLING	SWIFTLET	TIGER	TURACO	WAHOO	WOLF
SPARROW	SWINE	TIGLON	TURACOU	WALER	WOLFFISH
SPHINGID	SYNAPSID	TIGON	TURBIT	WALLABY	WOLVES
SPIDER	SYRPHIAN	TIGRESS	TURBOT	WALLAROO	WOMBAT
SPIRULA	SYRPHID	TILAPIA	TURDINE	WALRUS	WOODCHAT
SPITZ		TILEFISH	TURKEY	WANDEROO	WOODCOCK
SPLAKE	TABANID	TIMARAU	TURTLE	WAPITI	WOODHEN
SPOROZOA	TABBY	TINAMOU	TUSKER	WARBLER	WOODLARK
SPRAT	TACHINID	TINEID	TUSSAH	WARMOUTH	WOODWORM
SPRUG	TADPOLE	TIT	TUSSAR	WARRAGAL	WOOLER
SQUAB	TAHR	TITLARK	TUSSEH	WARRIGAL	WRASSE
SQUID	TAIPAN	TITMAN	TUSSER	WARSAW	WREN
SQUILLA	TAKAHE	TITMOUSE	TUSSOR	WARTHOG	WRYNECK
SQUIRREL	TAKIN	TOAD	TUSSORE	WASP	
STAG	TALAPOIN	TOADFISH	TUSSUR	WAT	XERUS
STAGGARD	TAMANDU	TODY	TYEE	WATCH	
STAGGART	TAMANDUA	TOGUE	TZETZE	WATERDOG	YAGER
STAGGIE	TAMARAO	TOKAY		WAVEY	YAK
STAIG	TAMARAU	TOM	UMBRETTE	WAXBILL	YAPOCK
STALLION	TAMARIN	TOMCOD	UNAI	WAXWING	YAPOK
STARFISH	TAMPAN	TOMTIT	UNAU	WAXWORM	YAUD
STARLING	TANAGER	TOPCROSS	UNGULATE	WEAKFISH	YEANLING
STARNOSE	TANUKI	TOPLINE	UNIVALVE	WEASEL	YEARLING
STEED	TAPEWORM	TORO	URIAL	WEAVER	YEELIN
STEENBOK	TAPIR	TORSK	URODELE	WEBWORM	YETI
STEER	TARPAN	TORTOISE	URSA	WEEVER	YOWE
STEGODON	TARPON	TORTRIX	URUS	WEEVIL	YOWIE
STEINBOK	TARSIER	TOUCAN	UTA	WEKA	
STERLET	TATOUAY	TOURACO		WETHER	ZANDER
STILT	TAUTAUG	TOWHEE	VARMINT	WHAUP	ZEBRA
STINGRAY	TAUTOG	TRAGOPAN	VEALER	WHEATEAR	ZEBRASS
STINKBUG	TEAL	TREPANG	VEDALIA	WHELK	ZEBU
STIRK	TEAM	TRICHINA	VEERY	WHELP	ZENAIDA
STOAT	TEG	TRICLAD	VELIGER	WHIDAH	ZIBET
STOCKER	TEIID	TRITON	VENDACE	WHIMBREL	ZIBETH
STONEFLY	TELEDU	TROCHIL	VERDIN	WHINCHAT	ZOEA
STORK	TELEOST	TROGON	VERMIN	WHIPPET	ZOEAE
STRIPER	TENCH	TROILUS	VERVET	WHIPRAY	ZOEAL
STROBILA	TENIA	TROOP	VESPID	WHIPTAIL	ZOIC
STRONGYL	TENREC	TROOPIAL	VICEROY	WHIPWORM	ZOOID
STUD	TERCEL	TROTTER	VICUGNA	WHITEFLY	ZOOIDAL
STUDFISH	TERCELET	TROUPIAL	VICUNA	WHITING	ZOOLATRY
STURGEON	TEREDO	TROUT	VIPER	WHITRACK	ZOOLOGY
SUCKFISH	TERMITE	TRUEBRED	VIREO	WHITTRET	ZOOMANIA
SUCKLING	TERN	TSETSE	VISCACHA	WHYDAH	ZOOMETRY
SUMPTER	TERRAPIN	TUATARA	VIVERRID	WIDGEON	ZOOMORPH

| ZOONOSIS | ZOOPHILY | ZOOPHYTE | ZOOTOMY | ZORILLA | ZORILLO |
| ZOOPHILE | ZOOPHOBE | ZOOSPERM | ZORIL | ZORILLE | ZYZZYVA |

COMPUTER

ABORT	CABLE	DAEMON	DUPLEX	FORK	INPUT
ACCESS	CACHE	DAISY	DUPLEXER	FORMAT	INSERT
ACOUSTIC	CAPTURE	DAMPING	DYADIC	FORMULA	INTEGER
ACTUATOR	CARD	DATA	DYNAMIC	FORUM	INVALID
ADAPTER	CARRIAGE	DATABANK		FRY	INVOKE
ADDRESS	CASSETTE	DATABASE	ECHO	FUNCTION	
ALIGN	CATALOG	DATUM	EDIT	FUZZY	JACK
ALLOCATE	CATHODE	DEADLOCK	ELITE		JITTER
ANALOG	CHAD	DEBUG	ELLIPSIS	GARBAGE	JOB
ANALYSIS	CHANNEL	DECIMAL	EMBEDDED	GATE	JOBNAME
ANALYST	CHAT	DECODER	EMULATE	GENDER	JUMP
APPEND	CHILD	DEFAULT	EMULATOR	GIGABIT	JUMPER
ARCHIVE	CHIP	DEGAUSS	ENABLE	GIGABYTE	JUSTIFY
AVATAR	CHUNK	DELETE	ENCIPHER	GLITCH	
	CIPHER	DELIMIT	ENCODE	GLOBAL	KERN
BACKBONE	CIRCUIT	DENSITY	ENGINE	GOPHER	KERNEL
BACKUP	CLEAR	DESKTOP	ENTER	GRABBER	KEY
BANK	CLICK	DEVICE	ENTITY	GRAPHIC	KEYPAD
BASIC	CLIENT	DIALECT	ENTRY	GRID	KEYWORD
BATCH	CLOBBER	DIALOG	ESCAPE	GULP	KILOBAUD
BAUD	CLOCK	DIGIT	EXECUTE	GUTTER	KILOBIT
BETA	CLONE	DIGITAL	EXIT		KILOBYTE
BINARY	CLOSE	DIGITIZE	EXPORT	HACK	KLUDGE
BINIT	CLUSTER	DINGBAT	EXTRACT	HACKER	KLUGE
BIOCHIP	COAXIAL	DISABLE		HALFTONE	
BIT	CODE	DISC	FALLOUT	HANG	LABEL
BLOCK	CODEC	DISCRETE	FANFOLD	HARDWARE	LAPTOP
BLOWUP	CODER	DISK	FATHER	HARDWIRE	LASER
BOARD	COLLATE	DISKETTE	FAULT	HASH	LAYOUT
BOMB	COMMAND	DISPLAY	FAX	HASHING	LEADING
BOOT	COMPILE	DOCUMENT	FEEDBACK	HAT	LEAPFROG
BRANCH	COMPILER	DOMAIN	FETCH	HEAD	LEXICON
BREAKOUT	COMPUTE	DOT	FICHE	HELP	LINEAR
BROWNOUT	COMPUTER	DOWN	FIELD	HERTZ	LITERAL
BUBBLE	CONNECT	DOWNLOAD	FILE	HIT	LOAD
BUCKET	CONSOLE	DOWNTIME	FIRMWARE	HOME	LOCAL
BUFFER	CONSTANT	DRAFT	FLAG	HOOK	LOCKOUT
BUG	CONTROL	DRAG	FLAME	HOST	LOCKUP
BULLET	COPY	DRIVE	FLAMER	HOT	LOG
BUNDLE	CORE	DRIVER	FLASH	HYBRID	LOGGED
BUNDLING	COUNTER	DROP	FLICKER		LOGIC
BURN	CRASH	DRUM	FLIPPY	ICON	LOGICAL
BURST	CRUNCH	DUMB	FLOPPY	IMAGE	LOGO
BURSTER	CRYSTAL	DUMMY	FLOW	IMAGING	LOOP
BUS	CURSOR	DUMP	FOLDER	IMPACT	LOOPHOLE
BYTE	CYCLE	DUPE	FONT	INDEX	

MACRO	PALETTE	QUAD	SCALE	SOUND	THERMAL
MAGNETIC	PARALLEL	QUANTIZE	SCAN	SOURCE	THIMBLE
MAILBOX	PARENT	QUANTUM	SCANNER	SPACE	THREAD
MANAGER	PARITY	QUERY	SCHEMA	SPATIAL	TICK
MANUAL	PARK	QUEUE	SCRAP	SPEC	TILE
MASTER	PARSE	QUIT	SCRATCH	SPIKE	TILING
MATRIX	PASCAL	QWERTY	SCREEN	SPIKES	TOGGLE
MEDIA	PASS		SCRIPT	SPLAT	TOKEN
MEGABIT	PASSWORD	RANDOM	SCROLL	SPLINE	TONER
MEGABYTE	PASTE	RASTER	SCROLLING	SPOILER	TOOLBOX
MEMORY	PATCH	READ	SEAMLESS	SPOOL	TOUCH
MENU	PATH	READER	SEARCH	SPOOLING	TRACK
MERGE	PAUSE	READOUT	SECTOR	SPRITE	TRACTOR
MICRO	PERIOD	REAL	SECURITY	SPROCKET	TRAFFIC
MINI	PERSONAL	REALITY	SEED	STACK	TRAILER
MIRROR	PHASE	REBOOT	SEEK	STAR	TRAIN
MNEMONIC	PHYSICAL	RECORD	SEGMENT	STARTUP	TRANSFER
MODE	PICA	RECOVER	SELECT	STATIC	TRAVERSE
MODEM	PIN	REFORMAT	SEMANTIC	STATION	TREE
MODULATE	PIPE	REFRESH	SENSOR	STATUS	TRUNCATE
MODULE	PIRACY	REGISTER	SENTINEL	STEPPER	TUBE
MONITOR	PITCH	RELATION	SERIAL	STORAGE	TURNKEY
MOUNT	PIXEL	RELATIVE	SERVER	STREAMER	TURNPIKE
MOUSE	PLANAR	RELAY	SERVICE	STRING	TURTLE
	PLATEN	RELEASE	SERVO	STROBE	TUTORIAL
NESTING	PLATFORM	RELOCATE	SESSION	STROKE	TWEAK
NETWORK	PLATTER	REMARK	SETUP	STUB	TYPE
NEURAL	PLOT	REMOTE	SHELL	STYLI	
NIBBLE	PLOTTER	REPORT	SHIFT	STYLUS	UNDO
NODE	POKE	RESET	SHOUTING	SUBMENU	UNIPOLAR
NOISE	POLARITY	RESOURCE	SILICA	SUPPORT	UNPACK
NOTATION	POLLING	RESPONSE	SILICON	SURF	UNSET
NOTEBOOK	PORT	RESTART	SIMPLEX	SURGE	UNZIP
NULL	PORTABLE	RESTORE	SINE	SUSPEND	UP
NUMERIC	PORTRAIT	RETRACE	SINK	SWAP	UPDATE
	POST	RETRIEVE	SITE	SWITCH	UPGRADE
OBJECT	POWER	RETROFIT	SKEW	SWITCHED	UPLOAD
OCTAL	PRIMARY	RETURN	SLARE	SYMBOL	UPTIME
ODD	PRINT	REVERSE	SLASH	SYMBOLIC	UPWARD
OFFSET	PRINTER	REVERT	SLEEP	SYNC	USER
OPERAND	PRINTOUT	REWIND	SLEEVE	SYSOP	UTILITY
OPERATOR	PRIORITY	REWRITE	SLOT	SYSTEM	
OPTICAL	PROCESS	ROBOT	SMART		VALUE
ORPHAN	PROGRAM	ROBOTICS	SMILEY	TAB	VARIABLE
OUTPUT	PROJECT	ROLLBACK	SMOKE	TABLE	VECTOR
OVERFLOW	PROMPT	ROLLOVER	SMOOTH	TABLET	VERIFY
OVERLAY	PROTECT	ROOT	SNAIL	TAG	VERSION
OVERRIDE	PROTOCOL	ROTATE	SNAPSHOT	TAPE	VERTICAL
OVERRUN	PULL	ROUTER	SNOW	TARGET	VIDEO
	PULSE	ROUTINE	SOFT	TASK	VIEW
PACKET	PUNCH	RULER	SOFTWARE	TEMPLATE	VIRTUAL
PADDLE	PURGE	RUN	SOLAR	TERMINAL	VIRUS
PAGE	PUSH		SOLENOID	TERNARY	VOICE
PAGING	PUSHDOWN	SAVE	SORT	TEST	VOLATILE
PAINT	PUT	SCALAR	SORTER	TEXT	VOLUME

WAFER	WEB	WINDOW	WORM	YOKE	ZIP
WAIT	WHEEL	WIZARD	WRAP		ZONE
WAND	WIDEBAND	WORD	WRITE	ZAP	ZOOM
WARM	WIDOW	WORK		ZERO	ZOOMING

LEGAL

ABATOR	ATTESTER	CHARGE	DELATOR	EDICT	FINDING
ABEYANCE	ATTESTOR	CHATTEL	DELICT	EDILE	FINE
ABEYANY	AWARD	CITABLE	DEMESNE	ELEGIT	FINEABLE
ABEYANT		CITATION	DEMIURGE	EMPOWER	FIRMAN
ABJURE	BAIL	CITATOR	DEMPSTER	ENACT	FISCAL
ABJURER	BAILEE	CITE	DEODAND	ENACTIVE	FORGER
ACQUIT	BAILER	CITER	DEPONE	ENACTOR	FORGERY
ADDUCE	BAILIE	CLEMENCY	DEPONENT	ENACTORY	FORJUDGE
ADJUDGE	BAILIFF	COATTEST	DEPOSAL	ENDORSE	FRAUD
ADJURE	BAILMENT	CODICIL	DEPOSE	ENDORSEE	
ADOPT	BAILOR	COGNOVIT	DEPOSER	ENDORSER	GAVEL
ADOPTEE	BAILSMAN	COHEIR	DERAIGN	ENDORSOR	GET
ADULTERY	BATTERY	COLESSEE	DETAINER	ENFEOFF	GRAFT
AEDILE	BENCHER	COLESSOR	DETINUE	ENTAIL	GRANT
AFFIANT	BENEFICE	COMAKER	DEVISEE	ENTAILER	GRAVAMEN
ALDERMAN	BEQUEATH	CONVICT	DEVISER	EPHOR	GUILT
ALIAS	BEQUEST	COPYHOLD	DEVISOR	EPHORAL	GUILTY
ALIBI	BIGAMIST	COSIGN	DHARMA	EPHORATE	
ALIENEE	BIGAMOUS	COSIGNER	DHARMIC	ESCHEAT	HALACHA
ALIENER	BIGAMY	COTENANT	DICAST	ESCROW	HALACHOT
ALIENOR	BINDER	COUNSEL	DICASTIC	ESTATE	HALAKAH
ALIMONY	BREACH	COVENANT	DICTUM	ESTOP	HALAKHA
AMERCE	BRIBEE	CREDITOR	DIGAMIES	ESTOPPEL	HALAKHOT
AMICUS	BRIBERY	CRIME	DIGAMIST	ESTOVERS	HALAKIC
ANNUL	BRIEF	CRIMINAL	DIGAMY	ESTREAT	HALAKIST
APPELLEE	BURGLAR	CULPA	DISBAR	EVICT	HALAKOTH
APPELLOR	BURGLARY	CURIA	DISENDOW	EVICTEE	HEARING
ARBITER	BURGLE	CURTESY	DISHERIT	EVICTION	HEARSAY
ARCHON		CUSTODY	DISMISS	EVICTOR	HEIR
ARRAIGN	CADASTER	CUSTUMAL	DISSENT	EXECUTER	HEIRDOM
ARREST	CADASTRE	CUTCHERY	DISTRAIN	EXECUTOR	HEIRESS
ARRESTEE	CADI	CYPRES	DIVORCE	EXHIBIT	HEIRLESS
ARRESTER	CALENDAR		DOCKET		HEIRLOOM
ARRESTOR	CAMERA	DEBTOR	DOGE	FALSIFY	HEIRSHIP
ARROGATE	CAMERAL	DECEMVIR	DOGEDOM	FATWA	HELIAST
ARSON	CANON	DECERN	DOGESHIP	FEASANCE	HEREIN
ARSONIST	CANONIST	DECREE	DOMICILE	FELON	HEREINTO
ARTICLE	CAPIAS	DECREER	DOOMSTER	FELONRY	HEREOF
ASSAULT	CASEBOOK	DEED	DOTATION	FELONY	HEREON
ASSIGNEE	CASELOAD	DEEMSTER	DRAWEE	FEU	HERES
ASSIGNER	CASUS	DEFAULT	DROIT	FEUAR	HERETO
ASSIGNOR	CAVEAT	DEFENSE	DURESS	FIAR	HERETRIX
ASSIZE	CAVEATOR	DELATE	DUTY	FIAT	HEREUNTO
ATTEST	CHANCERY	DELATION	DUUMVIR	FINABLE	HEREUPON

HEREWITH	KADI	LIEN	PANDECT	REPLEVY	TIPSTAFF
HERITAGE		LIENABLE	PARCENER	REPRIEVE	TIPSTAVES
HERITOR	LACHES	LITIGANT	PARDON	RESCIND	TORA
HERITRIX	LARCENER	LITIGATE	PAROLE	RETAINER	TORAH
HOMICIDE	LARCENY		PAROLEE	REVERSAL	TORT
HORNBOOK	LAW	MAJORITY	PATENT	REVOKE	TORTIOUS
HOTCHPOT	LAWBOOK	MANDAMUS	PATENTEE	ROGATION	TRESPASS
HUSTINGS	LAWFUL	MAYHEM	PATENTOR		TRIABLE
HYPOTHEC	LAWGIVER	MEDIACY	PERJURE	SCILICET	TRIAL
	LAWMAKER	MISPLEAD	PERJURER	SEIZIN	TRIBUNAL
IMMUNITY	LAWSUIT	MISTRIAL	PERJURY	SEIZOR	TROVER
IMMURE	LAWYER	MITTIMUS	PIGNUS	SENTENCE	TRUST
IMPANEL	LAWYERLY	MITZVAH	PIGNORA	SERVICE	TRUSTEE
IMPLEAD	LEASE	MITZVOTH	PLEA	SETTLOR	TRUSTOR
IMPOUND	LEET	MORTMAIN	PLEAD	SHRIEVAL	
INDICT	LEGACY	MOTION	PLEADING	SHYSTER	USUFRUCT
INDICTEE	LEGAL	MOTIVE	PODESTA	SIGNEE	USURER
INDICTER	LEGALESE	MUFTI	POIND	SLAMMER	USURIES
INDICTOR	LEGALISE	MURDER	PRAECIPE	SLANDER	USURIOUS
INFEOFF	LEGALISM		PRAETOR	SOKE	USURP
INFRACT	LEGALIST	NOLO	PRECIPE	SOLATIUM	USURPER
INFRINGE	LEGALITY	NOMISM	PRELEGAL	SOLON	USURY
INHERIT	LEGALIZE	NOMISTIC	PRETRIAL	STATUTE	
INQUEST	LEGALLY	NONJUROR	PROBATE	STAY	VAKEEL
INSOMUCH	LEGATE	NONJURY	PROVISO	STRIKE	VAKIL
INTENT	LEGATEE	NONLEGAL	PROXY	SUABLE	VALIDATE
	LEGATING	NONPROS	PUNITION	SUABLY	VENIRE
JEOPARDY	LEGATOR	NONSUIT	PUNITIVE	SUBORN	VERDICT
JOINDER	LEGES	NOTARIAL	PUNITORY	SUBORNER	VOID
JOINTURE	LEGIST	NOTARIZE	PURVIEW	SUBPENA	VOIDANCE
JUDGE	LESSEE	NOTARY		SUBPOENA	
JUDGMENT	LESSOR	NOTICE	QUAESTOR	SUE	WAIVER
JUDICIAL	LEVY	NOVATION	QUASH	SUER	WARRANT
JURA	LEX	NUISANCE	QUESTOR	SUIT	WEREGILD
JURAL	LIBEL	NULLITY		SUMMONS	WERGELD
JURANT	LIBELANT		REBUTTAL	SUNNA	WERGELT
JURAT	LIBELEE	OATH	RECESS	SUNNAH	WERGILD
JURATORY	LIBELER	OBLIGOR	RECOVERY		WHEREAS
JURIDIC	LIBELIST	OFFENSE	RECUSAL	TALESMAN	WHEREAT
JURIST	LIBELLED	OPINION	RECUSANT	TALMUDIC	WHEREBY
JURISTIC	LIBELLEE	OPTIONEE	RECUSE	TEMPLAR	WHEREIN
JUROR	LIBELLER	ORDER	REDRESS	TENDER	WHEREOF
JURY	LIBELLING	OVERRULE	RELEASE	TERMOR	WHEREON
JURYMAN	LIBELOUS	OYER	REMAND	TERMTIME	WHERETO
JUS	LIBER	OYES	REMEDY	TESTACY	WILL
JUSTICE	LICENSE	OYEZ	REMISE	TESTATE	WRIT
	LICTOR		REPLEVIN	TESTATOR	

MEDICAL

ABASIA	ALLOPATH	APHASIA	AUXETIC	BUBOED	CHALAZIA
ABLATION	ALLOTYPE	APHASIAC	AXENIC	BUBONIC	CHANCRE
ABNORMAL	ALLOTYPY	APHASIC	AZOTEMIA	BULIMIA	CHARNEL
ABORNING	ALOIN	APHONIA	AZOTIZE	BULIMIAC	CHILDING
ABORT	ALOPECIA	APHONIC	AZOTURIA	BULKAGE	CHLOASMA
ABORTION	ALOPECIC	APHTHA		BULLA	CHOKE
ABREACT	ALPHOSIS	APLASIA	BACTERIN	BUNION	CHOLERA
ABROSIA	AMAH	APNEA	BANDAGE	BURSITIS	CHOREA
ABSCESS	AMENT	APNEAL	BANDAGER	BUTE	CHOREOID
ABSCISE	AMENTIA	APNEIC	BANE		CHRONAXY
ABSTERGE	AMNESIA	APNOEA	BANEFUL	CACHEXIA	CHRONIC
ACAPNIA	AMNESIAC	APNOEAL	BARBITAL	CACHEXY	CICATRIX
ACCIDIA	AMNESIC	APNOEIC	BARF	CADAVER	CITRININ
ACCIDIE	AMNESTIC	APOPLEXY	BEDSONIA	CAFFEINE	CLAVUS
ACEDIA	AMPUTATE	APRAXIA	BEDSORE	CALAMINE	CLINIC
ACHOLIA	AMPUTEE	APYRETIC	BERIBERI	CALISAYA	CLONE
ACIDEMIA	AMUSIA	ARYTHMIA	BEVOMIT	CALOMEL	CLONIC
ACIDOSIS	AMYLOID	ARYTHMIC	BIOLOGIC	CAMOMILE	CLONING
ACIDOTIC	ANAEMIA	ASCITES	BIOLYSIS	CANCER	CLONISM
ACIDURIA	ANAEMIC	ASCITIC	BIOLYTIC	CANCROID	CLONUS
ACNE	ANALGIA	ASCORBIC	BIOMETRY	CANELLA	CLUBFOOT
ACROTIC	ANALITY	ASEPSIS	BIONICS	CANITIES	CLUBHAND
ACROTISM	ANASARCA	ASEPTIC	BIOPLASM	CANKER	CLYSTER
ADENITIS	ANEMIA	ASPHYXIA	BIOPSIC	CANNULA	COELIAC
ADENOID	ANERGIA	ASPHYXY	BIOPSY	CANNULAE	COENURE
ADENOMA	ANERGY	ASPIRIN	BIOPTIC	CANULA	COENURUS
ADENOSIS	ANESTRUS	ASTASIA	BIOSCOPY	CANULAE	COHOSH
ADIPOSIS	ANEURISM	ASTATIC	BIOTOXIN	CANULATE	COLIC
ADIPOUS	ANEURYSM	ASTHENIA	BIOTYPE	CAPSID	COLICIN
ADNEXA	ANGINA	ASTHENIC	BIOVULAR	CAPSIDAL	COLICINE
ADYNAMIA	ANGINAL	ASTHENY	BISTOURY	CARATE	COLICKY
ADYNAMIC	ANGINOSE	ASTHMA	BLAIN	CARDIAC	COLIFORM
AFEBRILE	ANGINOUS	ASTIGMIA	BLASTOMA	CARDITIC	COLISTIN
AGENESIA	ANGIOMA	ATARAXIC	BLASTULA	CARDITIS	COLITIS
AGENESIS	ANKYLOSE	ATARAXY	BLEB	CARIES	COLLYRIA
AGNAIL	ANODYNE	ATAVISM	BLEEDER	CARSICK	COLOBOMA
AGNOSIA	ANOOPSIA	ATAVIST	BLIND	CARUNCLE	COLONIC
AGRAPHIA	ANOPIA	ATAXIA	BLISTER	CASCARA	COLOTOMY
AGRIA	ANOPSIA	ATAXIC	BLISTERY	CASTRATE	COLPITIS
AGRYPNIA	ANORETIC	ATAXY	BLOOD	CATARRH	COMA
AGUE	ANOREXIA	ATHEROMA	BLOODY	CATHETER	COMATIC
AILMENT	ANOREXIC	ATHETOID	BLUEBALL	CATLIN	COMATOSE
AIRSICK	ANOREXY	ATONY	BOLUS	CATLING	COMEDO
ALEXIA	ANOSMIA	ATOPY	BORAGE	CAUTERY	CONCUSS
ALEXIN	ANOXEMIA	ATRESIA	BOTULIN	CELIAC	CONDYLAR
ALEXINE	ANOXIA	ATROPHIA	BOTULISM	CENTAURY	CONDYLE
ALIENIST	ANTHRAX	ATROPHY	BRANK	CENTESIS	CONIOSIS
ALLELISM	ANTIPYIC	ATROPISM	BROMISM	CERATE	CONTAGIA
ALLERGEN	ANTISERA	AURIST	BROMIZE	CESAREAN	CONTUSE
ALLERGIC	ANURESIS	AUTOPSIC	BROMO	CESARIAN	CONVULSE
ALLERGIN	ANURIA	AUTOPSY	BRUXISM	CESTODE	COPREMIA
ALLERGY	APHAGIA	AUXESIS	BUBO	CESTOID	CORONER

CORPORA	DEADNESS	DIGOXIN	EARACHE	EXANTHEM	GOITRE
CORPSE	DEAF	DIHYBRID	ECBOLIC	EXCIDE	GOITROUS
CORPSMAN	DEAFEN	DILATANT	ECCRINE	EXCISE	GOUT
CORPUS	DEAFISH	DILATATE	ECDYSIS	EXCISION	GOUTIER
CORSE	DEAFLY	DILATE	ECRASEUR	EXCITANT	GOUTILY
CORYZA	DEAFNESS	DILATER	ECTHYMA	EXOCRINE	GOUTY
CORYZAL	DEATH	DILATION	ECTOPIA	EXOTOXIN	GRAVIDA
COSTIVE	DEATHBED	DILATIVE	ECZEMA	EXTUBATE	GRAYOUT
COUGH	DEATHCUP	DILATOR	EDEMA	EYECUP	GRIPPE
COUGHER	DEATHFUL	DILDO	EDUCABLE	EYEDNESS	GRIPPY
COXALGIA	DEATHLY	DILDOE	ELIXIR	EYEDROPS	GRIPY
COXALGY	DEATHY	DIOPTRIC	EMBALMER	EYESTONE	GUAIACUM
COXITIS	DEAVE	DIPLEGIA	EMBOLI	EYEWASH	GUAIOCUM
CREMAINS	DEBRIDE	DIPLOPIA	EMBOLISM	EYEWATER	GULOSITY
CREMATE	DECAY	DIPLOPIC	EMBOLUS	EYEWEAR	GUMBOIL
CREMATOR	DECAYER	DISBOWEL	EMBOWEL		GUMMA
CRICK	DECEASE	DISGORGE	EMEROD	FASTING	GURNEY
CROUP	DECEDENT	DISINTER	EMEROID	FATAL	GYNANDRY
CROUPILY	DEGERM	DISOMIC	EMESIS	FATALITY	GYNIATRY
CROUPOUS	DEMENT	DIURESES	EMETIC	FATALLY	
CROUPY	DEMENTIA	DIURESIS	EMPYEMA	FAVISM	HABITUS
CROWNER	DENGUE	DIURETIC	ENATION	FAVUS	HAKIM
CRUOR	DENTIST	DIZYGOUS	ENCYST	FEBRIFIC	HANGNAIL
CRYONICS	DERMOID	DOC	ENDEMIC	FEBRILE	HANGOVER
CRYPT	DESEX	DOCTOR	ENDEMISM	FEEBLE	HAPLOPIA
CUPPING	DESMOID	DOCTORAL	ENEMA	FELDSHER	HARELIP
CURARA	DETOX	DOOLEE	ENFEVER	FETICIDE	HEADACHE
CURARE	DETOXIFY	DOOLIE	ENTASIA	FETOLOGY	HEADACHY
CURARI	DEX	DOOLY	ENURESES	FIBROMA	HEALTH
CURARINE	DEXIE	DOPA	ENURESIS	FIBROSIS	HEALTHY
CURARIZE	DEXIES	DOPAMINE	ENURETIC	FISTULA	HEMAGOG
CURATIVE	DEXTRAN	DOSAGE	EPHEDRIN	FLACCID	HEMATIC
CURE	DEXTRIN	DOSE	EPIDEMIC	FLEAM	HEMATOMA
CURELESS	DEXTRINE	DOSER	EPILEPSY	FLU	HEMOLYZE
CURER	DEXTROSE	DOWNER	EPISTASY	FOOTSORE	HEMOSTAT
CURET	DEXY	DRESSING	ERETHISM	FOOTWORN	HEPATIC
CURETTE	DIABETES	DROPSY	ERGOTISM	FORCEPS	HEPATIZE
CURING	DIABETIC	DROWN	ERRHINE	FORCIPES	HEPATOMA
CYANOSED	DIAGNOSE	DROWND	ERYNGO	FROSTBIT	HERNIA
CYANOSIS	DIALLEL	DROWNER	ERYTHEMA	FURUNCLE	HERNIATE
CYANOTIC	DIALYSE	DRUG	ESCHAR		HEROIN
CYESES	DIALYSER	DUMB	ESTHESES	GALANGAL	HERPES
CYESIS	DIALYSIS	DWARFISM	ESTHESIA	GANGRENE	HERPETIC
CYSTIC	DIALYTIC	DYING	ESTHESIS	GASSING	HIC
CYSTITIS	DIALYZE	DYSEGENIC	ETHER	GAVAGE	HICCOUGH
CYSTOID	DIALYZER	DYSLEXIA	ETHICAL	GELSEMIA	HICCUP
CYTASTER	DIARRHEA	DYSLEXIC	ETIOLOGY	GENERIC	HIDROSIS
CYTOLOGY	DICHOTIC	DYSPEPSY	EUCAINE	GERMFREE	HIDROTIC
	DICROTIC	DYSPNEA	EUPEPSIA	GERMY	HIRUDIN
	DIE	DYSPNOEA	EUPEPSY	GIANTISM	HOSPITAL
DALTONIC	DIED	DYSTAXIA	EUPNEA	GLAUCOMA	HOWDIE
DANDRIFF	DIET	DYSTOCIA	EUPNOEA	GLEET	HUNGOVER
DANDRUFF	DIETARY	DYSTONIA	EUTROPHY	GLIOMA	HYDATID
DAPSONE	DIETER	DYSURIA	EVACUANT	GLUTTONY	HYDRAGOG
DEAD	DIETER		EVERTOR	GOITER	HYDROPS
DEADLY	DIETETIC				

PHTHISIC	PRURIGO	QUINSY	SCROGGY	SPLENT	TABID
PHTHISIS	PRURITUS	QUINTAN	SCURF	SPLINT	TALIPED
PHYLAXIS	PSILOCIN		SCURVY	SPRAIN	TALIPES
PHYSIC	PSILOSIS	RABIC	SEDATE	SPRUE	TENACULA
PHYSICAL	PSORALEN	RABID	SEDATION	SQUELA	TENESMIC
PIAN	PTERYGIA	RABIDITY	SEDATIVE	STANCH	TENESMUS
PILLBOX	PTOMAIN	RABIES	SEMICOMA	STANCHER	TENIASIS
PILULAR	PTOMAINE	RACHITIC	SEMIDEAF	STAPH	TENOTOMY
PILULE	PTOSIS	RACHITIS	SEMIMUTE	STARVE	TERATISM
PIMPLE	PTOTIC	RALE	SENEGA	STASES	TERATOID
PIMPLY	PTYALISM	RALPH	SENILE	STASIS	TERATOMA
PINKEYE	PUKE	RANULA	SENILELY	STENOSED	TERTIAN
PINTA	PULMOTOR	RASH	SENILITY	STENOSIS	TESTIS
PITH	PURBLIND	REAGIN	SENNA	STENOTIC	TETANAL
PLACEBO	PURPURA	REAGINIC	SENOPIA	STERILE	TETANIC
PLEURA	PURPURIC	REGORGE	SEPSES	STOUND	TETANIES
PLEURISY	PURULENT	REINJURY	SEPSIS	STREP	TETANISE
PLEXOR	PUS	RELAXANT	SEPTIC	STRESSOR	TETANIZE
POCK	PUSTULAR	RENOGRAM	SEPTICAL	STRUMA	TETANUS
POCKILY	PUSTULE	REOVIRUS	SEQUELA	STRUMOSE	TETANY
POCKMARK	PYAEMIA	RESECT	SERA	STRUMOUS	TETTER
POCKY	PYAEMIC	RHEUM	SEROLOGY	STUN	THEBAINE
PODAGRA	PYCNOSIS	RHEUMIC	SERPIGO	STUNT	THELITIS
PODAGRAL	PYCNOTIC	RHEUMY	SERUM	STUPE	THERAPY
PODAGRIC	PYELITIC	RHINITIS	SERUMAL	STUTTER	THIAZIDE
PODIATRY	PYELITIS	RHONCHAL	SETON	STYE	THROE
POISON	PYEMIA	RHONCHUS	SEXOLOGY	STYPSIS	THROMBUS
POLIO	PYEMIC	RICKETS	SEXTAN	STYPTIC	TIC
POLYOMA	PYGIDIUM	RIFAMPIN	SHAMAN	SUBTILIN	TIMOLOL
POLYPUS	PYIC	RINGWORM	SHAMANIC	SUBVIRAL	TINEA
POLYURIA	PYKNOSES	ROENTGEN	SICK	SUDATION	TINEAL
POLYURIC	PYKNOSIS	ROSEOLA	SICKBED	SUDATORY	TINNITUS
POSOLOGY	PYKNOTIC	ROSEOLAR	SICKEE	SUDOR	TISSULAR
POTION	PYODERMA	RUBELLA	SICKEN	SUDORAL	TOCOLOGY
POX	PYOGENIC	RUBEOLA	SICKIE	SULFA	TOMOGRAM
POXVIRUS	PYOID		SICKLY	SULFATE	TONICITY
PREEMIE	PYORRHEA	SANATIVE	SICKNESS	SULFUR	TOXAEMIA
PREGNANT	PYOSIS	SANICLE	SICKO	SULFURET	TOXAEMIC
PREMED	PYRETIC	SANIES	SICKOUT	SUNBURN	TOXEMIA
PREMEDIC	PYREXIA	SANIOUS	SICKROOM	SUNTAN	TOXEMIC
PREMIE	PYREXIAL	SANITISE	SINAPISM	SUPERFIX	TOXIC
PREMUNE	PYREXIC	SANITIZE	SMALLPOX	SURGERY	TOXICAL
PRENATAL	PYROGEN	SAPREMIA	SORE	SURGICAL	TOXICANT
PRESSOR	PYROSIS	SAPREMIC	SORENESS	SWAYBACK	TOXIN
PRETERM	PYURIA	SARCOMA	SPASM	SWEATBOX	TOXINE
PRIAPISM		SCABIES	SPASTIC	SYCOSES	TOXOID
PROBANG	QUAALUDE	SCALL	SPECIFIC	SYCOSIS	TRACHOMA
PROCAINE	QUARTAN	SCALPEL	SPECULAR	SYNDROME	TRANK
PRODROME	QUASSIN	SCAR	SPECULUM	SYPH	TRANQ
PROGERIA	QUEASY	SCIATICA	SPEW	SYPHILIS	TRAUMA
PROGNOSE	QUEAZY	SCIRRHUS	SPEWER	SYRINGE	TREPAN
PROPHAGE	QUININ	SCLEROMA	SPINAL		TREPHINE
PROVIRAL	QUININA	SCOLIOMA	SPLENIA	TABES	TRIAGE
PROVIRUS	QUININE	SCROFULA	SPLENIUM	TABETIC	TRISMIC

TRISMUS	TURPETH	URINEMIA	VARIX	VIRULENT	WEN
TROCAR	TUSSIS	URINEMIC	VARUS	VIRUS	WENNISH
TROCHAR	TUSSIVE	UROLITH	VASOTOMY	VITILIGO	WENNY
TROCHE	TWINBORN	UROLOGIC	VENIN	VITRIOL	WHITLOW
TROPHIC	TWINGE	UROLOGY	VENINE	VOLVULUS	WINDBURN
TROPIN	TWINNING	UROSCOPY	VENOGRAM	VOMICA	WOOPS
TROPINE	TYLOSIN	UVEITIC	VENOM	VOMIT	WORKUP
TUMEFY	TYMPANY	UVEITIS	VERATRIN	VOMITER	
TUMID	TYPHOID	UVULITIS	VERRUCA	VOMITIVE	XANTHOMA
TUMIDITY	TYPHOSE		VIOMYCIN	VOMITO	XEROSIS
TUMIDLY	TYPHOUS	VACCINA	VIRAL	VOMITORY	XEROTIC
TUMOR	TYPHUS	VACCINAL	VIRALLY	VOMITOUS	XYSTER
TUMORAL		VACCINE	VIREMIA	VOMITUS	
TUMOROUS	ULCER	VACCINEE	VIREMIC	VULVITIS	ZEDOARY
TUMOUR	ULCERATE	VACCINIA	VIRICIDE		ZOOGLEA
TURGENCY	ULCEROUS	VAGOTOMY	VIRILISM	WALLEYE	ZOOGLEAL
TURGENT	URAEMIA	VALGOID	VIRION	WART	ZOOGLOEA
TURGID	URAEMIC	VALGUS	VIROID	WARTLIKE	ZOSTER
TURGIDLY	UREDO	VARICOSE	VIROLOGY	WARTY	
TURGOR	UREMIA	VARIOLA	VIROSIS	WEBFEET	
TURISTA	UREMIC	VARIOLAR	VIRUCIDE	WEBFOOT	

MILITARY

ABRI	ARBALIST	BAILOUT	BORDURE	CAPTOR	CHOPPER
ACELDAMA	ARBELEST	BALLISTA	BOWMAN	CAPTURE	CIPHONY
ADMIRAL	ARCHER	BANZAI	BOWYER	CARABIN	CITADEL
AGA	ARM	BARBICAN	BREN	CARABINE	CIVIE
AGGER	ARMADA	BARBUT	BRISANCE	CARBINE	CIVILIAN
AGGRESS	ARMAMENT	BARD	BRISANT	CARNAGE	CIVVY
AGHA	ARMATURE	BARESARK	BULWARK	CASCABEL	CLAXON
AIDMAN	ARMET	BARRAGE	BURGONET	CASCABLE	CLAYMORE
AIRBURST	ARMIES	BASINET	BUSHIDO	CASEMATE	CODE
AIRPOWER	ARMIGER	BASTION	BYRNIE	CASERN	CODEBOOK
ALCAIDE	ARMIGERO	BATTALIA		CASERNE	COLONEL
ALCAYDE	ARMOR	BATTLE	CADET	CASHIER	COMBAT
ALCAZAR	ARMORER	BAZOOKA	CAISSON	CASQUE	COMMANDO
AMBUSH	ARMORY	BEVOR	CALIBER	CASUALTY	CONELRAD
AMTRAC	ARMOUR	BILLET	CALIBRE	CATAPULT	CONQUER
AMTRACK	ARMOURER	BILLETER	CALIBRED	CAUDILLO	CONQUEST
ANABASIS	ARMOURY	BINNACLE	CAMAIL	CAVALRY	CONVOY
ANGARIA	ARMY	BIRDFARM	CAMION	CHAMFRON	COPTER
ANGARY	ARQUEBUS	BLAM	CAMISADE	CHANFRON	CORDON
ANLACE	ARSENAL	BLOWGUN	CAMISADO	CHAPE	CORNETCY
ANLAS	ASSAGAI	BLOWPIPE	CAMPAIGN	CHASSEUR	CORPORAL
ANTIAIR	ASSAIL	BLOWTUBE	CANNON	CHAUSSES	CORPS
ANTINUKE	ASSAULT	BLOWUP	CANNONRY	CHEDDITE	CORPSMAN
ANTITANK	ASSEGAI	BOLA	CAPONIER	CHEDITE	CORSELET
ANTIWAR	ATLATL	BOLAS	CAPTAIN	CHEVERON	CORVET
ARBALEST	AZON	BOMBLOAD	CAPTIVE	CHEVRON	CORVETTE

COSSACK	ENCRYPT	FOIN	HELIO	MAILLESS	PENTOMIC
COUTER	ENFILADE	FOOTSLOG	HILT	MANCIPLE	PERDU
CROSSBOW	ENLIST	FORT	HIPPARCH	MANGONEL	PETARD
CUIRASS	ENLISTEE	FORTRESS	HOLSTER	MANTELET	PETRONEL
CUISH	ENLISTER	FOXHOLE	HOPLITE	MANTLET	PEYTRAL
CUISSE	ENSIFORM	FRAG	HOTLINE	MARCH	PEYTREL
CULET	ENSIGN	FRAGGING	HOWITZER	MARCHER	PHALANX
CULVERIN	ENSIGNCY	FROGMAN	HUMVEE	MARTELLO	PICKEER
CUTLAS	EQUERRY	FUSIL	HUP	MARTIAL	PIKE
CUTLASS	EQUITES	FUSILEER	HUSSAR	MEDEVAC	PIKEMAN
	ESCUAGE	FUSILIER		MESSMAN	PLATOON
DAH	EVZONE		IMPI	MESSMATE	PLEBE
DEADEYE	ECHELON	GANTLOPE	INDUCT	MILITARY	POILU
DEBOUCH	ELINT	GARRISON	INDUCTEE	MILITIA	POMPOM
DEBOUCHE	EMBATTLE	GARROTE	INDUCTOR	MIQUELET	PRIVATE
DEBRIEF	ENCAMP	GARROTTE	INFANTRY	MORION	PROLONGE
DECIPHER	ENCEINTE	GENERAL	INROAD	MORSE	PSYWAR
DECODE	ENCODE	GHAZI	INSIGNEE	MUDCAP	
DECURIES	ENCODER	GISARME	INSIGNIA	MUNIMENT	RADAR
DECURION	ENCRYPT	GLAIVE	INTERN	MUNITION	RADIOMAN
DECURY	ENFILADE	GORGET	INTERNEE	MUSKET	RADOME
DEFENCE	ENLIST	GREAVE	INTERWAR	MUSKETRY	RADWASTE
DEFILADE	ENLISTEE	GRENADE	IRONCLAD		RAINOUT
DEMOB	ENLISTER	GUERILLA		NAPALM	RANKER
DEPLOY	ENSIFORM	GUN	JAMBE	NAUMACHY	RAPIER
DESTRIER	ENSIGN	GUNBOAT	JAMBEAU	NAVIES	RATO
DETENTE	ENSIGNCY	GUNFIGHT	JANISARY	NAVY	RAVELIN
DETONATE	EPAULET	GUNFIRE	JANIZARY	NONCOM	REARWARD
DISARM	EQUERRY	GUNFLINT	JARHEAD	NONWAR	REB
DISHELM	EQUITES	GUNFOUGHT	JAWAN	NUKE	REBELDOM
DISTAFF	ESCUAGE	GUNLOCK	JAYGEE		RECCE
DISTAVES	EVZONE	GUNNER	JEMADAR	ORDNANCE	RECRUIT
DIT		GUNNERY	JEMIDAR	OUTFLANK	REDAN
DIVEBOMB	FALCHION	GUNPLAY	JERRICAN	OUTGUN	REDCOAT
DOGFACE	FALLBACK	GUNPOINT	JERRY	OUTPOST	REDEPLOY
DOGFIGHT	FALLOUT	GUNROOM	JERRYCAN	OUTWAR	REDOUBT
DOGTROT	FASCINE	GUNSHIP	JEZAIL	OVERKILL	REG
DOT	FAULD	GUNSHOT	JINGAL		REGIMENT
DOUGHBOY	FEDAYEE	GUNSMITH	JINGALL	PACIFISM	RETIARII
DOVISH	FENCIBLE	GUNSTOCK		PACIFIST	REVEILLE
DRAFT	FIRE	GYRENE	KAMIKAZE	PALIKAR	REVOLVER
DRAFTEE	FIREARM		KERNE	PALLETTE	RIFLEMAN
DRAGOON	FIREBASE	HACKBUT	KLEPHT	PANDOOR	RIFLERY
DRUMFIRE	FIREBOMB	HAGBUT	KNIGHTLY	PANDOUR	RIFLING
DUD	FIRELOCK	HALBERD	KRIS	PANOPLY	RITTER
DUSTOFF	FLAK	HALBERT		PANZER	
	FLAMEOUT	HANDGUN	LAAGER	PAULDRON	SABATON
ECHELON	FLANCARD	HANGFIRE	LANCER	PAVIS	SABER
ENCODER	FLATTOP	HAUBERK	LANGRAGE	PAVISE	SAGUM
ENCODE	FLYBOY	HAWKISH	LANGREL	PAVISER	SALIENT
EPAULET	FLYBY	HAYWARD	LEAGUER	PAYGRADE	SALLET
ELINT	FLYOVER	HEADHUNT	LEGION	PEACENIK	SALVO
EMBATTLE	FLYPAST	HEAUME	LONGBOW	PELE	SANGA
ENCAMP	FOEMAN	HELICOPT	LOOIE	PELTAST	SANGAR
ENCEINTE	FOILSMAN	HELILIFT		PELTATE	SAPPER

SARGE	SOLDIERY	SWORD	TOPKICK	VIGIL	WARWORN
SCALADE	SOLLERET	SWORDMAN	TORPEDO		WATERLOO
SCALADO	SORTIE		TRIPWIRE	WAR	WEAPONRY
SCIMETAR	SOWAR	TACE	TROOPER	WARCRAFT	WHIZBANG
SCIMITAR	SPAHEE	TAMPION	TRUCE	WARDROOM	WILCO
SCIMITER	SPAHI	TARGE	TSUBA	WARFARE	WINGMAN
SCRAMJET	SPEAR	TASSE	TUCHUN	WARHEAD	WINGOVER
SCUTAGE	SPEARER	TASSET	TWIBIL	WARISON	WOMERA
SERGEANT	SPEARMAN	TEARGAS	TWIBILL	WARLESS	WOMMERA
SERJEANT	SPONTOON	TELEMAN		WARLIKE	WOOMERA
SHAKO	SQUAD	TENAIL	UHLAN	WARLORD	
SHOGUN	SQUADRON	TENAILLE		WARMAKER	YARDBIRD
SHOOTOUT	STALAG	TESTUDO	VAMBRACE	WARPLANE	YATAGAN
SHOTGUN	STINKPOT	THANE	VANQUISH	WARPOWER	YATAGHAN
SHRAPNEL	STRAFE	TOLEDO	VEDETTE	WARRED	
SKIRMISH	STRAFER	TOMPION	VELITES	WARRING	ZOUAVE
SNIPE	SUBDEPOT	TONLET	VENTAIL	WARRIOR	
SNIPER	SUTLER	TOPEE	VESICANT	WARSHIP	
SOLDIER	SWABBIE	TOPI	VETERAN	WARWORK	

NAUTICAL

ABAFT	BARGEMAN	BODKIN	CAIQUE	CLEW	DAHABEAH
ABEAM	BARQUE	BOGAN	CAISSON	CLUBHAUL	DAHABIAH
ABOARD	BARRATER	BOLLARD	CANAL	COASTING	DAHABIEH
AFT	BARRATOR	BOLTROPE	CANALLER	COBLE	DAHABIYA
AFTMOST	BARRATRY	BOSUN	CANOE	COCKBILL	DAVIT
AHOY	BARRETOR	BOTEL	CANOEIST	COCKBOAT	DEADWOOD
AHULL	BARRETRY	BOTTOMRY	CAPTAIN	COCKPIT	DEBARK
AIRBOAT	BATEAU	BOUSE	CARACK	COIL	DECKHAND
ALEE	BATTEAU	BOWSPRIT	CARAVEL	COMPASS	DECKING
AMIDSHIP	BEACH	BOXHAUL	CARINATE	CONN	DEMERSAL
ANCHOR	BEAM	BRAIL	CARLINE	CORACLE	DHOW
APORT	BECKET	BREAM	CARLING	CORDELLE	DIAPHONE
ARGOSY	BELAY	BRIG	CARRACK	CORSAIR	DINGEY
ARK	BENTHAL	BRINY	CARVEL	CORVET	DINGHY
ARMADA	BENTHIC	BROACH	CASSETTE	CORVETTE	DINGY
ASDIC	BENTHOS	BUGEYE	CAT	COX	DINK
ASEA	BERTH	BULKHEAD	CATBOAT	COXSWAIN	DISMAST
ASHORE	BIBB	BUMBOAT	CATFALL	CREW	DOCK
ASTERN	BIDARKA	BUMKIN	CATHEAD	CREWLESS	DOCKAGE
AWASH	BIDARKEE	BUNTLINE	CATSPAW	CREWMAN	DOCKER
AWEATHER	BILANDER	BUOY	CATTED	CREWMATE	DOCKHAND
AWEIGH	BILGE	BUOYAGE	CAULK	CROJIK	DOCKLAND
	BIREME	BUOYANCE	CAULKER	CRUISE	DOCKSIDE
BACKOUT	BOATEL	BUOYANCY	CAULKING	CRUISER	DOCKYARD
BACKSTAY	BOATHOOK	BUOYANT	CHANDLER	CURAGH	DOGGER
BAIDARKA	BOATMAN	BURGEE	CHANTEY	CURRACH	DOGWATCH
BAREBOAT	BOATSMAN	BURTON	CHANTIES	CURRAGH	DORIES
BARGE	BOATYARD		CHINE	CURRENT	DORY
BARGEE	BOBSTAY		CHOPPY	CUTWATER	DOWNHAUL

DOWNWIND	GABBARD	JACKSTAY	LOGBOOK	ONSHORE	RATLIN
DRAGLINE	GABBART	JACKY	LONGBOAT	OOMIAC	RATLINE
DRAGNET	GALE	JAYGEE	LONGSHIP	OOMIACK	RATTLING
DRAIL	GALIOT	JETSAM	LORAN	OOMIAK	RAZEE
DRIFT	GALLEASS	JETSOM	LUFF	ORLOP	RECHART
DRIFTAGE	GALLEON	JETTISON	LUGGER	OROMETER	REDOCK
DROGUE	GALLEY	JIBB	LUGSAIL	OUTBOARD	REEF
DROMON	GALLIASS	JIBBOOM	LUMPER	OUTHAUL	REEFER
DROMOND	GALLIES	JIBE	LUNAR	OUTPORT	REGATTA
DUGOUT	GALLIOT	JIBER		OUTSAIL	RESAIL
DUNNAGE	GANGWAY	JOHNBOAT	MAINMAST		RESHIP
	GANTLINE		MAINSAIL	PARRAL	RHUMB
EARING	GARBOARD	KAIAK	MAINSTAY	PARREL	RIBBAND
EASTER	GARVEY	KAYAK	MAINTOP	PATAMAR	RIGGING
EASTERLY	GENOA	KAYAKER	MAKEFAST	PATTAMAR	RIPTIDE
EASTING	GONDOLA	KAYAKING	MANROPE	PEDALO	RIVAGE
EASTWARD	GRAPLIN	KEDGE	MARINA	PELAGIC	ROBAND
EDDY	GRAPLINE	KEEL	MARINER	PELORUS	ROBBIN
EUPHROE	GRAPNEL	KEELAGE	MARITIME	PHAROS	ROGER
EURIPUS	GUNKHOLE	KEELBOAT	MARLINE	PIGBOAT	ROW
EXEC	GUNROOM	KEELHALE	MARLING	PILOTAGE	ROWBOAT
	GUNWALE	KEELHAUL	MAST	PILOTING	ROWLOCK
FAIRLEAD	GUYOT	KEELLESS	MASTHEAD	PINKEY	RUDDER
FALTBOAT	GYBE	KEELSON	MASTLESS	PINNACE	
FELUCCA	GYROSTAT	KELSON	MATELOT	PIRACY	SAILBOAT
FERRIAGE		KETCH	MAYDAY	PIRAGUA	SAILER
FERRY	HAAF	KEVEL	MIDSHIP	PIRATE	SAILOR
FERRYMAN	HADAL	KEVIL	MIDSHIPS	PIRATIC	SALTIE
FID	HALLIARD	KILLICK	MIDWATCH	PIROGUE	SALVOR
FIREBOAT	HALYARD	KILLOCK	MIZEN	PIROQUE	SAMPAN
FIREROOM	HANK	KYAK	MIZZEN	POLE	SANDBAR
FLAGSHIP	HARPING		MONOHULL	POLYNYA	SCEND
FLATBOAT	HATCHWAY	LAGAN	MOONSAIL	PONTON	SCHOONER
FLEMISH	HAULYARD	LAGEND	MOOR	PONTOON	SCHUIT
FLOATAGE	HAWSE	LANDFALL	MOORAGE	PORT	SCOW
FLOATEL	HAWSER	LANDING	MOORING	PORTAGE	SCUBA
FLOTA	HEADRACE	LANIARD	MUTINEER	PORTHOLE	SCULL
FLOTAGE	HEADSAIL	LANYARD	MUTINOUS	PORTLESS	SCULLER
FLOTILLA	HEADSTAY	LARBOARD	MUTINY	PRAM	SEABAG
FLOTSAM	HEADWAY	LASCAR		PRATIQUE	SEABEACH
FLUYT	HEADWIND	LATEEN	NAUMACHY	PRAU	SEABED
FLYBOAT	HELM	LATEENER	NAUTICAL	PROW	SEABOOT
FOGHORN	HELMLESS	LAVEER	NAVAID	PUNT	SEABORNE
FOLDBOAT	HELMSMAN	LEADSMAN	NAVAL	PUNTER	SEACOCK
FOOTROPE	HOMEPORT	LEE	NAVICERT	PURSER	SEACRAFT
FOREBODY	HOY	LEEBOARD	NAVIES		SEADOG
FOREBOOM		LEEWARD	NAVY	QUANT	SEADROME
FOREDECK	ICEBOAT	LEEWAY	NEAP	QUAY	SEAFARER
FOREMAST	INBOARD	LIFEBOAT	NERITIC	QUAYAGE	SEAFLOOR
FOREPEAK	INHAUL	LIFELINE	NORTHING	QUAYSIDE	SEAFRONT
FORESAIL	INHAULER	LIGAN			SEAGIRT
FORESTAY	IRONCLAD	LIGHTER	OAR	RACEWAY	SEAGOING
FOREYARD	ISOBATH	LIMEY	OARLOCK	RAFT	SEAMAN
FRIGATE	ISOTACH	LINER	OARSMAN	RAFTSMAN	SEAMARK
FUTTOCK		LOCKAGE	OFFSHORE	RANDAN	SEAMOUNT

SEAPORT	SOFAR	STUNSAIL	TIDEWAY	UNDERTOW	WHERVE
SEASICK	SONAR	SURFBOAT	TOMBOLO	UNDERWAY	WHITECAP
SEATRAIN	SONARMAN	SURFY	TOPMAST	UNDOCK	WINDAGE
SEAWARD	SONDER	SURGE	TOPSAIL	UNMOOR	WINDWARD
SEAWAY	SONOBUOY	SURGING	TOPSIDE	UNSHIP	WORKBOAT
SEXTANT	SPAR	SURGY	TORPID	UPHROE	
SHALLOP	SPARLIKE	SWABBIE	TOWBOAT	UPWIND	XEBEC
SHANGHAI	SPARRED	SWIFTER	TOWLINE		
SHANTEY	SPARRING		TOWPATH	VANE	YACHT
SHIPLOAD	SPENCER	TAFFAREL	TRAWLER	VANG	YACHTER
SHIPMAN	SPILING	TAFFEREL	TRIMARAN	VEDETTE	YACHTING
SHIPMATE	SPONSON	TAFFRAIL	TRIREME	VESSEL	YACHTMAN
SHIPSIDE	SPRIT	TANKER	TRYSAIL	VIDETTE	YARDARM
SHIPWAY	STAITHE	TANKSHIP	TSUNAMI	VIKING	YAW
SHIPYARD	STAYSAIL	TARTANA	TUGBOAT		YAWL
SHORAN	STEAMER	TELEMAN	TYE	WAISTER	
SICKBAY	STEEVE	TEXAS		WARDROOM	ZEBEC
SKEG	STEEVING	THOLEPIN	UMIAC	WATERAGE	ZEBECK
SKIFF	STEMSON	TIDAL	UMIACK	WATERMAN	ZONETIME
SKIPPER	STERN	TIDELAND	UMIAK	WATERWAY	
SKYSAIL	STERNSON	TIDELESS	UMIAQ	WHARF	
SLATCH	STERNWAY	TIDELIKE	UNANCHOR	WHARFAGE	
SLIPWAY	STOWAWAY	TIDEMARK	UNDERSEA	WHEELMAN	
SLOOP	STRAKE	TIDERIP	UNDERSET	WHERRY	

PERFORMING ARTS

ACCENT	ANGEL	AUBADE	BAROQUE	BONGOIST	CADENCY
·ACROBAT	ANIMATO	AUDITION	BARRE	BOUFFE	CADENT
ACTABLE	ANTHEM	AUTEUR	BARYTONE	BOURDON	CADENZA
ACTOR	ANTIMASK		BASS	BOURREE	CAKEWALK
ACTRESS	APPLAUD	BACKBEAT	BASSI	BOUSOUKI	CALLBACK
ADAGIO	APPLAUSE	BACKDROP	BASSIST	BOUZOUKI	CALLIOPE
AGITATO	APRON	BACKER	BASSO	BOW	CALYPSO
AGON	ARCO	BAGPIPE	BASSOON	BOWING	CAMEO
AGONES	ARIA	BAGPIPER	BATON	BRASS	CANCAN
AIR	ARIETTA	BALLAD	BATTERIE	BRAVA	CANSO
ALASTOR	ARIETTE	BALLADE	BATTU	BRAVO	CANTATA
ALLEGRO	ARIOSE	BALLADRY	BAYADEER	BRAVURA	CANTICLE
ALLONGE	ARIOSO	BALLET	BAYADERE	BUFFO	CANTO
ALMA	ARMONICA	BALLON	BEAT	BUFFOON	CANTOR
ALMAH	ARPEGGIO	BALLONNE	BEBOP	BUGLE	CANTUS
ALME	ARSES	BANDORA	BEGUINE	BUGLER	CANZONET
ALMEH	ARSIS	BANDORE	BELL	BUNRAKU	CAPO
ALPHORN	ARTIST	BANDSMAN	BERCEUSE	BURLESK	CARILLON
ALT	ARTISTE	BANJO	BLUESMAN	BUSKER	CARIOCA
ALTHORN	ARTISTRY	BANJOIST	BLUESY	BUZUKI	CARNEY
ALTO	ASIDE	BARD	BODHRAN		CARNIE
ALTOIST	ASSAI	BARDIC	BOLERO	CABARET	CARNIVAL
AMOROSO	ATABAL	BARITONE	BOMB	CACHUCA	CARNY
ANDANTE	ATONAL	BARKER	BONGO	CADENCE	CAROL

CAROLER	CLARINET	DEEJAY	FIFER	GRACIOSO	JUGGLER
CAROLLER	CLARION	DERRY	FIFTH	GRAND	JUGGLERY
CAROLLING	CLAVE	DESCANT ·	FIGURANT	GRAVE	
CAST	CLAVIER	DIAPASON	FIGURE	GRAZIOSO	KABUKI
CASTANET	CLEF	DIATONIC	FILM	GRIOT	KALIMBA
CASTRATO	CLOG	DIRGE	FILMABLE	GUIRO	KANTELE
CAVATINA	CLOWN	DISCANT	FILMDOM	GUITAR	KARAOKE
CELEB	CLOWNERY	DISEUSE	FILMER		KAZACHOK
CELESTA	CLOWNISH	DITTY	FILMGOER	HABANERA	KAZATSKI
CELESTE	COACTOR	DIVA	FILMIC	HAM	KAZATSKY
CELLIST	COAUTHOR	DOLCE	FILMLAND	HAMARTIA	KAZOO
CELLO	CODA	DOLOROSO	FINALE	HAMMY	KEY
CEMBALO	COLORIZE	DOWNBEAT	FINALIS	HARMONIC	KEYBOARD
CHACONNE	COMBO	DRAMA	FIPPLE	HARMONY	KITHARA
CHAINE	COMEDIAN	DRAMATIC	FLAMENCO	HARP	KLEZMER
CHAMADE	COMEDY	DRAMEDY	FLAT	HARPER	KOLO
CHANSON	COMIC	DRESSER	FLAUTIST	HARPIST	KOTO
CHANT	COMICAL	DRUM	FLOP	HAUTBOIS	KRUMHORN
CHANTER	COMP	DRUMBEAT	FLUTE	HAUTBOY	
CHANTEY	COMPERE	DRUMHEAD	FLUTER	HEAVY	LANCIERS
CHANTOR	COMPOSER	DRUMMER	FLUTIST	HELICON	LANDLER
CHASSE	CONCERT	DRUMROLL	FLYMAN	HEMIOLA	LARGANDO
CHEVALET	CONCERTO	DUET	FOIL	HEMIOLIA	LARGO
CHIMES	CONGA	DUETTIST	FOLKIE	HEPCAT	LEGATO
CHIVAREE	CONTINUO	DUI	FOLKY	HERO	LEGGIERO
CHIVARI	CORANTO	DULCET	FORTE	HEROINE	LEGIT
CHOIR	CORNET	DULCETLY	FORZANDO	HIT	LEGONG
CHOIRBOY	CORYPHEE	DULCIANA	FOUETTE	HOOF	LENTANDO
CHORAGUS	COSTUME	DULCIMER	FRET	HOOFER	LENTO
CHORAL	COTHURN	DUMKA	FUGAL	HORN	LIBRETTO
CHORALE	COTHURNI	DUO	FUGATO	HORNIST	LIED
CHORALLY	COULISSE		FUGUE	HORNPIPE	LIGATURE
CHORD	COUPE	EMCEE	FUGUIST	HULA	LOGE
CHORDAL	COURANT	ENCORE	FURIOSO	HUMORIST	LULLABY
CHOREGUS	COURANTE	ENSEMBLE		HYMENEAL	LUTANIST
CHORIC	COURANTO	EPILOG	GAGAKU	HYMN	LUTE
CHORINE	COURU	EPILOGUE	GALLIARD	HYMNIST	LUTENIST
CHORUS	COWBELL	EPITASIS	GALOP	HYMNODY	LUTHIER
CIMBALOM	CROON	ETUDE	GALOPADE		LUTIST
CINEAST	CROONER	EXEUNT	GAMBA	ICTUS	LYRE
CINEATE	CROTCHET	EXODOS	GAMELAN	IMPROV	LYRICISE
CINEMA	CRUMHORN	EXTRA	GAVOT	INGENUE	LYRICIZE
CIRCUS	CRWTH		GAVOTTE	INTERVAL	LYRICIST
CITHARA	CUE	FADING	GEEK		LYRIST
CITHER	CYMBAL	FADO	GEISHA	JAZZ	
CITHERN	CYMBALER	FALSETTO	GERMAN	JAZZLIKE	MADRIGAL
CITHREN	CYMBALOM	FANDANGO	GIGA	JAZZMAN	MAESTOSO
CITOLA	CZARDAS	FANFARE	GIGUE	JESTER	MAESTRO
CITOLE		FANTASIA	GITTERN	JETE	MAGE
CITTERN	DANCE	FANTASIE	GLEE	JINGLE	MAGI
CLAP	DANCER	FARCE	GLEEMAN	JIVE	MAGIAN
CLAPPER	DANSEUR	FERMATA	GLISSADE	JONGLEUR	MAGICIAN
CLAQUE	DANSEUSE	FIDDLE	GOBO	JOTA	MAGUS
CLAQUER	DEADPAN	FIDDLER	GONG	JUBA	MALLET
CLAQUEUR	DEBUT	FIFE	GOOMBAY	JUG	MANDOLA

MANDOLIN	MOVIEOLA	OVERACT	PRELUDE	ROOT	SHOWMAN
MARACA	MOVIOLA	OVERTONE	PRESA	ROSIN	SHTICK
MARCATO	MRIDANGA	OVERTURE	PRESCORE	ROTTE	SHTIK
MARCH	MUDRA	OVERWORD	PRESTO	ROULADE	SIDEMAN
MARIACHI	MUM		PRIMO	RUBATO	SIDESHOW
MARIMBA	MUMMER	PAINISM	PRODUCER		SINFONIA
MARQUEE	MUMMERY	PANDORA	PROGRAM	SACBUT	SING
MASKING	MUSE	PANDORE	PROMPTER	SACKBUT	SINGER
MASQUE	MUSETTE	PANDURA	PROPMAN	SAGBUT	SINGSONG
MATINEE	MUSIC	PANPIPE	PROTASIS	SALPINX	SIRVENTE
MAXIXE	MUSICAL	PANTO	PSALTERY	SALSA	SISTRUM
MAZOURKA	MUSICALE	PARLANDO	PSALTRY	SAMBAR	SITAR
MAZURKA	MUSICIAN	PARLANTE	PUNKER	SAMBUCA	SITARIST
MBIRA	MUTE	PARODOS	PUPPET	SAMBUKE	SITCOM
MEASURE		PARTERRE	PUPPETRY	SAMISEN	SKA
MEDIANT	NABE	PARTITA		SANTIR	SKETCH
MEGASTAR	NATURAL	PAS	QUARTET	SANTOUR	SKIFFLE
MELISMA	NAUTCH	PASSAGE	QUAVER	SANTUR	SKIP
MELODEON	NEUM	PASSE		SARABAND	SKIT
MELODIA	NEUME	PATRON	RAGA	SARDANA	SLUR
MELODIC	NOCTURNE	PAVAN	RAGTIME	SAROD	SMASH
MELODICA	NOH	PAVANE	RAP	SARODE	SOAPER
MELODISE	NONET	PAVILLON	RASE	SARODIST	SOL
MELODIST	NOODLE	PAVIN	RATTLE	SAX	SOLFEGE
MELODIZE	NOTATION	PEDAL	RAVE	SAXHORN	SOLFEGGI
MELODY	NOTTURNO	PEDALIER	REBEC	SAXTUBA	SOLO
MENO	NUDIE	PEGBOX	REBECK	SCALE	SOLOIST
METER		PIANIST	RECITAL	SCAT	SONATA
MEZZO	OATER	PIANO	RECORDER	SCENA	SONATINA
MIME	OBLIGATO	PIANOLA	REED	SCENARIO	SONG
MIMESIS	OBOE	PIASABA	REEDMAN	SCHERZO	SONGBIRD
MIMIC	OBOIST	PIBROCH	REFRAIN	SCORE	SONGBOOK
MIMICKER	OCARINA	PICCOLO	REGAL	SCRIM	SOPRANO
MIMICKING	OCTAVE	PIERROT	REGGAE	SECONDO	SORDINE
MIMICRY	OCTET	PIPE	REGISTER	SEGNO	SORDINO
MINSTREL	OCTETTE	PIPER	RELEVE	SEGUE	SOUL
MINUET	ODEON	PIQUE	REPRISE	SEMITONE	SOUNDBOX
MIRLITON	ODEUM	PIT	REQUIEM	SEMPLICE	SOUNDMAN
MODAL	OFFBEAT	PITCH	REST	SEMPRE	SOURDINE
MODALITY	OFFKEY	PIU	REVERB	SENNET	SPICCATO
MODE	OFFSTAGE	PLAGAL	REVUE	SEPTET	SPINET
MODERATO	OLIO	PLAYACT	REVUIST	SERENADE	SPINTO
MOLTO	ONSTAGE	PLAYBILL	RHAPSODY	SERENATA	STACCATO
MONODY	OOMPAH	PLAYBOOK	RHYTHM	SERPENT	STAFF
MORCEAU	OPERA	PLAYDATE	RHYTHMIC	SEXTET	STANZA
MORCEAUX	OPERATIC	PLAYER	RICERCAR	SFORZANDO	STARDOM
MORDENT	OPERETTA	PLAYLET	RIDOTTO	SFORZATO	STASIMON
MORRIS	OPUS	PLECTRUM	RISER	SHANTEY	STAVE
MOSSO	ORATORIO	PLIE	RITARD	SHARP	STEP
MOTET	ORGAN	PLOT	ROADIE	SHAWM	STOOGE
MOTIF	ORGANIST	POCO	ROADSHOW	SHOFAR	STRAIN
MOTIVE	OSSIA	POINTE	ROCK	SHOWBIZ	STRAWHAT
MOTIVIC	OSTINATO	POLKA	ROLE	SHOWBOAT	STRETTO
MOVEMENT	OTTAVA	POSTLUDE	ROMANTIC	SHOWCASE	STRING
MOVIEDOM	OUD	POSTSYNC	RONDO	SHOWGIRL	STRIPPER

STROPHE	TALKIE	TIMBAL	TROUPING	UPBOW	VIVACE
STROPHIC	TAMASHA	TIMBALE	TRUMPET	UPRIGHT	VOCAL
STRUM	TAMBOUR	TIMBRE	TRYOUT	UPSTAGE	VOCALIST
STRUMMER	TAMBOURA	TIMBREL	TUBA	USHER	VOCODER
STUNTMAN	TAMBUR	TIME	TUBAIST	UT	VOICING
SUBBASS	TAMBURA	TIMPANO	TUBIST		VOLANTE
SUBITO	TANTARA	TOCCATA	TUCKET	VALSE	VOLE
SUBTONIC	TANTO	TOESHOE	TUMMLER	VEEJAY	VOLTI
SUITE	TARDO	TONETTE	TUNE	VEENA	
SUPE	TELEFILM	TONGUING	TUNING	VEHICLE	WALTZ
SWELL	TELEPLAY	TONIC	TURKEY	VELARIUM	WARBLE
SWING	TEMPI	TOUCH	TURN	VELOCE	WARHORSE
SYMPHONY	TEMPO	TOUR	TURNOUT	VENUE	WEEPIE
SYNTH	TENOR	TRAGEDY	TUTTI	VERITE	WIND
SYRINX	TENORIST	TRAGIC	TUTU	VIBIST	WOODWIND
	TENOUR	TRAGICAL	TWEEDLE	VIBRATO	WOOFER
TABLA	TENUTO	TREBLE	TWEETER	VIGOROSO	
TABLEAU	THEATER	TREMOLO	TWOFER	VILLAIN	ZANZA
TABOR	THEATRE	TRIAD	TYMBAL	VILLAINY	ZAPATEO
TABORER	THEME	TRIANGLE	TYMPAN	VINA	ZARZUELA
TABORET	THEORBO	TRIGON	TYMPANO	VIOL	ZILL
TABORIN	THEREMIN	TRILL	TYPECAST	VIOLA	ZITHER
TABORINE	THESPIAN	TRIO		VIOLIN	ZITHERN
TABOUR	THRENODE	TRIPLET	UKE	VIOLIST	ZYDECO
TABOURER	THRENODY	TRITONE	UKELELE	VIOLONE	
TABOURET	THRUM	TROMBONE	UKULELE	VIRGINAL	
TACET	THRUMMER	TROUPE	UNISON	VIRTUOSA	
TALA	TI	TROUPER	UPBEAT	VIRTUOSO	

SPORTS

ABSEIL	ATHLETE	BAREBACK	BLOOPER	BRACER	CABER
ACE	AUDIBLE	BASEBALL	BLUELINE	BRASSIE	CABESTRO
ACROBAT	AXEL	BASELINE	BOARD	BREAK	CABRESTA
AEROBICS		BASEMAN	BOBBLE	BRIDLE	CABRESTO
AGGRO	BACKBEND	BAT	BOBSLED	BRIDLER	CADDIE
ALPINISM	BACKCAST	BATBOY	BOCCE	BRIDOON	CADDY
ALPINIST	BACKHAND	BATSMAN	BOCCI	BUCKAROO	CAESTUS
ANGLE	BACKLASH	BEANBALL	BOCCIA	BUCKAYRO	CAGER
ANGLER	BACKSPIN	BENCH	BOCCIE	BUCKER	CAMEL
ANGLING	BACKSTOP	BIATHLON	BODYSURF	BUCKEROO	CANCHA
APAREJO	BACKUP	BIKEWAY	BOGEY	BUCKTAIL	CANOE
APPEL	BAFF	BIKINI	BONSPELL	BULGER	CANOEIST
AQUACADE	BAFFIES	BIRDER	BONSPIEL	BULLDOG	CANTER
ARBALEST	BAFFY	BIRDIE	BOOGIE	BULLPEN	CANTLE
ARBALIST	BALKLINE	BIRDING	BOWL	BULLRING	CAPEWORK
ARBELEST	BALL	BIRL	BOWLER	BUNKER	CAPIOLE
ARCHER	BALLGAME	BIRLER	BOWLING	BUNNY	CARACOL
ARCHERY	BALLHAWK	BIRLING	BOWMAN	BUNT	CARACOLE
ARENA	BALLPARK	BLACKOUT	BOWSHOT	BUSHER	CAROM
ARMLOCK	BARBELL	BLOOP	BOWYER		CARROM

CAST
CATAPULT
CATCH
CATCHER
CAVER
CAVING
CELLAR
CESTA
CESTI
CESTUS
CHAQUETA
CHARRO
CHEAT
CHEATER
CHEERLED
CHRISTIE
CHRISTY
CHUKKAR
CHUKKER
CHUTIST
CIRCUIT
CLEAT
CLOP
COACH
COACHER
COCKSHY
COHOLDER
COLISEUM
COLORMAN
COMEBACK
COOLDOWN
CORRIDA
COX
COXSWAIN
CRAGSMAN
CRAMPIT
CRAMPON
CRAMPOON
CRAWL
CREEL
CREW
CRICKET
CROSSBAR
CROSSBOW
CROSSE
CUP
CURL
CURLER
CURLING
CYCLE
CYCLER
CYCLING
CYCLIST

DAP
DEADLIFT
DEADLOCK
DECISION
DEDANS
DEFEND
DEFENDER
DEFENSE
DEKE
DEMIVOLT
DEUCE
DIB
DIBBING
DIBBLE
DIBBLER
DINGER
DINK
DIPNET
DISCI
DISCUS
DISMOUNT
DIVE
DIVER
DOBBER
DOPESTER
DORMIE
DORMY
DOWNHILL
DRESSAGE
DRIBBLE
DRIBBLER
DROPKICK
DROPSHOT
DUCKPIN
DUGOUT
DUKE
DUMBBELL

EARPLUG
ENDURO
EPEE
EPEEIST
EXACTA

FADEAWAY
FAENA
FAIRLEAD
FAIRWAY
FALCONER
FALCONRY
FALLAWAY
FARRIER
FASTBALL
FAULT

FENCE
FENCER
FENCING
FIELD
FIELDER
FIN
FINESSE
FISHGIG
FISHHOOK
FISHLINE
FISHNET
FISHPOLE
FISTIC
FIVEPINS
FIX
FIZGIG
FLETCHER
FLEW
FLIPPER
FLY
FLYTIER
FOIL
FOILSMAN
FOIN
FOOTBALL
FOOTHOLD
FOOTING
FOOTRACE
FOOTWORK
FOREHAND
FORFEIT
FORKBALL
FORTY
FORWARD
FOUL
FRONTON
FULLBACK
FUNGO
FYKE

GAFF
GAINER
GAIT
GALLERY
GALLOP
GALLOPER
GAMASHES
GAMBADE
GAMBADO
GAMER
GATE
GAUNTLET
GIDDAP
GIDDYAP

GIDDYUP
GIG
GILL
GILLNET
GIMMIE
GNARLY
GOAL
GOALIE
GOALPOST
GOALWARD
GOGGLES
GOLF
GOLFER
GOLFING
GOOGLY
GREEN
GREMMIE
GREMMY
GRIDDER
GROUNDER
GYM
GYMKHANA
GYMNASIA
GYMNAST

HAAF
HACK
HALFBACK
HALFTIME
HANDBALL
HANDOFF
HARDBALL
HARDBOOT
HAYMAKER
HEADER
HEADLOCK
HEADPIN
HEAT
HELMET
HOCKEY
HODAD
HODADDY
HOMEBRED
HOMER
HOOPSTER
HORSEMAN
HOSEL
HOST
HOTDOG
HURDLE
HURDLER
HURLER
HURLEY
HURLING

INBOUND
INFIELD
INNING
IRON

JACKPOT
JAM
JAMMER
JAVELIN
JAYVEE
JEREED
JIBBER
JIG
JIGGER
JIUJITSU
JIUJUTSU
JOCK
JOCKETTE
JODHPUR
JOG
JOGGER
JUDO
JUDOIST
JUDOKA
JUJITSU
JUJUTSU

KABAR
KARATE
KART
KARTING
KATA
KAYAK
KAYAKER
KAYAKING
KAYO
KEBAR
KEGELER
KEGLER
KEGLING
KENDO
KICKBALL
KICKOFF
KLISTER
KNUCKLER

LACROSSE
LANGLAUF
LAP
LARIAT
LASSO
LASSOER
LATERAL
LATIGO

LAYUP
LEGER
LEISTER
LINESMAN
LINEUP
LINKMAN
LINKSMAN
LOB
LOFTER
LOGGETS
LONGBOW
LONGE
LONGLINE
LORIMER
LOVE
LUGE
LUGER
LUTZ

MAILLOT
MANEGE
MARATHON
MASHIE
MASHY
MASSE
MATADOR
MATCH
MATCHUP
MIDFIELD
MIDIRON
MINICAMP
MINISKI
MISCUE
MISHIT
MISPLAY
MITT
MOCHILA
MOGUL
MOUND
MUDDER
MUFF
MULETA
MUSH
MUSHER
MUTUEL

NATANT
NATATION
NATATORY
NELSON
NET
NIBLICK
NINEPIN
NOBBLE

NOBBLER	POSTGAME	RIPOSTE	SITUP	SPURGALL	TRACK
NOCK	POSTRACE	ROADWORK	SITZMARK	SQUAD	TRAINER
NONTITLE	POWDER	RODEO	SIXTE	SQUASH	TRAPBALL
NORDIC	PREGAME	ROLLOUT	SKATE	SQUID	TRAPEZE
NOSEBAG	PRELIM	ROOKIE	SKEET	STADIUM	TRAPPING
NOSEBAND	PREMEET	ROSIN	SKEETER	STANDOFF	TRAVERSE
	PRERACE	ROSTER	SKEIN	STEM	TRAWL
OFFSIDE	PROETTE	ROUGH	SKI	STIRRUP	TREBLE
OFFTRACK	PROMOTE	ROVER	SKIABLE	STOCCADO	TRIFECTA
OLYMPIAD	PROMOTER	ROWER	SKIBOB	STOCCATA	TROLL
ON	PSYCH	ROWING	SKIING	STRIKE	TROTLINE
ONSIDE	PUCK	RUGBY	SKIJORER	STROKE	TROUNCE
OUTCURVE	PUGILISM	RUGGER	SKIORING	SULKY	TRUDGEN
OUTFIELD	PUGILIST	RUNBACK	SKITTLE	SUMO	TRUDGEON
OVERHAND	PUNTO	RUNLESS	SKIWEAR	SUPERFAN	TRYOUT
OVERSPIN	PUSHBALL	RUSHING	SKYBOX	SURF	TUBE
OVERTIME	PUSHUP		SKYDIVE	SURFER	TUCK
	PUTOUT	SABER	SKYDIVER	SURFING	TUMBLING
PADDLE	PUTT	SABRE	SLALOM	SWAM	TURFMAN
PADDOCK	PUTTER	SACK	SLAM	SWEEP	TURFSKI
PALESTRA		SADDLE	SLED	SWIM	TURNHALL
PALFREY	QUARTE	SADDLER	SLEDDER	SWIMSUIT	TWINIGHT
PALOOKA	QUARTER	SADDLERY	SLEDGE	SWIMWEAR	
PAR	QUINELA	SALCHOW	SLEEPER	SWINGMAN	UMP
PARAKITE	QUINELLA	SANDLOT	SLEIGH	SWUM	UMPIRAGE
PARRY	QUINIELA	SAVATE	SLEIGHER		UMPIRE
PASE	QUINTAIN	SCATBACK	SLICE	TAILBACK	UNDERCUT
PASS	QUINTE	SCHUSS	SLOTBACK	TANDEM	UNDERDOG
PASSADE	QUIRT	SCHUSSER	SLUG	TAPADERA	UNITARD
PASSADO	QUIVER	SCLAFF	SLUGFEST	TAPADERO	UPFIELD
PELOTA		SCLAFFER	SLUMP	TEAM	UPSET
PENALTY	RACE	SCORE	SNAPBACK	TEAMMATE	
PENNANT	RACING	SCOREPAD	SNATCH	TEAMWORK	VARSITY
PESADE	RACKET	SCORER	SNELL	TEE	VAULT
PIAFFER	RACQUET	SCRUB	SNIGGLE	TELEMARK	VAULTER
PICADOR	RAH	SCRUM	SNORKEL	TENNIS	VIGORISH
PICKOFF	RAILBIRD	SCUBA	SNOWPLOW	TENNIST	VOLLEY
PIKE	RALLY	SCULL	SNOWSHOE	TENPIN	VOLLEYER
PIOLET	RALLYE	SCULLER	SOARING	THINCLAD	VOLTE
PISCARY	RAPPEL	SECONDE	SOCCER	THIRTY	VORLAGE
PISCATOR	RASSLE	SEED	SOFTBALL	THRUST	
PISTE	REDSHIRT	SELLE	SOKOL	THRUSTER	WAGER
PITCH	REF	SEMIPRO	SOMERSET	TIE	WAHINE
PITCHER	REFEREE	SEPTIME	SORING	TILTYARD	WAIVER
PITCHOUT	REGATTA	SERVE	SOUTHPAW	TIPCAT	WARMUP
PITON	REIN	SERVER	SPELUNK	TITLIST	WARSLE
PIVOTMAN	REINSMAN	SERVICE	SPIRAL	TOEHOLD	WARSLER
PLATOON	REMATCH	SET	SPITBALL	TOPSPIN	WARSTLER
PLAYDOWN	REPLAY	SETLINE	SPITTER	TOREADOR	WEAKSIDE
PLAYER	RESERVE	SHAG	SPORT	TORERO	WEBBING
PLAYOFF	RETURN	SHANK	SPOTTER	TORO	WEDEL
POINTMAN	RIATA	SHINNEY	SPREAD	TOSSUP	WEDELN
POLO	RINGER	SHUTOUT	SPRINT	TOUCHE	WEDGE
POLOIST	RINGSIDE	SIDELINE	SPRINTER	TOURING	WICKET
POMMEL	RINK	SIDESPIN	SPUR	TOURNEY	WIDE

WIDEOUT	WINGER	WOODY	WRESTLE	XYST	YOKOZUNA
WINDSURF	WIPEOUT	WORKOUT	WRESTLER	XYSTOS	
WINDUP	WOOD	WRASSLE		XYSTUS	ZONE
WINGBACK	WOODIES	WRASTLE